Introduction to Government and Binding Theory

Introduction to Government and Binding Theory

Liliane Haegeman

BLACKWELL
Oxford UK & Cambridge USA

Copyright © Liliane Haegeman 1991

First published 1991

Reprinted (twice) 1992

Blackwell Publishers
108 Cowley Road, Oxford, OX4 1JF, UK

Three Cambridge Center
Cambridge, Massachusetts 02142, USA

British Library Cataloguing in Publication Data
A CIP catalogue record for this book is available from the British Library.

Library of Congress Cataloging in Publication Data
Haegeman, Liliane M. V.
  Introduction to government and binding theory/Liliane Haegeman.
    p.   cm.
  Includes bibliographical references and index.
  ISBN 0–631–16562–2   ISBN 0–631–16563–0 (pbk.)
  1. Government-binding theory (Linguistics)   I. Title.
P158.2.H34   1991   90–37174
415—dc20   CIP

Typeset in 10 on 13 pt Sabon
by TecSet Ltd, Wallington, Surrey
Printed in Great Britain

This book is printed on acid-free paper

Contents

Preface

The purpose of this book is to provide an introduction to the mainline version of Government and Binding Theory, or GB-theory, using as a basis Noam Chomsky's more recent writings. Starting from the ideas developed in the *Lectures on Government and Binding* (1981), the book will include the most important notions and concepts of *Some Concepts and Consequences of the Theory of Government and Binding* (1982), *Knowledge of Language* (1986a) and *Barriers* (1986b). Some of the concepts that were used earlier in the development of generative grammar but have become less relevant will occasionally be referred to and reference will also be made to some of the more recent developments of the theory. The aim of the book is not to make the reader familiar with all the literature published within the GB framework, but rather to enable him to read this literature himself, to understand it and to evaluate it independently.

The book is aimed at intermediate students in linguistics. A general introduction to generative syntax is presupposed. Roughly, the reader would be expected to be familiar with notions such as competence, performance, informants and linguistic intuition, grammaticality, acceptability, autonomy of syntax, etc. and to be able to parse sentences using the tree diagram representation and the labelled bracketing format. The book presupposes some understanding of terms such as constituent, phrase, grammatical function, lexical category, etc., but this does not mean that such concepts and terms will be taken for granted entirely. On the contrary, part of the aim of the book will be to give the concepts and terms with which the reader is familiar more precise content by offering a coherent theoretical background.

The book should be usable both in the classroom and for private study. It consists of twelve chapters each dealing with a particular component of the theory. Each chapter will contain a number of exercises which allow the reader to test the knowledge acquired in the chapter.

As a basis for the organization of the book I have chosen to start from the projection principle: i.e. the idea that all syntactic structure is projected from the lexicon. This idea is introduced in the first chapter. Starting from this initial premise the book then discusses the distribution of overt material (chapters 2 to 4) and of non-overt material (chapters 5 to 9). Chapter 10 offers an introduction to Chomsky's book *Barriers* (1986b); chapters 11 and 12 illustrate the application of the theory developed in the book to some problems in the syntax of Germanic and Romance languages respectively.

Clearly, a book like this one cannot be written in a vacuum, and in this preface I can only mention a fraction of the people who have influenced the development of the book directly or indirectly.

I wish to thank my publishers for giving me the opportunity to write an introductory course book.

The manuscript of the book has developed on the basis of my own teaching at the English Department of the University of Geneva. Earlier versions of the book were used in manuscript form for students of English linguistics in the second and third year syntax programme at the University of Geneva (1988–90), as well as at the University of Bern (1988–89). The comments of my students have been of invaluable help for the rewriting of my book and I wish to use this opportunity to thank them for their enthusiastic help and patience with a manuscript that often was far from perfect.

As a teacher I owe thanks to my students, but I also owe tremendous thanks to my own teachers, especially to Neil Smith who helped me find a direction for my own research and teaching in linguistics, to Michael Brody who introduced me specifically to generative grammar, and to Henk van Riemsdijk who introduced me to the linguistic community in Europe and in the United States.

I also wish to thank the many colleagues in Geneva and elsewhere who have helped me not only by commenting on and making suggestions for parts of the book but also by being just good friends: Genoveva Puskas, Ian Roberts, Manuela Schoenenberger, Bonnie Schwartz, Andy Spencer, Sten Vikner, Richard Watts and Mariette Wauters.

Thanks are also due to Neil Smith, Noel Burton-Roberts and an anonymous reader who went painstakingly through an earlier manuscript and pointed out to me its many flaws and shortcomings. I hope that the current version of the book will not disappoint them too much.

Two friends merit special mention. Sylvie Ferioli was always willing to help me out on the practical side of typing and printing, and supported me patiently and good-humouredly at the moments when I became overwhelmed by various anxieties and worries. Corinne Grange has helped me and encouraged me throughout the whole period of my teaching in Geneva. She was one of the most enthusiastic and loyal students I have had, and she has become a colleague with whom I have been able to discuss any major or minor problems in the book. Her cheerful mood helped me across bad spots where I felt like abandoning the project entirely. I owe her special thanks for the substantial time that she invested in the rereading of the pre-final version of the text.

Thanks are also due to Ruth Kimber for the editorial work on the book and to Philip Carpenter, who followed the development of the book and gave me valuable comments throughout.

Obviously none of the people mentioned above can be held responsible for the final version of the book, for which I assume full responsibility.

Thanks are finally due to Hedwig De Pauw for reminding me that there is more to life than generative syntax.

Liliane Haegeman
Geneva

Introduction:
The Chomskian Perspective on
Language Study

Contents

Introduction

1 **Linguistics: the science of language**

2 **The native speaker: grammaticality and acceptability**
   2.1   Descriptive adequacy
   2.2   Grammaticality and acceptability
   2.3   The grammar as a system of principles and rules

3 **Knowledge of language: universal and specific properties of language**
   3.1   Explanatory adequacy and language acquisition
   3.2   Universal grammar
   3.3   Parameters and universal grammar
   3.4   Language learning and language acquisition

4 **The generative linguist**

5 **Language acquisition: some speculation**

6 **Purpose and organization of the book**
   6.1   General purpose
   6.2   Organization

7 **Exercises**

Introduction

The aim of this book is to offer an introduction to the version of generative syntax usually referred to as Government and Binding Theory. I shall not dwell on this label here; its significance will become clear in later chapters of this book.

Government–Binding Theory is a natural development of earlier versions of generative grammar, initiated by Noam Chomsky some thirty years ago.[1] The purpose of this introductory chapter is not to provide a complete discussion of the history of the Chomskian tradition. A full discussion of the underpinnings of the generative enterprise would in itself be the basis for a book.[2] What I shall do here is offer a short and informal sketch of the essential motivation for the line of enquiry to be pursued. Throughout the book the initial points will become more concrete and more precise.

By means of footnotes I shall also direct the reader to further reading related to the matter at hand. Much of the primary literature will be hard to follow for the reader who has not worked his[3] way through the book, but I hope that the information will be useful for future reference.

1 Linguistics: the Science of Language

When asked to indicate one prominent feature that distinguishes human beings from animals, many would probably say that this feature is 'language'. Even though animals may have communication systems, none of these systems is as rich or as versatile as the language used by humans. Language is human-

---

[1] For a survey of the development of the theory see van Riemsdijk and Williams (1986). This work should be accessible once chapter 7 has been covered.

[2] The reader will find a good introduction about generative grammar in general introductions to linguistics such as Akmajian, Demers and Harnish (1979), Fromkin and Rodman (1988), Lightfoot (1982), Smith and Wilson (1979), etc. These works should be accessible at this point. For more advanced introductions the reader is referred to Chomsky (1965, 1981a, b, c, 1982, 1986a, 1988), but reading them should be postponed until after chapter 7 of this book, at which point we shall have covered most of the technical issues that are discussed.

[3] My use of the pronoun *his* for referents which may be either male and female follows the conventions of English grammar and I hope that the female readers of this book will not feel offended by it.

specific.[4] This means that an understanding of the mechanisms of human language may lead us to understand, at least partly, what it is that distinguishes man from animals. Linguistics, the study of language, may give us an insight into the human mind.

Leonard Bloomfield defined linguistics as the science of language (Bloomfield, 1935). Like all scientists, linguists will aim at formulating the general rules and principles for the data with which they are faced. Linguists try to formulate generalizations about linguistic data, i.e. language.[5]

There are various ways of approaching the study of language. I assume the reader is familiar with the traditional view of language study, where the focus is often on the study of one specific language, say English. A linguist studying English will try to characterize the rules or principles that determine the formation of English sentences. The goal will be to provide a systematic description of English sentence formation, the grammar of English. The description will have to account for data such as the following:

1a   Agatha Christie has written many books.
1b   I don't like detective stories.

The sentences in (1) are **well formed**. They contrast with the sentences in (2), which are **ill formed**.

2a   *Agatha Christie many books written has.
2b   *I detective stories like.

Well formed sentences are constructed according to the rules of English grammar: they are **grammatical**. The sentences in (2) are not formed according to the rules of the grammar of English: they are **ungrammatical**, as indicated by the asterisks.

When writing a grammar, the linguist will not stop at merely listing examples with the appropriate grammaticality judgements. A simple catalogue of sentences may be an interesting basis for discussion but it will not satisfy the goal of scientific research. In addition to describing the data, the linguist will formulate general principles which will be applicable to further data. In-

---

4   In their introduction to linguistics Akmajian, Demers and Harnish (1979) present a fairly comprehensive discussion of the differences between human language and animal language.

5   Robins (1979) and Newmeyer (1980, 1983) offer good surveys of the development of linguistics. These books will offer a broader background to situate the theory we are discussing here in its historical context.

formally, a linguist might account for the ungrammaticality of (2), for instance, by proposing that in English verbs precede their direct objects. A first hypothesis might be that English sentences are constructed according to the SVO pattern: subject precedes verb, verb precedes object. Let us call this the SVO hypothesis. Having formulated this hypothesis on the basis of a limited number of data, the linguist will test it on the basis of further data. The SVO hypothesis will predict, for instance, that (3a) and (3b) are grammatical; but as it stands the hypothesis also predicts that (3c) and (3d) are ungrammatical: the objects, *detective stories* and *which stories* respectively, precede the subjects:

3a Jeeves is baking a cake.
3b John has bought a new car.
3c Detective stories, I don't like.
3d Which stories do you like?

Either the SVO hypothesis itself will have to be modified in the light of the data in (3c) and (3d) or one or more extra rules are needed which interact with the original hypothesis to account for the grammaticality of (3c) and (3d). We might, for example, formulate a rule of topicalization which allows one to move a direct object to the beginning of the sentence to account for (3c). In addition we might formulate a rule for question formation which states (i) that you move the questioning element (*which stories*) to the initial position of the sentence, and (ii) that you invert subject and auxiliary (*do*) (cf. (3d)).

The total of all the rules and principles that have been formulated with respect to a language constitutes the grammar of that language. A grammar of a language is a coherent system of rules and principles that are at the basis of the grammatical sentences of a language. We say that a grammar **generates** the sentences of a language.

A first requirement for any grammar is that it provides a characterization of the language it describes, i.e. the grammar must be able to distinguish those strings of words which are sentences of the language from those which are not sentences of the language in question. Such a grammar will be **observationally adequate**.

2   The Native Speaker: Grammaticality and Acceptability

2.1   Descriptive Adequacy

It is not only linguists that have the ability to judge English sentences. Every native speaker of English knows intuitively that the sentences in (1) and (3) are acceptable and that those in (2) are not. Moreover, every native speaker of English produces a large number of grammatical sentences and understands the English sentences that he comes across. The native speaker may not be able to state the rules and principles that underlie the sentences he produces, but he has an unconscious or tacit knowledge of such principles; he has internalized a grammar of the language.

The native speaker's tacit knowledge of the grammar of his language is the focus of enquiry for the linguist working in the Chomskian tradition. We say that a grammar reaches descriptive adequacy if it goes beyond the statement of rules to describe the facts and provides an account for the native speaker's intuitions.

Let us consider some examples. We have proposed that (3c) and (3d) could be generated by a rule that moves the direct object leftward to the beginning of the sentence. Now consider the examples in (4), which are not acceptable (hence the asterisk):

4a   *Detective stories, I wonder if he likes.
4b   *Where do you wonder if he lives?

To account for the unacceptability of (4a) we might propose that the rule that moves the direct object in (3c) must be constrained: the direct object cannot move across *if*.

Similarly, when we consider (4b) we might propose that the rule of question formation must also be constrained: the questioning element (*where*) must not move across *if*. At this point we have reached observational adequacy: we provide an account for the facts. However, if we stop at this point we are missing a significant generalization. The ungrammaticality of (4a) and (4b) is due to the same constraint. A **descriptively adequate** grammar will not simply provide an analysis for (3c) and (3d) and for the deviance of (4a) and (4b), but it will try to capture the relation between (4a) and (4b) and formulate a general principle to explain why both (4a) and (4b) are felt to be unacceptable. Such a principle may be that no element in English must be moved across *if*. This general rule will also predict that the examples in (5) are ungrammatical, whereas those in (6) are grammatical:

5a *Where* do you wonder *if* Emsworth has hidden the Empress?
5b *Which detective* do you wonder *if* Emsworth will invite for Sunday lunch?
5c *To Bill*, I wonder *if* he will give any money.

6a *Where* has Emsworth hidden the Empress?
6b *Which detective* will Emsworth invite for Sunday lunch?
6c *To Bill*, he won't give any money.

The general constraint which blocks movement of an element across *if* will be taken to be part of the native speaker's internal grammar.

A descriptively adequate grammar will not only state rules to describe the linguistic data, but it will contain the general principles that enable the native speaker to produce and interpret sentences in his language and decide on the acceptability of sentences. Such a grammar is an explicit formulation of the tacit linguistic knowledge of the native speaker, his internal grammar.

The shift of focus from language itself to the native speaker's knowledge of language is a prime feature of the Chomskian tradition. Both the generative linguist and the traditional linguist will be constructing grammars, i.e. systems of rules that underlie the sentences of a language. But the generative linguist conceives of his grammar as a reflex of the native speaker's competence. The grammar is a representation of the speaker's internal linguistic knowledge.

2.2 Grammaticality and Acceptability

At this point we turn to the notions of 'grammaticality' and 'acceptability'. 'Grammaticality' is a theoretical notion. A sentence is grammatical if it is formed according to the grammar of English as formulated by the linguist. 'Acceptability', on the other hand, is the term which characterizes the native speaker's intuitions about the linguistic data. Consider (7):

7a Bill had left. It was clear.
7b [That Bill had left] was clear.
7c It was clear [that Bill had left].
7d Once that it was clear [that Bill had left], we gave up.
7e Once that [that Bill had left] was clear, we gave up.

(7a) contains two independent sentences. In (7b) the bracketed sentence *Bill had left* is the subject of the complex sentence *that Bill had left was clear*. We say that *Bill had left* is a subordinate clause. It is introduced by *that*, a subordinating conjunction. Similarly, in (7c) *that Bill had left* is a subordinate clause. In (7d) the sentence (7c) is a subordinate clause in a complex sentence. A grammar must include a rule to generate complex sentences in which one clause is part of another one.

Let us turn to (7e). The sentence is odd for most native speakers: it is not acceptable. However, this sentence is formed according to the same principle that we posited to account for the formation of (7b)–(7d), i.e. that one sentence may become part of another sentence. Hence (7e) would be **grammatical**: it is formed according to the rules of the grammar, though it is not acceptable.

Faced with intuitions such as that for (7e) the linguist might decide to modify the rules of the grammar he has formulated in such a way that sentence (7e) is considered to be ungrammatical. He may also decide, however, that (7e) is grammatical, and that the unacceptability of the sentence is due to independent reasons. For instance, (7e) may be argued to be unacceptable because the sentence is hard to process. In the latter case the unacceptability is not strictly due to linguistic factors but is due to the more general mechanisms used for processing information.

The native speaker who judges sentences cannot decide whether the sentence is formed according to the rules of the grammar. He only has intuitions about acceptability. It is for the linguist to determine whether the unacceptability of a sentence is due to grammatical principles or whether it may be due to other factors. It is the linguist's task to determine what it is that makes (7e) unacceptable.

This entails that there may be disagreement between linguists as to whether certain unacceptable sentences are grammatical or not. The disagreement is not one of conflicting judgements of the sentence (although these may also exist), but it is one of analysis. The linguist will have to determine to what degree the unacceptability of a sentence is to be accounted for in terms of the grammar. All the linguist has to go by, though, is the native speaker's intuitions about language, and these, as argued above, are the result of the interaction between his internal grammar and other factors.

In this book we focus on the linguistic knowledge of the native speaker. We restrict our attention to his internal grammar. Obviously, the interaction between the grammar and other mental processes is also an interesting area of research, but it is not the topic of this book.

2.3   *The Grammar as a System of Principles and Rules*

One approach to formulating a grammar of a language would be to suppose that the speaker's internal knowledge of English, i.e. his internal grammar, is no more than a huge check-list of grammatical sentences. Speakers could be thought to 'check' any sentence they come across against this internal inventory. Sentences which match a sentence in the list would be said to be grammatical, those that do not are ungrammatical. Depending on the degree of deviance of such ungrammatical sentences we could rank the sentences for ungrammaticality. A grammar of a language would then be simply a list of sentences.

But it must be immediately obvious that listing all the grammatical sentences of a language is an impossible task and also that it misses the point.

Cataloguing all the grammatical sentences of English is first of all impossible because there is an infinite number of English sentences. In addition, there are other objections to such a listing enterprise. We stated above that linguistics is the scientific study of language. From such a perspective the listing of linguistic data is not enough. We expect general principles to explain the data.

For the generative linguist who tries to provide a representation of the native speaker's internal knowledge of a language a mere listing of sentences would never achieve descriptive adequacy: it could never account for the native speaker's knowledge of the language. Human beings – in our example speakers of English – have finite memories: we often forget things we have heard (perhaps unfortunately). Given that the capacity of our memories is finite, it would be absurd to claim that human beings are able to store all potential sentences of the language, an infinite set. It is thus inconceivable that the native speaker's internal linguistic knowledge consists in an inventory of sentences. We must assume that human beings are somehow equipped with a finite system of knowledge which enables them to construct and interpret an infinite number of sentences. This finite system of principles is what we referred to loosely above as the internal grammar of the language. The generative linguist will try to render explicit the finite system of rules and principles that make up the native speaker's competence. In our example, the rule which prohibits moving elements across *if* will be able to account for the unacceptability of (4) and (5).

3   Knowledge of Language: Universal and Specific Properties of Language

3.1   *Explanatory Adequacy and Language Acquisition*

Suppose that we have achieved our goal and that we have provided an explicit characterization of the system of general rules and principles of English sentence formation and which we assume is a representation of the native speaker's tacit knowledge of his language, in our example English. Our grammar will then have reached both observational and descriptive adequacy. Now another important and indeed fascinating question arises. We would like to determine how native speakers of a language, in our example English, come to possess the knowledge of their language. We shall say that a theory reaches **explanatory adequacy** if it can account for the fact that the principles of the internal grammar can get to be known to speakers.

This question is obviously intriguing since millions of people are native speakers of English without being able to formulate any of the rules of the grammar of their language. And all these people had learnt English more or less by the age of six. On the other hand, millions of people do not speak English at all but are fluent speakers of French, Italian, Japanese or any of the other languages that exist.

It would not be reasonable to argue that speakers of English are taught everything they know about their language. Native speakers are not formally taught, for instance, to judge the sentences in (4) and (5) above, and yet they will all agree on their unacceptability. How then do they attain this knowledge? To illustrate the same point, let us consider the following examples, taken from Chomsky (1986a: 8):

8a   I wonder who [the men expected to see them]
8b   [The men expected to see them]

Both (8a) and (8b) contain the string *the men expected to see them*. In (8a) the pronoun *them* can be interpreted as referring to *the men*; in (8b) it cannot. The difference in interpretation of the pronoun is not something that is formally taught and there is no overt indication in the sentences to signal the difference. Still, all native speakers of English have the intuition; non-native speakers of English too will never interpret the pronoun *them* in (8b) as referring to *the men* even though this is not part of their formal tuition in English.

Given that neither formal teaching nor overt evidence seems to be the source of the native speaker's intuitions, it is proposed that a large part of the native speaker's knowledge of his language, i.e. the internal grammar, is innate. The idea is that human beings have a genetic endowment that enables them to learn language. It is this innate capacity for language learning common to all human beings that the generative linguist tries to characterize. Of course, it would be unreasonable to posit that some individuals – those that will become native speakers of English – are born with a specific grammar of English and that others – those that will end up speaking Japanese as their first language – are born with the grammar of Japanese readily stored in their minds. Human beings with normal mental faculties are able to learn *any* human language. The innate linguistic endowment must be geared to any human language and not to just one.

3.2   Universal Grammar

Let us discuss some examples to try to clarify all this a little. We have introduced one generalization about English: the SVO hypothesis. The data in (7) have led us to formulate another hypothesis: any grammatical English sentence can apparently be embedded and become a subordinate clause in a complex sentence. Let us refer to this as the embedding principle.

9   **Embedding principle**[6]
    A grammatical sentence can become a subordinate clause in a complex sentence.

The embedding principle tries to render explicit part of the tacit knowledge of the native speaker. This principle would be taken to be part of the grammar of English, hence available to the native speaker. But this principle is not one that is particular to the grammar of English, it is not **language-specific**. Rather, the embedding principle is part of the grammar of all human languages. Thus in French too we find sentences such as (10a) embedded in (10b):

10a   Maigret a abandonné l'enquête.
      Maigret has abandoned the enquiry.

---

6   As the reader will see later, the embedding principle is not in fact part of our grammar. The fact that sentences can be embedded can be deduced from the principles of sentence formation discussed in chapters 1 and 2.

10b Lucas a annoncé que Maigret a abandonné l'enquête.
    Lucas has announced that . . .

The reader who knows other foreign languages will be able to apply this principle to those languages.

The embedding principle is a **universal**[7] principle. Principles that hold of all languages are said to be part of **universal grammar,** or UG for short. Informally, UG is a system of all those principles and rules that are common to all human languages, this means languages as different as English and French or Japanese.

A hypothesis adopted by generativists of the Chomskian tradition is precisely that universal grammar is innate to the human species. UG is a genetic endowment: we are born equipped with a set of universal linguistic principles. To quote Chomsky himself: 'Universal grammar may be thought of as some system of principles, common to the species and available to each individual prior to experience' (1981b: 7).

If we assume that there is such an innate linguistic endowment the task of attaining the knowledge of a specific grammar, say English, is facilitated. Someone learning English would not have to learn the embedding principle. It is innate; it is part of one's genetic endowment.[8]

Universal grammar is the basis for acquiring language. It underlies all human languages. All and only human beings are equipped with UG and they are all able to learn languages. Other systems (say, dogs or television sets) are not equipped with UG and therefore will not be able to learn human languages. The linguistic endowment characterized as UG is species-specific.

3.3 Parameters and Universal Grammar

The innate linguistic endowment UG is not sufficient to enable one to speak a language. If all we needed was UG then human beings would be able to speak any language wherever they were born and in whatever circumstances they grew up. The native language is that spoken by the child's immediate environment. It would be inconceivable, for instance, that a child growing up

---

[7] The principle might have to be reformulated and reinterpreted in the light of further data and in view of other hypotheses of our linguistic theory (for an example see the discussion of word order patterns in German in chapter 11).

[8] The reader may wonder why, if the principle is innate, children do not start using complex sentences straight away. However, it is conceivable that the development of the internal grammar interacts with a general maturation process. We leave this problem aside here.

in a community where only English is spoken could become a native speaker of Japanese. Human beings usually master one language with native competence and they have a hard time learning other languages later in life. It is a well-known fact that achieving complete mastery of second or third languages in adulthood is exceptional.

While certain grammatical principles and rules are universal, there is also a lot of variation between different languages. The grammar of English differs in important respects from that of, say, Japanese. Hence, if you 'know' the grammar of English, this will not entail that you 'know' the grammar of Japanese. In (1) we illustrated some simple English sentences and we saw that English sentences exhibit SVO word-order. In Japanese, on the other hand, the object precedes the verb; Japanese is SOV:

11 John ga   Mary o   but-ta.
    John particle   Mary particle   hit-past
    (Kuno, 1973: 3)

English and Japanese are similar in that sentences contain components such as subjects, objects and verbs. But they differ in the way these elements are ordered. The SVO hypotheses which we postulated as part of English grammar cannot be an absolute linguistic universal: it is part of the grammar of English (and of other languages) but not of that of Japanese. It is language-specific. How does the child learning English attain this rule? We could envisage the following scenario. The linguistic endowment UG makes available, among other things, the notions 'subject', 'object', 'verb'. Let us propose that these are universal concepts, available in all human languages.

Subject, verb and object will be linearly ordered. When learning a language the child will have to decide which is the word-order pattern characteristic of his language. We say that there exists a **parameter** along which languages vary: let us call it the word-order parameter. Individual languages will illustrate different 'settings' or 'values' of the parameter. The child's task is to figure out what the particular value of the parameter in question is for the language he is learning. The different word-orders of English and Japanese are the result of **parametric variation**. Another example of parametric variation is discussed in section 4.

The child must construct his internal grammar of English. To achieve this task he uses, on the one hand, the universal notions and principles of UG and the choices that it makes available, and on the other hand he uses the data of his linguistic experience, in our example the English sentences he hears. Sentences such as those in (1) will provide evidence to the child that in English subject precedes verb and verb precedes object. A sentence such as that in (11) will enable the child exposed to Japanese data to decide that Japanese is SOV.

Exposure to linguistic material is an essential ingredient in the child's learning process. The child will need the linguistic experience to start constructing the internal grammar of his language and thus to attain the knowledge of a language. Without exposure the child would not be able to construct his internal grammar: he would not know, for instance, whether to pick SVO or SOV. UG is crucial in the organization of the primary linguistic experience. UG determines the way the child will interpret and organize the language he is exposed to. In our example, UG would be said to make available the concepts subject, object and verb, and the word-order parameter, and the child will fix the setting of the parameter. We have now postulated two properties of UG:

(i)   UG contains a set of absolute universals, notions and principles which do not vary from one language to the next.

(ii) There are language-specific properties which are not fully determined by UG but which vary cross-linguistically. For these properties a range of choices is offered by UG. One parameter along which languages vary concerns word-order.

We have already said that absolute universal principles need not be learnt. But even with respect to the mastery of language-specific properties very little 'learning' is involved under the hypothesis outlined above. For those principles that are parametrized, the available options are given by UG. Attaining linguistic knowledge consists in fixing the parameters.

From this point of view, we conclude that the mastery of a language is not really the result of learning. Rather, being equipped with UG (with its parameters) and exposed to a language, the child cannot but construct the grammar of the language he is exposed to. For this reason the term 'learning' is often replaced by the term 'acquisition'.

In addition, the exposure to language will also equip us with a vocabulary, the words of the language to which we are exposed. Even if we have an innate knowledge of the principles of language we must inevitably learn the lexicon of the language, the words and their meaning, in order to be able to put this knowledge into operation. Thus an English child will have to learn all the words in the sentences above, and indeed many more. And we go on learning new words throughout our lives. Similarly a French child will learn the French lexicon, etc.[9]

---

[9]   The acquisition of the vocabulary of a language is also a matter of interest. For some introductory discussion the reader is referred to Lightfoot (1982: 121–2).

To sum up so far: human beings are born equipped with some internal unconscious knowledge of grammar: UG. UG is a set of universal principles of language, some of which parametrized. Via the input of the experience of one particular language this knowledge can be implemented. The acquisition process is 'triggered' by the exposure, the child's linguistic experience.

Exposure will also enable the child to learn the vocabulary of the language.[10] The view of language acquisition in terms of parameter setting is the basis of current work in the generative tradition.

3.4 *Language Learning and Language Acquisition*

Our ability to speak a language is based partly on the innate principles and parameters available in UG, partly on the triggering experience of exposure to a specific language. On the basis of these components we develop a grammar of one (or more) specific languages: the 'core grammar' of such a language.

Schematically we can represent the generative view of language acquisition as follows:

12
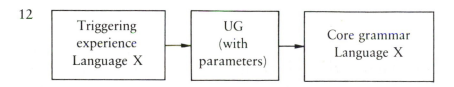

The exposure to some language, say English, will activate the innate principles of universal grammar. The child will fix the choices to be made for the language in question, for instance, that the object follows the verb, and will also learn the vocabulary of the language. To quote Chomsky:

> Endowed with these principles, a system provided with adequate experience will develop a grammar of the peculiar and specific sort characteristic of human language ... Lacking these principles, a system will develop no grammar or some different system. The telephone exchange, for example, has 'heard' much more English than any of us, but lacking the principles of universal grammar ... it develops no grammar of English as part of its internal structure. (1981b: 8)

---

[10] The reader will find a very accessible discussion of the acquisition process in Lightfoot (1981, 1982). For further information the reader should consult Chomsky (1981a, b and c) and the literature cited there. However, Chomsky's work will be hard to read at this stage and the reader is advised to postpone reading these works until he has worked through chapters 1–7 of this book.

By the age of six a child exposed to English will have constructed the grammar of his language. This does not mean that no further development of his knowledge of language is possible. For instance, we go on learning new words throughout our lives. In addition we also learn certain less usual constructions of the language. These exceptional or marked patterns of the language are not taken to be part of the **core grammar** of the language, they belong to the **marked periphery** of the grammar and may be acquired later. The native speaker will also have to learn all of the social or cultural conventions associated with his language, for instance, that certain words belong to a very high style whereas others are informal. These conventions are not part of the grammar, they belong to the more general domain of human behaviour.

The aim of generative syntacticians is to develop a theory of language that is a model of the acquisition of language. Linguists want to provide an explicit formulation of the three components of (12): (i) the principles of UG and the parametric variation across languages, (ii) the triggering experience needed to activate the principles of UG, and (iii) the core grammar of specific languages as it derives from these interacting components. A theory that can account for these three components will be said to have reached explanatory adequacy.

4   The Generative Linguist

The research programme as sketched here briefly and roughly is one that has been motivating linguistic research for the past thirty years and has given rise to many challenging results. The programme is indeed still developing.

It may be useful to repeat that the ultimate aim of generative linguistic theory is not to describe the details of one specific language, but rather to formulate the underlying principles that determine the grammars of human languages. These grammars are seen as representations of the native speaker's knowledge. In the course of their enquiry, linguists will examine data drawn from individual languages, of course, but the investigator will always bear in mind the interacting components in (12).

The generative linguist who tries to characterize knowledge of a language, say English, will wish to do two things: (i) he needs to determine what properties of English are universal, and (ii) what properties are English-specific and how these relate to the parameters of UG.

It must by now have become clear that by simply looking at English and only that, the generative linguist cannot hope to achieve his goal. All he can do is write a grammar of English that is observationally and descriptively adequate but he will not be able to provide a model of the knowledge of the native speaker and how it is attained. The generativist will have to compare English with other languages to discover to what extent the properties he has identified are universal and to what extent they are language-specific choices determined by universal grammar. Even when his main concern is some aspect of the grammar of English the linguist will have to go outside this one language and engage in contrastive work.

Work in generative linguistics is therefore by definition comparative. Generative linguists often do not focus on individual languages at all: they will use *any* human language to determine the general properties of UG and the choices it allows. Data from a language spoken by millions of people are just as important as data from a dialect spoken by only a couple of hundred people. Both languages are human languages and are learnt in the same way.

5 Language Acquisition: Some Speculation

Let us try to think a little more about language acquisition as represented in (12) above. A first proviso is in place: we are only looking at language acquisition from a linguistic point of view. We abstract completely away from any other psychological aspects involved in language acquisition. We also leave aside the mastery of social conventions concerning language use.

How does a child construct the grammar of his language? By hypothesis the child comes to the task equipped with UG: a set of universal principles and rules some of which are parametrized.

We illustrate these parameters with another example. Speakers of Italian will learn that in their language the pronominal subject of a sentence need not be expressed, while for French and English, speakers need to learn that the subject of a sentence is expressed, even if it is pronominal:

13a   Ho   incontrato il   commisario Maigret.
    Io ho   incontrato il   commisario Maigret.
    I have   met   the inspector   Maigret
13b   *Ai rencontré le commissaire Maigret.
    ^{OK}J'ai rencontré le   commissaire Maigret.
    I have met   the inspector   Maigret
13c   *Have met inspector Maigret.

In (13a) we see that in Italian the subject pronoun *io* ('I') may be left unexpressed. In (13b), the French example, the sentence is ungrammatical if the subject pronoun is not expressed. In English too (13c) will be ungrammatical in normal conversation.[11]

Whether the subject of a sentence must be expressed overtly or not is subject to parametric variation. Learners of specific languages have to fix the choice, the setting of the parameter. Let us call it the **null subject parameter**. The null subject parameter is positively set in Italian. It is negatively set in English and French.[12]

14a **Null subject parameter**
    Subject pronouns may be dropped.
14b Parameter settings: null subject parameter:
    French   −
    English −
    Italian +
    etc.

Fixing the parameter is easy enough for the Italian child. Data such as sentence (13a) will trigger the positive setting for the parameter. But how can an English child who hears only examples with overt subjects deduce that sentences such as (13c) are impossible? After all, it might be a mere accident that he is only faced with sentences with full pronouns? The problem described here is that of **negative evidence**: how do you conclude that something is not possible merely on the basis that you have not met with any occurrences of it?

One proposal to solve this problem is as follows. As a starting point observe that with respect to the realization of sentences with pronouns as subjects, Italian is a 'bigger' language than English. For every English sentence with a pronoun as its subject, there is the additional option in Italian of leaving the pronoun unexpressed:

[11]   In certain areas of usage the subject may be non-overt in English too:

   (i)   Wish you were here.
   (ii) Had a nice day at the swimming pool.

   (i) is typical of informal writing, (ii) could be a sentence taken from a diary. These sentences are acceptable within certain registers but not generally. We shall say that they are not part of the **core grammar** of English but belong to the marked **periphery**. For some discussion see Haegeman (1990).

[12]   Chapter 8 of this book contains a discussion of this parameter.

15   *English:*   She is ill.
             *Is ill.
16   *Italian:*   Lei è malata.
             È malata.

The sentences with pronoun subjects in English are a subset of those possible in Italian. For each sentence in English there are two Italian equivalents:

17

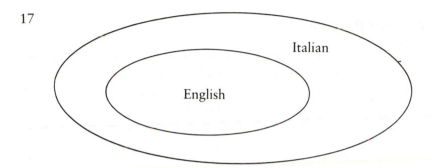

Some linguists have suggested that when constructing his internal grammar and fixing the values of the parameters, the child starts out with the minimal assumption. He starts from that parameter setting which produces the 'smallest' language. In our concrete example this would mean that all children start out assuming that the null subject parameter is negatively set, which will produce a language in which sentences without subjects are excluded.

The idea then is that the child will only opt for the setting which produces a bigger language, in our case a language in which sentences without visible subjects are allowed, if he is given positive evidence. The English child will not be given evidence to suggest that his language is positively specified for the null subject parameter; the Italian child will. Hence only the Italian child will reset the parameter.[13]

Work in this direction is very much in progress but it is important to mention it because it ties in directly with the general motivation of generative research in language. Recently, linguists in the generative tradition have also

---

[13]   An account in which language acquisition is related to the notions of sets and subsets is developed by Manzini and Wexler (1987). The reader should not attempt to read this text until he has studied chapter 7. For a different view on the acquisition of the null subject parameter the reader is referred to Hyams (1986, 1989).

started to investigate whether the model of first language acquisition that they advocate could be applied to the acquisition of a second language.[14]

6   Purpose and Organization of the Book

6.1   General Purpose

In this book I provide a survey of some of the main results of generative research over the past thirty years. The book is not an absolute beginner's book. The reader is expected to have some background in linguistics, specifically in syntax. He should, for instance, be able to parse sentences and be familiar with the tree diagram representation, and with the basic terminology of syntax. Notions such as sentence, clause, noun, verb, subject, object, etc. are presupposed. I assume therefore that the reader has had some introductory course to syntax or that he has read some introductory works.[15] However, in order to guarantee that we have a common starting-point, I shall often recapitulate the basic notions. It will also be shown how traditional concepts are used and reinterpreted within the framework of Government and Binding Theory.

The aim of the book is to offer a general introduction. I shall not go into all the complexities and details of ongoing research. Rather, I wish to familiarize the reader with the basic concepts used. I hope that the book will encourage the reader to turn to the primary literature himself and discover some of the more intricate problems. The references in the footnotes will provide indications of further reading.

Although the examples in the book will be taken primarily from English, this book is not a grammar of English. English is used as just one example of human language and we shall often discuss other languages. We shall try to decide what sort of internal grammar native speakers of English have at their disposal and to determine what it is that makes a sentence acceptable or unacceptable, what sort of grammatical principles can be advocated and to

---

[14]   For a survey of work in this area see Flynn and O'Neill (1988) and Pankhurst, Sharwood Smith and Van Buren (1988).

[15]   I am thinking of works such as Akmajian and Heny (1975), Akmajian, Demers and Harnish (1978), Burton-Roberts (1986), Fromkin and Rodman (1988), Huddleston (1976), Jacobs and Rosenbaum (1970), Smith and Wilson (1979), Wekker and Haegeman (1985) to mention only a few.

what extent these are universal or language-specific. In some sense we are like linguistic detectives. The linguistic data are like the clues a detective is given when starting his enquiry. He has to piece these data together, construct hypotheses, check these and ultimately he may discover the explanation for the evidence he has assembled. To remind the reader of this task I have chosen to illustrate the data with examples in which literary detectives play a prominent role. At the end of the book I hope that the reader will have become a competent linguistic detective himself.

6.2 Organization

The book is divided into twelve chapters. The first ten chapters provide the basic outline of the theory. Each chapter is followed by a one-page summary of the main ideas and by a set of exercises. The exercises have a dual purpose. First, they will enable the reader to check if he has understood and assimilated the basic concepts introduced in the chapter. The empirical range of the discussion is broadened: many exercises will include a discussion of data drawn from languages other than English.

Second, the exercises will be used to draw the reader's attention to theoretical or empirical problems not touched upon in the chapter. Often a problem introduced by way of an exercise in an earlier chapter is then picked up in the discussion of a later chapter. Alternatively, the exercises will direct the reader to areas for further reading or for further research.

The last two chapters of the book show how the theory can be applied to the analysis of specific languages. Chapter 11 discusses data from Germanic languages; chapter 12 discusses data from Romance languages.

Footnotes will mainly be used to direct the reader to further reading. The footnotes will also indicate at which point in the book the reader should be able to tackle the literature in question.

7 Exercises

Exercise 1

Consider the following sentences. None of them is fully acceptable but they vary in their degree of deviance. If you are a native speaker of English try to rank the sentences for acceptability. Wherever you can, try to construct an acceptable sentence modelled on the one you are judging. If you are not a native speaker of English you may attempt to carry out the task described above but it may be difficult. Another way of approaching this exercise is to ask some native speakers to do the exercise and compare their answers.

1   Which man do you know what John will give to?
2   Which man do you wonder when they will appoint?
3   Who do you wonder which present will give?
4   Which present do you wonder who will give?
5   Which man do you wonder whether John will invite?
6   Which man do you wonder whether will invite John?
7   Which man do you wonder what will give to John?
8   Which man do you wonder when will invite John?

Native English speakers are basically in agreement on the ranking of sentences 1–8. The judgements formulated are not the result of formal tuition. English grammar classes do not pay attention to sentences like 1–8. It is quite likely that speakers have never come across such sentences. In other words, they have not acquired the intuitions on the basis of overt evidence. On the contrary, given that the sentences above are judged as unacceptable, one does not expect them to be part of the linguistic data that we are exposed to.

On the basis of the judgements, try to classify the examples and formulate some principles that might account for the relative acceptability. You may find the discussion of examples (3), (4) and (5) in the text of some help. In chapter 7 and following we shall discuss the sentences above and similar ones. We shall assume that they are ungrammatical and we shall attempt to formulate the rules and principles at work.

Exercise 2

If you are a native speaker of a language other than English translate the sentence above in your own language, keeping as close to the English models as you can, and rank them for acceptability. Try to formulate some principles to explain the degree of acceptability.

If you have access to judgements on the English data and on data in other languages, see if the same degree of acceptability of the examples could be explained by the same principle(s).

1   The Lexicon and Sentence Structure

Contents

Introduction and Overview

In the Introduction we saw that a grammar of a language is a coherent system of rules and principles which determines the formation of the sentences of a language. The basic unit with which a grammar is concerned is the sentence. A grammar will specify what the components of the sentence are, how they interact, in which order they occur, etc. Partly, the rules formulated will be of a universal nature; partly, they will have to be parametrized to bring out language-specific properties of individual languages.

Grammars have nothing to say about units higher than the sentence, such as the paragraph, the discourse exchange, the text, etc. Such higher units will be the object of another type of enquiry.[1]

In this chapter we consider the relation between the structure of the sentence and the words that make up the sentence. We shall see that sentence structure is to a large extent determined by lexical information. As pointed out in the Introduction, it is assumed that the reader is familiar with the basic techniques and terminology of sentence parsing.

Chapter 1 is organized as follows: section 1 provides a brief discussion of the central concepts of sentence structure; section 2 focuses on the relation between lexical items and sentence structure; section 3 discusses the predicate–argument structure of sentences and introduces theta theory; section 4 sums up the link between lexical items and sentence structure and introduces the projection principle; section 5 explores the application of theta theory, concentrating on clausal arguments, expletive (non-argument) pronouns and auxiliary verbs; section 6 discusses the general constraint that sentences must have subjects; and in section 7 we consider the properties of the subject theta role.

1 The Units of Syntactic Analysis

In this section we briefly recapitulate the basic notions of syntactic structure that will be the starting point for our discussion. Consider the following example:

---

[1] For an interesting approach to the study of sentences in discourse see Sperber and Wilson (1986) and Kempson (1988), who examines the link between Sperber and Wilson's theory of utterance interpretation and formal syntax.

1   Jeeves will meet his employer at the castle.

(1) is a grammatical English sentence. When we look for its component parts, the constituents, the units that perhaps come to mind first are the words of the sentence: sentence (1) contains eight words. But, as anyone familiar with traditional techniques of sentence parsing knows, words are not the **immediate constituents** of a sentence. Rather, they are the **ultimate** constituents. The words of the sentence are organized hierarchically into bigger units called **phrases**. In the framework of generative syntax the constituent structure of a sentence is represented in one of the following formats: by means of the tree diagram format as in (2a), by means of phrase structure rules or rewrite rules as in (2b), or by means of labelled brackets as in (2c).[2]

2a

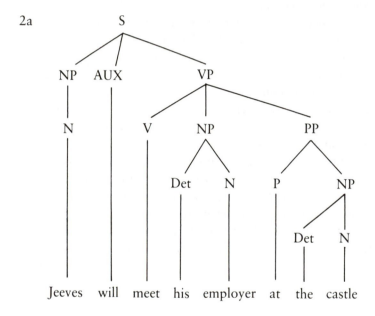

2b   i   S ⟶ NP – AUX – VP
       ii   NP ⟶ (Det) – N
       iii VP ⟶ V – NP – PP
       iv   PP ⟶ V – NP
       v   N ⟶ *Jeeves, employer, castle*
       vi   V ⟶ *meet*

---

[2] For an introduction to parsing see Burton-Roberts (1986), Fromkin and Rodman (1988) and Wekker and Haegeman (1985).

vii   AUX $\longrightarrow$ *will*
viii   P $\longrightarrow$ *at*
 ix   Det $\longrightarrow$ *the, his*

2c   [S [NP [N Jeeves]] [AUX will] [VP [V meet] [NP [Det his] [N employer]]
     [PP [P at] [NP [Det the] [N castle]]]]]]

Representations such as those in (2) give us information concerning the
structure of (1). They indicate, for instance, that the string *his employer* is a
syntactic unit, a **constituent**. It is a **noun phrase** (NP), a constituent whose
main element or **head** is the noun (N) *employer*. Analogously, the constituent
at the castle is a **prepositional phrase** (PP); the head of this PP is the preposition
at, which is followed by an NP, *the castle*. The constituent *meet his employer*
at the castle is a **verb phrase** (VP), whose head is the verb *meet*, which is
followed by two NPs: the NP *his employer* and the PP *at the castle*.

   The structural representations in (2) allow us also to describe syntactic
operations that may affect sentence (1). Consider (3):

3a   At the castle, Jeeves will meet his employer.
3b   His employer, Jeeves will meet at the castle.
3c   Meet his employer at the castle, Jeeves will (indeed).

   The sentences in (3) are intuitively felt to be variations upon sentence (1);
they are all paraphrases of (1). In order to capture the similarity between the
sentences in (3) and that in (1) we shall assume that all these sentences have the
same **underlying structure**, represented in (2). In each of the sentences in (3)
one of the constituents identified in (2) has been moved to the beginning of the
sentence, or **preposed**. Thus in (3a) the PP *at the castle* has been moved, in (3b)
the NP *his employer* is preposed, in (3c) the VP, *meet his employer at the*
castle, is preposed. The possibilities for preposing elements of a sentence can be
seen to be structure-based. Only constituents of the sentence such as NP and
VP can be preposed. One cannot indiscriminately prepose any random string
of words in the sentence:[3]

3d   *Employer at the, Jeeves will meet his castle.
3e   *Meet his, Jeeves will employer at the castle.

---

[3] For a formal discussion of operations such as preposing, see chapters 6 and 7.

Another operation that affects sentence constituents is the one that forms questions. If we form questions on the basis of (3) we see that again the constituent structure represented in (2) plays a crucial role.

We distinguish two types of questions: **yes–no questions** and **constituent questions**. The classification adopted is based on the type of answer expected. (4a) is a *yes–no* question: in normal circumstances we expect *yes* or *no* as an answer. The other questions in (4) are **constituent questions**: the answer to the question will be a constituent.

4a   Will Jeeves meet his employer at the castle?
4b   Who will Jeeves meet at the castle?
4c   Where will Jeeves meet his employer?
4d   What will Jeeves do?
4e   Who will meet his employer at the castle?

Yes–no questions are formed by moving the auxiliary (here, *will*) to sentence-initial position. Constituent questions are formed by means of a substitution process. Each of the sentence-initial question-words such as *who*, *where*, *what* in (4) substitutes for one of the constituents identified in (2): in (4b) *who* substitutes for the object NP *his employer*.[4]

Operations such as preposing and question formation thus provide evidence for the role of phrase structure in syntax.

2   Words and Phrases

Although words are not the immediate constituents of the sentence, they play an important role as the ultimate building blocks of the sentence.

Words belong to different **syntactic categories**, such as nouns, verbs, etc., and the syntactic category to which a word belongs determines its **distribution**, that is, in what contexts it can occur. Normally, one cannot easily interchange words of one category for words of another. If you were to replace the verb *meet* by the semantically-related noun *appointment* in (1) you would no longer obtain a grammatical sentence:

5   *Jeeves will appointment his employer at the castle.

---

[4]   Chapter 7 contains a detailed discussion of the formation of questions.

The grammar of English, and indeed of any language, will have to have access to the categorial information attached to lexical items since this information plays a part in the formation of sentences.

We assume that the categorial information is also available to the native speakers of the language: they will agree that (5) is unacceptable and that the unacceptability is due to the inappropriate use of the N **appointment**. We postulate that speakers of a language are equipped with an internal 'dictionary', which we shall refer to as the mental lexicon, or lexicon, which contains all the information they have internalized concerning the words of their language. As seen above, this mental lexicon will have to contain, among other things, information on syntactic categories. We assume that each word of the language known by a speaker will be listed in his mental lexicon with its categorial specification. For instance, a native speaker of English will presumably have a lexicon containing the following information:

6a *meet*:   verb
6b *employer*:   noun
6c *castle*:   noun
6d *at*:   preposition
6e *the*:   determiner
6f *his*:   determiner
6g *appointment*: noun

As we suggested in the Introduction, it would not make sense to claim that the native speaker's lexical knowledge, i.e. the mental lexicon, is entirely innate. If lexical knowledge were completely innate, then human beings would have to be born equipped with the lexicons of all known or possible human languages. Rather, we assume that the lexicon of a language is learnt by each native speaker. The speaker learns the words of the language and what category they belong to. But this does not imply that he comes to this learning process totally unprepared. We assume that UG, our innate knowledge of language, contains, for example, the notion of syntactic category. When exposed to the words of a particular language, speakers will have some expectation as to which categories to discover. We shall not speculate further here as to the sort of knowledge this involves.

Lexical information plays a role in sentence structure because the syntactic category of a word determines its distribution. Let us take as an example sentence (1) and consider its syntactic representation (2a). In the tree diagram (2a) the word *appointment* will not be inserted in a position dominated by the node V because only verbs can be inserted under a node V, the same observation would apply to the other words in the sentence. Looking at the tree diagram from top to bottom we can say that the **terminal category labels** such as N, V, etc. restrict which lexical elements can be inserted.

Looking at the tree from bottom to top, we see that the words that are inserted at the bottom of the tree determine the structure of the sentence. The inserted words will determine the syntactic category of the **head** of the phrase and hence they will ultimately determine the category of a phrase, the **phrasal category**. For instance, in our example (2a) the inserted N *employer* will be the head of a phrase of the type NP and not of a VP. Chapter 2 provides a more detailed discussion of the principles that regulate sentence structure.

Clearly, the mere matching of lexical and phrasal categories is not sufficient to produce a good sentence. For instance, the random insertion of nouns in the slots provided for them in (2) produces odd results in (7b) and (7c):

7a Jeeves will meet his employer at the castle.
7b ? Jeeves will meet his castle at the meeting.
7c ? Jeeves will meet his castle at the employer.

The question arises whether (7b) and (7c) are ungrammatical: is their oddness due to a violation of a grammatical rule or principle? When asked to explain what is displeasing in (7b), a native speaker will say that (7b) is bizarre because the verb *meet* is followed by the string *his castle*. The oddness is due to the fact that the concept 'meet' usually involves an interaction between two animate participants, while 'his castle' refers to an inanimate entity which does not normally qualify to take part in an action of the type 'meet'. But if we were to endow the concept 'castle' with animacy the oddness would be removed. In a fairy tale where castles take a walk (7b) would become acceptable. What is wrong with (7b) is not a grammatical issue; its strangeness relates to our general knowledge of the world. Issues of language use which hinge on the interaction of the grammar with extra-linguistic information such as that just described must not be integrated in a grammatical description. Grammars do not contain principles and rules about our beliefs about the world around us. (7b) may therefore be seen as grammatical but as bizarre in view of our encyclopaedic knowledge of castles as inanimate objects.

Let us return to sentence (1), repeated here as (8a), and its tree diagram representation (2a) repeated here as (8b):

8a Jeeves will meet his employer at the castle.

8b

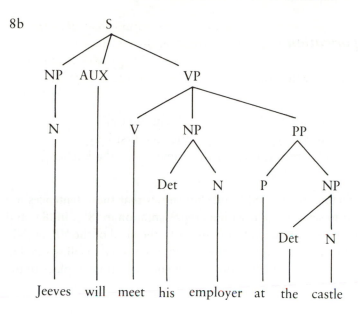

Jeeves will meet his employer at the castle

It is clear that some of the phrasal constituents of this sentence are more essential to the sentence than others. The PP *at the castle*, which specifies the place of the event, can be left out without any harm, but the NP *his employer* cannot.

8c Jeeves will meet his employer.
8d *Jeeves will meet at the castle.

In the next section we shall try to account for the obligatory nature of certain constituents in a sentence.

3 Predicates and Arguments

In this section we explain which constituents of a sentence are minimally required, and why. We first provide an informal discussion and then develop a formal approach known as theta theory.

3.1   *Subcategorization*

Consider the following sentences:

9a   Maigret will [$_{VP}$ imitate [$_{NP}$ Poirot] [$_{PP}$ with enthusiasm]].
9b   Bertie will [$_{VP}$ abandon [$_{NP}$ the race] [$_{PP}$ after the first lap]].
9c   Miss Marple will [$_{VP}$ reconstruct [$_{NP}$ the crime] [$_{PP}$ in the kitchen]]

The labelled bracketing in (9a), (9b) and (9c) shows that these sentences are structurally similar to sentence (8a) with its representation in (8b). In (8a) and in each of the sentences in (9) the VP contains a V, the head of the VP, an NP, the direct object, and a PP. In each of these the PP is optional (as illustrated in (8c) and in (10)): it provides information as to the manner, time or place of the event expressed in the sentence:

10a   Maigret will imitate Poirot.
10b   Bertie will abandon the race.
10c   Miss Marple will reconstruct the crime.

In the traditional literature on parsing, optional phrasal constituents such as the PPs in (8a) and (9) are called **adjuncts**.[5] While the PPs in the examples above are optional, we see that the VP-internal NPs are not:

11a   *Maigret will imitate.
11b   *Bertie will abandon.
11c   *Miss Marple will reconstruct.
11d   *Jeeves will meet.

This does not mean, however, that each English sentence contains just one VP-internal NP, as (12) shows:

12a   Hercule is dithering.
12b   Wooster gave Jeeves the money.

---

[5] In chapters 8 and 9 we shall turn to a more technical definition of the notion adjunct, as it is used in the Government and Binding literature.

Inserting an NP into the VP of (12a) renders the example ungrammatical:

13a Hercule is dithering *the crime/*Agatha.

On the other hand, in (12b) the verb *give* must be followed by two NPs, or alternatively by an NP and a PP:

13b *Wooster gave Jeeves.
13c Wooster gave [NP the money] [PP to Jeeves].

In traditional grammar the requirement that there should be or not be one or more NPs inside the VP is seen as a property of the verb involved. At least three classes of verbs are traditionally distinguished: transitive, ditransitive and intransitive verbs.[6] If a VP has a transitive verb as its head, one NP (the direct object) is required: the verb takes an NP-**complement**. If a VP has a ditransitive verb as its head, two NPs or an NP and a PP (the direct object and the indirect object) are required. If a VP contains an intransitive verb as its head then no NP-complement is allowed. Whether a verb belongs to the group of transitive, ditransitive or intransitive verbs is treated as an idiosyncratic property of the verb.

Native speakers of English would agree on the judgements given for the sentences in (12) and (13). This means that they too must have internal knowledge of the principles that decide on the type of VP in which a verb may appear. The subclassification of verbs must constitute part of their lexical knowlege. Let us therefore integrate the information on verb classes in the mental lexicon which we have posited as part of the internal knowledge of the native speaker.

One way of encoding the information on the complement structure of the verb is by associating it directly with the lexical entry of the verb in question. This would lead to the following (partial) lexicon:

14a *meet*:   verb; transitive
14b *imitate*:   verb; transitive
14c *reconstruct*: verb; transitive
14d *abandon*:   verb; transitive

---

[6] For discussion of the classification of verbs in the traditional literature, see Aarts and Aarts (1982), Burton-Roberts (1986), Huddleston (1984) and Quirk et al. (1985).

14e *dither*: verb; intransitive
14f *give*: verb; ditransitive

The child acquiring English will have to learn not only the syntactic category of the words of his language, but also the subcategory the verbs belong to. Exposure to English sentences containing these verbs will offer positive evidence of this information: the verb will occur in the appropriate syntactic environment. The child exposed to a sentence like (15a) will thus be able to conclude that *sleep* is intransitive and will assign it the property 'intransitive' in its lexical entry (15b):

15a Mummy is sleeping.
15b *sleep*: verb; intransitive.

In the Chomskian tradition the notions transitive, intransitive, etc. are encoded in distributional frames. Verbs are classified according to the type of VP in which the verb typically occurs. For example, the verb *meet* requires an NP-complement; its VP will contain an NP. This requirement can be represented as follows:

16 *meet*: V, [——— NP].

(16) shows in which syntactic frame the verb *meet* can and must be inserted: *meet* is inserted in front of an NP. The verbs are characterized on the basis of the frames in which they occur. *Dither*, for instance, does not take any complement:

17 dither: V, [———]

The frames that identify subcategories of verbs are called **subcategorization frames**. We say that *meet* **subcategorizes for** or **selects** an NP.

3.2 Argument Structure and Thematic Structure

All we have done so far is classify verbs according to whether they require any VP-internal NP. We have not really attempted to explain anything. On the contrary, we have implied that the subcategorization frame of a verb, i.e.

whether it is transitive or intransitive, etc. is an unexplained **primitive** property of the grammer, i.e. a property which does not follow from anything else. However, this seems intuitively wrong. Whether a verb is transitive or not is not a matter of mere chance; it follows from the type of action or state expressed by the verb, from its meaning.

A verb like *imitate* expresses an activity that involves two participants: the active participant, the person who imitates, and the passive participant, the person or thing that is imitated. In Government and Binding Theory this intuitive idea of 'participants in an activity' has been formalized on the basis of the approach commonly adopted in logic. In this section we first look briefly at the logical system of representation, then we apply it to language in terms of the general notion of argument structure and of the more refined notion of thematic structure.

3.2.1 ARGUMENT STRUCTURE IN LOGIC

Logicians have long been concerned with formulating representations for the semantic structure of sentences, or more correctly propositions.[7] In the notation of formal logic, (18a) is assigned the representation (18b):

18a Maigret imitates Poirot.
18b A (m,p)
     where A = 'imitate', m = 'Maigret' and p = 'Poirot'.

(18a) contains the NPs *Maigret* and *Poirot*, two referring expressions, i.e. expressions which serve to pick out an entity, a person, a thing, from those things we are talking about, the universe of discourse. It also contains a predicate *imitate*. The predicate does not refer to a person or thing but rather defines some relation between the referring expressions. In the logical notation in (18b) we see that the **predicate** 'imitate' takes two **arguments**, represented by m (for Maigret) and p (for Poirot). Predicates that require two arguments are **two-place** predicates. The transitive verbs of traditional syntax correspond approximately to the two-place predicates of logic. The arguments of a predicate are realized by noun phrases in our example: in (18a) the subject NP is one argument and the object NP is the second argument of the verb *imitate*.

Intransitive verbs correspond to **one-place** predicates: they take only one argument.

---

[7] For an introduction to logic written specifically for the linguist see Allwood et al. (1977).

19a   Maigret stumbled.
19b   S (m)

   where S = 'stumble' and m = 'Maigret'.

3.2.2   ARGUMENT STRUCTURE IN NATURAL LANGUAGE

Using the basic idea of formal logic outlined above, we can say that every predicate has its argument structure,[8] i.e. it is specified for the number of arguments it requires. The arguments are the participants minimally involved in the activity or state expressed by the predicate.

We could use a metaphor to summarize this: predicates are like the script of a play. In a script a number of roles are defined and will have to be assigned to actors. The arguments of a predicate are like the roles defined by the script of a play. For an adequate performance of the play, each role must be assigned to an actor. It will not do either to miss out on a part in the play or to have actors on the stage who have no part to play. Adjuncts might be compared to the parts in the script which are not central to the play.

We first discuss the argument structure of verbs and its relation to subcategorization frames. Then we also turn briefly to the argument structure of adjectives, nouns and prepositions.

The argument structure of the verb determines which elements of the sentence are obligatory. If a verb expresses an activity involving two arguments, there will have to be at least two constituents in the sentence to enable these arguments to be expressed. This conceptually-defined argument structure can partly replace the classification of verbs in terms of either transitivity labels or subcategorization frames described above. If a speaker knows the meaning of the verb *meet*, in other words if he knows what activity is expressed, he will also know how many participants are involved and hence how many arguments the verb takes. 'Meet' involves two participants, and hence will be expected to take two arguments. If one argument is realized as the subject of the sentence (cf. section 6 for discussion), it follows that *meet* will select one VP-internal complement.

This does not mean that we can conclude that the verb *meet* necessarily subcategorizes for an NP. After all, the arguments might have been realized by categories other than NP.[9] The argument structure of the verb predicts the number of constituents needed but not necessarily their type. Let us assume for the moment that the type of constituent which realizes the argument must be lexically encoded. We can improve the lexical representation of verbs by

---

[8]   For a more careful statement see section 5.3 where we discuss the difference between auxiliaries and main verbs.

[9]   We return to this point in sections 5.1 and 7.1.

specifying their argument structure, which is derived from their meaning, and the specification of the realization of the arguments. This notation replaces the labels transitive, intransitive and ditransitive, or the subcategorization frames illustrated in (14) and (16)–(17) respectively.[10] We shall represent the arguments the verb takes by arabic numerals.

20a *meet*:	verb;	1	2	
		NP	NP	
20b *imitate*:	verb;	1	2	
		NP	NP	
20c *reconstruct*:	verb;	1	2	
		NP	NP	
20d *abandon*:	verb;	1	2	
		NP	NP	
20e *give*:	verb;	1	2	3
		NP	NP	NP
		NP	PP	NP[11]
20f *dither*:	verb;	1		
		NP		
20g *smile*:	verb;	1		
		NP		

Recall that in addition to the arguments of the verb, sentences may also contain adjuncts, constituents providing additional information, for instance with respect to manner, place, time, etc.

[10] There is an important distinction between subcategorization frames and argument structure. Subcategorization frames only specify the complements of the verb, i.e. the constituents that are obligatory inside the VP. The subject NP need not be mentioned in the subcategorization frame because all verbs have subjects, hence the property of having a subject does not create a subcategory of V, whereas the presence of objects does.

The argument structure lists all the arguments: it also includes the subject argument which is realized outside the VP. The thematic structure of the verb (see section 3.2.3) also lists *all* the arguments.

[11] *Give* allows for two types of realizations of its arguments:

(i)   I gave Bill the money.
(ii) I gave the money to Bill.

The representation in (20e) in the text serves to indicate that the second argument of *give* is either realized as an NP (i) or as a PP (ii). As (ii) and (iii) show, a PP must follow the VP-internal NP. We turn to the relative order of VP-internal constituents in chapter 3.

(iii) *I gave to Bill the money.

In some cases it is less easy to determine the argument structure of predicates. Consider the following pairs of sentences:

21a Hercule bought Jane a detective story.
21b Hercule bought a detective story.

(21a) contains the verb *buy* with apparently three arguments. The argument *Jane* can be omitted, but as a result the meaning of the sentence changes subtly: in the unmarked context (21b) will be taken to mean that Hercule bought the detective story for himself. The action expressed in (21b) still implicitly involves someone for whom the book is bought. (21b) seems to contain an unexpressed or **implicit argument**. We shall encode the fact that some arguments may be left implicit by putting them in parentheses.

22 *Buy:* verb;   1   (2)   3
                   NP NP   NP

So far we have only illustrated the argument structure of verbs. Other lexical categories too have an argument structure. Consider (23):

23a Poirot is restless.
23b Jeeves is envious of Bertie.
23c Jeeves envies Bertie.

In (23a) the predicate *restless*, an adjective, takes one argument. *Restless* is a one-place predicate. The adjective *envious* in (23b) takes two arguments analogously to the verb *envy* in (23c), which is semantically and morphologically closely related to the adjective. (23b) and (23c) are near-paraphrases. The respective arguments of the verb *envy* in (23c) are realized by the two NPs *Jeeves* and *Bertie*. The arguments of *envious* are realized by an NP and by a PP headed by *of*. At this point we merely note that the second argument of the adjective cannot be realized by a straight NP but that it requires the presence of the preposition *of*. The reason why this should be so is treated in chapter 3.

23d *Jeeves is envious Bertie.

We cannot freely add new referring expressions to the sentences in (23):

24   *Poirot is restless of the case.

Unlike verbal arguments, the arguments of adjectives can often be left implicit:

25a *Poirot envies.
25b Poirot is envious.

(25b) will be understood as meaning 'Poirot is envious of someone.' We shall again encode the argument structure of adjectives in the lexical information:

26a *envious*: adjective;   1   (2)
                            NP   PP
26b *restless*: adjective;   1
                            NP

  The argument structure of lexical items is not always uniquely fixed. Take for instance the adjective *conscious* in the following examples:

27a Miss Marple is conscious of the problem.
27b Sir Galahad is conscious.

We distinguish two argument structures for the adjective *conscious. Conscious* is either a two-place predicate (27a) or a one-place predicate (27b). It would not do to say that the second argument of *conscious* is left implicit in (27b) in the way that we argued that the second argument of *envious* in (25b) was implicit. In (25b) the adjective *envious* has the same meaning as in (23b), whereas there is a semantic difference between (27a) and (27b). In (27a) *be conscious* is near-synonymous with *know, be aware*. In (27b) it means 'not be in coma'. Depending on the meaning of the predicate we assume that a different argument structure is associated with it:

28a *conscious$_1$*: adjective;   1   2
                                  NP   PP
28b *conscious$_2$*: adjective;   1
                                  NP

*Conscious*₁ will be parallel to *know* or *aware*:

29a *know*: verb;   1   2
                            NP   NP
29b *aware*: adjective;   1   2
                            NP   PP

Let us turn to nouns. Consider the following groups of examples:

30a Poirot will analyse the data.
30b *Poirot will analyse.
30c *There will analyse the data.

31a Poirot's analysis of the data was superfluous.
31b The analysis of the data was superfluous.
31c The analysis was superfluous.

In (30) the verb *analyse* requires two arguments. The noun *analysis* is semantically and morphologically related to the verb *analyse* and on the basis of (31a) we assume it has the same argument structure.

32a *analyse*: verb;   1   2
                             NP   NP
32b *analysis*: noun;   (1) (2)
                             NP   PP

The two arguments of *analysis* are realized overtly in (31a); in (31b) the agent of the activity is left unexpressed and in (31c) both arguments are unexpressed. It is a typical property of nouns that both their arguments may be unrealized.

  Prepositions too can be argued to have argument structure. The preposition *in*, for instance, will have two arguments; the preposition *between* will have three:

33a John is in London.
33b *in*: preposition;   1   2
                            NP   NP
33c Florence is between Milan and Rome.
33d *between*: preposition;   1   2   3
                               NP   NP   NP

3.2.3 THETA THEORY

Let us consider the argument structure of the verb *kill*.

34a Maigret killed Poirot.
34b *kill*: verb; 1 2
                    NP NP

In (34a), the two argument-NPs *Maigret* and *Poirot* are intuitively felt to stand in different semantic relationships with the verb. The argument-NP *Maigret* in the subject position refers to the entity that is the **AGENT** of the activity of killing. The argument NP *Poirot*, the direct object, expresses the **PATIENT** of the activity. We used the metaphor of the script of a play when discussing argument structure of predicates. A script of a play defines not only the number of parts to be assigned, hence the number of actors involved, but also what characters are involved, it specifies which roles these actors have to play. The more specific semantic relationships between the verb and its respective arguments may be compared with the identification of the characters in a play script.

In the literature the more specific semantic relationships between verbs and their arguments are referred to in terms of **thematic roles** or **theta roles** (θ-**roles**) for short. We say that the verb *kill* takes two arguments to which it assigns a theta role: it assigns the role **AGENT** to the subject argument of the sentence, and the role **PATIENT** to the object argument. The verb **theta-marks** its arguments. Predicates in general have a **thematic structure**. The component of the grammar that regulates the assignment of thematic roles is called **theta theory**.

Although many linguists agree on the importance of thematic structure for certain syntactic processes, the theory of thematic roles is still very sketchy. For example, at the present stage of the theory there is no agreement about how many such specific thematic roles there are and what their labels are. Some types are quite generally distinguished. We discuss them informally here.

35a AGENT/ACTOR: the one who intentionally initiates the action expressed by the predicate.
35b PATIENT: the person or thing undergoing the action expressed by the predicate.
35c THEME: the person or thing moved by the action expressed by the predicate.
35d EXPERIENCER: the entity that experiences some (psychological) state expressed by the predicate.

35e BENEFACTIVE/BENEFICIARY: the entity that benefits from the action expressed by the predicate.

35f GOAL: the entity towards which the activity expressed by the predicate is directed.

35g SOURCE: the entity from which something is moved as a result of the activity expressed by the predicate.

35h LOCATION: the place in which the action or state expressed by the predicate is situated.

The inventory above is very tentative. Other authors amalgamate the roles PATIENT and THEME under the one role of THEME.

35i THEME$_2$: the entity affected by the action or state expressed by the predicate.

We shall usually use the term THEME in this second interpretation.
   The thematic roles are illustrated in (36):

36a Galahad gave the detective story to Jane
     ACTOR   THEME   BENEFACTIVE/GOAL
36b Constance rolled the ball towards Poirot
     ACTOR   THEME   GOAL
36c The ball rolled towards the pigsty.
     THEME   GOAL
36d Emsworth sent the parcel to the aged relative.
     ACTOR   THEME   BENEFACTIVE/GOAL
36e Madame Maigret had been cold all day.
     EXPERIENCER
36f Madame Maigret was afraid.
     EXPERIENCER
36g Poirot bought the book from Maigret.
     ACTOR   THEME SOURCE
36h Maigret is in London.
     THEME LOCATION

   The identification of thematic roles is not always easy, as the reader can verify for himself. However, intuitively the idea should be clear, and we shall be drawing on this rather intuitive approach to theta theory in subsequent discussion.

The information as to the semantic relationship between the predicate and its arguments is part of the lexical knowledge of the native speaker and should hence also be recorded in the lexicon. Rather than merely specifying the number of arguments of a predicate, one may envisage a representation which specifies the type of semantic roles of these arguments. In Government and Binding Theory this is represented by means of a **thematic grid**, or **theta grid**, which is part of the lexical entry of the predicate. *Kill* would be given the lexical representation in (37a):

37a *kill*: verb

AGENT	PATIENT

(37a) specifies that *kill* **assigns** two thematic roles (AGENT and PATIENT). We deduce that the verb is a two-place predicate, which requires two arguments to which these roles can be assigned. Some linguists propose that the syntactic category realizing the thematic role should also be specified in the theta grid of a predicate (cf. section 7.1 for discussion).

37b *kill*: verb

AGENT NP	PATIENT NP

Consider some examples:

38a Maigret killed the burglar.
38b *Maigret killed.
38c *Maigret killed the burglar the cellar.

We see that two arguments and no more than two are needed. In (38b) the absence of the second NP renders the sentence ungrammatical: the second theta role cannot be assigned. In (38c), conversely, one extra NP is added to the sentence. This NP cannot be assigned a thematic role because *kill* only assigns two roles, which are already assigned to the subject-NP and to the object-NP respectively. In (38d) we have inserted the preposition *in*. The sentence is grammatical: the preposition *in* assigns the thematic role of LOCATION to the NP *the cellar*.

38d Maigret killed the burglar in the cellar.

One criterion for judging whether a sentence is grammatical is that the thematic roles associated with its predicate(s) must be assigned to arguments, these arguments must be structurally realized. Conversely, the referring NPs in the sentence must bear some semantic relation to a predicate. This semantic relation can be established via the assignment of thematic roles.

Each syntactic representation of a sentence is scanned for the predicate(s) it contains. Each predicate is tested with respect to its argument structure. Its arguments must be realized. More specifically the predicate is tested for its thematic roles: each role must be assigned to an argument.

Let us take as an example a sentence containing the predicate *kill*. *Kill* assigns the thematic roles of AGENT and PATIENT, hence it requires two arguments. When the theta roles can be assigned to arguments we say that they are **saturated** and we mark this by checking off the theta role in the thematic grid of the predicate. In order to identify the assignment of the respective thematic roles to the corresponding arguments, NPs are identified by means of an index, a subscript:

39a Maigret$_i$ killed the burglar$_j$.
39b *Maigret$_i$ killed.
39c *Maigret$_i$ killed the burglar$_j$ the cellar$_k$.

We shall not discuss the subscripting convention here. We hope that the intuitive idea is clear: an NP refers to an individual or an object and is identified by the referential index. Two NPs with the same index are said to be **co-indexed:** they are interpreted as referring to the same entity.[12]

40a Maigret$_i$ said that he$_i$ was ill.
40b Maigret$_i$ hurt himself$_i$.

[12] We return to a more detailed discussion of co-indexation in chapter 4.

In order to show how the theta roles of a predicate are assigned we enter the index of the argument to which the thematic role is assigned in the appropriate slot in the theta grid. For (39a) the saturation of the thematic roles can be represented as in (41):

41   *kill*:   verb

AGENT NP	PATIENT NP
i	j

If we try to do the same for (39b) we see that one of the slots in the thematic grid will remain unfilled: one thematic role is not assigned. Conversely, in (39c) there is one referential index which cannot be entered on the grid, hence cannot be assigned a thematic role.

42a   *kill*:   verb

AGENT NP	PATIENT NP
i	?

42b   *kill*:   verb

AGENT NP	PATIENT NP	adjunct
i	j	k?

In (42a) corresponding to (39b) the thematic role of PATIENT is not assigned or not saturated. In (42b), corresponding to (39c), the argument NP *the cellar* with the referential index *k* fails to be assigned a thematic role.

The requirement that each thematic role of a predicate must be assigned and that there must be no NPs that lack a thematic role is summed up in the **theta criterion**:

43   Theta criterion
43a Each argument is assigned one and only one theta role.
43b Each theta role is assigned to one and only one argument.

So far we have only discussed NP arguments. But other constituents may also be arguments: consider, for instance, (44a) and (44b):

44a The police announced the news.
44b The police announced that the pig has been stolen.

In (44a) *announce* is associated with two arguments, which will be assigned their thematic roles. The role AGENT is assigned to *the police*; THEME to *the news*. In (44b) the THEME role is assigned to a subordinate clause: *that the pig has been stolen*. Clauses too can thus be arguments of the predicate. We return to the issue in more detail in section 5.1.

Given the wide diversity among authors on the labelling of thematic roles and their definitions it would be a difficult enterprise to fix the types of roles and their number. Even if we are unable to pin down the exact nature of the different roles involved we are usually quite clear as to how many arguments a predicate requires in a given reading. Hence, instead of specifying the exact type of thematic role for each predicate, we shall often merely list the number of arguments, identifying their roles by numbers rather than by role labels. Thus for the verb *kill* we shall use the following lexical representation, unless we need to refer explicitly to the thematic label.

45   *kill*:   verb

1 NP	2 NP

The numerals 1 and 2 represent the thematic roles assigned by the verb whose labels need not concern us.

Recent research[13] suggests that it might not be necessary or desirable to refer to the thematic labels in the syntax, and that indeed the representation in (45)

---

[13] See Belletti and Rizzi (1988). This will not, however, be accessible to the novice.

is the one we need. We do not go into that discussion here and we refer the reader to the literature.

4   The Projection Principle

Let us sum up what we have done so far. We have seen that the lexical items which are the ultimate constituents of a sentence play an important part in its syntactic representation.

Section 2 shows that the lexical category of the head of a phrase determines the category of the phrase. Secondly, we have seen in section 3 that the thematic structure of a predicate, encoded in the theta grid, will determine the minimal components of the sentence. This idea that lexical information to a large extent determines syntactic structure is summed up in the projection principle:

46   **Projection principle**
 Lexical information is syntactically represented.

The projection principle will play an important role throughout this book.

5   The Assignment of Thematic Roles

In this section we look at the assignment of thematic roles in the syntax. We focus on three areas: section 5.1 discusses clausal arguments; section 5.2 discusses expletive pronouns, and section 5.3 considers the difference between lexical verbs, or main verbs, and auxiliaries.

5.1   *Clausal Arguments*

We have seen that the obligatory constituents of a sentence are determined by the semantic properties of the predicates (verbs, adjectives) and we have mainly discussed examples in which NP-arguments were involved. Sentences too may be arguments of a predicate.

47a Miss Marple has announced the news.
47b Miss Marple has announced that Poirot has left.

In (47a) the verb *announce* takes two arguments, realized by the NPs *Miss Marple* and *the news* respectively. In (47b) the arguments are realized by an NP and by the clause [*that Poirot has left*]. Consider also the following examples:

48a The robbery surprised all the inhabitants of Blandings.
48b [That the pig was stolen] surprised all the inhabitants of Blandings.

49a Jeeves' decision is very unfortunate.
49b [That Jeeves should be leaving] is very unfortunate.

50a Poirot asked three questions.
50b Poirot asked [whether anyone had seen the pig].

51a Maigret believes the story about the burglary.
51b Maigret believes [that the taxi driver is lying].

52a Constance is aware of the problem.
52b Constance is aware [that the pig is in danger].

The verb *surprise* takes two arguments. In (48a) both arguments are realized by NPs; in (48b) one argument is realized by a clause. Similarly, in (49a) the one argument of the adjective *unfortunate* is realized by an NP and in (49b) it is realized by a clause. In (50) and (51) we find further alternations between NPs and clauses as realizations of arguments. In (52) one of the arguments of the adjective *aware* is realized by an NP contained in a PP in (a) and by a clause in (b).

We conclude that the theta grid of predicates will not always specify a unique category to which a theta role can be assigned but will allow for a choice. We do not go into this property in any detail here.

Let us consider clausal arguments a little more closely:

53a [That Galahad had left] is very surprising.
53b [For Galahad to have left] is very surprising.

54a Maigret$_i$ believes [this story]$_j$.
54b Maigret$_i$ believes [that the taxi driver is innocent]$_j$.
54c Maigret$_i$ believes [the taxi driver to be innocent]$_j$.
54d Maigret$_i$ believes [the taxi driver innocent]$_j$.

In (53) we see that the adjective *surprising* takes one argument, to which it assigns a thematic role. The argument is realized by a **finite** clause in (53a): the verb *had* is finite, it is inflected for the past tense and the clause is introduced by the **complementizer** *that*. In (53b) the argument of the main predicate is realized by a non-finite clause: *have* is in the infinitive and the sentence is introduced by the complementizer *for*. We return to the general principles of sentence structure in chapter 2.[14]

In (54a) both arguments of *believe* are realized by NPs. In (54b) one of the arguments of *believe* is realized by a finite clause. As the bracketing indicates, the corresponding argument is realized by a non-finite clause in (54c).

The bracketing in (54c) is meant to show that we consider *the taxi driver* to form a constituent with *to be innocent*. The justification for this analysis is essentially one of analogy. If we compare the sentences (54b) and (54c) we see that they are very similar in meaning. In (54b) the verb takes two arguments: one argument which is realized by the subject NP, and one argument which is realized by a sentence. On the basis of examples like (54a) and (54b) we deduce that the lexical entry of *believe* has the following theta grid:

55   *believe*:   verb

1 NP	2 NP/S

In (54a) the arguments are saturated as in (56), where *j* is the index of an NP. In (54b), similarly, the saturation of the arguments can be represented as in (56), with *j* now seen as the index of a subordinate clause.

[14] Koster (1978b) provides arguments that what looks like a clausal subject is not a clause in the subject position. We refer the reader to Koster's own work. However, the article will not be readable until we have worked through chapter 7.

56   *believe*:   verb

1 NP	2 NP/S
i	j

Given the close similarity in meaning between (54b) and (54c), the minimal assumption is that the verb *believe* in (54c) is the same as that in (54b) and has the same theta grid. While in (54b) the second argument is associated with a finite clause, in (54c), the second argument is associated with a non-finite clause.[15] Again the theta roles in (54c) are saturated as in (56), with *j* standing for a non-finite clause.

(54d) is also very close in meaning to (54b) and (54c), so we postulate that the verb *believe* is unaltered and has the theta grid in (55). Given this assumption, we need to assign to (54d) a structure that allows the saturation of the argument-roles 1 and 2. The bracketing in (54d) will do that adequately.

It is not immediately obvious how to label the structure [*the taxi driver innocent*]. In the traditional literature on parsing, the term 'verbless clause' is sometimes used. This term serves to indicate that we have a constituent which has a propositional meaning, i.e. the same sort of meaning as a full clausal structure has, but it lacks any verb forms. In (54d) the constituent [*the taxi driver innocent*] corresponds to the sentence [*the taxi driver to be innocent*] in (54c). In both sentences the NP *the taxi driver* is the subject of the predicate expressed by the AP *innocent*. In the Government–Binding literature, constituents such as [*the taxi driver innocent*] are called **small clauses**. We return to their structure throughout the book.

Non-finite clauses and small clauses are not normally[16] found as independent clauses: they can only be subordinate to some other main predicate. The italicised constituents in (57) are all small clauses:

---

[15] Note, however, that in this particular example, the non-finite clause cannot be introduced by the complementizer *for*. We shall return to this issue in chapters 2 and 3.

[16] Small clauses seem to be in frequent use in certain registers, such as informal notes or telegrams (i) or newspaper headlines (ii):

(i)   Mother in hospital.
(ii)   Hijackers under arrest.

Register-specific syntactic properties have not often been studied in the generative framework (see Haegeman, 1987, 1990; and Massam and Roberge, 1989).
We also find small clauses in colloquial expressions such as:

(iii)   What? Me angry?

57a I consider *John a real idiot.*
57b The chief inspector wants *Maigret in his office.*
57c Emsworth got *Galahad in trouble.*

It is evident that the small clauses are of different types. In (57a) the small clause consists of an NP *John* and a second NP *a real idiot.* The first NP acts as a subject to the second one. In (57b) and (57c) the small clause is composed of an NP and a PP, where the NP is the subject with respect to the PP predicate.[17] That the italicized strings in (57) are constituents is supported by the fact that other material associated with the main verb of the sentence cannot occur internally to what we have called the small clause:

58 *The chief inspector wants [Maigret [very much] in his office].

In (58) the degree adjunct *very much*, which modifies the verb *want*, cannot intervene between the subject and the PP predicate of the small clause.

5.2 Expletives

Section 5.1 shows that not all arguments of a predicate are necessarily realized as NPs. In this section we shall see that the reverse also holds: some NPs in the subject position of the sentence are not assigned a thematic role, hence are not arguments.

5.2.1 *IT* AND EXTRAPOSITION

The obligatory presence of certain constituents in a sentence can be accounted for in terms of the argument structure of the predicate of a sentence. Let us now extend our analysis to some further data:

59a The burglary surprised Jeeves.
59b That the pig had been stolen surprised Jeeves.
59c It surprised Jeeves that the pig had been stolen.

---

[17] For a discussion and further motivation of the analysis of small clauses, see Stowell (1983). However, this work will only become accessible once chapter 8 has been covered.

From (59a) and (59b) we deduce that *surprise* takes two arguments. Neither of these can be omitted:

60a *The burglary surprised.
60b *Surprised Jeeves.
60c *That the pig had been stolen surprised.

Surprise will be associated with the thematic grid (61):

61   *surprise*:   verb

1	2
NP/S	NP

We cannot insert another NP in these sentences since this would not be able to be assigned argument status as it would not receive a theta role from *surprise*.

62a *The burglary surprised Jeeves *it*.
62b *That the pig had been stolen surprised Jeeves *it*.

In (62a) or (62b) the NP *it* cannot be assigned a thematic role and thus the sentence violates the theta criterion (43). The theta criterion specifies that theta roles are assigned uniquely. Hence one could not, for instance, propose that in (62a) theta role 1 is assigned both to the subject NP *the burglary* and to the NP *it*.

Now let us look at (59c) repeated here as (63a):

63a It surprised Jeeves that the pig had been stolen.

(63a) is a paraphrase of (59b). We deduce that *surprise* in (63a) has the theta grid given in (61) with two theta roles to be associated with two arguments. How are these arguments realized? If we capitalize on the equivalence between (63a) and (59b) then the easiest thing would be to say that in both (59b) and (63a) one theta role, say 1, is assigned to the clause [*that the pig had been stolen*] and the other one, 2, to *Jeeves*. This hypothesis leaves us with the

NP-constituent *it* in the subject position of (63a) unaccounted for. This NP is not optional:

63b   *Surprised Jeeves that the pig had been stolen.

On the other hand, *it* cannot be assigned a thematic role since *surprise* only assigns two thematic roles already saturated as described above.

One element in the discussion is that the choice of a filler for the subject position in (63a) is very limited: indeed no other NP (pronominal or not) can fill the position:

64a   *This* surprised Jeeves that the pig had been stolen.
64b   *He* surprised Jeeves that the pig had been stolen.

Moreover it is not possible to question the element *it* in (63a):

64c   *What* surprised Jeeves that the pig had been stolen?

In fact, the pronoun *it* in (63a) contributes nothing to the meaning of the sentence, (63a) being a paraphrase of (59b). *It* is not a referring expression: it does not refer to an entity in the world, a person or an object; it cannot be questioned.

On the basis of these observations we formulate the hypothesis that *it* plays no role in the semantic make-up of the sentence and that its presence is required in (63a) simply for some structural reason. The relevant explanation for the presence of *it* in the subject position in (63a) will be shown to be that English sentences must have an overt subject (see section 6 and chapter 2 for more discussion). We propose that the pronoun *it* in (63a) acts as a mere slot-filler, a dummy pronoun without semantic contribution to the sentence; it is a place-holder for the otherwise unfilled subject position.

In the literature such a dummy pronoun is often called an **expletive** pronoun. The term **pleonastic** *it* is also used. Expletives are elements in NP positions which are not arguments and to which no theta role is assigned. Note that, unlike adjuncts, expletives contribute nothing to the sentence meaning.

In an example like (63a) it is sometimes said that the sentential subject is **extraposed** and that it is **in construction with** an expletive. (65) contains some more examples of extraposition patterns. The extraposed clause and the expletive are italicized:

65a *It worries Maigret that Poirot should have left.*
65b *It is unfortunate that Poirot should have said that.*
65c *It is out of the question that Jeeves should be fired.*
65d *I consider it odd that Poirot should have left.*

The expletive *it* cannot just appear in any type of sentence. Consider for instance the following pair:

66a An announcement about the robbery worried Maigret.
66b *It worried Maigret an announcement about the robbery.

(66b) shows that the expletive *it* cannot become the place-holder for an extraposed NP.[18]

5.2.2 *THERE* AND EXISTENTIAL SENTENCES

Now let us turn to another sentence pattern which poses problems for our theory outlined so far.

67a Three pigs are escaping.
67b There are three pigs escaping.

In (67a) the predicate 'escape' has one argument, realized by the NP *three pigs*. In (67b) the sentence contains one more element: the pronominal *there*, which occupies the subject position. First note that *there* is not an adjunct of place. In (67b) *there* cannot be questioned like other place adjuncts by means of *where*:

68a I saw Bill there last week.
      Where did you see Bill last week?
      There.
68b *Where are three pigs escaping? There.

Also, unlike the place adjunct, *there* in declarative (67b) cannot be omitted freely:

---

[18] A good survey of the literature on extraposition can be found in Williams (1980). For different views see also Bennis (1986), Grange and Haegeman (1989) and Postal and Pullum (1988).

69a I saw Bill last week.
69b *Are three pigs escaping.

But *there* does not really contribute anything to the meaning of (67b), which has the same meaning as (67a). Again the data suggest that *there* is required for structural reasons: it fills up the subject position. As was the case with the pronominal *it* discussed before, we call *there* an expletive. In contrast with *it*, *there* is used to replace NP-subjects which have been moved to the right in the sentence, and it cannot replace clausal subjects:

69c *There surprised Jeeves [that the pig had been stolen].

The construction with *there* has many intriguing properties. For instance the *there*-construction is only allowed if the moved subject NP is indefinite. There are also heavy restrictions on the type of verb that can occur in this construction. Transitive verbs, for instance, are disallowed.[19]

70a *There are the three pigs escaping.
70b *There saw three children the pigs.

5.2.3 CONCLUSION

We have seen that there are two pronouns in English, *it* and *there*, that can be used without being assigned a thematic role. They are expletives filling the subject position for structural reasons. We turn to those structural reasons presently.

Expletives always turn up in the subject position of the sentence, i.e. the NP position for which the verb does not subcategorize. Indeed the theory outlined so far predicts that expletives will never turn up in subcategorized positions. Expletives are elements lacking a theta role. The positions a verb subcategorizes for are determined by the thematic structure of the verb. Whenever a verb requires a complement NP, this is because the verb has a theta role to assign to the NP. Inserting an expletive NP in an object position would miss the point, because the expletive element would not be able to receive the theta role. In (71) we find a pronoun *it* as the object of *believe*, but this pronoun is not an

---

[19] For the discussion of the *there*-construction, see Belletti (1988), Milsark (1974, 1977) and Stowell (1978). These texts will be accessible after chapter 6 has been covered.

expletive: it is assigned a thematic role by the verb. In such examples *it* can substitute for other NPs:

71   Poirot believes it/this/this story/the announcement.

The prediction of the theory outlined is thus that expletives can only occur in NP positions that are not subcategorized for, i.e. the subject position of the sentence.[20]

5.3   Main Verbs and Auxiliaries

So far we have implied that all verbs assign thematic roles. However, it is well known that the class of verbs can be divided into two sets: (a) lexical verbs or main verbs like *eat, sleep, walk*, and (b) auxiliaries: *be, have, do*, and the modal auxiliaries *will, shall, can, may, must, ought*. All these elements are inflected for tense:[21]

72	*Verb*	*Present tense*		*Past tense*
a	*eat*	eat	eats	ate
b	*sleep*	sleep	sleeps	slept
c	*walk*	walk	walks	walked
d	*be*	am/are	is	was/were
e	*have*	have	has	had
f	*can*	can	can	could
g	*do*	do	does	did

Auxiliary verbs have some special properties distinguishing them from lexical verbs. In (73) and (74) we have paired sentences containing a lexical verb in (a) and an auxiliary in (b). The reader can check that auxiliaries and main verbs behave differently in negative and interrogative patterns:

73a   John eats chocolate.
    *John eatsn't chocolate.
    John doesn't eat chocolate.

[20]   See Postal and Pullum (1988) for a different view.
[21]   In the present tense, verbs and the auxiliaries *have* and *be* are also inflected for person and number. Modals are not inflected. For a history of the development of modals see Lightfoot (1979).

73b John has eaten chocolate.
John hasn't eaten chocolate.
*John doesn't have eaten chocolate.

74a John eats chocolate.
*Eats John chocolate?
Does John eat chocolate?
74b John has eaten chocolate.
Has John eaten chocolate?
*Does John have eaten chocolate?

The negation element *n't* follows the auxiliaries (cf. (73b)), whereas it must precede the lexical verb (cf. 73a)). In a *yes–no* question the auxiliary and the subject of the sentence are inverted (see chapter 2 for discussion). Lexical verbs do not invert with their subjects: in both negative sentences and in questions the auxiliary *do* is needed. Now let us consider the thematic structure of auxiliaries and main verbs.

75a Poirot accuses Maigret
75b Poirot has accused Maigret.
75c Poirot is accusing Maigret.
75d Poirot does not accuse Maigret.

In (75a) the assignment of the thematic roles of *accuse* is straightforward: one thematic role will be assigned to the NP *Poirot* and the other one to *Maigret*. In addition to the lexical verb *accuse*, (75b) contains the perfective auxiliary *have*. The sentence is grammatical, which must mean that all thematic roles of the predicate(s) are assigned and that all referring NPs in the sentence have a thematic role assigned to them. Given that there are just as many NPs present in (75b) as in (75a), we are led to conclude that the auxiliary *have*, though morphologically like a verb in that it is inflected for tense, person and number, does not assign any thematic roles of its own. If *have* did assign any thematic roles then we would expect (75b) to contain one or more NPs in addition to those in (75a), which would be assigned the thematic roles of the auxiliary. The same argument can be applied to the auxiliaries *be* in (75c) and *do* in (75d). We conclude that auxiliaries do not assign thematic roles.

A related problem appears in connection with the copula *be* in (76) (cf. example (54)).

76a Maigret$_i$ believes [that the taxi driver is innocent]$_j$

76b   Maigret$_i$ believes [the taxi driver to be innocent]$_j$
76c   Maigret$_i$ believes [the taxi driver innocent]$_j$

In (76) *believe* assigns one theta role to *Maigret* and it assigns the second one to the bracketed clausal constituents. We are concerned with the internal predicate argument structure of the clausal argument. In the discussion above we have argued that the finite complement clause in (76a), the non-finite one in (76b) and the small clause in (76c) all basically mean the same thing: in all of them the property *innocent* is ascribed to the referent of the NP *the taxi driver*. We have also seen that adjectives, like verbs, have an argument structure. Let us first turn to (76c). Inside the small clause *the taxi driver innocent* the NP *the taxi driver* must have been assigned a thematic role, by virtue of clause (43a) of the theta criterion. We deduce that the NP is assigned a thematic role by *innocent*. The adjective will have the thematic grid (77):

77   *innocent*:   adjective

In the small clause in (76c) the theta role is assigned to the NP *the taxi driver*. With respect to (76a) and (76b) *innocent* must also be able to assign its thematic role and by analogy with (76c) we assume that it assigns it to the NP *the taxi driver* and hence we conclude that the copula *be*, like auxiliaries, does not assign any thematic roles. Interestingly, the copula *be* also has the other syntactic properties of the auxiliaries:

78a   The taxi driver is innocent.
78b   The taxi driver isn't innocent.
78c   Is the taxi driver innocent?

The formal differences between main verbs on the one hand and auxiliaries and the copula *be* on the other are matched by a semantic property: neither auxiliaries nor the copula *be* assign thematic roles.[22]

---

[22] See Pollock (1989) for an explanation. This article is very advanced and should not be tackled until the whole of this book has been covered.

6 The Extended Projection Principle (EPP)

Our discussion reveals that sentence constituents may be required for two reasons.

In the first place, the argument structure and the theta grid of the predicate determine the minimal composition of the sentence. Sentence structure is thus partly lexically determined. This property of syntactic representations is summed up in the projection principle ((46), section 4).

Secondly, expletive elements are required to fill the subject position in certain constructions (section 5.2). The structural requirement which necessitates the insertion of expletives is that sentences must have subjects.[23] This requirement is not one that is specific to individual lexical items, but it is a general grammatical property of all sentences. In this respect the structural requirement that sentences have subjects is an addition to the projection principle. Not only must lexical properties of words be projected in the syntax, but in addition, regardless of their argument structure, sentences must have subjects. The latter requirement has come to be known as the **extended projection principle** (EPP) (79). The phrase structure rules of our grammar (cf. (2b)) will specify that every sentence has a subject. (We return to a discussion of phrase structure in chapter 2.)

79 **Extended projection principle**
    S $\longrightarrow$ NP – AUX – VP

Consider (80):

80a Maigret accused Poirot.
80b *Accused Poirot Maigret.

In both (80a) and (80b) the two arguments of *accuse* are realized by the NPs *Maigret* and *Poirot*. The ungrammaticality of (80b) follows from the extended projection principle (79): the subject position is not filled. Insertion of the expletive *there* is not possible because *there* cannot be associated with definite NPs and also it cannot be used with transitive verbs. Similarly, *it* cannot be inserted since this expletive cannot be in construction with an NP.

---

[23] In chapters 5–8 we shall see that the subject may be non-overt.

81a *There accused Maigret Poirot
81b *It accused Maigret Poirot.

7   Thematic Roles: Further Discussion

7.1   The Syntactic Realization of Theta Roles

Linguists do not agree about the extent to which the syntactic category with which a thematic role is associated must be signalled in the thematic grid. It has been noted, for instance that the role ACTOR is always realized as an NP. NP could be said to be the **canonical realization** of ACTOR. Research is in progress to determine whether such canonical realizations can be generalized and what type of exceptions arise. In our discussion we shall often omit the specification of the syntactic category to which a thematic role is assigned and use representations such as (82). This convention is adopted for convenience' sake and implies no decision with respect to the issue discussed here.

82   *kill*:   verb

1	2

7.2   The Subject Theta Role

With respect to the assignment of thematic roles we have treated arguments in the subject position in the same way as arguments in the object position. For instance in (83) we would have said that both the NP *Maigret* and the NP *the taxi driver* are assigned a theta role by the verb *accuse*.

83   Maigret accused the taxi driver.

Two related observations are often advanced in the literature for treating subject arguments as different from object arguments. On the one hand, the choice of the object affects the thematic role of the subject while the choice of the subject argument does not affect the role of the object, and on the other hand, there exist 'object idioms' with the subject as a free argument while there are no subject idioms with a free object.[24]

In (84) we see how the choice of the object may determine the theta role of the subject:

84a John broke a leg last week.
84b John broke a vase last week.

In both (84a) and (84b) the verb *break* takes an NP-complement. The choice of the complement determines the thematic role of the subject: while in (84b) *John* could be considered ACTOR, in (84a) this is not the case: John is the one who undergoes the event. Consider also (85). While in (85a) the literal meaning of the verb *kill* is intended, the other three examples are idioms with free subjects. The idiomatic interpretation of the sentence depends on the combination of the verb *kill* and its object.

85a kill an insect
85b kill a conversation
85c kill a bottle (i.e. empty it)
85d kill an audience (i.e. wow them)
(examples from Bresnan, 1982: 350).

The theta role assigned to the subject is assigned **compositionally**: it is determined by the semantics of the verb and other VP constituents. Roughly, the verb assigns an object role first, the resulting verb-argument complex will assign a theta role to the subject. The subject argument is as it were slotted in last.

If a predicate assigns a thematic role directly to some constituent we shall say that the predicate **theta-marks** the constituent **directly**. If the predicate theta-marks an argument compositionally we call this **indirect theta-marking**.

---

[24] A discussion of the grammatical functions in the Government and Binding framework is found in Marantz (1981). For a discussion of some problems raised by the approach, see Bresnan (1982).

As mentioned above there is no agreement as to whether the difference between the types of theta roles should be considered as syntactically relevant. However, most linguists agree that the thematic role assigned to the subject must somehow be set apart from the other thematic roles. One quite popular proposal due to Edwin Williams (1981)[25] is that the argument which must be realized in the subject position and hence will be theta-marked indirectly is singled out lexically. The lexical entry for the predicate signals explicitly which argument must be outside the VP. Given that this argument is projected onto an NP outside the VP, it is referred to as the **external argument** and conventionally the external argument is indicated in the thematic grid by underlining:

86   *accuse*:   verb

1	2

Theta roles assigned to internal arguments will be referred to as **internal** theta roles; that assigned (indirectly) to the external argument is often referred to as the **external** theta role. (Cf. chapter 6, sections 3 and 5 for further discussion.)

8   Summary

In this chapter we have considered the extent to which sentence structure is determined by lexical properties. As a basis for the formation of sentences we have adopted the projection principle:

[25] Williams (1981) shows the relevance of the distinction between external and internal theta role for the domain of morphology. See also exercise 6.

In chapter 6 (section 5) we shall see the importance of setting off internal theta roles from external ones. We shall also discuss an alternative approach to the status of the subject-NP.

1   **Projection principle**
Lexical information is syntactically represented.

The type of lexical information with which we have been mainly concerned in this chapter is the thematic structure of the predicate, i.e. the number and types of arguments which the predicate takes. The thematic structure associated with lexical items must be saturated in the syntax, as stated in the theta criterion:

2   **Theta criterion**
2a   Each argument is assigned one and only one theta role.
2b   Each theta role is assigned to one and only one argument.

The theta roles of a predicate are represented in a grid-format. The assignment of thematic roles is registered by means of referential indices which are associated with thematic roles.

Independently of the argument structure of the main predicate, it is a general property of sentences that they must have subjects. This property is stated in the extended projection principle (EPP):

3   **Extended projection principle**
    S $\longrightarrow$ NP – AUX – VP

In order to satisfy the EPP, so-called expletives may have to be inserted in the subject position of a sentence. Expletives are pronouns such as *it* and *there* in English which are not assigned a thematic role.

9   Exercises

Exercise 1

We have seen that lexical verbs are specified for the number and types of theta roles they assign: *work* assigns one thematic role (AGENT), *destroy* assigns two (AGENT, THEME) and *give* assigns three (AGENT, THEME, BENEFICIARY). Provide five more examples for each type of verb.

Exercise 2

Discuss the argument structure of the verbs in the following sentences:

1 Poirot promised Maigret the job last week.
2 Emsworth is walking the dogs.
3 That Poirot had left disappointed the crowd immensely.
4 The huge pig frightened the spectators.
5 I have received the books this morning.

Exercise 3

The following examples illustrate how arguments of predicates can be realized in different ways. Discuss the syntactic realization of the arguments for the examples.

1a I prefer very much that the students should leave first.
1b I prefer very much for the students to leave first.
1c I prefer the students out of the way.
1d I prefer linguistics to literature.
1e I prefer the students to leave first.

2a I want hot chocolate.
2b I want my coffee to be piping hot.
2c I want my coffee piping hot.
2d I want the students out of my office.

Exercise 4

Sentences 1–10 below are all grammatical. On the basis of the examples establish the theta grid for the main verb of each sentence:

1 Mary is eating an apple.
2 John is washing the dishes.
3 The baby is drinking a glass of whisky.
4 John has never met Mary.
5 The President is kissing his wife.
6 The professor is writing a book on syntax.
7 The new secretary pleases all the students.
8 This analysis leads us to an unexpected conclusion.

9   Poirot smokes a pipe.
10   Joan is shaving her legs.

It is not necessary to give the label for each role identified; the number of arguments is the most important property to establish.

Now consider the following examples. They are also all grammatical. What problems do they raise for your treatment of the examples 1–10?

11   The children are eating.
12   Mary is washing.
13   John drinks.
14   These two students have never met.
15   The professor and his wife were kissing.
16   My father writes.
17   Joan is easy to please.
18   This analysis led to quite unexpected conclusions.
19   Poirot is smoking.
20   John is shaving.

Exercise 5

From sentences 11–20 in exercise 4 we conclude that certain thematic roles can be implicit. In (a) below, for instance, *eat* has an understood object, which would correspond to the explicit object in (b):

a   The children are eating.
b   The children are eating lunch.

This is not a general property of transitive verbs, though:

c   The children are devouring their food.
d   *The children are devouring.

Consider the following paired examples. Again in variant (a) there seems to be one more argument present than in variant (b). Try to characterize the semantic relation between the two sentences. You are not asked to give a very technical discussion, but simply to provide a description of the difference and/or similarity between the examples:

1a   Mary is cooking dinner.
1b   Dinner is cooking.

2a Maigret opened the door.
2b The door opened.
3a Poirot does not grow artichokes.
3b The artichokes are not growing.
4a Maigret has arrested the criminal.
4b The criminal has been arrested.
5a Mary is eating too much cake.
5b Mary is overeating.
6a Poirot was smelling the envelope.
6b Your feet smell.
7a Maigret is washing his shirts.
7b These shirts wash well.
8a They are closing down the new cinema already.
8b The new cinema is closing down already.
9a Poirot is reading the announcement.
9b Poirot is reading.
10a The guard marched the prisoners round the square.
10b The prisoners marched round the square.

Provide a classification of the examples above according to the variation in their thematic structure.

Exercise 6

It is generally accepted that morphological processes may affect thematic structure.[26] Consider the following examples:

1a I understand his position.
1b His position is understandable.
2a This shirt is too wide.
2b He has widened the shirt.
3a They arrest the criminal.
3b The criminal has been arrested.
4a Their activities are not regular.
4b They are regularizing the activities.
5a He read the book.
5b He reread the book.

Discuss the impact, if any, of the affixation of *-able*, *-en*, *-ed*, *-ize*, and *re-* on the thematic structure of the stems to which they attach. For each

[26] Williams (1981) contains an important discussion about the interaction of morphology and thematic structure.

affix, provide five more examples of the affixation process and check whether your conclusion holds.

Exercise 7

The following text belongs to the **register** of instructional writing: it is a recipe. Consider the thematic structure of the verbs in the text and try to identify which syntactic properties characterize this register:

> Beat two eggs and leave for three minutes. Add milk and mix thoroughly. Cover with grated chocolate. Bake in a moderate oven for 20 minutes. Serve immediately.

The sentences below are other examples of the register of instructional writing. Do they pattern like those in the preceding text?

1   Cross now.
2   Shake well before using.
3   Open here.
4   Push.

As you can see it is typical of the register of instructional writing that complements of verbs can be left implicit. Consider the interpretation of the implicit objects in the preceding examples. Discuss what enables people using this register to leave the objects of verbs implicit and how the reader can interpret these sentences correctly.[27]

Exercise 8

Discuss the assignment of thematic roles and the problems, if any, raised for the theta criterion by the following examples:

1   John, I really don't like him.
2   Which detective will Lord Emsworth invite?
3   Which book do you think Poirot will read first?

[27] For discussion see Haegeman (1987) and Massam (1989). Both articles will be accessible after reading chapter 8.

4   Which assistant do you think will reveal the secrets?

5   The new assistant appears to have revealed the secrets.

6   Which articles did Poirot file without reading?

7   *Italian*
Ho   visto Maria.
have [1sg, pres] seen Maria
'I have seen Maria'.

8   *Spanish*
Lo vimos   a Juan.
him see [1pl, pres] to Juan
'We see Juan'.

9   *French*
Quel   livre a-t-il   acheté?
Which book has he bought?

10   Quel   livre Poirot a-t-il acheté?
which book Poirot has-he bought
'Which book has Poirot bought?'

Exercise 9

Although it is not always possible to define the nature of the thematic roles assigned by the verbs, the role of ACTOR/AGENT is one that is fairly well understood. In (i) below, for instance, the subject NP *Poirot* is assigned the AGENT role and in its passive variant (ii) AGENT is assigned to an NP inside a PP introduced by *by*:

1   Poirot bought the pigs.

2   The pigs were bought by Poirot.

There are certain adjuncts which seem to require the presence of an AGENT in the sentence:

3   Poirot bought the pigs deliberately.

4   Poirot bought the pigs to annoy his mother.

5   *Poirot liked England deliberately.

6   *Poirot liked England in order to annoy his mother.

Adjuncts such as *deliberately* and *in order to annoy his mother* cannot modify predicates such as *like*. This is because these adjuncts imply intentionality, a notion which is not easily compatible with involuntary activities or states such as 'liking'. Consider the following examples: what conclusions can you draw with respect to the thematic structure of the predicates in the sentences?[28]

1a The enemy sank the ship deliberately.
1b The ship was sunk by the enemy deliberately.
1c The ship was sunk deliberately.
1d The ship sank.
1e *The ship sank deliberately.

2a We sold the books to raise money.
2b These books will be sold by the schools to raise money.
2c These books will be sold to raise money.
2d These books sell well.
2e *These books sell well to raise money.

[28] For discussion see Hale and Keyser (1986, 1987) and Roberts (1987). These texts presuppose the contents of chapter 6.

2 Phrase Structure

Contents

Introduction and overview

Introduction and Overview

In chapter 1 we established that the lexical properties of words, the ultimate constituents of the sentence, determine to a large extent the composition and the structure of the sentence. In this chapter we shall be looking more closely at the structural properties of syntactic representations.

We shall discuss a theory of phrase structure, X-bar theory, which aims at bringing out the common properties of the different types of syntactic constituents such as NP, VP, etc. We shall see that the theory applies both to phrasal constituents and to clausal constituents.

In section 1 we give an overview of the basic notions of phrase structure which we have been assuming so far. In section 2 we develop X-bar theory on the basis of phrasal categories VP, NP, AP, PP. In section 3 we extend the application of X-bar theory to the clausal constituents S and S'. In section 4 we deal with the structural relation c-command and define the notion government in terms of c-command. In section 5 we introduce the binary branching hypothesis and its relevance for acquisition. In section 6 we discuss the idea that syntactic features rather than lexical categories are the syntactic primitives.

1 Syntactic Structure: Recapitulation

Consider (1a) with its tree diagram representation (1b):

1a Poirot will abandon the investigation.

1b

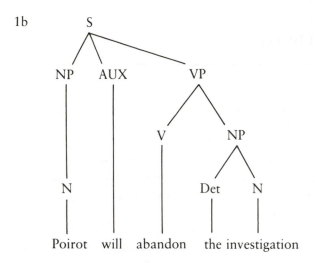

In (1a) the presence of the NPs *Poirot* and *the investigation* is required by the argument structure of the predicate *abandon*:

2   *abandon*: V

<u>1</u>	2

The presence of the subject NP is also required by the extended projection principle (chapter 1 (79)) which requires that sentences have subjects.

The syntactic categories of phrasal constituents such as VP, NP, etc. are also lexically determined: the VP is a constituent whose **head** is a V or which is **headed by** a V, NP is headed by an N, a PP is headed by a P and an AP is headed by an A. The different types of phrases are illustrated in (3), where the head of the phrase is italicized. For each phrasal category we provide a tentative phrase structure rule. The asterisk to the right of a constituent indicates that one or more such constituents are possible, parenthesized constituents are not always present. Obviously, the presence of a constituent may be required because of the argument structure of the head, as discussed in chapter 1.

3a VP $\longrightarrow$ V — (NP) — (PP*)
    abandon the investigation after lunch
    work in the garden
    leave his house
    return

3b NP $\longrightarrow$ (Det)—(AP*) — N — (PP*)
    Poirot
    the *investigation*
    the Belgian *detective*
    the *detective* with the funny accent

3c AP $\longrightarrow$ (Adv)—A — (PP*)
    interested
    very *interested*
    conscious of the problem
    entirely *aware* of the circumstances

3d PP $\longrightarrow$ (Adv)—P — NP
    in France
    immediately *after* the investigation
    on the Orient Express

When talking about tree diagrams it is useful to have a number of technical terms available to describe the relations between the elements in a tree. We shall briefly recapitulate the basic technical terminology which will be used throughout the book to describe structural relations.

First we can think of the vertical relations between the elements in a tree. We use the term *dominance* to characterize such relations.

4 **Dominance**
    Node A dominates node B iff A is higher up in the tree than B and if you can trace a line from A to B going only downwards.

In (1b) S dominates the NP *Poirot*, AUX, the VP, and indeed all other material inside the sentence. VP dominates the NP *the investigation*, but it does not dominate the NP *Poirot*, since it is not possible to trace a line from VP to the NP *Poirot* going only downwards.

It is sometimes useful to distinguish a more specific type of dominance. Consider the relationship between S and AUX, for example. S dominates AUX, and moreover, there is no intervening node between S and AUX: this is called **immediate dominance**. S also dominates the NP *the investigation* but it does not immediately dominate this NP.

We can also look at the tree diagram from a horizontal perspective and describe the left–right ordering of constituents in terms of **precedence**.

5   Precedence

Node A precedes node B iff A is to the left of B and A does not dominate B or B does not dominate A.

In (1b) AUX, for instance, precedes VP. VP does not precede AUX, since VP is to the right of AUX. Also, even though S is to the left of VP in our tree diagram, S does not precede VP because it dominates it.

Again we can distinguish precedence from **immediate precedence**: if a node A precedes a node B and there is no intervening node, then A immediately precedes B. AUX immediately precedes VP, the NP *Poirot* precedes the VP, but does not immediately precede it.[1]

In (1b) the NP node dominating *Poirot* is **non-branching**: there is only one line which starts at NP and goes downwards (in our example to N). The node S is **branching**, three lines originate from S and go downwards to NP, AUX and VP respectively. We return to a discussion of branching nodes in section 5.

Among the NP positions in a syntactic representation we distinguish those like the subject position or the object position which are occupied by arguments from those which are occupied by adjuncts. The former are called **A-positions**; the latter **A'-positions** (i.e. A-bar positions). We shall often need to refer to this distinction in later chapters.

Let us now focus on the structure of VP. VP immediately dominates V and NP. If we compare the tree diagram representation of syntactic structure with genealogical trees, then it is as if both V and NP are children of the same parent. Linguists refer to this relationship as one of **sisterhood**: V and the object NP are **sisters**. Similarly, we can say that VP is the **mother** of the NP *the investigation*.

The verb *abandon* has a close connection with its object, witness the fact that the object cannot be omitted. In languages with rich case systems the choice of verb may sometimes determine the morphological case of the following NP. In German, for instance, *helfen* ('help') takes a DATIVE complement while *sehen* ('see') takes an ACCUSATIVE:[2]

---

[1] It has been proposed that all relations in tree diagrams must be able to be described in terms of dominance and precedence relations. For some formal discussion, see Lasnik and Kupin (1977). Alternative proposals are found in Goodall (1987), Haegeman and van Riemsdijk (1986) and Zubizarreta (1985). These works are very advanced.

[2] We discuss the notion of case in chapter 3.

6a Ich helfe dem Mann.
   I help the-DATIVE man
6b Ich sehe den Mann.
   I see the-ACCUSATIVE man

Using terminology from traditional grammar we shall say that the verb **governs** the object, and more generally that the head of a phrase governs the complement. The element which governs is called the **governor**; the element that is governed is called the **governee**.

At this point we shall not try to give a very precise definition. Let us propose that government by a head is based on sisterhood.[3]

7 **Government** (1)
   A governs B if
   (i)   A is a governor;
   (ii) A and B are sisters.
   Governors are heads.

In (1b) *abandon*, the governor, is the head of the VP and the direct object, the governee, is its sister. V does not govern the subject NP *Poirot*: V is not a sister of the NP. If X is a head and it governs Y then X **head-governs** Y.[4] All the constituents governed by a node constitute the **governing domain** of that node. In our example VP is the governing domain of V.

In our discussion of external and internal arguments in chapter 1 (section 7.2), the question might have been raised why arguments of a verb should be realized inside the VP. One possible answer is that the verb can only assign an internal theta role to NPs or clauses that it governs. Hence an NP attached somewhere outside the governing domain of the verb would not be able to receive an internal theta role from the V.[5] When a V governs an element and assigns an internal theta role to it we say that it **theta-governs** this element. In (1b) the V *abandon* **theta-governs** the object *the investigation* though not the subject *Poirot*.

---

[3] Throughout the book we shall offer more and more refined definitions of government. In addition to government by a head, as discussed here, we shall also introduce government by a phrase in chapter 8.
[4] We return to the notion government in section 4 below.
[5] The assignment of theta roles will turn out to be more complex than is suggested in this section. The reader is referred to chapter 6.

2   The Structure of Phrases

In this section we examine the structure of the phrases, VP, NP, AP and PP. Our aim is to discover the common properties of these four phrase types. On the basis of our analysis we shall be able to replace the four phrase structure rules in (3) by one simplified and general rule. We shall start the discussion with the VP and then extend it to NP, AP and PP.

2.1   The Verb Phrase

2.1.1 LAYERED VPs

So far we have discussed phrases in terms of two components: the head, a lexical category, and the projection, a phrasal category. Phrasal categories are headed by lexical categories. Schematically, VPs, for example, are constituents with the following structure:

8a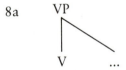

where...stands for non-head material in the VP, obligatory or optional. An alternative way of representing the structure of a phrase is by using the format of **rewrite rules** or **phrase structure rules**.

8b   VP ⟶ V – ...

Consider (9):

9   Miss Marple will [$_{VP}$ read the letters in the garden shed this afternoon].

Along the lines of the representation in (3a) sentence (9) will be represented as in (10):

10

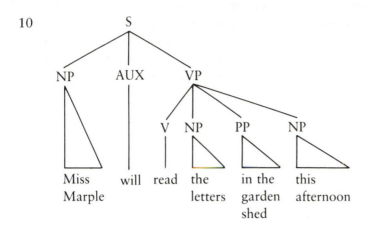

The structure of the VP in (10) is **flat**: there is no internal hierarchy between the constituents of V: all VP–internal constituents are treated as being on an equal footing. Such a flat structure might not be the best representation of the VP, however. Consider, for instance, the following examples, which are all intuitively felt to be related to (9):

11a Miss Marple will read the letters in the garden shed this afternoon and
     Hercule Poirot will do so too.
11b Miss Marple will read the letters in the garden shed this afternoon and
     Hercule Poirot will do so tonight.
11c Miss Marple will read the letters in the garden shed this afternoon and
     Hercule Poirot will do so in the garage tonight.

In (11), *do so* in the second conjunct substitutes for some part of the first conjunct. In (11a) *do so* substitutes for the entire VP *read the letters in the garden shed this afternoon*. In chapter 1 we have adopted the idea that substitution is structure-determined: only constituents can be substituted for by an element. From this point of view, the representation in (10) is unproblematic: *do so* replaces the entire VP, a constituent.

In (11b) *do so* substitutes for only part of the VP: *read the letters in the garden shed*, and in (11c) it picks up an even smaller part of the VP: *read the letters*. If we maintain the hypothesis that substitution is structure-determined, then it will be hard to reconcile the data in (11b) and (11c) with the representation in (10). On the basis of (10) substitutions affecting VP could be expected to affect either the top-node VP, i.e. the entire VP (as in (11a)), or each of the VP–internal constituents, that is to say V or NP or PP. But the structure does not allow for treating the strings *read the letters in the garden shed* or *read the letters* as constituents. There is no node which exhaustively dominates *read the letters*, for example. In order to maintain our hypothesis that substitution affects constituents only we need to redesign the tree diagram in (10) and elaborate the structure of its VP:

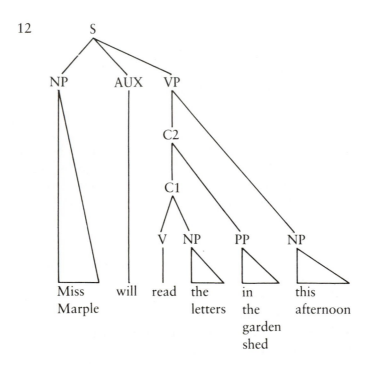

The VP in (12) has more internal structure than that in (10): it is hierarchically organized. The string *read the letters* is represented as a constituent, provisionally labelled C1 and can serve as a unit to be substituted for by *do so*. The same holds for *read the letters in the garden shed*, labelled C2. Unlike (10), (12) is compatible with the substitution data in (11).

We may wonder about the category of C1 and C2 in (12). Following our informal analysis above, we are tempted to say that, being headed by a V (*read*), they are projections of V, i.e. a type of VP. But on the other hand, they do not constitute the full VP or the **maximal VP** of the sentence. The projections of V, C1 and C2 are themselves dominated by verbal projections. C2 is dominated by VP and C1 is dominated by C2 and by VP. Projections of V that are dominated by more comprehensive projections of V are called **intermediate projections** of V. The highest projection of V, the node labelled

VP in our diagram, is the **maximal projection**. The maximal projection is not normally dominated by a projection of the same category.[6] The intermediate projections of V, are labelled **V-bar**, or **V'**.

13

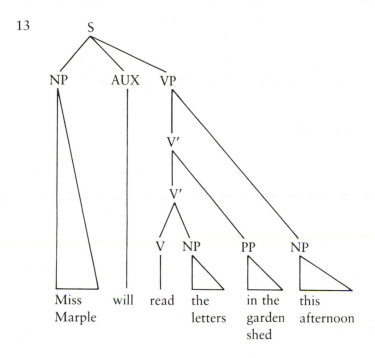

In (13) VP has a **layered** structure. There are different levels of projection. The direct object NP, *the letters*, is a complement of the verb, it is theta-governed by the verb. This NP combines with the head to form the lowest V', the first projection in (13). In the case of **do so** substitution we see that the minimal unit affected by substitution is the first projection of the type V'. *Do so* cannot simply replace V without the direct object:

14   *Miss Marple will read the letters in the garden shed this afternoon and Hercule Poirot will do so the diaries in the garage after dinner.

In (13) the verb projections that dominate the lowest V' are also labelled V'. The PP *in the garden shed* and the NP *this afternoon* are adjuncts; they combine with a V' to form another V'. Adjuncts are optional constituents and

---

[6] We return to the notion of maximal projection in chapters 7, 9 and 10.

they can be repeated: the level V′ is **recursive**. The node labelled VP in (13) is in fact another V′: it dominates V′ and an adjunct. (13) suggests that the maximal projection of V is thus the highest V′ which is not dominated by another V-projection. This, however, turns out to be inadequate. Consider (15):

15a   The detectives have all read the letters in the garden shed after lunch.
15b   All the detectives have read the letters in the garden shed after lunch.
15c   They have?
15d   *They have all?
15e   The policemen have all done so too.

In (15a) the VP is similar to that of our earlier examples, but it is preceded by the quantifier *all*. *All* relates to the subject NP *the detectives*: (15a) is closely related to (15b). (15c) is an example where the VP of the sentence is deleted. Interestingly, VP-deletion affects *all*, and *all* cannot be stranded, witness the ungrammaticality of (15d). We conclude that *all* is part of the VP. On the other hand, in (15e) *do so* substitutes for the string *read the letters in the garden shed this afternoon*, a V′. This means that *all* must be structurally independent from this V′. *All*, the quantifier, is not an adjunct of time or place like the post-verbal PPs. It is not recursive, there can only be one quantifier to the left of V. In order to distinguish VP-adjuncts, which combine with V′ to form V′, from the quantifier which combines with the highest V′ to form the full VP, we identify the position occupied by the quantifier *all* as the specifier position. The specifier dominated by VP is often represented as [Spec,VP]. [Spec,VP] combines with V′ to form a V″ projection.[7] V″ is the highest V–projection, which we equate with VP. For typographical reasons we shall usually replace V″ by VP.

[7] The analysis of *all* as occupying the VP specifier position is based on work by Sportiche (1988a). Sportiche's account introduces further modifications of phrase structure which we shall discuss in chapter 6 (section 5).

16

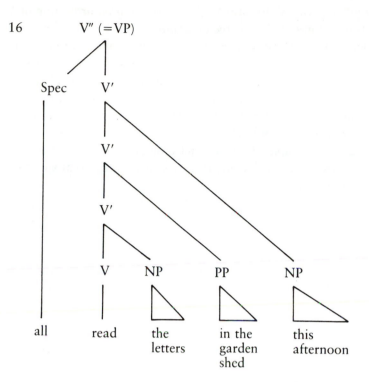

Schematically, English VPs are formed according to the following format:

17a

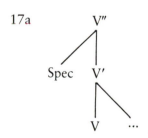

17b V″ ——➤ Spec – V′

　　 V′ ——➤ V – …

A complement combines with a V to form a V′. Adjuncts combine with V's to form higher V's. A V-projection may hence contain several V′ nodes.

The specifier combines with V′ to form V″. V″ is the maximal projection of V and corresponds to VP in our earlier tree diagrams.

Let us consider some further examples of VP structures. We must point out that often there may be no overt specifier in the VP of a given sentence, as seen in our earlier examples, or the VP may contain no adjuncts or no complements. We shall assume that the three levels, V, V′ and V″ are available for *any* VP in English, even if there is no overt material to attach to the different levels; the structure in (17) applies to every VP.[8]

Let us first return to example (9), which lacks the pre-verbal specifier. The representation (13) will be revised as in (18): there is no pre-verbal specifier; VP (or V″) is non-branching.[9]

18

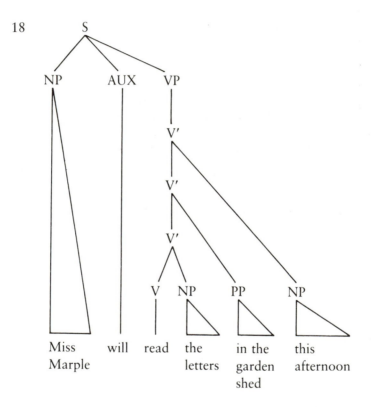

In (19a), there is again no specifier and also there is no direct object NP, *sleep* being intransitive. The lowest V′ is non-branching. *After lunch* is an

---

[8] For some discussion of this problem the reader is referred to Chomsky's discussion (1986b: 2–4).
[9] Another option would be to say that [Spec, VP] dominates a node which is not lexically filled. I shall not discuss this alternative here.

adjunct, which combines with the lowest V′ to form another V′. V″ is also non-branching. The representation of (19a) will be as in (19b):

19a Miss Marple will sleep after lunch.

19b

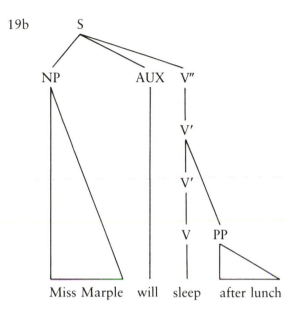

(20a) lacks a specifier and VP-adjuncts, we represent its structure in (20b):

20a Poirot will clean his motorbike.
20b

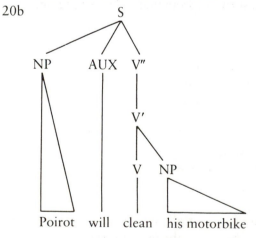

Finally, it is also possible that a VP simply dominates a verb and that there are no specifiers, adjuncts or complements. This is illustrated in (21a) with the representation in (21b):

21a Miss Marple will return.

21b

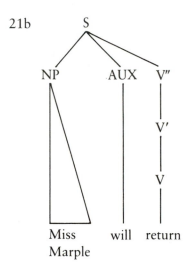

2.1.2 THE ORDER OF CONSTITUENTS

The projection schema for VPs developed so far is based solely on English examples; it is too rigid to apply universally. We have already seen that the word-order in Japanese differs considerably from that in English, for instance. Consider the following examples:

22a John ga   Mary o   but- ta.
         nominative   accusative   past
         particle   particle   tense
     John   Mary   hit
     'John hit Mary.'
22b John ga   Mary ni   hon o   yat-ta.
             nom   dative   acc.   past tense
     John   Mary   book   give
     'John gave Mary a book.'
22c John ga   Mary to   kuruma de   Kobe ni   it-ta.
     John   Mary with car   by   Kobe to   go-past
     'John went to Kobe by car with Mary.'
(from Kuno, 1973: 3, 5).

Japanese is an SOV language: the verb follows objects and adjuncts (Kuno, 1973: 3). Clearly, if we wish to devise a universal schema for V-projections then the order of the constituents in (17) is too rigidly fixed: (17) only allows for VO. It would be desirable to have a schema which allows both the order OV and the order VO and which relies on some other principle to account for language-specific orderings. We shall adopt this hypothesis here and propose the following projection schema for V:

23a

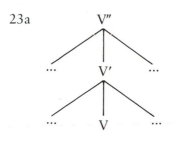

23b V″ ⎯⎯⎯▶ Spec; V′
    V′* ⎯⎯⎯▶ V′ ; XP
    V′ ⎯⎯⎯▶ V; XP

In (23a) the ellipses dominated by V″ stand for the potential specifier, those dominated by V′ for adjuncts or for complements. In (23b) Spec stands for the specifier, XP stands for adjuncts or complements. The semi-colon between the constituents in (23b) serves to indicate that they are not linearly ordered. The order of V and its complement XP, for instance, will be fixed according to language-specific options. V′* in (23b) allows for recursion of V′, indicated by the asterisk *.[10]

2.1.3 EXTENDING THE PROPOSAL

One question that immediately comes to mind is whether the hierarchical structure of VP proposed in section 2.1 can be extended to the other phrasal categories. If this were possible, we might be able to replace the four phrase structure rules in (3) by a single schema. Clearly, for reasons of economy, a theory which has one generalized schema for phrasal categories of various types is to be preferred to one in which distinct phrases are constructed on the basis of different schemata. If we are able to develop one general format, this

---

[10] For further discussion of adjuncts and phrase structure rules the reader is referred to chapter 7.

will mean that we have brought out the common properties between the phrases, a generalization which is lost if we adopt four unrelated phrase structure rules.

In the following sections we turn to the other lexical categories. In section 2.2 we discuss noun phrases, in section 2.3 adjective phrases and in section 2.4 prepositional phrases. We shall see that the projection schema developed for VP can be applied to all the categories examined.

2.2   *Noun Phrases*

Consider (24a):

24a the investigation of the corpse after lunch

Tentatively we might draw a flat structure for (24a) along the lines suggested by phrase structure rule (3b):

24b

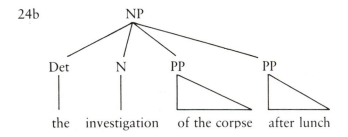

But (24b) is observationally inadequate since it fails to throw light on the *one*-substitution data in (25).

25   The investigation of the corpse after lunch was less horrible than the one after dinner.

In (25) *one* substitutes for the string *investigation of the corpse* but this string is not a constituent in the representation (24b): it is not exhaustively dominated by one node. A closer look at the data argues for a layered structure of NP by analogy with that of VP. On the one hand, *one* in (25) substitutes for the string *investigation of the corpse*, strongly suggesting that this string should be exhaustively dominated by one node in the syntactic representation. On the other hand, we can compare the NP (24a) with the VP of (26):

26   The police will [$_{VP}$ investigate the corpse after lunch].

It is intuitively attractive to argue that the relationship between the N *investigation* and the PP *of the corpse* in (24a) is like that between the verb *investigate* and its object NP *the corpse* in (26). Both the V *investigate* and the N *investigation* have a thematic relation with the NP *the corpse*. We return to the role of *of* in chapter 3.

If the relation between the V *investigate* and its complement NP *the corpse* is intuitively felt to be like that between the N *investigation* and the NP *the corpse*, then we would miss a generalization if we were to treat the NP structure as unrelated to the VP structure. One way of integrating NPs in the format established so far is to propose the following structure for the NP (24a):[11]

27

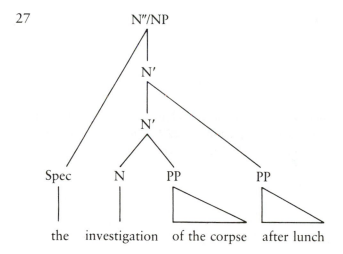

[11]   We shall usually replace N″ by NP for typographical reasons. In recent work it has been proposed that the head of NP is not N but rather the determiner. NP is reinterpreted as DP. This analysis has come to be known as the DP-hypothesis. The reader is referred to Abney (1987) for motivation. However, Abney's work should only be tackled after this book has been worked through.

The lowest N′ projection dominates N, the head of the phrase and its complement.[12] An adjunct combines with N′ to form another N′. Adjuncts are typically PPs as in (24a) or relative clauses, as in (28) below.[13] The specifier of NP, a determiner, combines with the topmost N′ to form the maximal projection, N″ or NP.

28a   a book [that I wrote]

28b

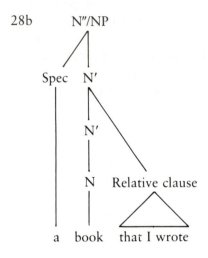

Like VPs, NPs may lack overt specifiers, complements or adjuncts, but we still generate the three levels of projection. In (29a), for instance, there is neither a complement nor an adjunct. In the syntactic representation (29b) N′ is non-branching.

29a   this book

---

[12] As mentioned before, the reason why complements of N must be realized as PP will be discussed in chapter 3.

[13] We shall address the internal structure of relative clauses in chapters 7 and 8.

29b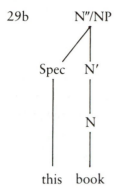

In English, the head noun precedes its complement and adjuncts, but again this is not a universal property.[14] To give but one example: in Japanese, relative clauses precede the head N:

30a *English:*
a book [that I wrote]
30b *Japanese:*
[watakusi ga kaita] hon
I wrote   book
(Kuno, 1973: 234).

Demonstrative pronouns, i.e. specifiers, also precede the head N in Japanese:

[14] Indeed in English too the complement NP may appear before the head noun:

   (i)   The painting of Saskia.
  (ii)   Saskia's painting.

We can compare the relation between (i) and (ii) to that between an active sentence (iii) and its passive parallel (iv):

 (iii)   Rembrandt painted Saskia.
 (iv)   Saskia was painted by Rembrandt.

We discuss passivization in chapter 6.

31   kono hon
     this book
(Kuno, 1973: 235)

In order to allow for cross-linguistic variation in word-order we shall have to assume a very general phrase structure schema along the lines of (23b) for VP, which does not impose a strict ordering on the constituents of the phrase:

32   N″ ⟶ Spec; N′
     N′* ⟶ N′; XP
     N′ ⟶ N; XP

For each of the PS-rules the order is fixed according to the language in question.

2.3   Adjective Phrases

Looking at APs it seems entirely reasonable to extend the layered analysis of VP and NP above and to distinguish different levels of projection:

33a   Jeeves is [$_{AP}$ rather envious of Poirot].

33b

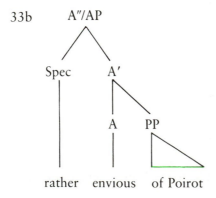

Like the verb *envy*, the adjective *envious* is a two-place predicate. In (33a) the subject NP *Jeeves* realizes one argument, the PP *of Poirot* contains the second argument. We discuss the role of the preposition *of* in chapter 3. The projection A' dominates the lexical head *envious* and its complement.

As was the case for VP, the order of the AP constituents varies cross-linguistically: adjectives may precede their complements as in English, or they may follow them, as in German:

34a Er ist des Französischen   mächtig.
     he is the French (GENITIVE) able
     'He has a command of French.'
34b Er ist seinen Grundsätzen   treu.
     he is his   principles (DATIVE) faithful
     'He is faithful to his principles.'

In (34), the adjectives *mächtig* and *treu* follow their NP complements. We assume that the relative order of the adjective and its complement is a language–specific property.[15]

2.4 Prepositional Phrases

PPs too can be assimilated to the schema proposed so far. Prepositions usually require an NP complement.

35a across [NP the bridge]
     with [NP a knife]
35b right across [NP the bridge]

Using the pattern adopted for VP, NP and AP as a model, we can propose the following structure:

---

[15] For a discussion of the GENITIVE the reader is referred to chapter 3, specifically section 3.2.1.2.

   Often authors try to derive the word–order variation between different languages from other principles of the grammar. One possibility, for instance, is to argue that heads assign their thematic role in one direction only. If V in English assigns the theta role to the right then we expect that the object NP must follow V.

36   P″/PP

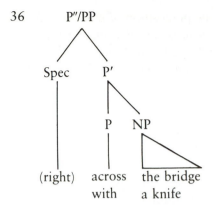

Spec   P′

          P   NP

(right)   across   the bridge
          with   a knife

Again the ordering of P and the complement is not universally fixed. In Japanese, elements corresponding to English prepositions follow their comple- ments and are referred to as postpositions (see (22c)). Let us use the label P to indicate both pre- and postpositions.

2.5   X-bar Theory

From the discussion above it appears that for all lexical categories (N,V,P,A) the format of phrasal projection can be represented by means of the layered representation. (37) summarizes the discussion:

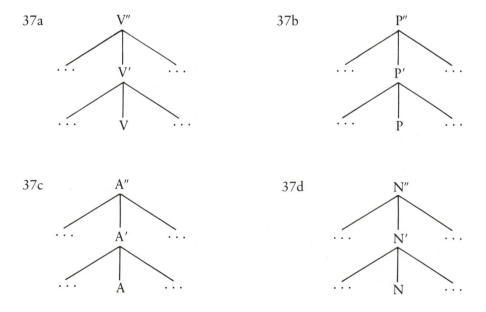

37a   V″

               V′

               V

37b   P″

               P′

               P

37c   A″

               A′

               A

37d   N″

               N′

               N

This means that we no longer need four different phrase structure rules, as suggested in (3). Abstracting away from the category of the head we arrive at the following schema:

38

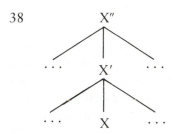

where X stands for N, V, A or P. Our grammar need not contain four schemata, but only one. The general format for phrase structure is summarized in the following PS-rules:

39a X″ $\longrightarrow$ Spec; X′
39b X′* $\longrightarrow$ X′; YP
39c X′ $\longrightarrow$ X; YP

The part of the grammar regulating the structure of phrases has come to be known as X-bar theory.[16] X-bar theory brings out what is common in the structure of phrases. According to X-bar theory all phrases are headed by a lexical head. In the terminology of traditional linguistics we say that all phrases are **endocentric**. The lexical head of the projection is a **zero projection** (X^0). X-bar theory distinguishes two levels of projection. Complements combine with X to form X′ projections (39c); adjuncts combine with X′ to form X′ projections (39b). The specifier combines with the topmost X′ to form the maximal projection X″ (39a). For convenience' sake we usually replace X″ by XP.[17]

While it is assumed that the layered projection schema in (39) is universal, we have already seen that the order of constituents with respect to the head of the projection is not universally fixed. We assume that some other principle of

[16] The theory has developed as a result of proposals by Chomsky (1970).
[17] For an early discussion of the theory and its application to English, see Jackendoff (1977). However, note that many of Jackendoff's proposals have been subject to major revisions. For a survey of the origins and development of X-bar theory, the reader is referred to Stuurman (1985). Muysken (1983) offers a reinterpretation of the theory in terms of features (see section 6).

the grammar accounts for the various constituent orders.[18] The specific phrase structure rules for one language, say English, can be derived from the general schema in (39) and the, as yet to be specified, principle which fixes the relative order of head, complements, adjuncts and specifiers. Language-specific phrase structure rules need not be stated separately since they follow from other, more general, principles.

We have also seen that there are differences between the internal structures of the phrases. For instance, V and P take NP complements, while N and A do not take NP complements. Such differences will be explained by independent mechanisms of the grammar. In chapter 3, for instance, we shall see that case theory explains that nouns and adjectives cannot take NP complements.

As the reader will observe, the result of our discussion is that the construction-specific phrase structure rules in (3) are broken down into several separate general rules and principles which capture what is common between the different phrases.

If we can treat phrase structure universally in terms of this general projection schema (39), then we may further assume that the child learning a language need not construct this schema as part of its grammar. The principles of X-bar theory will be part of UG, they are innate.[19]

On the other hand, UG does not fix the order of constituents. The ordering constraints found in natural languages vary cross-linguistically and they thus have to be learnt by the child through exposure. Very little data will suffice to allow the child to fix the ordering constraints of the language he is learning. A child learning English will only need to be exposed to a couple of transitive sentences to realize that in English verbs precede their complements.

[18] It is often proposed that there is a correlation between the ordering of the head and its complement and adjuncts in VP, PP, AP, etc. For instance, it is often proposed that languages which have OV order also have postpositions and adjectives that follow their complements. This is by no means a universal property. See Greenberg (1963, 1978) for some discussion.

[19] There is a lot of discussion as to whether (39) is indeed universal. It is sometimes argued that certain languages are not subject to the hierarchical organization in (39). Languages which are not subject to the hierarchical organization are called **non-configurational** languages. If we adopt the view that certain languages are not hierarchically organized but are basically 'flat', then we must give up the idea that (39) is universal and we must introduce some parameter to distinguish configurational languages subject to (39) from non-configurational languages.

One example of a language which has been claimed to be non-configurational is Hungarian (see Kiss, 1981) and another is Warlpiri (see Hale, 1983). Maracz and Muysken (1989) contains a series of recent papers on the configurationality issue in various languages.

3   The Structure of Sentences

3.1   *Introduction: the Problem*

So far we have achieved quite an interesting general approach to phrase structure: for all the phrasal categories we have developed the hypothesis that they are structured according to the X-bar schema (39). Nothing has been said about the larger unit of syntactic analysis, the sentence.

We start our discussion on the basis of the bracketed clause in (40):

40   They will wonder [whether Poirot will abandon the investigation].

In (40) the bracketed string is a constituent composed of sentence (1) of this chapter preceded by the **complementizer** *whether*. Assuming that the string *Poirot will abandon the investigation* is a syntactic unit, a sentence, the bracketing in (40) can be refined to set this sentence off from the complementizer. In standard generative syntax the simple sentence *Poirot will abandon the investigation* is labelled S and this S together with the complementizer is labelled S'.[20] Omitting details of the internal structure of VP (hence the triangle), (41a) has the representation in (41b):

41a   They will wonder [$_{S'}$ whether [$_S$ Poirot will abandon the investigation]].

41b

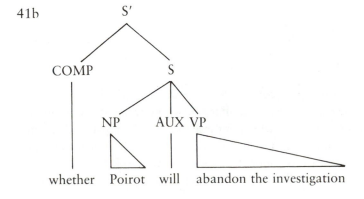

---

[20] The PS rule S' $\longrightarrow$ COMP – S is due to Bresnan (1970).

As it stands this representation is not an instantiation of the X′ schema (39). If S′, as the name suggests, is a projection of S, then this is an odd projection. In the X′-schema, phrasal projections project from their heads, words of the type N, V, etc. In (41) the labelling suggests that S′ is a projection of a higher level unit, S. S does not look like a projection of a head either. S has three immediate constituents: two are phrasal themselves (NP and VP) and one is an auxiliary.

One possibility would be to say that S′ and S are not endocentric categories but **exocentric** ones: they are not projections of heads but are somehow composed of several units next to each other. This would mean that our grammar will have to include the projection schema (39) and in addition one or more schemata to account for the structure of S and S′. Such a grammar will suggest that there is little or nothing in common between the structure of the phrasal constituents such as NP, VP, etc. and that of clausal constituents. This proposal will also entail that the child learning the language will have to differentiate the two types of structures and apply each to the relevant categories.

It would, of course, be more attractive if the structure of clauses could be assimilated to the schema in (39), thus generalizing the X-bar schema to all types of constructions. If this were possible, one X-bar format would apply both to phrases and to clauses and the child would operate with one schema rather than several.

A closer look at the structure of clauses will allow us to extend the schema in (39) to sentence structure. In section 3.2 we discuss the structure of S. We shall see that it is reasonable to argue that S is headed by the constituent indicated by AUX and relabelled I for INFL and that it is organized along the lines in (39). In section 3.3 we turn to S′ for which we shall argue that it is headed by the complementizer, C, and again follows the schema in (39).

3.2   *S as a Projection of INFL*

3.2.1   AUX AND TENSE

In (41b) S has three immediate constituents: the subject NP (*Poirot*), the VP (*abandon the investigation*) and the auxiliary (*will*). Looking at the X′ format in (39) we can ask ourselves first which of these three could in principle qualify as a head. One possibility presents itself: *will* is a word, a lexical unit. This observation might tempt us to adopt the hypothesis that *will*, i.e. AUX, is the head of S.[21] The analysis will extend automatically to sentences containing

---

[21]   In Jackendoff (1977) it was proposed that S was headed by V. This proposal was abandoned later (cf. Hornstein, 1977). See also Abney (1987) for discussion.

other modal auxiliaries such as *can, may, must, shall* and can also be applied to sentences containing the aspectual auxiliaries *have* and *be.*

One problem for this proposal arises immediately: if AUX is the head of S, then what do we do with sentences without overt auxiliary such as (42)?

42   Poirot abandoned the investigation.

At first glance one might adopt the following syntactic representation:

43

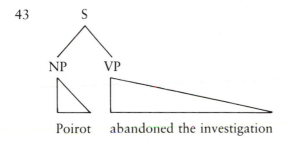

Poirot   abandoned the investigation

In (43) it would not be at all clear which lexical category is to head S. It turns out that there are empirical arguments against the representation (43). Consider the examples in (44):

44a   Abandon the investigation, Poirot did indeed.
44b   What Poirot did was abandon the investigation.

In (44a) the verb *abandon* and its direct object NP *the investigation* have been preposed and the past tense affix is left behind on an auxiliary (*did*). If we assume that only constituents can move, we must conclude that *abandon the investigation* is a constituent which is relatively independent from the past tense. Such an interpretation of the structure of the sentence is difficult to reconcile with (43) where tense is an integral part of the VP. The pseudo-cleft construction in (44b) illustrates the same phenomenon: *abandon the investigation* is separated off from its past tense.

These data suggest strongly that at a more abstract level of representation the inflectional element tense cannot be part of the VP, but must be generated separately from it. In (41) the tense specification of the sentence is separate from VP and it is associated with the AUX node (*will* is the present tense of the auxiliary, *would* is the past tense). AUX in (41b) is the site on which tense is realized.

Let us capitalize on this observation and posit that in all sentences, with or without overt auxiliaries, tense is located under a separate node which we shall from now on label **INFL**, for **inflection**. We return to the label in the section below. In sentences with an auxiliary which is inflected for tense (such as (41)) the tensed auxiliary is generated under INFL. INFL replaces AUX. In sentences without overt auxiliary we propose that tense is an independent category dominated by INFL. Under this analysis, the relevant part of (41a) will have the structure (45a) and (42) will have the structure (45b):

45a

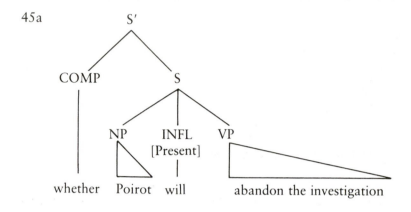

45b

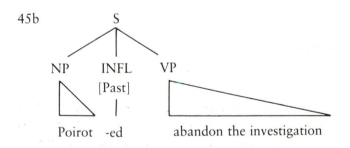

In (45b) INFL is specified for past tense and dominates the *-ed* affix. VP is a constituent separate from the past tense. Hence we expect that VP may move independently of the tense ending. Being an affix, the past tense ending cannot be left unattached, it must be attached to the verb. We shall assume that in (45b) the past tense morphology is lowered onto the verb.[22]

[22] In sentences with the auxiliary *do* this auxiliary will appear under INFL and pick up the tense ending.

3.2.2 AGREEMENT

We have proposed that there is a separate node INFL which dominates tense in English. However, as the label suggests, INFL is a node which is taken to dominate all verbal inflection, i.e. including person and number properties.

In English the inflectional properties of verb conjugation are minimal, but other languages have richer paradigms of conjugation. Person and number agreement, which is present in other languages, often does not have any morphological realization in English. Compare the following data from English, French and Italian. For each language we give the conjugation for present and past tense and at the bottom of each column we indicate the total number of distinct forms:

46a   *English*

Present tense	*Past tense*
I speak	I spoke
you speak	you spoke
he speaks	he spoke
we speak	we spoke
you speak	you spoke
they speak	they spoke
2 forms	*1 form*

46b   *French*

je parle	je parlais
tu parles	tu parlais
il parle	il parlait
nous parlons	nous parlions
vous parlez	vous parliez
ils parlent	ils parlaient
5 forms	*5 forms*[23]

---

[23]   In French there are five forms if we take orthography into account. However, for many verbs (such as *parler* in (46b)), first person singular, second person singular and third person verb forms sound the same.

46c *Italian*

io parlo	io parlavo
tu parli	tu parlavi
egli parla	egli parlava
noi parliamo	noi parlavamo
voi parlate	voi parlavate
essi parlano	essi parlavano

6 forms   *6 forms*

The overt agreement properties of English verbs are heavily reduced: regular verbs have in fact only two distinct forms for the present and one form only for the past tense. The verb *be* shows some more overt inflection:

47
I am	I was
you are	you were
he is	he was
we are	we were
you are	you were
they are	they were

3 forms   *2 forms*

Though the overt realization of agreement for person and number is restricted in English, we assume that there is **abstract** agreement, AGR, which is often not morphologically realized. The difference between English and French or Italian is not taken to be that English lacks AGR, but rather that the abstract AGR has fewer morphological realizations. It is sometimes said that Italian and French AGR are 'stronger' than English AGR. We return to the relevance of the agreement paradigms above for syntactic representations in chapter 8.

We now propose that INFL dominates not only the tense feature of the verb but also its agreement properties, ([AGR] for short).[24]

---

[24] In recent work (Pollock, 1989) it has been proposed that INFL should be split up into two components, Tense and AGR, which each head one projection. The reader is referred to Pollock's work for discussion. The article should not be tackled until we have studied syntactic movement (chapters 7 and 8).

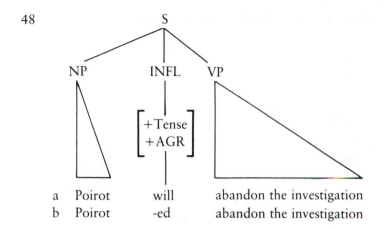

48
a   Poirot   will   abandon the investigation
b   Poirot   -ed   abandon the investigation

3.2.3   INFINITIVAL CLAUSES

In the previous sections we have examined finite or tensed clauses. Let us now turn to infinitival clauses.

Tensed clauses are specified as having an INFL containing the features [+Tense] and [+AGR]. Infinitives typically lack tense marking and agreement. They are [−Tense] and [−AGR]. We can represent the subordinate clause in (49a) by the structure in (49b).[25] We assume that *to* in infinitives corresponds to the verb inflection.

[25]   If we analyse the content of INFL in terms of the features [± AGR] and [± Tense] there ought to be four combinations:

[+AGR]
[+Tense]

[+AGR]
[−Tense]

[−AGR]
[+Tense]

[−AGR]
[−Tense]

So far, we have illustrated only the combination [+AGR, +Tense] in finite clauses and [−AGR, −Tense] in infinitivals. Raposo (1987) discusses agreeing infinitivals in Portuguese, a case of [+AGR, −Tense]. Stowell (1982) argues that certain infinitives in English are [−AGR, +Tense]. We refer the reader to the literature for discussion.

49a I did not expect [Poirot to abandon the investigation].

49b

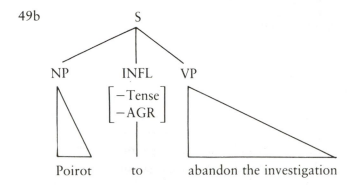

3.2.4 THE STRUCTURE OF IP

We have based the distinction between finite and infinitival clauses on the content of the node INFL, the features [±Tense] and [±AGR]. In other words, the type of clause is determined by the type of INFL. We propose that INFL, a category of the zero level, is the head of S. If we assume that S is headed by INFL it follows that S, like other phrasal categories such as VP, is endocentric: it is a projection of I, **IP**.

The next question to ask is whether we can fully assimilate IP to the X′-schema in (39) with its three levels of projection. The category INFL dominates material such as verbal inflection, infinitival *to*, aspectual auxiliaries and modals. Tense endings will end up on V; auxiliaries and infinitival *to* are followed by a verb. Since V heads VP, it seems reasonable to argue that I takes a VP as its complement to constitute the I′ projection.

In (39) the specifier of the phrase combines with the topmost X′ to form X″. In the case of sentences we propose that the subject of the sentence occupies the specifier position, it combines with the I′ projection to form I″ or IP. (50a) illustrates this idea by means of a tree diagram representation for the sentences discussed above. (50b) provides a set of phrase structure rules. Again the ordering of the constituents varies cross-linguistically and need not be stated in the PS-rules.[26]

---

[26] We shall see in chapter 11 that while English has the order SIVO, Dutch and German are assumed to have SOVI.

50a

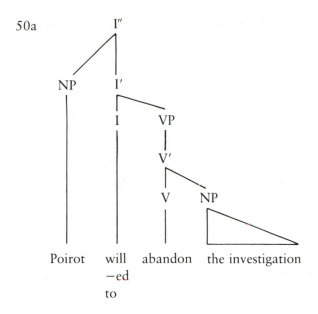

Poirot   will   abandon   the investigation
          −ed
          to

50b   I″ ⟶ Spec; I′
      I′ ⟶ I; VP

What is traditionally referred to as the subject of the sentence is the NP immediately dominated by IP, i.e. the NP in the specifier of IP position. This position is often indicated by [**Spec, IP**] or by [**NP, IP**]. The reader will observe that the grammatical function 'subject' is not a **primitive** notion in Government and Binding Theory: it is not a simple or unanalysed concept of the theory. Rather, 'subject' (and 'object' as well) is defined in terms of syntactic configurations; it is a derivative notion based on more elementary concepts in the theory.

Note that there is a distinction to be drawn between phrasal projections of lexical categories and a projection of I. N, V and the other lexical heads we have encountered, belong to what are called open classes. Open classes do not only have a large number of members, but new members may be freely added.[27] Closed classes are groups of a restricted number of elements to which new elements cannot be added.

---

[27] Prepositions constitute a relatively closed class too, but new prepositions or complex prepositions may be added to the language (cf. *because of, in spite of*). We shall continue treating prepositions as part of the lexical categories.

We have proposed that the head of S is INFL. INFL dominates the inflectional morphology of the verb, affixes and infinitival *to*, which are not independent lexical categories or 'words'. The only lexical elements, 'words', that can be dominated by INFL are the aspectual auxiliaries *have* and *be* and the modals. The latter constitute a closed class composed of the following elements: *will, can, may, shall, must* and possibly *dare, need, used* and *ought*. The aspectual and modal auxiliaries in English often correspond to inflectional affixes in other languages. The English perfect is formed with the auxiliary *have*, but Latin uses an inflection (51a). While English uses the modal *shall* or *will* for expressing futurity, Latin again uses a tense ending (51b):

51a *English*   *Latin*
     I have loved   amavi
51b I shall love   amabo

Because INFL does not dominate open class lexical heads, we shall say that it is a **non-lexical** head.

3.3 *S' as a Projection of C*

3.3.1 C AS THE HEAD OF CP

We have now assimilated the structure of S to the X'-schema. In this section we try to extend the format to S'.

Observe that the nature of the unit as a whole, the type of sentence, is determined by the nature of the complementizer:

52a I will ask [whether [Poirot will abandon his investigation]].
52b I will say [that [Poirot will abandon his investigation]].

The subordinate clause in (52a) is interrogative, that in (52b) is declarative. The difference between the two is signalled by the choice of complementizer introducing the clause, *whether* vs. *that*. In other words, the complementizer determines the type of clause. Because the complementizer is a word, a lexical item, this suggests that we treat the complementizer, represented as C, as the head of S'. Complementizers do not constitute an open class: the four complementizers that introduce subordinate clauses in English are *that, if, whether, for*. Analogously to the discussion of I, we say that the projection of C is a projection of a non-lexical head.

Complementizers such as *whether, if, that* and *for* introduce a sentence (IP): C takes an IP-complement. The choice of the type of IP is determined by the choice of C. The complementizers *that* and *if* select a finite clause as their complement; *for* selects an infinitival clause and *whether* selects either type of clause:

53a I think [that [Poirot   abandoned the investigation]].
                           *to abandon
53b I expect [for [Poirot   to abandon the investigation]].
                          *abandoned
53c Jane wonders [whether [Poirot   abandoned the investigation]].
                                    [to abandon the investigation]].

All the bracketed clauses in (53) have the structure in (54):

54

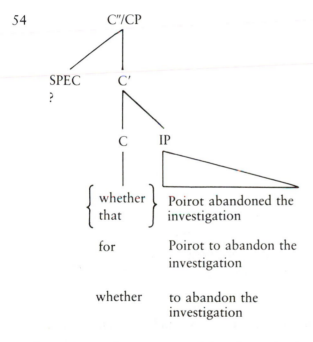

At this point we have no material to insert in the specifier position of CP, [Spec,CP]. We consider this point in the next section.[28]

---

[28] In standard English *for* must be absent when the infinitival clause lacks an overt subject NP:

(i)   *It was hard for to abandon the investigation

Other dialects of English, though, allow *for to* sequences to some degree (see Carroll, 1983; Henry, 1989).

3.3.2   HEAD-TO-HEAD MOVEMENT

Let us consider the following examples:

55a   Poirot will abandon the investigation after lunch.
55b   Will Poirot abandon the investigation after lunch?
55c   When will Poirot abandon the investigation?

(55a) is a declarative sentence which will be assigned the structure (56a):

56a   CP

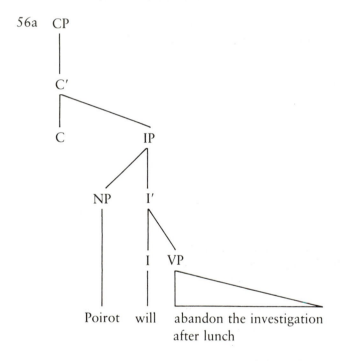

There is no overt complementizer in the sentence and we assume that the head of CP is empty.

(55b) is a direct *yes–no* question characterized by the inversion of subject and auxiliary.[29] How can this order be derived? Various possibilities come to mind. An option that we shall explore here, and that will be elaborated in chapters 7 and 11, is that the auxiliary *will* is moved from its position in I to the position C. In other words, we assume that (55b) has two syntactic

[29]   We discuss the different types of questions in chapter 7.

representations. In one, the **underlying** structure, the modal *will* occupies the position dominated by I, as in (56a). In the second representation, the **derived** structure, the modal is moved from under I to the position dominated by C. Movement from one head position (in our case I) to another one (C) is called **head-to-head movement** and will be illustrated more extensively in chapters 7 and 11.

56b

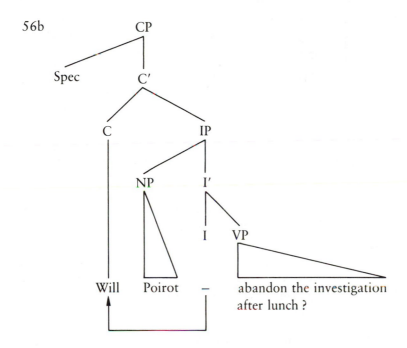

(55c) is a constituent-question or *wh*-question. The auxiliary *will* precedes the subject. We assume again that, as was the case in (56b), it has moved under C. In addition, the interrogative constituent *when*, which corresponds to the time adjunct *after lunch* in (55a) and (55b), precedes the auxiliary. We assume that *when* is moved from the sentence-internal position occupied by time adjuncts in (56a) and (56b) to a position preceding C. Without going into the details of the analysis here (see chapter 7), it is clear that the X′-schema as set up offers us a position for *when* to move to: it can be inserted under the specifier-node of CP, [Spec, CP] for short, a position left unoccupied in the earlier examples:

56c

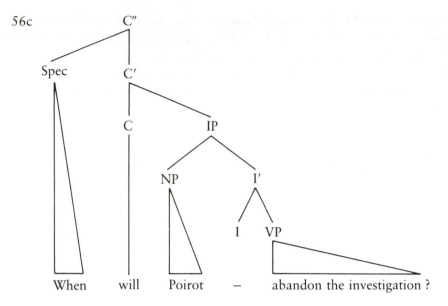

The question might be asked whether there are additional arguments for the claim that the auxiliary in (55b) and (55c) really goes to the position of C, the position occupied by the complementizer in subordinate clauses.

One argument in favour of this analysis is that it predicts that the complementizer and the inverted auxiliary can never co-occur since they would have to sit in the same slot. This prediction is borne out:

57a *I wonder $\begin{cases} \text{will whether} \\ \text{whether will} \end{cases}$ Poirot abandon the investigation.

57b *When that will Poirot abandon the investigation?

A parallel question is whether it is reasonable to propose that question words such as *when* move to [Spec, CP]. In main clause questions they overtly precede the inverted auxiliary, but in subordinate clauses in English *wh*-words do not co-occur with the complementizers *that* or *whether*.

Information from languages other than English and information from the earlier stages of English provide some evidence here.

In some French and Italian dialects, subject-auxiliary inversion is not obligatory in direct questions. When the auxiliary has not inverted with the subject, C is available and we predict that the complementizer is free to occupy the C position. This prediction is borne out.

58a   Quoi que tu as fait? (Quebec French)
       what that you have done (Cf. Koopman, 1983: 389)
       'What have you done?'
58b   Chi che t'è vest? (Italian Romagnolo dialect; cited in Poggi, 1983)
       who that you have seen
       'Whom have you seen?'

In (58a) *quoi* is in [Spec, CP], and *que* is dominated by C. The auxiliary *as* does
not invert with the subject. Similarly *chi* in (58b) is in [Spec, CP], and the
complementizer *che* appears under C. The auxiliary *è* is again in the IP-internal
position. While the overt complementizer may co-occur with the moved
wh-element in the dialects cited above, it cannot co-occur with an inverted
auxiliary. This is predicted if we assume that both complementizer and the
inverted auxiliary are dominated by C and if we also assume that a head
position is normally occupied by one head only.[30]
   Consider also the subordinate clauses in (59):

59a   Je me demande [quoi que tu fais].
       I wonder   what that you do
       (Quebec French; cited by Koopman, 1983: 389)
59b   Men shal knowe [who that I am] (1485, Caxton R67).
       (Lightfoot, 1979: 322)
59c   *Men shall know who that I am.

Quoi in (59a) precedes *que*, the complementizer. We again assume that *quoi* is
in [Spec, CP] and that *que* is dominated by C. The same pattern is found in
earlier stages of English as shown in (59b). (59c), the word for word
translation of (59b), is ungrammatical in modern English. We return to the
syntactic structure of questions in chapter 7.

3.3.3   THE STRUCTURE OF CP

We have proposed that the structure of S′ can be assimilated to the X′-format
in (39) in the following way:

60a   C″ ⟶ Spec; C′
60b   C′ ⟶ C; IP

[30]   In certain languages a V head may incorporate a head N, thus creating a complex
       lexical unit dominated by V and consisting of V and N. This is apparently not
       possible in the case of C and V. For a discussion of incorporation the reader is
       referred to Baker (1988).

C dominates the lexical complementizer or an auxiliary (in sentences with subject-auxiliary inversion). C combines with IP to form C'. C' in turn combines with a specifier to form the maximal projection C" or **CP**. The position [Spec, CP] is the position to which interrogative constituents are moved.

3.4   Summary: X'-theory and Non-lexical Categories

In section 3 of this chapter we have applied the X'-format, developed in section 2 for phrasal constituents, to the clausal constituents, S (i.e. IP or I") and S' (CP or C"). The X'-format will allow us to describe the structure of main and dependent clauses and of various types of questions.

We have now reached the important conclusion that all syntactic structure is built on the basis of the X'-format (39). This means that no special phrase structure rule needs to be stated for specific constituents and that when acquiring the language, the child will only need access to (38) to be able to construct both phrasal and clausal constituents.

3.5   Small Clauses: a Problem

In chapter 1 we introduced another clause type in addition to tensed clauses and infinitival clauses: small clauses.

61a   I consider [Maigret an inspector of great value].
61b   Maigret considers [the taxi driver entirely innocent].
61c   I consider [your proposal completely out of the question].

The bracketed strings are constituents, as shown in chapter 1. The idea was that in (61a), for instance, *Maigret* is the subject of the predicate *an inspector of great value* exactly like in sentence (62):

62   Maigret is an inspector of great value.

We raised the question as to the category label of these constituents. In the traditional literature they are called verbless clauses; we called them **small clauses**. Let us consider the syntactic representation of the bracketed strings. We choose (61a) but the discussion also applies to the other two examples.

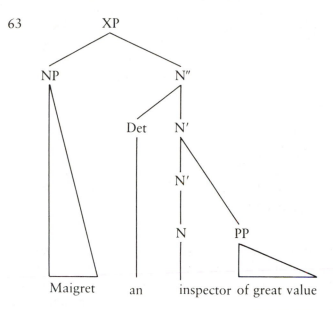

63

What is the category of XP? XP dominates N″, a maximal projection. Linguists have argued (see Stowell, 1983) that XP is another NP, a sort of super-projection of the head N *inspector*. The NP *Maigret* is **adjoined** to the maximal projection, the NP *an inspector of great value*. We return to adjunction structures in chapters 7, 8 and 9.

4 Structural Relations

We discussed the structural relations dominance, precedence, and government in section 1. In this section we discuss the structural relation c-command. We shall also return to the notion government and try to define it in terms of c-command. To illustrate the role of the notion c-command in the theory, we first consider agreement patterns.

4.1 *Agreement Patterns*

Let us examine some examples of agreement patterns. Consider the NP in (64a):

64a
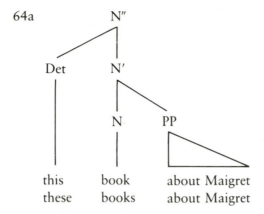

this	book	about Maigret
these	books	about Maigret

It is well known that demonstrative pronouns in English agree in number with the head of the immediately dominating NP. Agreement is overtly realized: *this* is singular, *these* is plural. Other determiners such as the definite article or possessive pronouns do not exhibit overt morphological agreement:

64b the book/the books
     my book/my books

In languages other than English specifier-head agreement between determiners and the head nouns in NPs is more extensively realized morphologically:

65a *French*

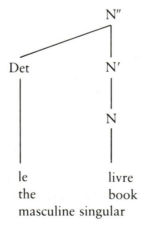

le	livre
the	book
masculine singular	

les   livres
the   books
masculine plural

la   voiture
the   car
feminine singular

les   voitures
the   cars
feminine plural

mon   livre
my   book

mes   livres
ma   voiture
mes   voitures

65b *German*

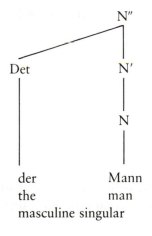

der   Mann
the   man
masculine singular

die   Männer
the   men
masculine plural

die   Frau
the   woman
feminine singular

die   Frauen
the   women
feminine plural

das   Kind
the   child
neuter singular

die   Kinder
the   children
neuter plural

The cross-linguistic variation of the overt inflection of NP determiners displayed in (64) and (65) is reminiscent of that discussed with respect to verbal inflection. In French and German NP determiners have rich overt agreement for the nominal features gender and number. The English system is impoverished, though there are traces of overt agreement. We shall assume that even in the absence of overt agreement, English head nouns and their specifiers agree in number and gender. The difference between French and English does not lie in the presence or absence of agreement as such, but rather in the morphological realization of this agreement.

Let us turn to subject–verb agreement. Consider some French examples first:

66a Poirot abandonne l'affaire.
     'Poirot abandons the case.'
66b Les inspecteurs abandonnent l'affaire.
     'The inspectors abandon the case.'
66c Nous abandonnons l'affaire.
     'We abandon the case.'

In French the verb ending is determined by the person and number of the subject. I and [NP, IP] agree with respect to the relevant nominal features.

67

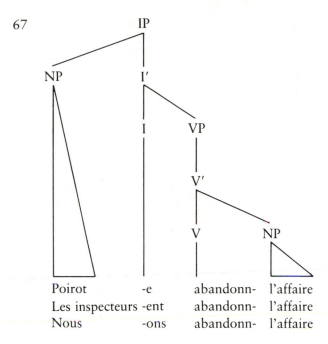

Poirot	-e	abandonn-	l'affaire
Les inspecteurs	-ent	abandonn-	l'affaire
Nous	-ons	abandonn-	l'affaire

In English there is little overt agreement, but again we have adopted the assumption that INFL is specified for abstract [AGR] in (68):

68a Poirot abandons the investigation.
68b The inspectors abandon the investigation.
68c We abandon the investigation.

Tree diagram (69) is the English analogue of (67):

69

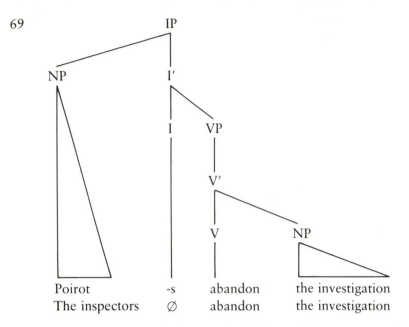

Poirot	-s	abandon	the investigation
The inspectors	∅	abandon	the investigation

If we compare the tree diagrams (64a), (67) and (69) we find a parallelism in the configurational relations between the agreeing constituents. In all three examples the phrasal head agrees with its specifier. This type of agreement is called **specifier-head agreement**. Head and specifier share features such as number, gender, person. Languages vary with respect to the extent to which agreement between specifier and head in IP and NP are morphologically realized.

In the literature it has been proposed that agreement between specifier and head be represented by means of a subscript[31] on the agreeing elements:

70a these$_i$ books$_i$ about Maigret
70b ces$_i$ livres$_i$ sur Maigret

The reader might conclude from the discussion above that agreement only affects the pair specifier-head, and also that it must necessarily affect this pair. Both these conclusions would be too rash.

It is not true that agreement only affects the specifier-head relation. Consider the following example from West Flemish, a dialect of Dutch:[32]

[31] Sometimes a superscript is used.

(i) these^i books^i

[32] For a discussion of Germanic word–order, see chapter 11.

71a ... [$_{C''}$ [$_{C'}$ da [$_{I''}$ den inspekteur da   boek gelezen eet]]].
       that   the inspector that book read   has
71b ... [$_{C''}$ [$_{C'}$ dan [$_{I''}$ d'   inspekteurs da   boek gelezen een]]].
       that   the inspectors that book read   have

In (71) the perfective auxiliary *eet/een* agrees in number and person with its subject *den inspekteur/d'inspekteurs*, illustrating specifier-head agreement. Furthermore, the complementizer *da* agrees in number and person with the subject and with the inflection: *da* is third person singular, *dan* is third person plural. The head of the CP, C, agrees with the head (and the specifier) of its complement IP.

On the other hand, we cannot claim that every element in [Spec, NP] must agree with the head noun:

72a the detective's book
72b the detectives' book
72c the detective's books
72d the detectives' books

In (72) the number of the head N *book* is independent of the number of the GENITIVE phrase preceding it. It is normally assumed that in English the GENITIVE phrase occupies [Spec, NP]:

73

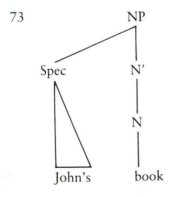

One argument for this assumption is that in English a pre-nominal GENITIVE and a determiner are incompatible, while a pre-nominal determiner and a post-nominal *of*-phrase may co-occur:

74a *this John's book
     *a John's book

74b   a book of John's
      this book of John's

In the case of pre-nominal GENITIVE specifiers the features of the phrase in
[Spec, NP] vary independently of those of the head noun.

   In the next section we shall try to define a unifying relation to characterize
the pairs of agreeing constituents discussed.

4.2   C-command and Government

4.2.1   C-COMMAND AND THE FIRST BRANCHING NODE

Consider the following representations where co-subscripted nodes indicate
agreement:

75a   French

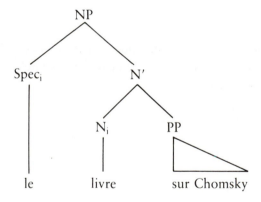

75b

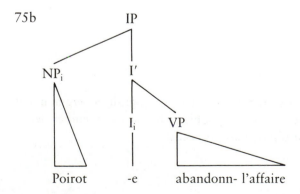

75c West Flemish

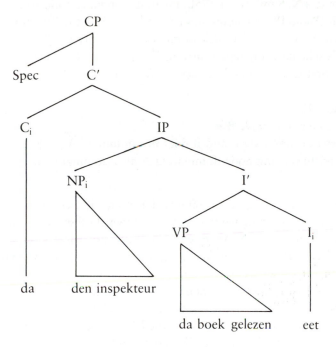

In (75a) and (75b) we have specifier-head agreement as discussed above, but the agreement of C and the lower constituents in (75c) cannot be defined in terms of specifier-head agreement. When we consider the geometrical relations between agreeing pairs of element it appears that one agreeing element is always higher in the tree than the element it agrees with.

76

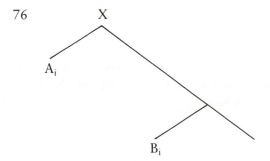

In all the representations in (75) X, the first branching node dominating A, the highest member of the agreeing pair, also dominates B, the lowest member of the agreeing pair. A itself does not dominate B and B does not dominate A.

In (75a) the first branching node dominating the determiner is NP (N″) and this node also dominates N. Similarly, in (75b) the first branching node dominating the subject NP is IP and IP also dominates I. Finally, in (75c) the first branching node dominating C is C′, which also dominates the subject NP and I. The relation which is schematically represented in (76) is one that has been labelled **c-command** (as first discussed and defined by Reinhart, 1981):

77   **C-command (1)**
     Node A c-commands node B iff
     (a)   A does not dominate B and B does not dominate A; and
     (b)   the first branching node dominating A also dominates B.

     Given a node A it is easy to determine which nodes it c-commands. The procedure is as follows: starting from A we move upward till we reach the first branching node dominating A; then we move downwards following the branches of the tree and every node that we find on our way is c-commanded by A, regardless of whether we move rightward or leftward.
     In diagram (75a), for instance, [Spec, NP] c-commands all the nodes dominated by NP. The total of all the nodes c-commanded by an element is the **c-command domain** of that element. In (75a) the NP is the c-command domain of the determiner. In (75b) the subject NP c-commands the entire IP; IP is the c-command domain of the subject. In (75c) C c-commands all the material dominated by C′. C′ is the c-command domain of C. The c-command domain of an element is of necessity a constituent, given that it consists of all the material dominated by one node, hence the term c(= constituent)-command. Note in passing that under the definition in (77) a node A always c-commands itself: it will always be possible to start from node A, go up to the first branching node and return then to node A. Nothing in the definition prevents one from returning via the same route.[33]

4.2.2   GOVERNMENT

At this point let us return to our definition of government (7) in terms of sisterhood. Recall that we restrict our attention to government by heads. According to (7) A, a head, governs B in (78).

78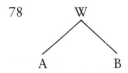

---

[33] Chomsky (1986b: n 12) discusses some other ramifications of the definition of c-command. The reader is referred to this work for discussion.

From our discussion of c-command above it follows that A, the governor, c-commands B, the governee; and conversely, B, the governee, c-commands A, the governor. Government could be defined as a relationship of 'mutual c-command'.

79 **Government** (2)
    A governs B iff
    (i)   A is a governor; and
    (ii) A c-commands B and B c-commands A.

We assume that governors are heads. Below and in later chapters we shall refine the notion of government considerably.

4.2.3 M-COMMAND AND GOVERNMENT

Let us consider the following VP structures:

80a VP

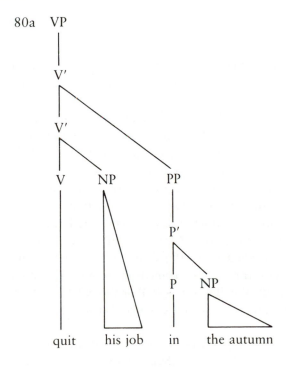

80b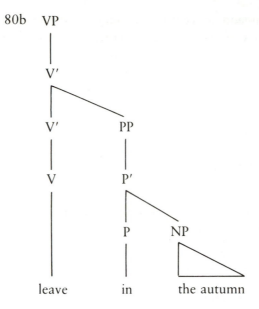

If we adopt our definitions of c-command (77) and government (79) above the relation between V and the PP *in the autumn* in (80a) is quite different from that between V and the PP *in the autumn* in (80b), although in both cases the PP is a time adjunct.

In (80a) the V *quit* c-commands the NP *his job*, which it governs and indeed theta-governs. Following our definitions, the V *quit* does not c-command or govern the time PP *in the autumn*. V does not c-command the PP because the first branching node that dominates it is the lower V', which does not dominate the PP. V does not govern PP because it does not c-command it.

In (80b), the V *leave* c-commands the PP *in the autumn*: the first branching node dominating V is the topmost V', which also dominates the PP. PP also c-commands V since the first branching node dominating PP is the higher V', which also dominates V. We conclude that in (80b) V and the PP *in the autumn* c-command each other. If government is defined in terms of mutual c-command, V will govern the PP. V will not govern P or the NP *the autumn* since there is no mutual c-command relation. V c-commands P and NP; P and NP do not c-command V.

We are thus led to conclude that V governs and c-commands the PP *in the autumn* in (80b) and it fails to do so in (80a). This seems a rather unsatisfactory state of affairs: intuitively one feels that both verbs, *quit* and *leave*, have the same relation to the PP *in the autumn*.

In the literature the definitions of government and c-command have been discussed extensively.[34] On the basis of various empirical and theoretical considerations which we shall not go into here, it has been proposed that in configurations like those in (80) the V should uniformly govern the PP in both (a) and (b). This will capture our intuition that the relation between V and PP is the same in the VPs in (80a) and (80b). In order to arrive at this conclusion, both the notions of c-command and of government have been reformulated in terms of maximal projections.

In *Barriers*, a work to which we return in chapter 10, Chomsky (1986b: 8) proposes the following definition of c-command:

81 **C-command (2)**
    A c-commands B iff A does not dominate B and every X that dominates A also dominates B.

For the choice of X in (81) two options are considered. When X is equated with the first branching node we obtain the c-command definition given in (77). This structural relation is sometimes referred to as **strict c-command**. Alternatively, X is interpreted as a maximal projection. Under the latter interpretation of (81), A **m-commands** B.

Let us apply this definition to (80). V c-commands the NP *his job* in (80a) but not the PP *in the autumn*. On the other hand, V m-commands both the NP *his job*, the PP *in the autumn* and also the preposition *in* and the NP *the autumn*. P c-commands the NP the *autumn*, and P also m-commands the NP *the autumn*. However, P does not c-command V: P', the first branching node dominating P, does not dominate V. P does not m-command V either: there is a maximal projection PP which dominates P and does not dominate V.

In (80b) V c-commands PP (unlike in (80a)), and it also m-commands the PP, the head P and the NP inside the PP. The relation between V and P is identical to that in (80a).

Using the notion of m-command Chomsky (1986b: 8) proposes that government be defined as follows:

82 **Government** (3)
    A governs B iff A m-commands B and no barrier intervenes between A and B.
    Maximal projections are barriers to government.
    Governors are heads.[35]

---

[34] Aoun and Sportiche (1983) discuss examples like those discussed here.
[35] At this point we only look at government by heads. In chapter 8 government by a maximal projection will also be considered.

In both (80a) and (80b) the verbs, *quit* and *leave* respectively, govern the PP *in the autumn*. PP being a maximal projection, the V will not be able to govern into PP. Hence, the verbs in (80a) and in (80b) m-command the NP *the autumn* but they do not govern it.

Our new definition of government (82) is intuitively more satisfactory since it allows us to establish the same relation between V and the PP (80a) and (80b). We adopt (82) from now on. The definition will be further modified in chapter 3. We return to the notion barrier in subsequent chapters and especially in chapter 10. As before, when a head governs a constituent and assigns it a thematic role, we say that the head theta-governs the constituent.

5   Learnability and Binary Branching: Some Discussion

In this chapter we have looked at the geometry of tree diagrams. We started out from a tree like (83) which we later replaced by (84) for various empirical and theoretical reasons.

83

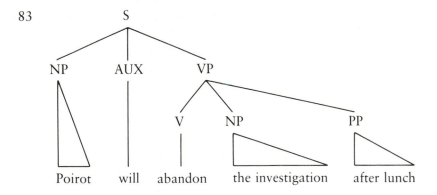

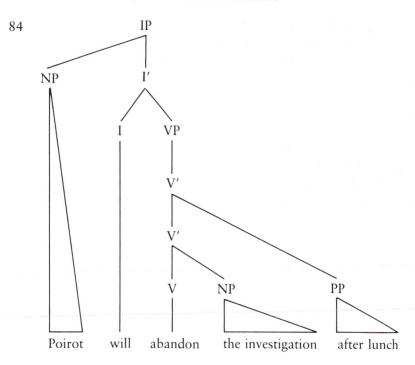

84

If we look at the configurational properties of the two trees there is one important contrast to which we have not paid much attention. In (83), with its flat structure, branching nodes are of different types: there are binary branching nodes, such as PP, which dominate two elements, and there are ternary branching nodes, such as VP or S, which dominate three constituents. If we added more constituents to VP we could end up with four-way or five-way branching nodes. In (84) all branching nodes are **binary branching**.

In the course of this chapter the change from the first type of structure to the second was motivated on empirical and theoretical grounds, but there are further advantages to adopting a grammar which allows only the second type.

The reader may point out that such a grammar is more aesthetically satisfying, though aesthetics may be a minor preoccupation for linguists.

A grammar which allows only binary branching nodes is more **constrained** than a grammar which freely allows any type of branching node: in the former type of grammar lots of imaginable representations are ruled out in principle. A more constrained grammar is preferred for reasons of economy and elegance and it will also be preferred if we think of the ultimate goal of linguistic theories in the generative tradition (as discussed in the Introduction).

Remember that linguists wish to account for the fact that children acquire language very fast and at an early age. In order to explain their fast acquisition we posit that children are genetically prepared for the task, that they have an innate set of principles which enable them to construct the core grammar of their language on the basis of the data they are exposed to.

One component of the child's internalized knowledge of the language, the internal grammar, will concern phrase structure. Theories of phrase structure such as X'-theory attempt to represent the native speaker's internal knowledge of phrase structure.

Let us now compare two theories of phrase structure which differ in one respect. Theory A liberally allows any type of branching (binary, ternary, etc.) Theory B allows only binary branching.

A child faced with linguistic data will have to decide on their phrase structure. Here are a few sentences that a child learning English might hear:

85a Daddy sleeps.
85b Mummy is working.
85c Mummy must leave now.

Theory A and Theory B assign the same structure to (85a):

86

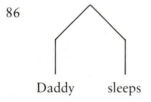

Daddy   sleeps

For the structure of (85b) Theory A offers three options:

87a

87b

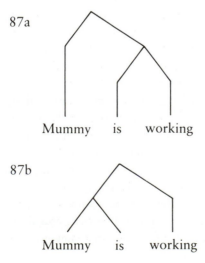

Mummy   is   working

Mummy   is   working

87c

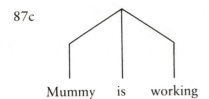

Mummy   is   working

Theory B only allows (87a) and (87b).

For (85c) Theory A offers eight possibilities:

88a

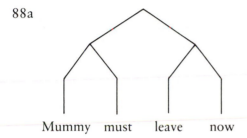

Mummy   must   leave   now

88b

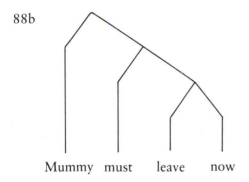

Mummy   must   leave   now

88c

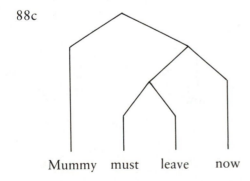

Mummy   must   leave   now

88d

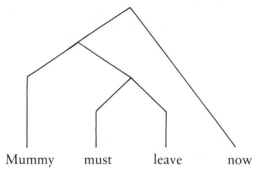

Mummy   must   leave   now

88e

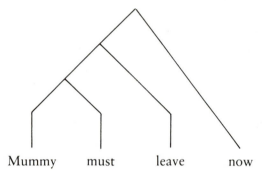

Mummy   must   leave   now

88f

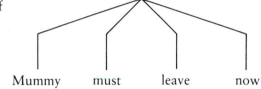

Mummy   must   leave   now

88g

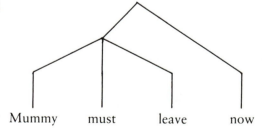

Mummy   must   leave   now

88h

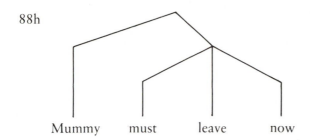

Mummy   must   leave   now

Theory B, which only allows binary branching, excludes the last three options (88f, g, h).

A child equipped with a UG that implements only binary branching will have fewer decisions to make when assigning syntactic structure to the data he is exposed to than a child equipped with a less constrained UG which allows ternary or four-way branching. It is easy to see that the more elements are involved the more choices are available, and hence that the unconstrained theory will consistently offer more choices than the binary branching theory and hence will make the child's task of deciding on the structure harder. For structuring three elements Theory A offers 50 per cent more possibilities than Theory B (three for A, two for B). For four elements Theory A offers 60 per cent more choices, with eight structures as opposed to five. The more elements there are the larger the discrepancy between the choices offered by Theory A and those by Theory B. You are invited to check for yourself what options would be available in the case of there being five elements.

If the ultimate goal of our grammar is to account for language acquisition, then it will be natural to aim for the more restricted type of grammar in which fewer decisions have to be made by the child. Fewer choices will automatically mean more speed in the construction of the core grammar of the language acquired. Nowadays most linguists working in the generative tradition tend to adopt some version of the binary branching framework.[36]

---

[36] Readers interested in theoretical and empirical implications of the binary branching hypothesis should consult work by Kayne (1984), who is one of the first proponents of the strict binary branching approach in the Government and Binding framework.

The binary branching hypothesis raises some important questions which we shall not go into here. One concerns the structure of double object patterns. Consider (i):

(i) John gave Mary the money.

A representation like (ii) is compatible with the binary branching hypothesis:

(ii)

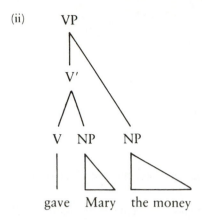

See Kayne (1984) and Larson (1988). Larson (1988) also offers a survey of the recent discussion.

Another issue is the structure of coordinate phrases such as (iii).

(iii)   the man and the woman

Often these are assigned a ternary branching structure:

(iv)

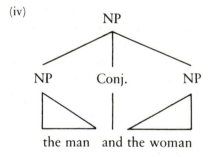

For a discussion of coordinate patterns, see Goodall (1987), who also offers a survey of the literature.

Given the high degree of technicality the books listed above should only be consulted after chapter 8 has been covered.

6   Features and Category Labels

So far we have been assuming that the building-blocks of sentences are lexical categories such as N, V, etc. and that these are syntactic **primitives**. Primitives are 'simple', they cannot be further decomposed with respect to their syntactic behaviour.[37] However, not all linguists agree that the simplest syntactic units are words or lexical categories such as N, V, etc.

An analogy with phonology is in order. One might say that phonology is concerned with the study of phonemes, such as /b/ and /d/. Phonologists have proposed, however, that the simplest units, the primitives, at the phonetic/phonological level are not the phonemes. If we restrict our discussion to the level of phonemes we cannot bring out the commonality between the different sounds. For instance, we cannot capture the fact that both /b/ and /d/ are voiced and that both are plosives. It is proposed that the phonemes can be decomposed into smaller component parts, the distinctive **features**. The features bring out the commonality between the sounds and allow us to set up classes of phonemes. For example, the sounds /b/ and /d/ are composed of the following features:[38]

89   /b/   /d/
    [+voice]   [+voice]
    [+plosive] [+plosive]
    [+bilabial] [+alveolar]

The features listed in (89) make up a **feature matrix**. The commonality between /b/ and /d/ is brought out by the fact that their feature matrices share the features [+voice] and [+plosive]. Their difference is related to the third feature.

Following the example of phonologists, who consider the distinctive features as the primitives of phonology, syntacticians propose that the lexical categories N, V, etc. are not syntactic primitives but should be seen as complexes of syntactic features. These syntactic features themselves will be the basic building-blocks, the primitives of syntactic structure.

---

[37] We are not concerned here with the analysis of words into phonemes. Such a decomposition is not syntactically relevant and concerns the phonological component of the grammar. Apart from the identification of verb inflection, we shall not be concerned with the decomposition of words into morphemes either.

[38] For some introductory literature to the notion of features in phonology, see Fromkin and Rodman (1988).

The features that are often taken to constitute the lexical and phrasal categories are [±noun] ([±N]) and [±verb] ([±V]). The lexical categories can be decomposed into their features:

90a noun: [+N, −V]
90b verb: [−N, +V]
90c adjective: [+N, +V]
90d preposition: [−N, −V]

As in (89), the features in (90) bring out the commonality between the categories which contain the same feature. Anticipating the discussion in chapter 3, it is, for instance, argued that the fact that both verb and preposition may assign case to their complement would be related to their feature [−N]. Conversely, the fact that neither N nor A can assign structural case would be due to their shared feature [+N].

There is no clear agreement about the feature composition of C and I at this point. With respect to I we have already mentioned that it contains the features [±Tense] and [±AGR]. We shall not go deeper into this issue.[39]

7 Summary

In this chapter we have concentrated on syntactic structure. In section 2 we have proposed that a uniform projection schema, the X-bar format, can be developed for all phrasal categories. Phrases are hierarchically structured projections of their heads.

1 XP ⟶ Specifier; X′
    X′* ⟶ X′; YP
    X′ ⟶ X; YP.

The X-bar format allows us to bring out the commonality between the different types of phrases. The traditional phrase structure rules for specific

---

[39] The reader interested in the theory of features should consult the literature. For the decomposition of the lexical categories, see Chomsky (1970) and Stowell (1981). Muysken (1982) extends the use of features to include the levels of projection X°, X′ and X″. Muysken and van Riemsdijk (1986) offer a survey of some of the problems concerning syntactic features. See also Rizzi (1990).

phrases, say VP, are reduced to more elementary notions. The hierarchical organization of the phrase is captured by X'-theory, the relative ordering of constituents will have to be related to some other principle of the grammar.

Section 3 shows that the X-bar schema can be extended to the clausal constituents: S is reinterpreted as a projection of INFL, with the subject NP in the specifier position. S' is reinterpreted as a projection of C.

2

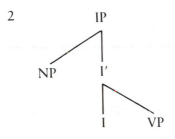

3

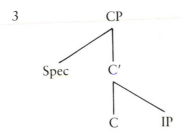

In section 4 we introduce the structural relations c-command and m-command, and we redefine government in terms of these notions.

4 C-command

A c-commands B iff A does not dominate B and every X that dominates A also dominates B.

When X is equated with the first branching node, A **c-commands** B. When X is interpreted as a maximal projection, A **m-commands** B.

5 Government

A governs B iff A m-commands B and no barrier intervenes between A and B.
Maximal projections are barriers to government.
Governors are heads.

We have considered the importance of the binary branching hypothesis especially in the light of language acquisition (section 5) and we have looked at the proposal that syntactic features should replace lexical categories as syntactic primitives (section 6).

8   Exercises

Exercise 1

Using the X-bar model draw a tree diagram for the following sentences:

1   Poirot will meet the new governess in the foyer of the opera.
2   Miss Marple cleaned the knife carefully with a handkerchief.
3   Maigret is quite fond of his assistant.
4   The announcement of the news on local radio surprised all the students of linguistics from England.
5   She has decided that owners of big cars without children should pay tax.

Exercise 2

In this chapter we have defined structural notions such as government, c-command and m-command. Consider the tree diagram below. Try to decide which elements are c-commanded by I, C and V, and which elements are m-commanded by them. Try to determine which elements are governed by I, by C and by V (a) when government is defined in terms of sisterhood, and (b) when government is defined in terms of m-command.

1

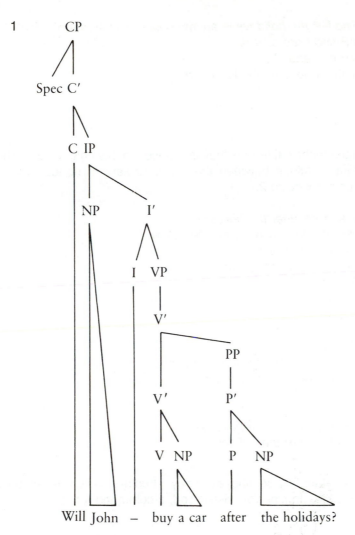

CP
Spec C'
C IP
NP I'
I VP
V'
PP
V' P'
V NP P NP
Will John – buy a car after the holidays?

Exercise 3

On the basis of the tree diagram in exercise 2 decide which of the following statements are true and which are false:

1   IP dominates CP.
2   IP immediately dominates the subject NP.
3   IP is a sister of C.
4   V and the NP *a car* are sisters.
5   V head-governs the PP *after the holidays*.
6   The NP *the holidays* is a constituent of IP.

7   The NP *the holidays* is an immediate constituent of VP.
8   VP and I are sisters.
9   VP precedes I.
10   V theta-governs the NP *a car*.

Exercise 4

Using the technical terminology introduced in this chapter describe the structural relations between the following sets of nodes in the tree diagram in exercise 2.

1   V and PP *after the holidays*.
2   PP *after the holidays* and NP *a car*.
3   NP *John* and VP.
4   NP *John* and NP *a car*.
5   IP and C'.
6   C and I.
7   C and NP *John*.
8   I and NP *a car*.
9   V and NP *John*.
10   V' and the PP *after the holidays*.
11   P and the NP *the holidays*.
12   V and P.
13   C and VP.
14   VP and the NP *the holidays*.
15   I and the NP *the holidays*.

For each pair, try to find as many structural relations as possible (precedence, dominance, sisterhood, c-command, etc.).

3 Case Theory

Contents

Introduction and Overview

In chapter 1 we discussed the component of the grammar that regulates the assignment of thematic roles to arguments. This component is called theta theory. Chapter 2 deals with the component of the grammar that regulates phrase structure, X-bar theory. These two chapters suggest that the grammar we are building has a modular structure: it contains different components or **modules**. In this chapter we consider another module of the grammar: **case theory**.

Case theory accounts for some of the formal properties of overt NPs and integrates the traditional notion of case into the grammar. Though the discussion focuses on case in English we shall occasionally refer to examples from German.

In section 1 we introduce the notion abstract case as distinct from morphological case. Abstract case is a universal property, while the overt realization of abstract case by means of morphological case varies cross-linguistically. Section 2 is concerned with the distribution of NOMINATIVE and ACCUSATIVE case in English. In this section we introduce the case filter, the requirement that all overt NPs be assigned abstract case. In section 3 we introduce the difference between structural case and inherent case. In section 4 we consider the adjacency requirement on case assignment. Section 5 describes the properties of passive sentences. Section 6 discusses the hypothesis that the case filter can be derived from theta theory.

1   Morphological Case and Abstract Case

Consider the examples in (1):

1a   The butler attacked the robber.
1b   [That the butler attacked the robber] is surprising.
1c   [For the butler to attack the robber] would be surprising.

(1a) is a simple sentence, containing two NPs, *the butler* and *the robber*. In (1b) the simple sentence (1a) is used as the subject clause of an adjectival predicate (*surprising*). In (1c) we find the non-finite parallel of (1a) used as the subject of the adjectival predicate.

In chapter 1 we saw that NPs realize the arguments of the predicate of the sentence and are theta-marked, directly or indirectly. In (1) the verb *attack* assigns two theta roles. This information is encoded in the lexical entry of *attack*. Following our convention adopted in chapter 1, we indicate the relevant theta roles by numbering and ignore for the most part the specific label. Occasionally, we shall consider the thematic relations more carefully.

2   *attack*:   verb

<u>1</u>	2

Let us replace the argument NPs in (1) by the corresponding pronouns:

3a   *He* attacked *him*.
3b   That *he* attacked *him* is surprising.
3c   For *him* to attack *him* would be surprising.

Depending on their positions in the sentences, the third person pronouns appear in different forms. When the pronoun is the internal argument of *attack* it takes the form *him*. Adopting the terminology of traditional grammar we call this form the **ACCUSATIVE case**. When the third person pronoun is the external argument of *attack* it takes either the form *he* or the form *him*. The latter form is again the ACCUSATIVE case of the pronoun; the form *he* will be called the **NOMINATIVE case**. Pronouns thus can be seen to have different case forms: *he* is NOMINATIVE, *him* is ACCUSATIVE. A third case form found in English NPs is the **GENITIVE**, illustrated in (3d) and (3e).

3d   *The butler's* coat was too big.
3e   *His* coat was too big.

In English, the overt morphological realization of case in full lexical noun phrases is restricted to the GENITIVE case. As can be seen in (1), NOMINATIVE and ACCUSATIVE are not realized overtly in modern English full NPs, though these case forms were overtly marked in earlier stages of the language.[1] Adjectives and determiners, which also used to have case forms in earlier stages of the language, equally do not have distinct overt case forms any more.

The overt distinction of NOMINATIVE and ACCUSATIVE forms in modern English is still to be found in the pronoun system, though even there we find several examples of case syncretism: two case forms having the same morphological realization. Table (4) illustrates the overt realization of the case forms in NPs: in (a) we find the full lexical NPs, in (b) we list the pronouns. As can be seen NOMINATIVE and ACCUSATIVE are the same for the pronouns *you* and *it*.

4   English overt case forms

		NOMINATIVE	ACCUSATIVE	GENITIVE
a	*Lexical NPs:*			
		the man	the man	the man's
		the good man	the good man	the good man's
b	*Pronominal NPs:*			
	1 sg	I	me	my
	2 sg	you	you	your
	3 sg masc	he	him	his
	3 sg fem	she	her	her
	3 sg neut	it	it	its
	1 pl	we	us	our
	2 pl	you	you	your
	3 pl	they	them	their

Other languages, like Latin or German, have a morphologically rich case system where distinct cases are overtly marked on nouns, adjectives, determiners, etc. as well as on pronouns. Consider, for instance, the following Latin examples:

5a Caesar Belgas   vincit.
    Caesar Belgians beats
    'Caesar beats the Belgians.'

---

[1] An interesting discussion of the development of the English case system is found in van Kemenade (1986) and Lumsden (1987). Both works should be accessible when chapter 7 has been covered.

5b Belgae   Caesarem tement.
    Belgians Caesar   fear
    'The Belgians fear Caesar.'

In (5a) the NP *Caesar* is in the NOMINATIVE case and the NP *Belgas* is ACCUSATIVE. Conversely, in (5b) *Belgae* is NOMINATIVE and *Caesarem* is ACCUSATIVE.

From German we give the following examples:

6a Der   Mann/Student   hat   den   Lehrer   gesehen.
    the   man/ student   has   the   teacher seen
    NOMINATIVE   ACCUSATIVE
6b Der   Lehrer   hat   den   Mann/Studenten   gesehen.
    the   teacher has   the   man/student   seen
    NOMINATIVE   ACCUSATIVE

In German case forms are overtly realized on the determiner system of NPs and also on a certain class of nouns (cf. the ACCUSATIVE form *Studenten* in (6b)).

Although English does not have the overt case-marking that we find, for example, in Latin and in German, it has the remnants of an overt case system, as seen in the pronominal system. We therefore do not wish to say that English lacks case. Rather, following our discussion of agreement in chapter 2, we postulate that English has a fully-fledged system of **abstract case**, similar to that in Latin or German. We assume that abstract case is part of universal grammar. However, we shall say that the abstract case-marking in English is often not morphologically realized. The degree of morphological realization of abstract case varies parametrically from one language to another.

The concept of abstract case is an important part of Government and Binding Theory. Based on work by Vergnaud (1985), Chomsky and his followers have developed a theory of case, **case theory**. As we shall see (section 6) attempts have been made to relate case theory to other components of the grammar, notably theta theory. We first look at some examples of English case forms and try to show how case theory can be developed on the basis of those.

2 Structural case: NOMINATIVE and ACCUSATIVE

In this section we concentrate on the distribution of NOMINATIVE and ACCUSATIVE case forms. We discuss GENITIVE case in section 3.

As can be seen in (3), the NOMINATIVE case (*he*) is reserved for the NP in the subject position of finite clauses. The ACCUSATIVE case (*him*) is used both for the object NP of a transitive verb ((3a), (3b) and (3c)) and for the subject NP of an infinitival subordinate clause (3c).[2] We also find ACCUSATIVE case realized on the NP complement of a preposition.

7   Jeeves moved towards him/*he.

Adopting the concepts of traditional grammar, we can say that subjects of finite clauses have NOMINATIVE case and that NPs that are complements of prepositions or verbs as well as NPs that are subjects of infinitival clauses appear in the ACCUSATIVE. But this informal system needs some discussion. At this point we have provided a list of occurrences without trying to relate the distribution of the case forms to other properties of the sentences in question. Recall that we argued in the Introduction that lists offer no insight in the phenomena that are listed.

2.1   Complements: ACCUSATIVE

Let us first look at the complements of transitive verbs and prepositions. Following traditional accounts of case we might say that transitive verbs and prepositions **assign** ACCUSATIVE case to the NP they govern. They **case-mark** an NP which they govern. Thus in (8) the V and the P will case–mark the complement NPs. In this view, heads assign case.

---

[2] The subject of infinitival clauses used as main clauses is assigned either NOMINATIVE (i) or ACCUSATIVE (ii):

(i)   He go there? Impossible.
(ii) Him attack Bill? Never.

Sentences such as (i) and (ii) are clearly marked. They cannot be used to start a conversation, rather they will be used to echo a preceding utterance. The source of the case on their subjects is a matter for further research.

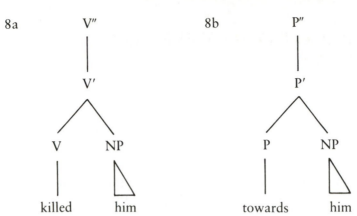

8a   V″ ... killed him

8b   P″ ... towards him

As we shall see in section 2.2 and the subsequent sections, the conditions of case assignment are partly structural: case is assigned under government. A verb cannot assign ACCUSATIVE case to an NP outside the VP such as the subject:

9a   *Him found the evidence.

In (9a) the V *find* does not govern the subject NP. We shall refine the definition of government in (17) and (18) below.

The possibility of case assignment is also a function of the type of verb, i.e. the governor. Only transitive verbs and prepositions assign case. Intransitive verbs like *wander* or *overeat* cannot assign case to a complement NP:

9b   *He wandered them.
9c   *He overate them.

Nouns and adjectives also do not assign ACCUSATIVE case (see discussion in section 3).

9d   *Poirot's attack him
9e   *Poirot is envious him

We shall classify transitive verbs and prepositions as ACCUSATIVE **case assigners.**[3]

---

[3]   In chapter 2, section 7, we pointed out that the ability of a category to assign case has sometimes been related to the presence of the feature [−N]. Prepositions and verbs are [−N], nouns and adjectives are [+N] (see Stowell, 1981).

2.2   Subjects: *NOMINATIVE and ACCUSATIVE*

2.2.1   NOMINATIVE SUBJECTS

Subjects of finite clauses have NOMINATIVE case (cf. (3a)). Let us try to link the presence of NOMINATIVE to some case assigning head in the sentence, just as we have linked the presence of ACCUSATIVE to government by a transitive verb or a preposition.

One important element in the discussion is that whereas subjects of finite clauses are NOMINATIVE, subjects of infinitivals have ACCUSATIVE case (cf. (3c)).

In chapter 2 we claimed that the distinction between finite and non-finite clauses can be characterized in terms of the feature composition of the head of the clause, INFL or I. In finite clauses, INFL is [+Tense, +AGR]. In non-finite clauses, INFL has the feature specifications [−Tense, −AGR]. This enables us to associate the occurrence of NOMINATIVE case with the INFL of a finite clause, which is marked for [+Tense] and [+AGR]. We leave it open here whether it is Tense or AGR that is responsible for the NOMINATIVE case.

Consider now a tree diagram representation for (3a).

10

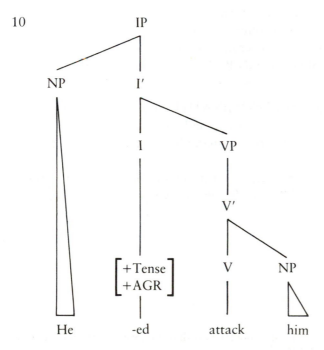

While the various definitions of government discussed in chapter 2 have equally satisfying results when we analyse (8), these definitions of government will give different results with respect to the diagram in (10).

If we were to adopt the definition of government in terms of sisterhood, or mutual c-command, then it would not be possible to argue that I governs the subject, [NP,IP], in (10). The first branching node dominating I is I' and I' fails to dominate [NP,IP].

On the other hand, [NP,IP] is inside the projection of I: it is immediately dominated by IP, the maximal projection of I. If we adopt the definition of government in terms of m-command, finite I governs [NP,IP] and we can say that finite I case-marks the subject NP.

Let us return to the definition of government[4] given in chapter 2. In (11a) we repeat the definition, in (11b) we analyse it into its component parts:

11a **Government** (chapter 2, (82)).

A governs B iff A m-commands B and no barrier intervenes between A and B.

Maximal projections are barriers to government.

Governors are heads.

11b **Government**

A governs B iff   (i)   A is a governor;

(ii)   A m-commands B;

(iii) no barrier intervenes between A and B.

Governors are lexical nodes (V,N,P,A) and tensed I.

With respect to the assignment of NOMINATIVE case, the governor we are concerned with is I (containing [+Tense] and [+AGR]) and the relevant maximal projection is IP. In (10) IP dominates both the governor I and the governed node [NP,IP], *he*.

Let us consider the problems raised by a definition such as (11). Consider case-marking inside VP and PP as in (8) above. We give only the syntactic representation of VP.

12a Poirot killed him.

---

[4] Recall that we are at this point only concerned with head-government. In chapter 8 we shall turn to government by phrases.

12b
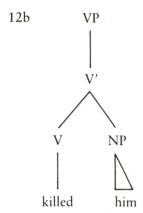

13a   Jeeves moved towards him/*he.

13b
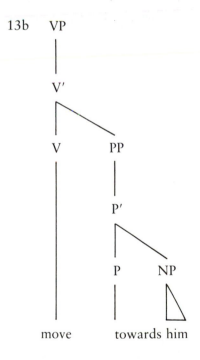

The definition of government in (11) at first glance does not pose any problems: V and P clearly govern their complements in (12) and (13). A closer look at (13) reveals that the definition in (11) may give rise to a problem, though. On the basis of (11), we might argue that the verb *move* also governs the complement of the preposition: *him*. The question could be raised if it really is the preposition *towards* that case-marks *him*, or if it could be the verb *move*.

Consider the following examples from German:[5]

14a dass er einen Roman schreibt.
        that he a   novel writes
        'that he writes a novel.'
14b dass er mit einem Bleistift schreibt.
        that he with a   pencil   writes
        'that he writes with a pencil.'
14c *dass er mit einen Bleistift schreibt.

In (14a) the direct object NP *einen Roman* is assigned ACCUSATIVE case by the transitive verb *schreiben*. In (14b), the complement of *mit* is assigned DATIVE. It cannot be assigned ACCUSATIVE, as seen in (14c). The structure of the VP in (14b) will be analogous to that of (13):

14d

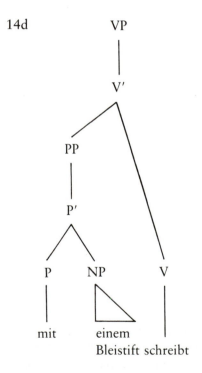

Given that (14c) is ungrammatical we conclude that the verb *schreiben*, although potentially an ACCUSATIVE case assigner (14a), cannot assign ACCUSATIVE to the complement of *mit* in (14b). We will have to deduce that the PP is a barrier for government by the verb.

A similar problem arises in (10) repeated here for the reader's convenience as (15):

15

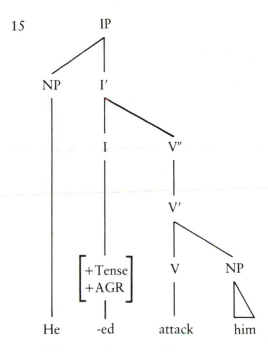

The first maximal projection dominating I is IP, which also dominates the object NP. We assume that I assigns NOMINATIVE case. Clearly we do not wish to say that I will be able to assign NOMINATIVE case to the object of the verb, given the ungrammaticality of (16):

16   *He attacked he.

The problem is that unless we define exactly which categories are barriers, the formulation in (11b) allows for multiple governors. In order to exclude this possibility we have to specify that PP is a barrier for government by V in (13) and (14b) and that VP is a barrier for government by I in (15). We would like to say that an m-commanding head which is closest to a constituent actually governs it and prevents other heads from governing the same constituent. Let us say that the closer head defines its maximal projection as a barrier for government by another head. P in (14d) is 'closer' to its complement NP than V, and hence P will govern the complement NP and PP is a barrier for government from I. In order to exclude multiple governors and to define maximal projections as barriers, we shall introduce the notion **minimality** into the definition (11b): (11b) is reworded as (17) with the minimality clause spelt out in (18).

17   Government (adapted[6] from Rizzi, 1990: 6)
    A governs B iff   (i)   A is a governor;
                    (ii)   A m-commands B;
                 (iii)   minimality is respected.
    Governors are the lexical categories and tensed INFL.

(17(ii)) specifies the structural relation, m-command, between a governor and its governee. But not all potential governors are governors. The minimality condition (17(iii)) will ensure that only the closest potential governor will actually count as a governor. The minimality condition is defined as follows:

18   **Minimality** (adapted from Rizzi, 1990: 7)
    A governs B iff there is no node Z such that
         (i)   Z is a potential governor for B;
    and (ii)   Z m-commands B;
    and (iii)   Z does not m-command A.

The joint definitions (17) and (18) may at first look rather complex. As mentioned, the main purpose is to exclude multiple governors for an element B. Let us check how multiple government is excluded in (14d), repeated here for convenience as (19). We have indicated the relevant nodes with A, B and Z:

---

[6] At this point the notion barrier is defined in terms of minimality and need not be stated in the definition of government. We return to a discussion of barriers in chapter 10.

19

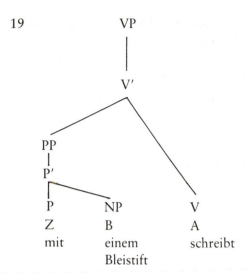

Both V(= A) and P (= Z) m-command the NP *einem Bleistift* (= B). Hence, according to (17(ii)), both V and P are in the right structural relation with respect to the NP and fulfil the structural condition to count as governors for the NP. But by minimality, (17(iii)), P is the actual governor. P is a node like Z in (18) and V is like A. (i) P is a potential governor, (ii) P is m-commanded by V but itself does not m-command V. Informally we can say that P is a closer governor than V and thus wins.

With respect to head-government we have arrived at the situation that each head determines a domain of influence into which outside heads cannot govern: the maximal projection of the head is the **governing domain**. In our tree diagram P determines as its governing domain PP, its maximal projection. Outside heads such as V cannot govern into this maximal projection. Maximal projections constitute **barriers** for outside head-government by virtue of the minimality condition in (18).[7]

On the basis of the amended definitions of government in (17) and of minimality in (18) we guarantee that, in (15), INFL will govern the subject NP uniquely and will be able to assign NOMINATIVE case to it; V governs the

---

[7] A word of caution is in order here. At this point of the discussion we are concentrating on head-government and we see that it might be possible to dispense with the term **barrier** in the definition of government by the addition of the minimality condition (18). Maximal projections are barriers for head-government because they will contain the minimal governor for a specific node. In later chapters (especially chapters 9 and 10) we shall also consider other governors and we shall have to reintroduce the notion barrier in addition to the minimality condition. Rizzi (1990) has further refined the notions barrier and minimality. See his work for discussion. The book should not be tackled until we have finished chapter 10.

direct object NP uniquely and can assign ACCUSATIVE. The maximal projection of V constitutes the barrier for government from the outside.[8]

2.2.2 THE SUBJECT OF INFINITIVAL CLAUSES

2.2.2.1 For as a Case-marker We repeat (3c) with its tree diagram representation in (20):

20a [For him to attack him] would be surprising.

20b

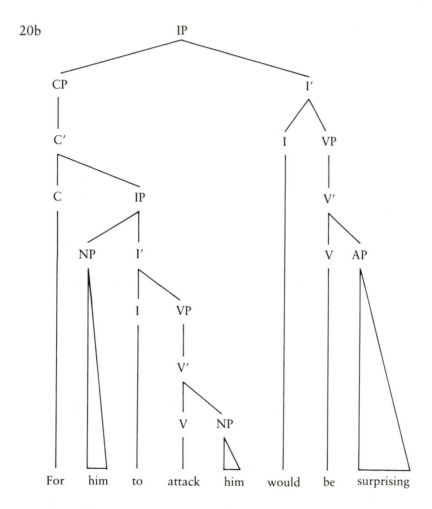

[8] In recent work (Sportiche, 1988b) it has been proposed that the subject in English is assigned NOMINATIVE by virtue of specifier-head agreement rather than by a governing head.

How do we account for the ACCUSATIVE case of the subject NP of the infinitival clause? One possible answer would be to argue that it is the infinitival I (*to*) that is responsible for case-marking the NP subject. This is unlikely in view of the following examples.

21a *[Him to attack Bill] would be illegal.
21b [That he should have attacked Bill] was surprising.

22a *I prefer very much [him to go now].
22b I prefer very much [that he should go now].

In (21a) and (22a) we have an infinitival subordinate clause. In each example the infinitive marker *to* is present but the sentence is not grammatical. In contrast, (21b) and (22b) contain a finite subordinate clause; the head of the clause, I, assigns NOMINATIVE case to the subject NP. Potentially, there might be different ways of explaining the ungrammaticality of (21a) and (22a), but a significant point to take into consideration is that the sentences are saved by the insertion of *for* as the complementizer of the non-finite clause:

23a [For him to attack Bill] would be illegal.
23b I prefer very much [for him to go now].

Alternatively, the sentences are rescued by the omission of the overt subject of the infinitival clause. In chapter 5 we discuss the status of the subject position (indicated with a dash) in the infinitival clauses in (24).

24a [– To attack Bill] would be illegal.
24b I prefer very much [– to go now].

Let us try to relate these groups of examples. It seems as if it is the presence of the element *for* under C that enables the overt NP subject *him* to survive. When *for* is absent the subject pronoun must also disappear (24). Which property of *for* could be used to explain these phenomena?

In (23), the preposition *for* occupies the head position of CP. We call *for* in such examples a **prepositional complementizer**. *For* is a preposition, hence an ACCUSATIVE case assigner (see sections 2.1 and 2.2.1). We shall argue that the role of *for* is indeed to case-mark the subject *him*. The next question is why there should be any need for such a case on the NP.

Let us postulate that there is a requirement that all overt NPs must be assigned abstract case, the **case filter**.

25   Case filter
Every overt NP must be assigned abstract case.

This requirement is called a filter because it 'filters out' any construction containing an overt NP which is not assigned case. We assume, from now on, that the case filter applies to *all* overt NPs. The reader may observe that a filter such as (25) does not explain anything. It merely states that a certain type of construction is ungrammatical, without attempting to explain why this should be so. In section 6 we shall try to link the case filter to other principles of the grammar.

(21a) and (22a) are ungrammatical, but can be saved either by insertion of the case assigner *for* or by omission of the overt subject. Our hypothesis will be that (21a) and (22a) are ungrammatical because *to*, the non-finite I of the infinitival clause, cannot assign case to the [NP,IP]. Finite I, which is [+Tense, +AGR], assigns NOMINATIVE case and contrasts with non-finite I which is [−Tense, −AGR] and does not assign case. (21a) and (22a) are ungrammatical because they violate the case filter.

The case filter has nothing to say about the subject of the infinitives in (24) since these sentences lack an overt NP subject (see chapters 5 and 8 for the discussion of infinitival clauses without overt subject).

The prepositional complementizer *for* in (23) case-marks the subject NP of the infinitival clause: (23) passes the case filter and is grammatical. However, caution is needed with respect to such an analysis of (23). We have said that case is assigned under government. Hence we would like to be able to say that the case assigner *for* governs *him*, the subject of the clause which it introduces. Consider (26):

26

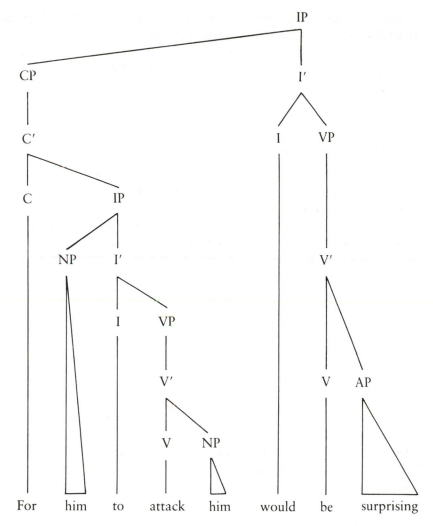

The question is whether the head of CP, *for*, can govern into IP, its complement. I in the subordinate clause is itself a head and thus a potential governor. We expect that it will define a governing domain IP, and, by the minimality condition, *for* should not be able to govern into that (see (17(iii)) and (18) above). While I is the head of a maximal projection, IP, we are forced to claim that infinitival IP is not a barrier for outside governors. Let us try to see why infinitival I should not define a governing domain. Observe that I, the head of IP, is non-lexical (cf. chapter 2) and that it is negatively specified for the features [Tense] and [AGR]. Informally, we could perhaps say that non-finite I is 'too weak' to define a barrier for outside heads, it loses out on stronger outside heads. With the stipulation that I does not define a barrier for outside governors, *for* will be able to govern into IP and to assign ACCUSATIVE case to the subject NP of the subordinate clause.

Our definition of government in (17) must equally ensure that in (26) the finite inflection of the main clause (past tense third person singular) will not be able to govern into the lower clause to case-mark its subject as NOMINATIVE:

27   *For he to attack Bill was illegal.

We only need to assume that by minimality (18) *for* will define a governing domain CP, hence CP is a barrier to outside governors. Though the main clause I is a head and hence a potential governor, it will lose out against the closer governor, the preposition *for*, which is the head of CP, a maximal projection. In chapter 10 we return to the discussion and modification of the notions barrier and government.

2.2.2.2 Exceptional Case-marking   Continuing the examination of subjects of infinitives in English, we turn to (28):

28   John believes [him to be a liar].

In (28) *believe* takes an infinitival clause as its internal argument. The first question we may ask is which label to assign to the bracketed string: is the relevant constituent an IP (I″) or a CP (C″)? One argument in favour of the IP hypothesis is that it is not possible to insert the complementizer *for*, which is typical for infinitival clauses, in front of the subordinate clause:[9]

29a   *John believes for him to be a liar.
29b   *John believes very much for him to be a liar.

(28) will have the syntactic representation (30):

---

[9] *Believe* may also take a finite CP as its complement:

(i) I believe [$_{CP}$ that [$_{IP}$ he is a liar]].

30

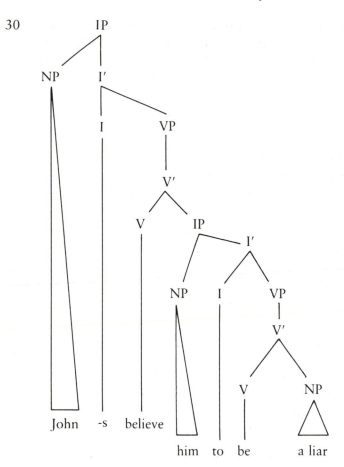

The question we address here is how *him* can satisfy the case filter, i.e. be assigned (ACCUSATIVE) case. Our hypothesis (see the discussion of (21) and 22)) was that infinitival I is not a case assigner. The obvious candidate for case-marking *him* in (30) is the transitive verb *believe*:

31   I believe this story.

In (31) *believe* case-marks the NP *this story*. On the basis of our previous discussion it is plausible that *believe* can assign case to *him*, the subject of the complement IP. *Believe* is separated from *him* by a maximal projection, infinitival IP. By assumption, infinitival IP will not constitute a barrier for outside government and hence *believe* can assign case to the relevant NP.

The situation in which a verb like *believe* can govern into an IP and assign case to its subject NP is often referred to as **exceptional case–marking** abbreviated as ECM. The 'exceptionality' is related precisely to the fact that maximal projections normally constitute barriers for case assignment from the outside.

As a final illustration consider the following examples:

32a I know [IP John to be the best candidate].
32b I don't know [CP whether [IP – to go to the party]].
32c *I don't know [CP whether [IP John to go to the party]].

(32a) is parallel to (30). *Know* takes an IP complement, governs into the maximal projection IP and case-marks *John*.

In (32b), the presence of *whether* indicates that we have an infinitival clause of the type CP. In this example, there is no overt subject in the infinitival clause (see chapter 5 for non-overt subjects in infinitival clauses), thus the case filter (25) does not come into play with respect to the subject NP of the lower clause.

In (32c) *know* again takes a clausal CP complement (witness the presence of *whether*). In this example the infinitival clause contains a lexical NP subject *John*. The sentence is ungrammatical because it violates the case filter. Infinitival *to* is assumed to be unable to assign case. The potential case assigner *know* is separated from the relevant NP by the maximal projection CP, which is a barrier (see also the discussion in chapter 10).

2.2.2.3 Small clauses In chapters 1 and 2 we have briefly discussed examples of small clauses, illustrated in (33).

33a Maigret considers [AP the taxi driver [AP entirely innocent]].
33b I consider [NP Maigret [NP an inspector of great value]].
33c I consider [PP your proposal [PP completely out of the question]].

Given the case filter the subject NPs of the small clauses in (33) must be case-marked. The small clauses themselves do not contain a case-marker. Consider, for instance, the simplified syntactic representation of (33a):

34

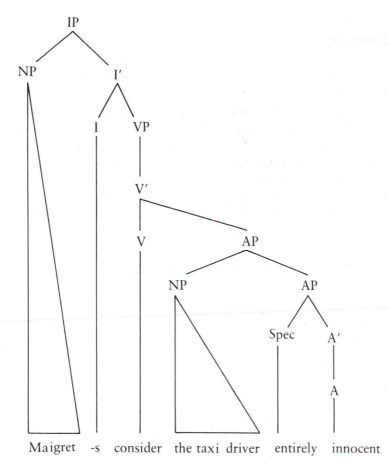

Maigret   -s   consider   the taxi driver   entirely   innocent

We adopt the proposal discussed in chapter 2 that small clauses are 'super-projections' of the category of their predicate. In (34) the small clause consists of an AP (*entirely innocent*) which combines with an NP *the taxi driver*. We shall see in section 3 that adjectives are not case assigners in English. We propose that the verb *consider* case-marks the subject of the small clause, the NP *the taxi driver*. Again we must assume that the small clause AP is not a barrier for an outside governor.

At this point it becomes clear that the definition of barrier is not going to be easy. Maximal projections such as VP and PP were argued to be barriers, CP too was argued to be a barrier. On the other hand, infinitival IP and small clauses were said not to be barriers. At the moment these distinctions sound like *ad hoc* stipulations. In chapters 9 and 10 we shall develop a more principled account for the concept.

2.3   Summary

To sum up this section: we have argued that overt NPs are subject to the case filter; they must be assigned abstract case. We have discussed two instances of abstract case: NOMINATIVE and ACCUSATIVE. NOMINATIVE is assigned by finite I, ACCUSATIVE is assigned by prepositions and verbs. In order to explain the case assignment to subjects of infinitival clauses we have adopted two hypotheses: (i) non-finite I is not a case assigner, (ii) infinitival IP is not a barrier to outside government.

We have proposed that a head can assign case to an NP which it governs. In our discussion we have reconsidered the definition of government and introduced the minimality condition.

3   Adjectives and Nouns

3.1   Of-insertion

So far we have looked at case assignment by finite I – NOMINATIVE – and by verbs and prepositions (including *for*) – ACCUSATIVE. Nouns and adjectives are not case assigners in English:

35a   Poirot envies Miss Marple.
35b   *Poirot is envious Miss Marple.
35c   Poirot is envious of Miss Marple.
35d   *Poirot's envy Miss Marple
35e   Poirot's envy of Miss Marple

All the examples in (35) contain a main predicate morphologically and semantically related to the verb *envy*. In (35a) *envy*, the verb, is used; in (35b) and (35c) we find the related adjective *envious*; in (35d) and (35e) the noun *envy*.

Let us consider how the case filter (25) applies to these examples. In (35a) case assignment is straightforward: *Poirot* is assigned NOMINATIVE by the finite inflection and *Miss Marple* is assigned ACCUSATIVE by the transitive verb *envy*.

(35b) is ungrammatical. If we compare it with the grammatical (35a) the only difference is that we have replaced the verb *envy* by the adjective *envious*. Apparently (35b) can be rescued by the insertion of the preposition *of* as seen in (35c). How can we account for these data?

This situation is reminiscent of that discussed in section 2.2.2.1. We saw there that the prepositional complementizer *for* rescued sentences (21a) and (22a) and we argued that *for* was needed in order to guarantee that the subject NP of the infinitival clause would receive case.

We shall try to explain the ungrammaticality of (35b), without *of*, and the grammaticality of (35c), with *of*, also in terms of the case filter. If adjectives like *envious* cannot case-mark their complement then (35b) is ruled out by the case filter since the NP *Miss Marple* will not be assigned case.

We also posit that English has a default procedure to rescue sentences like (35b) which consists of inserting the preposition *of* in front of the NP. We refer to this procedure by the term *of*-**insertion**. Like any other preposition, *of* can assign ACCUSATIVE case and thus will avoid a case filter violation: in (35c) *Miss Marple* is case-marked by *of*.

Let us turn to (35d) and (35e). First of all we see that these NPs contain a GENITIVE NP, *Poirot's*, in front of their head N. We shall not discuss GENITIVE assignment in the pre-nominal position. Let us assume that there is an element POSS in the specifier position of NPs which is able to assign GENITIVE to the NP in that position.[10]

We turn to the post-nominal complement of *envy*, the NP *Miss Marple*. Analogously to (35b) and (35c), we shall try to account for the ungrammaticality of (35d) and the grammaticality of (35e) in terms of case theory. If nouns fail to assign case to their complements (35d) violates the case filter. *Of*-insertion in (35e) enables the complement NP to receive case.

3.2   *Failure of Of*-insertion

We have considered case assignment as a structural property of verbs, prepositions and INFL. We have assumed that these heads are case assigners and will case-mark any NP they govern. We have also postulated that infinitival I is not a case assigner and that infinitival IP is transparent for outside government, hence for outside case-marking.

Let us now again turn to predicates with clausal complements.

---

[10]   The interested reader is referred to the discussion in Chomsky (1986a: 190) and the references cited there. See also Abney (1987).

36a I believe [that [John is honest]].
36b my belief [that [John is honest]]
36c I believe [John to be honest].
36d *my belief [John to be honest]
36e *my belief [of John to be honest]

37a Emsworth is proud of [the pig].
37b *Emsworth is proud [the pig].
37c Emsworth is proud [that [the pig has won]].
37d *Emsworth is proud [the pig to have won].
37e *Emsworth is proud [of the pig to have won].

In (36a) the verb *believe* takes a tensed CP as its complement. The subject of the lower clause *John* is assigned NOMINATIVE case by the finite INFL.

In (36b), similarly, the noun *belief* takes a finite CP complement and the same mechanism of case assignment applies. (36c) exemplifies ECM: the verb *believe* governs into the complement IP and assigns ACCUSATIVE to *John*. In (36d) we see that ECM is not possible with nouns. The ungrammaticality of this example is expected if we assume that nouns are not case assigners. However, we have seen that in other examples in which noun heads fail to assign case, a default mechanism of *of*-insertion applies to rescue NPs which would otherwise end up caseless (see (35) above). As (36e) shows, *of*-insertion cannot rescue (36d).

A similar pattern is found with the adjectival complementation in (37). (37a) illustrates obligatory (cf. (37b)) *of*-insertion. In (37c) the subject of the finite complement clause will be assigned NOMINATIVE by the finite inflection. In (37d) the adjective takes an IP complement. By assumption, infinitival IP is not a barrier for government by the adjective *proud* but this is not sufficient to save the construction since adjectives are unable to assign case. Again, as was the case for noun complements, the default mechanism of *of*-insertion (operative in (37a)) can apparently not be used to save (37d)).

In *Knowledge of Language* Chomsky (1986a) offers an explanation for the fact that *of*-insertion is not allowed in (36e) and (37e). Chomsky's solution uses a contrast between two types of case assignment. So far we have assumed that all case was dependent on purely structural relations. Specifically we assumed that the structural relation government is a sufficient condition for case-marking.

Chomsky distinguishes two types of case assignment: **structural** case assignment, which depends solely on government, a configurational property, and **inherent** case assignment, which is dependent on two conditions: (i) theta role assignment and (ii) government:

38 **Inherent case condition**

If A is an inherent case assigner, then A assigns case to an NP if and only if A theta-marks the NP.

(Chomsky, 1986a: 194)

Chomsky proposes that nouns assign GENITIVE case inherently and that rather than assigning structural case, as we implied previously, *of* is the overt reflex of an inherent GENITIVE case. In English an inherent GENITIVE in the complement of NP or AP is realized by means of a preposition *of* which assigns ACCUSATIVE case. There is thus a mismatch between the abstract GENITIVE case assigned inherently by the noun, and the overt realization by means of a preposition which assigns ACCUSATIVE.[11]

The inherent case condition (38) entails that nouns such as *envy* or *belief* and adjectives such as *proud* will only be able to assign the inherent GENITIVE to NPs which they also theta-mark. The NP *the pig* can be assigned inherent case in (37a) because it is theta-marked by the A *proud*. On the other hand, in the examples where the noun *belief* and the adjective *proud* take a sentential complement the noun or adjective cannot assign GENITIVE case to the subject of the complement clause since the noun or adjective does not assign a theta role to the relevant NPs. In (36d), for instance, the noun *belief* assigns a theta role to the entire clausal complement and not to the NP *John*.

The distinctive property of inherent case is that it is sensitive to thematic relations and to the structural condition of head government. Structural case, in contrast, is merely subject to structural requirements and is blind to thematic relations. If a structural case assigner governs an NP it can case-mark it whatever its thematic relation with that NP. We return to further discussion of inherent case in section 5.4.

3.3 *Inherent Case in German: Some Examples*

It is generally assumed that inherent case is rather restricted in English (see Kayne, 1984), but other languages have a more developed system of inherent case. The DATIVE and GENITIVE in German are also assumed to be instances of inherent case. In this section we briefly illustrate DATIVE and GENITIVE in German:

39a Sie hilft ihm.

she helps him (DATIVE)

---

[11] The interested reader is encouraged to read Chomsky (1986a: 186–204), which contains an accessible discussion of GENITIVE in English.

39b Er ist seinen   Grundsätzen   treu.
     he is his   principles (DATIVE) faithful (Haider, 1984: 68).
39c Er schreibt   mit   einem   Bleistift.
     he writes   with a   pencil (DATIVE)
40a Sie gedachte   vergangener Freuden.
     she remembered past   joy (GENITIVE)
40b Dieser Mann muss des Französischen mächtig sein.
     this man must French (GENITIVE)   in command be
     (Haider, 1984: 68)
40c das Lied des   Kindes
     the song of the   child (GENITIVE)

Whether a verb, adjective or preposition assigns DATIVE or GENITIVE has
to be learnt for each individual item. Hence this property is arguably part of its
lexical entry. We shall assume DATIVE and GENITIVE are assigned inherently. This means that these cases are associated with internal theta role
assignment. Let us try to be a little more precise. Suppose we say that the
inherent DATIVE case of *helfen* ('help'), for instance, is associated with the
internal theta role in the lexicon. The lexical entry for *helfen* is then as in (41):

41   *helfen*:   verb

$\underline{1}$	2 DATIVE

In our discussion of passivization below (section 5) we shall provide some
support for the distinction between inherent case and structural case.

We have already mentioned that languages vary with respect to the overt
morphological realization of abstract case. Another distinction to be made
between languages is in terms of the extent to which heads assign inherent
case. Roberts (1983) shows convincingly that language change may also be
related to changes in the degree to which inherent case is available in the
language.

4 Adjacency and Case Assignment

Consider the following examples:

42a Poirot speaks [$_{NP}$ English] fluently.
42b *Poirot speaks fluently [$_{NP}$ English].
42c Poirot sincerely believes [$_{IP}$ English to be important].
42d *Poirot believes sincerely [$_{IP}$ English to be important].
42e Poirot believes sincerely [$_{CP}$ that English is important].

In (42a) the verb *speak* takes an NP complement *English* and VP further includes an adjunct *fluently*. The NP *Poirot* is case-marked by the finite INFL; the NP *English* is case-marked by the transitive verb.

In (42b) the constituents of the sentence are not altered and yet the sentence is ungrammatical. The only contrast with (42a) is that the V *speak* and the complement NP *English* are no longer next to each other or **adjacent**.

A similar pattern is found in (42c) and (42d). In both sentences *believe* takes an IP complement. In (42c) the verb *believe* case-marks the subject NP of the lower clause (*English*) and the sentence is grammatical, while in (42d) the non-adjacency of the verb and the NP to which it should assign structural case leads to ungrammaticality. It would not be reasonable to argue that the verb *believe* or verbs in general must be adjacent to their internal argument: (42e) shows that the clausal complement of *believe* can be separated from the verb by the adverbial *sincerely*.

The data in (42) have led linguists to propose that government is not a sufficient condition for case assignment in English and that a further structural requirement is that the case assigner and the element to which case is assigned should be adjacent.[12] The **adjacency requirement** predicts that case asssigners must not be separated from the NPs which they case-mark by intervening material and hence that (42b) and (42d) are ungrammatical. In (42b) the verb *speak* would not be able to case-mark the NP *English* because there is intervening material. Hence the NP *English* will violate the case filter (25). In (42d) the verb *believe* must case-mark the subject of the non-finite clause, hence ought not be separated from it. Again the NP *English* violates the case filter.

The adjacency requirement has nothing to say about (42e). On the one hand, a finite clause does not need to be case-marked. The case filter applies to NPs,

---

[12] Cf. Stowell (1981), who is at the origin of this proposal.

not to clauses. On the other hand, the subject of the finite clause, the NP *English*, will satisfy the case filter because it receives NOMINATIVE from the finite I.

In the examples in (43) the interaction of the case filter and the adjacency requirement on case assignment will again account for the judgements given. We leave the reader to work out these examples.

43a I prefer [the boys to leave first].
43b *I prefer very much [the boys to leave first].
43c I prefer very much [for [the boys to leave first]].
43d I prefer very much [that [the boys should leave first]].

It might appear as if the adjacency requirement on case assignment cannot be a linguistic universal. Consider, for instance, the following German examples:

44a dass Poirot diesen   Roman   nicht   kennt.
    that Poirot this   novel   not   knows
    'that Poirot doesn't know this novel.'
44b dass Maigret dieses   Buch gestern   gekauft   hat.
    that Maigret this   book yesterday bought   has
    'that Maigret bought this book yesterday.'

However, the examples in (44) are compatible with a theory that makes case assignment dependent on adjacency, as will be shown in chapter 11.[13]

---

[13] Similar data are found in French:

(i) Poirot parle   souvent le   français.
     Poirot speaks often   the French
     'Poirot often speaks French.'

These data too can be made compatible with the case-adjacency requirement if we adopt the analysis proposed in recent work by Pollock (1989). The reader should not attempt to read Pollock's work until we have covered chapter 10.

5   Passivization: Discussion

This section contains an introductory description of passive sentences. We return to the discussion of passive in chapter 6. At this point we mainly wish to alert the reader to the salient features of passive and their relation to case theory.

5.1   *Passivization and Argument Structure*

Let us return to some of the earlier examples of case assignment.

45   Italy beat Belgium in the semi-finals.

According to the case filter (25) all overt NPs in the sentence above must be assigned case. The reader can verify that the case filter is satisfied in (45). Now consider (46), the passive pendant of (45).

46   Belgium were beaten in the semi-finals.

The effects of passivization will be familiar from the traditional literature. First, passivization affects the morphology of the verb: in (46) the verb *beat* turns up in its participial form and is accompanied by the auxiliary *be*.

Furthermore, in the passive sentence the agent of the activity is not expressed by an NP in an A-position. If we wish to refer to the AGENT of the action we need to use an adjunct PP headed by the preposition *by*, which itself carries the notion of AGENTIVITY.

47   Belgium were beaten *by Italy* in the semi-finals.

In (47) *by* assigns the theta role AGENT to the NP *Italy*. That the AGENT role need not be expressed in (46) is rather puzzling. In chapter 1 we introduced the projection principle which posits that syntactic structure is determined by lexical properties. We also adopted the theta criterion requiring that each theta role associated with a predicate be assigned to some argument (an NP or a clausal complement). In (45) the main predicate is the verb *beat* whose argument structure is given in (48):

48   *beat*:   verb

<u>1</u>	2

(45) satisfies the theta criterion and the projection principle. The NP *Italy* is assigned the external theta role (1) – AGENT – and the direct object NP *Belgium* is assigned the internal theta role (2) – PATIENT.

The situation in (46) is less clear. We clearly have the same predicate *beat* which has the same meaning as in (45) and thus should have the theta grid (48).

In (46) there is only one argument to theta-mark, the NP *Belgium*, the subject of the sentence. Intuitively, it seems wrong to assign the external AGENT role to the NP *Belgium*. In (46), just as in (45), the NP *Belgium* does not refer to the AGENT of 'beat', i.e. the entity that initiates the activity, but rather to the one that undergoes it, i.e. this NP is assigned the PATIENT role. Thus we conclude that the AGENT role (1) is not assigned to an NP in an A-position. It will be taken as a crucial property of passive verbs that they fail to assign the external theta role to an NP in an A-position.

However, in (46) we 'feel' that there is an implied AGENT, someone beat Belgium. Jaeggli (1986) and Roberts (1987) propose that the AGENT role is not absent in passive sentences, rather, they claim, it is **absorbed** by the passive morphology on the verb. The external theta role cannot be assigned to an NP in an A-position because it is absorbed by the passive ending. When the AGENT needs to be expressed overtly, it is expressed by means of an adjunct PP with *by*, as in (47).

Let us look at some more examples:

49a   Everyone believes that Bertie is a liar.
49b   It is widely believed that Bertie is a liar.

The properties associated with passivization and discussed with respect to (46) also obtain in (49):

(i)   the verb occurs in a participial form (*believed*) with *be*.
(ii)   the external theta role is not assigned to an NP.

In (49b) the subject position is occupied by *it*, an expletive, i.e. an element lacking a theta role (cf. the discussion of expletives in chapter 1). The expletive is allowed in the subject position precisely because the external theta role of *believe* is not assigned to an NP in this position.[14]

5.2 Case Absorption

If we compare (46) and (49b), the question arises why we could not also introduce an expletive in the subject position of a passive sentence like (46) and leave the complement NP in the VP-internal position:

50a *It was beaten Belgium.
50b *There was beaten Belgium.

The difference between (50) and (49b) is minimal: in the ungrammatical (50), the verb assigns the internal theta role to the NP *Belgium*, in (49b) the internal theta role is assigned to a clausal complement *that Bertie is a liar*. But what could explain their different status? The ungrammaticality of (50a) may be explained because *it* as an expletive is in construction with clauses and not with NPs (see chapter 1). Let us turn to (50b). In our account NPs have one crucial property that distinguishes them from clauses: NPs need case. Let us capitalize on this difference and try and explain the ungrammaticality of (50b) in terms of case theory. We shall assume that a passivized verb loses the ability to assign structural ACCUSATIVE case to its complement.[15] In chapter 6 we link the absorption of the external theta role to the absorption of structural case.

Given the assumption that passive verbs absorb structural case the ungrammaticality of (50b) follows. The object NP *Belgium* will not be able to receive ACCUSATIVE case from the verb *beaten*. Hence (50b) violates the case filter: the object NP fails to be case-marked. Given this assumption, (50a) will also be ruled out for case reasons: here too the NP *Belgium* cannot be assigned ACCUSATIVE case.

---

[14] We have said that in passive sentences the external theta role is implicit. Following Jaeggli (1986) and Roberts (1987) we say that the external theta role is absorbed by the verb morphology. This means that it is 'present' in the sentence. Some evidence for this proposal is that the adverbial *widely* in (49b) seems to modify the implicit external theta role of *believed*.

[15] In work by Jaeggli (1986) and Roberts (1987) it is proposed that the passive morphology absorbs the case because it also absorbs the thematic role. The relation between case and theta role is discussed in section 6 below.

The only way to rescue these sentences is to allow the complement of the verb to receive case in another position in the sentence. The obvious candidate is the [NP,IP] position to which NOMINATIVE case is assigned by the finite INFL. The [NP,IP] position is available in passive sentences because the external argument of the predicate, which is associated with the [NP,IP] position in active sentences, is not assigned to an NP in an A-position. The object NP is thus moved to the subject position. Movement of the clausal complement of *believe* to the subject position is also possible:

51   [CP That Bertie is a liar] is widely believed.

This movement is not obligatory, given that clausal arguments are not subject to the case filter.[16] Movement of an NP from the object to the subject position in passive sentences is obligatory because this is the only way that such NPs can pass the case filter.[17]

Consider the examples in (52):

52a   I believe [Emsworth to have attacked Poirot]

52b   I believe [Poirot to have been attacked]

---

[16] Koster (1987) provides important evidence that the clause in (51) is not in the specifier position of IP. The reader is referred to Koster's own work for discussion.

[17] The reader may have observed that one may find passive sentences where the NP which receives the internal theta role is not in the [NP,IP] position:

(i)   There were attacked [NP no fewer than three robbers].

If the passive verb is unable to assign case, how then does the bracketed NP pass the case filter? The answer to this question is complex and involves a discussion of the existential construction with *there*. One approach would be to adopt Belletti's (1988) account. Belletti proposes that passive verbs absorb the capacity to assign structural case, but that they may nevertheless assign an inherent PARTITIVE case. She argues further that the fact that only indefinite NPs are allowed in patterns such as (i) is related to the fact that such NPs would have PARTITIVE case. The reader is referred to Belletti's own work for discussion.

52c   *It was believed Emsworth to have attacked Poirot

52d   It was believed that Emsworth had attacked Poirot

$$\overline{|\text{NOM}|}$$

(52a) illustrates ECM. In the non-finite subordinate clause the external argument of *attack* is assigned ACCUSATIVE by *believe*, and the internal argument *Poirot* is assigned ACCUSATIVE by the active V *attacked*.

In (52b) the verb *attacked* is passive. The external argument is not expressed. We have proposed that passive verbs cannot assign ACCUSATIVE. Hence, in order to pass the case filter the NP *Poirot* must be **moved** to the [NP,IP] position of the non-finite clause where it can be assigned ACCUSA-TIVE case by the verb *believe*. We return to movement operations in section 6.2 and in chapters 6 and 7.

The ungrammaticality of (52c) is due to the same reason as that in (50b): the passive verb *believed* is unable to assign case, hence the NP *Emsworth*, subject of an infinitival clause, violates the case filter.

The reader can verify for himself that (52d) passes the case filter.

5.3   The Properties of Passivization

Let us summarize the major syntactic properties of passivization so far established. We return to them at length in chapter 6 where we discuss the movement of the object NP in much greater detail. Passivization has the following properties:

(i)   the verb morphology is affected;
(ii)   the external theta role is absorbed;
(iii) the structural case of the verb is absorbed;
(iv)   the NP which is assigned the internal theta role of the passive verb moves to a position where it can be assigned case;
(v)   the movement of the NP is obligatory in view of the case filter;
(vi)   the movement of the NP is allowed because the subject position is empty.

The question arises whether these properties are in any way related, i.e. if one property can be said to be dependent on, i.e. explained by, another property. If this is not the case then we must assume that a child acquiring a language will have to learn all six properties above one by one.

As mentioned above, Jaeggli (1986) and Roberts (1987) have proposed that properties (i) and (ii) can be linked by saying that the external theta role of the passivized verb is absorbed by the passive morphology. In chapter 6 we shall see that property (iii) can be linked to property (ii). The reader can check that (iv) is a consequence of the combination of (i), (ii) and (iii) and the case filter. Similarly, (v) and (vi) follow from property (iii), the case filter and the fact that the subject position is empty because there is no external argument (ii).

The connection between the properties listed above is important. It means that a child acquiring a language will not have to learn all the properties above. Once (i) and (ii) are established, for instance, all the other properties can be deduced. If we adopt the proposal, due to Jaeggli (1986) and to Roberts (1987), that (i) and (ii) are also related, then all a child needs to do is identify the passive morphology (i).

As it stands we have treated the properties listed above as specific to the passive construction. Chapter 6 will show that these properties are not only found in passive sentences, they are not construction-specific, but they can be found in other types of sentences.

5.4   Passive and Inherent Case

5.4.1   GERMAN

We have introduced the contrast between inherent and structural case in section 3. In this section we provide some further illustration of the difference between the two types of case. We shall see that passivization of a verb affects its potential for assigning structural case but does not have any effect on the inherent case assigning properties.

Consider the following examples:

53a Sie sieht ihn.
                ACCUSATIVE
     She sees him.
53b Er   wird gesehen.
     NOMINATIVE
     He   is   seen.
53c *Ihn   wird gesehen.
     ACCUSATIVE
     him   is seen

54a Sie hilft   ihm.
            DATIVE
      She helps   him.
54b *Er   wird   geholfen.
      NOMINATIVE
      He is   helped.
54c Ihm wird geholfen.
      DATIVE
      him is   helped

55a Sie gedachte   vergangener Freuden.
                        GENITIVE
      She remembered past   joy.
55b Vergangener Freuden wurde gedacht.
      GENITIVE
      past   joy   was   remembered
(Examples from Haider, 1984: 68)

The examples in (53) are predicted by the properties of passivization discussed above: passive *gesehen* absorbs the external theta role assigned to *Sie* in (53a) and it cannot assign ACCUSATIVE case. Hence (53c) is out: there is no ACCUSATIVE to assign. In (53b) the internal argument NP of *gesehen* is assigned NOMINATIVE by INFL.

(54) and (55) show that apparently only ACCUSATIVE is absorbed: DATIVE and GENITIVE survive under passivization. In order to explain this property of German we shall use our hypothesis (section 3.3) that the DATIVE and GENITIVE in German (54) and (55) are instances of inherent case.

Passivization alters the theta grid for the verb in that it absorbs the external theta role. But, crucially, this need not affect the properties of the internal theta role. We assume that inherent case, which is associated with the internal theta role, is unaffected by passivization. If DATIVE is an inherent case then the pattern in (54) is accounted for. If GENITIVE case is inherent then the pattern in (55) follows.[18]

5.4.2 THE DOUBLE OBJECT CONSTRUCTION IN ENGLISH: DISCUSSION

If it is a property of inherent case that it survives passivization then it could be argued that GENITIVE is not the only inherent case in English. Consider (56).

---

[18] For a discussion of the German case system, see Haider (1984) and the references cited there.

56a   I gave John a book.
56b   John was given a book

In this chapter, we have not said anything about verbs like *give* in (56a) which appear to take two internal arguments. These are subject to much discussion.[19] The question we address here is how both VP-internal NPs in (56a) are assigned case.

From passive (56b) we deduce that the NP *John* must receive structural case in the active sentence (56a): in the passive sentence it loses its ACCUSATIVE and is assigned NOMINATIVE. English contrasts in this respect with many other languages where the indirect object cannot be nominativized in the passive.

57   *German*
57a   Ich gab ihm ein Buch.
       I gave him (DATIVE) a book
57b   *Er wurde ein Buch gegeben.
       he (NOMINATIVE) was a book given
57c   Ihm wurde ein Buch gegeben.
       him (DATIVE) was a book given

58   *French*
58a   Je donne un livre   à Jean.
       I give a   book   to Jean
58b   Je lui   donne un livre.
       I to-him give   a   book
58c   *Jean/Il est donné un livre.
       Jean/he is given a book

Kayne (1984) argues that English has lost inherent DATIVE case and that the indirect object in (56a) is assigned a structural ACCUSATIVE through the intermediary of the verb. In French and German the idea would be that the indirect object receives DATIVE and that passivization does not affect DATIVE.

The direct object *a book* in (56) is a problem, though. If it is assigned a structural ACCUSATIVE by the active verb *give* in (56a) then it is not obvious why the ACCUSATIVE is not affected by the passivization. If the NP *a book* is

[19] Some important references are Czepluch (1982), Kayne (1984) and Larson (1988).

not assigned ACCUSATIVE by the verb, then what is its case? One approach would be to say that in (56a) the direct object is inherently case-marked and this would lead us to expect that it retains its case when the head that theta-marks it is passivized (56b).[20]

6 Visibility

6.1 Explaining the Case Filter

The case filter (25) applies to all overt NPs and filters out those overt NPs that lack abstract case. Remember that case can be either structural or inherent. Linguists have tried to explain this filter by relating it to other properties of the grammar. One hypothesis is based on the observation that, following the theta criterion, argument NPs must be assigned a theta role. The idea is then that a predicate can only assign a theta role to NPs that are **visible**. Abstract case renders an NP visible.[21]

Under this view, the case filter is no longer an independent property of the grammar. Rather it **derives** from the **visibility requirement** on NPs. This property in itself is related to theta theory: in order to be recognized as an argument of some predicate an NP must be made visible. Invisible NPs cannot be assigned a theta role. Hence, sentences in which we have argument NPs without case violate the theta criterion. Returning to our metaphor of the play, we could say that the argument NPs must be made visible by means of case in the way that the characters playing a part in a performance must be made recognizable by their outward appearance. If all actors looked identical we would not be able to tell who is playing which part. NPs are **licensed** by virtue of their case properties.

---

[20] The issue of the double object construction is a very interesting one and we cannot go into all the details of the discussion here. The reader is referred to work by Chomsky (1981a: 170–1), Czepluch (1982), Haegeman (1986b), Kayne (1984), Roberts (1983), Larson (1988) and the literature cited by these authors. Most of these texts will be accessible once we have covered chapter 6.

[21] Chomsky (1981: 170–83) discusses the link between visibility and case. This section will be accessible once we have read chapter 8.

Baker (1988) proposes that the visibility requirement be replaced by a requirement of morphological identification, or m-identification. This can be achieved by case–marking. Baker also suggests other ways of m-identifying an NP. See Baker's work for discussion. The book presupposes most of the content of this book.

6.2   *Movement and Chains (Introduction)*

The visibility hypothesis sketched in section 6.1 raises further questions with respect to passive sentences. We shall introduce the issue here and return to it in chapter 6.
    Consider:

59   [$_{IP}$ Poirot   [$_{I'}$ will [$_{VP}$ be attacked -]]]

         ↑ NOM

The major properties of passivization are listed in section 5.3. However, on closer inspection there remain important problems.
    Our hypothesis developed so far is that in (59) *Poirot* is assigned NOMINATIVE case by the finite INFL. We assume that it is theta-marked by the (passive) verb *attacked*, the head of VP.
    In chapter 1 we postulated, though, that internal theta roles are assigned under government. In (59) there is no way that we can claim that the verb *attacked* governs the NP *Poirot* in the subject position. The question is how the verb *attacked* can theta-mark *Poirot*.
    We have introduced the idea that abstract case is a condition on theta-marking. In (59) *Poirot*, the internal argument of *attacked*, cannot remain inside the VP because it would fail to be assigned case, the passive verb having lost its capacity for assigning the structural ACCUSATIVE case. If *Poirot* lacks case, it is not visible and therefore cannot receive a theta role from the verb. Hence *Poirot* must move in order to be case-marked and become visible. We conclude that the NP *Poirot* is forced to move to [NP,IP] and thus to leave the VP-internal position in which it can receive its (internal) theta role.
    We seem to be in a bit of a crux: on the one hand, *Poirot* should sit inside the VP to receive the internal theta role from *attacked*, and, on the other hand, it must move out of the VP to become visible and to be able to be theta-marked. What we seem to want to say is that the NP *Poirot* must be present inside the VP headed by *attack*, in order to be assigned the internal theta role, and that it also must be moved out of the VP to the subject position where it can be assigned NOMINATIVE case. This looks like a desperate situation: we want *Poirot* to be in two positions simultaneously: a position in which it can be theta-marked, or a **theta position** for short, and a position in which it can be case-marked, a **case position**. However, the situation can be rescued. We sketch the solution informally below and return to it in greater detail in chapters 6 and 8.

In order to maintain the idea that the internal theta role is assigned under government and the hypothesis that NPs are visible by virtue of being assigned case, we shall capitalize on the fact that the NP is moved. *Poirot* starts out as the object of *attacked*. In a way, *Poirot* IS the object of *attacked*. Then the NP *Poirot* is moved to the subject position. At this point *Poirot* IS the subject of the sentence. As will be shown extensively in chapter 6, we are led to conclude that there are two levels of syntactic representation for (59): one before the movement and one after. When *Poirot* has left the object position there remains an unfilled position or a gap inside the VP of (59).

We shall assume that the moved NP and the gap remain linked. *Poirot* is as it were chained to the VP-internal slot which it has deserted. The link between the two positions is referred to as a **chain**. We shall provisionally represent the vacant position by an *e*, for empty. We indicate that two positions are part of a chain by **co-indexation**. In chapter 6 we return to representations such as (60).

60    $[_{IP}$ Poirot$_i$ $[_{I'}$ will $[_{VP}$ be attacked e$_i]]]$

We now propose that the internal theta role of *attacked* is not assigned to the NP *Poirot* as such, or to the vacated position indicated by *e* in (60), but that it is the chain consisting of the vacant position *e* and the subject NP which will be assigned the theta role. The chain of two elements is represented as follows: <NP, *e*>.

In order to incorporate the ideas of visibility and chain formation we reformulate the theta criterion (chapter 1) in terms of chains.

61   **Theta criterion**
      Each argument A appears in a chain containing a unique visible theta position P, and each theta position P is visible in a chain containing a unique argument A.
(Chomsky, 1986a: 97)

Let us assume that theta roles are assigned to positions, theta positions. One possibility is that an argument A appears in the theta position P. In this case it picks up the theta role in its position. We could say there is a one-member chain. This situation is illustrated in (62):

62    $[_{IP}$ The robber$_j$ $[_{I'}$ -ed $[_{VP}$ attack   Poirot$_j]$

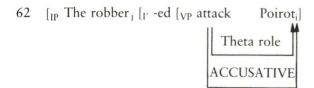

In (62) *Poirot*$_i$ is governed by *attack*. The NP is in its theta position and can pick up the theta role directly. The NP *Poirot* is in a chain with only one element, *<Poirot*$_i$*>*.

Alternatively, an argument NP has been moved out of P. It will form a chain with the vacated position and it will pick up the theta role assigned to the position P via the chain.

This second possibility is illustrated in (60). In this example, the relevant argument NP is *Poirot*. The NP is the internal argument of *attack*, but it has left the theta position in order to pick up NOMINATIVE case in the subject position. The moved NP forms a chain with the vacated position: *<Poirot*$_i$*, e*$_i$*>*. The chain is visible thanks to the NOMINATIVE case assigned to the highest position and is thus able to receive the internal theta role from *attacked*.

63   [$_{IP}$ Poirot$_i$ [$_{I'}$ will [$_{VP}$ be attacked   e$_i$]]]

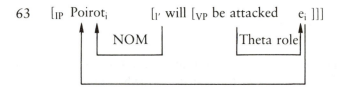

From this, admittedly sketchy, discussion, the reader can see that 'empty positions' count as much in our theory as positions that are filled. This issue will become central from chapter 5 onwards. In chapter 6 we return in great detail to passivization.

7 Summary

Case theory is the module of the grammar concerned with the distribution of NPs.

The case filter imposes a requirement on the licensing of NPs:

1 **Case filter**
   Every overt NP must be assigned abstract case.

We distinguish abstract case from morphological case (section 1) and we distinguish two types of abstract case: structural case (NOMINATIVE and ACCUSATIVE (section 2)) and inherent case (the English GENITIVE and the German DATIVE and GENITIVE (section 3)). While structural case is subject to the requirement that the case assigner govern the NP which it case-marks, an inherent case assigner must govern and theta-mark the NP which it case-marks. The important role of government with respect to case assignment has led us to reformulate the definition of government including the minimality condition:

2   **Government** (adapted from Rizzi, 1990: 6)
    A governs B iff

   (i)   A is a governor;
   (ii) A m-commands B;
   (iii) minimality is respected.

Governors are the lexical categories and tensed INFL.

3   **Minimality** (adapted from Rizzi, 1990: 7)
    A governs B iff there is no node Z such that

          (i)   Z is a potential governor for B;
   and (ii)   Z c-commands B;
   and (iii) Z does not c-command A.

A further requirement on case assignment is the adjacency condition (section 4).

It is a property of passive verbs that they do not assign the external theta role to an NP in an A-position and that they lose the ability to assign structural case. However, passive verbs retain their capacity to assign case inherently (section 5).

It is proposed that the case filter is not an independent principle of the grammar but can be related to theta theory via a visibility condition: in order to be theta-marked, an NP needs to be visible; in order to become visible an NP needs to be case-marked. In order to maintain the requirement that an NP can only be theta-marked if visible, i.e. when case-marked, we need to introduce the notion chain, which establishes a link between a theta position and a case position. The theta criterion is now defined in terms of chains.

4   **Theta criterion**
Each argument A appears in a chain containing a unique visible theta position P, and each theta position P is visible in a chain containing a unique argument A.
(Chomsky, 1986a: 97)

8   Exercises

Exercise 1

Consider the examples below. How do the NPs acquire case?

1   John left the university at noon.
2   I expect him to have written the letter by Friday.
3   For Jane to have bought the house is rather remarkable.
4   It is odd that Bill should have refused the offer.
5   Rembrandt's picture of Saskia is remarkably well preserved.
6   I want my coffee boiling hot.
7   For him to have agreed to the proposal is surprising.
8   Children should not treat their parents in this way.
9   I want these demonstrators in jail by tomorrow.
10   She thinks that Poirot will abandon the investigation.
11   Poirot is anxious for the children to return to town soon.
12   Miss Marple is aware of the problems.
13   Miss Marple has been contradicted by the inspectors.
14   Maigret gave his pipe to Janvier.
15   The book was given to the best student in the class.

Exercise 2

Consider the examples below. To what extent does case theory explain the contrasts in grammaticality?

1   Poirot preferred very much for the detectives to destroy the evidence.
2   Poirot believed Watson to be incompetent.
3   Poirot preferred the police to destroy the evidence.
4   *Poirot preferred very much the police to destroy the evidence.

5 *Anyone to destroy the evidence would be regrettable.
6 *I consider very much John to be a good candidate.
7 They consider Maigret entirely incompetent.
8 *It is considered Maigret entirely incompetent.

Exercise 3

It has been proposed (see section 6.1) that NPs need case because they need to be visible in order to receive a theta role. Discuss the problems raised for this approach by the following examples.[22]

1 It is regrettable that John has left.
2 I consider it to be regrettable that John has left.
3 *I consider very much it to be regrettable that John has left.
4 It is thought that it is regrettable that John has left.
5 They thought it regrettable that John had left.
6 *It is thought it regrettable that John has left.
7 There won't be many people at the meeting.
8 I don't expect there to be many people at the meeting.
9 *I expect very much there to be many people at the meeting.

Exercise 4

In section 4 we propose that structural case assignment is subject to an adjacency condition. This requirement will cause problems for the examples below. Discuss these problems.

1 You should drink after every meal a glass of boiling hot milk with honey.
2 Which detective would you like to invite?
3 On the wall was hanging a large picture of Napoleon.
4 *French*
   Quels livres a   acheté Jean?
   which books   has   bought Jean
   'Which books has John bought?'
5 *Dutch*
   Jan koopt altijd   oude   boeken.
   Jan buys   always   old   books

---

[22] For discussion see Davis (1986).

6   *Dutch*
    Jan heeft waarschijnlijk   die   oude boeken gisteren   gekocht.
    Jan has   probably   those old   books yesterday bought
7   *Dutch*
    Oude   boeken   heeft   Jan   nog   nooit   gekocht.
    old   books   has   Jan   yet   never   bought
8   *German*
    Diesen Studenten   hat   er   nicht   gesehen.
    this   student   has   he   not   seen
9   *German*
    Diesem Studenten   hat   er   nicht   geholfen.
    this   student   has   he   not   helped
    DATIVE
10 He often arrived late.

Exercise 5

Discuss the assignment of case in the examples below. Which problems, if any, do they raise for case theory, discussed in chapter 3? Try
to provide a classification of the types of problems that arise. As you
can see, the problems are often not language-specific. In subsequent
chapters some of the problems that you identify here will be solved very
easily. Others, though, are a persistent problem for the theory.

1   John being in hospital, his wife has signed the cheques.
2   Poirot is coming back this week.
3   You should hold the pen this way.
4   The detective and his wife are coming back soon.
5   I saw him in the courtyard, his hands in his pockets.
6   Detective stories, I have never liked them.
7   Agatha Christie I have never liked.
8   Poirot smokes cigars and Maigret a pipe.
9   There remain different problems.
10 *French*
    Quand Pierre est-il   arrivé?
    when Pierre is-he   arrived
11 *West Flemish* (a dialect of Dutch)[23]
    Jan peinst da- ze   zie   dienen boek a   gelezen eet.
    Jan thinks that she she   that   book already read   has
    'Jan thinks that she has already read that book'.

---

[23] For a description of West Flemish, see Haegeman (forthcoming).

Zie is the stressed form of the third person singular pronoun. The form *ze* is a weak form of the third person singular pronoun which attaches to the complementizer.

12 Mee zie dat hus te verkopen is alles veranderd.
    With she that house to sell is everything changed
          NOM
    'Everything has changed because she has sold that house'

13 *German*
    Ich weiss dass es Hans gestern gekauft hat.
    I know that it (DO) Hans yesterday bought has

14 *French*
    Il est arrivé un accident grave hier.
    it is arrived an accident bad yesterday
    'Yesterday there occurred a bad accident.'

15 Il a voulu acheter le livre hier.
    he has wanted buy the book yesterday
    'He wanted to buy the book yesterday'

16 Il l'avait déjà acheté hier.
    he it had already bought yesterday
    'He had already bought it yesterday'

17 *Italian*
    Gianni aveva voluto comprare il libro ieri.
    'Gianni had wanted to buy the book yesterday.'

18 Gianni aveva voluto comprarlo ieri.
    Gianni had wanted buy it yesterday
    'Gianni had wanted to buy it yesterday'.

19 Gianni l'aveva voluto comprare ieri.
    Gianni it had wanted buy yesterday
    (= 18)

20 Comprati gli stivali, Maria è partita.
    bought the boots, Maria is gone
    'Having bought the boots, Maria left'

Exercise 6

In descriptive grammars the terms NOMINATIVE case and ACCUSATIVE case have sometimes been replaced by 'subject-form' and 'object-form' respectively. On the basis of our discussion in chapter 3, consider whether these labels are appropriate.

Exercise 7

In this chapter we have assumed that both infinitival IP and the small clause boundary do not constitute barriers for outside government and hence allow for their subjects to be case-marked by a governing verb:

1   I expect [$_{IP}$ you to be in my office at four].
2   I expect [$_{sc}$ you in my office at four].

We leave aside the issue whether *sc* in (2) is a projection of P. What problems do the following sentences pose for treating small clauses and non-finite clauses identically with respect to case-marking.[24]

3   For workers to be angry about pay is really undesirable.
4   *Workers to be angry about pay is really undesirable.
5   Workers angry about pay is a situation which we must avoid.

---

[24] For a discussion of small clauses, see Stowell (1983). This paper will be accessible once we have covered chapter 8.

4 Anaphoric Relations and Overt NPS

Contents

Introduction and Overview

So far we have been looking at formal properties of sentences. We saw that the obligatory constituents of a sentence are required by the projection principle, the extended projection principle and theta theory (chapter 1). We have formulated an articulated theory of phrase structure, X-bar theory (chapter 2), and we have discussed the distribution of the case forms of NPs as regulated by case theory (chapter 3).

In this chapter we turn to some aspects of the interpretation of noun phrases. The module of the grammar regulating NP interpretation will be referred to as the **binding theory**. The reader will by now see why the particular theory we are presenting here is called Government and Binding Theory. In this chapter the concept binding comes in. Government has already been shown to be a structural property which is involved in syntactic processes such as theta-marking and case-marking, and in the present chapter too, government will be of primary importance. The version of the binding theory that we shall develop here is mainly based on work by Chomsky.[1]

The binding theory is the module of the grammar that will be responsible for assigning an appropriate interpretation to the italicized NPs in sentences like the following:

1a *Poirot* admires *him*.
1b *Bertie* hurt *himself*.
1c *Bertie* said that *he* felt rather ill.
1d *Bertie* expected *him* to feel a little better.
1e *He* expected *Bertie* to feel a little better.
1f *He* thought that *Bertie* looked miserable.

Three types of NPs are distinguished:

(i)   full noun phrases such as *Poirot, Bertie*, etc.;

---

[1] For an accessible introduction see Chomsky (1988a). Chomsky has developed the theory in work published throughout the eighties (1980, 1981a, 1982, 1986a). Most of these studies are very advanced. Higginbotham (1980, 1983, 1988) offers important discussion and alternative proposals for the binding theory. Again these works are very advanced and should not be tackled until the reader has worked his way through this book.

(ii) **pronouns** such as *he* and *him*, etc.;

(iii) **reflexive** elements such as *himself*, etc.

A full nominal expression such as *Poirot* refers independently. Such an NP selects a referent from the universe of discourse, the things we know and talk about. The use of the full NP indicates that there is, or is thought to be, an entity which is identifiable by the NP. We can say informally that a lexical NP is able to select a referent by virtue of its inherent properties.

Pronouns, on the other hand, do not inherently select a referent from the universe of discourse. Consider, for instance, the interpretation of the pronoun *he/him*. In (1a) all we know is that *him* refers to an entity that is characterized by its nominal features [+ singular] and [+ male]. The features of gender and number restrict the entities picked out by a pronoun, but they do not allow us to identify a uniquely specified referent from the universe of discourse. The pronoun *him* will merely select a subgroup from the wider domain of entities which we might want to talk about. On the other hand, we cannot freely choose any entity which is male as a referent for *him* in (1a): *him* cannot be used to refer to Poirot.

At this point we are talking about the interpretation of a pronoun in a sentence without any context. As soon as (1a) is contextualized we shall have a clearer idea as to the referent of the pronoun *him*. For instance, in the context (2) the most natural interpretation will be for *him* to refer to the same entity as that referred to by *Jeeves*.

2 A And what about Jeeves?
   B Poirot admires him.

Our grammar need not account for the fact that *him* in (2) will probably be taken to refer to the entity denoted by *Jeeves*. This interpretation is not a function of the properties of sentence (1a), rather it derives from the use of the sentence for communicative purposes and it arises in a specific context. Interpretive matters which depend on the context outside the sentence are not regulated in a sentence grammar but are dealt with in the domain of study that is concerned with utterance interpretation. This area of study is often referred to as pragmatics.[2]

On the other hand, the fact that *him* and *Poirot* cannot be coreferential in

---

[2] For an interesting account of the interpretation of utterances in context the reader is referred to work by Sperber and Wilson (1986).

(1a) is a matter of the grammar. It is the natural interpretation of the sentence independently of context.[3]

(1b) contains two NPs: *Bertie* and the reflexive element *himself*. Regardless of further contextualization, the reference of the reflexive is determined: the reflexive must refer to the subject *Bertie*; its interpretation is grammatically determined. The discussion above shows that the interpretation of NPs in a sentence will be at least partly constrained by the grammar. The binding theory aims at providing an explicit formulation of the grammatical constraints on NP interpretation in argument positions or A-positions. It is a theory of **A-binding**.[4] We shall develop three principles, one for each type of NP. Principle A will deal with reflexives and will impose that they are linked to, or **bound by**, an NP in an A-position within a certain domain, which we shall define as precisely as possible in this chapter. Principle B will impose that pronouns should not be linked to an NP in an A-position in the same domain. Principle C will determine that expressions like *Poirot* must not be linked to an NP in an A-position.

Section 1 deals with the interpretation of reflexives and also defines the concepts binding, subject/SUBJECT, accessibility and governing category, which we shall need throughout the chapter. Section 2 shows that reciprocals obey the same constraint as reflexives. Reciprocals and reflexives will be grouped under the label anaphor. Section 3 deals with the interpretation of pronouns. Section 4 deals with referential NPs. Section 5 is a summary of the rules of NP interpretation: the binding theory. The formulation of the binding theory in this section is essentially that of Chomsky (1981a). In section 6 we discuss some problems for the binding theory. In section 7 we reinterpret the classification of NPs in terms of the binary features [± anaphor,

---

[3] The grammatical principle that *him* and *Poirot* cannot be coreferential in (1a) may be overridden in special discourse contexts. Consider:

(i) Everyone admires Poirot. I admire him, you admire him and Poirot certainly admires him.

Examples such as these are referred to as accidental coreference and are discussed in Evans (1980).

[4] This means that we shall not be looking at the interpretation of NPs in A'-positions. For example, we have nothing to say about topicalized NPs such as *Jeeves* in (i) and (ii):

(i) Jeeves, Poirot doesn't like.
(ii) Jeeves, nobody likes him.

Jeeves occupies an A'-position, a non-argument position. We deal with the role of A'-positions in chapter 7.

± pronominal] and we reformulate the binding theory in terms of these features, following proposals in Chomsky (1982). In section 8 we discuss the problem of circularity of co-indexation.

1   Reflexives

In this section we formulate the rule of interpretation of reflexives such as *himself*.

1.1   Binding and Antecedent

Consider (3):

3a   Poirot hurt himself.
3b   *Miss Marple hurt himself.

In (3a) the reflexive picks up its reference from the subject NP *Poirot*. The NP on which a reflexive is dependent for its interpretation is the **antecedent** of the reflexive. We indicate that *himself* and *Poirot* have the same referent by means of **co-indexation.**[5]

4a   Poirot$_i$ hurt himself$_i$.

The reflexive and its antecedent must agree with respect to the nominal features of person, gender and number. Lack of agreement leads to ungrammaticality in (4b), (4c) and (4d).

---

[5]   The reader will recall that in chapter 3 we used co-indexation to link the elements in a chain.

(i)   Poirot$_i$ was attacked e$_i$

In (i) *Poirot* and the empty element *e* form a chain, $<Poirot_i, e_i>$. The internal theta role of *attacked* is assigned to the chain. In the text-example (4a) *Poirot* and *himself* each have their own theta role. We have here two one-member chains: $<Poirot>$ and $<himself>$. For a discussion of some constraints on co-indexation, see section 8 of this chapter.

4b *Poirot$_i$ hurt herself$_j$.
4c *Poirot$_i$ hurt themselves$_i$.
4d *Poirot$_i$ hurt myself$_i$.

The requirement that a reflexive and its antecedent agree with respect to their nominal features follows from the fact that the reflexive depends for its interpretation on the antecedent, i.e. the reflexive and its antecedent share their referent. It would be rather odd to find that a reflexive has the property [+ male], for instance, thus constraining the selection of the referent to a male entity, and is co-indexed with an antecedent which itself has the property [− male]. There would be a contradiction in the specification of the relevant properties for the selection of the referent. The agreement constraint explains the ungrammaticality of (3b).

5a = 3b *Miss Marple$_i$ hurt himself$_i$.

In order to circumvent the agreement constraint one might think of an interpretation in which the reflexive and the subject NP are independent in reference as illustrated in (5b), but such an interpretation is unavailable:

5b *Miss Marple$_i$ hurt himself$_j$.

Because reflexives lack independent reference they must have an antecedent. Reflexives must be **bound by an antecedent**. The antecedent is the **binder** of the reflexive. Throughout this section we shall make the notion 'binding' more precise.

In all our examples so far, the antecedent of the reflexive has been a full lexical NP. Pronouns may also function as antecedents for reflexives, as indicated in (5c): *he* is the antecedent of the reflexive:

5c He$_i$ has hurt himself$_i$.

1.2 *Locality Constraints*

Let us consider in more detail the relation between the reflexive and its antecedent.

6a   Poirot$_i$ hurt himself$_i$.
6b   *Poirot$_i$ thinks that Miss Marple hurt himself$_i$.

In (6a) *himself* is bound by *Poirot*, as indicated by co-indexation. In (6b) binding is apparently not possible. The problem seems to be that the distance between *himself$_i$* and its antecedent *Poirot$_i$* is too large: *Poirot* is too far away from the reflexive. Consider the grammatical (6c) where *Poirot* and the reflexive are closer to each other and where the NP *Poirot* can bind the reflexive:

6c Miss Marple thinks that Poirot$_i$ has hurt himself$_i$.

We conclude that reflexives need an antecedent (with which they agree with respect to the features of person, gender and number) and that the antecedent must not be too far away from the reflexive. In a sense to be made more precise, the antecedent must be found in some **local domain**, the **binding domain**. The reflexive must be **locally bound**. Needless to say, we must now try to define what this local domain for reflexive binding can be, i.e. what it means to say that a reflexive must be locally bound.

From the examples in (6) we might provisionally conclude that reflexive and antecedent must be in the same clause.[6] In the literature a condition which specifies that two elements, the reflexive and its antecedent, must be in the same clause has been referred to as the **clause-mate condition**. The **binding domain** for reflexives would thus be said to be the clause. In (6a) and in (6c) the antecedent is sufficiently local; in (6b) the NP *Poirot* is outside the clause which contains the reflexive and cannot function as an antecedent.

Let us extend our data-base now to check whether the locality constraint we have set up is adequate to account for all the data. Following our discussion in the introduction of this book, we shall adopt the following procedure. Having formulated a **hypothesis** – the clause-mate condition on reflexive interpretation – on the basis of a limited set of **data**, we **test** the hypothesis by applying it to different data. If the hypothesis fails we try to improve it, either by modifying the hypothesis itself, or by adding to it auxiliary hypotheses which take care of the problematic issues. Consider (7a):

7a   *I expect [$_{IP}$ himself$_i$ to invite Poirot$_i$]

---

6 Following chapter 2, the term clause is used to refer to IP, both embedded and non-embedded.

(7a) shows that the clause-mate condition is not sufficient to allow for binding of a reflexive. In (7a) both the reflexive and the antecedent appear in the non-finite clause (IP), but the reflexive cannot be bound. We might propose that in addition to being a clause-mate, the antecedent must (as the name suggests) precede the reflexive. This would entail that (7a) is ungrammatical and (7b) is grammatical. But this also predicts that (7c) is grammatical, contrary to fact:

7b   Poirot$_i$ invited himself$_i$.
7c   *Poirot$_i$'s sister invited himself$_i$.

In both (7b) and (7c) the reflexive and the antecedent are clause-mates, they are inside the same local domain of the clause. But the reflexive *himself* in (7c) cannot be successfully bound by the presumed antecedent *Poirot*, which occupies the specifier position of the subject NP *Poirot's sister*. Compare the ungrammatical (7c) and the grammatical (7d):

7d   [$_{IP}$ [$_{NPj}$ [$_{NPi}$ Poirot]'s brother] invited himself$_j$].

As shown by the indexation the antecedent of *himself* in (7d) is not NP$_i$, *Poirot*, but rather NP$_j$, *Poirot's brother*, which contains NP$_i$.

We must refine our rule for the interpretation of reflexives to account for the examples above. In order to establish the structural relations between antecedent and reflexive we shall analyse the tree diagram representations corresponding to the above examples. Before reading the discussion below, try to draw the representations for the examples in (7) as an exercise. For each tree, examine the configurational relations between the antecedent and the reflexive and try to determine which relation is the one that allows binding.

1.3   Structural Relations between Antecedent and Reflexive

(8) gives the tree diagram representations for the examples in (7). For each of the examples above circle the reflexive and the antecedent in preparation of the discussion.

8a

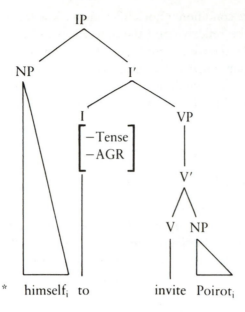

8b

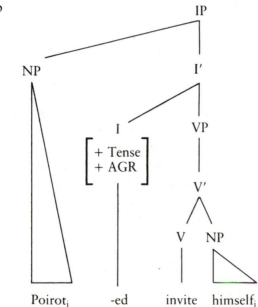

8c

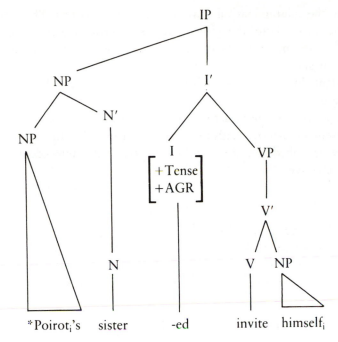

8d

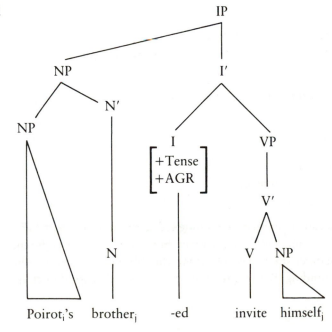

If we compare the ungrammatical (8a) with the grammatical (8b) a first observation is that in the latter the antecedent is somehow 'higher' up in the tree than the reflexive. The reader can check that this observation also applies to the other examples. But the fact that an antecedent is somehow higher in the tree is not sufficient. In (8c) *Poirot* is higher than *himself* and still it cannot serve as its antecedent.

A careful comparison of the structural relations between antecedents and reflexives in the sentences above leads us to the conclusion that the relation is one that we have described as c-command in chapter 2: the antecedent must c-command the reflexive.

9   **C-command**
   A node A c-commands a node B iff
   (i)   A does not dominate B;
   (ii)   B does not dominate A;
   (iii) the first branching node dominating A also dominates B.

The reader can verify for himself that in all of the grammatical examples in (8) the relevant relation holds.[7]

Let us now try to formulate the constraint on the interpretation of reflexives.

10   **Principle of reflexive interpretation** (1)
   A reflexive must be bound by a clause-mate antecedent.

Binding is defined in terms of c-command as in (11):

11   **Binding**
   A binds B iff
   (i)   A c-commands B;
   (ii)   A and B are co-indexed.

(10) says that a reflexive must be co-indexed with an antecedent NP, i.e. a reflexive cannot have independent reference but depends for its reference on the binder. Remember that we focus on the binding by antecedents in A-positions, or **A-binding**. Binding from A'-positions is discussed in chapter 7.

[7] There are potential problems with the definition when we consider the following examples:

(i)   I presented Watson$_i$ with a picture of himself$_i$.

The VP of this sentence will have the following structure:

(ii)

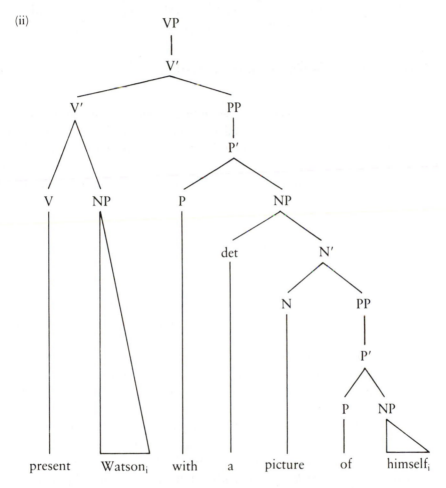

The antecedent *Watson* fails to c-command the reflexive *himself*. The first branching node dominating *Watson* is V′, which does not dominate the reflexive. One possibility would be to modify the rule for the interpretation of the reflexive and to replace c-command by m-command, which would also cover (i) above. (Cf. also Jackendoff, 1972: 163–77). Chomsky (1986: 8) gives arguments for retaining the c-command definition as stated in the text. Chomsky's discussion uses notions which we cover in chapter 6 of this book. We shall retain the definition in terms of c-command in our text.

1.4   The Domain of Reflexive Binding

1.4.1   GOVERNORS

An examination of further examples with reflexives shows that principle (10) is too powerful. It rules out grammatical sentences such as (12):

12   Poirot$_i$ believes [$_{IP}$ himself$_i$ to be the best].

It is easy to see that the relation between *himself* and *Poirot* does not satisfy (10). *Poirot*, the antecedent, does indeed c-command *himself* (cf. (11)), but they are not clause-mates. While *himself* is contained in the lower infinitival clause, *Poirot* is outside it. In order to accommodate examples such as (12), we shall need to extend the domain in which a reflexive can be bound. However, we should be careful not to extend the domain too much given (13):

13a   *Poirot$_i$ believes [$_{CP}$ that [$_{IP}$ himself$_i$ is the best]].
13b   *Poirot$_i$ believes [$_{NP}$ Miss Marple's description of himself$_i$]].

In (13a) the reflexive does not have a clause-mate antecedent and the sentence is ungrammatical. As predicted by (10), we cannot link the reflexive *himself* to the NP *Poirot*. The domain in which the reflexive must be bound apparently IS the clause containing it. On the other hand, in (13b) the reflexive *himself* cannot be linked to the antecedent *Poirot* even though they are clause-mates.

Let us look at (12) first. This is an example of an ECM construction described in detail in chapter 3, section 2.2.2.2. Recall that an essential property of ECM constructions is that the subject of a lower clause is governed (and case-marked) by an outside governor. In (12) *himself* is case-marked by the verb of the matrix clause, *believe*. Precisely the fact that the reflexive is governed by the verb *believe* apparently allows us to extend the domain in which we may look for an antecedent. Let us attempt a reformulation along these lines:

14   **Principle of reflexive interpretation** (2)
     A reflexive must be bound inside a clause that contains it and its governor.

The reformulation extends the local domain in which we find an antecedent for a reflexive in those cases in which the reflexive is governed from a higher clause. (14) will still rule out (13a) because the maximal projection CP is a barrier for government by an outside head.

Unfortunately, our new formulation (14) is still inadequate. It is too weak: as the reader can check for himself (14) fails to exclude (13b). The binding domain for the reflexive should be the entire clause, but apparently *himself* cannot be bound by the subject of the clause, the NP *Poirot*.

1.4.2 SUBJECTS

It looks as if the domain for binding of the reflexive in (13b) ought to be restricted to the NP [*Miss Marple's description of himself*] which contains a governor (the preposition *of*) for the reflexive. However, a general restriction of the binding domain to NPs would in turn be too powerful: it would give the correct result in (13b) but at the same time it would exclude the grammatical (13c):

13c Poirot believes [$_{NP}$ any description of himself].

The difference between (13b) and (13c) lies in the composition of the NP which contains the reflexive. In (13b), the bracketed NP contains an NP in its specifier position: *Miss Marple*. This NP receives a theta role from the N *description*. Indeed, when we compare (13b) with (13d) we see that the NP is analogous to a subject NP:

13d Miss Marple has described herself.

Recall that the subject NP of a finite clause occupies the specifier position of IP, [Spec, IP]. Analogously, we shall say that the NP in the [Spec, NP] position is the subject of an NP. In (13c) the specifier position of the NP is not occupied by an NP but rather by *any*. This suggests that the fact that there is a subject inside an NP determines the domain in which the reflexive can be bound. Consider furthermore that in (13e) the subject of the NP itself binds the reflexive:

13e Miss Marple believes [$_{NP}$ Poirot$_i$'s description of himself$_i$].

1.4.3 COMPLETE FUNCTIONAL COMPLEX

At this stage there are several ingredients to incorporate in our rules for the binding of reflexives. Apart from the c-command constraint we need to determine exactly how far away we allow ourselves to look for an antecedent, i.e. what constitutes its binding domain. The major factors that come into play are the following:

(i)   clauses and NPs containing a reflexive may but need not serve as binding domains for the reflexive;
(ii) the presence of a subject serves to delimit a binding domain;
(iii) the governor of the reflexive plays a role in defining the binding domain.

The factors listed in (i) and (ii) are not independent: both NPs and clauses have subjects, the latter obligatorily. Let us try to amalgamate all the conditions above into one formulation:

15   **Principle of reflexive interpretation** (3)
     A reflexive must be bound in the minimal domain containing it, its governor and a subject.

The domain defined by (15) is 'complete' in the sense that it contains all the functions determined by the projection principle. It contains the head of a projection, the governor, i.e. the predicate which assigns the theta roles, the governed elements, i.e. the complements, to which the internal theta roles are assigned, and the subject, to which the external theta role is assigned. For this reason Chomsky (1986: 169–72) refers to the domain defined by (15) as a **complete functional complex** (CFC).[8]

At this stage we ought to verify whether our third hypothesis (15) is still adequate for the examples treated so far. We repeat them here and invite the reader to check:

16a   = 7a   *I expect [$_{IP}$ himself$_i$ to invite Poirot$_i$].
16b   = 7b   Poirot$_i$ invited himself$_i$.
16c   = 3b   *Miss Marple$_i$ hurt himself$_i$.
16d   = 5c   He$_i$ has hurt himself$_i$.
16e   = 6b   *Poirot$_i$ thinks [$_{CP}$ that [$_{IP}$ Miss Marple hurt himself$_i$]].
16f   = 7c   *Poirot$_i$'s sister invited himself$_i$.
16g   = 7d   Poirot's brother$_i$ invited himself$_i$.
16h   = 12   Poirot$_i$ believes [$_{IP}$ himself$_i$ to be the best].
16i   = 13a   *Poirot$_i$ believes [$_{CP}$ that [$_{IP}$ himself$_i$ is the best]].
16j   = 13b   *Poirot$_i$ believes [$_{NP}$ Miss Marple's description of himself$_i$].

---

[8] For some discussion of CFC see Giorgi (1987).

16k = 13c   Poirot$_i$ believes [$_{NP}$ any description of himself$_i$].
16l = 13e   Miss Marple believes [$_{NP}$ Poirot$_i$'s description of himself$_i$].

In order to determine the binding domain for the reflexive you should proceed as follows: (i) find the governor of the reflexive, (ii) find the closest subject. The smallest IP or NP containing these two elements will be the binding domain in which the reflexive must be bound, i.e. co-indexed with a c-commanding (and agreeing) antecedent.

If you test the rule in (15) carefully on the data in (16) you will find that (15) is rather successful. One problematic case remains: (16i). Here the relevant governor will be the lower I, and the first subject we meet is the main clause subject *Poirot* but (16i) is ungrammatical with the higher subject as an antecedent for the reflexive. One rash conclusion might be to dispense with the requirement that there be a subject, but this will not do in view of examples such as (16j) and (16l) and the examples in (17) where the binding domain for the reflexive is the lowest IP, which contains a governor (*like*) and a subject, the NP *Miss Marple*:

17a *Poirot$_i$ believes [$_{IP}$ Miss Marple to like himself$_i$ too much].
17b Poirot believes [$_{IP}$ Miss Marple$_i$ to like herself$_i$ too much].

In the next section we reconsider examples like (16i) and try to improve upon our formulation so that those too can be included. The reader should be warned that the argumentation is rather complex and that the solutions proposed here are provisional and rather controversial. Current work in Government and Binding Theory tries to reduce the complexities of the account given below.

1.4.4   SUBJECT AND BIG **SUBJECT**

Let us return to the problem raised by (16i) repeated here as (18):

18   *Poirot$_i$ thinks [$_{CP}$ that [$_{IP}$ himself$_i$ is the best detective]].

The reflexive *himself* needs to be bound. On the basis of our last formulation of the principle of reflexive interpretation it is unexpected that the subject of the main clause *Poirot* cannot function as the binder for the reflexive. It is clear that the binding domain as defined is too large: it should be restricted to the tensed clause.

It would be possible, of course, to set up an *ad hoc* rule that tensed clauses are always binding domains. However there are two objections to this solution. On the one hand, such a **stipulation** would do no more than describe the facts without any explanation. This objection is conceptual in nature: a theory of grammar should explain rather than state the facts. Second, there is an empirical objection: additional data show that the *ad hoc* constraint would be too powerful, it would exclude grammatical sentences:

19   Poirot$_i$ thinks [$_{CP}$ that [$_{IP}$ a picture ot himself$_i$ will be on show at the exhibition]].

In the grammatical (19) the reflexive *himself* is bound outside the tensed clause.

In order to circumvent these problems Chomsky (1981a: 209) proposes to reconsider the notion subject when used to define binding domains. In our discussion so far, we have used the term rather informally to refer to subjects of clauses, tensed and infinitival, and to the subject of NPs. We have assumed that both the NP in [Spec, IP] and that in [Spec, NP] are subjects. It turns out that a distinction must be drawn between the subjects of finite clauses and those of non-finite ones and NPs.

In chapter 2 we saw that different clause types are characterized by the composition of their inflection, I, the head of the projection. The I node of tensed clauses is specified for the features [+ Tense] and [+ AGR]. [+ AGR] encodes the agreement properties of the subject: it contains the number and person features of the subject. Consider the paradigm for Italian verb conjugation given also in chapter 2:

20a   (io)   parlo
      I   speak
20b   (tu)   parli
      you   speak
20c   (lei)   parla
      she   speaks
20d   (noi)   parliamo
      we   speak
20e   (voi)   parlate
      you   speak
20f   (essi)   parlano
      they   speak

As discussed briefly in the Introduction, a pronominal subject in Italian may be left unexpressed. (20a) *parlo* will be understood as 'I speak'; the pronoun *io* is usually left unexpressed.[9] This is related to the fact that Italian has a rich inflectional system which allows us to recover the subject from the verbal inflection. The AGR features on the verb pick up the features of the subject. The absence of rich morphology in English disallows for the subject pronoun to be unexpressed.

Although the inflectional endings in English are morphologically impoverished, we have adopted the idea that in English AGR is also specified abstractly for the agreement features of the subject. For both Italian and English we propose that subject and verb agree, as shown by co-indexation:

21a   io$_i$ parlo$_i$
21b   I$_i$ speak$_i$

In other words, AGR in I picks up the nominal features of the subject. This equation between AGR and the subject has led Chomsky to propose that AGR is 'like the subject'. In order to distinguish AGR with its subject-like properties from the NP in the subject position (the NP position dominated by IP), Chomsky refers to the AGR of finite clauses as **SUBJECT**, the big subject.

On the basis of this proposal Chomsky then argues that for the definition of the binding domain for a reflexive SUBJECT can count as the 'subject' mentioned in (15). This means that in (18) the finite subordinate clause contains the reflexive, its governor (I) and a SUBJECT (AGR) and will constitute the binding domain in which the reflexive must be bound.

The reader may wonder about the validity of this step which looks like a makeshift device to rescue the principle developed so far. One argument in favour of the proposal of treating AGR as a SUBJECT is that intuitively what we have been calling the 'subject' is the 'most prominent' NP-position in IP (Chomsky, 1981a: 209). The subject NP c-commands the entire clause. But AGR itself is a bundle of nominal features (person, number) contained in INFL or I, the head of IP. AGR can in this way be argued to be at least as

---

[9] The pronoun *io* will be expressed when it receives special emphasis. In chapter 8 we shall propose that the non-overt subject of (20a) is syntactically represented: it is an empty category, which we shall indicate as *pro*. Chomsky (1981a: 65) proposes that whenever there is an option between having an overt pronoun and a non-overt one, the non-overt one is chosen 'where possible'. He refers to this principle as the **Avoid Pronoun Principle**. He leaves it open whether this principle is a grammatical principle or a conversational principle of 'not saying more than is required'.

'prominent': even if it is not an NP position AGR can be identified as a SUBJECT. Non-finite sentences also contain an I node, but their inflection is negatively specified for AGR. The absence of the nominal agreement features on infinitives entails that there will be no SUBJECT in infinitivals. Only an NP subject, an NP dominated by IP, can qualify. Hence:

22a *Poirot$_i$ believes [$_{IP}$ Miss Marple to like himself$_i$ too much].
22b Poirot$_i$ believes [$_{IP}$ himself$_i$ to be the best detective].

In (22a) the binding domain for the reflexive *himself* must be restricted to the lower clause which contains a governor *like* and a subject, the NP *Miss Marple*. In (22b) the binding domain is the main clause which contains a governor – the verb *believe* – and a subject *Poirot*. In contrast with (18) the lower I is [−AGR] hence cannot count as SUBJECT.

Small clauses will behave like infinitival IPs: they contain a subject, but lacking all verb forms they also lack finite AGR:

23a Poirot considers [$_{sc}$ Watson$_i$ entirely responsible for himself$_i$].
23b Poirot$_i$ considers [$_{sc}$himself$_i$ responsible for the damage].

In (23a) *himself* can only take *Watson* as an antecedent. The governor of *himself* is the P *for* and the subject is *Watson*, the subject of the bracketed small clause. The small clause will count as the binding domain. In (23b), the small clause does not contain a SUBJECT, lacking finite AGR, and the binding domain for the reflexive is extended to the higher clause. *Poirot* binds the reflexive. If small clauses are considered as maximal projections (see discussion in chapters 2 and 3), then the notion subject could be defined as the NP dominated by the maximal projection, [NP,XP]. Clausal subjects are [NP,IP], subjects of NPs are [NP,NP] and small clause subjects are [NP,XP], with XP of the same category as the predicate of the small clause.

According to our latest definition of the binding domain all finite clauses should of necessity be binding domains for reflexives, since they all contain a SUBJECT by definition. (19) raises problems. As discussed above, *himself* can be bound outside the lower clause. This phenomenon has come to be known as 'long-distance binding'.

1.4.5 ACCESSIBLE SUBJECT AND THE *i*-WITHIN-*i* FILTER

Let us start from examples (18) and (19), repeated here as (24) for convenience' sake, for our final revision of the rule of reflexive interpretation.

24a *Poirot_i thinks [_{CP} that [_{IP} himself_i is the best detective]].

24b Poirot_i thinks [_{CP} that [_{IP} [_{NP} a picture of himself_i] will to be on show]].

In (24a) the binding domain for the reflexive can be defined on the basis of the notions governor and SUBJECT. The inflection on *is*, third person singular, serves as the SUBJECT for the reflexive *himself*.

However, being a SUBJECT is not sufficient. Chomsky proposes that in order for an element to be able to count as a subject/SUBJECT to determine the binding domain of a reflexive it must be an **accessible** subject/SUBJECT for that reflexive. A subject/SUBJECT is accessible for a reflexive if it is possible to co-index it with this reflexive.

25   **Accessible subject/SUBJECT**
     A is an accessible subject/SUBJECT for B if the co-indexation of A and B does not violate any grammatical principles.

Chomsky (1981a: 211–2) proposes that one of the grammatical principles that should be considered is the *i*-within-*i* filter:

26   **The *i*-within-*i* filter.**
     *[_{Ai} . . . B_i . . .]

The goal of the filter is to avoid circularity in reference. In section 8 we discuss some examples of circularity.[10]

In (24a) the co-indexation of the reflexive and the SUBJECT is unproblematic: *himself* and AGR in *is* can be co-indexed without violating (25).[11] Thus AGR is an accessible SUBJECT. Moreover I is the governor of *himself*. The binding domain of *himself* will be the lower clause.

In (24b) matters are different. The reflexive *himself* is contained inside the subject of the lower clause. In order to find its binding domain we need (i) a governor and (ii) an accessible subject/SUBJECT. The governor of *himself* is *of*, the preposition. Now we need an accessible subject/SUBJECT. The first element to try would be the NP subject of the lower clause: [_{NP} *a picture of*

---

[10] For some discussion of accessibility and the problems it raises the reader is referred to Bouchard (1985) and Lasnik (1986). An alternative approach for examples like (24b) is found in Williams (1982).

[11] Indeed *himself* and SUBJECT (AGR) are co-indexed by virtue of subject-verb agreement.

himself]. In order for this NP to be accessible we must be able to co-index it with the reflexive:

27   [$_{NP_i}$ a picture of [$_{NP_i}$ himself]]

This co-indexation is banned because it would violate the *i*-within-*i* filter (26).

Let us see if the AGR of the lower clause could count as an accessible SUBJECT. Given that the entire NP in (24b) is the subject NP of the sentence it is co-indexed with AGR by virtue of its person and number agreement through AGR in I. The co-indexation of *himself* with AGR would again violate the *i*-within-*i* filter. *Himself* would be co-indexed with AGR and AGR in turn is co-indexed with the NP *a picture of himself*. Co-indexation is transitive: if A is co-indexed with B, and B is co-indexed with C, then A is also co-indexed with C. In our example *himself* would be co-indexed with AGR, AGR is co-indexed with the NP *a picture of himself*, hence *himself* ends up being co-indexed with the NP:

28   [$_{NP_i}$ a picture of [$_{NP_i}$ himself]]   AGR$_i$

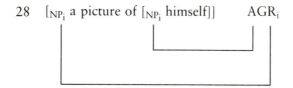

In other words, no accessible subject/SUBJECT is available inside the finite lower clause. We need to extend the domain for the binding of the reflexive to the next clause up: here the subject *Poirot* or the SUBJECT, AGR, can qualify: co-indexation with *himself* would not lead to a violation of the *i*-within-*i* filter.

The long-distance binding of the reflexive shown here is a result of the constraint on subject/SUBJECT accessibility. Given that the finite lower clause does not contain an accessible subject/SUBJECT the binding domain is enlarged to comprise the next higher clause.

One word of caution is in place here. The co-indexation proposed to determine whether a subject/SUBJECT is accessible is not to be taken as an actual co-indexation. Rather, what Chomsky means is that a subject/SUBJECT is accessible if co-indexation would not give rise to any violations. He obviously does not wish to imply that one must co-index the reflexive with the subject NP and therefore assume that they have the same referent.[12]

---

[12]   Aoun (1986) extends the notion of accessibility to propose a modification of the binding theory. This work should be accessible as soon as chapter 8 has been covered.

On the basis of the discussion we need yet again to modify our principle for the interpretation of reflexives:

29　**Principle of reflexive interpretation** (4)
　　A reflexive must be bound in the minimal domain containing it, its governor and an accessible subject/SUBJECT.

In the literature the binding domain defined in (29) is often referred to as the **governing category** (GC).[13]

1.5　*Reflexive Interpretation: Summary*

Throughout this section we have been trying to elaborate a set of principles that regulate the interpretation of reflexives. Starting from a small set of data which we have extended throughout the discussion, we have gradually arrived at a more complex proposal with maximal coverage. Let us summarize the results of our findings here:

30　**Principle of reflexive interpretation**
　　A reflexive must be bound in the minimal domain containing it, its governors and an accessible subject/SUBJECT.

31　**(A-) binding**
　　A A-binds B iff
　　(i)　A is in an A-position;
　　(ii)　A c-commands B;
　　(iii)　A and B are co-indexed.

32　**C-command**
　　A node A c-commands a node B iff
　　(i)　A does not dominate B;
　　(ii)　B does not dominate A;
　　(iii)　the first branching node dominating A also dominates B.

[13] For further discussion and modification of the binding theory, see Aoun (1986), Brody (1985) and Manzini (1983). For a discussion of the cross-linguistic variation with respect to the definition of the governing category and with respect to possible antecedents, see work by Manzini and Wexler (1987). This work also attempts at providing an explanation of how the cross-linguistic variation is acquired. For the literature mentioned here it will be best to wait until we have finished chapter 8 before you attempt to read the texts.

33 **Subject/SUBJECT**
    a   Subject: [NP,XP].
    b   SUBJECT corresponds to finite AGR.

34 **Accessible subject/SUBJECT**
    A is an accessible subject/SUBJECT for B if the co-indexation of A and B
    does not violate any grammatical principles.

35 The *i*-within-*i* filter
    $*[_{A_i}...B_i...]$

2   Anaphors: Reflexives and Reciprocals

Up till now we have concentrated exclusively on the interpretation of reflexives
such as *himself*. Reflexives do not refer independently, they receive their
referential interpretation by virtue of being bound by an antecedent.

   Reciprocals such as *each other* can be shown to be subject to the same
interpretative constraints as reflexives.

36a   The students$_i$ attacked each other$_i$.
36b   *The student$_i$ attacked each other$_i$.
36c   *Each other are ill.

Reciprocals are inherently plural and hence need a plural antecedent for their
interpretation. In (36b) the singular NP *the student* cannot act as the relevant
binder for the reciprocal. In (36c) there is no binder available. In (36a) the
reciprocal *each other* is bound by the subject NP and this sentence is
grammatical. A survey of a number of examples with reciprocals shows that
their interpretation is parallel to that of reflexives (cf. the examples listed in
(16) for parallel constructions with reflexives):

37a   *I expect [$_{IP}$ each other$_i$ to invite the students$_i$].
37b   The students$_i$ invited each other$_i$.
37c   *The student$_i$ invited each other$_i$.
37d   They$_i$ have invited each other$_i$.

37e *The students$_i$ think [$_{CP}$ that [$_{IP}$ Miss Marple invited each other$_i$]].

37f *The students$_i$' sister invited each other$_i$.

37g Poirot's brothers$_i$ invited each other$_i$.

37h The students$_i$ believe [$_{IP}$ each other$_i$ to be the best].

37i *The students$_i$ believe [$_{CP}$ that [$_{IP}$ each other$_i$ are the best].

37j *The students$_i$ believe [$_{NP}$ Miss Marple's description of each other$_i$].

37k The students$_i$ believe [$_{NP}$ any description of each other$_i$].

37l Miss Marple believes [$_{NP}$ the students$_i$' description of each other$_i$].

We leave it to the reader to check the application of the principle of binding for reflexives to the examples above. From now on we use the general label **anaphor** to refer to the referentially-dependent NP types: reflexives and reciprocals. We can then generalize the principles and definitions established for reflexives to cover all anaphoric NPs.

38 **Interpretation of anaphors**
An anaphor must be bound in the minimal domain containing it, its governor and an accessible subject/SUBJECT.

If we use the term **governing category** to refer to the binding domain described above then we can abbreviate (39):

39 **Interpretation of anaphors**
An anaphor must be bound in its governing category.

3 Pronouns

So far we have not achieved a great deal with respect to the inventory of NPs given in the introduction to this chapter. Only anaphors have been dealt with. In this section we turn to the second type of NP: pronouns. Consider the interpretation of the pronoun in (40a):

40a Poirot had hurt him.

40b Poirot had hurt himself.

It is obvious that the interpretation of pronouns differs from that of reflexives. The pronoun *him* in (40a) must refer to an entity different from the subject NP *Poirot*, while a reflexive in the same position (40b) must refer to the entity denoted by *Poirot*. Whereas the reflexive must be bound in (40b), the pronoun must be **free**. The first question to address is whether the domain in which pronouns must be free is identical to that in which anaphors must be bound, i.e. the governing category – from now on GC – defined above.

If the binding domains were identical, we would expect that whenever we find a reflexive bound by some antecedent X we should find that a pronoun in the same position must not be bound by an NP in the position X. Moreover in those cases where reflexives are ungrammatical because no antecedents are available in their binding domain, pronouns should still be possible since the pronoun does not need an antecedent.

Let us again refer to the data for reflexives in (16) and check whether the prediction sketched above holds. In each of the examples in (16) we replace the reflexive by a pronoun.

41a I expect [$_{IP}$ him$_j$ to invite Poirot$_i$].
41b Poirot$_i$ invited him$_j/*_i$.
41c Miss Marple$_i$ hurt him$_j$.
41d He$_i$ has hurt him$_j/*_i$.
41e Poirot$_i$ thinks [$_{CP}$ that [$_{IP}$ Miss Marple hurt him$_i/_j$]].
41f Poirot$_i$'s sister invited him$_i/_j$.
41g Poirot$_i$'s brother$_j$ invited him$_j/*_i$.
41h Poirot$_i$ believes [$_{IP}$ him$_j/*_i$ to be the best].
41i Poirot$_i$ believes [$_{CP}$ that [$_{IP}$ he$_i/_j$ is the best]].
41j Poirot$_i$ believes [$_{NP}$ Miss Marple's description of him$_i/_j$].
41k Poirot$_i$ believes [$_{NP}$ any description of him$_j/*_i$].
41l Miss Marple believes [$_{NP}$ Poirot$_i$'s description of him$_j/*_i$].

We shall not go through all the examples here. The reader is invited to compare the sentences above with the treatment of the examples with reflexives in (16). Let us just consider some examples.

In (41a) the pronoun is possible in the subject position of the non-finite clause. The corresponding example with the reflexive (16a) was ungrammatical because reflexives must be bound and there is no binder in the main clause of (16a). It appears from this example that pronouns need not be bound. In (41b) we see that indeed pronouns must not be bound, i.e. pronouns must be **free** where reflexives must be bound. *Him* is only possible in (41b) when there is no binder in the clause. Comparing (16b) and (41b) we see that where a reflexive and a pronominal are possible, their interpretations differ. The same point is illustrated in (41d). (41e) shows that the delimitation of the binding domain for pronouns corresponds to that of reflexives: pronouns must be free in their governing category, but they may freely be co-indexed with NPs outside that domain. Thus in (41e) co-indexation of *him* and *Poirot* is acceptable. (41f) illustrates that binding must be defined in terms of c-command. The pronoun *him* in this example can be co-indexed with *Poirot* in the same sentence because the NP *Poirot* does not c-command the pronoun. Remember that, according to our definition, binding is not merely co-indexation but it is co-indexation plus c-command.

We encourage the reader to go through the remaining examples himself. It will become abundantly clear that the constraint on the interpretation of pronouns is the converse of that on anaphors. Let us formulate the constraint as follows:

42   **Interpretation of pronouns**
     A pronoun must be free in its governing category;

   where the **governing category** is the minimal domain containing the pronoun, its governor and an accessible subject/SUBJECT; and where **free** is not bound.

It may not be superfluous to remind the reader that the principles we are setting up here concern A-binding. Consider for instance (43):

43   Poirot$_i$, Miss Marple doesn't like him$_i$.

Nothing prevents the pronoun *him* from being bound by the NP *Poirot*. In (43) *Poirot* is not in an A-position, but in an A'-position. The binding between *Poirot* and the pronoun *him* is not A-binding but A'-binding.[14]

In section 6 we return to the distribution of pronouns and reflexives in English.[15]

---

[14] The construction in (43) has come to be known as left-dislocation: a constituent (here the NP *Poirot*) is adjoined to the left of IP and is picked up by a co-indexed pronoun. We return to adjunction in chapter 7.

[15] For cross-linguistic variation, the reader is referred to Manzini and Wexler (1987).

4   Referential Expressions

So far we have discussed two types of NPs: anaphors and pronouns. Both of these share the property that they lack inherent reference; anaphors need an antecedent for their interpretation and pronouns do not require an antecedent. Pronouns inherently specify certain properties of the referent; for a complete determination of the referent contextual information is needed.[16]

Referential expressions, or R-expressions, constitute the third class of NPs. As their name indicates these elements are inherently referential: expressions such as *Poirot* and *the detective* select a referent from the universe of discourse. Given that R-expressions have independent reference, they do not need an antecedent; in fact they do not tolerate binding from another element. Let us look at some examples:

44a   Poirot$_i$ attacked him$_{j/*i}$.
44b   Poirot$_i$ says that he$_{i/j}$ is leaving.
44c   He$_i$ says that Poirot$_{j/*i}$ is leaving.
44d   His$_i$ brother$_k$ likes Poirot$_{i/j*k}$ very much.

For by now familiar reasons the pronoun *him* in (44a) and the R-expression *Poirot* must have different referents: both are free. In (44b) the pronoun *he* may be bound by *Poirot* since *Poirot* is outside the GC of *he*, the domain in which pronominals must be free. While the NP *Poirot* binds the pronoun *he* (outside its GC), the reverse does not hold: *he* does not c-command *Poirot*, so even if the two NPs are co-indexed *he* does not bind *Poirot* according to our definition of binding: *Poirot* is free.

In (44c) the order of pronoun and R-expression is reversed compared to (44b). In this example *he* and *Poirot* must not have the same referent: *he* selects an entity distinct from that referred to by *Poirot*. If *he* and *Poirot* were to be co-indexed in this example then the NP *Poirot* would be bound by the pronoun and this is not allowed.

A further extension of (44c) shows that no matter how far the potential binder is located with respect to the R-expression, binding is prohibited.

44e   *He$_i$ says [$_{CP}$ that Miss Marple thinks [$_{CP}$ that Jeeves claimed [$_{CP}$ that Poirot$_i$ is leaving]]].

---

[16]   For a discussion of the role of context in the interpretation of pronouns the reader is referred to Kempson (1988a, 1988b).

In (44e) three clause boundaries intervene between the R-expression *Poirot* and the pronoun, but still co-indexation is not possible. This is predicted: in (44e) too the pronoun *he* would bind the NP *Poirot* if it were co-indexed with it and this would violate the constraint which we have postulated above. Note in passing that the pronoun must not be co-indexed with the NP *Jeeves* for the same reasons.

In (44d) both pronoun (*his*) and R-expression occur in the same sentence and coreference is possible. As the reader can verify for himself, the grammaticality of the example is predicted: the pronoun *his* does not bind the R-expression since it does not c-command it. The NP *his brother* as a whole must, obviously, not bind the NP *Poirot*.

From the examples above we conclude that R-expressions do not tolerate any A-binding: they must be free. In contrast to pronouns which must be free locally, but may be bound outside their GC, R-expressions must be free everywhere.

45   **Principle of interpretation of R-expressions**[17]
        R-expressions must be free everywhere.

5   The Binding Theory

In this chapter we have considered in some detail the interpretation of the three types of NP: anaphors, pronouns and R-expressions. Anaphors need a local antecedent; pronouns may have an antecedent, but must be free locally; R-expressions must be free. The three principles of NP interpretation that we have established are commonly referred to as the binding theory.

---

[17] Evans (1980: 356–7) provides examples where Principle C apparently can be overridden by conversational principles:

  (i)   I know what John and Bill have in common. John thinks that Bill is terrific and Bill thinks that Bill is terrific.
  (ii)   Who loves Oscar's mother? I know Oscar loves Oscar's mother, but does anyone else?
  (iii) Everyone has finally realized that Oscar is incompetent. Even Oscar has realized that Oscar is incompetent.

For discussion of such examples the reader is referred to Evans' own work (see also Evans 1982).

46   **Binding theory**[18]
Principle A
An anaphor must be bound in its governing category.[19]
Principle B
A pronoun must be free in its governing category.
Principle C
An R-expression must be free everywhere.

In the literature the terms Principle A, etc. are always used to refer to these principles of the binding theory.

[18] An alternative formulation for the binding theory is developed in Higginbotham (1983) who uses linking rather than co-indexation to show referential dependence.

(i)

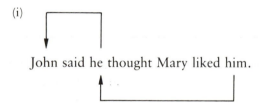

John said he thought Mary liked him.

(Higginbotham 1983: 401).

One advantage of the arrow notation is that it is directional. In (i) the arrows show that *him* depends on *he*, and that *he* depends on *John*.
    Co-indexation is not directional:

(ii)   John$_i$ said that he$_i$ thought that Mary liked him$_i$.

[19] In its present format (46) Principle A says nothing about what happens if an anaphor lacks a GC. Consider:

(i)   *Each other's pictures upset Mary.
(ii)   *Each other's pictures would please their professors.

The ungrammaticality of these examples is accounted for by Chomsky (1981a: 220) who stipulates that the root sentence will count as the GC for a governed element. Hence in (i) and (ii) above Principle A will be violated.

6 Discussion Section: Problems in the Binding Theory

The binding theory predicts that if both a pronoun and an anaphor are possible in a position they have different readings: the pronoun will be free and the anaphor will be bound. There are some problems with this prediction which we illustrate in this section.

6.1 Implicit Arguments

Consider the application of the binding theory in the following examples (taken from Chomsky, 1986a: 166ff):

47a They$_i$ told [$_{NP}$ stories about each other$_i$].
47b *They$_i$ told [$_{NP}$ my stories about each other$_i$].
47c *They$_i$ told [$_{NP}$ stories about them$_i$].
47d They$_i$ told [$_{NP}$ my stories about them$_i$].

48a They$_i$ heard [$_{NP}$ stories about each other$_i$].
48b *They$_i$ heard [$_{NP}$ my stories about each other$_i$].
48c They$_i$ heard [$_{NP}$ stories about them$_i$].
48d They$_i$ heard [$_{NP}$ my stories about them$_i$].

The data in (47) are accounted for by the binding theory. In (47a) and (47c) the sentence is the GC for the anaphor *each other* and the pronoun *them* respectively. The anaphor is bound by the subject NP *they* in (47a), hence the sentence is grammatical. In (47c) the pronoun is bound, hence violates Principle B of the binding theory, and the sentence is ungrammatical. In (47b) and (47d) the bracketed NP is the GC for the reflexive and the pronoun respectively. Recall that it is the presence of the subject *my* in the specifier position of NP in (47b) and (47d) which determines that the object NP is the GC. In (47b) the anaphor is not bound in its GC, hence the sentence is ungrammatical. Conversely the pronoun is free in the grammatical (47d).

(48a), (48b) and (48d) are analogous to (47a), (47b) and (47d) respectively and follow from the binding theory. (48c) raises a problem: the pronoun *them* is co-indexed with a c-commanding NP. If the GC of the pronoun is the entire sentence, as suggested by (48a) and the structurally parallel (47c), then the grammaticality of the sentence is unexpected.

An explanation suggests itself on the basis of the interpretation of (48c) in comparison with (47c), specifically in terms of who does the story-telling. In (47c), 'they', referred to by the subject NP, tell the stories. In (48c) someone else tells the stories. Let us assume, following Chomsky (1986a: 167), that there is an **implicit subject** inside the NPs. We shall represent this by the abbreviation SU.

49a = 47c   *They$_i$ told [SU$_i$ stories about them$_i$].
49b = 48c   They$_i$ heard [SU$_i$ stories about them$_i$].

If the implicit subject counts as a subject to determine the GC for the pronoun, then the pronoun in (49a) is bound in the GC, while that in (49b), is free. (49a) violates the binding theory. The reader will no doubt remark that the analysis introduces another problem. In order to account for the grammaticality of (48a) we must assume that Principle A of the binding theory is respected. In other words *each other* must be bound in its GC, and the GC must be the entire sentence. Clearly, in this example we cannot propose that the implicit subject of *stories* counts as a subject to determine the GC:

50 = 48a   *They$_i$ heard [$_{NP}$ SU$_j$ stories about each other$_i$].

The asterisk in (50) refers to the syntactic representation of the sentence. If we postulate an implicit subject SU$_j$ for the NP *stories about each other*, then this NP will be the GC for *each other* and (48a) ought not to be grammatical, contrary to fact. Chomsky concludes that the 'presence of the implicit argument as subject is optional' (1986a: 167). Clearly the issue raised here is still subject to research.[20]

[20] A similar type of example is illustrated in (i):

(ia)   They$_i$ saw a snake near them$_i$.
(ib)   They$_i$ saw a snake near themselves$_i$.

If the pronoun *them* in (ia) has the same GC as the reflexive *themselves* in (ib), then it is unexpected that they may both be co-indexed with *they*. It is sometimes proposed that in (ia) the PP *near them* is the predicate phrase of a small clause whose subject is non-overt. In (iia) we represent the non-overt subject as PRO (cf. chapter 5). (iia) is roughly analogous to (iib):

(iia)   They$_i$ saw a snake$_j$ [PRO$_j$ near them$_i$]
(iib)   They saw a snake which was near them.

In (iia) PRO, the subject of the small clause, is co-indexed with *a snake* (cf. (iib)). The bracketed small clause is the GC for the pronoun which will duly be free in its GC and may be bound by *they*.

6.2   *Possessive Pronouns and Anaphors*

Consider (51):

51a   The children$_i$ like [$_{NP}$ each other$_i$'s friends].
51b   The children$_i$ like [$_{NP}$ their$_i$/$_j$ friends].

Contrary to expectation the anaphor *each other's* and the possessive pronoun *their* can both be bound by the NP *the children* in (51). *Their* seems to act both as the possessive form of a pronoun (when not bound by *the children*) and as that of a reflexive.

Let us first try to determine the GC for the application of the binding theory. In (51a) and in (51b), the anaphor and the pronoun are governed by the head N of the NP (*friends*). The GC needs to contain a governor and a subject. One possibility would be to say that the specifier of the NP is the subject. This means that the GC is the bracketed NP itself. On this assumption the binding theory is violated in (51a) since the anaphor would not be bound in its GC. An alternative is to discount the subject of the NP as the relevant subject, since it is itself occupied by the item to be considered (anaphor or pronoun) and to extend the GC to the clause. On this assumption, (51a) is as expected but the grammaticality of (51b) is not explained. The problem is that in the two sentences above two different types of GC are needed: in (51a) we need to refer to the entire clause as the GC; in (51b) we need to refer to the NP as the GC.

In recent work Chomsky (1986a) proposes that the binding theory should be modified slightly to accommodate the phenomena above. The discussion will be kept rather informal here.[21] Chomsky proposes that the binding domain of an NP is the domain containing a governor and a subject in which the NP COULD satisfy the binding theory.

Let us apply this to (51b) first. The first potential binding domain for the pronoun is the NP. It contains a governor and a subject (the pronoun itself in [Spec,NP]). And indeed the NP will be the actual binding domain since the pronoun can be free in this NP. Binding from outside will thus be permitted.

In (51a) matters are different. In the first potential binding domain, the NP, principle A could not be satisfied since there is nothing inside the NP that could potentially bind the anaphor. Needless to say, the anaphor cannot bind itself. Given that the NP does not contain a position that could potentially bind the anaphor, we must take the next category up that satisfies the definition of GC:

---

[21]   For further details the reader is referred to Chomsky's own discussion (1986a: 170ff).

the sentence.[22] Chomsky's proposal thus explains that both an anaphor and a pronoun may appear in [Spec,NP] with the same type of co-indexation.

Although this seems a plausible solution to the problems raised for the English data in (51) it will not be possible to generalize it since not all languages pattern like English.

52a *Chinese*

Zhangsan$_i$ kanjian-le [ziji$_i$/ta$_i$ de shu].
Zhangsan   see- aspect self/him of book
'Zhangsan$_i$ saw his$_i$ book.'
(from Huang (1983), cited in Burzio (1989))

52b *Malayalam*

Mohan$_i$ [tante$_i$/awante$_i$ bhaaryaye] nulli.
Mohan self's/he's wife pinched
'Mohan$_i$ pinched his$_i$ wife.'
(from Mohanan (1982), cited in Burzio(1989))

53a *Latin*

Ioannes$_i$ sororem suam$_i$/eius $_j$/$_{*i}$ vidit.
Ioannes$_i$ sister self$_i$'s/his $_j$/$_{*i}$ saw
'Ioannes saw his sister.'
(from Bertocci and Casadio (1980), cited in Burzio (1989))

53b *Russian*

On$_i$ uze rasskazal mne o svoei$_i$/ego$_j$/$_{*i}$ zizni.
he$_i$ already tell me about self$_i$'s/his$_j$/$_{*i}$ life
'He had already told me about his life.'
(from Timberlake (1979), cited in Burzio (1989))

53c *Danish*

Jorgen$_i$ elsker sin$_i$/hans$_j$/$_{*i}$ kone.
Jorgen$_i$ loves self$_i$'s/his$_j$/$_{*i}$ wife
'Jorgen loves his wife.'
(from Pica (1984), cited in Burzio (1989)).

---

[22] Further and more extensive modifications of the binding theory are discussed in Chomsky's own work (1986a: 174–7). The discussion presupposes chapters 5, 6 and 12 of this book.

The languages illustrated in (52) and (53) have both a possessive reflexive and a possessive pronominal. As we have seen (51b) English lacks a possessive reflexive.

Languages which have a possessive reflexive show two patterns. One group of languages behaves like Chinese in (52): both the reflexive possessive and the pronominal possessive can occur in the [Spec,NP] position and be locally bound. This would be accounted for under Chomsky's modification of the binding theory discussed above. On the other hand, in the Indo-European languages illustrated in (53) the possessive reflexive and the pronominal reflexive in a [Spec,NP] have distinct interpretations: the reflexive possessive will be locally bound, the pronominal possessive will be locally free. In (53a), for instance, only *suam* can be used to refer to the subject NP *Ioannes*. Chomsky's modified binding theory referred to above will not account for the data in (53). But the binding theory as discussed in this chapter and summarized in (46) will.

7 NP Types and Features

7.1 *NPs as Feature Complexes*

In section 5 the binding theory was formulated as (46), repeated here as (54):

54 **Binding theory**
   Principle A
   An anaphor must be bound in its governing category.
   Principle B
   A pronoun must be free in its governing category.
   Principle C
   An R-expression must be free everywhere.

Chomsky (1982: 78–89) proposes that the three types of NPs should be reconsidered. In chapter 2, section 7, we discussed the problem of determining the simplest units, the primitives, of syntactic theory. We proposed that syntactic categories such as N, V, P and A were to be replaced by features matrices. The category N, for instance, would be reinterpreted as composed of two features: [+N] and [−V].

Analogously, Chomsky proposes that the three NP-types, anaphor, pronoun and R-expression, are not syntactic primitives. Rather they can be broken down into smaller components. Categories which are subject to principle A are characterized by the feature [+**anaphor**]. Categories subject to principle B are [+**pronominal**]. Reflexives and reciprocals are specified positively for the feature [±anaphor] and negatively for the feature [±pronominal] and can thus be represented by the following feature matrix:

55a   Reciprocals and reflexives:
       [+anaphor, −pronominal]

Conversely pronouns are specified as in (55b):

55b   Pronouns
       [−anaphor, +pronominal]

R-expressions are neither pronominal nor anaphoric:

55c   R-expressions
       [−anaphor, −pronominal]

The purpose of the features is again to bring out commonalities between types of NP by means of shared features. In (55a) and (55b) anaphors and pronouns are shown to share no features at all. Pronouns (55b) and R-expressions (55c) are both [−anaphor]; anaphors (55a) and R-expressions (55c) are both [−pronominal].

7.2   The Binding Theory in Terms of Features

The binding theory can be reformulated in terms of the feature specifications of NPs.

56   **Binding theory**
      Principle A
      An NP with the feature [+anaphor] must be bound in its governing category.

Principle B
An NP with the feature [+pronominal] must be free in its governing category.

R-expressions will not be subject to these principles since they are negatively specified for the features in question. Given that they are inherently referential, the fact that they have to be free need not be stated in the binding theory since binding by another referential element would contradict the fact that they are independently referential.

7.3   The Last NP

The treatment of NPs in terms of features leaves us with an interesting problem. The features proposed for NP types are **binary** features: an NP is either positively or negatively specified for the two features. If we have two features each specified either positively or negatively we expect to find four NP-types:

57a   [+anaphor,   −pronominal]
57b   [−anaphor,   +pronominal]
57c   [−anaphor,   −pronominal]
57d   [+anaphor,   +pronominal]

The first three have been associated with anaphors (reflexives and reciprocals), pronouns and R-expressions respectively. What about the fourth category?

Consider (57d) with respect to the revised binding theory in (56). An element which is [+anaphor] must be bound in its GC. An element which is [+pronominal] must be free in its GC. (57d) is thus subject to contradictory requirements: it must at the same time be bound and free in its GC. This seems impossible. One way out would be to find an element that lacks a GC. If there is no GC, then neither Principle A nor B will apply.

In what circumstances could an element lack a GC? The obvious possibility that comes to mind is for an element to be generated in a position where the definition of GC cannot be met. An element might lack a GC if it does not have a governor. This seems at first sight impossible. If an overt NP lacks a governor then this NP will not be able to be case-marked either. Hence an ungoverned overt NP is predicted to be ruled out by virtue of the case filter (see chapter 3).

It follows that there will be no overt NP corresponding to (57d), the feature matrix [+anaphor, +pronominal].

Note that we are here talking only about overt NPs. If we were to admit non-overt elements then it is conceivable that an element corresponding to (57d) could be found. A non-overt NP would not be subject to the case filter which applies to overt NPs. If an NP could be allowed to be caseless, the absence of a governor would not be problematic.[23] In such a situation a GC could not be established and there would not be any contradictory application of Principle A and Principle B. In chapter 5 we will argue for the existence of such non-overt NPs corresponding to the feature specification in (57d). Anticipating the discussion, this element will be called PRO. However, as soon as we admit that there are non-overt NPs of the type (57d), we are led to the question: what about (57a)–(57c): are there any non-overt correlates to anaphors, pronouns and R-expressions? We return to this issue in chapters 6, 7 and 8.

8   Appendix: Circularity

In the discussion we make use of the *i*-within-*i* filter (26), following Chomsky (1981a: 212), to deal with certain binding facts. As it stands, the filter may sound like an *ad hoc* device to solve residual problems. In this section we try to give some content to the filter.

Consider the interpretation of the NPs in (58):

58a   Hercule Poirot likes Agatha Poirot very much.
58b   He likes her very much.
58c   Hercule Poirot likes his wife very much.
58d   Her husband likes Agatha Poirot very much.
58e   Her husband likes his wife very much.
58f   His wife saw Hercule, her husband (cf. Higginbotham, 1983: 405).

Let us assume the following situation: the person referred to by the NP *Hercule Poirot* is married to the referent of the NP *Agatha Poirot*.

In (58b) we have replaced the full lexical NPs occurring in (58a) by their pronominal substitutes. *He* replaces *Hercule Poirot*; *her* replaces *Agatha*

---

[23] See Exercise 5 for another complication though.

Poirot. The interpretation of (58b) is straightforward. In order to establish the referent of the pronouns we need to know with which NP they are coreferential. The context, linguistic or otherwise, should provide us with the necessary information to recover these NPs.

In (58c) we replace the NP *Agatha Poirot* by the NP *his wife*. Continuing to assume that Hercule is married to Agatha the interpretation of (58c) is also unproblematic. When faced with an utterance like (58c) we need to determine what the referent of the NP *his wife* will be. In order to establish the referent of *his wife* we need to determine the referent of *his*, the pronoun. In this example *his* is coreferential with *Hercule Poirot*. Let us, following by now standard procedures, indicate this interpretation by co-indexation:

59   Hercule Poirot$_i$ likes [his$_i$ wife]$_j$ very much.

In this annotated sentence *his* and *Hercule Poirot* both bear the index *i*, indicating coreference. Obviously, the NP *his wife* has a distinct index, *j*, since the referent of this NP is different from the referent of *Hercule Poirot*. The arrow linking *his* and *Hercule Poirot*[24] is supposed to indicate the referential dependency.

In (58d) we replace the NP *Hercule Poirot* by the NP *her husband*, with an effect similar to that in (58c). In order to establish the referent of *her husband* we need to establish the referent of *her*. Analogously, we can express the referential relations inside (58d) by means of co-indexation:

60   [Her$_i$ husband]$_j$ likes Agatha Poirot$_i$ very much.

The interpretation of sentence (58e) raises an interesting problem. In (58b) two NPs had been replaced by a pronoun: *he* = *Hercule Poirot*, *her* = *Agatha Poirot*. In (58c) one NP is replaced by another coreferential NP, containing a possessive pronoun, similarly in (58d). The interpretation of (58e) suggests that we cannot apply the substitutions used in (58c) and (58d) simultaneously. (58e) is grammatical but it can only have the interpretation where one person's husband likes another person's wife. In other words the co-indexation in (61) is excluded.

---

[24] The linking arrows are introduced for expository reasons.

61 *[Her$_i$ husband]$_j$ likes [his$_j$ wife]$_i$ very much.

The question is why this should be? A related question is why (58f) is grammatical.

Let us return for a moment to (60) (= 58d). There are two NPs for which we need to establish the referent: *her husband* and *Agatha Poirot*. To establish the referent of the NP *her husband* we need to establish who *her* refers to. In order to interpret *her* we look for a possible antecedent, in this case *Agatha Poirot*.[25]

62   Her$_i$ husband   Agatha Poirot$_i$

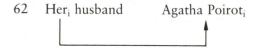

Let us try to apply the same procedure to (58e): here there are two NPs, both containing a possessive pronoun in their specifier: *her husband* and *his wife*. The interpretation of the first NP follows the strategy described above. Let us assume that *her* refers to the second NP. The second NP in turn contains a pronoun. In order to determine what the referent of the second NP is we need to determine what the pronoun *his* refers to. For the interpretation of this pronoun, we could try to link it to the first NP:

63

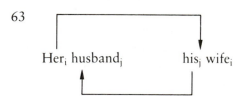

Her$_i$ husband$_j$ his$_j$ wife$_i$

As (63) shows, this leads to a vicious circle. In order to determine the referent of the first NP we need to turn to the second one; in order to determine the referent of the second one we need to return to the first one, etc. Such circularity is apparently not tolerated in natural language. Hence the specific reading imposed on (58e).

(58f) is grammatical since there is no vicious circularity: the NP *his wife* depends for its interpretation on the NP *Hercule* (Higginbotham, 1983: 405):

64

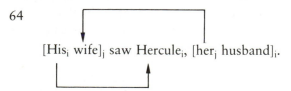

[His$_i$ wife]$_j$ saw Hercule$_i$, [her$_j$ husband]$_i$.

[25] We leave aside the irrelevant interpretation where *her* refers to someone different from Agatha Poirot.

Another instance of circularity is found in (65c):

65a She$_i$ took her$_i$ suitcase from the rack.
65b She$_i$ is [my$_j$ cook]$_i$.
65c *She$_i$ is [her$_i$ cook]$_i$.

In (65a) the pronoun *her* refers to the entity denoted by the subject. In (65b) the predicate NP *my cook* shares the index *i* of its subject: *She = my cook*. In (65c) it is not possible to co-index both the possessive pronoun *her* and the entire NP *her cook* with the subject. In other words, we cannot interpret the predicate NP *her cook* as being coreferential with the possessive pronoun *her* in its specifier. This reading can only be rendered by the alternative in (66), where the co-indexed pronoun *her* is itself contained inside another phrase (*her own*).

66   She$_i$ is [[[her$_i$] own] cook$_i$].

In order to express the coreference between *her* and the containing NP *her cook* in (65c) we would use co-indexation:

67a   [her$_i$ cook]$_i$

The circularity is clear. In order to establish the reference of *her* we need to establish the reference of the entire NP; in order to establish the referent of the entire NP we need to know who *her* refers to.

67b
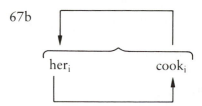
her$_i$ cook$_i$

As the reader can check, the *i*-within-*i* filter (26), repeated here as (68), rules out the circular co-indexation in (67a), since it rules out a construction where A contains B and where A and B share the same index.

68   **The *i*-within-*i* filter**
       *[$_{Ai}$ . . . B$_i$ . . .]

However, care must be taken when we formulate the filter. Consider (69) (example from Higginbotham, 1980: 706).

69   Mary$_i$ is [$_{NP_i}$ [$_{NP_j}$ [$_{NP_i}$ her] cook's] best friend].

In (69) the subject NP *Mary* and the predicate NP *her cook's best friend* are co-indexed. Inside the predicate NP the NP *her cook* bears the index *j*, distinct from the index of the predicate NP as a whole. But the pronoun *her* itself is co-indexed with *Mary* and hence with the predicate NP without resulting in ungrammaticality. We conclude that if (B) in (68) is embedded inside another maximal projection the filter is not valid. This explanation can also be used to explain the grammaticality of (66).

9   Summary

This chapter formulates the binding theory, the module of the grammar which regulates the interpretation of NPs. In its first formulation the binding theory contains three principles each of which regulates the interpretation of one NP-type.

1   **Binding theory**
    Principle A
    An anaphor must be bound in its governing category.
    The term anaphor covers reflexives and reciprocals.
    Principle B
    A pronoun must be free in its governing category.
    Principle C
    An R-expression must be free everywhere.

We have defined the following concepts which are used extensively in the binding theory:

2   **A-binding**
    A A-binds B iff
      (i)   A is in an A-position;

   (ii)   A c-commands B;
   (iii)   A and B are co-indexed.

3 C-command
A node A c-commands a node B iff
  (i)   A does not dominate B;
  (ii) B does not dominate A;
  (iii) the first branching node dominating A also dominates B.

4 Governing category
The governing category for A is the minimal domain containing it, its governor and an accessible subject/SUBJECT.

5 Subject/SUBJECT
  a   Subject: [NP,XP].
  b   SUBJECT corresponds to finite AGR.

6 Accessible subject/SUBJECT
A is an accessible subject/SUBJECT for B if the co-indexation of A and B does not violate any grammatical principles.

7 The *i*-within-*i* filter
  $^*[_{Ai} \ldots B_i \ldots]$

We have also proposed an alternative classification of NP-types on the basis of their feature composition.

8a   Anaphors: [+anaphor, −pronominal]
8b   Pronouns: [−anaphor, +pronominal]
8c   R-expressions: [−anaphor, −pronominal]

We have proposed a reformulation of the binding theory in terms of these features:

9 Binding theory
Principle A
An NP with the feature [+anaphor] must be bound in its governing category.

Principle B
An NP with the feature [+pronominal] must be free in its governing category.

In section 8 we discuss circularity and co-indexation.

10 Exercises

Exercise 1

Illustrate Principles A, B and C of the binding theory with examples of your own, providing three examples for each principle.

Exercise 2

Consider example (16a) in the text in the light of the binding theory developed in this chapter. How do you explain its ungrammaticality?

*I expect [himself$_i$ to invite Poirot$_i$]

Exercise 3

Consider the following examples. Does the binding theory explain the judgements we indicate?

1 *I arranged for myself to win.
2 *They would be happy for themselves to win.
3 *They recognized the necessity for themselves to leave.
4 *John requests that himself leave soon.
5 *For himself to win will amuse John.
6 *John longs for Mary to date himself.
7 We hate it for pictures of ourselves to be on sale.
8 *They expected that discussion about themselves would take place later.
9 My mother$_i$ says that for her$_i$/*herself to read so many comic books is a waste of time.

10 A picture of himself astonished John.
11 This is a picture of myself which was taken years ago.
12 John showed Mary pictures of themselves.
13 Unflattering descriptions of himself have been banned by our president.
14 *Himself astonished John.
15 Joan$_i$ recognized the necessity for her$_i$ to leave.

Discuss each example separately. Then try to classify the examples according to the problems they raise, if any. The examples and judgements indicated are taken from Nakajima (1984). This author reformulates the binding theory using COMP (C) as a subject. The reader is referred to his work for discussion and interpretation.[26] Discuss to what extent Nakajima's approach can account for the data above.

The examples (10)–(13) pose problems for our theory as well as for a theory which counts COMP as a SUBJECT. NPs like those in (10)–(13) which are headed by an N like *picture*, *rumour*, *story* etc. are referred to as *picture*-NPs.

Recall that *picture*-NPs were used extensively in the discussion of the binding domain for reflexives. Mohanan (1985: 641) points out the following contrast:

16 The boys thought that each other's pictures were on sale.
17 *The boys thought that each other's girlfriends were pretty.

The binding theory (46) will account for the data in (16) using the notion of accessible subject, but has no way of accounting for the structurally parallel (17). Mohanan (1985: 642, n 5) considers it a weakness of the binding theory (46) that the *i*-within-*i* filter is introduced for the definition of accessible subject/SUBJECT and GC to deal specifically with examples with *picture*-NPs, which are in many ways exceptional (1985: 641–2).[27]

---

[26] It will be preferable to postpone reading Nakajima's article until chapters 5, 6 and 7 have been covered.
[27] Mohanan (1985: 641) refers to Prewett (1977) for a detailed description of *picture*-NPs.

Exercise 4

Consider the interpretation of the R-expressions in the following sentences.

1   I saw the President on TV last night and the poor fellow looked tired.
2   The President said that the poor fellow was tired.
3   I met Bill and the guy looked desperate for company.
4   Bill believes the guy to be desperate for company.

NPs such as *the poor fellow* and *the guy* seem to act like pronouns. In (1) the NP *the poor fellow* can be replaced by *he*. Such NPs are often referred to as **epithets**. On the basis of the examples above and further examples which you construct yourself, decide which binding principles, if any, these epithets obey.

Exercise 5

In the final section of this chapter we tentatively suggest that there might be non-overt NPs which are not subject to the case filter. Discuss the implications for such a proposal in the light of the visibility principle discussed in chapter 3.

Exercise 6

Chinese offers some intriguing data for the binding theory. Consider the examples below and discuss the problems that they raise:

1   Zhangsan$_i$ shuo ziji$_i$ hui lai.
              say   self   will come
    'Zhangsan said that himself will come.'
2   Zhangsan$_i$ shuo ziji$_i$ you   mei you   qian   mei guanxi.
                say self have not have money not matter
    'Zhangsan said that whether himself has money or not didn't matter.'
    (examples from Aoun, 1984: 16–17).
3   Yuehan$_i$ renwei Mali xihuan   ziji$_i$.
    John   think Mary like   self
    'John thinks that Mary likes himself.'
    (example from Lasnik and Uriagereka, 1988: 122)

Would the binding theory as described above predict these data?

Chinese lacks verb inflection for person and number. One might propose that INFL in Chinese does not contain AGR. Huang (1982) uses this observation to explain the data above. A reflexive in the subject position of a clause will never have an accessible SUBJECT, i.e. AGR, in its own clause: the GC is automatically extended to the higher clause.

Exercise 7

In his description of Japanese Kuno (1973: 294) presents the following examples. The reflexive *zibun* in Japanese is invariant for person and number, but it can be used in a genitive form. On the basis of the examples try to decide whether the reflexive *zibun* is subject to the same constraints as an English reflexive. Discuss any problems you meet.

1   John ga Mary$_i$ o zibun$_i$ no   uti   de korosita.
   John   Mary   'herself' genitive house in   killed.
   'John killed Mary in her own house.'

2   John ga Mary$_i$ ni zibun$_i$ no   uti   de hon o yom-sase-ta
   John   Mary   herself -GEN house in   book   read causative
   'John made Mary read books in her own house.'

3   John$_i$ wa, Mary ga zibun$_i$ o korosoo to sita toki,   Jane to nete ita
   John   Mary   himself kill-try   did when Jane with sleeping was
   'John was sleeping with Jane when Mary tried to kill him' (literally: himself).

4   Zibun$_i$ ga baka na koto ga John$_i$ o kanasimaseta
        fool   is   that   saddened
   'The fact that he (himself) is a fool saddened John.'

5   Mary ga zibun$_i$ o aisite inai   koto ga John$_i$ o gakkarisaseta
   Mary   loving is not that   John   distressed
   'The fact that Mary does not love him distressed John.'

6   John$_i$ wa Mary ga zibun$_i$ o aisite iru koto o sitte ita
                    is loving that   knowing was
   'John knew that Mary loves him ('himself').'
   (examples: Kuno, 1973: 293–313)

Observe that we proposed that like Chinese, Japanese lacks AGR. Will this help in explaining the data above?[28]

Exercise 8

Consider the following examples: what problems, if any, do they raise for the binding theory as developed in this chapter?

1   *Icelandic*
    Jon$_i$ segir [ad   Maria   elski   sig$_i$/hann$_i$]
    Jon says that   Maria   loves (subj)   self/him
    'Jon$_i$ says that Maria loves him$_i$.'
    (from Anderson (1986), cited in Burzio (1989)

2   *Dutch*
    Hij$_j$ hoorde [mij over   zich$_i$/hem$_i$ praten].
    He heard   me about self/him   talk
    'He$_i$ heard me talk about him$_i$.'
    (from Everaert (1986), cited in Burzio (1989))

As the reader can check, the sentences above contain anaphors which are apparently bound outside what, according to our definition, would be their GC (the bracketed string). Anaphors which allow this type of binding are referred to in the literature as **long-distance anaphors**.[29]

Exercise 9

The following example illustrates the problem of referential circularity. (Haik, 1983: 313). Discuss its interpretation:

1   His wife told her daughter that her father was angry.

---

[28] For a description of the Japanese data the reader is referred to Kuno's own text (chapter 5). For a comparison between Japanese and other languages see also Manzini and Wexler (1987). The latter text presupposes familiarity with chapters 5–8.

[29] The reader is referred to the works cited for a detailed discussion of the data. For Italian see also Giorgi (1984).

5   Non-overt Categories: PRO and Control

Contents

Introduction and Overview

So far we have been dealing mainly with the NP constituents of sentences. Their occurrence, distribution and interpretation are subject to various principles and sub-theories of grammar such as the projection principle (chapter 1), the theta criterion (chapter 1), the extended projection principle (chapter 1), X-bar theory (chapter 2), case theory (chapter 3) and the binding theory (chapter 4).

In this chapter we turn to a non-overt NP, i.e. an NP which appears to be syntactically active, hence syntactically represented, but which has no overt manifestation. This non-overt NP will be indicated as PRO and is characterized by the feature composition [+ anaphor, + pronominal]. We alluded to this NP in chapter 4 (section 7.3). Other types of non-overt NPs will be discussed in chapters 6, 7 and 8.

In section 1 we show that the non-overt subject of infinitival clauses is syntactically represented. In section 2 we show that the NP PRO has the features [+ anaphor, + pronominal]. The non-overt NP PRO may be referentially dependent on, or controlled by, another NP in the sentence. The distribution and interpretation of PRO is regulated by the module of the grammar known as control theory. In section 3 we examine the distribution of PRO. We see that it occurs in ungoverned positions and we derive this property from its feature composition as discussed in section 2. In section 4 we discuss some of the main properties of control. In section 5 we offer illustrations of control in different types of syntactic environments.

1   The Non-overt Subject of Infinitivals

1.1   Understood Arguments

For each of the following examples, consider how the different sub-theories of grammar discussed so far determine the distribution and interpretation of NPs.

1a   This$_i$ would be regrettable.
1b   [$_{CP}$ That Poirot$_j$ should abandon the investigation$_k$]$_i$ would be regrettable.
1c   Poirot$_j$ should abandon the investigation$_k$.

From (1a) we deduce that *regrettable* is a one-place predicate: it requires the presence of one argument, realized by the NP *this*. In (1b) the argument of *regrettable* is realized as a finite clause: *that Poirot should abandon the investigation*. The predicate *abandon* in the subordinate clause in (1b) – and in the corresponding main clause (1c) – is a two-place predicate with an external argument, the AGENT of the activity, realized by *Poirot* in both (1b) and (1c), and an internal argument, realized here by the NP *the investigation*. (2a) represents the argument structure of *regrettable*; (2b) that of *abandon*.

2a   *regrettable*:   adjective

1
i

2b   *abandon*:   verb

1	2
j	k

Following our discussion so far, the subject position in the sentences in (1) must be syntactically represented for two reasons. First, given the projection principle and the theta criterion, arguments associated with predicates must be syntactically represented. The external arguments of the predicates *regrettable* and *abandon* are realized by an element in the subject position. Secondly, we also know that in all clauses there must be a subject position because of the extended projection principle (EPP).

With predicates that select an external argument one cannot satisfy the EPP by simply inserting an expletive in the subject position since this move would block the realization of the external argument:

1d   *There abandoned the investigation.

Now let us turn to (3):

3   [$_{IP}$ To abandon the investigation] would be regrettable.

(3) is a complex sentence containing a non-finite subordinate clause. The infinitival clause *to abandon the investigation* in (3) realizes the external argument of *regrettable*. We now focus on the structure of the bracketed infinitival clause.

The subordinate clause has as its main predicate the verb *abandon*. On the basis of (1b) and (1c) we have established that *abandon* is a two-place predicate with an external and an internal argument (cf. (2b)). Although the non-finite clause lacks an overt subject NP, its interpretation suggests that the external argument, the AGENT of *abandon*, is present. Consider (4):

4a   [To abandon the investigation in order to save money] would be regrettable.
4b   [To abandon the investigation without giving an explanation] would be regrettable.

We shall not go into the syntactic structure of the examples in (4) here. We concentrate on their interpretation. In (4a), the non-overt AGENT of the activity of 'saving money' in the purpose clause is interpreted as identical to the AGENT of 'abandon the investigation' in the main clause.[1] Similarly, in (4b) the AGENT of *giving an explanation* is taken to be identical to that of *abandon the investigation*. We conclude that the external argument of *abandon the investigation* is 'understood'.

The question may be raised whether the understood argument of *abandon* is also syntactically represented. Compare (5a) and (5b):

5a   The investigation was abandoned to save money.
5b   To abandon the investigation to save money would be regrettable.

[1] Note that purpose clauses may also have overt subjects:

(i)   We shall abandon the investigation in order for you to save money.

In (i) the subject of the purpose clause is *you*. It does not depend on the subject of the higher clause for its interpretation.
    It is only when the subject of the purpose clause is not overt that it depends on the higher subject for its content. We return to the interpretation of non-overt subjects later.

(ii)   We shall abandon the investigation in order to save money.

In both examples in (5) the AGENT of *abandon* is understood and will be interpreted as identical to the agent of *save money* in the purpose clause. However, in (5b) the AGENT is not simply understood, we shall see that it is also syntactically represented by an NP-position. Consider (6):

6a *The investigation was abandoned together.
6b To abandon the investigation together would be regrettable.

In (6a) the presence of *together* renders the sentence ungrammatical, in (6b) it does not. Why should this be? The data in (7) suggest that in general *together* is related to a plural NP in an A-position:

7a *Watson left together.
7b The detectives left together.
7c *I saw Watson together.
7d I saw the detectives together.

(6a) is ungrammatical because there is no plural NP in an A-position to be linked to *together*. Although the AGENT of passive *abandoned* is understood, it is not able to count as the relevant NP to link up with *together*. Since (6b) is grammatical it must be the case that *together* can be related to some NP in an A-position. The NP *the investigation*, being singular, cannot satisfy this requirement. Intuitively, *together* is related to the external argument of the predicate *abandon* of the infinitival clause (6b) in the same way that it would be related to the overt subject of the finite clause in (8a).

8a Poirot and Watson have abandoned the investigation together.
8b *Poirot has abandoned the investigation together.

We conclude that the understood subject of the non-finite clause in (6b) and (3) is syntactically represented as an NP position. This conclusion leads us to argue that syntactic positions may be present though not phonetically realized. We shall advance further arguments for this conclusion in the following sections.

1.2   The Extended Projection Principle

On the basis of the interpretation of (6b) we have proposed that in the infinitival clause there is an understood external argument of the verb *abandon* which is represented syntactically as a non-overt NP. In fact, the extended projection principle forces us to assume that there is indeed a subject position. According to the EPP all sentences, all I-projections, must have subjects:

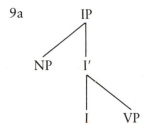

9a

If the EPP is applied to (3) then we are forced to conclude that its syntactic representation will be like in (9b), with a non-overt NP in the subject position [Spec,IP].

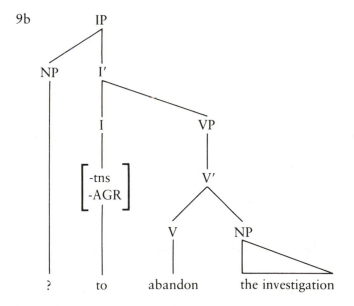

9b

We consider the properties of this non-overt NP in this chapter.

First consider that the sentence we are discussing is closely similar in structure to (10a) which contains an infinitival clause with an overt subject (10b/10c).

10a For Poirot to abandon the investigation would be regrettable.
10b [CP For [IP Poirot [I' to [VP abandon the investigation]]]]

10c

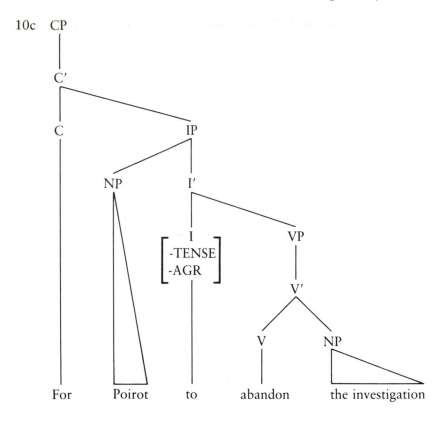

In (10a) the subject of *abandon* is the R-expression *Poirot*. This NP has a specific referent, an individual known by the name *Poirot*. In our earlier example (3), though, the non-overt subject of *abandon* does not have inherent reference. Its interpretation is like that of a pronoun, either a specific pronoun (which would be recovered from the context) or generic *one*:

10d   For $\left\{\begin{array}{c} \text{you} \\ \text{him} \\ \text{them} \\ \text{one} \end{array}\right\}$ to abandon the investigation would be regrettable.

In the literature the non-overt subject of the infinitival clause is represented by the element PRO:[2]

---

[2] PRO is often called 'big PRO', in contrast with 'small pro' which we discuss in chapter 8.

11   CP

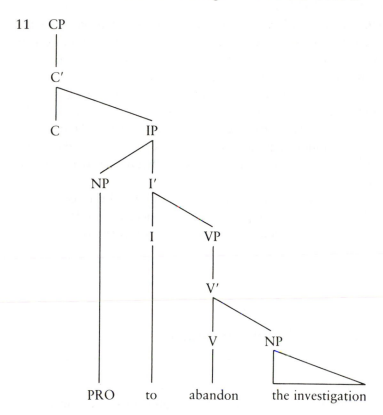

The difference between PRO and the pronouns in (10d) is that the latter have phonetic content and the former does not. PRO is a non-overt NP. This means that the EPP can be satisfied by non-overt material. By analogy with (10c), we also assume that the complementizer position in (11) is present though not filled by any overt elements. Below we give further support for this hypothesis.

1.3   The Binding Theory

In this section we shall advance arguments to motivate the existence of the non-overt syntactically active NP PRO. Consider:

12   [[$_{IP}$ To identify oneself]] would be wrong.

Following our discussion above we assume that the subject of *identify* is the non-overt element PRO. The direct object of *identify* is an anaphor, the reflexive *oneself*. As discussed extensively in chapter 4, Principle A of the binding theory (chapter 4, (46)) states that anaphors must be bound in their governing category. Given that (12) is grammatical, we deduce that Principle A is not violated. If we postulate that the infinitival clause has a non-overt subject, PRO, this subject can act as the binder of the reflexive. The governing category of *oneself* will be the lower non-finite clause. The clause contains the governor of *oneself*, the verb *identify*, and it contains a subject, PRO. It is clear that without the assumption that there is a non-overt subject in the lower clause, it will be hard to see how Principle A of the binding theory could be satisfied in the sentence.

Let us from now on adopt the hypothesis that in infinitival clauses without overt subject NP, the subject is represented syntactically by PRO. In the remainder of this chapter we look in some more detail at the properties of PRO.

2   PRO: Pronominal and Anaphoric

We have posited that infinitival clauses without overt subjects must have a non-overt subject represented as PRO. Using the arguments outlined in section 1, the same element will be taken to occupy the subject position in the infinitival clauses in (13). The reader is invited to consider for himself the motivation for the presence of PRO:

13a   Poirot is considering [$_{CP}$ whether [$_{IP}$ PRO to abandon the investigation]].

13b   Poirot needed a lot of courage [in order [$_{IP}$ PRO to abandon the investigation]].

13c   Poirot was glad [$_{CP}$ [$_{IP}$ PRO to abandon the investigation]].

In (13a) the infinitival clause is an object clause; it is the complement of the verb *consider*. In (13b) an infinitival clause is used as an adjunct; the clause is a purpose clause. In (13c) the infinitival clause is the complement of an adjective *glad*.

As the reader will have been able to verify, the projection principle, the theta criterion and the EPP, offer arguments for positing the presence of PRO. However, the interpretation of PRO in (13) differs from that in the (3), repeated here for convenience' sake as (13d):

13d [$_{CP}$ [$_{IP}$ PRO to abandon the investigation]] would be regrettable.

In (13d) PRO is roughly equivalent to a pronoun. Let us say that PRO is 'pronominal'. Depending on the context PRO may be taken to refer to a specific referent ('you', 'they', etc.) or it may be interpreted as equivalent to the arbitrary pronoun *one*. In (13a), (13b) and (13c) on the other hand, PRO, the subject of the infinitive, will normally be understood as 'Poirot'. In these examples PRO is like an anaphor: it is dependent on another NP for its interpretation.

In terms of the features introduced in chapter 4 (section 7) we might conclude on the basis of the two types of interpretations assigned to PRO in (13) that PRO is both pronominal (cf. (3) and (13d)) and anaphoric (13a–c): PRO is an NP with the feature matrix [+ anaphor, + pronominal].

In the examples where PRO is interpreted as referentially dependent on another NP in the same sentence, as is the case in (13a), (13b) and (13c), we say that it is **controlled** by that NP.

> The term **control** is used to refer to a relation of referential dependency between an unexpressed subject (the **controlled** element) and an expressed or unexpressed constituent (the **controller**). The referential properties of the controlled element ... are determined by those of the controller. (Bresnan, 1982: 372)

In (13a–c) PRO is **controlled** by the main clause subject NP *Poirot*. As has become our practice, we indicate the referential dependency between controller (*Poirot*) and controlled element (PRO) by co-indexation:

14a Poirot$_i$ is considering [whether [PRO$_i$ to abandon the investigation]].

14b Poirot$_i$ needed a lot of courage [in order [PRO$_i$ to abandon the investigation]].

14c Poirot$_i$ was glad [[PRO$_i$ to abandon the investigation]].

In the cases where PRO is not subject to control by another NP and refers freely, as in (13d), PRO can also have an arbitrary reading: this is **arbitrary** PRO. This occurrence of PRO is sometimes represented as follows: PRO$_{arb}$.

14d [[PRO$_{arb}$ to abandon the investigation]] would be regrettable.

PRO may also be dependent on implicit arguments:

15a The operation was abandoned [PRO to save money].
15b [PRO to control yourself] is very advisable.

In (15a) PRO is not arbitrary in reference. Rather it is controlled by the implied AGENT of *abandoned*. In (15b) PRO is controlled by the implied BENE-FACTIVE:

15c PRO to control yourself is very advisable (for you).

We assume that the non-overt subject NP of infinitival clauses is syntactically represented as PRO, with the feature matrix [+anaphor, +pronominal]. We now have to determine what the conditions of the occurrence of PRO are, in which contexts it is admitted or **licensed** and how its content, its interpretation, is determined. The module of the grammar which regulates the distribution and the interpretation of PRO is called control theory. We turn to the main aspects of control theory in the remaining part of this chapter.

3 The Distribution of PRO

3.1 *The Data*

In this section we study the distribution of PRO. We shall examine whether this element is necessarily restricted to subject positions of infinitivals. Would it be possible to find PRO as the subject of a finite clause? Can PRO be found in a direct object position? We may also wonder whether every infinitive could have a PRO subject. A glance at the data in (16)–(18) suggests that the answer to all three questions is negative:

16a *Poirot$_i$ wondered [$_{CP}$ whether [$_{IP}$ PRO$_i$ to invite PRO]].
16b *Poirot wondered [$_{CP}$ whether [$_{IP}$ he should invite PRO]].

17a *[$_{IP}$ PRO should invite the sergeant].
17b *Poirot$_i$ wondered [$_{CP}$ whether [$_{IP}$ PRO$_i$ should invite someone]].

18a *Poirot$_i$ preferred very much [$_{CP}$ for [$_{IP}$ PRO$_i$ to destroy something]].

18b *Poirot$_i$ believed [$_{IP}$ PRO$_i$ to be the best detective]].

(16) shows that the non-overt element PRO cannot be used as a direct object.[3] The ungrammaticality of the sentences is due to the presence of PRO in the object position of *invite*. If we replace PRO by an overt NP the sentences become grammatical:

19a Poirot$_i$ wondered [$_{CP}$ whether [$_{IP}$ PRO$_i$ to invite her]].

19b Poirot wondered [whether [$_{IP}$ he should invite her]].

(17) suggests that PRO cannot appear as the subject of finite clauses, whether they be main clauses (17a) or subordinate ones (17b). If we replace PRO by an overt NP the sentences in (17) become grammatical:

20a [$_{IP}$ You should invite the sergeant].

20b Poirot$_i$ wondered [$_{CP}$ whether [$_{IP}$ he should invite someone]].

(18) finally provides evidence that although PRO may be the subject of some infinitival clauses, not every infinitival construction allows PRO as its subject.

These facts need to be explained. Recall that the ultimate goal of linguistic theory is to provide an explanation for language acquisition. We assume that the child acquiring a language will have to construct a grammar which allows for sentences containing the non-overt NP represented as PRO. The child will also have to construct a grammar which is constrained enough so as to allow only grammatical sentences. The grammar should not generate, for instance, (16), (17) and (18).

One can, of course, try to think of many hypotheses why PRO should not be able to turn up in the examples above. One approach would be to devise three separate statements banning PRO from (i) being the object of a transitive verb (16), (ii) being the subject of a finite clause (17) and (iii) being the subject of certain, yet to be determined, infinitivals (18). But this would be merely providing a list of three descriptive stipulations and such a list does not explain anything. A list would also suggest that these three constraints on the occurrence of PRO are three independent principles of UG which a child must learn one by one. It would clearly be preferable if we could explain the three

---

[3] For non-overt NPs that may occur in object position the reader is referred to chapters 6, 7, 8 and 12.

properties mentioned in terms of one or more other properties which are independently established. We turn to an explanation for the restrictions on the distribution of PRO in the next section.

3.2   *PRO and Overt NPs*

Let us see if we can find a property common to the illegitimate occurrences of PRO in (16), (17) and (18) and oppose these examples to legitimate occurrences of PRO such as those in (21).

21a   Poirot$_i$ preferred very much [PRO$_i$ to invite the sergeant].
21b   [PRO to invite the policeman] would be regrettable.

   One characteristic that sets off the illegitimate occurrences of PRO in (16)–(18) from the legitimate ones in (21) is that in the former an overt NP can replace the illegitimate PRO and lead to grammaticality (as shown in (22)–(24)) while this is not possible for the legitimate occurrences of PRO (25).

22a cf. 16a Poirot$_i$ wondered [$_{CP}$ whether [$_{IP}$ PRO$_i$ to invite *anyone*]].
22b cf. 16b Poirot wondered [$_{CP}$ whether [$_{IP}$ he should invite *anyone*]].

23a cf. 17a *You* should invite the sergeant.
23b cf. 17b Poirot$_i$ wondered [$_{CP}$ whether [$_{IP}$ *he*$_i$ should invite someone]].

24a cf. 18a Poirot$_i$ preferred very much [$_{CP}$ for [$_{IP}$ *the detectives*$_j$ to destroy something]].
24b cf. 18b Poirot$_i$ believed [*Watson*$_j$ to be the best detective].

25a cf. 21a *Poirot$_i$ preferred very much [$_{CP}$ [$_{IP}$ *the police*$_j$ to invite the sergeant]].
25b cf. 21b *[$_{CP}$ [$_{IP}$ *Anyone* to invite the policeman]] would be regrettable.

   The ungrammaticality of the examples in (25) can be explained in terms of case theory (see chapter 3). In (25a) the NP *the police* will not be case-marked by the verb *prefer*, because it is not adjacent to the verb. In (25b), there is no case assigner to case-mark the NP *anyone* in the subject position of the infinitival clause. The insertion of the prepositional complementizer *for* saves the sentences:

26a Poirot preferred very much [cp for [ip the police to invite the sergeant]].
26b [cp For [ip anyone to invite the policeman]] would be regrettable.

The overt NP subject of the infinitival clause in (26) cannot be replaced by PRO:

26c *Poirot preferred very much [cp for [ip PRO to invite the sergeant].
26d *[cp For [ip PRO to invite the policeman]] would be regrettable.

In (26a) and (26b) *for* governs the relevant NPs and will assign them ACCUSATIVE case. We deduce from these observations that PRO in (21) occurs in an ungoverned position. From the ungrammaticality of (26c) and (26d) we conclude that PRO must not be governed.

If PRO must be ungoverned, then it cannot alternate with overt NPs and the ungrammaticality of the examples in (16)–(18) follows. Consider the italicized NPs in (22)–(24). We know from our discussion of case theory in chapter 3 that overt NPs must be case-marked and that case is assigned under government. We conclude that the relevant NPs in (22), (23) and (24) are governed. In (22) the object NP is governed by the verb *invite*. In (23) the subject NP of the finite clause is governed by INFL. The subject of infinitival clause in (24) is case-marked by the prepositional complementizer *for* in (24a) and by the verb *believe* (ECM) in (24b). In (21) PRO is legitimate and it does not alternate with overt NPs. Being ungoverned, overt NPs would not be able to be case-marked.

Let us briefly return to example (12), repeated here as (27a) with its syntactic representation (27b):

27a To identify oneself would be wrong.

27b

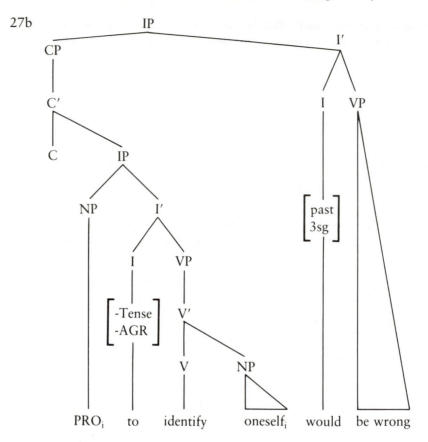

If we want to say that PRO is ungoverned we must assume that the head of IP, I, does not govern PRO. Note that this is a case of a 'weak' I, i.e. one that is negatively specified for both [Tense] and [AGR] features. Perhaps we can say that I is not strong enough to govern PRO.

In our representation in (27b) we also posit that there is a C-projection. We may wonder whether the C-projection is needed. Suppose that there were no C-projection and that the representation of (27a) were (27c).

27c

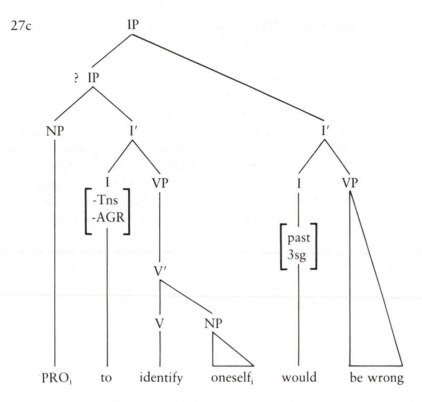

PRO is the subject of an infinitival clause. We have just adopted the hypothesis that infinitival I is not strong enough to govern PRO. Recall that we also assume that the projection of this 'weak' infinitival I is not a barrier for outside government (see the discussion in chapter 3). In the representation (27c), PRO, the subject of the lower IP, will be governed by an external governor, specifically the finite inflection of the higher clause, which is a governor (see chapter 3). We conclude that representation (27c) is inadequate and must be rejected in favour of (27b). In (27b) PRO is ungoverned: infinitival I is not a governor, by assumption, and CP is a barrier to government, being a maximal projection.[4]

3.3   *PRO must be Ungoverned: the PRO Theorem*

Our hypothesis with respect to the distribution of PRO is that its occurrence is restricted to ungoverned positions. PRO is admitted or **licensed** if it is

---

[4]   At this point we are operating with a provisional definition of the notion barrier. We return to the notion extensively in chapters 9 and 10.

ungoverned. It follows that PRO is in complementary distribution with overt NPs. Where PRO is allowed, overt NPs are excluded; where overt NPs are allowed, PRO is excluded.

This analysis is an improvement on the previous one in which we simply stipulated that PRO does not occur (i) in object positions, (ii) as the subject of finite clauses, and (iii) as the subject of certain infinitival clauses. Three stipulations are now seen to follow from one general constraint: PRO must be ungoverned. But what we have achieved so far is still only a generalization which describes the restricted occurrence of PRO. It is not an explanation. In comparison with our earlier discussion, all we have obtained is a more general stipulation: we have replaced three separate constraints by a single one. The remaining question is why PRO should be constrained to appearing only in ungoverned positions.

In the discussion of the interpretation of PRO in section 2 we assumed that PRO is specified as [+ anaphor, + pronominal]. Given our discussion in chapter 4 we expect this element, like all NPs, to be subject to the binding theory. In chapter 4, section 7 the binding theory was reformulated in terms of the features [± anaphor], [± pronominal]:

28   **Binding theory**
     Principle A
     An NP with the feature [+ anaphor] must be bound in its governing category.
     Principle B
     An NP with the feature [+ pronominal] must be free in its governing category.

According to its feature composition, PRO should be subject to both Principle A (it is [+ anaphor]) and to Principle B (it is [+ pronominal]). In other words, as discussed in chapter 4, section 7.3, PRO is subject to contradictory requirements: it must be both bound and free in its GC.

We hinted at a solution for this paradox in our earlier discussion in chapter 4, section 7.3. One possibility for elements with the features [+ anaphor, + pronominal] to be able to exist is if they are ungoverned. If an element is not governed, then it will not have a GC. We had developed the hypothesis that PRO is licensed when ungoverned. The requirement that PRO be ungoverned is not simply a stipulation that describes its distribution. It is a property that **derives** from the binding theory as set up independently and from the characterization of PRO as [+ anaphor, + pronominal].

The proposition that PRO must be ungoverned is referred to as the PRO theorem: it is not a self-evident truth, but it is deduced by a chain of reasoning on the basis of other accepted propositions.

Consider also the following contrast:

29a *John prefers [$_{CP}$ for [$_{IP}$ PRO to leave]].
29b *John doesn't know [$_{CP}$ if [$_{IP}$ PRO to leave]].
29c John doesn't know [$_{CP}$ whether [$_{IP}$ PRO to leave]].

The ungrammaticality of (29a) is related to the PRO theorem: *for*, the prepositional complementizer, governs PRO. The same explanation could be used to explain why (29b) is ungrammatical: *if* is the complementizer of indirect questions and governs PRO. However, the grammaticality of the apparently analogous (29c) is surprising. One possibility is simply to stipulate that *whether* is not a governor. Another possibility (suggested in Borer, 1989: 76) would be to assign the structures (30a) and (30b) to the infinitival clauses in (29b) and (29c) respectively:

30a

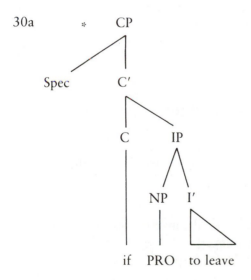

30b

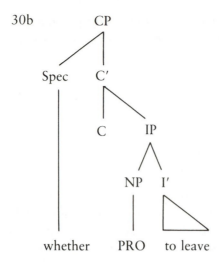

Contrary to our proposals in chapter 2, (30) differentiates between *if* and *whether*. *If* is a head, dominated by C; in (29b)/(30a) *if* will govern PRO. *Whether*, on the other hand, would not be dominated by C but is generated under [Spec, CP]. This analysis would mean that *whether* counts as a maximal projection. Recall that we have seen in chapter 2 that [Spec, CP] is occupied by maximal projections. *Whether* will not govern PRO in (30b)[5] according to our definitions.

3.4   *Other Non-finite Clauses and PRO*

So far we have seen that PRO occurs as the subject of infinitival clauses. However, it seems reasonable to extend its occurrence to other types of non-finite clauses:

31a   Poirot$_i$ remembers [PRO$_i$ abandoning the investigation].
31b   I$_i$ left [without [PRO$_i$ saying goodbye]].
31c   Poirot$_i$ died [[PRO$_i$ waiting for Miss Marple]].
31d   Poirot$_i$ arrived [PRO$_i$ angry].

In (31a) the verb *remember* has a gerundival clause as its complement, a clause headed by the gerund of the verb *abandon*. The structure of such clauses is

---

[5]   As we shall see in chapter 8 and following, *whether* would also not be an antecedent governor of PRO.

notably complicated.[6] Suffice it to say that, following earlier discussion, the verb *abandon* assigns two thematic roles and thus requires two arguments. We assume that the external argument is PRO. PRO is interpreted as referentially dependent on the main clause subject *Poirot*.

In (31b) we find a gerundival clause as the complement of a preposition (*without*). We do not discuss the structure of the PP headed by *without* or of the gerundival constituent. However, on the assumption that *say goodbye* needs an external argument we posit that the subject of the gerund is also PRO.

In (31c) the gerundival clause is an adjunct and is not governed by either a verb or a preposition. As the reader can see, PRO may again function as the subject.

Gerundival clauses are thus another environment where one could reasonably postulate the presence of PRO.

In (31d) we find PRO as the subject of a small clause. From (32) we deduce that *angry* assigns a theta role: the NP *Poirot* is assigned a theta role by the predicate *angry*. The bracketed string is a small clause complement of *thought*.

32 We thought [Poirot angry].

For (31d) we assume that the small clause has a non-overt subject. At this point the reader may well become suspicious. In chapter 3 we argued that small clauses are not barriers to outside government. In an example like (32) the subject of the small clause *Poirot* must be case-marked. In (32) we shall say that the verb *think* case-marks the subject of the small clause. On the other hand, we have argued that PRO is ungoverned. How can the subject of a small clause be governed in one context (32) and ungoverned in another (31d)? We return to this issue in chapter 10. At this point we merely draw the reader's attention to the fact that the small clause in (32) is a **complement** of *think*: *Poirot angry* is assigned a theta role by the lexical head *think*. The small clause *PRO angry* is an **adjunct** in (31d), it may be omitted.[7]

---

[6] There is a vast literature on gerunds. The reader is referred for example to work by Abney (1987), Johnson (1988), Milsark (1988), Reuland (1983) and to the references cited there.

[7] For a different interpretation of the adjunct small clause the reader is referred to Williams (1980).

4 Properties of Control

So far we have not dealt in any detail with the interpretation of PRO. We have merely established (in section 1.3) that sometimes PRO is controlled by an NP, sometimes it is controlled by an implicit argument, and sometimes it is not controlled at all and its interpretation is 'arbitrary'. In this section we give a brief survey of some of the central issues which control theory should deal with.[8] We discuss the contrast between obligatory and optional control (section 4.1), between subject control and object control (section 4.2). We also discuss the c-command requirement on control patterns (section 4.3) and we deal with the type of NP that can act as a controller (section 4.4).

4.1 *Obligatory Control and Optional Control*

In the literature on control two types are often distinguished: **optional control** as in (33), and **obligatory control,** as in (34):

33a John thought that it was important [[PRO to behave oneself/himself]].
33b John asked [how [PRO to behave oneself/himself]].

34a John tried [[PRO to behave himself/*oneself]].
34b John promised Mary [[PRO to behave himself/*herself/*oneself]].
34c John abandoned the investigation [[PRO to keep himself/*oneself sane]].
34d John was reluctant [[PRO to behave himself/*oneself]].
34e John told Mary [[PRO to behave herself/*himself/*oneself]].

In (33) control is optional. PRO may be controlled by *John* but it may also have an arbitrary interpretation as suggested by the fact PRO may bind either *himself* or *oneself*. In (34), on the other hand, PRO, must be controlled and cannot be arbitrary, as shown by the ungrammaticality of *oneself*.

---

[8] This section relies heavily on Chomsky (1986a: 124–31), on Manzini (1983) and on Williams (1980). Manzini (1983) integrates the theory of control into a revised version of the binding theory. Williams (1980) relates control to the more general notion of predication, i.e. the relation between subject and predicate.

4.2   Subject Control vs. Object Control

In the examples of obligatory control in (34) we see that sometimes the controller must be the subject (34a)–(34d), sometimes the object NP (34e). The former type is **subject control**, the latter is **object control**. Verbs like *try* and *promise*, which impose subject control are called verbs of subject control. Verbs like *tell* are verbs of object control.

Other examples of subject control are given in (35) and object control is further illustrated in (36). The phrase *on his/her/one's own* is linked to the PRO subject. We can infer which NP is the controller of PRO from the choice of possessive.

35a   Poirot_i decided finally [[PRO_i to go on his/*one's own]].
35b   Poirot_i was willing [[PRO_i to go on his/*one's own]].
35c   Poirot_i was eager [[PRO_i to go on his/*one's own]].

36a   Poirot_i ordered Miss Marple_j [[PRO_j to go on her/*his/*one's own]].
36b   Poirot_i instructed Miss Marple_j [[PRO_j to go on her/*his/*one's own]].
36c   Poirot_i allowed Miss Marple_j [[PRO_j to go on her/*his/*one's own]].

4.3   C-command and Obligatory Control

Consider the examples of obligatory control in (37):

37a   Poirot's sister promised Miss Marple [[PRO to behave herself/*himself]].
37b   Poirot ordered Watson's sister [[PRO to behave herself/*himself]].

In (37a) only the NP *Poirot's sister* can control PRO in the subordinate clause. The NP *Poirot* in its specifier position cannot function as a controller of PRO. Similarly, in (37b), only the entire NP *Watson's sister* can be a controller for PRO. There appears to be a configurational constraint on control similar to the constraints that define the antecedent for binding: in the case of obligatory control the controller must c-command the controlled element. The reader can verify that *Poirot* in (37a) or *Watson* in (37b) do not c-command PRO.

In the case of optional control the situation is different, as illustrated in (38):

38a [[PRO not to behave myself/himself/oneself]] would be wrong.
38b [[PRO to behave myself]] would be my pleasure.

In (38a) PRO is not controlled by anything in the sentence: it may be taken to have an arbitrary reading or it may be taken as referring to a specific referent which will have been established in the context. In (38b) PRO will be taken to be controlled by the specifier *my* of the NP *my pleasure*. The controller *my* in (38b) does not c-command PRO. Williams (1980) has argued that the c-command requirement distinguishes obligatory control from optional control.

4.4 *The Controller: Argument Control*

Consider the following examples:

39a Three accidents occurred after lunch.
39b There occurred three accidents after lunch.
39c No medical help was available on the premises.
39d There was no medical help available on the premises.
39e Three more accidents occurred without there being any medical help available on the premises.
39f There occurred three more accidents without there being any medical help available on the premises.
39g *There occurred three more accidents without PRO being any medical help available on the premises.

In (39a) *occur* takes one argument. In (39b) we have an example of an alternative sentence pattern in which the subject position of *occurred* is occupied by the expletive element *there*.[9] Expletives are non-argument elements which fill an NP position. The expletive subject is required for structural reasons (EPP).

Similarly in (39c), the subject of the sentence is the NP *no medical help* and in the paraphrase in (39d) the subject position is taken up by the non-argument *there*.

---

[9] Cf. chapter 1 for the notion expletive.

As can be seen in (39e) and (39f) *there* may also be the subject of a gerundival clause. However, (39g) shows that it is not possible for PRO in the subject position of the gerund to be controlled by an expletive *there* in the higher clause. We conclude from the examples that control by an expletive is not allowed: PRO must be controlled by an argument.

5   Control Patterns

In section 4 we have discussed some of the main properties of control. In this section we illustrate and discuss some types of control sentences. The following topics are discussed: (i) sentences with PRO as the subject of a complement clause (5.1), (ii) passivization and control (5.2), (iii) adjunct clauses with PRO subjects (5.3), (iv) subject clauses with PRO subjects (5.4).

5.1   *PRO in Complement Clauses*

Consider examples (35) and (36) repeated here as (40):

40a   Poirot$_i$ decided finally [[PRO$_i$ to go on his/*one's own]].
40b   Poirot$_i$ was willing [[PRO$_i$ to go on his/*one's own]].
40c   Poirot$_i$ was eager [[PRO$_i$ to go on his/*one's own]].
40d   Poirot$_i$ ordered Miss Marple$_j$ [[PRO$_j$ to go on her/*his/*one's own]].
40e   Poirot$_i$ instructed Miss Marple$_j$ [[PRO$_j$ to go on her/*his/*one's own]].
40f   Poirot$_i$ allowed Miss Marple$_j$ [[PRO$_j$ to go on her/*his/*one's own]].

When PRO is the subject of a declarative complement clause it must be controlled by an NP. Arbitrary PRO is excluded in (40). However, different properties obtain when the complement clause is interrogative. In (41) either subject control (41a) or arbitrary control (41b) is possible:

41a   John asked [$_{CP}$ how [$_{IP}$ PRO to behave himself]].
41b   John asked [$_{CP}$ how [$_{IP}$ PRO to behave oneself]].
(examples: from Manzini, 1983: 127)

As the term suggests, a controller must be present in the case of obligatory control. Certain verbs in English may take arguments optionally rather than obligatorily:

42a This analysis led the students to the wrong conclusion.
42b This analysis led to the wrong conclusion.

The direct object *the students* in (42a) is optional. We do not go into the discussion of this example here (see Rizzi, 1986a). Interestingly, *lead* may also act as an object control verb. In (43a) PRO as the subject of the complement clause of *lead* must be controlled. As expected, the direct object cannot be omitted.

43a This analysis led the students$_i$ [[PRO$_i$ to conclude for themselves/*oneself that Poirot was Belgian]].
43b *This analysis led [[PRO to conclude for oneself that Poirot was Belgian]].

Lead contrasts with *promise* which is a verb of subject control. In (44b) we see that the complement NP of *promise* can be omitted.

44a Poirot$_i$ promised Miss Marple$_j$ [[PRO$_i$ to go]].
44b Poirot$_i$ promised [[PRO$_i$ to go]].

Because *lead* is a verb of object control, the direct object must be present in order to control the subject of the infinitival clause. In the case of *promise*, the direct object is not required as a controller.[10]

5.2 Passivization and Control

When PRO appears as the subject of a complement of a transitive verb we may wonder what happens under passivization. With object control passivization is generally possible. The object of the active sentence becomes the subject of the passive sentence (see the discussion in chapter 3 and also chapter 6) and controls PRO.

---

[10] That an object controller cannot be omitted is known as **Bach's generalization**. We return briefly to the data in chapter 12.

45a Miss Marple$_i$ was ordered [[PRO$_i$ to go on her/*one's own]].
45b Miss Marple$_i$ was instructed [[PRO$_i$ to go on her/*one's own]].
45c Miss Marple$_i$ was allowed [[PRO$_i$ to go on her/*one's own]].

Subject control verbs do not pattern uniformly with respect to passivization. Consider the examples in (46) and their passive counterparts in (47):

46a They preferred to go.
46b They wanted to go.
46c They tried to go.
46d They decided to go

47a *It was preferred to go.
47b *It was wanted to go.
47c *It was tried to go.
47d It was decided to go.

Promise, in (48a) which takes an NP complement in addition to the clausal complement, cannot be passivized:

48a They promised Miss Marple to go.
48b *Miss Marple was promised to go.

The ungrammaticality of (48b) cannot be explained by saying that *promise* does not passivize in general as seen in (49) and (50).

49a Emsworth promised Miss Marple a new bicycle.
49b Miss Marple was promised a new bicycle.

50a Emsworth promised Miss Marple that she would get a new bike soon.
50b Miss Marple was promised that she would get a new bike soon.

In (48) *promise* is a subject control verb and it fails to passivize. One might think that the absence of the controlling NP renders (48) ungrammatical. But an overt expression of the agent of *promise* in a *by*-phrase does not rescue the sentence.

51 *Mary was promised by Emsworth [[PRO to go]].

In (51) the AGENT NP does not c-command PRO, as the reader can verify for himself. If we adopt the idea that in cases of obligatory control, the controller must c-command the controlled element (see section 4.3) then the ungrammaticality is explained. The data above also show that the passive subject cannot be the controller.[11]

There are many complexities in this area. Consider (52) (from Bresnan, 1980: 404), where *promise* is a control verb and does passivize:

52a   Mary was never promised [[PRO to be allowed to leave]].
52b   It was never promised to Mary [[PRO to be allowed to leave]].
52c   [[PRO To be allowed to leave]] was never promised to Mary.

In (52a) we see that the passive subject *Mary* can control PRO. Moreover, as the reader can verify, the NP *Mary* in (52b) and (52c) fails to c-command the PRO which it controls, suggesting that these are cases of optional control (cf. 4.3). The examples in (52) pattern like those in (53) (cf. Bresnan, 1980).

53a   Mary was never promised that she would be allowed to leave.
53b   It was never promised to Mary that she would be allowed to leave.
53c   That she would be allowed to leave was never promised to Mary.

5.3   PRO *in Adjunct Clauses*

PRO as the subject of adjunct clauses is also obligatorily controlled:

54a   John abandoned the investigation [[PRO to save money for himself/ *oneself]].
54b   John entered [without [PRO introducing himself/*oneself]].
54c   John hired Mary [[PRO to fire Bill]] (Manzini, 1983: 428).

In (54a) and (54b) PRO is controlled by the subject *John*, in (54c) either subject control or object control is possible.

---

[11] The fact that verbs like *promise* resist passivization is referred to in the literature as **Visser's generalization**. Various proposals to explain this phenomenon have been made.

5.4   PRO *in Subject Clauses*

In declarative complement clauses (cf. (40) vs. (41)) and in adjunct clauses PRO is obligatorily controlled. This is not the case when PRO appears in subject clauses. In (55a) we have an example of arbitrary control, in (55b) PRO is controlled by *Bill* which does not c-command it. In (55c) an NP from a higher clause (*Mary*) controls PRO. (55d) shows again that c-command is not obligatory (data from Manzini, 1983: 424, (36)–(39)):

55a   [[PRO to behave oneself in public]] would help Bill.
55b   [[PRO to behave himself in public]] would help Bill.
55c   Mary knows that [[PRO to behave herself in public]] would help Bill.
55d   [[PRO to behave himself in public]] would help Bill's development.

Various proposals have been formulated to deal with the data described in this section. However, at this stage no completely satisfactory control theory has been developed to cover all the complexities involved.[12]

6   Summary

This chapter focuses on a non-overt NP, represented as PRO, which occurs as the subject of non-finite clauses. After providing empirical and theoretical arguments for postulating such an empty category, we examine its distribution and its interpretation. The module of the grammar that regulates the occurrence and interpretation of PRO is called control theory.

The feature composition of PRO is argued to be [+anaphor, +pronominal], from which we derive the PRO theorem:

1   **PRO theorem**
    PRO must be ungoverned.

[12] The reader is referred to the literature for further discussion. See, for example, Bouchard (1984), Chomsky (1981a: 74–9; 1986a: 119–31), Koster (1984a), Manzini (1983) and the criticism in Mohanan (1985) and Williams (1980).

We say that PRO is **licensed** when it is ungoverned. This property allows us to predict that PRO does not alternate with overt NPs.

With respect to the interpretation of PRO we see that it is either controlled by an argument NP or it is arbitrary in interpretation. In some sentence patterns control is obligatory, in others it is optional. Both subject and object NPs may be controllers. In the case of obligatory control the controller must c-command the controlled element.

In the final section of the chapter we illustrate the occurrence of PRO in three syntactic environments: in complement clauses, in adjunct clauses and in subject clauses.

7   Exercises

Exercise 1

In this chapter we have shown that the complementary distribution of PRO and overt NPs can be related to considerations of case theory and binding theory. Hence a pattern such as that in (1) and (2) is expected:

1a   *I tried Bill to go.
1b   I tried to go.
2a   I believed Bill to be innocent
2b   *I believed to be innocent.

For each of the above examples provide a detailed syntactic representation and discuss the contrast in grammaticality between the paired examples. Consider which verb is a control verb and which an ECM verb. On the basis of examples such as those above one could conclude that a verb is *either* a control verb *or* an ECM verb.
      Now consider the following examples:

3a   I expect John to go first.
3b   I expect to go first.
3c   I want John to go first.
3d   I want to go first.

      How could one account for the grammaticality of all four examples? Would it be possible to maintain that a verb is either a control verb or an ECM verb?

Consider the following examples from West Flemish, a dialect of Dutch. We have provided syntactic annotations. Which problems do the examples pose for the theory?

4a   [Me [$_{IP}$ Marie da te zeggen]] is et al utgekommen.
      with   Marie that to say   is it all outcome
      'Because Marie said that, everything was revealed.'
4b   [Me [$_{IP}$ zie da   te zeggen]] . . .
      with   she that to say
      'Because she has said that, . . .'

Zie is the third person feminine singular NOMINATIVE pronoun.

4c   [Me [PRO$_i$ da   te zeggen]] ee Jan$_i$ t al verroan,
      with   that to say   has Jan it all betrayed
      'By saying that, John has given away everything.'

Exercise 2

Consider again the idea that PRO is ungoverned. What problems does this raise for our discussion of the visibility requirement on theta-marking discussed in chapter 3?[13]

Exercise 3

Consider the syntactic structure of the following sentences. Try to provide arguments for positing PRO whenever needed:

1   Cinderella needs time to clean the chimney.
2   Snow White ate the apple to please the witch.
3   The dwarfs intend to take a cleaner.
4   The dwarfs need a man who will do their washing.
5   The dwarfs need a man to do their washing.
6   Cinderella suggested going to the ball.
7   Prince Charming asked Cinderella to come along.
8   While waiting for the coach, Cinderella fell ill.

---

[13] The reader will see that explaining the case filter in terms of visibility is problematic. One possible way out is to argue that PRO is inherently case-marked. PRO would have a case specification as part of its feature composition. We shall not explore this possibility here. The occurrence of PRO is one issue that raises questions for reducing the case filter to visibility. See also Davis (1986).

9   When in doubt, ask a policeman.
10 Cinderella was happy to accept the offer.
11 I shall give you the examples, whenever relevant.
12 Moving house often means buying new furniture.
13 To err is human, to forgive divine.
14 Cinderella was anxious to try the shoes.
15 Utterly exhausted, Cinderella lay down on the bed.

Exercise 4

Consider the following pairs of sentences. The (b) sentences suggest a syntactic representation for the (a) sentences. Which arguments could be advanced against the representations?

1a I have eaten.
1b I have [$_{VP}$ eaten PRO].
2a This analysis led to a remarkable conclusion.
2b This analysis [led PRO [$_{PP}$ to a remarkable conclusion]]
3   *Italian*
    a Ho visto Luigi.
    b [$_{IP}$ PRO ho [$_{VP}$ visto Luigi]]. (Cf. chapter 8 for discussion of such Italian examples.)
4a Take three eggs and boil for two minutes.[14]
4b Take three eggs and [$_{VP}$ boil PRO for two minutes]].
5a They met after a party.
5b They met PRO after a party.
6a This book is too difficult for me to read.
6b This book is too difficult [$_{CP}$ for [$_{IP}$ me to read PRO]].
7a He is a man whom you like when you see.
7b He is a man [$_{CP}$ whom [$_{IP}$ you like PRO] [$_{CP}$ when [$_{IP}$ you see PRO]]]. (See chapter 8 for discussion.)
8a John is ill. I know.
8b John is ill. [$_{IP}$ I [$_{VP}$ know PRO]].
9a John opened the door and left.
9b John opened the door and [$_{IP}$ PRO left].
10 *Italian*
10a Questo conduce la gente a concludere che . . .
    This   leads   people   to conclude   that . . .
10b Questo conduce PRO   a concludere che . . .[15]

---

[14] The examples in (4) are from the register of instructional writing. See Haegeman (1987) and Massam and Roberge (1989) for discussion.
[15] For a discussion of examples such as (10) see Rizzi (1986) and chapter 12 of this book.

Exercise 5

So far we have illustrated cases of PRO being controlled by one antecedent NP. Identify the controller of PRO in the following examples.

1   Mary told John that it would be nice [PRO to go to the pictures together].
2   Mary told John that [PRO going to the pictures on their own] was out of the question.
3   Bill wanted Tom to approve the decision [PRO to swim across the pond together].
4   Bill wanted Tom to agree that it was time [PRO to swim across the pond together].
5   Bill's mother wanted Tom to agree that it was time [PRO to swim across the pond together].
     ((3), (4) and (5) from Chomsky, 1986a: 126 (147))

As suggested by the presence of *together* and *on their own*, PRO in the examples above must have a plural controller. The plurality is obtained by combining two NPs. The examples illustrate what are known as **split antecedents**. Do the split antecedents in these examples c-command PRO?

   Williams (1980) argues that split antecedents are only possible in the case of optional control. Using examples of your own, check whether this hypothesis can be maintained. You may base your examples on section 4.1.

6 Transformations: NP-Movement

Contents

Introduction and Overview

In this chapter we discuss the properties of NP-movement, which plays a part in the derivation of passive sentences and raising structures. We examine the characteristics of NP-movement and of the verbs that induce it. From our analysis it follows that each sentence is associated with two levels of syntactic representation: D-structure and S-structure. The relation between these levels will be discussed in this chapter.

In section 1 we give a general survey of movement transformations. In section 2 we concentrate on NP-movement as instantiated in passive sentences and in raising sentences. We shall discuss the arguments in favour of the assumption that a moved NP leaves a trace in its base-position. We shall also discuss raising adjectives. Section 3 focuses on the verbs which induce NP-raising. It will be argued that the case assigning properties of a verb depend on its argument structure. We discuss the distinction between two types of one-argument verbs: those with only an external argument ('intransitives') and those with only an internal argument ('unaccusatives'). In section 4 we examine the relation beween D-structure and S-structure and we discuss how the principles of grammar posited so far apply to these levels. In section 5 we shall briefly consider an analysis which proposes that subject NPs are base-generated in the specifier position of VP.

1 Movement Transformations

We have already touched upon the movement of constituents in interrogative and in passive sentences (cf. chapters 2 and 3). In this section we give a general survey of the movement transformations posited so far.

1.1 Passivization: Recapitulation

In chapter 3 we discussed the properties of passivization illustrated in (1a):

1a This story is believed by the villagers.
1b The villagers believe this story.

(1a) contains the passive form of the verb *believe*. Comparing (1a) with its active counterpart (1b), we see that the subject NP of the passive sentence, *this story*, corresponds to the internal argument of the active verb. In chapter 3 we proposed that in both (1a) and (1b) the NP *this story* is assigned the internal theta role by the verb. Internal theta roles are by definition assigned directly under government by the head. Hence, the NP *this story* in (1a) ought to be assigned its theta role under government by the verb *believe*, exactly as in (1b). As it stands, *believe* obviously does not govern the NP *this story* in (1a).

In order to maintain the parallelism between (1a) and (1b) and our hypothesis that internal theta roles are assigned directly by a governing head we developed a movement analysis relating the patterns in (1a) and (1b). We proposed that at some level of syntactic representation the NP *this story* IS the direct object of the verb *believe*:

2a [$_{IP}$ e [$_{I'}$ is [$_{VP}$ [$_{V'}$ believed [this story]]] by the villagers]]].

(2a) is called the **D-structure** of (1a). It encodes the basic thematic relations in the sentence as determined by the argument structure of the predicate, passive *believed*. In (1a) the external theta role of *believed* is not assigned to an NP in the subject position, but it is assigned to an NP in a *by*-phrase. Because of the extended projection principle the subject position in (2a) is generated but is not filled by an argument NP. The empty subject position is indicated by the symbol *e* for 'empty'. In the D-structure (2a) the object NP *this story* is VP-internal and is assigned an internal theta role directly by the governing verb.

In addition to the D-structure representation which reflects lexical properties, a sentence is associated with a second level of representation, **S-structure**, which is closer to the surface manifestation of the sentence, its **surface form**. At this point, we shall equate the surface form of the sentence with S-structure for expository reasons. In chapters 9 and 12 we shall see that S-structure is not necessarily identical with the surface form of a sentence. The S-structure of (1a) is (2b):

2b [$_{IP}$ This story$_i$ [$_{I'}$ is [$_{VP}$ believed [e$_i$]]] by the villagers]]

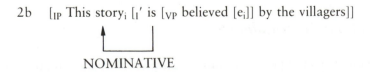

NOMINATIVE

In (2b) the NP *this story* has been moved from the VP-internal position to the subject position of the sentence. This movement is called **NP-movement**. As a result of movement, the VP-internal D-structure position of *this story* is left vacant or empty: it is a **gap** represented provisionally by *e*. We turn to a discussion of such empty positions in section 2. The link between the gap and the moved NP is indicated by co-indexation. The co-indexation allows us to 'reconstruct' the D-structure of the sentence.

The word-order of (2a) is referred to as the **underlying order**. The S-structure order in (2b) is called the **derived order**: it is an order which results from modifications of the D-structure. Similarly, the NP *this story* in (2b/1a) is referred to as a **derived subject**: it is not a D-structure subject of the sentence (2a). The D-structure position of the NP, i.e. the object position, is called the **base-position**. We say that the NP *this story* is **base-generated** in the object position of the passive V *believed*.

In our discussion in chapter 3 we related the movement of the NP from the object position to the subject position to case theory. For some reason (to which we return in section 3) passive verbs do not assign structural case to their complements. If the NP *this story* were to stay in the object position, it would violate the case filter, as seen in (2c):

2c *There is believed this story by the villagers.

In (2b), *this story* occupies the subject position, where it is assigned NOM-INATIVE case by INFL. Our analysis implies that the case filter must apply at S-structure (2b). At the level of D-structure (2a) the NP *this story* is in its base-position where it cannot be assigned case.

When discussing the syntactic structure of a sentence we shall from now on assume that there are two **levels of syntactic representation**: the D-structure and the S-structure. Both levels of representation encode syntactic properties of the sentence. The D-structure encodes the predicate-argument relations and the thematic properties of the sentence. The S-structure representation accounts for the surface ordering of the constituents. We return to the relation between the two levels in section 4.

1.2 Questions

1.2.1 SURVEY

In this section we briefly discuss the representation of the sentences in (3), concentrating on the questions (3b)–(3f).

3a Lord Emsworth will invite Hercule Poirot.

3b Will Lord Emsworth invite Hercule Poirot?
3c Lord Emsworth will invite whom?
3d Whom will Lord Emsworth invite?
3e I wonder [whether Lord Emsworth will invite Hercule Poirot].
3f I wonder [whom Lord Emsworth will invite].

(3a) is a declarative sentence. (3b) is a direct *yes–no* **question** (to be discussed in 1.2.2), (3c) is an **echo question** (to be discussed in 1.2.3), (3d) is a direct *wh*-**question** also referred to as a **constituent question** (to be discussed in 1.2.4). For completeness' sake (3e) and (3f) have been added. The bracketed strings in these examples are **indirect questions**: (3e) contains an indirect *yes–no* question; (3f) an indirect *wh*-question. Indirect questions will be discussed in chapter 7, where we return to a full discussion of questions.

From (3a) we infer the argument structure of the verb *invite*:

4   *invite*:   verb

1	2

In (3a) the external argument of *invite* is realized by the NP *Lord Emsworth* and the internal argument is realized by the NP *Hercule Poirot*. The D-structure of (3a) is given in tree diagram format in (5). The external argument of *invite* is syntactically represented by the NP in the subject position of the clause; the internal argument is syntactically represented by the direct object of the V, the NP dominated by V'.

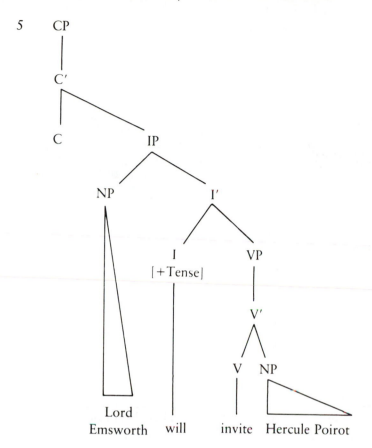

5

The S-structure representation of example (3a) is given in (6). It does not differ substantially from its D-structure (5). Recall that S-structure is the level at which structural case is assigned: I assigns NOMINATIVE to the subject NP and the verb assigns ACCUSATIVE to the direct object NP.

6   CP

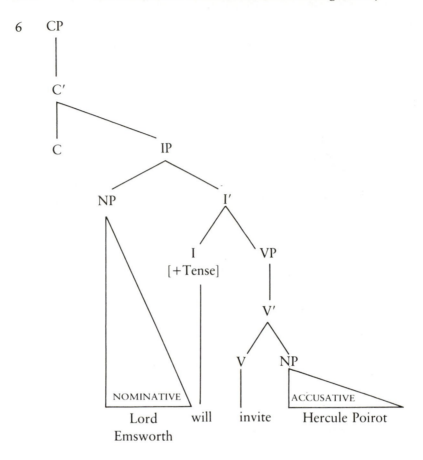

NOMINATIVE

ACCUSATIVE

Lord   will   invite   Hercule Poirot
Emsworth

A word of caution is in order at this point. We assume that ALL sentences have two levels of syntactic representation: D-structure and S-structure. In the case of passive sentences such as (1a) discussed above, the D-structure (2a) differs clearly from the S-structure (2b): a constituent has been moved. But, as indicated in (5), and (6) the difference between D-structure and S-structure may be minimal: in this example no movement has taken place and the two levels of representation will not differ in word-order.

1.2.2 *YES–NO* QUESTIONS

Questions such as (3b) are called *yes–no* questions for the obvious reason that one expects an answer such as *Yes* or *No*. Let us try to work out the syntactic representation of this question, bearing in mind that we need to consider both D-structure and S-structure.

In chapter 2 we saw that sentences are projections of I which in their turn are complements of C. Because they are always specified for tense we assume that modal auxiliaries like *will* are base-generated in the position dominated by I, as illustrated in (5) and (6) above. One potential problem for the representation of (3b) concerns the surface position of the modal auxiliary *will*, which in our example precedes the subject NP. We assume that the order exhibited in (3b) is not the underlying order of the sentence but a derived order, an order obtained as the result of moving an element. The D-structure position of *will* in (3b) will be as in (7). *Will* is dominated by I, the position which it also occupies in (5):

7

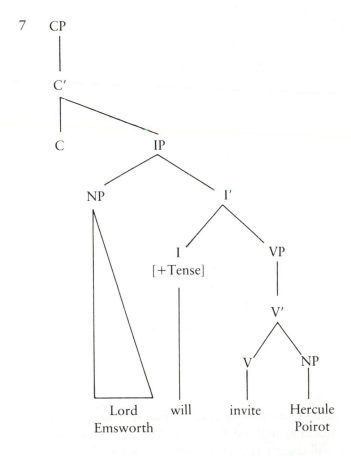

In our discussion in chapter 2 we proposed that the inverted order auxiliary-subject (cf. (3b)) arises from the fact that the modal auxiliary has been moved out of the base-position, where it is dominated by I, to the vacant position dominated by C. Under this analysis, the S-structure of (3b) is as in (8).

8   CP

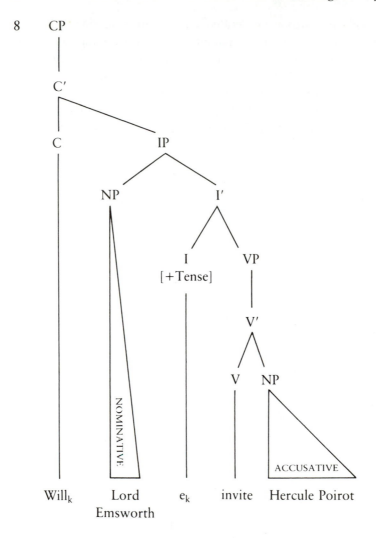

In (8) the gap resulting from moving *will*$_k$ is indicated by e_k. The link between the position vacated by *will* and the moved element is again indicated by co-indexation. We shall discuss verb movement in chapter 11.

1.2.3   ECHO QUESTIONS

(3c) is an echo question. It will be used as a reaction to a sentence such as (3a) by a speaker who wishes the interlocutor to repeat (part of) (3a). Echo questions are formed by simply substituting a **question word** (here *whom*) for a constituent. Interrogative constituents such as *whom* are called ***wh-***

constituents. *Whom* realizes the internal argument of *invite*. The D-structure of (3c) is as follows:

9 [$_{CP}$ [$_{IP}$ Lord Emsworth will [$_{VP}$ invite [$_{NP}$ whom]]]]?

Given that there is no reordering of constituents in echo questions the S-structure of (3c) will be like its D-structure:

10 [$_{CP}$ [$_{IP}$ Lord Emsworth will [$_{VP}$ invite [$_{NP}$ whom]]]]?

1.2.4 *WH*-QUESTIONS

Finally we turn to (3d), a *wh*-question. Unlike echo questions, which are used in the rather specific circumstances discussed above, ordinary *wh*-questions are freely used when a speaker needs some information. The *wh*-constituent *whom* questions one constituent. To (3d) one might expect answers such as 'Hercule Poirot', 'Lord Peter Wimsey', 'Bertie Wooster', 'his mother-in-law', etc. Let us again try to provide the D-structure and the S-structure representations of (3d).

The first question that we need to address here is how the arguments of *invite* are realized. As was the case in the preceding examples, the external argument is realized by the NP *Lord Emsworth*. By analogy with (3c) we would like to say that the internal argument of *invite* is the NP *whom*.

Two problems arise with respect to the internal argument NP. If internal theta roles are assigned directly under government, then, like (1a), (3d) raises the question of how *invite* assigns a theta role to *whom*, which it plainly does not govern. A second and related question concerns the form of *whom*. It is an ACCUSATIVE case. In chapter 3 we argued that ACCUSATIVE case is assigned at S-structure by a governing verb.

The D-structure of (3d) is no different from the D-structure of the echo question (3c) discussed in 1.2.3:

11 [$_{CP}$ [$_{IP}$ Lord Emsworth will [$_{VP}$ invite [$_{NP}$ whom]]]]?

At S-structure we assume that, as is the case in (3b), the modal *will* in (3d) is moved to the position dominated by C. As discussed in chapter 2, we further assume that *whom* is moved to the specifier position immediately dominated by CP, [Spec,CP]. The symbol e_i indicates the position vacated by *whom*$_i$. Co-indexation establishes the link between *e* and the moved constituent. Movement of question words is referred to as **wh-movement**.

12

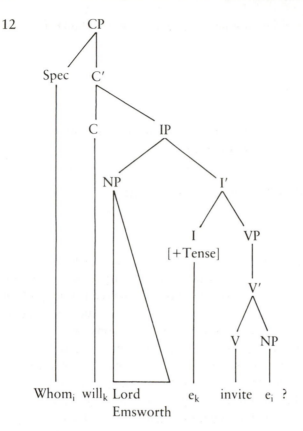

The problems raised concerning the theta-marking and case-marking of *whom* can now be solved. We will assume that the verb *invite* assigns its internal theta role to the VP-internal position e_i and that it also assigns ACCUSATIVE to this position. In chapter 7 we return in detail to the properties of *wh*-movement.

1.3 *Syntactic Representations*

Throughout the discussion in this chapter we have been assuming that sentences have two levels of syntactic representation:

(i) **D-structure**

This level encodes the lexical properties of the constituents of the sentence. It represents the basic argument relations in the sentence. External arguments are base-generated in the subject position relative to their predicate;[1] internal arguments are governed by the predicate in their base–position.

(ii) **S-structure**
This level reflects the more superficial properties of the sentence: the actual ordering of the elements in the surface string, and their case forms.

The two levels of syntactic representation are related to each other by means of movement transformations: elements which originate in some position at D-structure are moved elswhere at S-structure. Schematically our grammar thus looks as follows:

13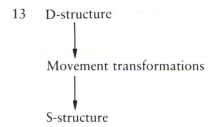
D-structure

Movement transformations

S-structure

In section 4 we shall consider the relation between D-structure and S-structure in more detail.

In the discussion above, we have distinguished three types of movement: (i) the movement of auxiliaries from I to C; (ii) *wh*-movement: the movement of *wh*-constituents to the specifier of CP (or [Spec,CP]); and (iii) NP-movement: the movement associated with passive in which an NP is moved to an empty subject position.[2] In this chapter we discuss NP-movement in more detail. In chapter 7 we turn to *wh*-movement, the discussion of movement from I to C is postponed till chapter 11.

Even at this preliminary stage of the discussion the reader can see that the three types of movements have a lot in common. In each of the movements you take an element and move it somewhere else. In the literature this operation is often referred to in general terms as '**move-α**', **move alpha,** that is 'move

---

[1] See section 5 for an alternative analysis of the NP in the canonical subject position, though.
[2] For different proposals concerning the levels of representation see for instance van Riemsdijk and Williams (1981), who posit a level between D-structure and S-structure, Zubizarreta (1987), who introduces a level of lexical structure and Koster (1987), who argues that only one level of representation is needed.

something'. The types of movements discussed can be differentiated on the basis of the **target** of movement, the element that is moved, and on the basis of the **landing site**, the position to which an element moves. Two targets are distinguished. Either we move a head of a projection to another head position: in (3b) and in (3d) *will*, the head of IP, moves to C, the head of CP. This is called **head-to-head-movement**. Alternatively, a maximal projection is moved, as illustrated by NP-movement in (1a), and by *wh*-movement in (3d). Chomsky (1986b) argues that in fact movement must be restricted to just these types: either we move a head or we move a full phrase. We return to a discussion of landing sites in chapters 7 and 8.

2   NP-movement

In this section we consider the mechanisms of NP-movement, concentrating mainly on the position vacated by movement: the trace (2.2). We shall see that NP-movement is found not only with passive verbs but also with so-called raising verbs (2.1) and raising adjectives (2.3).

2.1   *Introduction: Passive and Raising*

As a starting point let us consider the syntactic representations of passive sentences:

14a   This story was believed by the villagers.
14b   Poirot was believed to have destroyed the evidence.

We have already discussed (14a). The D-structure of (14a) is given in (15a) and the S-structure in (15b):

15a   [$_{IP}$ e [$_{I'}$ was [$_{VP}$ believed [$_{NP}$ this story] by the villagers]]].
15b   [$_{IP}$ [$_{NP}$ This story$_i$] [$_{I'}$ was [$_{VP}$ believed e$_i$] by the villagers]]].

In (15a) the NP *this story* is theta-marked directly by the verb *believed*. The subject position is empty since passive verbs do not assign an external theta role. In (15b) *this story* is moved to the subject position and case-marked by the finite inflection.

Let us consider (14b) which also contains passive *believed*. (14b) can be paraphrased by means of (16):

16   It was believed [$_{CP}$ that [Poirot had destroyed the evidence]].

In (16) the subject position of the main clause is occupied by an expletive, *it*, which is not assigned a theta role. Passive *believed* takes a sentential complement (the bracketed CP) as its internal argument.

Inside the subordinate clause, the verb *destroy* assigns an internal theta role to the NP *the evidence* and the NP *Poirot* is the external argument which is assigned the AGENT role: 'Poirot is the person who is engaged in the activity of destroying.' Note specifically that the verb in the main clause, *believed*, has no thematic relation with *Poirot*, the subject of the subordinate clause.

The thematic relations in (14b) are identical to those in (16). *Believed* takes as its internal argument a clausal complement, here infinitival. *Poirot*, the surface subject of the main clause, has a thematic relation (AGENT) with the predicate *destroy* in the lower infinitival clause. Again, *Poirot* has no thematic relationship with *believed*. We conclude that in (14b) *Poirot* is a derived subject which is assigned the external theta role of the lower verb *destroy*. On this assumption, the D-structure of (14b) will be (17a), where *Poirot* is base-generated as the subject NP of the infinitival clause:

17a   [$_{IP}$ e [$_{I'}$ was [$_{VP}$ believed [$_{IP}$ Poirot to have destroyed the evidence]]]].

Believed directly theta-marks the lower IP. *Poirot* is the external argument of *destroy*, the predicate of the lower infinitival clause. *Believed*, being passive, fails to assign structural case. If the NP *Poirot* were left in the subject position of the lower clause at S-structure it would not be case-marked. This explains the ungrammaticality of (17b):

17b   *It was believed Poirot to have destroyed the evidence.

A way of enabling the NP *Poirot* to pass the case filter is by moving it from the subject position of the lower clause to the subject position of the higher clause, leaving a co-indexed gap:

17c   [$_{IP}$ Poirot$_i$ [$_{I'}$ was [$_{VP}$ believed [$_{IP}$ e$_i$ to have destroyed the evidence]]]].

Consider now (18). The relation between (18a) and (18b) is exactly parallel to the relation between (16) and (14b).

18a   It seems [that [Poirot has destroyed the evidence]].
18b   Poirot seems to have destroyed the evidence.

(18a) shows that *seem* is like passive *believe*: it is a one-place predicate which takes a clausal complement. The subject position is not assigned a theta role and it is filled by the expletive *it*. We infer from (18a) that the thematic structure of *seem* is (18c):[3]

18c   *seem*:   V

1

Inside the complement clause, the NP *Poirot* in (18a) is the external argument of *destroy*.

The thematic relations in (18b) are identical to those in (18a). Again *seem* has the argument structure in (18c). The NP *Poirot* is the external argument of *destroy*. At D-structure *Poirot* is the subject of *destroy*, and the subject position of *seem*, which receives no theta role, is empty. (19a) is parallel to (17a) the underlying structure of (14b).

19a   [$_{IP}$ e seems [$_{IP}$ Poirot to have destroyed the evidence]].

Apart from its argument structure, *seem* shares another property with passive *believe*: it cannot assign structural case:

19b   *It/*there seems Poirot to have destroyed the evidence.

---

[3] To indicate that 1 is an internal argument it is not underlined. Recall that we adopted the convention that the external argument is underlined.

(19b) is ungrammatical for the same reason that (17b) is ungrammatical: the external argument of the verb *destroy* is caseless. In order to be able to be theta-marked by *destroy* the NP must be visible, and in order to be visible *Poirot* needs to be case-marked. Movement to the subject position of the main clause brings rescue. (19c) is the S-structure representation of (18b): *Poirot* is a derived subject. (19c) is again parallel to (17c).

19c [$_{IP}$ Poirot$_i$ [$_{I'}$ -s [$_{VP}$ seem [$_{IP}$ e$_i$ to have destroyed the evidence]]]].

(19c) is another example of NP-movement. Because the subject of the lower clause is raised out of the clause and moved into a higher clause, this movement is sometimes referred to as **NP-raising** or **raising**. Verbs such as *seem* which induce raising are called **raising verbs**.[4]

2.2 *Traces*

We have now discussed three examples of NP-movement. The relevant S-structures are given in (20):

20a [$_{IP}$ This story$_i$ [$_{I'}$ was [$_{VP}$ believed [e$_i$] by the villagers]]].
20b [$_{IP}$ Poirot$_i$ [$_{I'}$ was [$_{VP}$ believed [$_{IP}$ [e$_i$] to have destroyed the evidence]]]].
20c [$_{IP}$ Poirot$_i$ [$_{I'}$ -s [$_{VP}$ seem [$_{IP}$ [e$_i$] to have destroyed the evidence]]]].

In each of these examples we assume that there is a null element in the position vacated by the NP. Co-indexation is used to indicate that the null element and the NP in the matrix subject position are linked. In chapter 3 we introduced the term chain to refer to this link and we shall return to this terminology below. An empty category which encodes the base-position of a moved constituent is referred to as a **trace** and will be indicated from now on by *t*:

21a [$_{IP}$ This story$_i$ [$_{I'}$ was [$_{VP}$ believed t$_i$ by everyone]]].
21b [$_{IP}$ Poirot$_i$ [$_{I'}$ was [$_{VP}$ believed [$_{IP}$ t$_i$ to have destroyed the evidence]]]].
21c [$_{IP}$ Poirot$_i$ [$_{I'}$ -s [$_{VP}$ seem [$_{IP}$ t$_i$ to have destroyed the evidence]]]].

---

[4] For an early discussion of raising, see Postal (1974).

The moved element is called the **antecedent** of the trace. In the remainder of this section we go through the arguments for positing traces in syntactic representations.[5]

2.2.1   THETA THEORY

A first argument for traces of NP-movement was advanced in chapter 3 and is used in the discussion above. It is based on the discussion of the projection principle and theta theory on the one hand, and of case theory on the other hand.

In chapter 3 we introduced the idea that the case filter is not an independent principle of the grammar but that it derives from the visibility requirement for NPs: in order to be assigned a theta role an NP must be visible. Visibility of overt NPs is achieved via case-marking. Remember that internal theta roles are directly assigned to arguments by the governing head. An external theta role is assigned indirectly to the subject of clause containing the predicate.

In each of the S-structures in (21) the moved NP is visible: it is assigned NOMINATIVE. But the position to which the theta role is assigned is not the derived position but the base-position. In other words, for theta role assignment both the D-structure position and the S-structure position of the NPs in (21) are relevant. The D-structure position is indicated by the trace, it is the position to which the theta role is assigned. The S-structure position is case-marked.

This analysis allows us to maintain theta theory and the visibility principle as discussed in chapter 3. In chapter 3 (section 5.2 (61)) we cited Chomsky's reformulation of the theta criterion as in (22):

22 Theta criterion

22a   Each argument A appears in a chain containing a unique visible theta position P, and each theta position P is visible in a chain containing a unique argument A (Chomsky, 1986a: 97).

22b   A position P is visible in a chain if the chain contains a case-marked position (Chomsky, 1986a: 96).

The reader will be able to verify that the conditions for theta role assignment are fulfilled in the S-structures in (21). Consider, for example, (21b). The argument *Poirot* appears in a chain $<Poirot_i, t_i>$. The position occupied by

---

[5]   The reader will no doubt observe that the argumentation used in 2.2 is similar to that used to justify the presence of PRO in chapter 5, section 1. However, note that PRO does not result from movement. We return to a comparison of PRO and trace in chapter 8.

Poirot is called the **head** of the chain; that occupied by the trace is called the **foot** of the chain. The subject position of the non-finite clause, to which the external theta role of the lower verb is assigned, is a theta position. It is visible in the chain <*Poirot*$_i$, t$_i$> because the chain contains a case-marked position: the subject position of the main clause is assigned NOMINATIVE by the finite I. The reader can check that the same conditions obtain in (21a) and in (21c).

2.2.2 THE EXTENDED PROJECTION PRINCIPLE

In chapters 1 and 2 we discussed general principles of phrase structure and we introduced the requirement that sentences must have subjects (the EPP). The EPP requires that the non-finite IPs in (21b) and (21c) have a subject position. In the S-structures in (21b) and (21c) the subject position of the lower clause is occupied by the trace, an empty category (see also section 4.3 below).

2.2.3 LOCAL PROCESSES

In the following examples we find further arguments for positing a trace in the subject position of non-finite clauses such as (21b) and (21c).

23a [$_{IP}$ It seems [$_{CP}$ that [$_{IP}$ Poirot has been the best detective/*detectives]]].
23b *[$_{IP}$ Poirot thinks [$_{CP}$ that [$_{IP}$ these schoolchildren are a lousy detective]]].
23c [$_{IP}$ Poirot seems to have been the best detective].
23d [$_{IP}$ These schoolchildren seem to have been the best detectives].

24a It seems [that [the schoolchildren have left together]].
24b *The schoolchildren thought [that [Holmes had left together]].
24c The schoolchildren seem to have left together.
24d *Poirot seems to have left together.

25a It seems [that [Poirot has done the job his/*her/*my own way]].
25b *I thought [that [Poirot would do the job my own way]].
25c Poirot seems to have done the job his own way.
25d *Poirot seems to have done the job her own way.

26a It seems [that [Poirot has hurt himself/*herself]].
26b *I thought [that [Poirot had hurt myself]].
26c Poirot seems to have hurt himself.
26d *Poirot seems to have hurt herself.

In (23a) the predicate NP *the best detective* must be singular rather than plural. It agrees in number with the subject *Poirot*. (23b) suggests that agreement is clause-bound: *a lousy detective* cannot agree, for instance, with the subject of a higher clause. Without going into the details of agreement rules, let us assume that there is a **clause-mate condition on agreement**.

If we now turn to (23c) and (23d) it appears that the predicate of the infinitival clause agrees in number with the subject of the higher clause. Clearly, one might wish to modify the rule of agreement to allow for this possibility. But on the assumption that there are empty categories we do not need to change our agreement rule at all:

27    $[_{IP}$ Poirot$_i$ $[_{I'}$ -s $[_{VP}$ seem $[_{IP}$ t$_i$ to be the best detective]]]].

We assume that the NP *the best detective* agrees with the subject of the lower clause, t$_i$. This means that the trace carries the relevant properties of the antecedent NP, that is, for our example, number. In other words, so-called 'empty' categories are not devoid of properties: they are specified for syntactic features. The term 'empty' refers to the fact that these categories are not associated with phonetic material.

The discussion of the examples in (24)–(26) follows the same lines as that of (23). In (24) the adjunct *together* in the lower clause has to be linked to a clause-mate plural NP (cf. the ungrammaticality of (24b)).[6] For (24c), we assume that the moved NP *the schoolchildren* is related to *together* via its trace in the lower clause:

28    $[_{IP}$ The schoolchildren$_i$ $[_{I'}$ I $[_{VP}$ seem $[_{IP}$ t$_i$ to have left together]]]].

(25) suggests that there is a clause-mate constraint on the interpretation of the phrase *his/her . . . own way*. The possessive pronoun in this phrase is like an anaphor in that it is referentially dependent on an antecedent NP in the same clause with which it agrees in person, number and gender (cf. (25a,b)). By positing a trace in the position vacated by the NP *Poirot* we can relate the phrase *his own way* to a clause-mate.

29   Poirot$_i$ seems $[_{IP}$ t$_i$ to have done the job his$_i$ own way].

---

[6] Cf. the discussion of PRO in chapter 5, section 1.

(29) also shows that traces are fully specified for all the nominal features such as person, number and gender.

The examples in (26) should look familiar to the reader. (26b) illustrates a binding theory violation: the reflexive *myself* in the lower clause is not bound in its GC. If we maintain that *seem* takes a clausal complement whose subject position is occupied by a trace in (26c) then we can maintain the binding theory as formulated in chapter 4.

30   Poirot$_i$ seems [$_{IP}$ t$_i$ to have hurt himself$_i$].

In all the examples above the reasoning is identical. We establish that some rule or principle of grammar (binding, agreement, etc.) is best described in terms of a locality condition. In order to maintain the rule or principle in its simplest form we use the trace of a moved element as the relevant local element in the application of the rule or principle.

2.3   Some Properties of NP-movement

In this section we sum up our discussion of NP-movement so far. In section 2.3.1 we give a catalogue of properties which we have already come across, in section 2.3.2 we examine the configurational relation between the antecedent and the vacated position.

2.3.1   PROPERTIES OF A-CHAINS

(31) provides the typical examples of NP-movement which were the basis for our discussion.

31a   [$_{IP}$ This story$_i$ [$_{I'}$ was [$_{VP}$ believed t$_i$ by the villagers]]].
31b   [$_{IP}$ Poirot$_i$ [$_{I'}$ -s [$_{VP}$ seem [$_{IP}$ t$_i$ to have destroyed the evidence]]]].

As suggested above, a distinction is sometimes made between examples such as (31a), which are instances of **passivization**, and examples such as (31b), which are referred to as **NP-raising**.[7] Passivization moves an object NP to the subject position of the same clause; in raising patterns a subject NP is raised

---

[7] The term subject-to-subject raising is also used (cf. Postal, 1974).

from a lower clause to a higher clause. The terms raising and passivization are useful descriptive labels but the reader should not have the impression that passivization and raising are mutually exclusive. In (32a), discussed in section 2.1 as (14b), passive *believed* is a raising verb: the subject NP *Poirot* is moved from the lower infinitival clause to a higher clause. (32b) combines passivization in the lower infinitival IP and raising. This example will be discussed below (see (35b)).

32a $[_{IP}$ Poirot$_i$ $[_{I'}$ was $[_{VP}$ believed $[_{IP}$ t$_i$ to have destroyed the evidence]]]].
32b $[_{IP}$ This story $[_{I'}$-s $[_{VP}$ seem $[_{IP}$ t$_i$ to be believed t$_i$ by everyone]]]].

Let us make a provisional inventory of the common properties of all the examples of NP-movement illustrated here.

a   The moved element is an NP.
b   Movement is obligatory.
c   The landing site of movement is an empty position.
d   The landing site is an A-position.
e   The landing site is an NP-position.
f   The landing site of movement is a position to which no theta role is assigned. Let us call this a **theta-bar position** by analogy with an A-bar position.
g   The landing site of the movement is a position to which case is assigned. In our examples the landing site is the subject position of a finite sentence.
h   The site from which the element is moved is an NP-position to which no case is assigned.
i   Movement leaves a **trace**.
j   The trace is co-indexed with the moved element, the **antecedent**, with which it forms a chain. Because the head of the chain is an A-position, the chain created by NP-movement is called an **A-chain**.
k   The chain is assigned one theta role.
l   The theta role is assigned to the lowest position of the chain: the foot of the chain.
m   The chain is case-marked once.
n   Case is assigned to the highest position of the chain: the **head** of the chain.

The characteristics of A-chains listed above are not all independent. Let us consider some of them here.

That the NP moves obligatorily (a + b) in the examples discussed is due to the fact that it would otherwise be caseless and violate the case filter. Hence, we do not need to state that NP-movement is obligatory in the passive and raising sentences above.

Both statements (a) and (b) need some qualification. Consider (33):

33a Everyone believed [$_{CP}$ that Poirot would give up].
33b It was believed by everyone [$_{CP}$ that Poirot would give up].
33c [$_{CP}$ That Poirot would give up] was believed by everyone.

In (33a) active *believed* takes a clausal complement. In (33b) the verb is passivized; the complement has not moved. In (33c) the clausal complement is moved.[8] In this example movement affects CP rather than NP. We see that it is not obligatory: CPs, unlike NPs, are not subject to the case filter, hence CP may remain in its base-position in (33b).

Movement is to an empty position (c). Intuitively this is reasonable. Suppose an NP were to move into a position already occupied by another NP. Clearly this would result in some sort of a clash. The principles we have established so far enable us to account for this property.

Let us assume that there were a putative verb *HIT* which takes an external and an internal argument but which, unlike English *hit*, does not assign ACCUSATIVE case. We will project a D-structure like (34a):

34a [$_{IP}$ John [$_{VP}$ HIT Mary]].

In (34a) *Mary* is assigned the internal theta role of *HIT* and *John* is assigned the external theta role. The NP *Mary* will be caseless if left in place at S-structure. Suppose it were to move into the position occupied by *John*:

34b [$_{IP}$ Mary$_i$ [$_{VP}$ HIT t$_i$]].

Mary is assigned NOMINATIVE case and forms a chain with its trace. At S-structure *HIT* will assign its internal theta role to the visible chain <Mary$_i$, t$_i$>.

What about the external theta role? If *HIT* were to assign it to *Mary$_i$* then the chain <Mary$_i$, t$_i$> would have two theta roles in violation of the theta criterion (22). If *HIT* failed to assign its external theta role then again the theta criterion is violated since one theta role is now unassigned. We conclude that it

---

[8] We assume here that CP is moved to [NP,IP]. Koster (1978b) argues against this hypothesis.

is not possible for an NP to move into a position already occupied by another NP. This means that there can be no verb like *HIT*, which assigns both an external and an internal theta role and fails to assign case to its complement. We return to types of verbs in section 3 below.

The reader can work out for himself that movement of an NP will also have to be to a theta-bar position (cf. property (f)).

Do NPs always move to positions in which case is assigned? (see property (g)). Yes and no. Consider:

35a It seems [that [this story is believed by everyone]].
35b This story seems to be believed by everyone.

(35a) is straightforward: *seem* takes an internal clausal argument and lacks an external argument. *Believed* in the lower clause is passivized and assigns its internal theta role to the NP *this story*. We invite the reader to provide the D-structure and S-structure representations for (35a).

(35b) is a paraphrase of (35a). *This story* is the internal argument of *believed*. The subject position of *believed* is unoccupied at D-structure, though it must be present in view of the EPP. *Seem* also lacks an external theta role (cf. (35a)): the subject position of the higher clause is generated empty at D-structure:

36   [IPe [I'-s[VPseem [IPe to be believed this story . . .]]]]

In its VP-internal base-position, *this story* cannot be assigned case. Hence it will move. The subject position of the lower IP cannot serve as the ultimate landing site for the movement since this is also a caseless position: we have proposed that *seem* does not assign ACCUSATIVE case.

We might propose that the NP *this story* moves in one fell swoop to the subject position of the higher clause. This would mean that it can cross an IP. We shall see in section 4.5.2 that this is not possible for independent reasons. Consider (37a) with the S-structure (37b):

37a *John seems that it is believed by everyone.
37b *John$_i$ [I' -s [VP seem [CP that [IP it is believed t$_i$ by everyone]]]].

In (37b) the idea is that the lower subject position is filled by an expletive, and that the NP *John*, the internal argument of *believed*, is moved directly to the subject position of the higher clause where it receives NOMINATIVE case. The ungrammaticality of (37a) suggests that NPs cannot escape from their own clause and move to the subject position of a higher clause. Movement of an NP must be 'local' in a way yet to be made precise. Let us adopt this descriptive statement without further motivation for the moment and assume that the NP *this story* in (35b) moves first to the subject position of *be believed* and then to the subject position of the higher clause. There are two stages or **cycles** for the movement transformation. The first cycle for the operation of move-alpha (cf. section 1.3 for the term) is the lowest clause. The second cycle includes the next higher clause, and so on. We assume that each of these movements leaves a trace in the vacated site and that all traces are co-indexed with the antecedent, and thus with each other:

38   This story$_i$ seems [$_{IP}$ t$_i'$ to be believed t$_i$ by everyone].

STEP II
Higher cycle

STEP I
Lowest cycle

We shall say that movement of *this story* is **cyclic**: it goes step by step creating **intermediate traces** until we arrive at the final landing site. We indicate the intermediate trace with a prime notation. The chain created by NP movement in (38) has three members: <*this story*$_i$, t$'_i$, t$_i$>. The head of the chain is *this story*$_i$, the foot is the trace t$_i$.

Returning to our question concerning the landing site of NP-movement, we conclude that NP-movement ultimately moves the NP into a position which is case-marked: the head of the chain is case-marked (properties (m) and (n)). Indeed, this is only natural since we saw that the NP must move precisely to become case-marked (properties (a) and (b)).

The discussion of the properties of movement developed in this section is important from the point of view of language acquisition. We have proposed that a speaker of the language has some internal grammar. If our grammar is a representation of this internal knowledge then the properties of NP-movement which we have postulated must be 'known' to the native speaker. From the discussion it follows that the properties listed above do not have to be learnt one by one. They are descriptive statements which can be deduced from more general principles of the grammar. If a child has the general principles (theta theory, case theory, the projection principle, X-bar theory, etc.) at his disposal, the individual descriptive statements listed above follow. As an exercise we invite the reader to try to derive the remaining properties listed above on the basis of the theory established so far.

A word of caution is in order: in this section we deal with NP-movement exclusively. We shall see in chapter 7 and in chapter 11 that other types of movement have properties distinct from those listed above.

2.3.2   C-COMMAND

In section 2.3.1 we have looked at several examples of NP-movement for which we have identified a set of common properties. We have discussed examples in which NPs move from a VP-internal position to the subject position of a sentence, or instances where an NP is moved from a subject position of a lower clause to the subject position of a higher clause. Schematically NP-movement operates as in (39):

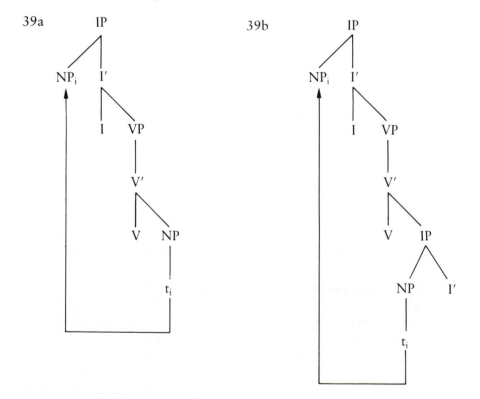

NPs are moved upwards. If we examine the configurational relationships between the antecedent and the trace in these representations we see that the antecedent **c-commands** the trace. We return to this property of movement in section 4.5.1.

2.4 Raising Adjectives

So far we have only looked at examples of NP-movement **induced** by raising verbs or passive verbs. In this section we show that adjectival predicates too may induce raising. Consider (40):

40a It is likely [$_{CP}$ that John will leave].
40b John is likely to leave.

The main clause subject position in (40a) is occupied by an expletive, hence we conclude that *likely* takes one argument, realized here as CP, and fails to assign an external theta role. In (40a), *John* is assigned a theta role by the lower verb *leave*. *John* has no thematic relation with the adjective *likely*.

(40b) is a paraphrase of (40a). *John* is again an argument of *leave*, and has no thematic relation with the adjective *likely*; in (40b) *John* is in a derived position. Its base-position is the subject position of the lower clause: (41a) is the D-structure representation of (40b) and (41b) its S-structure:

41a [$_{IP}$ e is likely [$_{IP}$ John to leave]].
41b [$_{IP}$ John$_i$ is likely [$_{IP}$ t$_i$ to leave]].

We have treated the adjective *likely* in exactly the same way as the raising verb *seem*. *Likely* is referred to as a **raising adjective**. Another example of raising adjectives is *certain* in (42).

42a It is certain that the weather will change.
42b The weather is certain to change.

One might infer that all modal adjectives are raising adjectives. This conclusion would be wrong, though. *Probable*, for instance, which is near-synonymous to *likely*, does not allow the subject of the lower non-finite clause to raise to the higher subject position:

43a It is probable that John will leave.
43b *John is probable to leave.

3   Burzio's Generalization

3.1   Case-Marking and Argument Structure

In the preceding section we mentioned two properties of passive constructions in English.

(i)   Absorption of the case assigning properties of the verb: a passive verb fails to assign structural case to the complement NP; this NP has to move to a position in which it can be case-marked.

(ii) Absorption of the external argument of the verb: the D-structure subject position is generated empty.

We have postulated that raising verbs are like passive verbs in that they (i) fail to assign structural case and (ii) lack an external argument.

Luigi Burzio (1986) has related these two properties by the descriptive generalization in (44a) which is schematically summarized in (44b):

44a **Burzio's generalization**

(i)   A verb which lacks an external argument fails to assign ACCUSAT-IVE case (Burzio, 1986: 178–9).

(ii) A verb which fails to assign ACCUSATIVE case fails to theta-mark an external argument (Burzio, 1986: 184).

44b T $\longleftrightarrow$ A (Burzio, 1986: 185)

Where T stands for theta-marking; A stands for ACCUSATIVE. The leftward placement of T is important: it represents the external theta role, assigned to the left of the VP in English.

In this section we look at Burzio's general classification of verbs. (45) gives a survey of three possible argument structures for verbs.

45a VERB 1:

1	2

45b VERB 2:

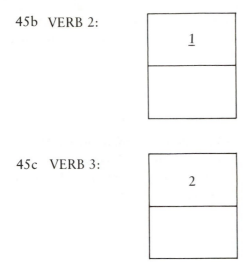

45c VERB 3:

A verb with the theta grid in (45a) is traditionally called a transitive verb: it is a verb which has two arguments and assigns two theta roles, e.g. *abandon* (which assigns the roles of AGENT and THEME) or *fear* (which assigns EXPERIENCER and THEME). Such a verb must be able to case-mark its complement NP. If a transitive verb failed to case-mark the object, then it would be like the putative verb HIT discussed in 2.3.1 above. We have seen that such verbs do not exist.

(45b) is the thematic grid of an intransitive verb: a verb which has only an external argument, such as *work* (which assigns the external role of AGENT). The D-structure and S-structure representations of sentences containing such intransitive verbs will be, schematically, as in (46a) and (46b) respectively:

46a $[_{IP}$ NP $[_{I'}$ $[_{VP}$ V$]]]$
46b $[_{IP}$ NP $[_{I'}$ $[_{VP}$ V$]]]$

We see that the S-structure is isomorphic in the relevant respects to the D-structure. According to Burzio's generalization verbs of this kind could case-mark a complement NP. Since these verbs lack an internal argument, they will not take an NP-complement, though, and their case-marking potential will not need to be activated.[9]

The third class of verbs with the theta grid (45c) is the one that we shall look into now. This class contains verbs which only have an internal argument. The most obvious examples of such verbs that we have already come across are

[9] Cf. the discussion of this point in Burzio's own work (1986: 184).

passive verbs. We have seen that as a result of passivization the external argument becomes suppressed. Verbs of the third class will be generated in a D-structure like (47a):

47a $[_{IP}$ e $[_{I'}$ $[_{VP}$ VERB$_{pass}$ NP]]]

Following Burzio's generalization, the VERB in (47a) cannot assign ACCU-SATIVE case to its complement. This is in line with our discussion: we have said that passive verbs fail to assign structural case. At S-structure the NP to which the internal theta role is assigned will have to move to the subject position to be case-marked:

47b $[_{IP}$ NP$_i$ $[_{I'}$ $[_{VP}$ VERB t$_i$]]]

Verbs which lack an external argument and therefore cannot assign ACCUSATIVE case to their complement-NP will from now on be referred to as **unaccusative** verbs. We shall see presently that not only passive verbs belong to this class.

The surface strings of the S-structures (46b) and (47b) will be similar, the trace in (47b) having no phonetic content. On the surface a sentence with an unaccusative verb of class 3 will look like a sentence with an intransitive verb of class 2. One of the important consequences of this analysis is that verbs that are one-place predicates in fact are to be divided into two groups: intransitive verbs with only an external argument (VERB 2) and unaccusative verbs with only an internal argument (VERB 3). We turn now to some empirical motivation from Italian for this claim.

3.2   *Unaccusatives in Italian*

Burzio's research relied initially on the study of Italian verbs and we shall discuss some of the essential data in this section. For further discussion the reader is referred to Burzio's own work (1986).

Consider the following examples:

48a   Giacomo telefona.
       Giacomo telephones.
48b   Giacomo arriva.
       Giacomo arrives.

Both *telefonare* and *arrivare* are one-argument verbs but a cluster of properties distinguishes them. We look at two of these properties here: *ne*-cliticization and auxiliary selection.

3.2.1 *NE-CLITICIZATION*

The basic facts of *ne*-cliticization in Italian are illustrated in the following examples:

49a Giacomo ha insultato due studenti.
     'Giacomo has insulted two students.'
49b Giacomo ne   ha   insultati   due.
     Giacomo of-them   has   insulted   two
     'Giacomo has insulted two.'

50a Giacomo ha parlato a due studenti.
     'Giacomo has spoken to two students.'
50b *Giacomo ne   ha   parlato   a due.
     Giacomo of them   has   spoken   to two
     'Giacomo has spoken to two.'

A noun head of an NP can become attached to a higher verb as *ne*, leaving its specifier behind. *Ne* is a clitic: a pronominal element which must be attached to a head. The attachment of *ne* to a verb head is referred to as **ne-cliticization**.[10] (50) shows that this is only possible if *ne* is extracted from a post-verbal NP: extraction from a PP produces ungrammaticality. (51) and (52) show that the conditions on *ne*-cliticization are more stringent:

51a Giacomo passa tre settimane a Milano.
     'Giacomo passes three weeks in Milan.'
51b Giacomo ne passa tre a Milano.

52a Giacomo resta tre settimane a Milano.
     'Giacomo stays three weeks in Milan.'
52b *Giacomo ne resta tre a Milano.

[10] For further discussion of clitics the reader is referred to chapter 12. For a discussion of *ne*-cliticization see also Belletti and Rizzi (1981).

Ne-cliticization from the NP *tre settimane* is allowed in (51b) and disallowed in (52b). The contrast between the two sentences lies in the function of the post-verbal NP. In (51a) *tre settimane* is a complement of the verb: a direct object. In (52a) the NP *tre settimane* is an **adjunct**. *Ne*-cliticization is restricted to NPs that are complements of V. Such NPs appear in the structure (53):

53

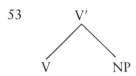

Before we discuss further data we need to add here that one typical property of Italian sentences is that the subject may appear either pre-verbally or post-verbally; the latter phenomenon is sometimes referred to as **free inversion**. (54b) illustrates free inversion in active sentences with transitive verbs:

54a Il   ragazzo ha   mangiato un   dolce (Belletti, 1988: 7).
    The   boy   has   eaten   a   sweet.
54b Ha mangiato un dolce il ragazzo.

The inverted word-order found in active sentences is also found in passive sentences.

55a Furono   arrestati molti   studenti.
    were   arrested   many   students
55b Molti studenti furono arrestati.

And similarly with one-argument verbs:

56a Molti   studenti   telefonano.
    many   students   telephone
56b Telefonano molti studenti.

57a Molti   studenti   arrivano.
    many   students   arrive
57b Arrivano molti studenti.

In (54b) the post-verbal subject *il ragazzo* follows the direct object NP *un dolce* and is assigned NOMINATIVE case.[11] Since the direct object position is occupied already, the inverted subject NP must be in a position somewhere outside the lowest V', which dominates V and its object-NP. Let us say that the post-verbal subject in (54b) is attached to or **adjoined** to VP (for some discussion of adjunction the reader is referred to section 4.1 below. A full discussion follows in chapter 7).[12]

In passive (55a) we cannot decide immediately whether the post-verbal NP *molti studenti* is inside or outside the lowest V'. Given its interpretation as the internal argument of the verb, *molti studenti* originates in the D-structure object position of *arrestati*. In (55b) the NP is a derived subject. It is moved to the subject position where it is assigned NOMINATIVE case by the finite inflection. In (55a) the NP occurs after the verb. The question is whether the NP in (55a) might still be in its D-structure position, i.e. dominated by V', or whether it is outside V'. Consider the following data of *ne*-cliticization:

58 Ne   furono   arrestati molti.
    of them   were   arrested   many

(58) shows that *ne* can be cliticized from the NP *molti studenti* in (55a). Given the properties of *ne*-cliticization discussed above, we infer that the relevant NP is in the object position (cf. (53)), the position dominated by V'.[13]

---

[11] Various proposals have been formulated to account for the NOMINATIVE case assignment to the post-verbal subject. See, for instance, Belletti (1988), Burzio (1986) and Rizzi (1982).

[12] Belletti (1987) proposes that I assigns NOMINATIVE case to the NP *il ragazzo* in (54b).

[13] Belletti (1988) proposes that the post-verbal NP in the passive sentence in (58) is assigned an inherent PARTITIVE case by the passive verb. Belletti's general thesis is that while passive verbs do not assign STRUCTURAL case they can assign an inherent PARTITIVE. Belletti proposes that PARTITIVE case is only compatible with indefinite NPs. For examples such as (i), where a definite NP occupies the post-verbal position, Belletti adopts the analysis proposed for (54b):

(i) Fu arrestato il professore.
     was arrested the professor
     'The professor was arrested.'

She proposes that the definite NP *il professore* is not in the position dominated by V', but is adjoined to VP where I can assign NOMINATIVE case. If we adopt the PARTITIVE hypothesis we will have to assume that only indefinite subjects can appear in the position dominated by V'.

59

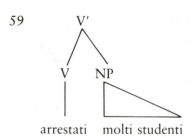

arrestati   molti studenti

An interesting contrast appears when we compare the one-argument verbs in (56) and (57), with respect to *ne*-cliticization:

56c   *Ne telefonano molti.
57c   Ne arrivano molti.

Consider first *telefonare* ('telephone') in (56). As in every Italian finite clause, the subject of the verb may appear either post-verbally or pre-verbally. From the impossibility of *ne*-cliticization (56c), we conclude that the inverted subject in (56b) does not occur in the position dominated by V', but is outside V'.

The situation for *arrivare* is quite different. Again both pre-verbal and post-verbal subjects are allowed but *ne*-cliticization from the post-verbal subject is possible (57c). This leads us to conclude that the NP *molti studenti* in (57b) occupies the position dominated by V'. In other words, the structure of (57b) is like that of passive (59):

60   [IP e I [VP [V' arrivare [NP molti studenti]]]]

Burzio proposes to assimilate verbs such as *arrivare* to the class of passive verbs. These verbs lack an external argument and their sole argument is internal. Thus both passive verbs and verbs such as *arrivare* are assumed to have the argument structure of VERB 3 above:

61   VERB 3:

2

At D-structure the subject position of sentences with these verbs remains unfilled:

62a [$_{IP}$ e furono [$_{VP}$ [$_{V'}$ arrestati [$_{NP}$ molti studenti]]]]
62b [$_{IP}$ e I [$_{VP}$ [$_{V'}$ arrivare [$_{NP}$ molti studenti]]]]

At S-structure there are two possibilities:

(i)   Either the complement of the verb is moved to the subject position to be assigned NOMINATIVE case. The subject is then a derived subject.

63a [$_{IP}$ Molti studenti$_i$ furono [$_{VP}$ [$_{V'}$ arrestati [$_{NP}$ t$_i$]]]].
63b [$_{IP}$ Molti studenti$_i$ I [$_{VP}$ [$_{V'}$ arrivare [$_{NP}$ t$_i$]]]].

Movement of the NP to the subject position leaves a co-indexed trace in the vacated position inside V'.

(ii) Alternatively, the object NP remains in its base-position. The null subject in (64) is non-thematic, it is a non-overt expletive.[14]

64a [$_{IP}$ e furono [$_{VP}$ [$_{V'}$ arrestati [$_{NP}$ molti studenti]]]]
64b [$_{IP}$ e I [$_{VP}$ [$_{V'}$ arrivare [$_{NP}$ molti studenti]]]]

Telefonare has a different argument structure. It has only an external argument.

---

[14] Non-overt expletives are not allowed in English:

(i)   *Arrived three students.
(ii) *Seems that John is ill.

The ungrammaticality of (i) and (ii) is due to the fact that pronominal subjects in English must be overt. In Italian a pronominal subject may be non-overt:

(iiia) *Speaks English.
(iiib) Parla inglese.

We discuss the nature of the non-overt subject in Italian in chapter 8.

65   VERB 2:

```
┌─────────────┐
│             │
│      1      │
│             │
├─────────────┤
│             │
│             │
│             │
└─────────────┘
```

The D-structure of sentences (56a) and (56b) will be:

66a [$_{IP}$ Molti studenti [$_{I'}$ I [$_{VP}$ telefonare]]]

Two S-structures are possible. Either the NP *molti studenti* stays in its base-position:

66b [$_{IP}$ Molti studenti [$_{I'}$ I [$_{VP}$ telefonare]]].

Alternatively, the subject appears in a post-verbal position outside V'. The [NP,IP] position is again occupied by a non-overt expletive.

66c [$_{IP}$e I [$_{VP}$ [$_{V'}$ telefonare] molti studenti]].

On the basis of the *ne*-cliticization facts we have concluded that there are two types of verbs which are traditionally called intransitive. Verbs like *telefonare* have an external argument; verbs like *arrivare* have just an internal argument. For the latter class of verbs Burzio's generalization predicts that although they have an internal argument they do not assign ACCUSATIVE case, exactly in the way that passive verbs fail to assign ACCUSATIVE. Verbs of the *arrivare* class are **unaccusatives**.

We have seen that whenever a verb allows *ne*-cliticization from what looks like an inverted subject NP, this NP must occur in the object position, the position dominated by V'. Such a verb will lack an external argument and will not assign ACCUSATIVE case. In (67) we give some more examples.

67a Ne   vengono   molti.
     of them   come   many
67b Ne   vanno   molti   al concerto.
     of them   go   many   to the concert

67c	Ne	tornano	molti.
	of them	return	many
67d	Ne	partono	molti.
	of them	leave	many
67e	Ne	muoiono	molti.
	of them	die	many
67f	Ne	cadono	molti.
	of them	fall	many
67g	Ne	entrano	molti.
	of them	enter	many

Though the class of unaccusative verbs is not easily defined (see Burzio's own work for discussion), it appears that it contains primarily verbs of movement and verbs that indicate some state or a change of state.

3.2.2   AUXILIARY SELECTION

We have seen that certain one-argument verbs have only an external argument, while others have only an internal argument to which they cannot assign ACCUSATIVE case. *Ne*-cliticization distinguishes these verbs. Another distinction is the choice of perfective auxiliary:

68a   Giacomo ha telefonato.
68b   Giacomo è arrivato.

Burzio proposes that the selection of the perfective auxiliary *essere* is dependent on the following condition:

69   *Essere* selection
     There is a chain between the subject position and the complement position of the verb (cf. Burzio, 1986: 55).

Following our discussion in 3.2 the S-structure representations of the examples in (68) will be as in (70):

70a   [$_{IP}$ Giacomo [$_{I'}$ ha [$_{VP}$ telefonato]]].
70b   [$_{IP}$ Giacomo$_i$ [$_{I'}$ è [$_{VP}$ arrivato t$_i$]]].

In (70b) *Giacomo* has moved to the subject position and has left a co-indexed trace. There is a chain between the moved NP and the vacated position. (70b) fulfils the condition for *essere* selection. In (70a) no movement is assumed and the condition for *essere* selection is not satisfied.

If we return briefly to the other examples of unaccusative verbs listed under (67) we see that these verbs also select *essere* as the perfect auxiliary:

71a   Roberto è venuto.
71b   Roberto è andato al concerto.
71c   Roberto è tornato.
71d   Roberto è partito.
71e   Roberto è morto.
71f   Roberto è caduto.
71g   Roberto è entrato.

Passive verbs are also unaccusative: they also meet the condition for *essere* assignment in (69):

72   Notevoli danni sono stati arrecati alla chiesa.
     Important damage has (lit. are) been caused to the church.

3.3   One-argument Verbs in English

Let us try to see if Burzio's analysis of the one-argument verbs carries over to English. We have already discussed the passive verbs. The crucial properties of these verbs are that (i) they fail to assign an external theta role, i.e. they lack an external argument, and that (ii) they do not assign ACCUSATIVE case to their complement. Can other verbs be considered unaccusatives along the lines of the Italian verbs of the *arrivare* group?

3.3.1   RAISING PREDICATES

Raising verbs also belong to the class of unaccusatives. Consider the S-structures in (73):

73a   [$_{IP}$ Poirot$_i$ [$_{I'}$ was [$_{VP}$ believed [$_{IP}$ t$_i$ to have destroyed the evidence]]]].
73b   [$_{IP}$ Poirot$_i$ [$_{I'}$ -s [$_{VP}$ seem [$_{IP}$ t$_i$ to have destroyed the evidence]]]].

We have discussed the derivation of (73a) and (73b) in section 1.1. The verbs *believed* and *seem* take one internal clausal argument and do not assign an external theta role to the subject position. For both verbs we have also said that they cannot assign an ACCUSATIVE case to the subject position of the lower infinitive.

We now see that the properties attributed to these verbs are captured by Burzio's generalization: passive and raising verbs lack an external argument and they consequently fail to assign ACCUSATIVE case.

3.3.2 VERBS OF MOVEMENT AND (CHANGE OF) STATE

We may wonder whether the English verbs of movement and (change of) state are like their Italian counterparts of the *arrivare* class. Remember two crucial features of verbs of the *arrivare*-class: they allow *ne*-cliticization from the post-verbal subject and they select *essere* as a perfect auxiliary. In present-day English there is no choice of auxiliary for the perfect, this being invariably *have*, and there is no equivalent to *ne*-cliticization, so the diagnostics introduced are not immediately applicable.

A consideration of the history of the language throws some light on the issue. While modern English uses only *have* as a perfective auxiliary, older stages of the language had both *have* and *be*. At those earlier stages verbs of movement and change of state like *come, go, return, grow, die, fall* formed their perfective forms by means of *be*:

74a Se   halga faeder   *waes*   inn agan.
  the holy father   was   in gone
  'The holy father had gone in'.
  (Quirk and Wrenn, 1957: 78)
74b *Is*   nu   geworden.
  (it) is   now   become
  'It has happened'.
  (Quirk and Wrenn, 1957: 79)

Present-day English still allows the form in (75) (cf. 74a):

75   Poirot is gone.

From earlier stages of the language we obtain indirect support for the idea that verbs of movement and change of state are unaccusative verbs like their Italian counterparts of the *arrivare* class.

Another argument can be obtained from present-day English and concerns the use of the expletive *there*. We have briefly discussed existential sentences such as (76) and (77) in chapter 1:

76a   Three men arrived at the palace.
76b   There arrived three men at the palace.

77a   Three students came to the party.
77b   There came three students to the party.

In (76a) the subject precedes the verb *arrived* while in the existential pattern (76b) it follows it and the expletive *there* occupies the [NP,IP] position. It is clear, though, that the existential pattern cannot be used with every verb in English.[15]

78a   Three men bought a book.
78b   *There bought three men a book.

79a   Three men slept in the room.
79b   *There slept three men in the room.

Transitive verbs are excluded (78b). Only a subset of one-argument verbs allows the construction, as indicated by the ungrammaticality of (79b). A closer look at these and other examples suggests the following descriptive generalization: the *there* construction is restricted to one-argument verbs of movement and (change of) state. In addition to the verbs given above, Burzio (1986: 159) mentions: *arise, emerge, ensue, begin, exist, occur, follow.* The Italian counterparts of these verbs (*sorgere, emergere, succedere, cominciare, esistere, accadere, seguire*) all pattern like *arrivare*.[16]

We shall follow Burzio in assuming that the English verbs of movement and of (change of) state listed above are also unaccusatives, i.e. fail to assign ACCUSATIVE case and lack an external theta role.

3.3.3 ERGATIVE-CAUSATIVE PAIRS

A group of verbs in English have properties which have led some linguists to treat them as unaccusatives.

[15]   See Belletti (1988) for a discussion of the existential construction. For further discussion of the existential construction in Germanic see Haegeman (forthcoming: chapter 4).
[16]   See Burzio (1986: 160–1) for discussion though.

80a   The enemy_i sank the boat_j.

80b   The boat_j was sunk.

80c   The boat_j sank.

The argument structure for active *sink* is given in (81a). We have specified the theta roles and we have entered the relevant indices in the theta grid of the verb to indicate which NP realizes which argument:

81a *sink*: verb

$\underline{1}$ AGENT	2 THEME
i	j

In (80b) passive *sink* has the argument structure (81b):

81b *sunk*: verb

2 THEME
j

For by now familiar reasons we propose (82a) as the D-structure and (82b) as the S-structure of (80b):

82a   [$_{IP}$ e [$_{I'}$ was [$_{VP}$ [$_{V'}$ sunk [$_{NP}$ the boat]]]]]

82b   [$_{IP}$ The boat$_j$ [$_{I'}$ was [$_{VP}$ [$_{V'}$ sunk [$_{NP}$ t$_j$]]]]].

In (80c) the NP *the boat* has the same thematic relation to the verb as in (80b): *the boat* is the THEME, the thing that is affected by the activity. One might assume that *sink* in (80c), although active, has an argument structure similar to that of a passive verb, i.e. that *sink* in (80c) is an unaccusative verb.

82c *sink*: verb

2 THEME
j

On this assumption, (80c) would have the D-structure (83a) and the S-structure (83b):

83a [IP e [I' past [VP [V' sink [NP the boat]]]]]
83b [IP The boatj [I' past [VP sink [NP ti]]]].

In (83a) the NP *the boat* is base-generated as the object of *sink*; at S-structure it becomes a derived subject. The two argument structures correlate with a semantic difference between two uses of *sink*. (80c) merely encodes that some object (the boat) is engaged in some activity (the sinking). In (80a) the external argument specifies who is responsible for the sinking: (80a) is equivalent to 'the enemy made the boat sink' or 'the enemy caused the boat to sink'. In view of the element of causation involved in the interpretation of *sink* in (80a), this use of the verb is referred to as the **causative** pattern.

There are two reasons for not referring to *sink* in (80c) as an unaccusative verb. First, unlike *arrive*, *sink* has a transitive pendant which does assign ACCUSATIVE:

84a The enemy sank the ship.
84b *I arrived the baby to the crèche.

Second, unlike the unaccusative verbs of movement and (change of) state mentioned above, *sink* does not appear in the *there*-construction:

85a There came three new sailors on board.
85b *There sank three ships last week.

On the basis of these two criteria it seems reasonable to argue that *sink* (and verbs which pattern like it) is not an unaccusative verb. Other verbs that pattern like *sink* are *open, close, increase, break, drop:*

86a Poirot opened the door.
86b The door opened.

87a Poirot closed the door.
87b The door closed.

88a The police have increased the activities.
88b The activities have increased.

89a Poirot broke the vase.
89b The vase broke.

90a The boy dropped the vase.
90b The vase dropped.

Rather than claiming that these verbs have the theta structure in (82c) we shall propose that they are intransitive verbs which project their THEME argument in the subject position at D-structure:

91   *sink*: verb

The D-structure of (80c) will not be as in (83a) but will be:

92   [IP the boatⱼ [I′ past [VP sink]]]

In this book the term unaccusative is used for passive verbs, raising verbs and verbs of movement and (change of) state, and we shall refer to one-argument verbs like *sink* as **ergatives**.[17] The classification of verbs as unaccusative/ergative is a matter of ongoing research. Many authors do not make any distinction between the terms, or consider verbs with transitive pendants like *sink*, which we label ergatives, as unaccusatives. The reader is referred to the literature for details.

4   Levels of Representation and Principles of the Grammar

In this chapter we have developed the hypothesis that all sentences are associated with two syntactic representations: D-structure and S-structure. In this section we discuss the relation between these levels and we shall give an overview of how the principles of grammar established in previous chapters apply to them.

4.1   The Structure Preserving Principle

There is an important constraint on the relation between syntactic representations: structures established at D-structure must be preserved at S-structure: transformations are **structure preserving**.

If a syntactic position is required at D-structure it will be present at S-structure as well. For instance, a position which is required by the projection principle at D-structure will also be present at S-structure. A position projected as a certain category at D-structure cannot change its category at S-structure: NP-positions remain NP-positions, I remains I, etc. A D-structure NP-position, for example, cannot be turned into a PP-position at S-structure. If we adopt the hypothesis briefly alluded to at the end of chapter 2 that syntactic category labels represent bundles of features ([$\pm$N], [$\pm$V]) then we conclude that features assigned at D-structure are preserved, i.e. they do not change. If NPs are furthermore assigned the features [$\pm$ anaphor; $\pm$ pronominal] then

---

[17]   In so doing we depart from Burzio's own analysis (1986) and we follow a suggestion in work by Belletti (1988: 4, 14), based on Hale and Keyser (1986, 1987). Obviously, the same type of analysis will also apply to the equivalents of the ergatives in other languages.

these features too are expected to be invariant between D-structure and S-structure. This point becomes relevant in chapter 8.

The structure preserving principle also has consequences for movement. One constraint which it imposes on movement is that phrasal projections must move into positions which are themselves labelled as phrasal projections. NPs, for example, must not move into positions dominated by lexical categories (such as N) or intermediate phrasal categories (N'). Heads such as I must move into other head positions.

Second, movement will have to respect syntactic categories. For example, NPs can move into NP-positions without problem, but they will not be able to move into a position labelled AP. This does not mean that NPs must move to NP-positions. Provided all other principles of the grammar are respected, NPs will also be allowed to move to positions which are not specified for a syntactic category (see the discussion of *wh*-movement in chapter 7). The structure preserving principle does not prevent that a moved element is given a new position at S-structure, a position that does not exist at D-structure, as long as the new position created respects the principles of phrase structure. Such a move would not violate the principle that structure must be preserved.

Consider, for instance, the example of free subject inversion in Italian, illustrated in (3.2.1) as (54) and repeated here as (93).

93a Il ragazzo   ha   mangiato un dolce.
     the boy   has   eaten   a   sweet.
93b Ha mangiato un dolce il ragazzo.

The VP of (93a) is as in (93c):

93c   VP

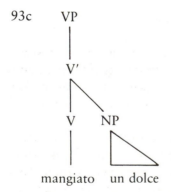

In (93b) the subject NP occurs post-verbally. We assume that the D-structure (93b) is like that of (93a), i.e. the VP contains the verb and its internal argument. At S-structure the subject NP must be moved somewhere to the right of the VP. It is proposed in the literature that the NP is **adjoined** to the VP node:

93d

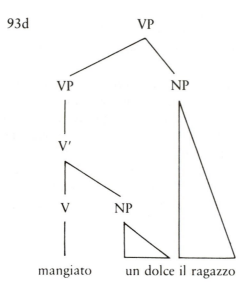

The S-structure in (93d) is not incompatible with the structure preserving principle: all structure assumed at D-structure (93c) is preserved unaltered. We return to adjunction structures in chapter 7.

4.2 The Theta Criterion

In 2.2.1 we discussed the application of theta theory to the two levels of representation.

D-structure is a representation of lexical properties. D-structure representations are subject to the theta criterion: all syntactic arguments of the predicates must be realized. Moreover we must not randomly generate arguments (say NPs) which cannot be associated with any predicate since they will fail to receive a theta role.

S-structure encodes the result of movement transformations. The structure preserving principle will also entail that movement leaves traces since positions created at D-structure must be preserved. Traces of movement form a chain with their antecedent. If we redefine the theta criterion in terms of chains (cf. (22)) we can maintain that the theta criterion also applies at S-structure, as discussed above.

4.3 The Extended Projection Principle

The EPP is another principle regulating syntactic structure which applies at all levels of syntactic representation: sentences must have subject positions, [NP,IP] positions, at all syntactic levels. It is important to point out here that the EPP imposes that the [NP,IP] position be generated. The EPP does not impose that this position be filled by overt elements: we have already seen that it may be filled by a trace or by PRO. Also, the EPP does not require that the [NP,IP] position be filled by arguments: we have seen that sometimes it is filled by an expletive element. Given the structure preserving principle discussed in 4.1 it follows that if the EPP forces us to generate an [NP,IP] position at D-structure, this position is also present at S-structure.

4.4 The Case Filter

Throughout this chapter we have been assuming that the case filter applies at S-structure (cf. section 1.1). NPs do not need to be assigned case at D-structure. Structural case is assigned at S-structure.

This does not mean that at D-structure NPs must be caseless. All we are saying is that case is not **checked** at D-structure. In chapter 3 we adopted the idea that inherent case is associated with theta roles as a lexical property. The German DATIVE in (94a) was taken to be an inherent case. The verb *helfen* is assumed to have the lexical structure in (94b):

94a Poirot hilft ihm.
     Poirot helps him-DATIVE

94b *helfen*: verb

1	2 DATIVE

If D-structure is a representation of lexical structure then we can assume that the DATIVE will be assigned to *ihm* at D-structure. As seen before, inherent case is unaffected by passivization.

94c Ihm wurde geholfen.
     him was helped
     'He was helped.'
94d *Er wurde geholfen.
     he (NOM) was helped

4.5 The Binding Theory

4.5.1 LEVEL OF APPLICATION

In chapter 4 we discussed the module of the grammar responsible for the interpretation of NPs: the binding theory. At that point in the discussion we were not worried about levels of representation. We simply looked at sentences, pretending there was a unique syntactic representation associated with them. Now life is more difficult: we have two levels of representation and we may well ask at which point the binding theory (BT) is supposed to apply.

In order to decide at which level the BT applies we examine the application of the BT in examples in which movement has taken place. We shall consider first the application of Principle A and then that of Principles B and C.

The standard example that is often used to illustrate the application of Principle A is (95).

95   They seem to each other to be intelligent.

The D-structure of (95) is (95a) and its S-structure is (95b):

95a [$_{IP}$ e seem to each other [$_{IP}$ they to be intelligent]].
95b [$_{IP}$ They$_i$ seem to each other$_i$ [$_{IP}$ t$_i$ to be intelligent]].

Principle A of the BT requires that anaphors such as *each other* be bound in their GC. The GC of *each other* is the matrix clause. In the D-structure (95a) *each other* cannot be bound in its GC since there is no NP available to bind it. The correct binding configuration arises at S-structure: the derived subject *they* can bind the anaphor:

95c [$_{IP}$ They$_i$ seem to each other$_i$ [$_{IP}$ t$_i$ to be intelligent]].

Belletti and Rizzi claim that (95) only shows 'that Principle A can be fulfilled at S-structure, not that it cannot be fulfilled at D-structure' (1988: 313). They include in the discussion examples such as (96):

96a Replicants of themselves seemed to the boys to be ugly.
     (from Johnson, 1985, quoted in Belletti and Rizzi, 1988: 316)
96b D-structure
     [IP e seemed to the boys [IP replicants of themselves to be ugly]]
96c S-structure
     [IP [Replicants of themselves]k seemed to the boys [IP tk to be ugly]].

In (96a) the reflexive *themselves* is referentially dependent on the NP *the boys*, hence we expect it is bound by it. At S-structure (96c) the anaphor is not c-commanded by the antecedent *the boys*, hence is not bound by it. Belletti and Rizzi argue that D-structure (96b) stands a better chance of satisfying Principle A. However, even here there will be problems. It is not immediately clear how the NP *the boys*, which is a complement of the preposition *to*, can c-command the reflexive even at D-structure. The reader can verify for himself that the first branching node dominating the NP *the boys* will be the PP node dominating *to the boys*. One might try to circumvent the problem by saying that the PP node somehow does not count.

96d

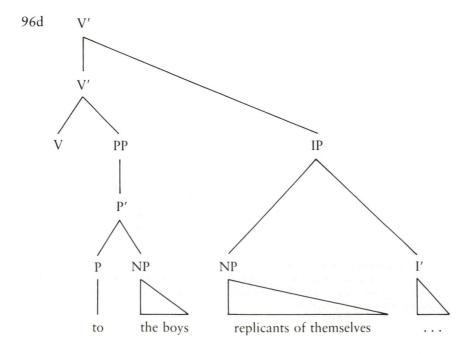

Another problem with the example is that it illustrates reflexives associated with what are called *picture*-NPs. Such NPs are known to be problematic for the BT.[18] Consider for instance (97):

97   This is a picture of myself which was taken years ago.

In (97) the reflexive *myself* lacks an antecedent and still the sentence is grammatical. Because of their special behaviour it is sometimes proposed that *picture*-NPs be treated separately from other NPs with respect to the BT. Rizzi and Belletti's argument that Principle A can be satisfied at D-structure is weakened because it relies on *picture*-NPs, which are problematic for the binding theory anyway.

Let us consider the application of Principle C. (98a) is ruled out on the interpretation indicated by the co-indexation: *Bill* must not be coreferential with *he* (Belletti and Rizzi, 1988: 318).

98a   *He$_i$ seems to Bill'$_i$s sister to be the best.

---

[18]   We have illustrated the problems with *picture*-NPs in chapter 4, exercise 3. For discussion of the data the reader is referred to work by Prewett (1977). Nakajima (1984) proposes that *picture*-NPs should be kept outside the BT. Mohanan (1985) contains a similar suggestion.

Consider the syntactic representations of the sentence:

98b D-structure

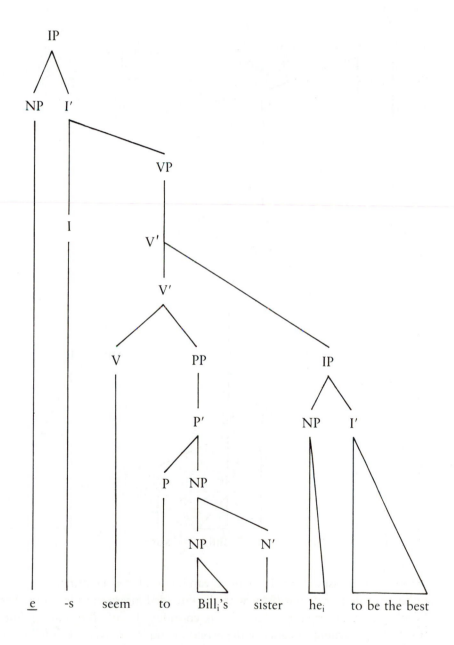

98c S-structure

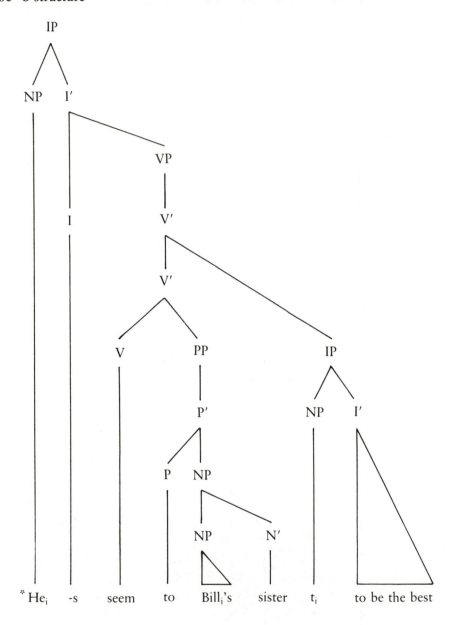

If we were to assume that Principle C can be fulfilled at D-structure it would not be possible to rule out (98a) with the intended interpretation on the basis of the BT. At D-structure (98b), *he*ᵢ is co-indexed with *Bill*ᵢ but (i) *Bill* is outside the governing category of the pronoun and, moreover, (ii) *Bill* does not c-command the pronoun, as the reader can verify on the tree diagram. The D-structure configuration (98b) is identical in the relevant respects to the structure of (99) where co-indexation between *Bill* and *he* is allowed:

99a   It seems to Bill$_i$'s sister that he$_i$ is the best man.
99b   D-structure/S-structure
      It seems to Bill$_i$'s sister [that [he$_i$ is the best man]].

We conclude that it is the S-structure representation (98c) which is ruled out by Principle C. *Bill$_i$*, an R-expression, is bound by *he$_i$* and this violates Principle C. This suggests that Principle C must be satisfied at S-structure.

The same reasoning can be applied to (100) to demonstrate that Principle B cannot be satisfied at D-structure either:

100   *He$_i$ seems to him$_i$ to be likely to be the best.

We leave the reader to work out the D-structure and S-structure of this example.[19]

On the basis of the discussion above, we conclude that Principles B and C apply to S-structure configurations. The evidence that Principle A can be fulfilled at D-structure is controversial.

4.5.2   THE FEATURE COMPOSITION OF NP-TRACES

Let us return to a point left unexplained in section 2.3.1 above. It was observed that example (37a), repeated here as (101), is ungrammatical:

101   *John$_i$ seems that it is believed t$_i$ by everyone.

Let us try to explain why this should be so.

We have seen that traces of NP-movement occupy an NP-position and can be said to have nominal features of gender, number and person. This means that these traces are in fact like non-overt NPs. In chapter 4 we propose that NPs are subject to the BT. The question to address is: which principle applies to traces of NP-movement, i.e. what type of NP are NP-traces? Recall that there were four types of NPs:

[19]   See Belletti and Rizzi (1988: 318).

102   Classification of NPs:

Type:	OVERT	NON-OVERT
[+anaphor, −pronominal]	anaphors	
[−anaphor, +pronominal]	pronouns	
[−anaphor, −pronominal]	R-expressions	
[+anaphor, +pronominal]		PRO (chapter 5)

The binding theory says that:
(i)   elements that are [+anaphor] must be bound in their GC.
(ii) elements that are [+pronominal] must be free in their GC.

Consider the typical examples of NP-movement: a passive sentence (103a) and a raising construction (103b):

103a   [John$_i$ is believed t$_i$ by everyone].
103b   [John$_i$ seems [$_{IP}$ t$_i$ to be the best]].

Which of the combinations of features listed in (102) would be appropriate to characterize the NP-traces in (103)?

Suppose the traces were considered to be R-expressions ([−anaphor, −pronominal]). Clearly this is not a good idea as the traces in (103) are co-indexed with a c-commanding NP in an A-position. If a trace of NP-movement were an R-expression it would violate Principle C.

Suppose the trace is [−anaphor,+pronominal], i.e. a pronoun. Again this will not do: the traces in (103) are bound in their GC. The reader will be able to work out that in both examples in (103) the antecedent *John* is contained in the GC of the trace.[20]

Could the trace be like the non-overt element PRO, [+anaphor, +pronominal] discussed in chapter 5? We have seen that such NPs are subject to contradictory requirements with respect to the BT. The only context in which PRO is licensed is when it is ungoverned. Clearly, the object position of the passive verb in (103a) is governed, and similarly, infinitival IP not being a barrier, *seem* will govern the trace in the subject position of the infinitival IP (103b).

---

[20] Remember that we stipulated in chapter 3 that infinitival IP is not a barrier for outside government, hence *seem* governs the trace in the subject position of the complement IP.

Finally, we are left with the category [+anaphor, −pronominal], subject to Principle A. This is rather a nice result. As the reader can verify for himself, the traces in (103) are bound in their GC: t_i is co-indexed with a c-commanding antecedent in its GC. NP-traces are like anaphors.

If we treat NP-traces as anaphors the ungrammaticality of (101) follows from the BT: t_i must be bound in its GC. The GC is the lower clause, containing a governor (*believe*) and a subject (*it* or the SUBJECT, AGR). In (101) the trace is not bound in its GC.

At this point it is clear that the term 'antecedent', which we introduced to refer to the moved NP, is not accidental. The moved NP behaves like an antecedent in that it **binds** the trace.The requirement that the moved NP should bind the trace will also account for some of the properties discussed in section 2.3. Recall that antecedents of NP-movement c-command their traces (see section 2.3.2). We have defined binding in terms of co-indexation with a c-commanding element in an A-position. The c-command relation between the moved NP and its trace follows if we assume that the trace must be bound by the moved element.

On the basis of the examples discussed above we have identified NP-traces as non-overt NPs of the type [+anaphor, −pronominal]. This means that in our inventory of NP types (102) we can pair them with overt anaphors:

104 Classification of NPs

Type:	OVERT	NON-OVERT
[+anaphor, −pronominal]	anaphors	NP-trace
[−anaphor, +pronominal]	pronouns	
[−anaphor, −pronominal]	R-expressions	
[+anaphor, +pronominal]		PRO

There are now only three gaps in the paradigm we have set up. The absence of overt elements which are [+anaphor, +pronominal] was motivated in chapter 4. We have as yet no non-overt elements which are [−anaphor, +pronominal] and [−anaphor, −pronominal]. In subsequent chapters we shall see that these latter types also exist so that we shall be able to arrive at a picture where all overt NP-types have a non-overt pendant. We return to the classification of non-overt categories in chapters 7 and 8.[21]

---

[21] The classification of NPs on the basis of the features given in (104) is discussed at length by Chomsky (1982).

5   Appendix: Subjects and Derived Subjects

So far we have assumed that unaccusative verbs induce NP-movement, hence that their subjects, i.e. NPs which occupy the [NP,IP] position, are derived subjects. In this section we consider a proposal which has been gaining ground in the literature where it is argued that subjects of transitive and intransitive verbs are base-generated in [Spec,VP]. This section is mainly based on Sportiche (1988a).

Consider the following French sentences:

105a   Tous les garçons   ont   lu   ce   livre.
       All   the boys   have read   this book.
105b   Les garçons   ont   tous lu   ce   livre.
       The boys   have all   read   this book.

(105a) and (105b) are paraphrases. In the literature it has often been proposed that they are syntactically related, in the sense that one is derived from the other. One possibility would be that (105b) derives from (105a). In (105b) the quantifier *tous* occupies the position which we have identified as [Spec, VP] (cf. chapter 2). If (105a) were closer to the underlying order of the sentence in (105b) then we would have to assume that *tous* is moved downwards from the subject position [NP, IP] into the VP.

Alternatively, we might assume that the NP *tous les garçons* originates in the [Spec, VP] position. Under this view both (105a) and (105b) involve movement. In (105a) the NP *tous les garçons* moves as a whole to the [NP,VP] position, in (105b) only the phrase *les garçons* moves, leaving the quantifier in the [Spec,VP] position. Roughly, the D-structure of the sentence in (105) would be (106) and their S-structures would be (107):

106

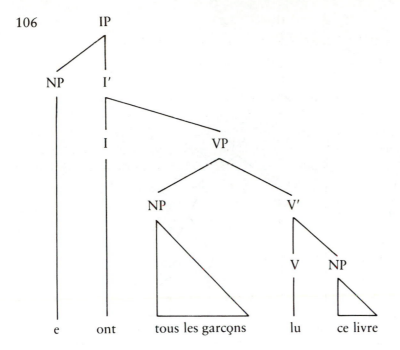

107a

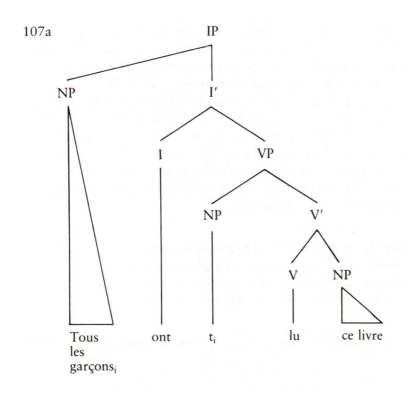

107b

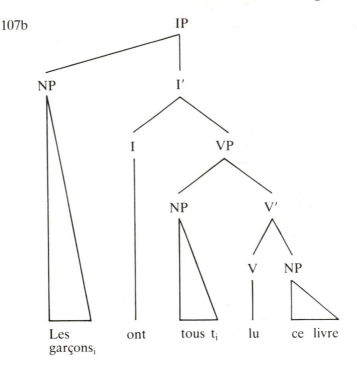

In (107b) *tous* is adjacent to the trace of the moved NP. The movements of the NPs in (107a) and (107b) are examples of NP-movement: an NP is moved to the subject position. Hence the trace of the moved NP is of the type [+anaphor, −pronominal] and subject to Principle A of the BT.

In his discussion of these sentences Sportiche (1988a) provides arguments that the relation between the trace and the moved NP is like that of an anaphor and its antecedent. In (107b) *tous* signals the position of the trace. *Tous* in (107b) is c-commanded by the related NP. The c-command relation is necessary, as illustrated by the ungrammaticality of (108b). In this sentence the NP *ces livres* does not c-command *tous*, hence it does not c-command its trace, which is assumed to be adjacent to *tous*.

108a L'auteur de tous ces livres a acheté cette maison.
      The author of all these books has bought this house.
108b *L'auteur de ces livres a tous acheté cette maison.
      *The author of these books has all bought this house.

Secondly, the quantifier must not be too far removed from the related NP:

109   *Les garçons lui ont demandé de [[PRO tous acheter ce   livre]].
      the   boys   him have asked   all   to buy this book

In (109) the NP *les garçons* cannot be related to the quantifier *tous* in the lower clause. Sportiche explains the ungrammaticality of (108b) and of (109) by arguing that the quantifier *tous* is adjacent to a trace of the moved NP and that the trace is a trace of NP-movement, subject to Principle A of the BT.

110a *L'auteur de [NPi ces livres] a tous ti acheté cette maison.
110b *[NPi Les garçons] lui ont demandé de [[PRO tous ti acheter ce livre]].

Sportiche (1988a)[22] proposes that indeed all subject NPs are base-generated in the [Spec, VP] position. Hence a sentence such as (111a) would have the D-structure (111b) and the S-structure (111c). Similarly the English example in (112a) would have the D-structure (112b) and S-structure (112c):

111a Les filles ont gagné le championnat.
      The girls have won the championship.

111b

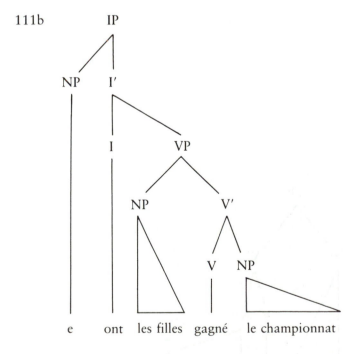

22 Similar proposals are discussed in Kitagawa (1986), Kuroda (1986), Koopman and Sportiche (1987) and Zagona (1982). We have based the discussion here on Sportiche (1988a) because this article is probably most readily available.

111c

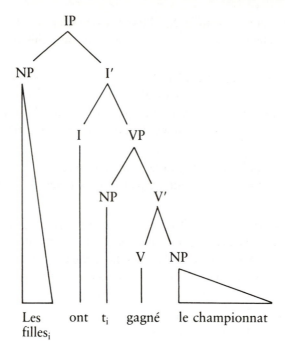

Les filles$_i$ ont t$_i$ gagné le championnat

112a The girls have won the championship.

112b

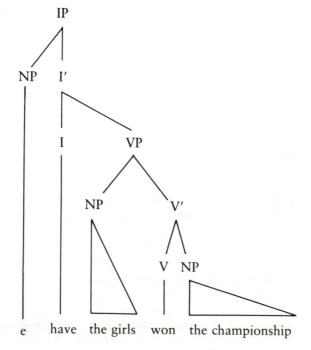

e have the girls won the championship

112c

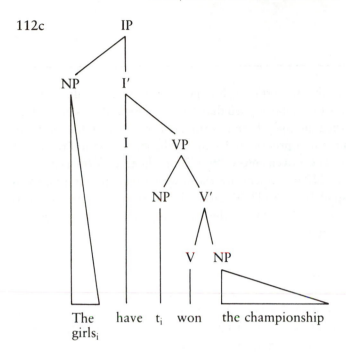

The proposal that all NPs found in [NP,IP] are derived subjects[23] obviously has considerable consequences for the theory of grammar outlined so far. For instance, the proposal entails that the [NP,IP] position is always empty at D-structure and is not theta-marked; in other words, it is a theta-bar position at D-structure. In addition we can no longer define the external argument of the predicate as that realized outside VP, since all subject NPs will have traces in [Spec,VP]. The classification of verbs discussed in section 3 of this chapter will also have to be revised. If [Spec,VP] is an NP position the question can also be raised whether all NP-movement must pass through it. All these and many other issues are subject to ongoing research. We shall not go into the problems here.

In the subsequent chapters of this book we shall not adopt the hypothesis that all NPs in the [NP,IP] position are derived subjects. We shall stick to the more traditional line developed so far. However, we encourage the reader to bear in mind the hypothesis when reading the following chapters.

---

[23] This statement may be too general though, as seen in Rizzi and Roberts (1989).

6 Summary

This chapter discusses the properties of NP-movement, which is illustrated in passive and raising stuctures. It is argued that NP-movement affects NPs which cannot be case-marked in their base-position. NP-movement leaves a co-indexed trace which is a non-pronominal anaphor, hence subject to Principle A of the binding theory. The moved antecedent NP and the trace form a chain.

Verbs which induce NP-movement are those which lack an external theta role and fail to assign ACCUSATIVE case. These verbs are referred to as unaccusative verbs. The link between the two properties of these verbs is expressed by Burzio's generalization:

1 **Burzio's generalization**
   (i)   A verb which lacks an external argument fails to assign ACCUSATIVE case (Burzio, 1986: 178–9).
   (ii) A verb which fails to assign ACCUSATIVE case fails to theta-mark an external argument (Burzio, 1986: 184).

The chapter also examines the relation between the two levels of representation: D-structure and S-structure. The structure preserving principle imposes severe restrictions on the effect of transformations. The theta criterion and the extended projection principle are argued to apply at both D-structure and at S-structure, while case theory and the binding theory apply at S-structure.

In the final section we discuss the proposal that all NPs in [NP, IP] are in a derived position and are base-generated in [Spec,VP].

7 Exercises

Exercise 1

Discuss the derivation of the following sentences. For each sentence provide a D-structure representation, an S-structure representation, and discuss the assignment of theta roles and of case.

1   The prisoners have been arrested.
2   Poirot seems to like the countryside.
3   George is thought to have been invited to Court.
4   They expect Bill to be arrested presently.
5   For Bill to have been arrested so soon was disappointing.
6   I expect that Poirot will be invited.
7   Not to have been invited to court was a real insult.
8   I expect to be invited.
9   John appears to have left.
10 John is likely to leave soon.

We know that subject NPs agree with INFL. At what level of representation will this agreement be determined?

Exercise 2

Consider the Italian examples below. Try to classify the italicized verbs on the basis of the selection of perfective auxiliaries (see section 3). The infinitive of the verb is given in parentheses. What problems, if any, do these examples raise?

1   Maria è già *partita* (partire).
    Maria is already left
2   Maria è *stata* malata (essere).
    Maria is been ill
3   Maria ha *guardato* se stessa nello specchio (guardare).
    Maria has watched herself   in the mirror
    'Maria has looked at herself in the mirror.'
4   Maria s'è *guardata* nello specchio.
    Maria herself has watched in the mirror

How could the verbs in the following French examples be classified?

5   Maria est déjà *partie* (partir).
    Maria is already left
6   Le bateau a *coulé* (couler).
    the ship has sunk
7   On   a   *coulé* le   bateau.
    they   have   sunk   the   ship
8   Maria a *travaillé* longtemps (travailler).
    Maria has worked for a long time

9 Maria a *été* malade (être).
  Maria has been ill

10 Maria s'est   *regardée* dans le   miroir (regarder).
   Maria herself is watched   in   the   mirror
   'Maria has looked at herself in the mirror.'

Discuss the classification of the verbs in the Dutch examples below.

11 Maria is al *vertrokken* (vertrekken).
   Maria is already left

12 Maria heeft lang   *gewerkt* (werken).
   Maria has a long time worked
   'Maria has worked for a long time.'

13 Maria heeft   dat   boek   *gekocht* (kopen).
   Maria has   that book   bought
   'Maria has bought that book.'

14 Maria is ziek *geweest* (zijn).
   Maria is ill   been
   'Maria has been ill.'

15 Maria heeft zichzelf in de spiegel *bekeken* (bekijken).
   Maria has   herself in the mirror   watched.

Exercise 3

Discuss the derivation of the following sentences:

1 They got Bill to accept the job.
2 Bill got to accept the job.
3 They got Bill into trouble.
4 Bill got into trouble.
5 They got all their friends invited.
6 All their friends got invited.
7 The robber got himself attacked by Jeeves.

What conclusions can you draw with respect to the argument structure of *get* in these examples?[24]

---

[24] For discussion see Haegeman (1987).

Exercise 4

We have said that both anaphors and NP-traces are assigned the features [+anaphor, −pronominal]. On the basis of examples that you will construct discuss the similarities and differences between the overt anaphor *himself* and NP-trace.

Exercise 5

Consider the following sentences. For each sentence we offer some possible syntactic representations. Which one is theoretically justified?

1a   John tried to go.
1b   [$_{IP}$ John$_i$ tried [$_{CP}$ [$_{IP}$ PRO$_i$ to go]]].
1c   [$_{IP}$ John$_i$ tried [$_{IP}$ t$_i$ to go]].

2a   John seems to be happy.
2b   [$_{IP}$ John$_i$ seems [$_{IP}$ t$_i$ to be happy]].
2c   [$_{IP}$ John$_i$ seems [$_{CP}$ [$_{IP}$ PRO$_i$ to be happy]]].

3a   John is happy to leave.
3b   John$_i$ is happy [$_{IP}$ t$_i$ to leave].
3c   John$_i$ is happy [$_{IP}$ PRO to leave].
3d   John$_i$ is happy [$_{CP}$ [$_{IP}$ PRO to leave]].

Exercise 6

The following sentences are ungrammatical. Why?

1   *John$_i$ seems that Mary likes t$_i$.
2   *John$_i$ seems that he$_i$ is believed t$_i$ to be happy.
3   *I$_i$ believe [$_{IP}$ PRO$_i$ to be happy].
4   *It is believed [$_{IP}$ John $_i$ to have been invited t$_i$].
5   *I$_i$ never cry when [$_{IP}$ PRO$_i$ watch a film].
6   *I$_i$ want [$_{IP}$ John to invite PRO$_i$].
7   *John$_i$ seems that [$_{IP}$ it appears [$_{IP}$ t$_i$ to be happy]].
8   *There hit John.
9   *John$_i$ invited t$_i$.
10   *Himself$_i$ seems to Bill$_i$ to be the best candidate.

Exercise 7

Consider (1). It is ambiguous: (1a) and (1b) are two paraphrases, with a clear difference in meaning. Try to provide the syntactic representations for (1) that bring out these readings.

1   John is certain to win.
1a   It is certain that John will win.
1b   John is certain that he will win.

Exercise 8

So far we have assumed that *seem* is a verb which selects only one internal argument. Discuss the problems raised for this hypothesis by the following example:

John seems as if he does not like Mary.

7 *Wh*-Movement

Contents

Introduction and Overview

In chapter 6, section 1 we gave a survey of various types of movement. Movement affects either heads or maximal projections. Chapter 6 discussed movement of NPs in passive and raising patterns. In this chapter we turn to *wh*-movement. We shall discuss the target of *wh*-movement, its landing site and the arguments for positing traces in the extraction site. We shall show that the subjacency condition imposes a constraint on the range of *wh*-movement and is subject to parametric variation. Using the subjacency condition as a diagnostic we show that English relative clauses are derived via *wh*-movement.

We continue our classification of empty categories, adding *wh*-traces which are of the type [−anaphor, −pronominal]. From our discussion it follows that heavy NP-shift and PP-extraposition from NP are also instantiations of *wh*-movement.

In section 1 we illustrate *wh*-movement in questions. Section 2 concerns the target of movement; section 3 the landing site. In section 4 we consider arguments for traces of *wh*-movement. In section 5 we describe some special properties of subject extraction. Section 6 deals with the subjacency condition on movement. In section 7 we turn to the typology of empty categories and in section 8 we discuss heavy NP-shift and PP-extraposition from NP.

1   *Wh*-movement: Some Examples

In chapter 6 section 1.2 we gave a brief analysis of *wh*-questions such as (1).

1   Whom will Lord Emsworth invite?

The *wh*-constituent *whom* is the internal argument of *invite*: it is VP-internal at D-structure. We also assume that the auxiliary *will* is base-generated under I.

2a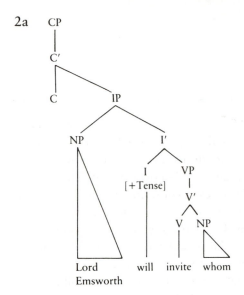

At S-structure, *will* is moved to the position dominated by C through head-to-head movement. Second, and more importantly for the present discussion, *whom* is moved to the sentence-initial position: [Spec,CP]. We postulated that, as was the case for NP-movement discussed in chapter 6, movement of *whom* leaves a co-indexed trace. Using the terminology familiar from chapter 6, we call the moved element *whom*$_i$ the **antecedent** of t$_i$.

2b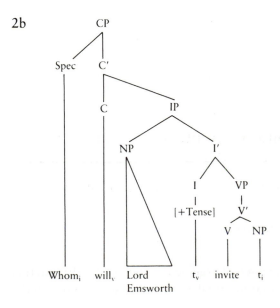

In this chapter we do not deal with the movement of the auxiliary and we concentrate on the movement of elements such as *whom*.[1]

2   The Target of Movement: *Wh*-Phrases

In this section we discuss some of the main properties of the constituent which undergoes *wh*-movement in interrogative sentences.[2] In each of the *wh*-questions in (3) a constituent is fronted:

3a   [What] will Poirot eat?
3b   [Which detective] will Lord Emsworth invite?
3c   [Whose pig] must Wooster feed?
3d   [Where] will Jeeves live?
3e   [When] will the detective arrive at the castle?
3f   [Why] must Wooster feed the pig?
3g   [To whom] will the police inspector give the money?
3h   [In which folder] does Maigret keep the letters?
3i   [How] will Jeeves feed the pigs?
3j   [How big] will the reward be?

From (3) it is clear that the target of *wh*-movement, the moved element, is a phrasal constituent. Various types of constituents can move: NPs (3a,b,c), adverb phrases (3d,e,f,i), PPs (3g,h) and APs (3j). As the reader can verify for himself, the moved element may be both an argument of the verb or an adjunct.[3]

The moved constituent in (3) will be referred to as a **wh-phrase** or a **wh-constituent**. The motivation for the label is transparent in (3a)–(3h): the moved constituent either consists of or contains a word beginning with *wh*-. In (3i) and (3j) the *wh*-questions are not introduced by a word which begins with *wh*-, but we can paraphrase the examples using a *wh*-phrase:

[1]   For a discussion of the movement of auxiliaries, see chapter 10. Verb movement in general is also discussed in chapter 11.
[2]   In sections 6 and 8 we shall see that the range of elements that undergo *wh*-movement includes non-interrogative elements.
[3]   In chapter 9 we shall see that the distinction between arguments and adjuncts is important.

4a   [In *what* way] will Jeeves feed the pigs?
4b   [Of *what* size] will he reward be?

The term *wh*-phrase will also be used to refer to the moved phrases in (3i) and
(3j).

Let us consider the structure of the *wh*-phrases more carefully. In (3a), (3d),
(3e), (3f) and (3i) the *wh*-element is itself the head of the moved phrase (cf.
(5a)). In (3b), (3c) and (3j) the *wh*-element is the specifier of the moved phrase
(5b). We turn to the PPs in (3g) and (3h) presently.

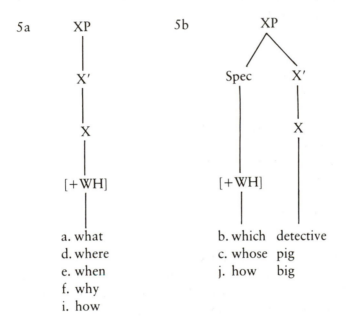

Since the nature of the phrase is determined by the nature of the head it
follows that a phrase containing an interrogative element as its head will be
characterized as an interrogative phrase or a *wh*-phrase for short. Let us say
that an interrogative word carries a feature [+WH]. We have discussed at
length the projection of phrases in chapter 2. The properties of the phrase are
determined by the properties of the head. If a head of a phrase is specified as
[+WH] the phrase will also be specified as [+WH]: the WH-feature **percolates**
from the head of the phrase to the maximal projection.

In (5b) the phrase XP whose [Spec,XP] contains a *wh*-word is interpreted as
an interrogative phrase or a *wh*-phrase. We conclude that the features of the
specifier also determine the features of the entire phrase. This should not
surprise us too much. We have already seen (in chapter 2) that there is often

agreement between head and specifier, for gender and number for instance. We can assume that features of the specifier may percolate to the maximal projection.[4]

In (3g) and (3h) the target of *wh*-movement is a PP. Ignoring irrelevant differences between them, the moved PPs are of the following form:

6

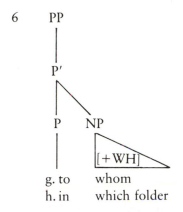

    g. to   whom
    h. in   which folder

The presence of a *wh*-phrase as the complement of the preposition apparently suffices to allow the PP to undergo *wh*-movement. We might propose that the [+WH]-feature of the NP percolates to the PP.

Compare (3g) and (3h) with the examples in (7):

7a [$_{NPi}$ Whom] will the police inspector give the money to?
7b [$_{NPi}$ Which folder] does Maigret keep the letters in?

In (7) the *wh*-phrase is moved out of the PP; the head of the PP is left behind. The phenomenon in which a preposition is left behind after its complement has been moved out is called **preposition-stranding**. The phenomenon where the preposition is moved along with the complement NP is referred to as **pied-piping**: the preposition is pied-piped with the NP. In English pied-piping of prepositions is always legitimate. P-stranding is restricted, as the following examples show:[5]

---

[4] Abney (1987) proposes that NPs should be reinterpreted as projections of the determiner. If this analysis were to be adopted it would obviously also follow that a phrase whose determiner is [+WH] is itself characterized as [+WH].
[5] See Hornstein and Weinberg (1981) and Kayne (1984) for discussion.

8a   ?*Which party did Poirot meet Maigret after?
8b   ?*Whose office did the inspectors discuss the crime in?

The possibility of preposition-stranding is subject to cross-linguistic variation, as illustrated in the following examples:

9a   *French*
    *Qui   as-tu   parlé   de?
    who   have you   talked   about
    'Who did you talk about?'
    vs. De qui as-tu parlé?
9b   *Italian*
    *Cui   hai   parlato   di?
    who   have you   talked   about
    vs. Di cui hai parlato?

The question that should be answered is what explains the difference between language with preposition-stranding, such as English, and languages without, such as Italian and French. Ideally the difference should be related to some difference in parameter setting between the languages.[6] We do not discuss this issue here.

3   The Landing Site of *Wh*-Movement

In this section we discuss where the element which is affected by *wh*-movement is moved to, i.e. its **landing site**.

3.1   *Long vs. Short Movement*

Consider the following example:

10   Whom do you believe [$_{CP_j}$ that [Lord Emsworth will invite]]?

---

[6] Kayne (1984), for example, relates the difference between English and other languages to the fact that in English prepositions assign structural ACCUSATIVE while in other languages prepositions assign an inherent case.

(10) is a complex sentence. *Believe* takes two arguments: the external argument is realized by its subject *you*, the internal argument is clausal (CP_j). We have already seen that *invite* takes two arguments. The external argument is realized by the NP *Lord Emsworth*. It seems natural to say that *whom* is the internal argument. On this assumption, the D-structure of (10) should be (11a).

11a

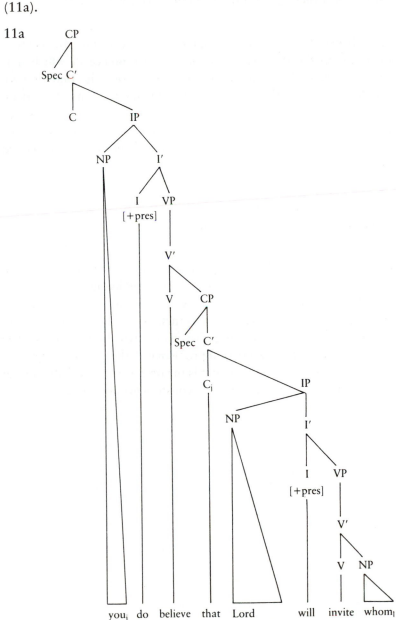

At S-structure *whom* is moved from the lower clause to the [Spec,CP] of the higher clause, leaving a co-indexed trace. In addition the auxiliary *do* is moved to C.

11b   Whom$_l$ do you$_i$ believe [$_{CP_j}$that [$_{IP}$ Lord Emsworth$_k$ will invite t$_l$]]?

The difference between our earlier examples such as (1) and (3), where a *wh*-element moves to the [Spec,CP]-position of the sentence in which it is theta-marked, and examples such as (11), where it moves beyond its own clause to the [Spec,CP] of a higher clause, is often made in terms of **short** vs. **long movement.**

We assume that the reader is familiar with the contrast between direct or **root** questions such as the ones discussed so far and indirect or embedded questions as illustrated in (12):

12a   He wonders [if [Lord Emsworth will invite Poirot]].
12b   I wonder [whom [Lord Emsworth will invite]].

One property that distinguishes root questions from embedded questions is that in the latter the auxiliary does not move: in (12) *will* has not inverted with the subject NP. The D-structure for (12a) will be as in (13). *Wonder* is a two-place predicate, which assigns its external theta role to *he*, the subject, and the internal theta role to the interrogative clause which it governs. The realization of the arguments of *invite* is unproblematic: the external argument is the subject NP and the internal argument is the object NP. The S-stucture of the sentence will also be as in (13) since no constituents are moved.

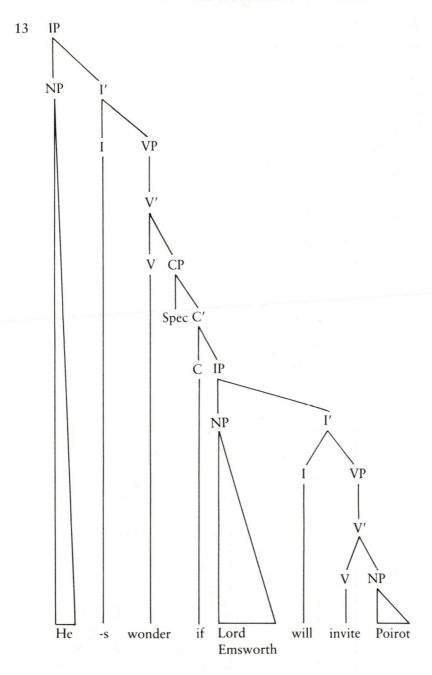

13

What about (12b)? Based on the preceding discussion we propose that the D-structure and the S-structure of (12b) are (14a) and (14b) respectively:

14a

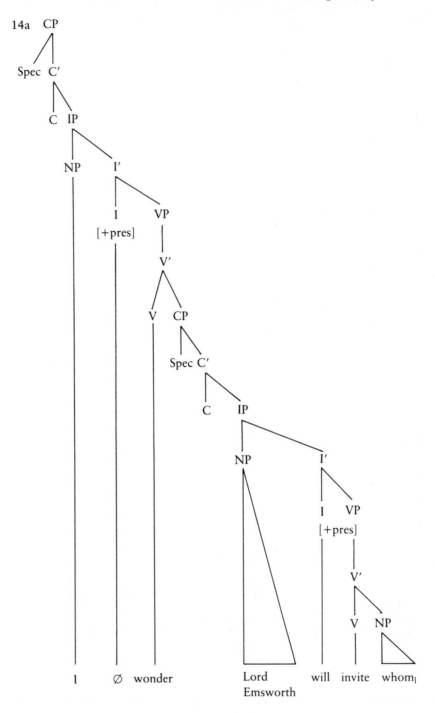

14b

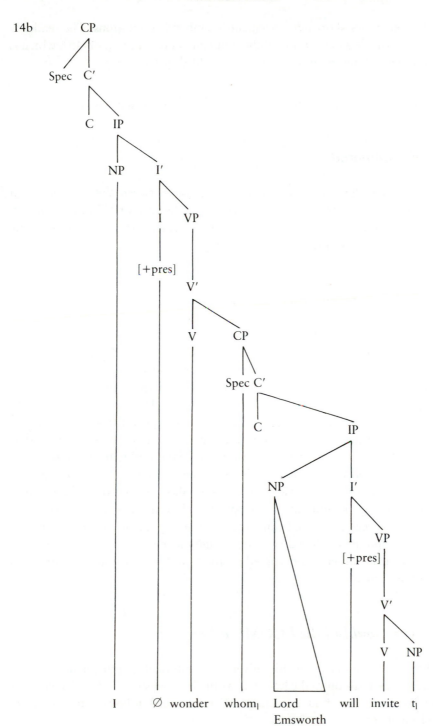

(14) exemplifies short *wh*-movement in embedded questions. The reader is invited to provide a description of the syntactic representation of (15), which is an example of long *wh*-movement in embedded questions:

15   I wonder whom they believe that Lord Emsworth will invite.

3.2   C-command

When we consider the configurational relation between the antecedent of *wh*-movement and the trace we see that, as in the case of NP-movement (cf. chapter 6, 2.3.2), the *wh*-antecedent c-commands its trace. We leave it to the reader to verify this in the preceding examples.

3.3   Wh-movement and Substitution

We have been assuming that the landing site of *wh*-movement is [Spec,CP]. The motivation for this proposal was discussed briefly in chapter 2.

A first and rather natural assumption is that an element moves into an unoccupied position. Remember that we adopted the structure preserving principle for transformations (chapter 6, section 4.1). Considering that *wh*-movement moves phrasal projections of different categories, it is not reasonable to claim that all these categorially distinct *wh*-constituents move to a position that is labelled for one specific category. Rather, the landing site for *wh*-movement must be a position which is not specified for the phrasal category. [Spec,CP] is just such a position: the phrase structure rules allow us to project the position but they do not identify it for a specific phrasal category. A non-filled [Spec,CP] can receive phrasal constituents of any syntactic category: NP, AP, etc. The proposal developed here treats *wh*-movement as substitution: the *wh*-phrase fills a hitherto unoccupied position. In this respect, *wh*-movement is like NP-movement.

3.4   The Doubly Filled COMP Filter

In chapter 2 we have already given an empirical argument for taking [Spec,CP], the position to the left of C, as the landing site of *wh*-movement: in many languages we find sequences of a *wh*-word followed by an overt complementizer:

16a *Dutch*

Ik	weet	niet	*wie*	*of*	Jan	gezien	heeft.
I	know	not	whom	whether	Jan	seen	has

'I don't know whom Jan has seen.'

16b *Flemish* (a dialect of Dutch)[7]

Ik	weet	niet	*wie*	*dat*	Jan	gezien	heeft.
I	know	not	whom	that	Jan	seen	has

'I don't know whom Jan has seen.'

16c *Bavarian German*[8] (see Bayer, 1984a and b)

I	woass	ned	*wann*	*dass*	da Xavea	kummt.
I	know	not	when	that	Xavea	comes

'I don't know when Xavea is coming.'

(Bayer, 1984a: 24)

16d *Early English:*

men shal wel knowe *who that* I am

'Men will know well who I am'.

(Caxton, 1485, R 67, in Lightfoot, 1979: 322).

In modern English there appears to be a restriction barring the occurrence of a *wh*-word in [Spec,CP] when the head of this CP is filled by an overt complementizer. In the literature this constraint is formulated as a filter: the **doubly filled COMP filter**.

17 **Doubly filled COMP filter**[9]

When an overt *wh*-phrase occupies the Spec of some CP the head of that CP must not dominate an overt complementizer.

The label doubly filled COMP was associated with the earlier analysis of clauses as S'. In this type of analysis the positions [Spec,CP] and C were not clearly distinguished. It was assumed that both the complementizer and the moved element in (16) were dominated by the node COMP. For (16a), for instance, the relevant S-structure would have been as in (18).[10]

---

[7] For discussion see Haegeman (forthcoming).

[8] For discussion of the Bavarian data, see Bayer (1984a, 1984b).

[9] The doubly filled COMP filter was first formulated in Chomsky and Lasnik (1977).

[10] There were a number of alternative proposals for the structure of (16). (18) is only one example. We shall leave these divergencies out of the discussion here since they have become obsolete.

18

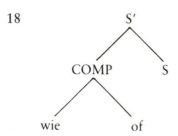

Following the convention in the current literature, we maintain the label doubly filled COMP filter here and reinterpret it according to the CP-analysis of clauses as suggested in (17).[11]

The hypothesis that the landing site of *wh*-movement is the position [Spec,CP], leads us to expect that only one element can be moved to occupy this position:

19a   John wondered which book Bill bought for whom.
19b   John wondered for whom Bill bought which book.
19c   *John wondered for whom which book Bill bought.
19d   *John wondered which book for whom Bill bought.

(19c) and (19d) will be ruled out by our grammar since two phrases would have to be moved to [Spec,CP]. Recall that we cannot move a phrase under C because C is a head position.

However, there are examples from Polish which are problematic (Lasnik and Saito, 1984: 280):

20   Maria zastanawiala się,   kto   co   przyniesie.
     Maria wondered   who   what   would bring
     'Maria wondered who would bring what.'

In (20) two *wh*-phrases occur sentence–initially. If one of them moves to [Spec,CP], the question arises where the second one will go. For such sentences we shall have to assume that a new position is created for a moved constituent. In the next section we shall discuss how such positions could be generated.

---

[11]   As it stands (17) is non-explanatory. It would, of course, be preferable if it could be derived from some general principle.

3.5 Adjunction

3.5.1 GENERAL DISCUSSION

Recall, first of all, our discussion of the structure preserving principle in chapter 6, section 4.1. We have seen that the structure preserving principle does not allow us to destroy existing structure by movement operations, but that it does not exclude that structure be added as long as the resulting representations are compatible with the principles of our grammar. We briefly discussed one example where new structure is generated: free subject inversion in Italian. In this section we shall discuss the proposal that *wh*-movement also creates a new position.

We shall first provide a general discussion of adjunction structures. Schematically D-structure representations are like (21):

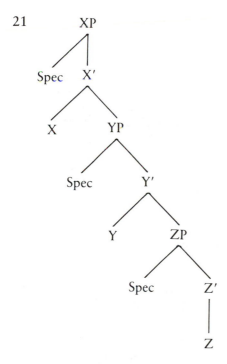

21

For the sake of generality, we leave aside which phrasal categories are involved and what their functions might be. Assume that the constituent ZP is going to be moved and that it cannot be moved INTO a position. This means we must create a new position for ZP. Following the discussion of *wh*-movement so far we assume that moved elements c-command their traces. Suppose ZP moves somewhere in the vicinity of the topmost node, XP.

22a

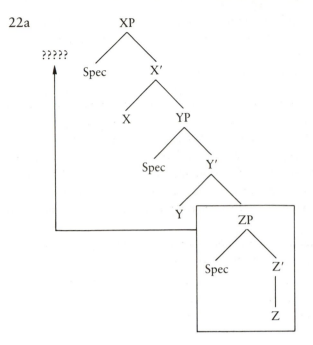

We need to create a node for the moved ZP but in doing so we must respect all the principles of the grammar, specifically the X-bar format for phrase structure. One option is to attach ZP in the following way:

22b

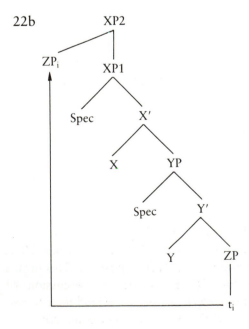

In (22b) a new node XP, identified for convenience' sake as XP2, is created, dominating the original XP, XP1, and the moved element is attached there. As mentioned briefly in chapter 6, section 4.1, this operation is referred to as **adjunction**. Adjunction respects our phrase structure theory: the new constituent XP is headed by X. The node XP created by adjunction is binary branching, etc.

Let us go into the relation between XP and ZP more carefully. There are two nodes XP. XP1 is the original maximal projection. It is sometimes called the **base maximal projection** or the **minimal maximal projection**. XP2 dominates the base maximal projection XP1 and the adjoined ZP.

ZP is dominated by the topmost maximal projection XP2, but it is not dominated by the base maximal projection XP1. YP in contrast is dominated both by XP1 and by XP2. In a way, YP is completely inside the projection of X, YP is **included** in the projection of X. ZP is only partly inside the projection of X, it is not fully part of the projection of X.

In chapter 2 we proposed that syntactic representations be described in terms of dominance and precedence. We may wonder whether the maximal projection of X in our adjunction structure above can be said to dominate the adjoined ZP. Roughly speaking, the answer is 'partly'. Let us adopt the proposal formulated by Chomsky (1986b: 7) based on May (1985) to define the notion **dominance**:

23   **Dominance**

A is dominated by B only if A is dominated by every segment of B.

A is ZP in our example, B is the maximal projection of X. The idea, informally, is that in (22b) the maximal projection of X is the combination of XP1 and XP2. ZP is not dominated by every **segment** of the maximal projection of X: ZP is dominated by the topmost XP2, but it is not dominated by the base maximal projection XP1.

Even though ZP is not dominated by the maximal projection of X, it is not entirely outside the maximal projection of X, being dominated by the topmost XP2. Because ZP is dominated by one segment of XP, we say that ZP is not **excluded** from XP. Following Chomsky (1986b) **exclusion** is defined as follows:

24   **Exclusion**

B excludes A if no segment of B dominates A.

Speaking metaphorically, we could say that a position created by adjunction is like a balcony: when on a balcony you are neither completely outside the room nor completely inside. You may, for instance, easily participate in conversations going on inside while at the same time get dripping wet if it is raining outside.

A restriction imposed on adjunction by Chomsky (1986b) is that phrases can only be adjoined to maximal projections and that adjunction can only be to non-arguments.

We have gone in some detail into the notion adjunction because it will be relevant also for section 8 below and for subsequent chapters.

3.5.2   *WH*-MOVEMENT AS ADJUNCTION?

Let us return to our problematic Polish example (20) repeated here as (25):

25   Maria zastanawiala się, [kto   co   przyniesie].
     Maria wondered   who what   would bring
     'Maria wondered who would bring what.'

The bracketed indirect question is introduced by two interrogative elements *co* ('what') and *kto* ('who'). Consider also (26) (from Lasnik and Saito, 1984: 238, example (11)).

26   Maria myśli [że   co [$_{IP}$ Janek   kupił t]]?
     Maria thinks that   what Janek   bought
     'What does Maria think that Janek bought?'

Since *co* follows the complementizer *ze* and precedes the subject *Janek* in (26), it obviously is not in [Spec,CP]. Let us assume that *co* is adjoined to IP. The relevant part of the structure of (26) would be (27).

27

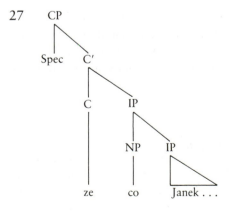

For (25) we propose that *co* is also adjoined to IP, and that *kto*, which precedes it, has been moved to [Spec,CP]:

28

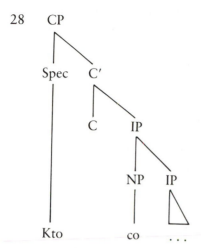

Note that neither (27) nor (28) violates the doubly filled COMP filter: in (27) the position dominated by C is occupied, but [Spec,CP] is not; in (28) [Spec,CP] dominates overt material but C does not.

An adjunction analysis of *wh*-movement in (27) and (28) will allow us to describe the Polish examples.[12] However, the Polish data differ crucially from the English data in that two *wh*-constituents may co-occur sentence-initially. In order to exclude two co-occurring *wh*-constituents in English and languages that behave like English we assume that *wh*-movement in English is NOT done by adjunction but by substitution: *wh*-elements must move to [Spec,CP].[13] Whether *wh*-movement may include adjunction is a matter of parametric variation.

---

[12] We give the Polish data for the purpose of exemplification. Other analyses may be conceivable (cf. Lasnik and Saito, 1984). The reader is referred to the literature. Chapter 9 of this book contains an introduction to the theory developed by Lasnik and Saito (1984) and familiarity with the contents of the chapter will help the reader to follow the article.

[13] In earlier versions of the theory an adjunction analysis had also been adopted for *wh*-movement in English (see Chomsky, 1980, 1981a), but for various reasons such an analysis has been abandoned. Lasnik and Saito (1984) still assume an adjunction analysis for English. I have reinterpreted their discussion in terms of substitution in the subsequent chapters of this book.

3.6   *Movement of Maximal Projections: a Comparison*

At this point it may be useful to summarize the discussion of movement so far and to compare the landing site of NP-movement, discussed in chapter 6, and that of *wh*-movement, discussed in this chapter.

29a   Poirot$_i$ will be invited t$_i$.
29b   Poirot$_i$ seems t$_i$ to be the best detective.

30a   Who/whom$_i$ do you think Lord Emsworth will invite t$_i$?
30b   Who$_i$ do you think t$_i$ is the best detective?

(29) illustrates NP-movement. An NP is moved to the subject position, an A-position. (30) illustrates *wh*-movement: a *wh*-element is moved to [Spec,CP], an A'-position. Based on the distinction in landing sites, we say that the chain created by NP-movement is an A-chain and that created by *wh*-movement is an A'-chain. We distinguish the antecedents of the two types of movement in terms of A-antecedent vs. A'-antecedent. The antecedent of NP-movement c-commands its co-indexed trace: we say that it **A-binds** the trace. In the case of *wh*-movement the antecedent also c-commands the co-indexed trace, but it occupies an A'-position: *wh*-antecedents **A'-bind** their traces (cf. section 7). In later sections of this chapter and in chapter 8, we offer further comparisons between the two types of movement.

4   Traces and *Wh*-Movement

Having looked at the landing site of *wh*-movement, the head of the A'-chain, let us now turn to the position from which the element is moved, the **extraction site** or the foot of the chain.

   As was the case for NP-movement, *wh*-movement is taken to leave a trace co-indexed with its A'-antecedent. Let us refer to traces of *wh*-movement as *wh*-traces and to traces of NP-movement as NP-traces. In this section we provide some arguments for postulating *wh*-traces. As the reader will observe our reasoning in this chapter is closely parallel to that used in chapter 6 to motivate NP-traces.

4.1 Theta Theory and the Projection Principle

One motivation for *wh*-traces is analogy: having posited that NP-movement leaves traces it seems reasonable to also adopt this proposal for *wh*-movement. A second argument comes from theta theory. In chapter 6, section 4.2, we argued that the theta criterion applies to all syntactic levels. Internal theta roles are assigned under government of the lexical head. In an S-structure representation such as (31) *invite* will not be able to theta-mark *whom*, but it will assign the internal theta role to its trace.

31   Whom$_i$ do$_v$ you t$_v$ believe that Lord Emsworth will invite t$_i$?

4.2 Agreement and Binding

In chapter 6, we provided some arguments for traces of NP-movement, based on the locality constraint on certain syntactic processes. The same type of argument can be advanced in favour of co-indexed *wh*-traces:

32a   Poirot thinks [the sergeants are lousy detectives/*is a lousy detective].
32b   Which sergeants$_i$ does Poirot think [t$_i$ are lousy detectives]?

33a   Poirot thinks [the sergeants have left together].
33b   Which sergeants$_i$ does Poirot think [t$_i$ have left together]?

34a   Poirot thinks [the sergeants have done the job their/*his own way].
34b   Which sergeants$_i$ does Poirot think [t$_i$ have done the job their/*his own way]?

35a   Poirot thinks [the sergeants have invited them for lunch].
35b   Who$_i$ does Poirot think [t$_i$ have invited them for lunch]?

In the (b)-examples above a *wh*-constituent has been moved from the lower finite clause to the [Spec,CP] of a higher clause. In all cases a subject NP is moved (we return to movement of the subject in section 5).

The finite verb in the lower clause is plural and must be plural for all the sentences above. This can only be explained if the subject of the verb is plural. We assume that subject-verb agreement is a local process, i.e. that each verb agrees with its own (clause-mate) subject. Under this assumption the co-indexed *wh*-trace in the lower subject position enables us to state the agreement rule in a maximally simple way. Note that this again means that traces have nominal features such as number and person.

In (32) the lower clause contains the copula *be* and a predicate NP. As (32a) shows, the predicate NP agrees in number with the subject of its clause. Postulating a co-indexed trace in (32b) allows us to maintain the idea that subject-predicate agreement is based on a clause-mate condition.

In (33) the lower clause contains the adjunct *together* which must be related to a clause-mate plural NP. The co-indexed trace resulting from *wh*-movement will serve as the relevant NP.

In (34a), the antecedent for anaphoric *their* in *in their own way* is local: it is the subject of the clause. *Poirot*, for instance, cannot serve as the antecedent to *his* in *in his own way* in the lower clause. Postulating a subject trace in the lower clause of (34b) allows us to state the anaphoric relation maximally simply.

In (35a) Principle B of the binding theory predicts that *them* in the lower clause cannot be coreferential with the NP *the sergeants* (see chapter 4 and the discussion of the level of application of Principle B in section 4.5). In (35b) *who* is not inside the GC of *them*. If we assume that there is a *wh*-trace co-indexed with *who* in the subject position of the lower clause then we predict that *them* must not be coreferential with *who*.

4.3 Case

4.3.1 *WH*-PRONOUNS AND CASE

We have seen that abstract case is not often morphologically realized in English. For the *wh*-element *what*, for instance, there is no overt difference between the NOMINATIVE and the ACCUSATIVE, as the following echo questions demonstrate:

36a I think that the castle will be destroyed.
36b You think that WHAT will be destroyed?

37a I think that Lord Emsworth will sell the pig.
37b You think that Lord Emsworth will sell WHAT?

The situation with *who* is different:

38a I think that Poirot will arrive first.
38b You think that WHO/*WHOM will arrive first?

39a I think that Lord Emsworth will invite Poirot.
39b You think that Lord Emsworth will invite WHO/WHOM?

In (38b) the echo question contains a *wh*-constituent in the lower subject position: only *who* is admitted, *whom* is disallowed. In (39b) the *wh*-constituent occupies the object position: both *who* and *whom* are possible in spoken English, in writing *whom* is used. Putting aside many complications with respect to the use of *who/whom* here, we assume that the NOMINATIVE case is morphologically realized as *who* and that the ACCUSATIVE is realized either as *who* or as *whom*. Given this assumption let us turn to (40):

40a Who/*whom$_i$ do you think t$_i$ will arrive first?
40b Who/whom$_i$ do you believe that Lord Emsworth will invite t$_i$?

In (40a) the moved *wh*-phrase is NOMINATIVE; in (40b) it is ACCUSATIVE. In English NOMINATIVE and ACCUSATIVE are assigned at S-structure and under government (see chapter 3 for discussion). Neither in (40a) nor in (40b) do the case assigners, the finite I and the transitive verb *invite* respectively, govern the moved *wh*-phrase. But the traces of *who* and *whom* are governed by the relevant case assigners. We adopt the idea that the trace of *wh*-movement is case-marked, allowing case to be realized on the antecedent. Again the case on the trace will make the theta position visible and will allow the predicate to assign its theta role.

4.3.2 *WH*-TRACE VS. NP-TRACE: MORE CONTRASTS

Let us briefly compare *wh*-traces and NP-traces with respect to the assignment of case.

41a Poirot$_i$ will be invited t$_i$.
41b Poirot$_i$ seems t$_i$ to be the best detective.

42a Who/whom$_i$ do you think Lord Emsworth will invite t$_i$?
42b Who$_i$ do you think t$_i$ is the best detective?

NP-traces are not assigned case. In (41a) the passive verb fails to case-mark its complement NP and in (41b) unaccusative *seem* is unable to case-mark the subject of the lower non-finite clause.

The *wh*-traces in (42) are case-marked: the verb *invite* in (42a) assigns ACCUSATIVE case to its complement; the finite I in (42b) assigns NOMINATIVE to the *wh*-trace in the subject position.

The situation of the antecedent of the trace is reversed: in the case of NP-movement the antecedent is assigned case. In the case of *wh*-movement the antecedent is not in a position to which case is assigned.

(43) summarizes the comparison between NP-movement and *wh*-movement so far.

43a NP-movement
     A-chain
     Antecedent (head of the chain):   +Case
     Trace (foot of the chain):   −Case
43b *Wh*-movement
     A'-chain
     Antecedent: −Case
     Trace: +Case

By simply inspecting the head or the foot of a chain we shall be able to identify the type of movement and its properties. Chapter 8 will offer a more detailed comparison between the two types of movement.

4.4 *Adjunct Traces*

So far we have only discussed *wh*-traces of arguments. However, adjunct phrases may also be subject to *wh*-movement:

44   When did you tell her that Bill is coming?

In the sentence-initial position of (44) we have the temporal adjunct *when*. *When* can be related to, or **construed with**, the activity expressed in the matrix clause, i.e. 'telling', or with that in the subordinate clause, 'coming'. The trace of the moved phrase will indicate which clause the time adjunct modifies (45b) and (45d) suggest the type of answer for each interpretation:

45a When$_i$ did you tell her t$_i$ that Bill is coming?
45b I told her yesterday that Bill is coming.
45c When$_i$ did you tell her that Bill is coming t$_i$?
45d I told her that Bill is coming tomorrow.

5   Subject Movement

In this section we turn to two problems related to *wh*-movement from subject position. Both phenomena will be described here and will be discussed in more detail in chapters 8, 9 and 10.

5.1   *Vacuous Movement*

Let us look at sentences in which the subject is questioned.

46a Who$_i$ do you think [t$_i$ will arrive first]?
46b Who will arrive first?

In (46a), an example of long subject movement, *who* has been extracted from the subject position of the lower clause, leaving a co-indexed trace. In (46b) matters are not so obvious. In the literature two contrasting proposals have been put forward: until recently it was generally assumed that, by analogy with object movement and long subject movement, the subject *wh*-phrase also moves in examples such as (46b). Under this view the S-structure representation of (46b) will be (47):

47   [$_{CP}$ Who$_i$ [$_{IP}$ t$_i$ will arrive first]]?

In contrast with the long subject movement in (46a), the effect of short movement in (46b) cannot be observed on the surface string, t$_i$ having no phonetic content. Movement transformations whose effects cannot be observed are referred to as instances of **vacuous movement.**

Chomsky (1986b: 48–54) argues that the vacuous movement analysis of *wh*-question such as (46b) may not be the optimal analysis. Apart from a

number of empirical arguments which we shall not discuss here,[14] Chomsky
advances an argument from language acquisition. The child who is acquiring a
language uses overt evidence for constructing the grammar and the syntactic
representations of sentences. The child acquiring English and faced with a
sentence like (46b) has no overt evidence for assuming that the subject *who* has
moved. An S-structure like (48) would be equally compatible with the
evidence:

48   [$_{CP}$ [$_{IP}$ Who will arrive first]]?

We shall not decide on either analysis here. Future research will no doubt
provide support for one analysis or the other (see also chapter 10, section 4.1).

5.2   The That-*trace Filter*

Consider the following examples:

49a   Whom$_i$ do you think [$_{CP}$ that [$_{IP}$ Lord Emsworth will invite t$_i$]]?
49b   Whom$_i$ do you think [$_{CP}$ [$_{IP}$ Lord Emsworth will invite t$_i$]]?

50a   *Who$_i$ do you think [$_{CP}$ that [$_{IP}$ t$_i$ will arrive first]]?
50b   Who$_i$ do you think [$_{CP}$ [$_{IP}$ t$_i$ will arrive first]]?

For most speakers[15] there is an asymmetry between the sentences in (49) where
an object phrase is extracted and those in (50) where a subject is extracted. In
(49) it does not matter whether the head of the lower CP is overtly realized or
not; in (50) we can only extract a subject from inside a lower clause provided
there is no overt complementizer. (50a) is ruled out in Chomsky and Lasnik
(1977) by means of a filter:

51   *That*-trace filter
     The sequence of an overt complementizer followed by a trace is
     ungrammatical.

---

[14]   We return to the issue in chapter 10. See also Chomsky (1986b: 48–54) and George
     (1980).
[15]   There is a lot of idiolectal variation which we shall not go into here. An interesting
     survey of intuitions is given in Sobin (1987). This paper presupposes also chapter 8.

As it stands, the filter does not explain anything: it merely states that the sequence *that*-t is ungrammatical. In chapters 8, 9 and 10 we shall see how a more principled account for the filter can be proposed. The filter is not universal though:

52 *Italian*
    Chi   credi   che   venga?
    who   you think   that   come (SUBJUNCTIVE)
    'Who do you think is coming?'

53 *French*
    a   *Qui crois-tu   que   viendra?
        who think you   that   will come
    b   Qui crois-tu   qui   viendra?
        who think you   'who' will come
        'Who do you think will come?'

54 *Dutch*
    %Wie   denk   je   dat   dat   boek   gekocht   heeft?
    who   think you   that   that   book   bought   has
    'Who do you think has bought that book?'

In Italian *che* may be used to introduce a sentence from which a subject has been extracted. However, this is not evidence against the *that*-trace filter. Recall that subject NPs in Italian may also occur post-verbally; it is hence conceivable that *chi* in the Italian example (52) is extracted from the post-verbal position.[16]

Like English, French does not allow the complementizer *que* to introduce sentences from which the subject has been moved. In (53a) we need to replace the complementizer *que* by the form *qui*. This has come to be known as the **que–qui rule** (Pesetsky, 1982), which we discuss in chapter 8, section 4.1.2.

In Dutch there is a lot of dialectal variation as indicated by the diacritic %: some dialects allow the sequence *dat*-trace, others do not.

---

[16] For (52) we could propose the following rough S-structure:

(i)   Chi$_i$ credi [$_{CP}$ che [$_{IP}$ e[$_{VP}$venga t$_i$]]]? (cf. chapter 6, section 3)

The empty subject position marked by *e* would be a non-overt expletive. For a full discussion of the Italian data the reader is referred to Rizzi (1982c).

Leaving aside the cross-linguistic variation and returning to English, we see that the *that*-trace filter in (51) can also account for the judgements in (55):

55a I would prefer Bill to come first.
55b Who would you prefer to come first?
55c I would prefer for Bill to come first.
55d *Who would you prefer for to come first?

The ungrammaticality of (55d) can be related to the ban on a sequence complementizer-trace:

55e Who$_i$ would you prefer [$_{CP}$ for [$_{IP}$ t$_i$ to come first]]?

6 Bounding Theory

6.1 Island Constraints

Consider (56), an example of long *wh*-movement:

56 [$_{CP}$ Which detective$_i$ did you say [$_{CP}$ that Jeeves thinks [$_{CP}$ that Lord Emsworth will invite t$_i$]]]?

The NP *which detective* is moved from the object position of *invite* and ends up in a [Spec,CP] of a higher clause. Research initiated by J. R. Ross in the 1960s (Ross, 1967) has shown that *wh*-movement is not unconstrained.
    Compare the grammatical sentences in (57) with ungrammatical (57d):

57a Poirot told me [$_{CP}$ when$_i$ [$_{IP}$ he had seen Miss Marple t$_i$]].
57b Poirot told me [$_{CP}$ who$_i$ [$_{IP}$ he had seen t$_i$ last week]].
57c [$_{CP}$ Who$_i$ did [$_{IP}$ Poirot tell you [$_{CP}$ that [$_{IP}$ he had seen t$_i$]]]]?
57d *[$_{CP}$ Who$_i$ did [$_{IP}$ Poirot tell you [$_{CP}$ when$_j$ [$_{IP}$ he had seen t$_i$ t$_j$]]]]?

In (57d) *who* is extracted from an indirect question, which is introduced by a moved element *when*. When we compare (57d) with the grammatical (57c) we infer that it is the presence of the *wh*-element *when* that blocks the movement.

On the basis of ungrammatical examples such as (57d), Ross concludes that extraction out of *wh*-questions must be blocked: *wh*-questions are **islands** for movement.

A similar constraint is illustrated in (58):

58a [CP Who_i did [IP he see t_i last week]]?
58b [CP Who_i did [IP Poirot claim [CP that [IP he saw t_i last week]]]]?
58c *[CP Who_i did [IP Poirot make [NP the claim [CP that [IP he saw t_i last week]]]]]?

In the ungrammatical (58c) the *wh*-phrase is extracted from inside a complex NP, an NP whose head N (*claim*) takes a sentential complement. Ross proposes that movement out of a complex NP is blocked. In the literature this constraint is often referred to as the **complex NP constraint**.

Indirect questions and complex NPs are islands for *wh*-movement. The ungrammatical examples above violate **island constraints** on movement. The question arises why there should be such islands and why certain constituents seem to allow movement and others do not.

6.2   Subjacency

In analyses of *wh*-movement an attempt has been made to provide a more general treatment of Ross's island constraints. This has led to the formulation of the **bounding theory**, another sub-component of the grammar which defines the **boundaries** for movement and thus determines how far an element can be moved. It has been proposed (Chomsky, 1973, and later work) that the constituents S and NP are boundaries for movement. In our terminology (see chapter 2) S corresponds to IP. This constraint on the distance of movement is known as the subjacency condition:

59 **Subjacency condition**
    Movement cannot cross more than one bounding node, where **bounding nodes** are IP and NP.

Let us consider how the condition applies to (57). In (57b), repeated here for convenience as (60a), only one bounding node (IP) is crossed and the sentence is grammatical:

60a Poirot told me [CP who_i [IP he had seen t_i last week]].

The problem in (57d), repeated here as (60b), is that *wh*-movement crosses two boundaries of the IP type, violating the subjacency condition:

60b   *[CP Who_i did [IP P. tell you [CP when_j [IP he had seen t_it_j]]]]?

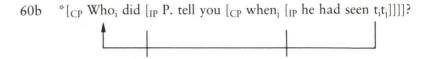

However, if only one bounding node can be crossed, how can we account for the grammaticality of (57c) repeated and annotated as (61a)?

61a   [CP Who_i did [IP Poirot tell you [CP that [IP he had seen t_i]]]]?

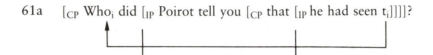

The ungrammaticality of (60b) is due to the presence of the *wh*-element *when* in the lower [Spec,CP]. In (61a) the corresponding position is not occupied by anything. We shall capitalize on this contrast and propose an alternative representation for the S-structure of (57c). In (61a) we assume that the *wh*-constituent has moved in one single leap from its base-position in the lower clause to the matrix [Spec,CP]. However, *wh*-movement in this example need not be a single step movement. Rather than assuming, as we do in (61a), that the *wh*-element moves in one single step from the complement position of *saw* to its final landing site, the matrix [Spec,CP], we could imagine that *who* moves first to the nearest vacant [Spec,CP]. From there, it moves on to the next vacant [Spec,CP] and so on. As we have been doing generally, we also assume that each movement of the *wh*-element leaves a trace. We refer to traces in between the lowest trace and the antecedent as **intermediate traces** (see chapter 6 for intermediate traces of NP-movement):

61b   [CP Who_i did [IP Poirot tell you [CP t_i that [IP he had see t_i]]]]?

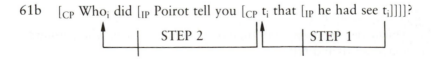

In (61b) each of the two steps is an application of *wh*-movement: a *wh*-phrase is moved to a [Spec,CP]. Each clause (CP) defines a domain of application for *wh*-movement, a syntactic domain in which *wh*-movement can apply or a **cycle**. We say that the movement is successive **cyclic**: it applies in successive cycles. We have seen in chapter 6 that NP-movement is also cyclic. In general it is assumed that transformations are subject to cyclicity: all transformations that are constrained to a lower cycle apply prior to those that involve higher cycles.

As the discussion of (61b) shows, the vacant [Spec,CP] of the subordinate clause serves as a sort of passway for movement: thanks to the availability of this position, movement out of the lower clause can go through. It is like an escape hatch. When this lower [Spec,CP] is filled, *wh*-movement will have to cross two IPs and violate the subjacency condition as is the case in (60b), where there is no escape hatch since the lower [Spec,CP] is occupied by *when*.

The reader might argue that the result achieved in (60b) could have been achieved in another way too. What if we were first to move *who* successive-cyclically to its landing site, the matrix [Spec,CP] and then subsequently move *when* to the lower [Spec,CP]. Let us consider this proposal in some detail. We assume that we can order the movements in such a way that *who* moves before *when* in (57d). Movement of *who* would give us the representation (60c). *When*ⱼ will then have to move to the lower [Spec,CP].

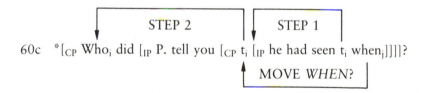

60c *[CP Whoᵢ did [IP P. tell you [CP tᵢ [IP he had seen tᵢ whenⱼ]]]]?

This procedure raises several problems.

The movement of *who* operates on the lower cycle, the lower CP, in Step 1, and then on the higher cycle, the higher CP, in Step 2. The subsequent movement of *when* applies only to the lower cycle, the lower CP. When we move *when* we return to a cycle which we had already 'used' and left in our movement of *who*. The analysis suggested in (60c) violates the cyclicity principle.

Secondly, consider the intended movement of *when*ⱼ in (60c). *When*ⱼ has to be moved to the intermediate [Spec,CP]. This position is occupied by the trace of the moved *who*ᵢ. If we allow *when* to move into this position, it will obliterate the trace (remember there is only one [Spec,CP]) and the A′-chain between the antecedent *who*ᵢ and its trace will be destroyed.

Now let us turn to (58c), a violation of what Ross called the complex NP constraint. In (62) we have charted the route that *wh*-movement could take in this example in order to make maximal use of available empty positions:

62   *[CP Who_i did [IP P. make [NP the claim [CP t_i that [IP he saw t_i

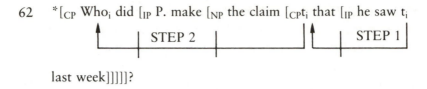

last week]]]]]?

Step 1 is perfectly legitimate: only one bounding node is crossed, IP. Step 2 is illegitimate: two bounding nodes, one NP and one IP, are crossed. (62) shows that complex NP violations can be reinterpreted in terms of the subjacency condition.

In our discussion we have represented each step of the various movements discussed by means of arrows. This was done for expository reasons. The S-structure representation of the sentences itself will record effects of movement: traces indicate the vacated positions and this includes both the D-structure position of the moved phrase and any intermediate steps of movement. By inspecting the distance in terms of bounding nodes between the antecedent and the traces we can determine if the movements respect the subjacency condition or not.

Summing up the discussion: *wh*-movement is subject to the subjacency condition (59). In order to allow for long movement we posit that movement is successive cyclic and that intermediate traces encode each step of the movement.

6.3   *Subjacency as a Diagnostic for Movement*

We propose that *wh*-movement is subject to the subjacency condition. Whenever the possible linking of an empty position and its antecedent can be seen to be subject to this condition we can conclude that *wh*-movement is involved (cf. van Riemsdijk, 1978b). In this section we consider two constructions for which a movement analysis has been proposed: left dislocation (6.3.1) and relative clause formation (6.3.2) and (6.3.3). Using the subjacency condition as a diagnostic we shall show that a movement analysis is not appropriate for left dislocation but that relative clauses are derived by means of *wh*-movement. In section 6.3.4 we shall see that NP-movement is also subject to the subjacency condition.

6.3.1   LEFT DISLOCATION: MOVEMENT AND COPYING?

(63) illustrates left dislocation:

63a   Simenon, I don't like him.

63b   Simenon, I always wonder when I discovered him.

In (63a) the NP *Simenon* is in a sentence-initial position. Let us assume it is adjoined to IP (for adjunction see section 3.4). The pronoun *him* is coreferential with the NP *Simenon*. One might propose that the NP *Simenon* IS the D-structure object of *like* and that it has been moved to the sentence-initial position. The pronoun *him* would then be seen as a pronominal copy inserted at the vacated site.

64a   [$_{IP}$ Simenon$_i$ [$_{IP}$ I don't like him$_i$]].

A closer look at the examples shows that a movement analysis is inappropriate. The distance between *Simenon$_i$* and *him$_i$* is not subject to the subjacency condition: in (64b) two bounding nodes (IPs) are crossed; indicated by #:

64b   Simenon$_i$, [$_{IP}$ I always wonder [$_{CP}$ when [$_{IP}$ I discovered him$_i$]]]
       #   #

This leads us to the conclusion that left dislocation is not the result of movement. The sentence-initial NP *Simenon* has not been moved from inside IP. We assume that the NP is present in the adjunction position at D-structure.

This conclusion is rather important, though. So far we have suggested that adjunction structures are created by *wh*-movement. The examples above lead us to the conclusion that adjunction structures can be base-generated, i.e. that they also occur at D-structure. At this point then, we must reconsider the discussion of phrase structure in chapter 2 and include adjunction structures. The X-bar schema has to be completed with the PS-rule in (65a), where the semi-colon means that order is irrelevant, allowing both right adjunction (65b) and left adjunction (65c):

65a   XP* ⟶ XP; YP
65b   XP* ⟶ XP – YP
65c   XP* ⟶ YP – XP

The X-bar format can then be summarized as in (66):

66a   XP* ⟶ XP; YP
66b   XP ⟶ Spec; X′

66c   X′*————→X′; YP
66d   X′ ————→ X; YP

6.3.2   RELATIVE CLAUSES AND *WH*-MOVEMENT

Consider the following example, with partial bracketing:

67   I know [$_{NP}$ the man [$_{CP}$ whom [$_{IP}$ Emsworth will invite]]].

(67) contains a complex NP with a relative clause: the head noun *man* is modified by a clause (CP). We focus on the internal structure of the relative clause here. Based on the presence of a tensed auxiliary (*will*) and a subject NP we propose that the relative clause is an IP preceded by the relative pronoun *whom*. This is strikingly similar to the structure of indirect questions. Let us assume that relative clauses are sentences, i.e. CPs, and that the relative pronoun *whom* occupies [Spec,CP]. Note that being a maximal projection *whom* could only occupy [Spec,CP], C being reserved for heads. The predicate of the relative clause, the verb *invite*, needs an internal argument. There is no overt element present but by analogy with our analysis of *wh*-questions we propose that *invite* is followed by a trace whose antecedent is *whom*. The complete S-structure of the relative clause in (67) is (68a) and its D-structure (68b):

68a   [$_{CP}$ whom$_i$ [$_{IP}$ Emsworth will [$_{VP}$ invite t$_i$]]]
68b   [$_{CP}$ [$_{IP}$ Emsworth will [$_{VP}$ invite whom]]]

This analysis claims that relative clause formation involves *wh*-movement. If this hypothesis is correct then the relative clause construction should be subject to the subjacency condition on movement (59).

69a   This is the man whom Emsworth claims that he will invite.
69b   *This is the man whom Emsworth told me when he will invite.
69c   *This is the man whom Emsworth made the claim that he will invite.

In (69a) long movement is allowed in relative clauses. (69b) is a violation of the *wh*-island constraint (cf. (57d)). (69c) contains a violation of the complex noun phrase constraint (cf. (58c)). The S-structure representations of the relevant NP in the sentences in (69) are given below.

70a [NP the man [CP whom_i [IP Emsworth claims [CP t'_i that [IP he will invite t_i]]]]]

The violations of subjacency in (69b) and (69c) will be signalled by means of the diacritic # on the brackets.

70b *[NP the man

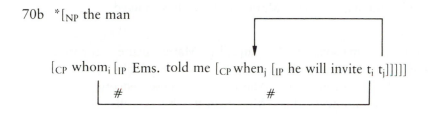

[CP whom_i [IP Ems. told me [CP when_j [IP he will invite t_i t_j]]]]]

70c *[NP the man [whom_i [IP Emsworth made [NP the claim [t'_i that

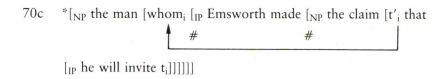

[IP he will invite t_i]]]]]]

Using the subjacency condition as a diagnostic we find confirmation that relative clause formation is indeed a result of movement. In chapter 10 we shall reformulate the subjacency condition in terms of the notion barrier.

As it stands the S-structure representations in (70) are not sufficient to allow us to interpret the relative clause. (70a), for example, does not indicate that *whom_i* is to be linked to *the man*. We assume that the interpretation of the relative pronoun is achieved through a rule of co-indexation where *the man* and *whom* end up having the same index. This co-indexation is used to represent the fact that the relative clause modifies or is 'predicated of' *the man*, it is a **predication rule**.[17]

6.3.3 RELATIVE CLAUSES AND RESUMPTIVE PRONOUNS

In the section above we have seen that relative clauses in English are derived by means of *wh*-movement. However, relative clauses need not be formed by

---

[17] For a discussion of predication the reader is referred to Williams (1980). It is proposed in the literature that the co-indexation rule does not apply at S-structure but at the level of logical form, LF, which is discussed in chapter 9. Further discussion of the predication rule is found in Chomsky (1982: 92–3) and Safir (1986).

means of movement. Consider the following examples from French, taken from Zribi-Hertz (1984).

71a Voici   l'homme$_i$ à qui$_i$ Marie   a   parlé t$_i$.
     here is   the man   to whom   Marie   has   talked
71b Voici   l'homme$_i$ que   Marie   lui$_i$ a   parlé.
     here is   the man   that   Marie   to him   has   talked

72a Voici   la   maison$_i$ à   laquelle$_i$ Marie   pense   encore t$_i$.
     here is   the   house   about   which   Marie   thinks still
72b Voici   la   maison$_i$ que   Marie   y$_i$ pense   encore.
     here is   the   house   that   Marie   of it   thinks still

73a Voici   le   courrier$_i$ qui$_i$ t$_i$ est   arrivé   ce soir.
     here is   the   mail   which   is   arrived tonight
73b Voici   le   courrier$_i$ qu'   il$_i$ est   arrivé   ce soir.
     here is   the   mail   that it   is   arrived   tonight

The (a)-examples above illustrate 'standard' French, the (b)-examples illustrate 'popular' French. The (a)-examples are straightforward illustrations of *wh*-movement: in (71a), for instance, the PP *à qui* is moved to [Spec,CP] and binds a trace in its extraction site. The (b)–example illustrates an alternative strategy for the formation of relative clauses. The relative clause is headed by the complementizer *que* and it contains a pronoun *lui* which is co-indexed (by the rule of predication) with the relativised NP *l'homme*. The pronoun which is related to the relativised NP is called a '**resumptive pronoun**'. Resumptive pronouns are interpreted like *wh*-traces.

English too has a substandard resumptive pronoun strategy for the formation of relative clauses. Zribi-Hertz (1984: 27) gives the following example (from Chomsky, 1982: 11, his (8b)).

74   the man who$_i$ John saw him$_i$

(74) differs from the French examples in that the resumptive pronoun *him* is associated with a *wh*-element in [Spec,CP]. Given that the pronoun occupies its base-position, we must conclude that the *wh*-element must be base-generated in [Spec,CP], i.e. it does not move to that position.[18] An important conse-

---

[18] For French we shall assume that the resumptive pronoun is related to a non-overt element in [Spec,CP]. Such non-overt elements will be discussed in chapter 8, section 4.

quence of this analysis is that because no *wh*-movement is involved, the subjacency condition should not come into play:

75   the man who$_i$ [$_{IP}$ they think [$_{CP}$ that [$_{IP}$ [$_{CP}$ if [$_{IP}$ Mary
                      #   #
      marries him$_i$]] then everyone will be happy]].

The resumptive pronoun *him* is inside a clause introduced by *if*. As (76) shows, such clauses are *wh*-islands:

76   *the man who they think that [$_{CP}$ if [$_{IP}$ Mary marries]] then everyone will be happy

For many speakers of English, the resumptive pronoun strategy is a way of avoiding subjacency violations.[19] (69b) and (69c) will be replaced by (77):

77a   This is the man$_i$ whom$_i$ Emsworth told me when he will invite *him$_i$*.
77b   This is the man$_i$ whom$_i$ Emsworth made the claim that he will invite *him$_i$*.

6.3.4   NP-MOVEMENT

If the subjacency condition is a constraint on movement, then we expect it will also apply to NP-movement. In (78), clearly, the subjacency condition is respected: in (78a) no bounding nodes are crossed; in (78b) one bounding node is crossed.

78a   John$_i$ was invited t$_i$ at Mary's house.
78b   John$_i$ seems [$_{IP}$ t$_i$ to have lost]].

Now consider the ungrammatical (79).

79   *John$_i$ seems [$_{CP}$ that [$_{IP}$ it is likely [$_{IP}$ t$_i$ to resign]]].

We assume that *John* originates as the subject of the lowest clause and has moved to the matrix subject position leaving a trace. (79) is an example of **super-raising**: an NP is raised across an intermediate clause. Super-raising gives

[19] For further discussion see Sells (1984) and Zribi-Hertz (1984: 27–8).

rise to ungrammaticality. The ungrammaticality of (79) could be explained in terms of a subjacency violation. In chapter 6, section 5, we argued that the ungrammaticality of (79) may also be explained as a violation of the BT: the trace in the lowest IP is not bound.

6.4   *The Subjacency Parameter*

Consider the following Italian NPs (Rizzi, 1982b: 50):

80a   tuo   fratello,   a   cui   mi   domando   che   storie
      your   brother,   to   whom   myself I-ask   which stories
      abbiano   raccontato
      they have told
      'your brother, to whom I wonder which stories they told'
80b   il   solo   incarico   che   non   sapevi   a chi
      the   only   change   that   not   you-knew   to whom
      avrebbero   affidato
      they would have   entrusted
      'the only charge about which you did not know to whom they would
      have entrusted it'
80c   la   nuova   idea   di Giorgio,   di cui   immagino che cosa
      the   new   idea   of Giorgio,   of which   I imagine what
      pensi
      you think
      'Giorgio's new idea, of which I imagine what you think'

The English equivalents of (80) are far less acceptable:

81a   *your brother, to whom I wonder which stories they told,
81b   *the only task which you ignore to whom they'd entrust
81c   *George's new idea, of which I can imagine what you think,

The reader will probably be able to identify the English examples in (81) as violations of the subjacency condition. In (81a), for instance, *to whom* has been extracted out of an embedded question introduced by *which stories*, crossing IP$_2$ and IP$_1$:

82 your brother [$_{CP}$ to whom$_i$ [$_{IP1}$ I wonder

                    #

    [$_{CP}$ which stories$_j$ [$_{IP2}$ they told t$_j$ t$_i$]]]]

                #

Apparently this type of extraction is allowed in Italian: omitting irrelevant details the S-structure of (80a) is (83). *A cui* has crossed IP$_2$ and IP$_1$, without any harm.

83 tuo fratello [$_{CP}$ a cui$_i$ [$_{IP1}$ mi domando

    [$_{CP}$ che storie$_j$ [$_{IP2}$ abbiano raccontato t$_j$ t$_i$]]]]

One possibility would be to claim that the subjacency condition is language-specific, like the doubly filled COMP filter, and does not apply in Italian. If this were true one would equally expect that extraction out of any type of indirect questions and out of complex NPs is freely possible, contrary to fact (example from Rizzi, 1982b: 51–4):

84 *tuo fratello, [$_{CP}$ a cui$_i$ [$_{IP}$ temo [$_{NP}$ la possibilità
    your brother to whom I fear   the possibility
    [$_{CP}$ t′$_i$ che [$_{IP}$ abbiano raccontato t$_i$ tutto]]]]]
      that   they have told   everything

Rizzi's proposal to account for the example given here is NOT that subjacency is irrelevant for Italian. Rather he proposes that the bounding nodes are parametrized, i.e. that different languages may have different bounding nodes. While we assume that in English NP and IP are the relevant bounding nodes, for Italian bounding nodes would be NP and CP. On the basis of this proposal the grammaticality of (80) follows: in each of the examples only one CP has been crossed (see (83)). The ungrammaticality of (84) is also predicted. In (85) we indicate the relevant bounding nodes by the diacritic #:

85 *tuo fratello, [$_{CP}$ a cui$_i$ [$_{IP}$ temo [$_{NP}$ la possibilità
                        #
    [$_{CP}$ t′$_i$ che [$_{IP}$ abbiano raccontato t$_i$ tutto]]]]]
    #

In (85) the PP *a cui* ('to whom') originates in the lowest clause: it is the complement of *raccontare* ('tell'). It is first moved to the lowest [Spec,CP], and then it has to move across CP and across NP, crossing two bounding nodes.

The subjacency parameter is one of the earliest formulated in the present theory.[20]

7   Binding Theory and Traces of *Wh*-Movement

7.1   *Typology of NPs*

In the discussion of *wh*-movement it has become clear that some of the *wh*-traces (86) have the status of NPs:

86a   Whom$_i$ will Lord Emsworth invite t$_i$?
86b   Which detectives$_i$ do you expect [t$_i$ to admire themselves most]?

The trace in (86a) occupies a position normally taken by an NP, it is case-marked by the verb and it is assigned a theta role. In (86b) the trace binds a reflexive with which it shares features of person, number and gender. If these *wh*-traces are NPs,[21] the next question is how they behave with respect to the BT. Or to put it differently: what type of NPs are those traces? In chapter 4 we identified four NP-types based on the features [± anaphor] and [± pronominal]:

---

[20]   For a discussion of the subjacency parameter in French the reader is referred to Sportiche (1981). Further discussion of the Italian data is found in Rizzi (1982b). For various modifications of the parameter see also Chomsky (1986b) and chapters 9 and 10.
[21]   Clearly, traces of PPs, for example, will not have the status of NPs but rather that of PPs.

87   Classification of NPs

Type:	OVERT	NON-OVERT
[+anaphor, −pronominal]	anaphors	NP-trace (chapter 6)
[−anaphor, +pronominal]	pronouns	?
[−anaphor, −pronominal]	R-expressions	?
[+anaphor, +pronominal]	— — — — —	PRO (chapter 5)

We have assimilated NP-traces with anaphors. Could we do the same for *wh*-traces? At first glance one might wish to say yes. After all, *wh*-traces need a c-commanding antecedent. But a more careful analysis shows that the correct answer is NO. The moved *wh*-constituent is co-indexed with its trace and c-commands it. Since the *wh*-constituent is in an A′-position, it does not A-bind its trace. We have said (section 3.5) that the moved *wh*-constituent A′-binds its trace. The BT developed in chapter 4 is about A-binding, i.e. binding from an A-position, and says nothing about A′-binding. The reader can verify for himself that the *wh*-trace is not A-bound by anything in its GC in the examples above.

We do not dwell too long on the question whether the *wh*-trace is like the null element PRO, discussed in chapter 5. It must be clear that the *wh*-trace is governed and PRO must not be governed.

Is the *wh*-trace then like a pronoun? Principle B of the binding theory says that pronominal elements must be free in their GC. In other words a pronoun may be bound by something outside the GC. If *wh*-traces were like pronouns they should have the same distribution. Let us try to construct an example:

88a   The detective$_i$ thinks [that [$_{IP}$ he$_i$ likes Bill best]].
88b   *Who$_i$ does the detective$_i$ think [t′$_i$ [$_{IP}$ t$_i$ likes Bill best]]?

In (88a) the pronoun *he* is allowed to be coreferential with the NP *the detective*, since the latter is outside its GC. In (88b) the lowest trace of *who*$_i$ occupies the position filled by the pronoun *he* in (88a). But in (88b) the natural answer is not that 'the detective thinks that he himself likes Bill best', i.e. that the NP *the detective* can be co-indexed with *who* and consequently with the trace of *who*; t$_i$ and the NP *the detective* must not be coreferential in (88b). If the trace of *wh*-movement were like a pronoun then the facts would be rather hard to explain.

Last but not least we turn to the final option: what if *wh*-traces were like R-expressions? Following Principle C of the binding theory they would have to be free everywhere. A brief look at the data above confirms that this is indeed the right answer. The fact that the trace of *who* in (88b) cannot be bound by *the detective* follows directly. The example is structurally parallel to (88c).

88c *He$_i$ thinks [that [$_{IP}$ John$_i$ likes him best]].

We can now identify one more null element in the table above: *wh*-traces are like R-expressions:

89   Classification of NPs

Type:	OVERT	NON-OVERT
[+anaphor, −pronominal]	anaphors	NP-trace
[−anaphor, +pronominal]	pronouns	?
[−anaphor, −pronominal]	R-expressions.	*wh*-trace
[+anaphor, +pronominal]	− − − − −	PRO

In the discussion we have distinguished the concepts A′-binding from A-binding, and A′-bound from A-bound. If we wish to refer to 'any' binding we can use the terms **X-binding** or **X-bound**. Traces must be X-bound.

By way of summary, let us look at some examples of movement in order to see how the BT applies.

90a   Who do you think is believed to be the best detective?
90b   *Poirot seems is the best detective.

We invite the reader to provide the S-structure and the D-structure for these examples before continuing to read. The sentences in (90) have S-structures (91a) and (91b) respectively:

91a   Who$_i$ do [$_{IP}$ you think [$_{CP}$ t″$_i$ [$_{IP}$ t′$_i$ is believed [t$_i$ to be the best detective]]]]?
91b   *Poirot$_i$ seems [$_{CP}$ t′$_i$ [$_{IP}$ t$_i$ is the best detective]].

(91a) contains a combination of NP-movement and *wh*-movement. *Who$_i$* originates as the subject of the lower infinitival clause. Being caseless – *believed* is passive – *who* moves to the subject position of the higher clause where it is assigned NOMINATIVE case. (In passing we draw the reader's attention to the fact that it is quite possible, as in (91a), that a *wh*-constituent undergoes NP-movement.) From this subject position who_i is then *wh*-moved to the matrix [Spec,CP], via the intermediate [Spec,CP]. The trace in the subject position of the infinitival clause has all the properties of an NP-trace: it is caseless, it is A-bound and like anaphors it is bound in its governing category. The trace in the subject position of *is believed* is a trace of *wh*-movement: it has case, it is A'-bound and like R-expressions it is not A-bound.

Let us turn to the ungrammatical (90b), whose S-structure is given in (91b). The idea is here that the NP $Poirot_i$ moves from the lower subject position of a finite clause to the subject position of the matrix clause VIA the intervening specifier of CP where it leaves an intermediate trace. The lower trace in the subject position of *is* has case and thus to all appearances is a trace of *wh*-movement. The lower trace is A'-bound from the intermediate [Spec,CP]: it is the foot of an A'-chain. The analysis implies that NPs can undergo *wh*-movement, a possibility independently allowed as we discuss in section 8.1. Admitting this possibility for the moment without further discussion, the representation (91b) is still problematic: the lower trace, being like an R-expression, must be free. In the example it is bound by the NP $Poirot_i$ in an A-position, the subject position of *seems*. (91b) violates the BT. Movement which goes from an A-position to an A'-position and back to an A-position is often referred to as **improper movement**.[22]

Let us briefly consider another derivation for (90b): take the S-structure representation (92), where we assume that the NP $Poirot_i$ moves directly from the lowest subject position to the matrix position, leaving a co-indexed trace.

92   *$Poirot_i$ seems [CP [IP t_i is the best detective]].

The trace in (92) is assigned NOMINATIVE by the finite INFL of *is*, so we conclude that it is a *wh*-trace. There are two problems with this derivation. First, a *wh*-trace should have an antecedent in an A'-position, which is not the case in (92), and second, it should not be A-bound, which it is.

On the other hand, suppose we were boldly to ignore the case diagnostic and assume t_i is an NP-trace. We only do this to our detriment. An NP-trace is subject to Principle A of the BT: it must be bound in its GC. The GC is the lower finite clause (see chapter 4 for the definition of the GC and for the role of AGR in particular) and clearly the trace is not bound there. Whatever syntactic

---

[22] The term is from May (1985).

representation we imagine for (90b) it will violate some principle of our grammar. (90b) has no legitimate syntactic representation and is ungrammatical.

7.2 Crossover

In the literature[23] the following examples have received a lot of attention (cf. (88b)):

93a *Who$_i$ does he$_i$ think t$_i$ left?
93b *Who$_i$ does he$_i$ think you saw t$_i$?
93c *Who$_i$ does he$_i$ see t$_i$?

The ungrammaticality was at one time attributed to the fact that *wh*-movement moves a constituent across a co-indexed pronoun. It was proposed that these examples are ruled out by the so-called **leftness condition**, reformulated here for expository reasons (Koopman and Sportiche, 1982: 140):

94a **Leftness condition**
     A *wh*-trace cannot be co-indexed with a pronoun to its left.

94b   *Who$_i$ does he$_i$ think t$_i$ left ?

The ungrammatical examples in (93) are usually described as illustrating **'strong crossover'** (SCO).[24] It is clear that such examples can also be explained in terms of the discussion in section 7.1: in all instances the *wh*-trace will be A-bound.

Now consider the contrast in (95). An example such as (95b) is referred to as **'weak crossover'** (WCO). The term is chosen because the ungrammaticality is less strongly felt than that illustrated in (93).

---

[23] See Koopman and Sportiche (1982: 148) and the references cited there.
[24] A first discussion of crossover is found in Postal (1971). This work is written in a pre-government and binding framework but it anticipates a lot of current discussion.

95a Who$_i$ loves his$_i$ mother?
95b *Who$_i$ does his$_i$ mother love t$_i$?

The contrast in grammaticality between the sentences in (95) can also be explained by the leftness condition (cf. Koopman and Sportiche, 1982: 140). The contrast in (95), however, does not follow from the BT. In (95b) the trace is not A-bound: the pronoun *his* does not c-command, hence does not bind, the *wh*-trace. We conclude that SCO follows from the binding theory but WCO does not. One proposal is to maintain the leftness condition. This will rule out both the examples in (93) and (95b). However, there is then some redundancy in our theory since (93) is ruled out both by the binding theory and by the leftness condition. The leftness condition and the BT do the same job in (93), this suggests that one of the two is superfluous. Restricting the leftness condition for WCO seems an *ad hoc* solution.[25]

8   Movement to the Right in English

So far we have been discussing only leftward movement of constituents in English: NP-movement takes a constituent to a c-commanding [NP,IP] and *wh*-movement takes an element to a c-commanding [Spec,CP]. In this section we illustrate two instances of rightward movement,[26] known as heavy NP-shift and PP-extraposition from NP. We shall see that these two are instances of *wh*-movement. Our discussion will entail that the term *wh*-movement is interpreted as movement to an A'-position.

---

[25] For an alternative analysis of weak crossover, the reader is referred to Koopman and Sportiche (1982). Further discussion of crossover and relative clauses is found in Safir (1986).

[26] The adjunction of the subject NP *Giacomo* to the VP in the Italian example (i) is another example of rightward movement:

(i) Ha visto il   dottore Giacomo.
     has seen the doctor Giacomo

8.1 Heavy NP-shift

In chapter 3 we discussed case assignment in English. On the basis of examples like those in (96) we postulated an adjacency constraint on ACCUSATIVE assignment.

96a Poirot speaks English badly.
96b *Poirot speaks badly English.
96c Bertie drinks whisky every night.
96d *Bertie drinks every night whisky.
96e Jeeves introduced him to the guests.
96f *Jeeves introduced to the guests him.

Certain examples seem to disprove the adjacency requirement on case assignment in English:

97a Jeeves introduced to the guests [$_{NP}$ the famous detective from Belgium].
97b My doctor told me to drink every night [$_{NP}$ two glasses of mineral water with a slice of lemon].

The bracketed NPs in (97) are internal arguments of the verbs (*introduce* and *drink* respectively) and are hence directly theta-marked. Theta theory specifies that direct theta-marking is achieved under government. Also, at S-structure the relevant NPs should be made visible by case. In order to account for the thematic relations between the verbs and their complements we assume that the sentence-final positions of the NPs in (97) are derived positions and that the D-structure of these sentences is as in (98):

98a Jeeves [$_{V'}$ introduced [$_{NP}$ the famous detective from Belgium]] to the guests.
98b My doctor told me to [$_{V'}$ drink [$_{NP}$ two glasses of mineral water with a slice of lemon]] every night.

The S-structure of these examples will be (99):

99a Jeeves [$_{VP}$ [$_{VP}$ [$_{V'}$ introduced t$_i$ to the guests] [$_{NPi}$ the famous detective from Belgium]].
99b My doctor told me to [$_{VP}$ [$_{VP}$ [$_{V'}$ drink t$_i$] every night] [$_{NPi}$ two glasses of mineral water with a slice of lemon]].

As is standard by now, we assume that moved elements leave a co-indexed trace. At first sight, one might wish to argue that the trace is an NP-trace: after all, an NP has been moved. This would mean that the chain created by movement is an A-chain whose head is in an A-position. But the traces in (99) are case-marked by the verb. NP-traces are ordinarily not assigned case. We need to determine whether the moved NP, i.e. the antecedent of the trace, is in an A-position or an A'-position. A-positions are positions in which arguments are generated, they are the positions which are assigned grammatical functions such as subject and object. It is obvious that the position occupied by the antecedent in (99) is not the object position, this being the position of the trace. Another property of NP-movement is that it substitutes an NP for an empty NP-position. The latter position is projected but unfilled at D-structure. That there should be an empty NP-position available (at D-structure) to which the NP could be moved is hard to defend. Why should such a position be projected at all?

We need to look carefully at the landing site of the movement illustrated in (99). At the end of the sentence there is no empty NP-position available and also there is no sentence-final categorially unspecified vacant position such as the sentence-initial [Spec,CP]. We conclude that the NP is moved to a position created for it. In other words the moved NP is **adjoined**. (See the discussion of adjunction in connection with structure preservation in chapter 6; and also section 3.4 above.) Let us assume that the moved NP is adjoined to VP producing a structure like in (100):

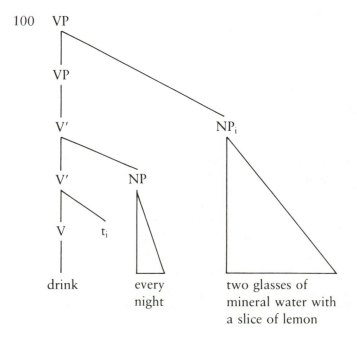

The moved NP$_i$ c-commands its trace, a desirable result since we have seen that both NP-traces and *wh*-traces are c-commanded by their antecedents. Obviously, the adjunction analysis is incompatible with the hypothesis that the chain <NP$_i$,t$_i$> is an A-chain. The adjoined position is an A'-position. We conclude that the chain created by the moved NP in our example is like the chain created by *wh*-movement. The trace is A'-bound. That the trace is assigned case is as expected.

If the empty category in the object position in (100) is indeed a trace created by movement – our hypothesis – then the link with its antecedent should be subject to the subjacency condition on movement. This is easy to check. In (101) we see that rightward movement of NPs must not cross more than one bounding node: NP$_i$ crosses its containing IP and in addition an NP-node and the result is ungrammatical:

101   *[$_{NP}$ The man [$_{CP}$ who$_j$ [$_{IP}$ t$_j$ drinks t$_i$ every night   ]]]

      # #

      bothers me [$_{NP_i}$ two glasses of mineral water with a slice of lemon].

We may wonder why the object NPs in (96) cannot be adjoined to the VP. What distinguishes the grammatical examples from the ungrammatical ones is that the moved NP in the grammatical examples is rather **heavy**. Apparently the adjunction of object NPs to the VP is only admitted with heavy NPs. A precise definition of the concept of heaviness has not been formulated but the intuitive idea is clear. Rightward movement of NPs as exemplified in (97) is called **heavy NP-shift**.

8.2   *PP-extraposition from NP*

In the examples below we concentrate on the bracketed NPs[27]:

102a   I read [$_{NP}$ a description [$_{PP_i}$ of Hockney's latest picture]] yesterday.
102b   I read [$_{NP}$ a description] yesterday [$_{PP_i}$ of Hockney's latest picture].

The sentences in (102) are paraphrases. The bracketed PP is the complement of the head N *description*. We shall assume that the D-structure of the examples corresponds to (102a) and that the surface order of (102b) is derived. The PP$_i$,

[27]   For more detailed discussion of the properties of extraposition of PPs from NPs see Coopmans and Roovers (1986), Guéron (1980) and Rochemont (1978).

of Hockney's latest picture, has been moved out of the NP and is adjoined to the right. Movement of constituents out of NPs is referred to as **extraposition**: PP_i is extraposed from the object NP.

Let us assume that extraposition leaves a co-indexed trace and that the extraposed constituent must c-command its trace. Analogously to the discussion of heavy NP-shift above it would not be reasonable to argue that the moved PP is inserted in an unfilled PP-position. As before we would have a hard time motivating that such a position is projected at D-structure. We conclude that the PP must be in an adjoined position.

Assuming that the extraposed PP in (102b) is in a derived position as a result of movement, we expect the subjacency effects illustrated in (103):

103 $*[_{NP_1}$ A translation $[_{PP}$ of $[_{NP_2}$ a description t_i $]$ $]$ $]$ has

          #   #

appeared $[_{PP_i}$ of Hockney's latest picture].

If PP_i is to be construed with the N *description* then it would have been extraposed out of NP_2 and subsequently out of NP_1. This is not a possible construal.

8.3 *Conclusion*

In section 8 we have illustrated two examples where a constituent is moved to the right: heavy NP-shift and PP-extraposition from NP. Both are assumed to involve adjunction. In both we have argued that the moved constituent is in an A'-position and heads an A'-chain. The trace of the moved element is A'-bound. We conclude that the trace is a *wh*-trace. From now on the term *wh*-trace is to be interpreted as a trace bound from an A'-position. This means that such a trace need not necessarily be bound by a *wh*-constituent, as illustrated in our examples. The term *wh*-movement will be used to refer to movement to an A'-position.

9 **Summary**

In this chapter we have discussed the properties of *wh*-movement. *Wh*-movement moves a constituent to an A'-position, leaving a co-indexed trace.

We have discussed the properties of the target of movement, of the landing site and of the trace. Typically *wh*-movement is involved in the formation of questions, where a *wh*-phrase is moved to [Spec, CP], but we have seen that it is also involved in the derivation of certain types of relative clauses, in heavy NP-shift and in PP-extraposition from NP. *Wh*-movement is subject to the subjacency condition:

1   **Subjacency condition**
     Movement cannot cross more than bounding node.

The bounding nodes are subject to parametric variation. In English IP and NP are bounding nodes; in Italian CP and NP are bounding nodes.
   In addition we discuss two filters which both involve the content of C:

2   **Doubly filled COMP filter**
     When an overt *wh*-phrase occupies the Spec of some CP the head of that CP must not dominate an overt complementizer.

3   ***That*-trace filter**
     The sequence of an overt complementizer followed by a trace is ungrammatical.

These filters are language-specific.
   Traces of NPs which are *wh*-moved are characterized as [−anaphor, −pronominal] and are subject to Principle C of the binding theory.
   In our discussion we have also paid attention to adjunction structures, illustrated in (4):

4   XP$_2$

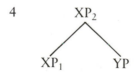

        XP$_1$ YP

In (4) YP is adjoined to XP$_1$. We have shown that adjunction may arise from movement as in heavy NP-shift, for example. However, left dislocation structures suggest that adjunction structures may also be base-generated. We have now extended our phrase structure rules to allow for adjunction:

5a   XP* $\longrightarrow$ XP; YP
5b   XP $\longrightarrow$ Spec; X'
5c   X'* $\longrightarrow$ X'; YP
5d   X' $\longrightarrow$ X; YP.

The relation between the adjoined element and the phrase to which it is adjoined has led us to redefine the notion **dominance** and also to introduce the concept **exclusion**:

6   **Dominance**
A is dominated by B only if A is dominated by every segment of B.

7   **Exclusion**
B excludes A if no segment of B dominates A.

10   Exercises

Exercise 1

Discuss the motivation for the intermediate traces in the following representations:

1a   Who$_i$ does the detective think [$_{CP}$ [t'$_i$ that [$_{IP}$ he likes t$_i$ best]]]?
1b   Who$_i$ does the detective think [$_{CP}$ t'$_i$ [$_{IP}$t$_i$ likes him best]]?

Exercise 2

Consider the following sentences which we have already given in the exercise to the Introduction of this book.

1   *Which man do you know what John will give to?
2   *Which man do you wonder when they will appoint?
3   **Who do you wonder which present will give?
4   *Which present do you wonder who will give?

5   *Which man do you wonder whether John will invite?
6   **Which man do you wonder whether will invite John?
7   **Which man do you wonder what will give to John?
8   **Which man do you wonder when will invite John?

Although none of the sentences above is entirely acceptable to all native speakers, the degree of unacceptability varies. The number of stars is relative to the degree of unacceptability: the less acceptable a sentence is the more stars it has. Try to account for the relative unacceptability of these sentences using the concepts developed in chapter 7. When discussing these sentences you should first of all determine their syntactic representations, D-structure and S-structure. Then you should try to identify which principle or principles are violated.

In your analysis you will no doubt discover that the extraction of a subject *wh*-constituent is consistently more difficult than that of an object. This type of asymmetry was discussed in terms of the *that*-trace filter. From the analysis of the examples above try to check whether the filter as formulated in the chapter is adequate and if not, try to reformulate it. In subsequent chapters we shall return to examples such as these above.

If you are a native (or near-native) speaker of a language other than English then check how translations of examples like those above fare in this language.

Exercise 3

In section 6.3.1 we have seen that an analysis of left dislocation in terms of movement and pronoun insertion is not consistent with our present version of the grammar. A structure that closely resembles left dislocation is topicalization:

1a   Detective stories, I have never liked them.
1b   Detective stories, I have never liked.

(1a) illustrates left dislocation, (1b) topicalization. On the basis of the example above and of the examples given below try to decide whether a movement analysis would be adequate to account for topicalization:

2a   ?*Detective stories, I wonder if he likes.
2b   *Detective stories, I wonder who reads.
2c   *Detective stories, I don't believe the rumour that they will ban.
2d   *Detective stories, I don't like linguists who read.

2e   Detective stories, I expect will be quite successful.
2f   **Detective stories, I expect that will be successful.
2g   **Detective stories, I wonder if will be successful.
2h   **Detective stories, I wonder when will be successful.

Exercise 4

Discuss the derivation (D-structure, S-structure and the various principles that determine them) of the following sentences:

1   Which detective do you think will invite Miss Marple?
2   This is the author whom I like best.
3   Which detective will be invited next week?
4   These are stories which are believed everywhere.
5   Which detective do you think seems to be nicest?
6   Which ships will the enemy sink first?
7   Which ships do you think will sink first?
8   Which sailors do you think will arrive first?

Exercise 5

Compare the properties of NP-movement and *wh*-movement on the
basis of section 2.3 in chapter 6, where we discuss the properties of
NP-movement. Make a list of similarities and differences between
A-chains and A'-chains. This exercise prepares you for the next
chapter.

Exercise 6

Consider the application of the binding theory in the following
examples:

1   Which pictures of himself will John sell?
2   Which pictures of each other do you think that your parents prefer?
3   Those are the pictures of himself which John likes best.
4   Every picture of him, John likes.

Do examples like these produce evidence for Rizzi and Belletti's (1988)
proposal that Principle A can be satisfied either at D-structure or at
S-structure?

Exercise 7

How can the grammaticality judgements of the following English examples be accounted for?

1   **Which book did you wonder when would be published?
2   *Who did Poirot tell you why he had interviewed?

How could we account for the fact that (1) is worse than (2)?
   Consider the following data from Italian (Rizzi, 1982b: 54–6). Can the subjacency parameter discussed in section 6.4 account for them?

3   Non so   proprio chi   possa avere indovinato a chi   affiderò
    not know really   who could have guessed   to whom I'll entrust
    questo incarico.
    this   task
    'I really don't know who might have guessed to whom I will entrust
    this task.'
4   *Questo incarico, che   non so   proprio chi   possa avere
     this   task,   which not know really   who could have
    indovinato a chi   affiderò,   mi sta   creando   un sacco
    guessed   to whom I'll entrust, me is   giving   a   lot
    di   grattacapi.
    of   trouble
    'This task, which I really don't know who might have guessed to
    whom I'll entrust, is giving me a lot of trouble.'
5   Il mio primo libro, che   credo   che tu   sappia a chi
    my   first   book, which I   believe that you   know to whom
    ho   dedicato,   mi   è   sempre   stato   molto   caro.
    I have dedicated,   to me is   always   been   very   precious
    'My first book, which I know that you know to whom I have dedicated
    has always been very dear to me.'
6   *Il mio primo libro, che   so   a chi   credi   che abbia
     my   first   book, which I know to whom you think that I have
    dedicato   mi   è   stato sempre   molto caro.
    dedicated, to me is been always   very   dear.

   Jaeggli (1981: 170) gives the following Spanish data:

7   *el unico encargo que   no sabias   a quién   iban a dar
    the only task   which you didn't know to whom they would give

8   *A quién no sabias   qué le   regalaron?
    to whom didn't you know what they had given
9   *tu hermano, a quièn me pregunto que historias le habran contado
    your brother, to whom I wonder   what stories they have told.

Assuming that the bounding nodes for subjacency may be parametrized (along the lines suggested by Rizzi), would the data above
suggest that the bounding nodes in Spanish are like in English or like in
Italian?

Exercise 8

In section 5.1 we discussed the vacuous movement hypothesis for
subject extraction. Consider the following examples from Chomsky
(1986b: 50, example (109)). According to Chomsky (1) is more acceptable than (2). Would this contrast in grammaticality throw any light on
the discussion in section 5.1?

1   He is the man to whom I wonder who knew which book to give.
2   He is the man to whom I wonder who John told which book to give.

In chapter 5 (section 3.3) we discussed the position of *whether* as being
possibly in [Spec,CP]. According to Chomsky (1986b: 50), example (3)
(his (110)) is more acceptable than (2) above.

3   He is the man to whom I wonder whether John told us which book to
    give.

Does this throw any light on the discussion in chapter 5?

8 An Inventory of Empty Categories

Contents

Introduction and overview

1 Null elements in English: an inventory
1.1 D-structure representations
1.2 Identification of null elements
1.3 Government
1.4 The binding theory and the classification of NP-types
    1.4.1 The typology of NPs
    1.4.2 NP-trace and PRO
    1.4.3 NP-trace and *wh*-trace

2 Null elements in a grammar
2.1 Formal licensing: the empty category principle
2.2 Subjacency and ECP
2.3 Some problems
    2.3.1 Adjunct movement and ECP
    2.3.2 Subject movement

3 Non-overt subjects: the *pro*-drop parameter
3.1 The gap in the paradigm: *pro*
    3.1.1 Null subjects in Italian
    3.1.2 Inflection and *pro*
    3.1.3 The typology of null elements: some discussion
3.2 Cross-linguistic variation: the *pro*-drop parameter
3.3 Licensing of *pro*
3.4 Discussion: the *pro*-drop parameter and the subset principle

Introduction and Overview

Chapters 5–7 introduced three types of non-overt NPs, PRO, NP-trace and *wh*-trace, and at this point it is useful to take stock of the various properties that we have attributed to these non-overt or null elements.

The first part of this chapter provides a survey of our discussion so far and extends our examination of the properties of null elements. We shall introduce an important principle which constrains the occurrence of traces: the empty category principle.

In the second part we look at some more data which will complete our inventory of null elements. We shall discuss evidence for a fourth null element, the zero pronoun *pro*. We also discuss the null operator.

Since much of this chapter is a revision and extension of the preceding part of the book, the reader should find this a relatively straightforward chapter which enables him to consolidate his knowledge and prepares him for the subsequent part of the book in which we shall further develop the grammar which we have been elaborating.

Section 1 contains an inventory of the empty categories discussed so far. Section 2 discusses the licensing of empty categories and the empty category principle. In section 3 we deal with the null element *pro*. Section 4 discusses non-overt antecedents of *wh*-traces and section 5 deals with the parasitic gap phenomenon.

1 Null Elements in English: an Inventory

The null elements introduced so far are exemplified in (1). (1a) illustrates PRO, (1b) illustrates NP-trace and (1c) illustrates *wh*-trace.

1a John$_i$ would prefer very much [[PRO$_i$ to invite Bill]].
1b [$_{IP}$ Bill$_i$ will be invited t$_i$].
1c [$_{CP}$ Whom$_i$ would [$_{IP}$ John prefer [$_{CP}$ t′$_i$ for [$_{IP}$ us to invite t$_i$]]]]?

The three null elements illustrated here all have an S-structure antecedent, an NP with which they are co-indexed, but the status of PRO is quite distinct from the status of traces. And similarly, NP-trace and *wh*-trace can be

differentiated. Let us discuss some of the distinctions between the null elements
here.

1.1 D-structure Representations

D-structure is a representation of the argument structure and the thematic
relations of the sentence. The D-structures corresponding to the S-stuctures in
(1) will be as in (2):

2a [$_{IP}$ John$_i$ would prefer very much [$_{CP}$ [$_{IP}$ PRO$_i$ to invite Bill]]].
2b [$_{IP}$ e will be invited Bill].
2c [$_{CP}$ [$_{IP}$ John would prefer [$_{CP}$ for [$_{IP}$ us to invite whom]]]]?

The D-structures (2b) and (2c) encode the underlying positions of the
arguments *Bill* and *whom* respectively. The S-structures (1b) and (1c) illustrate
the effect of the transformation move-α: *Bill* in (1b) and *whom* in (1c) have been
moved, leaving a trace.

Two comments are in order with respect to the examples. In (1c) there is also
an intermediate trace in the specifier position of the lower CP. We need to
postulate this trace in order to guarantee that the subjacency condition is
observed (see chapter 7, section 6). We discuss the status of intermediate traces
in chapters 9 and 10.

In the D-structure (2b) the empty subject position indicated by *e* is generated
because of the EPP. It is not assigned a theta role since passive verbs absorb the
external argument.

Let us turn to (1a) and (2a) which illustrate the occurrence of PRO. In (2a)
we see that PRO is a D-structure null element. This is an important feature
distinguishing PRO from the traces in (1b) and (1c) which arise at S-structure
as a result of movement.[1]

The reader should find it easy to work out for himself why PRO must be
present in the D-structure representation (2a). Let us follow the procedure we
have adopted for determining D-structure. In (1a)/(2a) there are two verbs:
prefer and *invite*. Both are two-place predicates requiring an external and an
internal argument.

---

[1] Authors who dispense with the distinction between D-structure and S-structure may
   assume one level of representation with traces. Zubizarreta (1987) is one example.
   For this author the lexicon itself contains levels of representation and gives rise to a
   projection of a syntactic level of representation with base-generated traces. The
   reader is referred to her work for discussion.

Given the projection principle, which holds at each syntactic level, the theta roles must be assigned, hence the arguments must be present, both at D-structure and at S-structure. At both levels of representation *prefer* theta-marks the NP *John* indirectly and the clausal complement (CP) directly.[2] *Invite* theta-marks PRO indirectly and *Bill* directly.

PRO is present at D-structure and has its own theta role, independently from the theta role of its antecedent, *John*. The position in which PRO is generated at D-structure is a theta position. The antecedent of PRO, *John*, also has a theta role. We have defined a chain as having one and only one theta position (see (22) in chapter 6); we conclude that PRO and its antecedent are part of two different chains. In (1a/2a) there are two one-member chains: $<John>$ and $<PRO>$. The content of the pronominal anaphor PRO is determined on the basis of the controller: *John*.

The traces ((1b) and (1c)) are members of chains and they share their theta roles with their antecedents. For example, in the D-structure (2b) the internal theta role of *invited* is assigned to the argument-NP *Bill*. At the corresponding S-structure (1b), the internal role of invited is assigned to the chain $<Bill_i, t_i>$.

1.2 Identification of Null Elements

A consideration of thematic properties of null elements helps us to identify the type of zero element we are dealing with: PRO or trace. So far our discussion suggests that D-structure null elements with thematic roles could only be PRO (but see section 3 below for a discussion of *pro*), traces being an S-structure phenomenon by definition.

At S-structure a null element with an antecedent may be either PRO or trace. If the antecedent and the non-overt element each have a theta role, they belong to separate chains, and the non-overt category will be identified as PRO. If the antecedent and the null element share a theta role they form a chain and the null element will be identified as a trace.

Since PRO has its own theta role it may also appear without an antecedent:

3a [CP [IP PRO to invite Poirot]] would be a mistake.

3b [CP [IP PRO to shave myself now]] would be painful.

---

[2] We ignore the hypothesis discussed in chapter 6 that all NPs in [NP,IP] are derived subjects and that external arguments are base-generated in [Spec,VP].

1.3   Government

In chapters 4 and 5 we discussed the status of the null element PRO and on the basis of the binding theory we deduced that this element must be ungoverned. In both (1a) and (3) PRO is indeed ungoverned: CP will constitute a barrier protecting PRO from government (but see the discussion in chapters 9 and 10 for modification of this proposal).

Let us turn to the traces in (1b) and (1c) respectively. We ignore the intermediate trace in (1c), to which we return in chapter 9. Both traces are governed by the verbs, *invited* and *invite* respectively. In section 2 below we shall argue that traces must be governed and we shall discuss this property in detail. The configurational property of government thus also distinguishes traces from PRO: traces must be governed and PRO must not be governed. Looking at S-structure zero elements we can decide on whether they are PRO or trace on the basis of their government properties: a governed empty category can only be a trace, an ungoverned one can only be PRO. In section 3 we identify another null element which is governed: *pro*.

1.4   The Binding Theory and the Classification of NP-types

1.4.1   THE TYPOLOGY OF NPS

We have established that the three null elements posited are specified for the features [±anaphor] and [±pronominal] in the following way:

4   Classification of NPs

Type:	OVERT	NON-OVERT
[+anaphor, −pronominal]	anaphors	NP-trace
[−anaphor, +pronominal]	pronouns	?
[−anaphor, −pronominal]	R-expressions	*wh*-trace
[+anaphor, +pronominal]	– – – – – – – – –	PRO

The importance of a chart like (4) should not be underestimated. What such a representation means is that labels such as trace or PRO are not primitives or unanalysable concepts of the theory. A term such as PRO is a shorthand term for a null element with the feature combination [+anaphor, +pronominal].

Though we shall go on using the terms PRO and trace in our discussion, the reader should bear in mind that these are used for convenience' sake and can be analysed in terms of more elementary properties.

Depending on the feature matrices of the NPs, they are subject to different principles of the BT. NP-traces are subject to Principle A, *wh*-traces to Principle C, PRO is subject to both Principles A and B, hence its special distribution (cf. discussion in chapter 5).

NP-trace and PRO both have the property of being [+ anaphor], in contrast with *wh*-traces. We compare PRO and NP-trace in section 1.4.2. NP-trace and *wh*-trace are [−pronominal], in contrast with PRO which is [+pronominal]. We compare traces in section 1.4.3.

1.4.2   NP-TRACE AND PRO

We have already seen that NP-traces MUST have an antecedent whereas PRO need not have one (see example (3)). Let us consider the relation between the antecedent and PRO or NP-trace. We shall look at the distance between the antecedent and the null element and we shall also consider the type of antecedent. Consider the following examples:

5a   John$_i$ believes [$_{CP1}$ that   [$_{IP1}$ [$_{CP2}$ [$_{IP2}$ PRO$_i$ to invite
         #   #

  Poirot]] would be a mistake]].

5b   John$_i$ told me [$_{CP1}$ that   [$_{IP1}$ it was not easy [$_{CP2}$ [$_{IP2}$
                 #   #

  PRO$_i$ to solve the problem]]]].

Between the antecedent *John* and PRO in (5) there are two IP nodes, marked as IP1 and IP2. These sentences do not violate the subjacency condition discussed in chapter 7: subjacency constrains movement and since no movement is involved in this example the distance between PRO and its antecedent is irrelevant.

We have seen in chapter 7 (section 6.3.4) that NP-movement is subject to subjacency, like all movement. The ungrammaticality of the super-raising example (6) can be explained as a subjacency violation:

6   *John$_i$ seems [$_{CP}$ that [$_{IP1}$ it is likely [$_{IP2}$ t$_i$ to resign]]].

The controller of PRO may be a subject (7a) or an object (7b), or it may be an implicit argument (7c):

7a John$_i$ prefers very much [$_{CP}$ [$_{IP}$ PRO$_i$ to invite Bill]].
7b I told John$_i$ [$_{CP}$ [$_{IP}$ PRO$_i$ to invite Bill]].
7c The house was sold [$_{CP}$ [$_{IP}$ PRO to save money]].

NP-movement moves an element to an A-position, leaving a trace in the base-position. In the case of NP-trace there will thus be a syntactically represented antecedent,[3] the moved element. The presence of an antecedent to bind the NP-trace is also imposed by the fact that NP-traces are subject to Principle A of the binding theory.

NP-movement cannot move an element to an object position. We do not need to state this as an independent principle though. Our theory as developed so far will account for the fact that NP-traces must not have object-NPs as their antecedents. NP-movement is substitution: we move an NP to a position that is empty at D-structure. With one-place predicates like passive *believed* the subject position of IP will be generated (due to the EPP) but empty. Suppose we wanted to move an element into an unoccupied object position. This would involve a derivation like that in (8) with a D-structure (8a) and an S-structure (8b). In order for such a derivation to be possible we would have to imagine that there is a putative verb *BELIEVE* which is like English *believe* in that it takes an external argument and a clausal complement but which differs from English *believe* in that we can also generate an object position.

8a NP1 BELIEVE [$_{NP2}$ e] [$_{IP}$ NP3 to VP]
8b NP1 BELIEVE [NP3] [$_{IP}$ t$_3$ to VP]

In (8a) NP3 is the D-structure subject of the lower IP; it is therefore (indirectly) theta-marked by the lower V and the position it occupies is a theta position. NP3 will be caseless: it cannot receive structural ACCUSATIVE from BELIEVE because it is not adjacent to it, it could not receive INHERENT case from BELIEVE since it has no thematic relation with the verb (cf. chapter 3 on

---

[3] In (7c) the implied AGENT of *sold* controls PRO in the purpose clause. We have argued that the implied AGENT is not syntactically represented, it cannot, for instance, be linked to *together*:

(i)   *The house was sold together.

case). At S-structure we propose that NP3 moves into the position NP2, where it can be assigned ACCUSATIVE by BELIEVE. But the question is what would allow NP2 to be generated in the D-structure (8a) in the first place? D-structure is the representation of thematic relations. VP-internal NPs specifically are projected to realize arguments. This means that in order to be projected NP2 must have a theta role, hence the position occupied by NP2 is a theta position, and the putative verb BELIEVE must be taken to assign one external theta role to NP1 and two internal ones, to NP2 and to the clausal complement IP respectively. If this is true then the chain $<NP3,t_3>$ created as a result of the movement of NP3 will be assigned two theta roles and will violate the theta criterion which states that there is a one-to-one relation between arguments, i.e. chains, and theta roles (see discussion in chapters 1, 3 and 6).

If NP2 were not assigned a theta role, i.e. if putative BELIEVE were like *believe* in that it has only one internal argument, realized by IP, then there could be no motivation for projecting the NP2 position at D-structure. Remember that the EPP forces us to project the [NP,IP] position even in the absence of an argument. But no such principle allows us to generate an unfilled [NP,V'] position at D-structure.

We conclude that there is no verb such as BELIEVE and that NP-movement to an object position is not possible.[4]

1.4.3   NP-TRACE AND *WH*-TRACE

NP-trace and *wh*-trace share the feature [−pronominal]. During the discussions in chapters 6 and 7 and the sections above we have already identified several properties that distinguish NP-traces from *wh*-traces. These concern the target of movement, the landing site, the trace. (9) is an inventory of the main properties.

---

[4] Derivations such as that sketched in (8) were proposed in earlier versions of the grammar where they were referred to as subject to object raising (SOR), in contrast with subject to subject raising (SSR). In the present version of Government and Binding Theory these derivations are ruled out on principled grounds.

9   Traces: survey of properties

	NP-trace	*wh*-trace
Category of target		
	NP	XP (NP,PP,etc.)
Landing site		
	A-position	A′-position
	by substitution	by substitution
		or adjunction
	NP-position	[Spec,CP] or
		adjoined position
Properties of antecedent		
Case	Yes	No
Chain	A-chain	A′-chain
Properties of trace		
Features	[+anaphor]	[−anaphor]
	[−pronominal]	[−pronominal]
Binding theory	A	C
Theta role	Yes	Yes
CASE	No	Yes (when target = NP)
Governed	Yes	Yes

Needless to say, all these properties are not independent of each other. We invite the reader to try and relate them in the way that we have done in the discussion of NP-traces in chapter 6.

2   Null Elements in a Grammar

If we assume that null elements are an actual component of the grammar of natural languages, we must assume that the language learner has the ability to posit such null elements in the representations he assigns to sentences. He needs to have arguments for positing these categories and ways of identifying them. The discussion above has shown that not any null category can appear anywhere, in the same way that overt categories too cannot be generated everywhere. We saw in chapter 3 that overt NPs must be assigned abstract case. Let us say that overt NPs must be formally **licensed** by case. Null elements too must be formally licensed. The learner must know and the grammar must specify (i) in what conditions these elements can occur and (ii) how they can be interpreted, i.e. how such null elements can be given semantic content.

The licensing of PRO has already been discussed. (i) PRO is restricted to occurring in ungoverned contexts. (ii) Its interpretation is determined by control theory.

In the next section we shall consider in what way traces are licensed. The two questions which we address are: (i) in which structural positions are traces allowed to occur and (ii) how are they given content? We shall return to the problem in Chapters 9 and 10.

2.1 Formal Licensing: the Empty Category Principle

In our survey of the properties of traces we have noticed that both NP-traces and *wh*-traces are governed. In Government and Binding Theory, government has been identified as the formal licensing condition for traces: traces must be governed. However, simple government will not suffice to license a trace: traces must be governed in a special way.

The discussion of the government requirement of traces starts out from the **subject-object asymmetry** exhibited in (10) and (11) and already discussed in chapter 7, section 5.1.

10a Whom$_i$ do [$_{IP}$ you think [$_{CP}$ t'$_i$ that [$_{IP}$ Lord Emsworth will invite t$_i$]]]]?
10b Whom$_i$ do [$_{IP}$ you think [$_{CP}$ t'$_i$ [$_{IP}$ Lord Emsworth will invite t$_i$]]]?

11a *Who$_i$ do [$_{IP}$ you think [$_{CP}$ t'$_i$ that [$_{IP}$ t$_i$ will invite Poirot]]]?
11b Who$_i$ do [$_{IP}$ you think [$_{CP}$ t'$_i$ [$_{IP}$ t$_i$ will invite Poirot]]]?

While objects can be freely extracted across overt complementizers, subjects can only be extracted from clauses without overt complementizers. This phenomenon was described in terms of the *that*-trace filter. The *that*-trace filter has been reinterpreted in the light of the government requirement for traces. The idea is that in order to be licensed, i.e. allowed to occur in certain positions, traces must be governed in a special way: they must be **properly governed**. Proper government can be achieved in two quite distinct ways: **theta-government** and **antecedent-government**. A head **theta-governs** a constituent if it both governs and theta-marks the constituent. Antecedent-government is government by a co-indexed maximal projection. At this point we extend our range of governors: either heads or maximal projections can be governors under the right conditions. The licensing condition that traces must be properly governed is known as the **empty category principle**:

12   **Empty category principle: ECP**
Traces must be properly governed.
A properly governs B iff A theta-governs B or A antecedent-governs B (cf. Chomsky, 1986b: 17).

A theta-governs B iff A governs B and A theta-marks B.
A antecedent-governs B iff A governs B and A is co-indexed with B.

The new definition of government in (13) incorporates both head- and antecedent-government. We shall discuss the notion barrier in chapter 10.

13   **Government**
A governs B iff
   (i)   A is a governor;
  (ii)   A m-commands B;
 (iii)   no barrier intervenes between A and B;
 (iv)   minimality is respected.
where governors are: (i)   heads,
   (ii)   co-indexed XPs.

14   **Minimality**
A governs B iff there no node Z such that
  (i)   Z is a potential governor for B;
 (ii)   Z m-commands B;
(iii)   Z does not m-command A.

Let us carefully consider the structures in which the relevant traces appear in the examples above on the basis of the partial tree diagram representations.

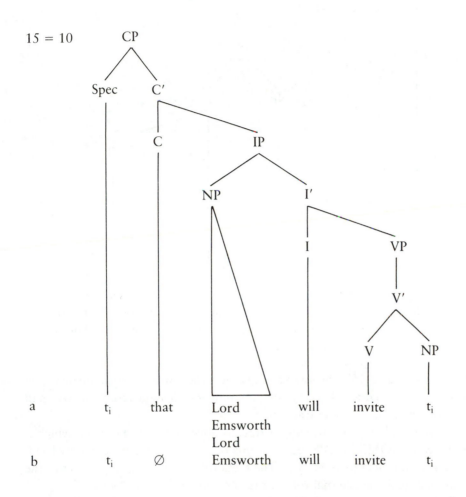

15 = 10

| a | t$_i$ | that | Lord Emsworth | will | invite | t$_i$ |
| b | t$_i$ | ∅ | Lord Emsworth | will | invite | t$_i$ |

16 = 11

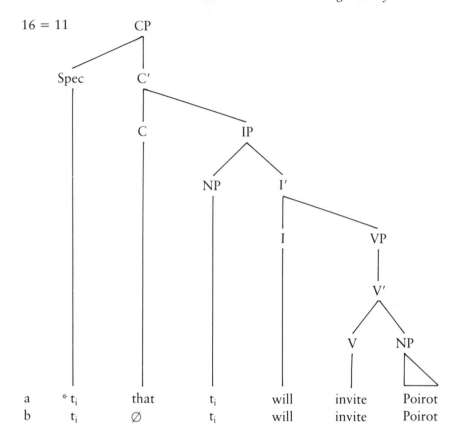

	Spec	C	NP	I	V	NP
a	* t$_i$	that	t$_i$	will	invite	Poirot
b	t$_i$	Ø	t$_i$	will	invite	Poirot

In (15a) and in (15b) the lowest trace is governed by the verb *invite* by which it is also theta-marked. This type of government is **theta-government**. We shall be looking at intermediate traces in chapter 9.

In (16a) and in (16b) the subject-trace is governed by INFL, from which it will receive NOMINATIVE case. But this trace is not theta-governed by INFL since it is not theta-marked by it. The theta role assigned to the subject of the lower clause is the external role of the verb *invite*.

Following our earlier discussion, let us adopt the hypothesis that even though finite INFL is a governor, it is defective. IP, its maximal projection, does not constitute a complete barrier for outside government (see chapter 9 and especially chapter 10, which deals exclusively with the notion barrier). If IP is not a barrier for government, the subject traces in (16a) and (16b) can be governed from outside. This would mean that the subject traces could be properly governed from the outside of IP. Proper government will only be possible by antecedent-government, though, since there is no theta-marker for the subject outside IP.

In (16a) the complementizer *that* intervenes between the trace in the subject position and the intermediate trace in [Spec,CP]. The complementizer is the head of CP, hence it is a potential governor. Assuming that IP is not a barrier for government, *that* governs into IP and will be able to govern the trace in the subject position.

The intermediate trace in the [Spec,CP] position is co-indexed with the trace in the subject position of IP and, assuming again that IP is not a barrier, the intermediate trace should thus be able to antecedent-govern the trace in the subject position.

We have a construction with two potential governors: the complementizer *that* and the intermediate trace. By minimality (14) the co-indexed trace in [Spec,CP] cannot govern the subject trace because the complementizer *that* is a Z in the sense of (14) and will be the governor of the trace in the subject position. But *that* is not a proper governor (12): *that* does not theta-mark the trace and hence does not theta-govern it; *that* is not co-indexed with the trace so it does not antecedent-govern it either. Without a proper governor, the subject trace violates the ECP. In (16b) there is no overt complementizer to interfere with the government from the intermediate trace. Again assuming that IP is not a barrier, the trace in [Spec,CP] can antecedent-govern the subject trace. The subject trace is properly governed.

On the basis of the subject-object asymmetries discussed, the ECP (12) has become established as a licensing condition on traces.

It may be useful to point out a contrast between the ECP and the anti-government constraint for PRO. That PRO must not be governed follows from its feature specifications as already discussed. The ECP, on the other hand, is conceived as a primitive of the theory of null elements. The ECP is a principle which, at the moment, does not seem to follow from anything else in the grammar.

Having established that the ECP formally licenses traces we now turn to the question how their content is recovered. There is a rather natural answer here. We have seen that traces must have an antecedent. The properties of the trace will be able to be recovered by virtue of the co-indexation with its antecedent.

In the next sections we illustrate the ECP and we turn to some problems.

2.2 Subjacency and ECP

Consider the judgements in (17) and (18).

17a ?What do you wonder when John bought?
17b *Who do you wonder when bought these books?

18a   ?What do you wonder who will read?
18b   *Who do you wonder what will read?

Although none of the sentences in (17) and (18) is perfectly acceptable, there is a marked decrease in the acceptability of the (b)-examples. If we turn to the S-structure representations of these sentences we can explain these intuitions:

19a   ?[$_{CP1}$ What$_i$ do [$_{IP1}$ you wonder [$_{CP2}$ when$_j$ [$_{IP2}$ John
            #   #
bought t$_i$ t$_j$]]]]?
19b   *[$_{CP1}$ Who$_i$ do [$_{IP1}$ you wonder [$_{CP2}$ when$_j$ [$_{IP2}$ t$_i$ bought
            #   #
these books t$_j$]]]]?

20a   ?[$_{CP1}$ What$_i$ do [$_{IP1}$ you wonder [$_{CP2}$ who$_j$ [$_{IP2}$t$_j$ will read t$_i$]]]]?
              #   #

20b   *[$_{CP1}$ Who$_j$ do [$_{IP1}$ you wonder [$_{CP2}$ what$_i$ [$_{IP2}$ t$_j$ will read t$_i$]]]]?
           #   #

All the examples above are violations of Ross's *wh*-island constraint. In more general terms they are subjacency violations. In (19a) *wh*-movement violates subjacency: two bounding nodes, IP1 and IP2, are crossed. In (19b) the subjacency condition is violated in a similar fashion, but the sentence is markedly worse. This is due to the fact that not only subjacency is violated but in addition the ECP is violated. The subject-trace in IP2 is not properly governed: it is not theta-governed nor is it governed by its antecedent *who$_i$*. This latter statement depends on the assumption that though the lower IP2 is not a barrier to outside government, the CP2 maximal projection that intervenes between the antecedent *who$_i$* and the trace in the lower IP2 is a barrier. We return to the notion of barrier in chapter 9 and especially in chapter 10.

In (20a) only subjacency is violated. All the traces are properly governed: the object-trace is theta-governed by the verb and the subject-trace is antecedent-governed by *who$_i$*.

In (20b) an ECP violation is added to a subjacency violation. The lower subject-trace is not governed: it is not theta-governed for obvious reasons and *what$_i$* in [Spec,CP2] is not its antecedent, hence cannot antecedent-govern it. Again the real antecedent of the subject-trace is too far away to antecedent-govern it.

2.3 Some Problems

In this section we turn to some problematic examples which our theory so far cannot handle. We shall deal with properties of adjunct traces and with subject extraction. These problems will be tackled more fully in chapters 9 and 10.

2.3.1 ADJUNCT MOVEMENT AND ECP

Consider (21), an example of short movement of a time adjunct:

21a I wonder [$_{CP}$ when$_i$ [$_{IP}$ John bought it t$_i$]].

If the ECP applies generally to traces then we expect that the trace of *when* is also subject to the ECP. In this section we consider the application of the ECP to adjuncts and we shall discover that here are some problems. We return to those in chapter 9.

As an optional time-adverbial, *when* is not theta-marked by the verb. So we shall not be able to claim that its trace is theta-governed by the verb. The only way for an adjunct-trace to be properly governed is by antecedent-government. In this way adjunct-traces are like subject-traces. (21b) is a partial tree diagram representation of the S-structure of (21a).

21b

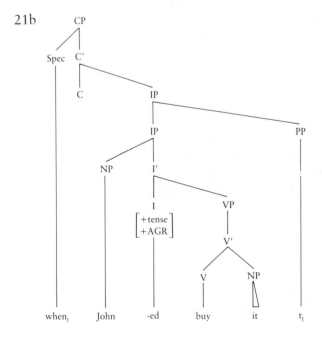

We propose that the time adjunct is base-generated in a position adjoined to IP (cf. chapter 7, section 5 and 5.1 on adjunction). That *when* should be adjoined as a modifier to IP seems intuitively defensible since *when* specifies the time and INFL contains the feature [±tense]. Given this assumption *when$_j$* will antecedent-govern its trace. Hence the ECP is respected.

The assumption that the trace of *when* is outside VP is rather crucial for our discussion. If the trace of *when* had been inside the VP,[5] then it could not have been governed by its antecedent, assuming that VP, unlike the defective I projection, is a barrier for outside government.

But even if the representation of (21a) as (21b) is plausible there are other examples that cannot be handled this way. Certain adverbial phrases must have their D-structure position inside VP and still allow extraction. (This point is raised at some length in Chomsky, 1986b: 19–20).

Consider (22) which is closely analogous to (21) and is equally grammatical. The only difference is that here a manner adverbial has been moved (cf. Chomsky, 1986b: 29, example (37)).

22   I wonder [$_{CP}$ how$_j$ [$_{IP}$ John will fix it t$_j$]].

Traces of manner adjuncts are not theta-governed by the verb. Consequently they can only respect the ECP through antecedent-government. Concerning the D-structure position of manner adverbials like *how* and the corresponding S-structure positions of their traces there is strong evidence that these adverbs are VP-constituents.

23a   What John will do is [$_{VP}$ fix the car clumsily].
23b   [$_{VP}$ Fix the car clumsily] is what they all do.
23c   [$_{VP}$ Fix the car clumsily] John surely did.

In the three examples above the manner adverbials behave as VP-constituents. In the pseudo-cleft sentences (23a) and (23b) the adverb *clumsily* is clefted with the VP. In (23c) the manner adverb is preposed along with the verb and its object. Under this analysis the S-structure representation of (22) would be (24): the trace of *how* is inside VP.

[5]   I.e. as assumed in chapter 2.

24

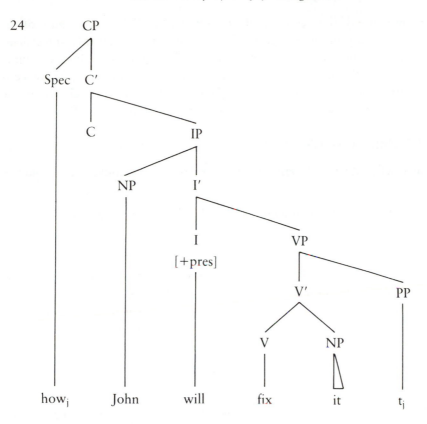

If (24) is the only representation available then the antecedent *how*ⱼ should not be able to antecedent-govern the trace tⱼ. The antecedent is separated from the trace not only by the defective I-projection but also by the V-projection. We have been assuming that VPs are barriers. For example, we assume that I cannot assign NOMINATIVE case to the complement of a verb, because VP is a barrier. It would be a rather drastic step to argue that VP is not a barrier.

Although adjunct traces and subject traces are similar in that they can only satisfy the ECP through antecedent-government, the two types of traces pattern differently with respect to long movement. Compare long subject *wh*-movement in (25) with long adjunct *wh*-movement in (26):

25a *Whoᵢ do [ᵢₚ you think [𝒸ₚ t′ᵢ that [ᵢₚ tᵢ will invite Poirot]]]?
25b Whoᵢ do [ᵢₚ you think [𝒸ₚ t′ᵢ [ᵢₚ tᵢ will invite Poirot]]]?

26a Whenᵢ do [ᵢₚ you think [𝒸ₚ t′ᵢ that [ᵢₚ Emsworth will invite Poirot tᵢ]]]?
26b Whenᵢ do [ᵢₚ you think [𝒸ₚ t′ᵢ [ᵢₚ Emsworth will invite Poirot tᵢ]]]?

The presence of the overt complementizer *that* in (25a) is the cause of the ungrammaticality of the sentence: the complementizer prevents antecedent-government of the subject trace by the intermediate trace. In (26a) the adjunct trace is in exactly the same relation to its antecedent and yet the sentence is grammatical. The ECP is respected in (26a), an unexpected conclusion in the light of our theory so far. We return to the problem in chapter 9.

2.3.2 SUBJECT MOVEMENT

Let us briefly return to (20a), repeated here as (27) for convenience' sake:

27   $[_{CP1}$ What$_i$ do $[_{IP1}$ you wonder $[_{CP2}$ who$_j$ $[_{IP2}$ t$_j$ will read t$_i]]]]$?
           #   #

We have proposed that the relative ungrammaticality of this example is due to a subjacency violation. However, such an analysis presupposes that the subject *wh*-element *who* is moved. An alternative S-structure of this example would be (28) in which *who* stays in the subject position.

28   $[_{CP1}$ What$_i$ do $[_{IP1}$ you wonder $[_{CP2}$ t$'_i$ $[_{IP2}$ who$_j$ will read t$_i]]]]$?

(28) does not violate any principles of the grammar. *What* has moved successive-cyclically, leaving an intermediate trace in the lower [Spec,CP]. The fact that the sentence is not perfectly acceptable must be explained (cf. chapter 10, 4.1).

3 Non-overt Subjects: the *Pro*-drop Parameter

3.1 *The Gap in the Paradigm:* pro

3.1.1 NULL SUBJECTS IN ITALIAN

Our classification of NPs rests on two features [±anaphor] and [±pronominal]. It is easy to see that on the basis of two features, each specified as either + or −, there are four possible combinations.

We have seen that for overt NPs only three of the four combinations are actually realized and we have discussed why the category [+anaphor, +pronominal] is excluded in principle (chapter 4).

For non-overt NPs we should ideally use the same system of classification and thus we also identify four possible combinations. So far we have only identified three and we have not discovered a non-overt corollary to the combination [−anaphor, +pronominal]. Indeed this was the situation that generative linguists had arrived at in the beginning of the 1980s. However, the gap in the paradigm of non-overt categories is not very fortunate. There is no reason why there ought not to be an empty category characterized by the features [−anaphor, +pronominal]. Such an element would be subject only to Principle B of the binding theory (cf. Chomsky, 1982: 78).

Turning to languages other than English, we find evidence for such an empty category. Consider the following examples from Italian:

29a Giacomo ha parlato.
     Giacomo has spoken.
29b e Ha parlato.
        has spoken
29c Giacomo ha detto [CP che [IP e ha parlato]].
     Giacomo has said that has spoken

In (29a) *parlare* assigns an external theta role to *Giacomo*. By analogy we assume that the same is true of the occurrence of *parlare* in (b) and (c). On the basis of the EPP we postulate that there is a subject position, [NP,IP], in all examples in (29). The projected subject position of *ha parlato* in (29b) is an NP-position which is not phonetically realized and to which the external theta role of the verb is assigned. We postulate that the [NP,IP]-position is occupied by a zero element. The question is: what are the properties of this zero NP?

The non-overt subject of (29b) is obviously not a trace, there being no antecedent. It would also not be very reasonable to assimilate *e* with PRO. Recall that PRO must be ungoverned and the finite inflection in (29b) and (29c) will presumably govern *e*.

The empty element in (29b) has definite reference: its interpretation is like that of an overt pronoun. Like a pronoun it may refer to an entity in the non-linguistic context (29b), or it may be co-indexed with an element in the linguistic context. In (29c) one possible interpretation is that the non-overt subject of *ha parlato* is identical to that of the overt subject of *ha detto*.

In other words, the non-overt subject in (29b) and (29c) is the missing non-overt NP that we have been looking for: it is a non-overt pronoun. The null element has the feature combination [-anaphor, +pronominal]. This final non-overt NP is represented by *pro*, 'small *pro*'. Again the label *pro* is only a shorthand label to single out the element with the specific feature combination given.

30a   *pro* Ha parlato.
30b   Giacomo ha detto che *pro* ha parlato.

3.1.2   INFLECTION AND *PRO*

In earlier discussion (chapter 2) we have already seen that any pronominal subject in Italian may remain unexpressed. We posit that the understood subject is syntactically represented by a non-overt pronominal. The subject pronoun is only overtly expressed when it is emphasized; *pro*, being a null element, can obviously not be stressed.

31a   io parlo   *pro* parlo
31b   tu parli   *pro* parli
31c   lei parla   *pro* parla
31d   noi parliamo   *pro* parliamo
31e   voi parlate   *pro* parlate
31f   essi parlano   *pro* parlano

Expletive pronouns in Italian are also realized as *pro*. Since they contribute nothing to the interpretation of a sentence, expletives will never be stressed, hence they will never be overt.[6]

32   *pro* Sembra che Gianni sia ammalato.
         seems   that Gianni is (subjunctive) ill

In (32) we assume that the subject position is filled by *pro*, which in this example is a non-overt expletive pronoun.

3.1.3   THE TYPOLOGY OF NULL ELEMENTS: SOME DISCUSSION

Let us complete our survey of NP-types:

---

[6] The same observation holds for *weather*-verbs such as *rain*, *snow*, etc. In Italian their subject is never overt.

33   Classification of NPs

Type:	OVERT	NON-OVERT
[+anaphor, −pronominal]	anaphors	NP-trace
[−anaphor, +pronominal]	pronouns	*pro*
[−anaphor, −pronominal]	R-expressions.	*wh*-trace
[+anaphor, +pronominal]	− − − − − − − − − −	PRO

Consider (34):

34   Ho   telefonato.
      (I) have   telephoned

Telefonare assigns an external theta role. The D-structure of (34) is (35a) and the S-structure (35b):

35a   *pro* Ho telefonato.
35b   *pro* Ho telefonato.

pro must be projected at D-structure because the external theta role of *telefonare* must be assigned. Like PRO, *pro* is present at D-structure. Even when coreferential with some antecedent, *pro* will not form a chain with the antecedent: both *pro* and the antecedent have their own theta role:

36   Giacomo$_i$ ha   detto   che   *pro*$_i$ ha   telefonato.
      Giacomo   has   said   that   (he)   has   telephoned

   The two null elements specified as [+pronominal] are both present at D-structure. Those specified as [−pronominal] are generated by movement. In contrast with PRO, which must be ungoverned, *pro* is found in governed positions: it alternates with overt pronouns which will have to occur in governed positions since they must be assigned case.

3.2   *Cross-linguistic Variation: the* **Pro**-*drop Parameter*

We have now established the existence of a fourth non-overt NP, with the features [−anaphor, +pronominal], *pro*. So far we have given examples from Italian. The English analogues of the Italian examples discussed above show that *pro* subjects are not a universal property of all human languages.[7]

[7] For a survey of a range of languages see Jaeggli and Safir (1989). Various articles in this volume propose alternative accounts to the one given in this book.

37a *Has spoken.
37b *John has said that has spoken.

It is intuitively clear what allows the subject to be unexpressed in Italian and disallows this in English. In Italian the verb inflection is rich. As discussed in chapter 2, there are six different present-tense forms in Italian, one for each person and number combination. This will allow one to identify the person and number of the subject even when the overt pronoun is absent. In English only third person subjects in the simple present can be identified on the basis of the verb inflection, English inflection is otherwise too poor to enable one to identify person and number of the subject on the basis of verb forms only.

Let us exploit this distinction and say that a rich INFL may identify an empty category in the subject position while a poor INFL fails to do so. In other words the grammatical features of the subject can be recovered from those of INFL, specifically from AGR, in languages with rich verb inflection. In English these features are not recoverable because its AGR is too poor. The identification of the subject features via AGR is represented by co-indexation:[8]

38   pro_i parlo$_i$

Languages which allow a pronominal subject to be left unexpressed are called **pro-drop languages**, they 'drop' the subject pronoun. Italian is a *pro*-drop language, English is not. This cross-linguistic variation is referred to as the **pro-drop parameter**. A child learning the language will have to discover whether the language he or she is exposed to is *pro*-drop or not. Clearly not very much overt evidence is needed to establish that subject pronouns can be left unexpressed. A child will have to set the *pro*-drop parameter either positively or negatively: the positive setting means that the language is a *pro*-drop language. For some discussion of the acquisition of *pro*-drop see the discussion of the subset principle in the Introduction of this book. We return briefly to the issue below.

Spanish is like Italian in that it allows null subjects, but French is like English in that it does not have null subjects.[9]

---

[8] The agreement between [NP,IP] and [I] is also often represented by co-superscripting:

(i)   pro^i parlo^i

[9] In chapter 12 we turn to other properties of Romance languages.

39   *Spanish*
39a   *pro* Vimos a Juan.
       Ø (We) see Juan.
39b   *pro* Baila bien.
       Ø (He/She) dances well.
39c   *pro* Estamos cansadisimos.
       Ø (We) are very tired.

40   *French*
40a   **pro* Voyons Jean.
       Ø (We) see Jean.
cf.   Nous voyons Jean.
40b   **pro*   Danse   bien.
       Ø (He/She)   dances   well
cf.   Il/elle danse bien.
40c   **pro*   Sommes très   fatigués.
       Ø (We)   are   very   tired.
cf.   Nous sommes très fatigués.

   Let us look at an interesting example from another language group: Modern Hebrew also allows the subject pronoun to be dropped:

41a   'Ani   'axalti   'et   ha-tapu'ax.
       I   ate-l-sg ACC   the apple
41b   'Axalti 'et ha-tapu'ax.

The *pro*-drop possibility in Modern Hebrew is restricted. Borer (1980, 1983) shows that it is not allowed in the present tense at all and that in main clauses with the future and past tenses it is restricted to first and second persons (Borer, 1986: 392):

42a   Hu 'axal   'et   ha-tapu'ax.
       he   ate-3sg ACC the apple
42b   *'Axal 'et ha-tapu'ax.
42c   'Ani/   'ata/ hu 'oxel   'et ha-tapu'ax.
       I/   you   he eat-sg the apple
42d   *'Oxel 'et ha-tapu'ax.

   Borer relates the *pro*-drop option in Modern Hebrew to the richness of inflection. In the present tense, only gender and number are overtly realized, person is not. The third person is the unmarked form in the other tenses too. The idea then is that not all types of inflection are strong enough to allow *pro*-drop.[10]

3.3   *Licensing of* Pro

Following our discussion of null elements we again ask (i) how *pro* is formally licensed, and (ii) how its content is recovered.

Rizzi (1986a) proposes that in *pro*-drop languages *pro* is subject to two requirements: (i) it is licensed under head-government: in the examples above the null element in the subject position is governed by INFL, a head; (ii) the content of *pro* is recovered through the rich agreement specification.

43   **The *pro*-drop parameter**
43a   *pro* is governed by X^0_y;
43b   Let X be the licensing head of an occurrence of *pro*: then *pro* has the grammatical specification of the features on X co-indexed with it.

Whether a language has any X^0 of type *y* licensing *pro* is a language-specific property. Also the choice of X^0 varies cross-linguistically. In English I is not a choice for X in (43a). Hence null elements cannot occur in subject positions. In Italian and Spanish I is a choice for X^0 in (43a).

Modern Hebrew poses a problem in that I can be a choice for X^0 but apparently only in a restricted way (see (42) above). In certain cases the features of the governing head of *pro* will not be sufficient and hence the content of *pro* cannot be recovered (see discussion above).

Another problem for this account is posed by languages such as Japanese and Chinese. Huang (1984) argues that Chinese allows null subjects, i.e. is a *pro*-drop language, in spite of the fact that it lacks AGR entirely. The same observation holds for Japanese and Korean. Huang's (1984) proposal is to argue that *pro* is possible either in languages with rich agreement or no agreement at all. This generalization does not hold universally, however, since mainland Scandinavian languages too lack overt AGR and still cannot be argued to be *pro*-drop languages (see Platzack, 1987). We shall not go into this problem here.[11]

---

[10]   The Hebrew data are more complicated once we also turn to subordinate clauses. With past and future tenses a null subject is obligatory in any grammatical person in a subordinate clause if this subject has an antecedent in the matrix clause. For discussion of these data and a new interpretation, see Borer (1989).

[11]   For discussion see Huang (1989) and Rizzi (1986a).

The reader will have observed that (43a) does not restrict the licenser of *pro* to inflection only and that in principle other types of heads could license *pro*. We return to this possibility in chapter 12, section 1.1.2.

3.4 Discussion: the Pro-drop Parameter and the Subset Principle

Let us return to the discussion of the acquisition of the *pro*-drop parameter which was briefly touched upon in the Introduction.

We saw that the question involves two components: how do Italian children, for instance, learn that their language is a *pro*-drop language and thus adopt the hypothesis that X^0 is I in (43a). And conversely, how do English children learn that their language is not a *pro*-drop language, and hence that I, for instance, is not a choice for X^0 in (43a).

Recall our informal discussion in the Introduction. The hypothesis is that when constructing a grammar a child starts out with the minimal hypothesis yielding the smallest language, i.e. the parameter allowing the smallest number of possibilities.

If we compare a language in which I licenses *pro* (43a) and one in which I is not a licenser of *pro*, we shall see that the former is 'bigger' than the latter. For every finite clause with a pronominal subject in English (44a), there are two Italian sentences (44b):

44a I speak.
44b (i) Io parlo, AND (ii) Parlo.

With respect to the *pro*-drop parameter, the smallest language will be the one which does not have any licenser for *pro*: in which there is no X^0_y (43a). Any choice of X^0 will increase the set of sentences generated by the grammar and will count as a marked option. Rizzi says: 'the decision to add a given head to the class of licensers is always justified by the primary data' (1986a: 55).

Under this hypothesis we speculate that a child learning a language starts out from a negative setting for the *pro*-drop parameter, i.e. with the assumption that no head is an X^0 in (43a). Overt evidence to the contrary will then fix the positive choice for X^0. Thus the Italian child will decide that X^0 in (43a) is I when exposed to sentences with a missing subject pronoun. A child learning

English will not come across evidence for the choice of I as a licenser of *pro* and will retain the minimal hypothesis (see also Rizzi, 1986a).[12]

4 Non-overt Antecedents of *Wh*-Movement

In this section we reconsider *wh*-movement structures. We shall see that it often happens that the antecedent of *wh*-movement is non-overt.

4.1 Relative Clauses

4.1.1 EMPTY OPERATORS AND OBJECT RELATIVES

In chapter 7 we have discussed the derivation of relative clauses. Consider:

45a This is [NP the man [CP whom John claims that he will invite]].
45b *This is [NP the man [CP whom John made the claim that he will invite]].
45c *This is [NP the man [CP whom John told me when he will invite]].

We established that these examples involve another instantiation of *wh*-movement since they are subject to the subjacency condition (see discussion in chapter 7). The S-structures of the sentences in (45) are given in (46). We indicate the subjacency violations by means of the diacritic # on the relevant bounding nodes.

46a the man [CP whom_i [IP John claims [CPt'_i that [IP he will invite t_i]]]].

46b *the man [CP whom_i [IP John made [NP the claim [t_i

[12] Attractive though this scenario may be, it poses problems. Hyams (1983, 1989) observes that the actual acquisition of English apparently involves an initial stage in which the child assumes English is a *pro*-drop language. The reader is referred to Rizzi (1986a: 526, n. 27) for discussion and a possible solution. For further discussion of the *pro*-drop parameter, see also Jaeggli and Safir (1989).

46c   that [$_{IP}$ he will invite t$_i$]]]]]
        *the man
        [$_{CP}$ whom$_i$ [$_{IP}$ John told me [$_{CP}$when [$_{IP}$ he will invite t$_i$]]]]

But there are other types of relative clauses which we have not discussed at all:

47a   I know [$_{NP}$ the man [$_{CP}$ that Lord Emsworth will invite]].
47b   This is [$_{NP}$ the man [$_{CP}$ that Lord Emsworth claims that he will invite]].

The bracketed CPs in (47) are modifiers of the head noun *man* and thus are relative clauses. However, it is not clear that *wh*-movement is involved since there is no overt *wh*-element in these sentences. On the other hand, we must postulate that the S-structure representations in (47) contain a null element as the object of *invite*, since this is required by the theta criterion and the projection principle:

48a   I know [$_{NP}$ the man [$_{CP}$ that Lord Emsworth will invite e]].
48b   This is [$_{NP}$ the man [$_{CP}$ that Lord Emsworth claims that he will invite e]].

What type of empty category is *e*? From the discussion so far there is not much choice. The *e* is governed and case-marked by *invite* and thus cannot be PRO (which ought to be ungoverned) or NP-trace (which normally is caseless). Two possibilities remain: *pro* or *wh*-trace. The former option is suspicious as we have posited that *pro* is not an option for English.[13] The latter option is more reasonable because we have seen that relative clauses with overt relative pronouns contain *wh*-traces, as illustrated in (46). If the *es* are traces resulting from *wh*-movement, we expect subjacency effects. In (49) we see that there are clear subjacency effects in relative clauses without overt relative pronoun:

49a   *This is the man that Lord Emsworth made the claim that he will invite e.
49b   *This is the man that Lord Emsworth told me when he will invite e.

---

[13]   We return to object *pro* in chapter 12.

To all appearances (49a) is a violation of Ross's complex NP constraint and (49b) is a violation of the *wh*-island constraint. One way of improving these examples is by sticking a resumptive pronoun in the object position of *invite*.

50a ?This is the man that Lord Emsworth made the claim that he will invite him.
50b ?This is the man that Lord Emsworth told me when he will invite him.

In order to account for the subjacency effects in (49) we shall posit that the relative clauses contain a non-overt antecedent, a non-overt *wh*-phrase, indicated by O. This element is the D-structure complement of *invite* and has moved to [Spec,CP] exactly like an overt *wh*-element would do, leaving a co-indexed trace.

51a I know [$_{NP}$ the man [$_{CP}$ O$_i$ that [$_{IP}$ Lord Emsworth will invite t$_i$]]].
51b This is [$_{NP}$ the man [$_{CP}$ O$_i$ that [$_{IP}$ Lord Emsworth claims that he will invite t$_i$]]].

O$_i$ is another null element. The literature is not very explicit about the nature of this element. For reasons to which we return in chapter 9 the element is called an **empty operator**. In the traditional literature this element is sometimes referred to as a zero relative pronoun. The null element O is the D-structure object of *invite*:

52a I know [$_{NP}$ the man [$_{CP}$ that Lord Emsworth will invite O]].
52b This is [$_{NP}$ the man [$_{CP}$ that Lord Emsworth claims that he will invite O]].

At S-structure O$_i$ is the antecedent of t$_i$, which it A'-binds. What type of empty category could O$_i$ be? Let us maintain the assumption that null elements are restricted to the four types as discussed previously. Clearly, O itself is not a trace: it is present at D-structure and it is the head of a chain at S-structure. O$_i$ has itself been moved.

An option adopted in work by Jaeggli (1981) is that O is PRO. The reader may object that in (52) O, as PRO, would violate the anti-government condition on PRO. But remember that we stated that the anti-government condition is not a primitive of our theory. It follows from the feature specification of PRO, which is [+anaphor, +pronominal] and thus subject to contradictory conditions of the binding theory. But the binding theory comes into play at S-structure. (52) are D-structure representations. Hence the fact that PRO would be governed will not lead to any problems.

At S-structure O is moved to [Spec,CP] (cf. (51)). Indeed, if we equate the null element O with PRO, it must be moved since otherwise it would remain in a governed position. In order to maintain the idea that O is PRO, we need to ensure that the S-structure position to which it is moved is ungoverned. This involves the plausible assumption that CP is a barrier for government, and also the less convincing assumption that the complementizer *that*, the head of CP, does not govern PRO, which occupies the specifier position of CP.[14] Clearly, more research is needed to substantiate the claim that O is PRO.

How is the content of the null antecedent in the relative clauses above recovered? Let us assume that like a relative pronoun, O receives its interpretation through the head that it modifies: we assume that O will be co-indexed with the relevant NP by the predication rule mentioned in chapter 7.

Finally we look briefly at the following examples:

53a I know [NP the man [CP [IP Lord Emsworth will invite]]].
53b This is [NP the man [CP [IP Lord Emsworth claims he will invite]]].

(53a) and (53b) are near-identical to (48a) and (48b). The only difference is that the complementizer *that* in the examples in (53) is absent. We do not need to say anything specific about these examples. They exploit a possibility generally available in English: the complementizer *that* may be omitted:

54a I think that Poirot is a decent detective.
54b I think Poirot is a decent detective.

4.1.2 SUBJECT RELATIVES

In (48) and (53) we have given examples of object relative clauses. Let us now turn to subject relatives:

55a the letter which will surprise Poirot
55b the letter that   will surprise Poirot

Adopting our analysis so far we have two possibilities for the S-structure of (55a): either *which* has moved vacuously, leaving a trace in the subject position (56a), or alternatively *which* is unmoved (56b):

56a the letter [CP which$_i$ [IP t$_i$ will surprise Poirot]]
56b the letter [CP [IP which will surprise Poirot]]

[14] We might stipulate that *that* only governs to the right as an *ad hoc* solution.

Remember that traces are subject to the ECP. In (56a) the ECP is satisfied: *which*$_i$ antecedent-governs its trace.

Let us turn to (55b). We adopt the analysis outlined in 4.2.1 and propose that an empty operator O$_i$ has moved:[15]

57   the letter [$_{C'}$ O$_i$ that [$_{IP}$ t$_i$ will surprise Poirot]]

But the S-structure (57) raises questions. In fact, this configuration is the one that was explicitly excluded by the old *that*-trace filter and that we have shown to be ruled out by the more general ECP. According to our discussion the trace in the subject position in (57) cannot be governed by its antecedent O$_i$ because there is an intervening complementizer *that*.

In order to account for the grammaticality of (57) and to preserve the ECP, Pesetsky (1982: 306) proposes that a special rule is involved in this construction. The rule has the effect of collapsing the empty operator in [Spec,CP] and the adjacent complementizer into one constituent which is assigned all the features of the operator:

58   **Complementizer contraction (English)**
      O$_i$ *that* ⟶ *that*$_i$

As a result of the contraction (58) the S-structure of (57) is as in (59):

59   the letter [$_{CP}$ that$_i$ [$_{IP}$ t$_i$ will surprise Poirot]]

That$_i$ will now be able to antecedent-govern the trace. Pesetsky's rule captures the intuition that the element *that* in examples like (57) is not quite the ordinary complementizer but that it also acts like a relative pronoun: *that* unites the properties of C and of the operator in [Spec,CP].

The rule as formulated in (58) predicts that the complementizer *that* can only be turned into a pronoun when it is adjacent to the null operator. The rule cannot apply to a sequence of an intermediate trace in [Spec,CP] and the adjacent complementizer:

60a   *a letter that John said that would surprise Poirot

---

[15]   If *0* is PRO then it must move because its base-position [NP,IP] is governed by I.

60b *[$_{NP}$ a letter [$_{CP1}$ O$_i$ that [$_{IP1}$ John said [$_{CP2}$ t$'_i$ that [$_{IP2}$ t$_i$ would surprise Poirot]]]]]

60c **Complementizer contraction**:

*[$_{NP}$ a letter [$_{CP1}$ that$_i$ [$_{IP1}$ John said [$_{CP2}$ t$'_i$ that [$_{IP2}$ t$_i$ would surprise Poirot]]]]]

Complementizer contraction may apply to the complementizer *that* which heads CP1 (cf. (60c)), but this does not save the sentence. The trace in the subject position of IP2 is not properly governed. The complementizer *that* in CP2 will continue to block government from the intermediate trace in [Spec,CP2]. The rule of complementizer contraction as formulated does not apply to CP2.

Pesetsky argues for the application of a similar rule to explain the alternation between *que* and *qui* in French.

61a l'homme que Maigret a arrêté
the man that Maigret has arrested

61b l'homme que je pense que Maigret a arrêté
the man that I think that Maigret has arrested

62a *l'homme qu'a été arrêté
the man that has been arrested

62b l'homme qui a été arrêté
the man who has been arrested

62c *l'homme que je pense qu'a été arrêté
the man that I think that has been arrested

62d l'homme que je pense qui a été arrêté
the man that I think who has been arrested

Que is the French equivalent of *that*. For the S-structure representations of (61) we propose a null operator analysis:

63a l'homme [$_{CP}$ O$_i$ que [$_{IP}$ Maigret a arrêté t$_i$]]

63b l'homme [$_{CP}$ O$_i$ que [$_{IP}$ je pense [$_{CP}$ t$'_i$ que [$_{IP}$ Maigret a arrêté t$_i$]]]]

We can explain the ungrammaticality of (62a) and (62c) in terms of an ECP violation. Consider the S-structures in (64):

64a *l'homme [$_{CP}$ O$_i$ que [$_{IP}$ t$_i$ a été arêté t$_i$]]
64b *l'homme [$_{CP}$ O$_i$ que [$_{IP}$ je pense [$_{CP}$ t'$_i$ que [$_{IP}$ t$_i$ a été arrêté t$_i$]]]]

The trace in the subject position of the lowest clause is not properly governed: the intervening complementizer *que* governs the subject and, being a closer governor, *que* prevents antecedent-government by the trace in [Spec,CP]. In the S-structures in (64) we have also indicated the trace of NP-movement in the complement position of *arrêté*. Needless to say this trace is properly governed by the verb and is unproblematic.

(62b) and (62d), conversely, are grammatical. The only difference between these examples and their ungrammatical pendants (62a) and (62c) is that *que* is replaced by *qui*. Pesetsky (1982: 308) proposes that the replacement of *que* by *qui* is the overt reflex of the application of complementizer contraction in French:

65 Complementizer contraction (French)

XP$_i$ *que* $\longrightarrow$ *qui$_i$* / $\underline{\qquad}$ [$_{IP}$ t$_i$

The effect of (65) is like that of the English contraction rule given in (58): it collapses a complementizer and an adjacent index-bearing element in [Spec,CP].

But (65) differs from (58) in some respects. The context for the application of (65), which is specified to the right of the oblique, is restricted: (65) only applies to a complementizer which governs a trace co-indexed with the constituent in [Spec,CP]. On the other hand, the French rule applies both to operators and to intermediate traces and it has an overt reflex. The S-structures of the grammatical examples in (62) are given in (66):

66a l'homme [$_{CP}$ qui$_i$ [$_{IP}$ t$_i$ a été arrêté t$_i$]]
66b l'homme [$_{CP}$ O$_i$ que [$_{IP}$ je pense [$_{CP}$ qui$_i$ [$_{IP}$ t$_i$ a été arrêté]]]]

As the reader can verify for himself, (65) applies to *que* in both examples since *que* occurs in the context specified by the rule. The higher *que* in (66b) is not adjacent to a subject trace co-indexed with O$_i$. Subsequent to the application of (65) the subject traces in (66) will be properly governed by the indexed complementizer *qui*. The alternation between *que* and *qui* in French is referred to as the *que–qui* alternation and the complementizer contraction rule for French is often referred to as the **que–qui rule**.[16]

---

[16] For some discussion see Jaeggli (1982), Koopman (1983) and Rizzi (1990). For another example of a similar rule see exercise 1 of this chapter.

4.2 *Further Examples of Empty Operators*

4.2.1 INFINITIVAL RELATIVES

Consider the following sentences:

67a I need a man whom I can love.
67b I need a man that I can love.
67c I need a man to love.

The derivation of (67a) is straightforward. Its S-structure is given without discussion in (68a):

68a I need [$_{NP}$ a man [$_{CP}$ whom$_i$ [$_{IP}$ I can love t$_i$]]].

(67b) is equally unproblematic: we assume that the null operator O$_i$ has been *wh*-moved:

68b I need [$_{NP}$ a man [$_{CP}$ O$_i$ that [$_{IP}$ I can love t$_i$]]].

(67c) is an example of an infinitival relative. We posit that analogously to the previous examples the object of *love* is a null operator that has been moved. In addition, the infinitival clause has a null element as its subject which we identify as PRO. PRO is controlled by the main clause subject *I*.

68c I$_j$ need a man [$_{CP}$ O$_i$ [$_{IP}$ PRO$_j$ to love t$_i$]].

4.2.2 INFINITIVAL ADJUNCTS

Another construction for which the null operator hypothesis has been advocated is given in (69):

69 John is too stubborn to invite.

The infinitival clause expresses a purpose. (69) is parallel in structure to (70):

70a John is too stubborn [$_{CP}$ for [$_{IP}$ us to invite him]].

70b John is too stubborn [$_{CP}$ for [$_{IP}$ us to invite]].

In (70a) the external argument of *invite* is *us*, the subject NP, and the internal argument is *him*, the direct object NP. For (70b) we assume that the complement of *invite* is a null element which is both governed and case-marked. The most obvious hypothesis is that it is a *wh*-trace, i.e. that it is an A'-bound zero element.[17]

71   John$_i$ is too stubborn [$_{CP}$ O$_i$ for [$_{IP}$ us to invite t$_i$]].

The reader can check for himself that it will not do to argue that the null element in the object position of *invite* is PRO because this would violate the anti-government condition on PRO. The NP-trace option is equally unlikely. On the one hand, the null element is assigned ACCUSATIVE case and NP-traces are caseless. On the other hand, if the null element were identified as an NP-trace it would be subject to Principle A of the binding theory: it would have to be bound in its GC. The GC for the NP in the object-position of *invite* is the lower clause: it contains both a governor (*invite*) and a subject (*us*). It follows that if we identified the null complement of *invite* as an NP-trace, this trace would be A-free and hence it would violate Principle A of the binding theory.

On the analogy of the sentences in (70) with that in (69) it is reasonable to postulate that both the subject and the object in (69) are non-overt categories. The subject of the infinitive is PRO; the object will be assumed to be a trace co-indexed with a moved zero operator:

72   John$_i$ is too stubborn [$_{CP}$ O$_i$ [$_{IP}$ PRO to invite t$_i$]]

The hypothesis that movement is involved in (71 = 70b) and (72 = 69) and not, of course, in (70a), can be tested if we check for subjacency effects:

73a John is too stubborn for us to even wonder when to invite him.
73b *John is too stubborn for us to even wonder when to invite.
73c *John is too stubborn to even wonder when to invite.

---

[17] We leave aside the option that *pro* occurs in the object position. We turn to object *pro* in chapter 12.

4.2.3 PRINCIPLE C AND OPERATOR BINDING

One potential problem has to be tackled here. We have seen that traces of *wh*-movement are like R-expressions and hence subject to Principle C of the binding theory: they must be free everywhere. In fact, Principle C appears at first sight to be violated in both (71) and (72) where the trace of the moved operator is co-indexed with John$_i$, a c-commanding NP in an A-position.

In his discussion of such examples Chomsky (1986a) proposes that Principle C of the binding theory should be reformulated as follows:

74 Principle C
 a An R-expression must be A-free in the domain of its operator.
 b An R-expression must be A-free.
 (Chomsky, 1986a: 86)

The term operator can be taken to be equivalent to the head of an A′-chain. Principle C is now stated as a disjunction: it contains two clauses either of which will apply. First, we apply clause (74a): it will apply to all R-expressions which are operator-bound, i.e. it applies to traces of movement. If (74a) does not apply, i.e. when the R-expression is not bound by an operator, we apply (74b).[18]

5 Parasitic Gaps

5.1 Description

This section deals with a quite unusual construction which has been the subject of much discussion in the literature.

75a Poirot is a man whom you distrust when you meet.
75b Poirot is a man that anyone that talks to usually likes.

[18] For further revisions of Principle C the reader is referred to Chomsky's own discussion (1986a: 98).

We focus solely on (75a). The analysis carries over to (75b). (75a) contains a complex relative clause with two verbs: *distrust* in the higher clause and *meet* in the time clause. Both verbs are two-place predicates which assign an external and an internal theta role. The question that we ask here is: how are the internal arguments realized? Adopting our by now familiar strategy we assume that the complements of the verbs are null elements:

76   Poirot is a man [$_{CP}$ whom [$_{IP}$ you distrust e$_1$ [$_{CP}$ when [$_{IP}$ you meet e$_2$]]]].

Let us try to identify the type of null element represented by e_1 and e_2 respectively. Both *es* in (76) occur in a governed position in which they are assigned ACCUSATIVE case. The most plausible option is to say that they are *wh*-traces. For e_1 this is reasonable enough: *e* would be a trace co-indexed with *whom* exactly like in (77):

77   Poirot is a man [$_{CP}$ whom$_i$ [$_{IP}$ I distrust t$_i$]].

E_2 is problematic. If it is co-indexed with an antecedent relative pronoun, then where is the pronoun? As far as the meaning goes, e_2 is interpreted as coreferential with e_1. One might want to say that, like e_1, e_2 is bound by *whom*, but this hypothesis raises problems.

On the one hand, extraction from adverbial clauses introduced by *when* normally leads to subjacency effects:

78   *Poirot is a man whom I yawn [when I see].

In addition the hypothesis that *whom* is the antecedent of e_2 and of e_1 means that it is the antecedent of two *es*. But it is not possible to argue that one element, *whom*, has been moved from the two distinct positions indicated by *e*. *Whom* should have one and only one D-structure position, either the position of e_1 or that of e_2.

An interesting observation is that e_2 in some sense depends for its existence on the presence of e_1. When we eliminate e_1 from the sentence, replacing it by a pronoun for instance, the sentence becomes less acceptable:

79   *Poirot is a man [$_{CP}$ whom$_i$ [$_{IP}$ you distrust him [$_{CP}$ when [$_{IP}$ you meet t$_i$]]]].

In (79) *whom* has been extracted from the *when*-clause, producing subjacency effects analogous to those in (78).

Non-overt elements like e_2, which depend for their existence on the presence of another null element have been labelled **parasitic gaps**. A parasitic gap is a null element whose presence must be licensed by another gap in the sentence.[19]

In the literature various proposals have been formulated to account for the occurrence of parasitic gaps and to identify the type of null element we are dealing with. It is not our purpose here to discuss all the analyses that have been proposed in detail. We shall merely introduce two different options that have been adopted in the literature.[20]

5.2　The PRO Hypothesis

Given that *whom* in our example (76) can only be extracted from one of the empty positions, say e_1, and hence fill the corresponding position at D-structure, it is assumed that the position of the parasitic gap, say e_2, is occupied by a theta-marked empty cateory at D-structure. So far we have been assuming that in English null elements present at D-structure are associated with the feature matrix [+pronominal, +anaphor], i.e PRO for short.

It has been proposed in the literature that the parasitic gap e_2 is PRO. PRO in (80a) would be controlled by the object of *distrust*. We represent this referential dependency by co-indexation. For our purposes it is irrelevant whether PRO is already co-indexed with *whom* at D-structure, or whether it gets co-indexed at S-structure only. Remember that the anti-government condition on PRO does not apply at D-structure.

80a　Poirot is a man [$_{CP}$ [$_{IP}$ you distrust whom$_i$ [$_{CP}$ when [$_{IP}$ you meet e_2]]]].

　　　　　　　　　　　　　　　　　　　　　　　　　　　　= PRO$_i$

At S-structure *whom* moves to [Spec,CP] and leaves a trace.

80b　Poirot is a man [$_{CP}$ whom$_i$ [$_{IP}$ you distrust t$_i$ [$_{CP}$ when [$_{IP}$ you meet e_{2i}]]]].

　　　　　　　　　　　　　　　　　　　　　　　　　　　*PRO$_i$/t$_i$

[19] Parasitic gaps were first discussed by Engdahl (1983) and Taraldsen (1981).
[20] See Chomsky (1982, 1986b) and Kayne (1984).

Let us turn to e_2 in (80b). It is a null element which is governed, and which is assigned ACCUSATIVE. Being governed, e_2 cannot be PRO. Through the index i e_2 is A′-bound by *whom*$_i$. At S-structure e_2 is an A′-bound empty category, i.e. it is like a *wh*-trace. In the literature elements that are A′-bound are often referred to as **variables** as we shall see in chapter 9.

The analysis outlined here has one important property: it allows for an *e* to be identified as one type of NP at D-structure and as another at S-structure. At D-structure the features of e_2 would have been [+pronominal, +anaphor], at S-structure they are [–anaphor, –pronominal]. In other words, the referential features of an NP are allowed to change. One might expect, contrary to fact, that other features could change between D-structure and S-structure: agreement features, tense features or categorial features (see chapter 2), for instance. Chomsky (1986b: 17) proposes that features assigned at D-structure remain constant. This is a strong argument against the PRO hypothesis as described here.

The hypothesis that e_2 is [–anaphor, –pronominal] at S-structure predicts correctly that parasitic gaps are subject to Principle C of the binding theory and therefore must not be A-bound.

81   *Poirot is a man [$_{CP}$ who$_i$ [$_{IP}$ t$_i$ runs way [when [you see e$_{2i}$]]]].

(81) illustrates a property that was discovered early on in the discussion of parasitic gaps: the so called **anti-c-command condition** on parasitic gaps. The co-indexed trace must not c-command the parasitic gap (81) nor must the parasitic gap c-command the co-indexed trace (82).[21]

82   *Poirot is a man [$_{CP}$ who$_i$ [$_{IP}$ e$_{2i}$ runs way [when [you see t$_i$]]]].

(82) violates the subjacency condition on movement and in addition the trace in the lower clause, itself [-anaphor, -pronominal], violates Principle C of the binding theory.

5.3   Parasitic Gaps are Traces

In Chomsky (1986b: 55) examples analogous to the following are discussed.

---

[21] See Chomsky (1982); also Chomsky (1986b) and Safir (1987) for discussion.

83   Poirot is a man who$_i$ I interviewed t$_i$ before
a   hiring e.
b   deciding to hire e.
c   ?wondering whether to hire e.
d   *wondering when to hire e.
e   *announcing the plan to hire e.
f   *expecting the announcement that they would hire e.
etc.

In (83) we adopt the hypothesis that *who* has been extracted from the object position of *interviewed* leaving a trace in its base-position. The gap in the object position of *hire* marked by *e* is a parasitic gap.

While (83a) and (83b) are fully acceptable, the other examples degrade in acceptability. The decrease in acceptability in (83) is strongly reminiscent of subjacency effects illustrated in (84):

84a   Which detective did you hire?
84b   Which detective did you decide to hire?
84c   ?Which detective did you wonder whether to hire?
84d   *Which detective did you wonder when to hire?
84e   *Which detective did you announce the plan to hire?
84f   *Which detective did you expect the announcement that they would hire?

We shall not go through all the examples here. The reader can verify the impact of the subjacency condition for himself. In (84) subjacency effects are entirely expected. These examples illustrate *wh*-movement in a straightforward way.

But if parasitic gaps are subject to subjacency then we are forced to conclude that they are also traces of movement. The question stated earlier reappears: what is the antecedent of the parasitic gap? Which element has been moved from the object position of *hire* giving rise to subjacency effects in (83)?

In our earlier discussion one option that we blatantly failed to explore is that parasitic gaps are traces of empty operators, the null element represented as 0 and discussed above. This is the option taken in Chomsky (1986b). (83a) is assigned the D-structure in (85a) and the S-structure (85b):

85a   Poirot is a man [$_{CP}$ [$_{IP}$ I interviewed who$_i$ [before [$_{CP}$ [$_{IP}$ PRO hiring 0$_j$]]]]].
85b   Poirot is a man [$_{CP}$ who$_i$ [$_{IP}$ I interviewed t$_i$ [before [$_{CP}$ 0$_j$ [$_{IP}$ PRO hiring t$_j$]]]]].

On the basis of the analysis proposed here the subjacency effects in parasitic gap constructions are entirely expected.

The proposal developed means that sentences with parasitic gaps contain two A'-chains: in (85b) one chain is composed of *who*$_i$ and its trace; the second is composed of 0_i and its trace. Chomsky (1986b: 63) proposes that for the correct interpretation of the parasitic gap and its operator, the two chains are united in a process of **chain composition**:

86   If C = $<x_1 \ldots x_n>$ is the chain of the real gap and C' = $<b_1 \ldots b_m>$ is the chain of the parasitic gap, then the 'composed chain' $<C, C'>$ = $<x_1, \ldots x_n, b_1 \ldots b_m>$ is the chain associated with the parasitic gap construction and yields its interpretation.

The A'-chain containing the parasitic gap will be assigned an interpretation by virtue of entering into a composed chain with the A'-chain of the real gap. If there is no real gap in the sentence the chain containing the parasitic gap will be uninterpreted and the sentence will not be grammatical. One of the components that will be part of the licensing conditions of parasitic gaps will be to define the conditions on chain composition. This is discussed in detail by Chomsky (1986: 54–68) and the reader is referred to the discussion there.

5.4   Conclusion

In section 5.2 and 5.3 we have compared two accounts of parasitic gaps: the PRO hypothesis and the trace hypothesis. Given that parasitic gaps show subjacency effects, the latter hypothesis is preferable.

The study of parasitic gaps is important not only because we are dealing with a rather complex phenomenon but also because of the marginal status of the data we are looking at. If we accept the account proposed here then parasitic gaps, though marginal, follow completely from principles established independently for the grammar. In other words we do not need a special component in our grammar to deal with such relatively marginal phenomena. Given that the properties of parasitic gaps are derived from principles of our grammar which are established independently, the child will not have to be exposed to actual parasitic gap sentences to acquire their properties. Rather, the properties of parasitic gap sentences follow from the grammar as it is. Indeed, given our grammar, parasitic gaps 'must' be possible.[22]

---

[22]   For a discussion of the learnability of parasitic gaps see also Chomsky (1982: 39). This work should be accessible to the reader at this point.

6 Summary

In this chapter we first give an inventory and description of all the null elements posited in previous chapters and their licensing conditions.

1a PRO, characterized by the feature matrix [+anaphor, +pronominal], must not be governed. Its content is determined by control theory.

1b Traces, which are [−pronominal], are subject to **empty category principle: ECP.**

2 **ECP**
   Traces must be properly governed.
   A properly governs B iff A theta-governs B or A antecedent-governs B.
   A theta-governs B iff A governs B and A theta-marks B.
   A antecedent-governs B iff A governs B and A is co-indexed with B.

Government is defined as in (3):

3 **Government**
   A governs B iff
   (i)   A is a governor;
   (ii) A m-commands B;
   (iii) no barrier intervenes between A and B;
   (iv) minimality is respected.
   where governors are: (i)   heads;
                          (ii) co-indexed XPs.

The content of traces is determined by their antecedents.

In addition we have identified the non-overt pronominal *pro*. The occurrence of *pro* is subject to parametric variation. The licensing conditions of *pro* are given in (4):

4 **The *pro*-drop parameter**
4a *pro* is governed by X^0_y;
4b Let X be the licensing head of an occurrence of *pro*: then *pro* has the grammatical specification of the features on X co-indexed with it.

We also discuss movement of null operators in various types of clauses (relatives, infinitival relatives, purpose clauses). The final section of the chapter describes the parasitic gap phenomenon which can also be interpreted as involving a null operator construction.

7 Exercises

Exercise 1

Another example of complementizer contraction with overt reflex is found in West Flemish, a dialect of Dutch which seems to have a type of rule similar in its domain of application to the French rule but with optional overt reflex. We invite the reader to work out the syntactic representations of the sentence and the formulation of the complementizer contraction rule.[23]

1a	den	vent	da	Valère		gezien	eet	
	the	man	that	Valère		seen	has	
1b	den	vent	da	Jan	zeid	da Valère	gezien eet	
	the	man	that	Jan	said	that	Valère	seen	has
1c	den	vent	dad	ier		geweest	eet	
	the	man	that	here		been	has	
1d	den	vent	die	ier		geweest	eet	
	the	man	who	here		been	has	
1e	den	vent	da	Jan	zei	dad	ier	geweest	eet
	the	man	that	Jan	said	that	here	been	has
1f	den	vent	da	Jan	zei	die	ier	geweest	eet
	the	man	that	Jan	said	who	here	been	has
1g	*den	vent	die	Jan	zei	dad	ier	geweest	eet
	the	man	who	Jan	said	that	here	been	has
1h	*den	vent	die	Jan	zei	die	ier	geweest	eet
	the	man	who	Jan	said	who	here	been	has

---

[23] For discussion of the West Flemish data see Bennis and Haegeman (1984) and Rizzi (1990). *Da* and *dad* are variants of the complementizer *da* ('that').

Exercise 2

In our discussion of (1) below we have assumed that the subject of the infinitival clause is PRO and that the object is a trace bound by an empty operator:

1   I_j need a man $[_{CP}$ 0_i $[_{IP}$ PRO_j to love $t_i]]$.

We now ask the reader to work out why it would not be possible to argue that the empty operator is in the subject position at D-structure and is subsequently moved to the [Spec,CP], while a null element PRO is generated in the object position where it remains throughout the derivation:

2   *I_j need a man $[_{CP}$ 0_j $[_{IP}$ t_j to love $PRO_i]]$.

Exercise 3

Consider the representation (1) below and discuss why it is not allowed in our grammar.

1   *Poirot is a man $[_{CP}$ $whom_i$ $[_{IP}$ you distrust t_i $[_{CP}$ when $[_{IP}$ you meet $t_i]]]]$.

Exercise 4

Consider text-example (75b), which we left undiscussed.

75b   Poirot is a man that anyone that talks to usually likes.

In the light of the preceding chapter discuss the D-structure and the S-structure representations of this sentence.

Text-examples (75a) and (75b) are the two typical instances of parasitic gap constructions: in (75a) the gap occurs in an adjunct clause, in (75b) it occurs inside a subject.

Exercise 5

Consider the example of super-raising (6), repeated here as (1). It was argued in chapter 6 that this example was a violation of the BT, the trace of *John* not being bound in its GC. In chapter 7 and in this chapter we also saw that the ungrammaticality of (1) can be explained as a subjacency violation. Consider whether other principles of the grammar can be used to rule out the example:

1   *John seems that it is likely to resign.

Exercise 6

In the earlier literature on *wh*-movement the text-examples (17) and (18) repeated here in (1) and (2) were considered as violations of the so-called **superiority condition** (Chomsky, 1973).

1a   ?What do you wonder when John bought?
1b   *Who do you wonder when bought these books?

2a   ?What do you wonder who will read?
2b   *Who do you wonder what will read?

The superiority condition was a constraint on the order of extracting *wh*-elements in sentences containing more than one *wh*-element. This condition says that if A is superior to B then any movement affecting A must take place on a lower cycle than that affecting B. **Superiority** is a structural notion defined in terms of c-command:

3   **Superiority**
     XP is superior to YP if XP and YP are in the same IP and XP c-commands YP.

Subjects are consequently superior to objects.
    First discuss to what extent the superiority condition is able to deal with (1) and (2) above. Next, consider whether the superiority condition is equivalent to the ECP.[24] You may use the examples in the text for this exercise.

---

[24] The overlap between the superiority condition and the ECP is discussed in Aoun, Hornstein and Sportiche (1981).

9 Logical Form and Phonetic Form

Contents

Introduction and Overview

So far we have mainly been looking at the formal properties of sentences and we have paid little attention to their interpretation. This chapter focuses on matters of sentence interpretation. We shall see that in order to arrive at an appropriate representation of the interpretation of quantifiers and *wh*-phrases we need to posit a level of representation in addition to D-structure and S-structure. This third level of representation is referred to as 'logical form' or LF. The transformation move-α maps S-structure onto LF.

Two examples of the application of move-α between S-structure and LF are discussed: *wh*-raising, exemplified in Chinese and in English, and quantifier-raising.

We show that LF representations are subject to the ECP, like any other level of syntactic representation. In our discussion of this point, we shall provide a more careful account of the application of the ECP. We provide evidence that the ECP applies to all traces, including intermediate traces. The new formulation of the ECP is applied to *wh*-raising and to quantifier-raising.

Section 1 introduces the level of LF. Section 2 shows that the ECP applies to LF and reformulates the ECP in terms of gamma-marking. Section 3 discusses the status of intermediate traces with respect to the ECP. Section 4 discusses examples of quantifier raising. Section 5 is a note on the parasitic gap phenomenon in the light of the discussion in chapter 9.

1 Operator and Variable

1.1 *The Interpretation of Quantifiers*

Consider the following sentences:

1a George saw William.
1b William saw everyone.
1c William saw someone.
1d William saw every policeman.

The interpretation of (1a) is straightforward: the subject NP *George* and the object NP *William* pick out referents from the universe of discourse and the predicate *see* relates these entities. In the notation of formal logic the interpretation of the sentence would be represented (roughly) as in (2a):

2a   S (g, w)

where S is the predicate 'see', and g and w represent *George* and *William*, the arguments. We ignore the role of the past tense here. (1b) contains a **quantifier**: *everyone*. As a first approximation of its interpretation, one might adopt a representation such as (2b) by analogy to (2a):

2b   S (w, e)

However, this representation misses an important point about quantifiers. Words like *everyone, no one*, etc. do not serve to pick out one specific entity of the universe of discourse. (1b) does not mean something like 'take the entity referred to by the NP "everyone" and assign to it the property that William sees it'. *Everyone* does not have a specific referent. Rather, (1b) means something like 'for every element you take, provided that this element is human, it is the case that William sees this element'. The internal argument of *see* in (1b) is variable and depends for its interpretation on the range of the quantifier. The variability of the interpretation of *everyone* is obvious if we think of two situations. In Situation A a teacher is speaking about her class. *Everyone* will be taken to indicate all the people present in the class. In Situation B a teacher is speaking about her colleagues. Here *everyone* will be taken to indicate all the colleagues.

Lexical NPs such as *William* or *George* do not have this variable interpretation. Whichever situation we think of, say A or B above, William picks out a particular person baptised with that name. Even if there actually should exist more than one person called William, in any given context (1b) will still be taken to apply to only one of them – the one that is contextually most accessible – and not to every single person called William. This means that the representation (2b) for (1b) is inadequate: it fails to represent the variable element in the interpretation of quantifiers. Logicians[1] use representations such as the following:

3a $\forall x \ (Hx \longrightarrow Swx)$

---

[1] See for example Allwood et al. (1977) for an introduction to logic written for linguists.

(3a) contains a conditional component, represented by the arrow, and can be paraphrased roughly as follows:

3b ∀x   (Hx ⟶ Swx)
   For all x it is the case that if x is human then William sees x.

The first part of the conditional, the part to the left of the arrow, restricts the selection of elements x to just humans.

   An alternative representation for the interpretation of the quantifier is (3c). Again we add a paraphrase:

3c ∀x,   x = H   (Swx)
   For all x, such that x is human, William sees x

The element x in the representations above represents the variable which depends on the element represented as ∀ for its interpretation. ∀ is the **universal** quantifier meaning 'all'. We call ∀ and **operator** and x a **variable bound** by the operator.

   The interpretation of a variable depends on the operator. Roughly, the logical representation of (1c) is something like (4):

4 Ex, (H = x) & (Swx)

E is the **existential** quantifier. (4) can be paraphrased as follows: 'there is an x, such that x is human and William sees x.'

   The interpretation of (1d) can be represented as in (5). Here the restriction on the variable x is more specific: only policemen are selected.

5 ∀x, x = P (Swx)

   We shall not go into the details of the rough logical representations here. Our sketch above should suffice to introduce the notions of variable and quantifier. For more detailed discussion the reader is referred to works on logic. The operator-variable notation has been introduced because we shall need it in our representation of sentence interpretation.

1.2 Wh-*phrases and Operators*

Consider the interpretation of the sentences in (6):

6a George saw William.
6b Who did George see?
6c Which policeman did George see?

The contrast between (6a) on the one hand and (6b) and (6c) on the other is close to that between (1a) and (1b,c,d) above. *Who* and *which policeman*, in (6b) and (6c) respectively, do not have a specific referent. (6b) and (6c) could be paraphrased as (7a) and (7b) respectively:

7a For which x, x is human, is it the case that George sees x?
7b For which x, x is a policeman, is it the case that George sees x?

From the paraphrases we see that the *wh*-phrases in (6b) and (6c) act like operators binding a variable *x*.

There is a striking parallel between (8a) the S-structure of (6b), in which the *wh*-phrase in [Spec,CP] binds a trace, and the representation (7a).

8a $[_{CP}$ Who$_i$ did $[_{IP}$ George see t$_i$]]?

Linguists (e.g. May, 1985) propose that the logico-semantic representations of sentences are to be modelled on their syntactic representations. The logico-semantic representation of (8a) is argued to be as in (8b), where the *wh*-constituent is treated as an operator binding a variable on the analogy of quantifier-variable binding discussed in section 1.1.

8b $[_{CP}$ Who$_i$ did $[_{IP}$ George see x$_i$]]?

This proposal entails that each sentence has not only a D-structure representation which encodes its lexical properties, etc. and an S-structure encoding the results of move-α but also a representation of its logico-semantic properties: its **logical form** or LF. LF is a level of syntactic representation because, as we shall see in this chapter, it is subject to the principles that govern syntactic representations, such as the projection principle or the ECP, discussed in chapter 8, section 2. The LF representation of a sentence is not identical to the semantic representation posited by semanticists and logicians; it is an intermediate step between S-structure representations and the semantic representations of the type advocated by semanticists. (6c) repeated here as (9a) will be assigned the S-structure in (9b) and the LF (9c):

9a   Which policeman did George see?
9b   [CP Which policeman_i did [IP George see t_i]]?
9c   [CP Which policeman_i did [IP George see x_i]]?

Our syntactic analysis of sentence structure will from now on have to consider three levels of representation: D-structure, S-structure and LF. Yet another level, **phonetic form**, or PF, will be discussed later in this chapter and in chapter 12.

As was the case with respect to D-structure and S-structure, S-structure and LF may be very similar, as can be seen in (9). In other cases, there will be quite an important difference between the levels. Anticipating the discussion in section 4 below consider for instance (10):

10a   **D-structure**
      [IP William [I'-ed [VP see everyone]]]
10b   **S-structure**
      [IP William [I'-ed [VP see everyone]]]
10c   **LF**
      [IP everyone_i [IP William [I'-ed [VP see x_i]]]]

Analogously to the standard logical representations discussed in section 1.1. it is proposed that quantificational elements should be treated as operators at LF which bind a variable.

In the LF representations adopted in the literature traces left by *wh*-movement are often replaced by *x* to indicate their status as variables, but this is not a generalized practice. In this chapter we shall often not replace the trace by *x*. However it is understood that being bound by an operator, the trace in the base-position is by definition a variable.

1.3   *Move-alpha and LF*

Consider the following Japanese examples taken from Lasnik and Saito (1984: 244):

11a John-wa   naze kubi-ni natta no?
    John-topic why was fired   *Question marker*
    'Why was John fired?'
11b Bill-wa [$_{CP}$ John-ga   naze kubi-ni natta tte] itta no?
    Bill-topic   John NOM   why was fired   C   said Q
    'Why did Bill say that John was fired?'

We do not enter into the details of the grammar of Japanese at all here. The relevant property is that, unlike English *why*, Japanese *naze* does not need to be moved to [Spec,CP]. The reader can see this quite clearly in (11b): *why* in the English translation of the sentence is extracted from the subordinate clause, but in Japanese *naze* remains in its base-position.[2] (12) gives further examples of questions in Japanese:

12a John ga dare   o butta   ka siranai.
          who ACC   hit   know not
    'I don't know who John hit.'
12b John wa, Mary ga dare o   kiratte-iru to sinwite-ita ka?
    John   Mary   whom ACC hating is   that believing was
    'Who did John believe that Mary hated?'
    (from Kuno, 1973: 13–16)
12c Watasi-wa John-ga nani-o   katta ka sitte iru.
    I-topic   John-NOM what-ACC ought Q   know
    'I know what John bought.'
    (from Lasnik and Saito, 1984: 235)

Although question words are not subject to syntactic movement in Japanese, the interpretation of *wh*-phrases is like that of such phrases in English. *Wh*-phrases such as *dare* ('who'), *dore* ('which'), *nani* ('what'), are not referential. (12a) means 'I don't know for which x, x human, it is the case that John hit x', and (12b) means: 'For which x, x human, is it the case that John

---

[2] The English translation of (11b) is ambiguous: *why* in [Spec,CP] may bind a trace in the matrix clause or in the lower clause. *Why* may be construed with the higher predicate or with the lower, asking for the reason of Bill's saying something or for the reason of John's being fired:

(i)   [$_{CP}$ Why$_i$ did [$_{IP}$ Bill say t$_i$ [$_{CP}$ that [$_{IP}$ John was fired]]]]?
(ii) [$_{CP}$ Why$_i$ did [$_{IP}$ Bill say [$_{CP}$ that [$_{IP}$ John was fired t$_i$]]]]?

In Japanese (11b) *naze* has not moved from its base-position. (11b) is unambiguous: *naze* asks for the reason of John's being fired.

believed that Mary hated x?' The LF representations of these sentences should also represent question words as operators binding variables. For (12a), repeated as (13a), we propose an LF representation such as (13b), where the *wh*-phrase is moved and binds a variable in its base-position. Following Lasnik and Saito (1984: 244, n. 15), we assume that operators are moved rightward because overt complementizers occur sentence finally in Japanese, but this is not important for the discussion.

13a John ga dare o butta ka siranai.
          who   hit   know not
    'I don't know who John hit.'
13b [[$_{IP}$ John ga x_i butta ka] dare-o$_i$ $_{CP}$] siranai.

Chinese is like Japanese in that there is no *wh*-movement of question words at S-structure:

14a Wo xiang-zhidao [$_{CP}$ [$_{IP}$ Lisi   mai-le   sheme].

        I wonder   Lisi   bought   what
    'I wonder what Lisi bought.'
    (Lasnik and Saito, 1984: 239)
14b Zhangsan wen   [shei mai le shu].
                ask   who   buy-Aspect book
    'Zhangsan asked who bought books.'
14c [Zhangsan xiangzin [shei   mai-le shu]].
                believe   who   buy-ASP book
    'Who does Zhangsan believe bought books?'
14d [Zhangsan zhidao [shei   mai-le shu]].
                know   who   buy-ASP book
    (i) 'Zhangsan knows who bought books.'
    (ii) 'Who does Zhangsan know bought books?'
    (b,c,d: Aoun, 1984: 18)

Again, at LF we represent *wh*-phrases as operators binding variables. The LF representation of (14a) will be (15a) and that of (14d), an example that is ambiguous between an interpretation as an indirect question (i) and as a direct question (ii), will have the two representations in (15b):

15a Wo xiang-zhidao [$_{CP}$ sheme$_i$ [$_{IP}$ Lisi mai-le x_i]]
15b (i) [Zhangsan zhidao [[shei]$_i$ [x_i mai-le shu]]]
    (ii) [[shei]$_i$ [Zhangsan zhidao [x_i mai-le shu]]]

Let us sum up the discussion so far. In Chinese and Japanese *wh*-phrases in interrogative sentences are not subject to *wh*-movement at S-structure. We assume that the *wh*-phrases are moved to an A′-position at LF, exactly parallel to the S-structure movement of *wh*-consituents in English.

S-structure is derived from D-structure through a movement transformation, move-α; LF also derives from S-structure via move-α. Our grammar is now a three-level model:

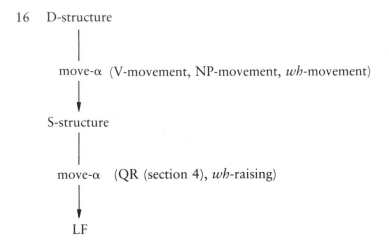

16   D-structure

       move-α (V-movement, NP-movement, *wh*-movement)

     S-structure

       move-α   (QR (section 4), *wh*-raising)

       LF

Before we move on, one other observation is important. The movement of *wh*-phrases to derive the LF representation in Chinese and Japanese questions clearly has no overt reflex. In the surface form of these sentences, the *wh*-phrase is in its base-position. The surface form of the sentence is hence not derived from the LF representation. Rather, the surface form of the sentence corresponds more closely to the S-structure. In Government and Binding Theory the separation of the superficial appearance of the sentence and its LF representation is obtained by positing that there is yet a further level of representation, which determines the superficial form of the sentence and is based on the S-structure representation. Hence we arrive at the model in (17):

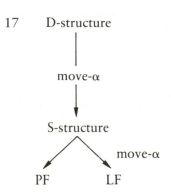

17   D-structure

       move-α

     S-structure

       move-α

   PF   LF

The representation that encodes the surface properties of the sentence is called **phonetic form** or PF (see also chapter 12). The model in (17) has come to be known as the **T-model.**[3]

1.4 *LF-movement in English:* wh-in situ

Consider the following English examples:

18a To whom did George give what?
18b Why did George see whom?

Both sentences in (18) contain two *wh*-phrases. We have seen previously (chapter 7) that it is not possible in English for two *wh*-phrases to be fronted in the same clause.[4] In the examples in (18) the second *wh*-phrase remains in its base-position, *in situ*. However, the unmoved *wh*-phrase is like any other *wh*-phrase: it lacks specific reference. It is desirable that all *wh*-phrases be treated as operators binding variables. In (18a) we are not merely questioning who was the receiver of the thing given, but we also question what is being given. The answer to a question like (18a) will treat the *wh*-phrases as a pair. One might expect answers like (19a) but not (19b) or (19c):

19a George gave the letter to Miss Marple and the postcard to William.
19b *To Miss Marple.
19c *The letter.

For the LF representation of the example in (18a) we propose that the *wh*-phrase which is *in situ* at S-structure is also moved to [Spec,CP] where it is associated for its interpretation with the phrase which had already been moved to [Spec,CP], by what is referred to as **wh-absorption**. The movement of a *wh*-element to adjoin to an already moved *wh*-element is often called **wh-raising**. This is not identical to NP-raising discussed in chapter 6. *Wh*-raising moves an element to an A'-position, while NP-raising as an instantiation of NP-movement moves an element to an A-position.

20 [$_{CP}$ what$_i$, to whom$_j$ [$_{IP}$ George gave x$_i$ x$_j$]]

---

[3] Other models have been proposed in the literature. The reader is referred to the discussion in Van Riemsdijk and Williams (1981), who propose a linearly organized model with an intermediate level between D-structure and S-structure.

[4] [Spec,CP] dominates only one position, and *wh*-adjunction to IP is argued to be excluded in English (unlike in Polish).

Given that there is only one position in [Spec,CP] we assume that *what* is moved to an adjoined position, adopting a modified version of Lasnik and Saito's (1984) analysis:

21

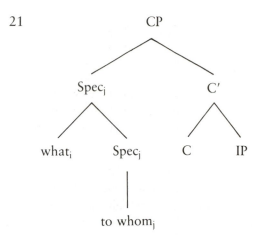

At S-structure *to whom$_j$* moves into [Spec,CP]. We assume that this element determines the index, *j*, of [Spec,CP]. The adjoined element *what* has no influence on the index of [Spec,CP]: *to whom$_j$* is the head of [Spec,CP].

Wh-raising is another instantiation of *wh*-movement to derive LF from S-structure, in other words it is another instantiation of move-α. As an LF operation, *wh*-raising has no overt reflex: it does not feed into PF (cf. (17)).

1.5 Wh-*movement and Parametric Variation*

The level of application of *wh*-movement is another instance of parametric variation. In English, *wh*-phrases can – and often must – be moved at S-structure;[5] in Chinese there is no *wh*-movement at S-structure.

---

[5] In French *wh*-phrases may move at S-structure or they may be left *in situ*:

  (i) Tu   as   dit   quoi?
         you have   said   what
         'What did you say?'
  (ii) A qui as-tu donné l'argent?
         to whom have-you given the money
         'To whom have you given the money?'
(see also Aoun et al., 1981).

22 Question formation

	English	Chinese/ Japanese
Move-α		
S-structure	YES	NO
LF	YES	YES

The overt evidence available will allow the child learning these languages to fix the parameter accordingly. Sentences such as (6b) and (6c) are easy to come by and will enable the child to opt for the presence of *wh*-movement at S-structure.

2   The ECP

2.1   *ECP effects at LF*

The reader may be sceptical about our proposal that LF is a level of syntactic representation derived from S-structure by move-α. However, there is good evidence that this syntactic level does indeed exist. In this section we show that LF is subject to the ECP.

2.1.1   SUBJECT–OBJECT ASYMMETRIES

There is a subject–object asymmetry with respect to multiple questions. Consider the following examples.

23a I don't remember who said what.
23b *I don't remember what who said.

In our discussion in chapter 8 we have seen that the ECP can explain S-structure subject–object asymmetries. Let us try to see if the ECP could also explain the difference between (23a) and (23b). The S-structure of the grammatical (23a) is given in (24a) and its LF representation in (24b). We omit irrelevant details for expository reasons:[6]

24a I don't remember [$_{CP}$ who$_i$ [$_{IP}$ t$_i$ said what]].
24b I don't remember [$_{CP}$ [$_{speci}$ what$_j$ [$_{Speci}$ who$_i$]] [$_{IP}$ t$_i$ said t$_j$]][7]

(23b) has the following representations:

25a I don't remember [$_{CP}$ [$_{Spec_j}$ what$_j$] [$_{IP}$ who$_i$ said t$_j$]].
25b I don't remember [$_{CP}$ [$_{Spec_j}$ who$_i$ [$_{Spec_j}$ what$_j$]] [t$_i$ said t$_j$]].

   Recall the proposal that the constituent first moved to [Spec,CP] assigns its index to [Spec,CP] and that any element subsequently adjoined to the indexed specifier of CP cannot transmit its index. The S-structure representations (24a) and (25a) do not violate any of the principles so far developed. Subjacency, theta theory, the case filter and the ECP are observed, as the reader can verify.
   Let us turn to the LF representations (24b) and (25b). The variables resulting from LF-movement are also traces. In order to keep our theory as general as possible we shall postulate that traces resulting from movement at LF are also subject to the ECP. This assumption provides us with a natural explanation for the ungrammaticality of (25b) in contrast with the grammaticality of (24b).
   (26a) is a partial tree diagram to represent (24b):

---

[6] In (24a) the assumption is that *who* is moved vacuously to [Spec,CP]. Alternatively *who* is not moved at S-structure and both *wh*-phrases move at LF. (23a) will then be grammatical if we adopt the LF representation in (24b).
[7] We represent traces at LF as *t*. Recall that often such traces are represented also as *x*.

26a

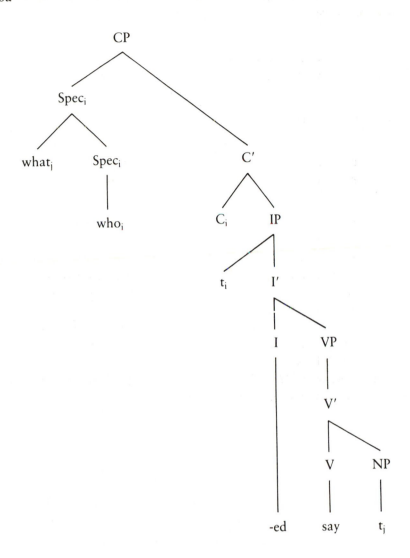

The variable co-indexed with *what*$_j$, i.e. t$_j$, is properly governed by the lexical verb *say*. The variable t$_i$ in the subject position is co-indexed with *who*$_i$ and with [Spec,CP]. Spec$_i$ c-commands t$_i$. It is separated from the variable by C′, which is non-maximal and thus not a barrier, and also by IP, which we posited is not a barrier. The subject trace, t_i is properly governed: it is antecedent-governed.[8]

26b

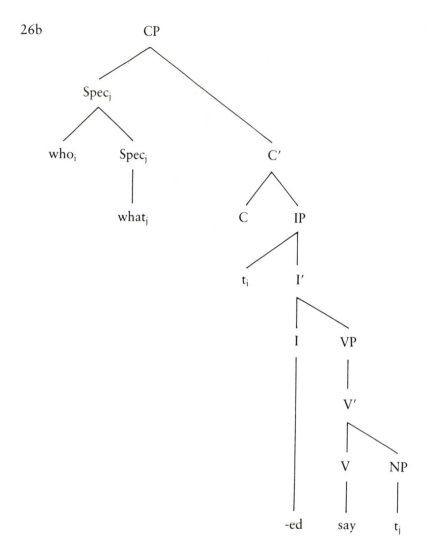

Consider (26b), the LF representation of (23b).

---

[8] A problem remains which we shall not go into here. Strictly speaking, *what$_j$* in the adjoined position might be said not to c-command its trace, hence not to A'-bind it. We shall assume that the operator *what$_j$* can bind its trace through being associated with *who*, as illustrated in the paired reading of the question (cf. section 1.4).

The variable t_i is properly governed by the verb; t_j, the trace of *who*$_j$, is not properly governed. Its antecedent is adjoined to [Spec,CP] but *who*$_j$ cannot transmit its index to the specifier and hence it will be prevented from governing the variable.

To sum up the discussion so far. We have posited that in addition to D-structure and S-structure there is a third level of representation, LF. This level derives from S-structure by move-α. One instantiation of move-α at LF is the movement of *wh*-elements which were not moved at S-structure. Evidence for the existence of a syntactic level of representation, LF, is the fact ECP effects are observed at LF.

2.1.2 COMPLEMENT VS. NON-COMPLEMENT AND ECP

We have been relating the ECP effects to subject-object asymmetries. This needs some further discussion.

Why do subjects differ from objects with respect to ECP? The answer is that subjects are not theta-governed, while objects are. Subject traces will always need to be antecedent-governed to satisfy the ECP.

It follows that other elements which are not theta-governed, such as adjuncts, will behave like subjects. Like subjects, they can only satisfy the ECP by antecedent-government. We expect that there will be an asymmetry between complements (theta-governed) and non-complements (antecedent-governed). Consider (27):

27a When did George do what?
27b *What did George do when?

(27a) will have an LF representation (28):

28 $[_{CP} [_{Spec_j} \text{what}_i [_{Spec_j} \text{when}_j]]$ did $[_{IP}$ George $[_{VP}$ do $t_i]]$ $t_j]]$?

In (28) the variable bound by *what*$_i$ is properly governed: it is theta-governed by the verb. The variable bound by *when*$_j$ is also properly governed: *when*$_j$ is the head of [Spec,CP] and antecedent-governs its trace.

In (27b) *what*$_i$ is the head of [Spec,CP] and *when*$_j$, which is *wh*-raised at LF, will not be able to antecedent-govern its trace. Given that this trace is not theta-governed by the verb either, it violates the ECP.

29 $[_{CP} [_{Spec_i} \text{when}_j [_{Spec_i} \text{what}_i]]$ did $[_{IP}$ George $[_{VP}$ do $x_i]]$ $x_j]]$?

The ECP thus accounts for the complement–adjunct asymmetries in questions such as (27a) and (27b). Postulating a syntactic level of LF representation enables us to account for a range of data without there being a need for additional principles. We merely apply the syntactic principles we have adopted previously for S-structure representations.

2.2   The Application of the ECP

In this section we return to the general discussion of the application of the ECP. Our analysis developed so far has a number of shortcomings, also pointed out in chapter 8 (section 2.3), which we shall try to amend here.

2.2.1   *THAT*-TRACE EFFECTS

As the reader will remember from chapter 8, the ECP allows us to dispense with the unexplained *that*-trace filter: (30b) is a violation of the ECP: t_i in the [NP,IP] position is not properly governed because *that* prevents the trace in [Spec,CP] from antecedent-governing it (cf. (31)).

30a   Who$_i$ do you think [$_{CP}$ t$'_i$ [$_{IP}$ t$_i$ came]]?
30b   *Who$_i$ do you think [$_{CP}$ t$'_i$ that [$_{IP}$ t$_i$ came]]?

31a   What$_i$ do you think [$_{CP}$ t$'_i$ [$_{IP}$ John likes t$_i$]]?
31b   What$_i$ do you think [$_{CP}$ t$'_i$ that [$_{IP}$ John likes t$_i$]]?
      (examples from Lasnik and Saito, 1984: 255)

If we assume that adjuncts also leave traces the grammaticality of (32b) is unexplained:

32a   Why$_i$ do you think [$_{CP}$ t$'_i$ [$_{IP}$ he left early t$_i$]]?
32b   Why$_i$ do you think [$_{CP}$ t$'_i$ that [$_{IP}$ he left early t$_i$]]?
      (Lasnik and Saito, 1984: 255)

The trace of the moved adjunct *why* must be antecedent-governed, not being theta-governed. In (32a) the intermediate trace, t$'_i$, can antecedent-govern the lowest trace as in (30a); but (32b) remains unexplained: how is it that the intervening *that* in C does not prevent antecedent-government as it does in (30b)?

In their analysis of the ECP Lasnik and Saito (1984) offer a way of dealing with the problem. Their proposal is further modified in Chomsky (1986b). We adopt Lasnik and Saito's proposal and Chomsky's account here.[9]

2.2.2 TWO ASSUMPTIONS

In order to solve the problems discussed above, Lasnik and Saito introduce two assumptions with respect to the application of the ECP.

2.2.2.1 *ASSUMPTION I: Level of gamma-marking* Consider (30), where the subject is extracted. Subjects are arguments and they are theta-marked by the verb, either indirectly or directly in the case of unaccusative constructions (see discussion in chapter 6). Subject argument NPs are hence required by the projection principle.

On the other hand, *why* in (32) is an adjunct, hence not required by the projection principle: the verb *leave* does not theta-mark *why*.

Roughly speaking, the idea that Lasnik and Saito propose is that adjuncts as it were come into full force at the level of LF only. Traces of adjuncts will be subject to the ECP only at that level and NOT at S-structure. Arguments, on the other hand, are present at S-structure where the projection principle requires them, and they are subject to the ECP at S-structure.

For determining whether the ECP is observed Lasnik and Saito propose a system of **gamma marking**, γ, is the Greek *g*, for government.

At S-structure we check argument traces for proper government. Those that respect the ECP are marked $[+\gamma]$, those that violate the ECP are $[-\gamma]$. At LF we re-check all variables for the ECP. Those variables that are the reflexes of S-structure argument traces will already have a gamma-mark. An element which is $[+\gamma]$ at S-structure will also be $[+\gamma]$ at LF. Gamma-marking at LF will thus concern two types of variables only: (i) variables which are reflexes of S-structure adjunct traces; (ii) variables of LF applications of move-α.

Positing this discrepancy for the level of gamma-marking might appear an *ad hoc* move, but it is crucial in Lasnik and Saito's (1984) proposal and we adopt it here.

Lasnik and Saito propose that the ECP must be satisfied at LF at the latest.

[9] The reader is advised to read through Lasnik and Saito's account in order to appreciate the range and complexity of the issue involved. We offer only a small fragment of the discussion.

This proposal comes down to a two-step procedure in the application of the ECP: (i) gamma-marking, (ii) checking the representation of a sentence at LF.[10]

The proposal that the feature assigned by gamma-marking is constant is in itself plausible. We have already seen that syntactic features do not change in the course of a derivation. For instance, a category which is recognized as a VP is not altered at S-structure. Nominal features such as gender, person and number do not change either: once an NP is singular, for instance, it will remain so. The features [±anaphor] and [±pronominal] also do not vary from one level to the next. This last property led us to abandon the PRO analysis of parasitic gaps in chapter 8.

2.2.2.2 ASSUMPTION II: Deletion at LF   In addition Lasnik and Saito (1984) also discuss the role of *that*. In English its role is minimal: it can easily disappear and a sentence will not change its meaning. Lasnik and Saito propose that at LF *that* is irrelevant because it does not contribute to the semantics of the sentence and may be deleted without altering the interpretation of the sentence. But when *that* is present in the surface string of the sentence, it must be present at PF and hence must be present at S-structure.

In fact Lasnik and Saito propose a slightly more general deletion process at LF: an element that does not contribute to the logico-semantic representation can be deleted at LF. To subsume move-α and delete-α they use the term affect-α.

2.2.3 APPLYING THE PROPOSAL

The combination of the two assumptions outlined above gives the right results for the analysis of (30) and (32).

In order to get used to the new components in our by now quite intricate grammar we shall go through all the examples in (30)–(32) repeated here for convenience as (33)–(35):

33a Who$_i$ do you think [$_{CP}$ t$'_i$ [$_{IP}$ t$_i$ came]]?
33b *Who$_i$ do you think [$_{CP}$ t$'_i$ that [$_{IP}$ t$_i$ came]]?

34a What$_i$ do you think [$_{CP}$ t$'_i$ [$_{IP}$ John likes t$_i$]]?
34b What$_i$ do you think [$_{CP}$ t$'_i$ that [$_{IP}$ John likes t$_i$]]?

35a Why$_i$ do you think [$_{CP}$ t$'_i$ [$_{IP}$ he left early t$_i$]]?

---

[10] This two-step procedure is perhaps reminiscent of the idea that while case-marking may apply both at D-structure (for inherent case) and at S-structure (for structural case), the case filter applies at S-structure.

35b Why$_i$ do you think [$_{CP}$ t'$_i$ that [$_{IP}$ he left early t$_i$]]?

In (33) and (34) arguments have been *wh*-moved. This means that there will be traces, which must be gamma-marked at S-structure (ASSUMPTION I). The object-trace in (34) is theta-governed by the verb *like* and the subject-trace in (33) must be antecedent-governed. This is possible in (33a) but prevented by the intervening *that* in (33b). As before we ignore intermediate traces to which we return in section 3. Gamma-marking for (33) and (34) is encoded in (36) and (37) respectively.

36a Who$_i$ do you think [$_{CP}$ t'$_i$ [$_{IP}$ t$_i$ came]]?
$$[+\gamma]$$
36b *Who$_i$ do you think [$_{CP}$ t'$_i$ that [IP t$_i$ came]]?
$$[-\gamma]$$

37a What$_i$ do you think [$_{CP}$ t'$_i$ [$_{IP}$ John likes t$_i$]]?
$$[+\gamma]$$
37b What$_i$ do you think [$_{CP}$ t'$_i$ that [$_{IP}$ John likes t$_i$]]?
$$[+\gamma]$$

At LF the traces are interpreted as variables bound by the *wh*-operator and they retain the gamma feature. When the ECP is checked at LF, (36b) will be rejected because it contains a trace which is $[-\gamma]$.

Now we turn to (35). Adjunct traces are not gamma-marked at S-structure, but rather at LF. According to ASSUMPTION II, the complementizer *that* may be deleted. This means that the LF representations of (35a) and (35b) will be identical and the trace of *why* satisfies the ECP as desired.

38 Why$_i$ do you think [$_{CP}$ t'$_i$ [$_{IP}$ he left early t$_i$]]?
$$[+\gamma]$$

Let us return to an earlier example to see if our adjusted theory applies appropriately. After all, we should not introduce auxiliary assumptions to rescue some examples and then find that our previous good results have become undone. (27) repeated here as (39), illustrates the asymmetry between complements and non-complements:

39a When did George do what?
39b *What did George do when?

The structures of both examples will contain traces. In the S-structure (40a) of (39a) there will be an adjunct-trace, so we need not worry about gamma-marking yet. In (40b), the S-structure of (39b), there will be a complement-trace and gamma-marking will apply.

40a $[_{CP} [_{Spec_j} when_j]$ did $[_{IP}$ George $[_{VP}$ do what$_i]$ $t_j]]$?
40b $[_{CP} [_{Spec_i} what_i]$ did $[_{IP}$ George $[_{VP}$ do $t_i]$ when$_j]]$?
$$[+\gamma]$$

At LF *wh*-raising applies to the second *wh*-phrase. Gamma-marking applies to all traces not gamma-marked yet:

41a $[_{CP} [_{Spec_j} what_i [_{Spec_j} when_j]]$ did $[_{IP}$ George $[_{VP}$ do $t_i]$ $t_j]]$
$$[+\gamma] [+\gamma]$$
41b $[_{CP} [_{Spec_j} when_j [_{Spec_i} what_i]]$ did $[_{IP}$ George $[_{VP}$ do $t_i]]$ $[t_j]]$
$$[+\gamma] [-\gamma]$$

In (41a) the variable resulting from *wh*-raising *what$_i$* is theta-governed by *do*: it is properly governed and assigned $[+\gamma]$. The trace left after S-structure movement of *when$_j$* is also properly governed since it is antecedent-governed.

In (41b) the variable bound by *what$_i$* retains its $[+\gamma]$ feature assigned at S-structure, but the variable resulting from *wh*-raising *when$_j$* is not properly governed: it is not theta-governed, being an adjunct-trace, and it cannot be antecedent-governed because *when$_j$* cannot govern it from its adjoined position in [Spec,CP].

Finally we discuss example (42).

42   Why do you wonder whom John will invite?

This example is grammatical if we interpret *why* as bearing on the reason for wondering. An answer could be: 'I wonder because I am concerned about the man's knowledge of French.' But (42) cannot have the reading in which *why* is connected with *invite*. Apparently we cannot represent this sentence as an example of long movement of *why* parallel to (43):

43   Why do you think that Emsworth will invite George?

(43) is ambiguous. *Why* can be interpreted with or **construed with** *think* or with *invite*.

We return to (43) below ((50a) in 3.2). Let us now concentrate on (42). The possible interpretation of (42) will have S-structure (44a) and LF (44b):

44a Why$_i$ do [$_{IP}$ you wonder t$_i$ [$_{CP}$ whom$_j$ [$_{IP}$ John will invite   t$_j$]]]?
                                                                    [+γ]
44b Why$_i$ do [$_{IP}$ you wonder   t$_i$ [$_{CP}$ whom$_j$ [$_{IP}$ John will invite   t$_j$]]]?
                                 [+γ]   [+γ]

This ought to pose no problems to the reader: the complement-trace is gamma-marked at S-structure and the trace of *why* is gamma-marked at LF.

(45) is the S-structure of (42) where *why* is construed with the lower clause:

45   *Why$_i$ do [$_{IP}$ you wonder [$_{CP}$ whom$_j$ [$_{IP}$ John will invite t$_i$ t$_j$]]]?

First of all note that the subjacency condition has been violated: *why* has crossed two bounding nodes IP. But it appears that the sentence is more than a mere subjacency violation. In order to assess the impact of subjacency let us first look at a simple example (46):

46   ?*Whom do you wonder why John will invite?

This sentence is ungrammatical but it can be interpreted: *whom* is the object of *invite*. (46) is an example of a subjacency violation, but the ECP is observed. Gamma-marking applies to the trace of *whom* at S-structure (47a) and to the trace of *why* at LF (47b).

47a Whom$_i$ do   [$_{IP}$ you wonder [$_{CP}$ why$_j$ [$_{IP}$ John will invite t$_i$ t$_j$]]]?
              #   #   [+γ]

47b Whom$_i$ do [$_{IP}$ you wonder [$_{CP}$ why$_j$ [$_{IP}$ John will invite   t$_i$ t$_j$]]]?
                                                              [+γ] [+γ]

In (42) *why* cannot be construed with the lower clause at all. This leads us to conclude that it cannot just be that subjacency is violated. Subjacency violations as in (46/47) do not lead to such strong effects. The S-structure and the LF representations of (42) with their gamma-features are given in (48a) and (48b) respectively.

48a   *Why$_i$ do [$_{IP}$ you wonder [$_{CP}$ whom$_j$ [$_{IP}$ John will invite   t$_j$ t$_i$]]]?
                                                                                  [+γ]

48b   *Why$_i$ do [$_{IP}$ you wonder [$_{CP}$ whom$_j$ [$_{IP}$ John will invite   t$_j$ t$_i$]]]?
                                                                                  [+γ] [−γ]

In the S-structure (48a) gamma-marking applies to the trace of *whom$_j$*. In the LF representation (48b) gamma-marking applies to the trace of *why*. *Why* is separated from its trace by two IP boundaries and one CP boundary. We conclude that the antecedent is too far removed from the trace to be able to antecedent-govern it. We need to make this conclusion more precise and we return to the matter in chapter 10.

Our discussion above illustrates a general phenomenon to which we shall return in the following sections: sentences that violate subjacency may give rise to unacceptability but those that violate ECP are much worse.

We invite the reader to check the modified account here with other examples of ECP effects discussed in this and the preceding chapter.

3   Intermediate Traces and the ECP

3.1   *The Problem*

We have not yet discussed the status of the intermediate traces created by movement. Clearly, the formulation of the ECP would be maximally simple if we could assume that it also applies to these traces. Otherwise we have to discriminate such traces from traces in base-positions, a complication of the theory which we then would have to explain. In this section we shall see that, like adjunct traces, intermediate traces at LF are subject to the ECP and must be antecedent-governed.

3.2 *Intermediate Traces and Antecedent-government*

Consider an S-structure representation (49a) and the corresponding LF representation (49b):

49a Whom$_i$ do [you think [t$'_i$ that [John will invite   t$_i$]]]?
                                                              [+γ]
49b Whom$_i$ do [you think   [that [John will invite   t$_i$]]]?
                                                              [+γ]

At S-structure the trace in the base-position is [+γ]: it is theta-governed by the verb. The intermediate trace is created in order to observe the subjacency condition (see chapter 7). Since the intermediate trace is not in an argument position, we expect it to behave like an adjunct trace. The trace is not theta-governed: *think* theta-marks the complement CP but not the trace in [Spec,CP]. In order to satisfy the ECP the intermediate trace will have to be antecedent-governed. According to ASSUMPTION I, the intermediate trace, which is a non-argument trace, could be gamma-marked at LF, like all adjunct traces. ASSUMPTION II allows elements which do not contribute to the logico-semantic representation of a sentence to be deleted at LF. The intermediate trace is such an element. In the LF representation (49b) the intermediate trace is accordingly deleted.

As a result, (49) is in a sense a non-example: at the level where we are checking the gamma-features of intermediate traces there are none left. This does not mean that the problem of intermediate traces is a non-problem, though.

Consider (50a) (= 43), in which an adjunct is extracted, with the S-structure (50b) and the LF (50c):

50a Why do you think that Emsworth will invite George?
50b Why$_i$ do [$_{IP}$ you think [$_{CP}$ t$'_i$ that [$_{IP}$ Emsworth will invite George t$_i$]]]?
50c Why$_i$ do [$_{IP}$ you think [$_{CP}$ t$'_i$ [$_{IP}$ Emsworth will invite George   t$_i$]]]?
                    [?]   [+γ]

The lowest trace of the moved adjunct *why* must be gamma-marked at LF: it must be assigned the feature [+γ], by virtue of being antecedent-governed. The question is how t$_i$ is antecedent-governed, by t$'_i$ or by *why*?

Compare (50) with (51). (51) was discussed in the previous section as (42). We consider only the impossible interpretation in which *why* is construed with the lower clause. We have already established that under this interpretation the sentence violates subjacency and, more importantly, the ECP.

51a *Why do you wonder whom John will invite?

51b Why$_i$ do [$_{IP}$ you wonder [$_{CP}$ whom$_j$ [$_{IP}$ John will invite t$_j$ t$_i$]]]?
$$[+\gamma]$$

51c Why$_i$ do [$_{IP}$ you wonder [$_{CP}$ whom$_j$ [$_{IP}$ John will invite t$_j$ t$_i$]]]?
$$[+\gamma][-\gamma]$$

The distance between *why* and the trace in the base-position in (51c) was said to be too great for antecedent-government. This distance is exactly the same in (50c). We conclude that antecedent-government of the trace in the base-position in (50c) is ensured not by *why* itself but by the intermediate trace, t'$_i$, which hence must not be deleted at LF.

If we postulate that the intermediate trace must be properly governed like any trace then in (50c) the intermediate trace must be antecedent-governed by *why*:

50d Why$_i$ do [$_{IP}$ you think t'$_i$ [$_{IP}$ Emsworth will invite George t$_i$]]]?
$$[+\gamma] \qquad\qquad\qquad\qquad\qquad [+\gamma]$$

At this point we should perhaps dwell one moment on the LF representations (50d) and (51c), repeated here for the reader's convenience as (52a) and (52b):

52a = 51c *Why$_i$ do [$_{IP}$ you wonder [$_{CP}$ whom$_j$ [$_{IP}$ John will invite t$_j$ t$_i$]]]?
$$[+\gamma] \ [-\gamma]$$

52b = 50d Why$_i$ do [$_{IP}$ you think [$_{CP}$ t'$_i$ [$_{IP}$ Emsworth will invite
$$[+\gamma]$$

George t$_i$]]]?
$$[+\gamma]$$

We attributed the impossibility of construing *why* with the lower clause in (52a) to the ECP, saying that *why* would be too far from its trace to antecedent-govern it. The distance between *why* is two IPs and one CP. On the other hand, we assume that *why* in (52b) can antecedent-govern the intermediate trace although it is separated from it by one IP and one CP. It looks as if we shall need to be very careful about defining which categories define barriers for government since blatantly neither CP nor IP can always constitute a barrier. This intricate matter is discussed in chapter 10.

There is, of course, another way of discussing this issue. That would be by claiming that intermediate traces do not need to be governed at all. Though such a step would complicate our formulation of the ECP it would not lead to any different predictions with respect to the examples discussed so far.

3.3 *Intermediate Traces must be Antecedent-governed*

In order to test whether intermediate traces are subject to the ECP, we need an example whose ungrammaticality can be attributed solely to the presence of an ungoverned intermediate trace. This is not an easy matter but let us try.

53   *Why do you wonder whom Bill thinks that John will invite?

(53) is grammatical if we interpret *why* as asking for the reason of the wondering, but *why* cannot be construed with either *think* or *invite*. As in the discussion of (42), we assume that the impossible readings are attributed to ECP effects since subjacency violations do not produce such strong effects. We shall only discuss the reading in which *why* is construed with *invite*, hence the asterisk.

The S-structure and LF representations of (53) are (54a) and (54b) respectively:

54a   *$[_{CP1}$ Why$_i$ do $[_{IP1}$ you wonder $[_{CP2}$ whom$_j$ $[_{IP2}$ Bill thinks $[_{CP3}$ t$'_i$ that $[_{IP3}$ John will invite   t$_j$ t$_i$]]]]]]?
          $[+\gamma]$

54b   *$[_{CP1}$ Why$_i$ do $[_{IP1}$ you wonder $[_{CP2}$ whom$_j$ $[_{IP2}$ Bill thinks $[_{CP3}$ t$'_i$ $[_{IP3}$
          $[-\gamma]$

          John will invite   t$_j$ t$_i$]]]]]]?
          $[+\gamma][+\gamma]$

In (54a) t$_j$ is marked $[+\gamma]$, being theta-marked by *invite*. In (54b) the lowest trace of *why* is properly governed by the intermediate trace, t$'_i$, in [Spec,CP3]. This means that this trace must be present at LF. If the intermediate trace in [Spec,CP3] were itself not subject to the ECP the sentence would only violate subjacency and this would not explain the strong unacceptability of the reading in which *why* is construed with the lower clause (CP3). Let us assume that the intermediate trace in [Spec,CP3] is subject to the ECP. Given that it is not in an argument position, proper government will have to be achieved by antecedent-government. But the trace is separated from the antecedent *why*ᵢ by two IPs and one CP. As seen above (52a), this distance is apparently too great for antecedent-government: the combination of the three maximal projections has the effect of creating a barrier.

If we assume that intermediate traces are subject to the ECP at LF then we have a way of explaining why the representation (54b) is ruled out. So far no other principle of our grammar is able to explain the strong ungrammaticality of this sentence.

An example that makes the same point is discussed in Chomsky (1986b: 11, example (22d)).

55   *How did Bill wonder [CP who [IP wanted [t′ [to fix the car t]]]]?

We invite the reader to work out why (55) is ungrammatical.

4   Quantifiers

In this section we turn to a second instantiation of move-α at LF. Research in this area is still very much in progress and the reader is referred to the literature.[11]

4.1   *LF Representations and the Scope of Quantifiers*

Consider the following example:

56   Mary likes everyone.

---

[11] As a starting point see May (1985). For more discussion of LF and its properties the reader is referred to Aoun et al. (1981), Aoun and Hornstein (1985), Haik (1983), Heim (1982), Higginbotham (1980 and 1988), Higginbotham and May (1981), Hornstein (1984), Hornstein and Weinberg (1988) and Koopman and Sportiche (1982).

The sentence contains a quantified NP: *everyone*. In section 1.1 we suggested that the LF of such sentences should reflect the fact that quantifiers are operators that bind variables. Roughly, one could paraphrase the sentence as 'for every person x it is the case that Mary likes x', or in the notation of logic:

57   $\forall x, x = \text{human} (L\ m, x)$

In (57) the quantifier is extracted out of the sentence leaving a variable in the extraction site. The LF representation of (58) reflects the logical properties:

58   $[_{IP} \text{Everyone}_i\ [_{IP} \text{Mary likes } t_i]]$

The quantifier *everyone* is an operator binding a variable. It is adjoined to IP[12] and leaves a trace in its base-position. The operation that adjoins the quantifier to IP is called **quantifier raising** or **QR** (May, 1985), and is another instantiation of the transformation move-α.

Consider (59), which has two interpretations:

59   Everyone likes someone.
   (i)   For everyone x, there is someone y, such that x likes y.
or   (ii)   There is someone y, such that everyone x, x likes y.

In (i) each person may like someone different, in (ii) there is one individual that is liked universally. In (i) *everyone* is said to have **wide scope**; it takes scope over *someone*; *someone* has **narrow scope**. In (ii) *someone* has wide scope; *everyone* has narrow scope.

The LF representations for the two interpretations of (59) would be (60a) and (60b) respectively:

60a $[_{IP} \text{everyone}_i\ [_{IP} \text{someone}_j\ [_{IP} t_i \text{ likes } t_j]]]$
60b $[_{IP} \text{someone}_j\ [_{IP} \text{everyone}_i\ [_{IP} t_i \text{ likes } t_j]]]$

Analogously with *wh*-raising at LF, we expect that quantifier raising may also give rise to ECP effects. In the next section we turn to some evidence of ECP effects with QR.

---

[12]   In section 4.3 this proposal is modified slightly and QR is also seen to adjoin to VP.

4.2   Subject–object Asymmetries and French Negation

French negative existentials such as *personne* ('no one') have the property that they are accompanied by a negative clitic *ne* (at least in the standard language):

61   Je n'aime personne.
    I not-like no one
    'I like no one.'

In the literature it has often been assumed that the element *ne* is an overt scope-marker. The LF representation of (61) will be:

62   [Personne$_i$ [$_{IP}$ je n'aime t$_i$]]

In other words: 'for no person is it the case that I love him or her'. The scope of the negative existential *personne* is the entire clause.

    An interesting contrast appears when we compare simple sentences with complex ones:

63a   Je n'ai invité personne.
     'I have not invited anyone.'
63b   Personne n'a téléphoné.
     'No one has telephoned.'

64a   J'ai demandé qu'on n'invite personne.
     'I have asked that they invite no one.'
64b   J'ai demandé que personne ne téléphone.
     'I have asked that no one telephones.'

65a   Je n'ai demandé qu'on invite personne.
     I have not asked that they invite anyone
     'There is no person such that I have asked that they invite him or her.'
65b   *Je n'ai demandé que personne téléphone.
     I have not asked that anyone telephone

    In the simple sentences in (63) the scope of *personne* is the containing clause as can be seen from the translation. In (64) the scope of the negation in the lower clause is restricted to the lower clause. Crucially for our purposes, the negation does not bear on the verb *demander* ('ask') of the main clause. In (65) *ne* is found in the matrix clause. It indicates that *personne* should have main clause scope and thus negate the verb *demander*. This works fine when *personne* is in the object position in the lower clause, but it fails when *personne* is in the subject position. We shall consider these two examples here in some detail.

In (65a) the negative existential *personne* has scope over the main clause. Whereas (64a) means that there is a request being made that no one should be invited, (65a) means that there has not been a request to invite any person. (64a) has the LF representation (66a) and (65a) has the LF representation (66b):

66a   [j'ai demandé [$_{CP}$ que [$_{IP}$ personne$_i$ [$_{IP}$ on n'invite t$_i$]]]
66b   [personne$_i$ [$_{IP}$ je n'ai demandé [$_{CP}$ que [$_{IP}$ on invite t$_i$]]]]

Correspondingly, the LF representation of (64b) will be (67a) and that of the ungrammatical (65b) – where *personne* takes scope over the higher clause – ought to come out as (67b):

67a   [J'ai demandé [$_{CP}$ que [$_{IP}$ personne [t$_i$ ne téléphone]]]
67b   *[personne$_i$ [$_{IP}$ je n'ai demandé [$_{CP}$ que [$_{IP}$ t$_i$ téléphone]]]]

The asymmetry between the two sentences in (65) is a typical subject–object asymmetry. Such asymmetries are usually related to the ECP. The idea is that (67b) is like a *that*-trace violation: *personne* in (67b) is not able to antecedent-govern its trace in the lower subject position.[13]

4.3   VP-adjunction of Quantifiers

In this last section we turn to one more example of quantifier interpretation. Consider the contrast between (68a) and (68b):

68a   Who does everyone like?
68b   Who likes everyone?

---

[13]   For more discussion of the scope facts in French the reader is referred to Kayne (1984) which should be accessible at this point in our discussion.

The first question is ambiguous: either there is one person liked by everyone, say Chomsky, or there are as many persons as there are entities associated with *everyone*. In the latter reading one could answer: Sten likes Tarald, Corinne likes Luigi, Ian likes Oswaldo, Bonnie likes Irene. In the first interpretation, *who* takes scope over *everyone*. In the second reading *everyone* takes wide scope. If we were to assume that QR only moves a quantifier to IP, as suggested so far, then (69a) would be the LF representation for (68a):

69a

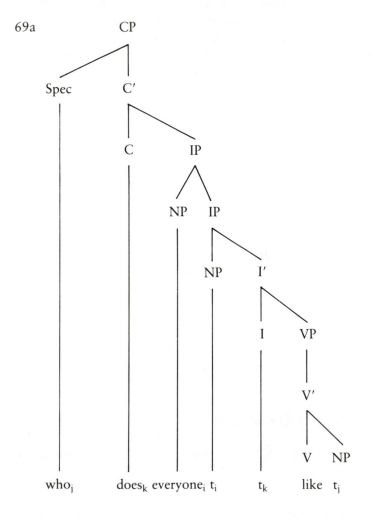

Everyone is adjoined to IP. Remember that adjunction creates a maximal projection on top of another one (see chapter 7). We have assumed that in order to be 'inside' – or dominated by – a maximal projection an element must be inside – or dominated by – ALL the maximal projections of that category.

In (69a) *everyone* is not **dominated** by IP in this sense, since it is only dominated by one segment of it, the higher IP. *Everyone* is, to use our metaphor, 'on the balcony'. *Everyone* is, however, dominated by CP and so is *who*. This means that in this representation *who*$_j$ and *everyone*$_i$ are dominated by exactly the same maximal projections. May (1985) proposes that when two quantifiers are dominated by exactly the same maximal projections either may take wide scope, hence the two readings associated with the sentence.

Adopting this analysis raises a problem for (68b). This sentence is unambiguous: *who* must have wide scope. To a question like (68b) the only possible answer is something like: 'Sten'. Sten would be an individual who likes everyone else. Suppose we apply QR as before and adjoin *everyone* to IP:

69b

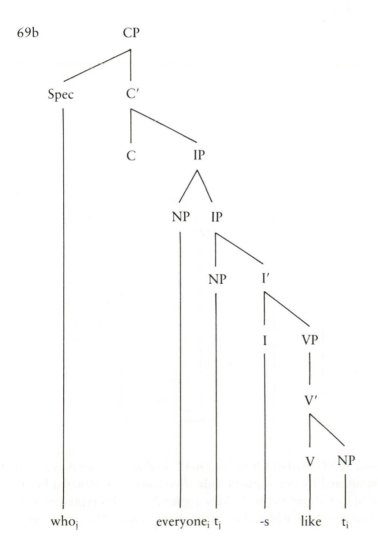

The reader can see that the relation between *who*$_j$ and *everyone*$_i$ is identical to that in (69a). Hence (69b) should lead us to say that (68b) is ambiguous, contrary to fact.

Robert May (1985) proposes that the LF representation of (68b) is not (69b) but (70):

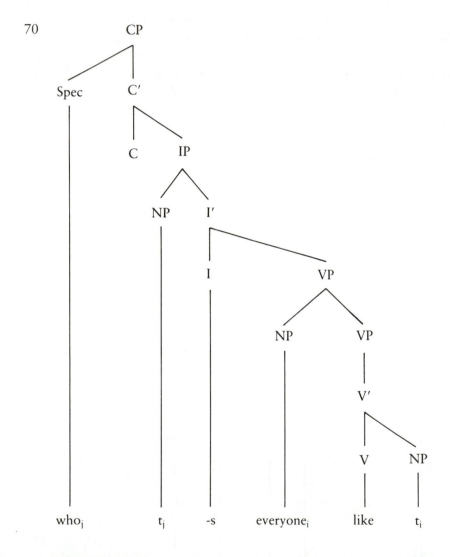

70

In (70) *everyone*$_i$ is adjoined to VP and not to IP. *Everyone*$_i$ is not dominated by VP, being dominated by one segment only. *Everyone*$_i$ is dominated by IP. *Who*$_j$ is dominated by CP and not by IP. May argues that in this representation the scope of *who* must be wider than that of *everyone*. The scope of a quantifier at LF will be determined by the maximal projection which dominates it. Adjunction to VP is not new in our theory. In chapter 6 we discussed free subject inversion in Italian as an instance of VP-adjunction, and in chapter 7 we discussed heavy NP-shift and PP-extraposition in those terms.

5 A Note on Parasitic Gaps

In chapter 8 we have discussed the phenomenon of parasitic gaps, i.e. gaps which are licensed by their occurrence in a sentence which contains another *wh*-trace.

71   Which books did John file t_i without reading e_i?

If parasitic gaps are licensed by another A'-bound gap, it might be the case that such a licensing gap occurs not at S-structure but at LF. A parasitic gap might be licensed by a gap resulting from LF movement of an operator, for example by the *wh*-raising of a *wh*-constituent which occupies its base-position at S-structure. (72), however, shows that parasitic gaps must be licensed at S-structure:

72   *Who read which articles without filing e?

Wh-raising would give us the LF representation (73) for the above example, but this clearly is not sufficient to license the parasitic gap indicated by *e*:

73   [Which articles$_j$ who$_i$] t_i read t_j without filing e_j.

We conclude that parasitic gaps are licensed at S-structure.[14]

---

[14] Section 9.5 will turn out to be relevant in our discussion of movement in Germanic languages in chapter 11.

6 Summary

In this chapter we have seen evidence for positing the level of logical form or LF. This is a level that represents the interpretation of scope-taking elements such as *wh*-phrases and quantifiers. We have illustrated two applications of move-α which mediate between S-structure and LF: *wh*-raising, which moves *wh*-constituents that were not moved to [Spec,CP] at S-structure, and quantifier raising, which adjoins quantificational elements to a dominating maximal projection, such as IP or VP.

Movement of elements between S-structure and LF creates traces which we have shown to be subject to the ECP. During the discussion we have refined our definition of the ECP, introducing the notion of gamma-marking. Following proposals in the literature (Lasnik and Saito, 1984) we assume that gamma-marking applies to argument traces at S-structure and to other traces at LF. Furthermore there is a free deletion process at LF.

We assume that the ECP is checked at LF and that intermediate traces are also subject to the ECP.

7 Exercises

Exercise 1

Discuss the S-structure and the LF representations of the following sentences and show how the ECP applies.

1 I told them [$_{CP}$ whom$_i$ [$_{IP}$ John will invite t$_i$]].
2 Whom$_i$ did you tell them [$_{CP}$ that [$_{IP}$ John will invite t$_i$]].
3 Whom$_i$ did you tell them [$_{CP}$ [$_{IP}$ John will invite t$_i$ where]]?

Exercise 2

In earlier versions of Government and Binding Theory (cf. Chomsky, 1981a: 250) proper government was interpreted either as lexical government or antecedent-government. A is a lexical governor for B if A head-governs B and A is a lexical category (N, V, A, P). In later versions (i.e. the one adopted here) lexical government has been replaced by theta-government. On the basis of examples (1) and (2) below, show that lexical government is not enough and that theta-government is required.

1 Why do you think Emsworth will invite Poirot?
2 Why do you wonder whom Bill thinks John will invite?

In (1) *why* can be interpreted as modifying both *think* and *invite*. In (2) *why* cannot be construed with *invite*.

Exercise 3

Discuss the contrast in grammaticality between the following sentences:

1 I don't know who said that Bill must retake which exam.
2 *I don't know which student said that who must retake the syntax exam.

Exercise 4

In the following examples the quantifier in the main clause takes scope over that in the subordinate clause. Provide the LF representations of these sentences.

1 Everyone believes that someone loves him.
2 Everyone believes that he loves someone.

On the basis of examples such as these it has been proposed that quantifier scope is clause-bound: QR does not normally raise quantifiers out of their clauses.

Does this hypothesis predict the fact that *everyone* in (3) can have scope over *someone*?

3 Someone believes everyone to be invited.

(3) contrasts with (4) where *everyone* cannot have scope outside the immediately dominating clause:

4   Someone believes that everyone will be invited.

The contrast between (3) and (4) is also found in (5) vs (6):

5   I expect that no one will come.
6   I expect no one to come.

In (5) the negation contained in *no one* cannot take scope over the main verb *expect*. (6) may have the interpretation: 'I do not expect anyone to come' or 'for no person is it the case that I expect them to come'. Try to identify the syntactic properties of the paired sentences that may influence the interpretations outlined.

Exercise 5

Consider the following French examples:

1   Jean a   trouvé beaucoup de livres.
    Jean has found   many   of books
    'Jean has found many books.'
2   Jean n'a pas trouvé de livres.
    Jean *ne* has not found   of books
    'Jean has not found any books.'
3   *De livres n'ont pas été   trouvés par Jean.
    Books *ne* have not been found   by Jean.
4   Beaucoup de livres ont été   trouvés par Jean.
    'Many   books have been found   by Jean.'
5   Jean ne veut   pas que tu   achètes de livres.
    Jean *ne* wants not that you buy   books
6   *Jean ne veut   pas que de livres soient achetés.
    Jean *ne* wants not that books   be bought

Kayne (1984) proposes that constructions of the form *de*. . .N be analysed as containing an empty category corresponding to the overt *beaucoup*:

7   [_{NP} e de livres]

How would this proposal enable us to account for the contrasts in acceptability among the examples above?

10   Barriers: an Introduction

Contents

Introduction and overview

Introduction and Overview

Throughout this book we have repeatedly referred to the concept of barrier. We have often talked about barriers for government, specifying at various points that certain maximal projections were or were not barriers for outside governors. We have also used the notion 'bounding node' with respect to the subjacency condition on movement: NP and IP are said to be bounding nodes; they impose limits on the distance a constituent can move.

Intuitively, it seems that the concepts 'barrier' and 'bounding node' are similar. Both serve to restrict the domain of application of grammatical processes. But so far we have treated these two concepts quite independently. For instance, we argue, on the one hand, that IP is defective and does not constitute a barrier for government, while, on the other hand, we have defined IP as a bounding node for subjacency.

In this chapter we formulate a definition of the notion barrier which can be used both in the definitions of government and proper government and in the definition of subjacency. The chapter is based exclusively on Chomsky's monograph *Barriers* published in 1986 (Chomsky, 1986b). *Barriers* has become the impetus to much current research in Government and Binding Theory.

It is not the purpose of this chapter to offer a complete discussion of the *Barriers* framework. The aim is to give an introduction to the general principles behind Chomsky's work and to render the current literature more accessible. For a fully-fledged account the reader should consult Chomsky's own work.[1]

Section 1 defines the notion barrier. In section 2 the subjacency condition is formulated in terms of barriers. In section 3 the ECP is reinterpreted in terms of barriers. Section 4 raises some remaining problems for *wh*-movement and section 5 introduces the extension of the barriers framework to NP-movement.

1   Maximal Projections: Transparent or Opaque?

In the course of our discussion we have explicitly or implicitly treated maximal projections as barriers for outside government, although many exceptions

---

[1] For modifications of the *Barriers* framework, see Rizzi (1990).

were allowed on a more or less *ad hoc* basis. Let us examine the areas in which we assumed government across maximal projections more carefully.

Government plays an important role in many syntactic processes. NPs are case-marked under government by the relevant case-marker (I,V,P); traces must be properly governed, a more restricted type of government. Whenever we can show that case is assigned or that a trace is governed from outside the maximal projection, we shall have to conclude that this projection is transparent for outside government. We shall first look at a range of data illustrating this point.

1.1 *Case-Marking and Proper Government*

1.1.1 INFINITIVAL IP

Consider (1).

1a I believe [$_{IP}$ him to be happy].
1b I prefer very much [$_{CP}$ for [$_{IP}$ him to leave first]].
1c John$_i$ is believed [$_{IP}$ t$_i$ to be happy].

(1a) is an example of exceptional case-marking (ECM): the subject NP of the lower infinitival clause is assigned ACCUSATIVE case by the matrix verb *believe* (see chapter 3 for discussion). This means that in (1a) IP cannot be a barrier for an outside governor. The same point applies to (1b), where *for* assigns ACCUSATIVE to *him*.

The ECP forces us to conclude that in (1c) too the lower IP is not opaque for an outside governor. The trace of the moved NP *John* must be properly governed to satisfy the ECP. It is clear that there is no proper governor inside the lower infinitival clause: the lower IP does not contain a theta-governor or an antecedent-governor for the trace. Hence the relevant governor must be outside IP. At this point we shall not discuss which element is the relevant governor in (1c). The verb *believed* is an unlikely candidate since this verb theta-marks and hence theta-governs the clause IP and not its subject. We return to examples like (1c) in section 5 below.[2]

1.1.2 FINITE IP

Finite IP too must not be an inherent barrier given the grammaticality of (2):

---

[2] For a full discussion of this example the reader is referred to Chomsky (1986b: section 11).

2a [$_{CP}$ Who$_i$ do [$_{IP}$ you think [$_{CP}$ t$'_i$ [$_{IP}$ t$_i$ left]]]]?
2b [$_{CP}$ When$_i$ did [$_{IP}$ he leave t$_i$]]?

In both examples the lowest traces must be properly governed and neither the trace of *who$_i$* nor that of *when$_i$* is theta-governed. We conclude that in both examples the antecedent in [Spec,CP] must be able to (antecedent-)govern the trace. This means that the IP projections in (2) cannot be barriers for outside government.

1.1.3 TRANSPARENT CP

Let us try to see if there are reasons for assuming that other maximal projections too are not barriers. Consider (3a) with the LF representation (3b).

3a When do you think that Emsworth will invite Poirot?
3b When$_i$ do [$_{IP}$ you think [$_{CP}$ t$'_i$ [$_{IP}$ Emsworth will invite Poirot t$_i$]]]?
  [+γ] [+γ]

Because we are dealing with adjunct traces, gamma-marking will only take place at LF. We assume that the complementizer *that* is freely deleted at LF (see chapter 9, section 2.2.2.2). In (3b) the lowest trace of *when* is antecedent-governed by the intermediate trace, t$'_i$, as expected if IP is not a barrier. The intermediate trace must also be properly governed (see chapter 9) and it can only be antecedent-governed. We are forced to conclude that *when* antecedent-governs the intermediate trace. This means that neither IP nor CP can constitute a barrier to government.

1.1.4 TRANSPARENT SMALL CLAUSES

Small clauses offer further evidence that maximal projections are not necessarily opaque for outside government:

4a I thought [$_{AP}$ John unhappy].
4b I thought [$_{NP}$ John a great friend].
4c I expect [$_{PP}$ John in my office].
4d I saw [$_{VP}$ John leave].

If we assume that the complements of the matrix verbs in (4) are maximal projections of the categories A, N, P and V respectively, we are led to conclude that government by an outside governor must be possible. The subject NPs of the small clauses must be able to be assigned ACCUSATIVE case by the matrix verbs.

The same reasoning is applicable when we look at the examples in (5) where a *wh*-phrase has been extracted from the subject position of a small clause. The ECP requires that the trace be properly governed. Again the proper governor will be outside the small clause:

5a   Who$_i$ did you think [$_{AP}$ t$_i$ unhappy]?
5b   Who$_i$ did you think [$_{AP}$ t$_i$ a great friend]?
5c   Who$_i$ do you expect [$_{AP}$ t$_i$ in your office]?

1.1.5   CONCLUSION

On the basis of data concerning ECM and ECP we have established so far that certain maximal projections must be transparent for outside government.

1.2   PRO

1.2.1   OPAQUE SMALL CLAUSES

The PRO theorem (chapter 5), in contrast, helps us to identify those maximal projections that must be barriers for outside government. Consider (6):

6   John arrived totally exhausted.

In (6) there are two predicates: the V *arrive* and the A *exhausted*. Both of these need an argument to which to assign their thematic role. If we assume that *arrive* assigns its thematic role to *John*[3] we shall need to posit a non-overt NP to which *exhausted* may assign its own thematic role (see discussion in chapter 5). A consideration of the properties of the non-overt subject of *totally exhausted* suggests that this is the null element referred to as PRO, which must be ungoverned at S-structure. We conclude that AP is opaque in (7): it is a barrier for outside government (from the verb or from I).

7   John arrived [$_{AP}$ PRO totally exhausted].

---

[3]   Being an unaccusative verb *arrive* assigns its theta role VP-internally (cf. chapter 6).

In (8) the same conclusion can be reached with respect to NP and PP:

8a John came home [$_{NP}$ PRO a wiser man].
8b John came home [$_{PP}$ PRO in a foul mood].

We conclude that maximal projections sometimes are barriers for outside government and sometimes are not. They are not barriers by definition. Barrierhood is a relative property which apparently is determined by the syntactic position in which the maximal projection appears.

1.2.2 OPAQUE CP

As another piece of evidence that maximal projections are sometimes opaque for outside government, consider the following example:

9 John decided [$_{CP}$ [$_{IP}$ PRO to see the movie]].
   (from Chomsky, 1986b: 11)

PRO must be ungoverned, so we are forced to conclude that either CP or IP is a barrier to government from the outside.

A similar conclusion is obtained when we consider (10a) which is ungrammatical when *why* is construed with *invite*. Under this interpretation (10a) has the LF (10b):

10a *Why do you wonder whom Bill thinks John will invite?
10b [$_{CP1}$ Why$_i$ do [$_{IP1}$ you wonder [$_{CP2}$ whom$_j$ [$_{IP2}$ Bill thinks [$_{CP3}$ t$'_i$ [$_{IP3}$
                                                                                        [$-\gamma$]

   John will invite   t$_j$ t$_i$]]]]]]]?
                    [$+\gamma$] [$+\gamma$]

Based on the discussion in chapter 9, the intermediate trace in [Spec,CP] is the offending trace: it violates the ECP (see the [$-\gamma$]). We assumed in chapter 9 that *why*$_i$ could not antecedent-govern the relevant trace because it was too far away. We conclude that though IP or CP are not absolute barriers for outside government, the combination of IP1, CP2, IP2 and CP3 is a barrier in this example.

1.3   Conclusion: Maximal Projections May or May Not be Barriers

We arrive at a problematic situation. On the one hand, we wish to say that maximal projections are not necessarily barriers for outside government (see the discussion in section 1.1), they are not intrinsically barriers. On the other hand, we need to assume that such projections are sometimes barriers for government (section 1.2). To add to the confusion, compare (9) with (11):

11   [$_{CP1}$ When$_i$ did [$_{IP1}$ John decide [$_{CP2}$ t$'_i$ [$_{IP2}$ PRO to fix the car t$_i$]]]]?

We need to assume that IP2 is not a barrier for outside government since t$'_i$ must govern t$_i$. Similarly we need to assume that *when* is able to antecedent-govern t$'_i$. Hence in (11) the combination of IP1 and CP2 is also not a barrier for government. But, on the other hand, we want to be able to say that PRO is ungoverned. Hence, the combination CP2 and IP2 ought to be a barrier for government.

One conclusion that appears to follow from the discussion so far is that IP is never a barrier on its own. Rather, it seems in certain circumstances to reinforce another maximal projection and form a barrier with it. In (11) the combination CP2 + IP2 is a barrier, whereas IP2 on its own is not. On the other hand, the combination IP1 + CP2 is not a barrier. Structurally the combination CP + IP seems to be a potential barrier. For (10) we could assume that the barrier for the government of the offending trace is constituted by CP2 + IP2.

This hypothesis will be confirmed in our analysis below, where we shall provide a more general justification.

1.4   Defining Barriers

In this section we shall provide a definition of the notion barrier. We shall see that certain maximal projections are barriers themselves, intrinsically, others become barriers by inheritance.

1.4.1   L-MARKING

Let us return to some of the small clause examples discussed previously:

12a I thought [$_{AP}$ John unhappy].

12b I thought [NP John a great friend].
12c I expect [PP John in my office at five].

13a John arrived [AP PRO totally exhausted].
13b John arrived [NP PRO a wiser man].
13c John arrived [PP PRO in a bad mood].

We see that sometimes AP, NP and PP are transparent (12), sometimes they are opaque (13). There is one important contrast between the two groups of examples. In (12) the relevant maximal projections are complements of the verbs *think* and *expect*; in (13) the maximal projections are adjuncts: they modify the VP but they are not arguments of the verb *arrive*. In (12) the lexical verbs govern the complements AP, NP and PP and theta-mark them: the verbs **theta-govern** the maximal projections. In order to refer to the special relation established between a lexical item and the complement which it governs and theta-marks, Chomsky introduces the term **L-marking**.

As a first hypothesis let us say that a maximal projection which is L-marked is transparent for an element contained in it, and that a maximal projection which is not L-marked is potentially opaque for an element contained in it. A maximal projection which is not L-marked is called a **blocking category** (BC).

14a **L-marking**
   A L-marks B iff A is a lexical category that theta-governs B. (Chomsky, 1986b: 15).
14b **BC**
   C is a BC for B iff C is not L-marked and C dominates B. (Chomsky 1986b: 14, def. (25)).

From the examples in (13) we might conclude that a BC is of necessity a barrier for outside government, but this conclusion is too rash. Consider (15):

15 When$_i$ do [IP1 you think [CP t'$_i$ that [IP2 John left t$_i$]]]?

IP2 is the complement of *that*. Even if one were to argue that the complementizer assigns a theta role to IP2, it is standardly assumed that the complementizer *that* is not a lexical category. One argument for this assumption is that *that* does not have any real semantic content and in fact in English *that* can be deleted, which is not true for other lexical categories. Thus IP2 is not L-marked by *that*. *Think* theta-marks CP, which is therefore L-marked. But *think* does not theta-mark IP2. Hence IP2 is not L-marked and a BC. In (15) t_i must be antecedent-governed by t'_i. We conclude that IP2, though a BC, is not a barrier for outside government.

Let us say that a maximal projection is an intrinsic barrier for an element contained in it if the maximal projection is a BC, exception being made for IP. We assume that the exception for IP is justified because IP is 'defective' in that its head is a bundle of syntactic features, [± Tense, ± AGR], which does not correspond to a word.

1.4.2 INHERITANCE

In section 1.1 we suggested that IP on its own would never be a barrier. On the other hand, an IP dominated by a CP was said to be a barrier. This is schematically represented in (16a), which corresponds to an example like (16b):

16a $[_{CP} \ldots [_{IP} \ldots]]$
16b John decided $[_{CP} [_{IP}$ PRO to see the movie]].

In (16b) *decide* L-marks CP. Hence CP is not a BC. IP is not L-marked; it is a BC. Remember that we argued that the BC IP on its own is not a barrier. It is the combination of IP and CP that results in the opacity. Chomsky (1986b) proposes that in our example CP becomes a barrier by virtue of the fact that it dominates a BC. CP is a barrier by inheritance. This leads us to the following definition for barrierhood:

17 A is a barrier for B iff (a) or (b):
    (a) A is a maximal projection and A immediately dominates C, C is a BC for B.
    (b) A is a BC for B, A is not IP.
    (cf. Chomsky 1986b: 14.)

In (16) A is CP, B is PRO, the relevant BC, C, is IP.

The notion government can be redefined integrating the notion barrier in (17). We distinguish between government by a head and antecedent-government:

18a **Government**
    X governs Y iff
        (i) X is either of the category A, N, V, P, I;
            or
            X and Y are co-indexed;

(ii)   X c-commands Y;

(iii)   no barrier intervenes between X and Y;

(iv)   minimality is respected.

18b   **Minimality Condition on Government**

There is no Z such that Z satisfies (i), (ii) and (iii) and X c-commands Z.

(18a(i)) allows for the two types of government. (18b), the minimality condition on government, serves to ensure that if two potential governors compete for government of Y then the closer one wins out.

1.5   *Unifying Subjacency and Government*

In the theory developed in *Barriers* (Chomsky, 1986b) the notion barrier is used in the definition of government and it is also used to replace the notion bounding node in the definition of subjacency. Informally, government cannot cross a barrier and movement must not cross more than one barrier.[4] In the subsequent sections of this chapter we turn to examples to illustrate the idea. Given the relative complexity of the discussion we shall give several examples to illustrate the same point. In this way we hope that the reader can familiarize himself with the theory. It is advisable that the reader try to analyse the examples before reading our discussion. Do not get discouraged if at first your own analysis contains certain lacunae. If you go through all the sentences we discuss here you will finally get the knack.

2   Subjacency and Barriers

In this section we see how the notion barrier can be integrated in the definition of the subjacency condition on movement.

2.1   *Movement and Adjunction*

2.1.1   SHORT MOVEMENT AND LONG MOVEMENT

We first look at the application of the notion barrier to the standard examples of subjacency. Let us say that movement must not cross more than one barrier.

---

[4] For a more careful formulation of the notion which does not appeal to counting barriers the reader is referred to Chomksy's own discussion (1986b: 30–1).

Consider (19):

19a When will John fix the car?
19b When do you think John will fix the car?

We discuss the examples one by one. The S-structure of (19a) is given in (20):

20   [$_{CP}$ When$_i$ will [$_{IP}$ John fix the car t$_i$]?

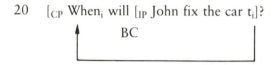

We assume that *when* is base-generated in a position outside VP. The movement of *when* crosses only IP. By our definitions IP is a BC (14b) but it is not a barrier (17b). In (20) *wh*-movement does not violate subjacency.

Now let us turn to (19b), whose S-structure is given in (21).

21   [When$_i$ do[$_{IP}$ you[$_{VP}$ think[$_{CP}$ t$'_i$[$_{IP}$ J will fix the car t$_i$]]]] ?

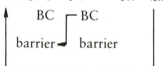

We do not consider the distance between the lower trace and the intermediate trace of *when*, which is the same as the distance between *when* and its trace in (20), but we concentrate on the distance between the intermediate trace and the antecedent *when*. Between *when* and t$'_i$ we find CP, a maximal projection which is L-marked hence not a BC. A second intervening XP is VP. VP is not L-marked, hence it constitutes a BC and a barrier (17b). The third maximal projection intervening between *when*$_i$ and t$'_i$ is an IP. IP is a BC. According to (17), IP is not a barrier intrinsically but it may become a barrier by inheritance if it dominates a BC. In (21) IP dominates the BC VP, hence IP is a barrier. In the representation (21) the movement of *when* crosses two barriers and ought to violate subjacency. But example (19b) is a perfectly natural example of long *wh*-movement and there are no subjacency effects.

In passing, we observe that given the present analysis (21) would also violate the ECP. The intermediate trace is not theta-governed and therefore must be antecedent-governed at LF (see discussion in chapters 8 and 9). If two barriers intervene between the trace and its purported antecedent it is not clear how antecedent-government could obtain. But there are no ECP effects in this example. Our analysis as developed so far thus raises problems for this example.

Indeed, other examples of *wh*-movement would at first sight also turn out to be subjacency violations under the analysis we have sketched in this chapter. Consider (22), a perfectly normal example of short object extraction:

22   Who$_i$ did   [$_{IP}$ John   [$_{VP}$ invite t$_i$]] ?

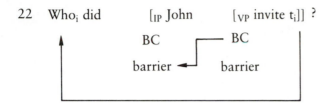

As the reader can verify, VP is a barrier (it is a BC) and IP becomes one by inheritance. But of course (22) does not violate the subjacency condition at all.

Either we shall have to abandon the formulation of subjacency in terms of barriers formulated above, or we must reconsider the definition of barriers, or we must try and think of alternative syntactic representations to replace (21) and (22).

2.1.2   VP-ADJUNCTION

The problem raised by (21) and (22) is due to the piling up of two BCs: IP, which is not an inherent barrier (by hypothesis), sits on top of another BC (VP) and ends up being a barrier by inheritance. But it is not obvious that the only syntactic representations for (19b) and (22) are the ones given above. In chapter 7 we discussed examples of heavy NP-shift, an instance of *wh*-movement in which the moved element is adjoined to a maximal projection, VP. (23a) has the partial S-structure (23b):

23a   My doctor told me to drink every night [$_{NP}$ two glasses of mineral water with a slice of lemon].

23b   VP

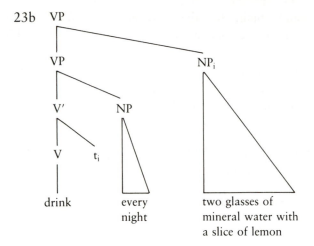

In chapter 9 we proposed that LF-movement of quantifiers may similarly adjoin an operator to VP. One example discussed there was (68b), repeated here as (24a) with the LF representation (24b):

24a Who likes everyone?

24b   CP

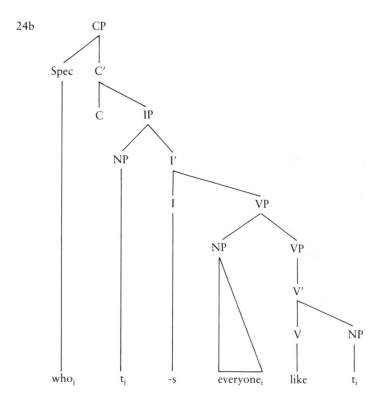

In the discussion of (24b) we adopted the idea[5] that the VP-adjoined constituent *everyone*ᵢ in (24b) is not dominated by VP because it is not dominated by both segments of VP. The position created by adjunction is a marginal position, neither inside nor outside the maximal projection to which adjunction takes place. We compared such a position to a balcony: when you're on a balcony you have not really left the room completely. Pursuing this idea let us say that the movement of *everyone* in (24b) does not cross the maximal projection VP, though it does cross one segment of it.

Let us now return to (22), repeated here in its initial analysis as (25a).

25a   Whoᵢ did [ₗₚ John [ᵥₚ invite tᵢ]]?

If we allow for a possibility of adjoining moved constituents to VP, then nothing stops us in principle from also carrying out the movement of *who*ᵢ to [Spec,CP] in two steps: first we adjoin *who*ᵢ to VP and then we move it to [Spec,CP]:

25b   Whoᵢ did   [ₗₚ John   [ᵥₚ t′ᵢ [ᵥₚ invite tᵢ]]]?

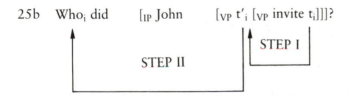

Step I is parallel to the adjunction we find in the case of heavy NP-shift in (23) and to the VP-adjunction by QR in (24). Step I does not strictly speaking cross VP: it crosses only one segment of it. No barriers are crossed and Step I does not violate subjacency. Step II does not strictly speaking 'cross' VP either: the topmost segment is crossed but not the lowest VP. Again then, this maximal projection does not come into play when we determine the barriers relevant to check for violations of subjacency. Step II does cross IP, a non-L-marked maximal projection, hence a BC (see 14b)). But, by hypothesis, IP is not a barrier inherently: IP only may become a barrier by inheritance. Following our definitions, IP in (25b) cannot become a barrier by inheritance for the VP-adjoined trace: between the VP-adjoined trace and IP there is only a segment of a maximal projection (the higher VP) but not a full BC. Step II also does not violate subjacency and our sentence is grammatical, a desirable result.

By using VP-adjunction, independently justified on the basis of heavy NP-shift examples and examples of QR, we can retain our reformulation of

---

[5] Due to May (1985).

subjacency in terms of barriers. The option of adjoining a constituent to VP is a way of circumventing the subjacency condition. The adjoined position is thus a sort of escape hatch. We shall exploit this option maximally in the discussion of the examples below.

Let us reconsider (19b) and its problematic representation in (21) repeated here as (26a):

26a   [When$_i$ do [$_{IP}$ you [$_{VP}$ think [$_{CP}$ t′$_i$ [$_{IP}$ J. will fix the car t$_i$]]]]]?

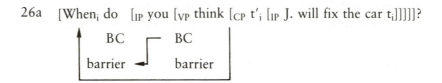

It is clear that the VP-adjunction analysis enables us to account for the grammaticality of our example in terms of subjacency:

26b   [When$_i$ do [$_{IP}$ you [$_{VP}$ t″$_i$ [$_{VP}$ think [$_{CP}$ t′$_i$ [$_{IP}$ J. . . . t$_i$]]]]]]?

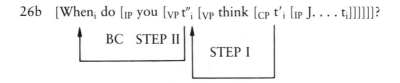

Step I crosses CP which is L-marked by *think* and hence not a BC. It does not 'cross' VP for reasons discussed above. Step II crosses IP which is not L-marked and thus a BC, but which on its own does not qualify for barrierhood. Hence neither step crosses a barrier and the sentence is all right for subjacency.

Note also that the intermediate traces will be antecedent-governed: both t′$_i$ in the lower [Spec,CP] and the VP-adjoined trace, t″$_i$, are antecedent-governed since no barrier intervenes.

2.2   *Island Violations*

Let us turn to some standard examples of subjacency violations and see if the theory developed so far is able to deal with them. We look at some extractions from *wh*-islands:

27a   ?Which man do you wonder when to meet?
27b   ?*Which man do you wonder when John will meet?

(27a) is marginal. It is an example of a weak subjacency effect: the *wh*-island created by the moved *when* is crossed. In our new system the sentence will have the following representation:

28 [CP Which man$_i$ do [IP you

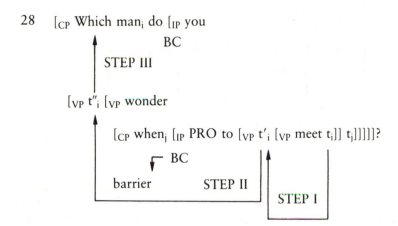

We have opted for VP-adjunction whenever possible. In our representation we assume that *when* originates outside VP. It can move to the lowest [Spec,CP] without problems. We do not discuss this movement at all.

Let us turn to the movement of the object NP *which man*. This adjoins first to the lower VP. The lower [Spec,CP] is occupied by the moved *when*, hence *which man* cannot move to it. In *Barriers* Chomsky bars adjunction to arguments. Adjunction of *which man* to CP is consequently also impossible. *Which man* moves on to the matrix VP. The third step of movement takes the element to the matrix [Spec,CP].

Step II crosses two maximal projections: IP and the lower CP. The former is not L-marked and thus a BC. Recall that IP is never a barrier of its own. The lower CP is a maximal projection which dominates a BC and thus, by (17a), it is a barrier – by inheritance – for the intermediate trace, t'_i. Step II of move-α crosses one barrier which gives a **weak** subjacency effect. (28) illustrates that a category which is L-marked, CP in our example, may still become a barrier by inheritance: CP is not a BC but it is still able to block government jointly with IP.

Now we turn to the representation of (27b), an example which is felt by many speakers, though not all, to be less acceptable. The question we ask now is whether there is a way of explaining that (27b) is felt to be worse than (27a).

The S-structure representation of (27b), annotated for movement and barriers, is (29):

29   ?* [CP Which man_i do [IP you

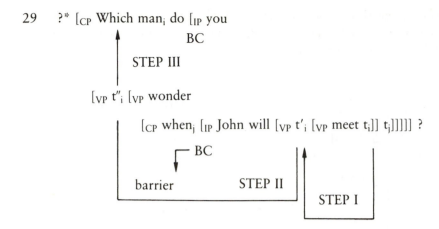

If you compare (29) with (28) you will find that the two S-structures are near-identical. Chomsky (1986b) proposes that a tensed clause, i.e. a tensed CP, is an additional barrier, though perhaps a 'weak barrier' for subjacency. Not all speakers share this intuition, the status of tensed CP as a barrier for subjacency is a matter of parametric variation.[6] If tensed CP is an extra barrier for subjacency then step II of *wh*-movement in (29) crosses two barriers rather than one and this explains why many speakers feel the sentence to be worse.

Following our discussion we can thus integrate the notion barrier into the subjacency condition:

30 **Subjacency condition**
    Movement must not cross more than one barrier.

Where barrier is defined in (17). For some speakers tensed CP is an additional barrier for subjacency in English.

The degree of unacceptability of sentences can now be linked to the degree to which (30) is violated: the more barriers are crossed the worse a sentence will become. If only one barrier is crossed we have a **weak** subjacency violation.

---

[6] Cf. chapter 7 for a discussion of the subjacency parameter.

3 ECP and Barriers

3.1 *Degree of Grammaticality: Subjacency and ECP*

In section 2 we have seen how the subjacency condition can be reinterpreted in the *Barriers* framework. In this section we consider ECP violations in the light of our definition of the notion barrier.

3.1.1 EXAMPLE 1: EXTRACTION FROM A RELATIVE CLAUSE

Consider:

31a   *Whom do you know [NP the date [CP when [IP Mary invited]]]?
31b   **When do you know [NP the man [CP whom [IP Mary invited]]]?

In (31a) the subjacency condition is violated: *whom* is extracted out of a complex NP, an NP whose head is modified by a relative clause. (31b) is ungrammatical in the reading in which *when* is construed with *invited*. In fact, (31b) is worse than (31a) – under the intended interpretation, that is – though they have a similar syntactic structure: in both extraction takes place from inside a complex NP. The S-structure of (31a), annotated to indicate move-ment, is (32a):

32a   *[CP Whom_i do [IP you

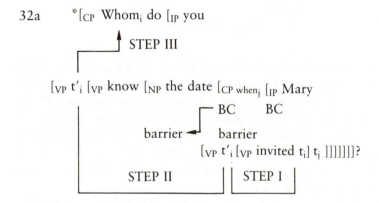

When_j moves to the lower [Spec,CP] crossing only the lower IP. This is a BC but not a barrier inherently.

In Step I *whom* adjoins to VP. This step does not cross any BC since it only crosses one segment of VP. Step II is problematic: *whom* moves and adjoins to the matrix VP. It crosses the lower IP, the lower CP, and NP. Which of these, if any, are BCs and/or barriers?

Starting from the lowest point, the embedded IP is a BC but it is not an intrinsic barrier. CP is a maximal projection which is not L-marked, hence a BC and hence a barrier. (Note that being on top of the BC IP, CP would become a barrier by inheritance anyway.) NP is a maximal projection which dominates a BC (CP) hence is also a barrier by inheritance. Thus in Step II *whom* crosses more than one barrier. Step III is unproblematic: only one IP is crossed.

(31a) will be a stronger subjacency violation than the example (27a) where only one barrier was crossed. This corresponds to our intuitive judgement of these examples.

Now we turn to (31b) which is felt to be worse than (31a). The S-structure representation of (31b) is (32b):

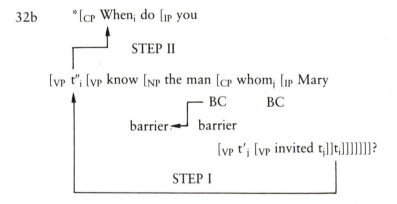

32b   *[_{CP} When_i do [_{IP} you

We do not deal with the movement of *whom*_j in detail, we simply adopt the analysis with VP-adjunction. We assume that *when* originates outside VP. *When* moves out of its base-position and will have to cross the lower IP, the lower CP and the NP to adjoin to the matrix VP. CP is a barrier, and so is NP, by inheritance (cf. the discussion of (32a)). Step II is identical to Step III in (32a) and we refer the reader to the discussion above. As far as subjacency is concerned, (32b) is no different from (32a). How come that (32b) is intuitively felt to be so much worse than (32a)?

At this point the ECP comes into play. The ECP states that traces must be properly governed. In chapter 9 we have developed a rather refined and complicated system of checking for proper government. Let us apply this to the examples above. In both examples there are two A'-chains, one headed by *when* and one headed by *whom*. Traces of arguments are subject to gamma-marking at S-structure, while traces of adjuncts are gamma-marked at LF. (33a) is the S-structure of (31a) with the relevant gamma-marking and in (33b) we produce the LF representation:

33a *[$_{CP}$ Whom$_i$ do [$_{IP}$ you [$_{VP}$ t''$_i$ [$_{VP}$ know [$_{NP}$ the date [$_{CP}$ when$_j$ [$_{IP}$ Mary [$_{VP}$
t'$_i$ [$_{VP}$ invited t$_i$]] t$_j$]]]]]]]?
[+γ]

33b *[$_{CP}$ Whom$_i$ do [$_{IP}$ you [$_{VP}$ know [$_{NP}$ the date [$_{CP}$ when$_j$ [$_{IP}$ Mary
[$_{VP}$ invited t$_i$] t$_j$]]]]]]?
[+γ] [+γ]

In (33a) the lowest trace of the object is properly governed being theta-governed by the verb. We do not gamma-mark any of the other traces: they are not in A-positions. At LF all traces are checked for gamma-marking. However, we may freely delete redundant material and we use this opportunity to delete the intermediate traces created by adjunction and the maximal projections which are created by the adjunctions. Now we are left with only one trace to gamma-mark: t$_j$. This trace is duly antecedent-governed by *when* in the lower [Spec,CP]: there are no intervening barriers.

Now let us turn to (31b). The S-structure with gamma-marking is (34a) and the LF representation (34b).

34a *[$_{CP}$ When$_i$ do [$_{IP}$ you [$_{VP}$ t'$_i$ [$_{VP}$ know [$_{NP}$ the man [$_{CP}$ whom$_j$ [$_{IP}$ Mary
BC
[$_{VP}$ t'$_j$ [$_{VP}$ invited t$_j$]] t$_i$]]]]]]]
[+γ]

34b *[$_{CP}$ When$_i$ do [$_{IP}$ you
BC
[$_{VP}$ t'$_i$ [$_{VP}$ know [$_{NP}$ the man [$_{CP}$ whom$_j$ [$_{IP}$ Mary
[+γ]   BC   BC
barrier   barrier
[$_{VP}$ [$_{VP}$ invited t$_j$]] t$_i$]]]]]]]
[+γ] [−γ]

(34a) raises no peculiar problems. The lowest t$_j$ is [+γ] being theta-governed by *invited*. In (34b), we must check the proper government of the traces. Being an adjunct-trace, t$_i$ can only be antecedent-governed. The intermediate trace t'$_i$, adjoined to the higher VP ought to take care of antecedent-government but this trace cannot antecedent-govern the lowest t$_i$, being separated from it by two barriers, CP and NP. Needless to say deleting t'_i is pointless since t_i is too far from the matrix [Spec,CP]. The intermediate t'_i itself satisfies the ECP, being antecedent-governed by *when*.

The difference in grammaticality judgements between (31a) and (31b) has nothing to do with subjacency. Both examples are violations of subjacency: two barriers are crossed. But (31b) is considerably worsened because the sentence also violates the ECP. This example illustrates another aspect of the relative grammaticality of sentences. Given that there are various principles of grammar which may be violated the sentence will worsen as more than one principle is violated. It also turns out that ECP violations are a cause of strong ungrammaticality.

3.1.2   EXAMPLE 2: EXTRACTION FROM AN ADJUNCT

Consider the contrast in (35):

35a Which man did Bill go to Rome to visit?
35b *Where did Bill go to Rome to work?

(35a) is acceptable, (35b) is unacceptable with *where* construed with the purpose clause.

The S-structure of (35a) is (36):

36   [CP Which man$_i$ did [IP Bill

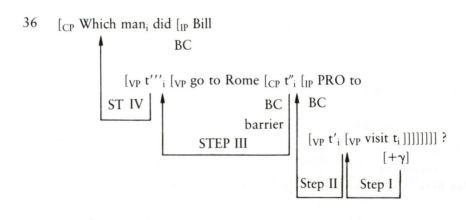

In (36) we maximally exploit the VP-adjunction option. Step I does not cross any BC/barriers, VP-adjunction provides the needed escape hatch. Step II crosses the lower IP, which is a BC but not a barrier on its own. Step III crosses the lower CP, the purpose clause. Purpose clauses are adjuncts: they are not

L-marked hence they are BCs and barriers. This means that Step III crosses one barrier. Remember that Step III does not cross the higher VP because it only crosses the lower segment VP. Step IV crosses only the higher IP, a BC but not an independent barrier.

(35a) is a weak subjacency violation: one barrier is crossed. As far as ECP is concerned, we see that the trace in the object position of *visit* is properly governed: it is [+γ] since it is theta-governed by the verb. We need not be concerned with the status of the intermediate traces at S-structure. Neither will we need to worry about them at LF since we can liberally delete them all.

The S-structure of (35b) is (37a) and its LF-representation is given in (37b):

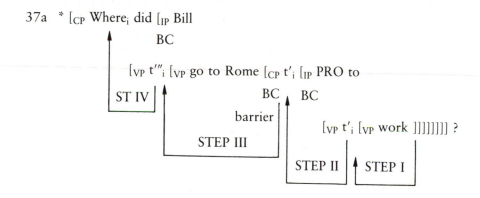

37a   * [$_{CP}$ Where$_i$ did [$_{IP}$ Bill

37b   [$_{CP}$ Where$_i$ did   [$_{IP}$ Bill
                    BC
    [$_{VP}$ t$'''_i$ [$_{VP}$ go to Rome [$_{CP}$ t$''_i$ [$_{IP}$ PRO to
       [+γ]   BC   [−γ] BC
                       barrier
   [$_{VP}$ t$'_i$ [$_{VP}$ work   t$_i$]]]]]]]]?
      [+γ]   [+γ]

We assume that the place adjunct originates inside VP but nothing hinges on this assumption. (37a) is in the relevant respects identical to (36): one barrier, the lower CP, is crossed by Step III, resulting in a weak subjacency violation. At S-structure no gamma-marking takes place since we have extracted an adjunct. Gamma-marking is done at LF, (37b). Since the lower CP is not L-marked, it is a barrier, and t$'_i$ in the lower [Spec,CP] cannot be antecedent-governed by a governor outside CP and violates the ECP. This explains the difference in grammaticality between (35a) and (35b): both violate subjacency weakly, but (35b) also violates the ECP.

3.1.3   EXAMPLE 3: EXTRACTION FROM A SUBJECT CLAUSE

Compare the following examples: in each an element is extracted from a subject clause.

38a   *This is a book which reading would be fun.
38b   **This is a pen with which writing would be fun.

Both sentences are felt to be unacceptable but (38b) is markedly worse. We go through the derivations of these sentences below. As the reader may by now anticipate the contrasting grammaticality will be related to the fact that (38b) violates not only subjacency, as does (38a), but also the ECP.

   The S-structure and LF-representations of the relevant NP in (38a) are as in (39a) and (39b) respectively. We assume without discussion that the gerund *reading* heads a NP.[7]

39a $[_{NP}$ a book $[_{CP}$ which$_i$ $[_{IP}$ $[_{NP}$ PRO $[_{VP}$ t$'_i$ $[_{VP}$ reading t$_i]]]$
                       BC   BC
                       barrier barrier $[+\gamma]$
      would . . .
39b $[_{NP}$ a book $[_{CP}$ which$_i$ $[_{IP}$ $[_{NP}$ PRO $[_{VP}$ reading   t$_i]]]$
                                                            $[+\gamma]$
      would . . .

In (39a) *which*, the object of *reading*, first adjoins to the gerundival VP and then moves to [Spec,CP]. Following Chomsky we assume (i) that adjunction to arguments is not possible and (ii) that *wh*-movement does not adjoin to IP in English. The movement of *which* crosses two maximal projections: NP and IP. NP is not L-marked: it is assigned an external theta role, but not under direct government by the verb. Hence NP is a BC and a barrier. IP is a maximal projection and it dominates a BC. IP will become a barrier by inheritance. The movement of *which* violates subjacency: it crosses two barriers. At S-structure the trace of *which* in the base-position is theta-governed by the verb *reading*, hence properly governed and $[+\gamma]$. At LF intermediate traces can be deleted and the trace of *which* is properly governed.

   In (40) we represent the S-structure and LF of (38b):

[7]   Cf. Aoun and Sportiche (1983: 219). See also Abney (1987)

40a [$_{NP}$ a pen [$_{CP}$ with which$_i$ [$_{IP}$ [$_{NP}$ PRO [$_{VP}$ t$'_i$ [$_{VP}$ writing t$_i$]]]
　　　　　　　　　　　　　　　　　　BC
　　　　　　　　　　　　　　barrier barrier

　　　would . . .

40b [$_{NP}$ a pen [$_{CP}$ with which$_i$ [$_{IP}$ [$_{NP}$ PRO [$_{VP}$ t$'_i$ [$_{VP}$ writing   t$_i$]]]
　　　　　　　　　　　　　　　　　　BC　　　　　　[$-\gamma$]　　　　　　[$+\gamma$]
　　　　　　　　　　　　　　barrier barrier

　　　would . . .

In (40a) the moved adjunct is first adjoined to the gerundival VP and then crosses NP and IP, identified as barriers above. The representation violates subjacency. At S-structure adjunct traces are not gamma-marked. At LF (40b) the intermediate trace of the moved adjunct, t$'_i$, cannot be antecedent-governed: the intervening barriers prevent the antecedent from governing the trace. Hence (40b) violates the ECP.

3.1.4 EXTRACTION FROM COMPLEMENTS

In (35) and (38) we illustrate two violations of what used to be known as the condition on extraction domains, or the CED.[8] This constraint bars movement out of subjects and out of adjuncts. In (38) the extraction is out of a subject and in (35) out of an adjunct. What unites the two examples is that an element is extracted from a category which is not directly theta-marked under government by a lexical head. Such extraction will always cross a BC and a barrier.

Furthermore when an adjunct is extracted from an adjunct clause or a subject clause, the ECP will be violated: the barrier(s) intervening between a trace and an antecedent will block antecedent-government. In the case of complement extraction no such ECP violation arises given that the complement will be theta-governed.

Extraction from L-marked categories is predictably better than extraction from adjuncts or subjects:

41a Which book would you recommend reading?
41b With which pen would you recommend writing?

The S-structure and LF representations of (41a) are (42a) and (42b) respectively:

[8] Cf. Huang (1982).

42a Which book$_i$ would [$_{IP}$ you [$_{VP}$ t$'_i$ [$_{VP}$ recommend [$_{NP}$ PRO
                BC
     [$_{VP}$ t$'_i$ [$_{VP}$ reading   t$_i$]]]]]]?
                [+γ]

42b Which book$_i$ would [$_{IP}$ you [$_{VP}$ recommend [$_{NP}$ PRO [$_{VP}$ reading   t$_i$]]]]?
                                                                        [+γ]

In (42a) *wh*-movement does not cross any barriers. In contrast with the
example illustrating extraction from a subject gerundival NP, (39a), the
gerundival NP in (42a) is L-marked and hence not a BC. The trace of *which
book* is theta-governed, hence [+γ] and at LF intermediate traces are deleted.
(41b) has the representations in (43):

43a With which pen$_i$ would [$_{IP}$ you
                BC
     [$_{VP}$ t$''_i$ [$_{VP}$ recommend [$_{NP}$ PRO [$_{VP}$ t$'_i$ [$_{VP}$ writing t$_i$]]]]]]?
43b With which pen$_i$ would [$_{IP}$ you
                BC
     [$_{VP}$ t$''_i$ [$_{VP}$ recommend [$_{NP}$ PRO [$_{VP}$ t$'_i$ [$_{VP}$ writing t$_i$]]]]]]?
       [+γ]   [+γ]   [+γ]

No additional problems arise with respect to the extraction of the adjunct. At
LF all traces are antecedent-governed.
    Finally, we invite the reader to turn to (44) which contains extractions from
wh-islands.

44a ?Which man do you wonder when to meet?
44b *With which pen do you wonder what to write?

(44a) corresponds to (27a) discussed in section 2.2. *Wh*-movement extracts an
object NP from a *wh*-island, created by the moved *when*. (45a) is the
S-structure of (44a):

45a [$_{CP}$ Which man$_i$ do [$_{IP}$ you [$_{VP}$ t$''_i$ [$_{VP}$ wonder [$_{CP}$ when$_j$ [$_{IP}$ PRO to [$_{VP}$ t$'_i$
                BC   barrier BC
     [$_{VP}$ meet t$_i$]]   t$_j$]]]]]]?
       [+γ]

The lower CP is a barrier by inheritance: it dominates the BC, IP. Thus (45a) weakly violates subjacency. Being theta-governed by *meet*, the trace of *which man*$_i$ is properly governed. At LF the trace of *when* is subject to gamma-marking, it is antecedent-governed, hence properly governed. Intermediate traces of *which man* can be deleted:

45b [$_{CP}$ which man$_i$ do [$_{IP}$ you
$$\qquad\qquad\qquad \text{BC}$$
[$_{VP}$ wonder [$_{CP}$ when$_j$ [$_{IP}$ PRO to [$_{VP}$ meet t$_i$ t$_j$]]]]]?
$$\qquad\qquad\qquad \text{BC} \qquad\qquad\qquad\qquad [+\gamma]\,[+\gamma]$$
$$\qquad\quad \text{barrier}$$

In (44b) there is a weak subjacency violation, as is the case in (44a), and in addition there is an ECP violation:

46a [$_{CP}$ With which pen$_j$ do [$_{IP}$ you[$_{VP}$ t$_j$ [$_{VP}$ wonder
$$\qquad\qquad\qquad\qquad \text{BC}$$
[$_{CP}$ what$_i$ [$_{IP}$ PRO to [$_{VP}$ t$_j$ [$_{VP}$ t$_i$ [$_{VP}$ write   t$_i$ t$_j$]]]]]]]]]]
$$\qquad \text{BC} \qquad\qquad\qquad\qquad\qquad [+\gamma]$$
$$\text{barrier}$$

We assume without discussion that both the PP and the NP may adjoin to the lower VP.[9] Movement of *what* does not cross any barriers; movement of *with which* crosses the lower CP barrier. The trace of *what* is properly governed via theta-government by *write*. For gamma-marking of the trace of the adjunct we need to turn to LF. The intermediate trace of *what* is deleted.

46b [$_{CP}$ With which pen$_j$ do [$_{IP}$ you
$$\qquad\qquad\qquad\qquad \text{BC}$$
[$_{VP}$ t''$_j$ [$_{VP}$ wonder
$$\;\; [+\gamma]$$
[$_{CP}$ what$_i$ [$_{IP}$ PRO to [$_{VP}$ t'$_j$ [$_{VP}$ write   t$_i$ t$_j$]]]]]]]]]
$$\qquad\quad \text{BC} \qquad\qquad\qquad [-\gamma] \qquad\qquad [+\gamma]\,[+\gamma]$$
$$\text{barrier}$$

(46b) violates the ECP: t'$_j$, adjoined to the lower VP, cannot be properly governed. Its antecedent, the trace, t''$_j$, adjoined to the higher VP, is separated from it by a barrier, CP.

[9] See discussion in Chomsky (1986b: 66).

3.2   Extraction: Summary

On the basis of the examples above we conclude that extraction from complements which are not islands is straightforward for both adjuncts and complements. On the other hand, extraction from complements which are islands leads generally to subjacency violations and in addition it results in ECP violations when adjuncts are extracted. Extraction from adjuncts will also lead to subjacency violations and in the case of adjunct extraction from adjuncts an ECP effect is added.

4   Discussion Section: Further Data

4.1   Subjects and the Vacuous Movement Hypothesis

We have claimed that extraction from *wh*-islands results in subjacency effects, with additional ECP effects if adjuncts are extracted. In previous discussion (chapter 7), however, we discussed the special problem of subject extraction. It was proposed that in questions like (47) it would be possible to assume that the subject *wh*-word remains *in situ*:

47a $[_{CP} [_{IP}$ Who likes John]]?
47b   I wonder $[_{CP} [_{IP}$ who likes John]].

If this analysis is correct, no *wh*-islands are created: [Spec,CP] is still available for movement.

48   ?What do you wonder who saw? (from Chomsky, 1986b: 48)

Assuming that *who* is unmoved, the S-structure of (48) is (49):

49   $[_{CP}$ What$_i$ do $[_{IP}$ you wonder $[_{CP}$ t$'_i$ $[_{IP}$ who$_j$ saw t$_i$]]]]?
           BC   BC   [+γ]

At LF *who*, an operator, needs to be moved to an operator position. Chomsky suggests it is moved to the lower CP, obliterating the trace of the moved *what*.[10] That (48) is not quite perfect may be due to the fact that at LF *who* moves into a [Spec,CP] into which another constituent has already moved.

The hypothesis that subject *wh*-constituents remain *in situ* at S-structure is interesting since it accounts for the contrast in grammaticality between (50a) and (50b).[11]

50a ?This is a paper that we need someone who understands.
50b *This is a paper that we need someone that we can intimidate with.

Chomsky considers (50b) as less acceptable than (50a). Consider the S-structure and LF representations of (50a):

51a a paper [$_{CP}$ 0$_i$ [$_{IP}$ we [$_{VP}$ t''$_i$ [$_{VP}$ need [$_{NP}$ someone [$_{CP}$ t'$_i$
                                   BC   BC
                                   barrier   barrier
   [$_{IP}$ who [$_{VP}$ t$_i$ [$_{VP}$ understands t$_i$]]]]]]]]]
   BC
51b a paper [$_{CP}$ 0$_i$ [$_{IP}$ we [$_{VP}$ need [$_{NP}$ someone [$_{CP}$ who$_j$
   [$_{IP}$ t$_j$ [$_{VP}$ understands t$_i$]]]]]]]

At S-structure, the zero operator, 0$_i$, can move through the lower [Spec,CP] crossing two barriers, NP and CP. (51a) violates subjacency. At LF, the subject relative *who*$_j$ covers the intermediate trace of 0$_i$ in the specifier position of the lower CP.[12]

(50b) is slightly worse than (50a). (52) is its S-structure.

52   a paper [$_{CP}$ 0$_i$ [$_{IP}$ we [$_{VP}$ t''$_i$ [$_{VP}$ need
                BC
     [$_{NP}$ someone [$_{CP}$ 0$_j$ that [$_{IP}$ we can
                BC   BC
     barrier   barrier
        [$_{VP}$ t'$_i$ [$_{VP}$ t'$_j$ [$_{VP}$ intimidate t$_j$ with t$_i$]]]]]]]]]]]].
               [+γ]   [+γ]

---

[10] The moved *who* will have to take the place of *what* in order to be able to transmit its index to [Spec,CP]. If the moved *who* were simply adjoined to the trace of *what* then it would not be able to antecedent-govern its trace. See chapter 9, section 1.4 (21) for discussion.
[11] See Chomsky (1986b: 51) and Chung and McCloskey (1983).
[12] Cf. the discussion of (49a) above.

In (52), the zero operator 0_i moves to the lowest [Spec,CP] crossing only IP. 0_i moves to the higher [Spec,CP] and crosses two barriers: CP, which is itself not L-marked and also inherits barrierhood from the lower IP, and NP, which inherits barrierhood from the CP. 0_i cannot move through the lower [Spec,CP]. The LF representation of (52) will cause no further problems: the relevant argument traces are already properly governed, and the intermediate traces can be deleted. The difference of acceptability between (50a) and (50b) could not be explained if we assume that *who* is moved at the S-structure (50a). As the reader can verify, under such an analysis both sentences would only involve identical subjacency violations.[13]

4.2 Noun Complement clauses

Consider the following sentences. (53b) is unacceptable if *when* is construed with the lower clause. We only discuss this reading.

53a ?Which car did John announce a plan to steal tonight?
53b *When did John announce a plan to steal Bill's car?

Using Ross's terminology we would classify both examples above as violations of the complex NP constraint. The *wh*-constituents have been extracted from inside a clause which is the complement of a N. In chapter 7, the complex NP constraint was reinterpreted in terms of subjacency. Let us examine these sentences in the *Barriers* framework. (54) is the S-structure of (53a):

54   [$_{CP}$ Which car$_i$ did [$_{IP}$ John [$_{VP}$ t'''$_i$ [$_{VP}$ announce [$_{NP}$ a
                     BC
     plan [$_{CP}$ t''$_i$ [$_{IP}$ to [$_{VP}$ t'$_i$ [$_{VP}$ steal t$_i$] tonight]]]]]]]]?
           BC   [+γ]

In this example the complement CP is L-marked by the head N, hence the CP is not a barrier. The NP itself is not a barrier either since it is also L-marked. But intuitively the example is not perfect. (cf. Chomsky, 1986b: 35).

Adjunct extraction from complex NPs is worse, as illustrated by (53b), which has the S-structure (55a):

---

[13] In *Barriers* Chomsky (1986b: 48–54) gives more examples where an analysis with a subject *wh*-constituent *in situ* at S-structure gives promising results.

55a [CP When_i did [IP John [VP t''_i [VP announce [NP a
　　　　　　BC
plan [CP t'_i [IP to [VP steal Bill's car] t_i]]]]]]]?
　　　BC

Again no barriers are crossed, but the sentence is still not acceptable. Chomsky suggests that there must be a barrier for movement in these examples and he proposes that the CP complement of the N *plan* may be such a barrier (see Chomsky, 1986b: 36).

Let us turn to the LF representation corresponding to the S-structure (55a). We need to consider LF because the trace of the moved *when* is an adjunct trace and can only be gamma-marked at LF.

55b [CP When_i did [IP John [VP t''_i [VP announce [NP a
　　　　　　BC　　　　　[+γ]
plan [CP t'_i [IP to [VP steal Bill's car] t_i]]]]]]]?
　　　[−γ]　　　　　　　　　　　　[+γ]

The lowest trace of *when* is properly governed by the intermediate trace, t'_i, in the lowest [Spec,CP]. The highest intermediate trace, t''_i, will be antecedent-governed by *when*. This leaves us to consider the gamma-feature of t'_i.

56

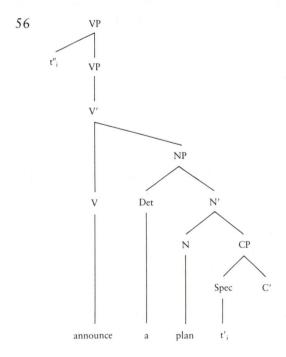

t''_i ought to antecedent-govern t'_i. It does indeed c-command t'_i but it is not the closest governor. The N *plan* governs CP and assigns it a theta role. Hence N L-marks CP. CP is neither a BC nor a barrier so N can govern inside CP and crucially it can govern the t'_i. This means that by minimality the antecedent trace, t''_i, loses out and will not be able to govern t'_i. Regardless of the status of CP with respect to subjacency, t'_i violates the ECP (cf. Chomsky, 1986b: 43). In noun complement clauses the N-head will always govern the CP complement, thus it will always prevent antecedent-government of material inside CP from the outside. It follows that adjunct extraction from N-complement clauses is impossible.[14]

5   A-Chains

So far we have applied the *Barriers* framework as developed by Chomsky (1986b) exclusively to examples of *wh*-movement, i.e. to A'-chains. In this section we turn to A-chains. We shall see that as it stands our theory faces serious problems when it comes to dealing with raising and passive constructions (cf. chapter 5). In the present section the problems will be raised and some suggestions for a solution to the problem are made. For extensive discussion and a complete analysis the reader is referred to Chomsky's own work (1986b: 68 ff) and to recent work by Pollock (1989).

(57) illustrates NP-movement:

57a   John will be invited.
57b   John is believed to have left.
57c   John seems to have left.

In each of these sentences the subject NP *John* is a derived subject. The S-structure representations of (57) are as in (58):

58a $[_{IP}$ John$_i$ will $[_{VP}$ be invited t$_i]]$.
58b $[_{IP}$ John$_i$ pres $[_{VP}$ be believed $[_{IP}$ t$_i$ to have left$]]]$.
58c $[_{IP}$ John$_i$ pres $[_{VP}$ seem $[_{IP}$ t$_i$ to have left$]]]$.

---

[14] Rizzi (1990) provides an alternative definition of minimality.

Consider (58a). *John* originates as the direct object of *invited* and moves to the subject position. It crosses the maximal projection VP which is a BC and a barrier. This would mean that sentences such as (57a) and (58a) contain a weak subjacency violation, hardly the result we expect for sentences as normal as those. Assuming that *invited* theta-governs the trace of *John*, the ECP is not violated.

The situation becomes worse in the case of raising sentences such as (57b) and (57c). Consider the S-structure (58c). *John* originates as the D-structure subject of the lower IP. It moves to the subject position and crosses IP, a BC though not a barrier, and VP, a BC and a barrier. Again (58c) ought to be a weak subjacency violation. The trace of *John* in (58c) can only satisfy the ECP through antecedent-government. The only potential antecedent is *John*, from which it is separated by a barrier, VP. In fact, the antecedent *John* will never be able to govern the trace in the lower infinitival clause since *seem* is always a closer governor and thus by minimality prevents *John* from governing the trace. It is hardly desirable that we should be forced to consider sentences like (57c) as ECP violations.

The reader might suggest that we use the escape hatch introduced in the case of *wh*-movement, where movement was allowed to go via VP-adjunction. However this solution is not possible in the case of A-chains. Consider, for instance, (57a/58a), the passive sentence. Suppose we allowed *John* first to adjoin to VP before moving to the subject position:

59   $[_{IP}$ John$_i$ will $[_{VP}$ t$'_i$ $[_{VP}$ be invited t$_i$]]].

In (59) the lowest trace, t$_i$, is bound by the intermediate trace, t$'_i$, which occupies an A'-position, the position created by VP-adjunction. Hence t$_i$ in (59) is like a *wh*-trace. It has the features [−anaphor, −pronominal] and is subject to Principle C of the binding theory. But t$_i$ is also A-bound by *John*. (59) illustrates a case of improper movement: movement from an A position to an A'-position and back to an A-position.[15] In *Barriers* (1986b: 68–80) Chomsky offers a solution to the problem raised here. I give a brief indication of the direction taken. The account is a rough approximation of the full story and the reader should also read the primary literature. The problem in the examples above is clearly the status of VP. VP is a maximal projection. It is not L-marked, hence a BC, hence a barrier.

In chapter 2 we discussed the structure of clauses and we suggested that I is the head of S, which we got to refer to as IP. As a head, I selects a V projection,

---

[15]   See chapter 7, section 6.1 for discussion.

VP. I is composed of agreement features and tense features. Tense features typically associate with VP. We could say that I theta-marks VP. This means that I governs VP and theta-governs VP. It does not mean that I L-marks VP, though, since we have argued that I is not a lexical category, but rather a bundle of grammatical features.

Another characteristic of IP is that the subject NP agrees with INFL for the features summed up as AGR: person and number. Let us say that I also 'agrees' with the head of the VP which it selects. After all, it is this verb which will finally be inflected for tense.[16] Let us indicate the V-I agreement through co-indexation. The subject NP and I also agree, we also co-index them.

60   John$_i$ [$_{I'}$ INFL$_i$ [$_{VP}$ works$_i$]]].

In a raising construction like (57c/58c) we would end up with the following pattern of indexing: the subject NP agrees with INFL, INFL agrees with the associated V:

61   John$_i$ INFL$_i$ seem$_i$ [$_{IP}$ t$_i$ to have left].

This co-indexation solves at least one of the problems raised: t$_i$ is now co-indexed with *seem$_i$*, which governs the trace. Hence the trace is governed by a co-indexed element, and this could qualify as antecedent-government.

Needless to repeat here, the analysis above is a very rough outline of the direction one could take to integrate A-chains into the *Barriers* framework. Research into the implications of the *Barriers* framework for the theory in general is still very much in progress and it would be impossible to attempt to give a definitive statement here.

---

[16] Cf. also the discussion in Pollock (1989).

6 Summary

In this chapter we have defined the notion barrier and integrated it in our theory. The definition of barrier is as follows:

1 A is a **barrier** for B iff (a) or (b):
   (a) A is a maximal projection and A immediately dominates C, C is a BC for B;
   (b) A is a BC for B, A is not IP.

Using (1) we define government as follows:

2a **Government**
   X governs Y iff
      (i)   X is either of the category A, N, V, P, I;
            or
            X and Y are co-indexed;
      (ii) X c-commands Y;
      (iii) no barrier intervenes between X and Y;
      (iv) minimality is respected.

2b **Minimality condition on government**
   There is no Z such that Z satisfies (i), (ii) and (iii) and X c-commands Z.

The subjacency condition is formulated in terms of barriers:

3 **Subjacency condition**
   Movement must not cross more than one barrier.

Barriers are defined as in (1). For some speakers tensed CP is an extra barrier for subjacency in English.
   We show that the ECP can also be reinterpreted in terms of the notion barrier.
   The *Barriers* framework applies quite straightforwardly to *wh*-movement. For NP-movement, we see that there are additional problems which require that co-indexation be extended.

7   Exercises

Exercise 1

Discuss (1) and (2) in terms of our new interpretation of the subjacency condition and the ECP:

1   Who does the detective think that he likes best?
2   Who does the detective think likes him best?

Exercise 2

Consider the following sentences from the exercise in the Introduction to this book, also discussed in exercise 2 in chapter 7. Using the *Barriers* framework developed in chapter 10, try to account for the relative acceptability of the examples below as indicated by the number of asterisks:

1a   *Which man do you know what John will give to?
1b   *Which man do you wonder when they will appoint?
1c   **Who do you wonder which present will give?
1d   *Which present do you wonder who will give?
1e   *Which man do you wonder whether John will invite?
1f   **Which man do you wonder whether will invite John?
1g   **Which man do you wonder what will give to John?
1h   **Which man do you wonder when will invite John?

When discussing these sentences you should first determine their syntactic representations. Then you should try to identify which grammatical principle or principles are violated.

Exercise 3

Compare (38a), repeated here as (1), with (2):

1   This is a book which reading would be fun.
2   This is a book reading which would be fun.

How does the contrast in grammaticality fall out from our discussion?

11 Aspects of the Syntax of Germanic Languages: Word-order Variation and Government and Binding Theory

Contents

Introduction and Overview

In this chapter we turn to some quite well-known data concerning word-order variation taken from two Germanic languages, Dutch and German. We shall describe the data and try to see how a syntactic theory like Government and Binding Theory can account for the phenomena.

The purpose of this chapter is to show how one can apply the theory developed so far to linguistic data. We shall discuss the hypothesis that German and Dutch are SOV languages in which the word-order typical of root clauses is achieved by a process of verb-movement: verb second. Verb-movement is an instantiation of head-to-head movement. The word-order variation of VP-constituents in German and Dutch will be attributed to the rule of scrambling.

Section 1 offers a survey of word-order variation in English. Section 2 discusses the word-order variation in Dutch and German. Section 3 discusses scrambling.

1   Movement Transformations in English: a Survey

In English declarative sentences the subject precedes the verb, whether this be a lexical verb or an auxiliary, while in certain direct questions the auxiliary verb precedes the subject:

1a   John will hit Mary.
1b   John hits Mary.
1c   Will John hit Mary?
1d   *Hits John Mary?
1e   Does John hit Mary?
1f   Whom will John hit?
1g   *Whom hits John?
1h   Whom does John hit?

The inverted order auxiliary-subject in (1c), (1e), (1f) and (1h) is achieved by moving the auxiliary from the position I, the head of IP, into C, the head of CP, by head-to-head movement. The D-structure of (1c), for example, will be as in (2a) and the S-structure will be as in (2b):

2a

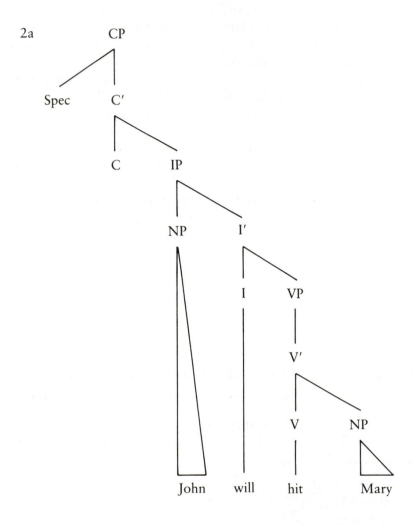

2b

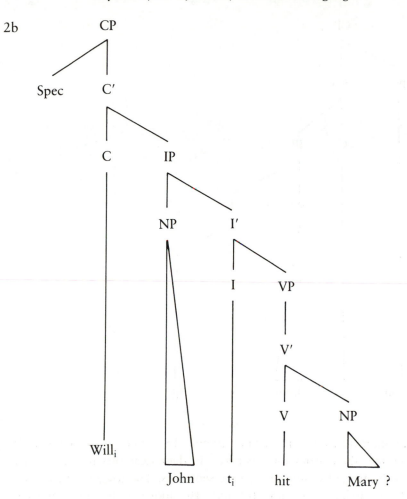

In (1f) the auxiliary has moved to C, as in (2b), and the *wh*-phrase *whom* has moved to [Spec,CP] by *wh*-movement. The S-structure of (1f) is as in (2c):

2c

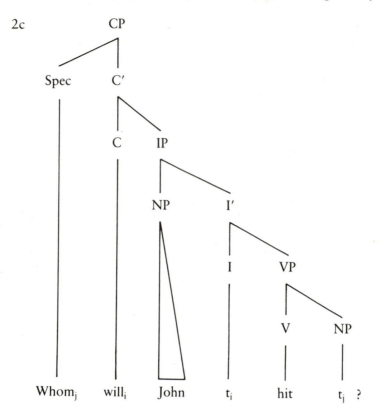

Whom$_j$ will$_i$ John   t$_i$ hit   t$_j$?

In English, lexical verbs like *hit* in (1d) and (1g) cannot be moved to C. We do not go into the reasons for this here.[1] In these examples the auxiliary *do* inverts with the subject in interrogative sentences. The **trigger** for the movement of the auxiliary in both (1e) and (1h) above is that the sentence is interrogative.[2]

---

[1] Pollock (1989) relates the impossibility of moving lexical verbs under I in English to the nature of the verb inflection. The reader is encouraged to read Pollock's work which offers some very important new insights.

[2] Subject-auxiliary inversion is also triggered by negative elements:

   (ia) On no account should you go there.
   (ib) Never before have I seen such a thing.

It is not obvious why preposing a *wh*-phrase or a negative phrase to [Spec, CP] should activate V to C movement. Perhaps, as suggested by Lightfoot (1989), this is due to the fact that once [Spec,CP] is activated the head must be filled lexically. Rizzi (1990: chapter 1) also provides discussion of the triggers for subject-auxiliary inversion.

Wh-movement of full phrases such as *whom* in (2c) was discussed fully in chapter 7 and subsequent chapters. Let us briefly turn to the movement of the auxiliary in the examples above. This type of movement instantiates movement of a head to a head-position. That a head moves to another head-position is expected under the general idea that syntactic structure must be preserved. Moreover, heads can only move to head-positions. If heads were to move under nodes dominating maximal projections, then the structure preserving constraint would be violated.

In chapter 8 we have proposed that traces must be properly governed. If the movement of *will* in (2b) leaves a trace then it should also be properly governed. In (2b) this is not problematic: the moved $will_i$ is the antecedent of the trace. $Will_i$ c-commands the trace and governs it: there is no barrier between $will_i$ and the trace, IP not being a barrier.

Now consider (3):

3a   Could you have done such a thing?
3b   *Have you could done such a thing?

The examples in (3) contain two auxiliaries, *could* and *have*. As can be seen from (3b) only *could* can move into the head-position of C. The S-structure of (3b) would be as in (3c), omitting irrelevant structure:

3c $[_{CP} [_{C'}$ have$_j$ $[_{IP}$ you could $[_{VP} t_j$ done such a thing]]]]?

The trace of *have* must be properly governed. Clearly the auxiliary is not theta-governed hence it will have to be antecedent-governed. Being the trace of a head, the trace of *have* must be governed by another head. In (3b) the antecedent of t_j is in the head position of C. However, t_j is separated from its antecedent by VP, which is not L-marked and hence a BC and a barrier. Moreover, IP is a BC which dominates VP and inherits barrierhood. Hence the antecedent *have* under C cannot govern its trace inside VP: head-to-head movement is local: it cannot skip an intervening head-position. A head of VP moves to I and then to C, but cannot leap directly from V to C.[3]

---

[3] See also the discussion of V-movement in Chomsky (1986b: 68–71). For important modifications of the barriers framework to accommodate and explain the strict locality of head-to-head movement and related issues the reader is referred to work by Rizzi (1990) and by Pollock (1989).

In chapter 7 we also discussed the rightward movement of the direct object in English referred to as heavy NP-shift.

4a You should [$_{VP}$ mix [$_{NP}$ two parts of water and three parts of wine] carefully].
4b You should [$_{VP}$ [$_{VP}$ mix t$_i$ carefully] [$_{NPi}$ two parts of water and three parts of wine]].

We argued that (4b) results from an application of move-α, where the moved NP is right-adjoined to the VP.

The discussion above gives us a survey of all the types of movement postulated so far: (i) movement of maximal projections, which are either moved under unoccupied maximal projection nodes or which adjoin to maximal projections, and (ii) movement of heads to head-positions. In the next sections we shall show how these types of movement can be used to account for the word-order variation in Germanic languages.

2   Word-order in Dutch and German

2.1   SOV and SVO?

In German (5) and Dutch (6) declarative sentences, the relative order of the verb and its complements seems to vary depending on whether the clause in which they appear is a root clause or a subordinate clause.

5a . . . dass Karl das Buch kauft.
        that Karl the book buys
    '. . . that Karl buys the book.'
5b Karl kauft das Buch.
    Karl buys the book
    'Karl buys the book.'

6a . . . dat Wim het boek koopt.
    . . . that Wim the book buys
    '. . . that Wim buys the book.'

6b Wim   koopt   het   boek.
 Wim   buys   the   book
 'Wim buys the book.'

On the basis of (5) and (6) one might be led to adopt the idea that Dutch/German declarative root clauses ((5b),(6b)) exhibit SVO word-order and that declarative subordinate clauses ((5a), (6a)) have SOV order. The question that arises is whether the two patterns are at all related, and if so, how. If the word-order patterns were not related it would be necessary to adopt two phrase structure rules for the German and Dutch VP.

7a   Root clauses   7b   Subordinate clauses

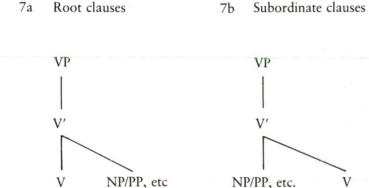

In (7) *NP/PP etc.* stands for the complements of the verb.

This proposal seems more like an *ad hoc* solution without much theoretical foundation, especially so if one does not explain why VP is head-initial in main clauses and head-final in subordinate clauses. Rather than trying to motivate (7), we shall assume that there is one underlying order for ALL Dutch and German sentences and word-order variations will be dealt with in terms of the application of move-α. In the literature various proposals have been formulated.[4] In this chapter we shall give a number of convincing arguments that in Dutch and German the SOV word-order, i.e. the word-order found in subordinate clauses, is the underlying order, i.e. that the Dutch and German VP is head-final (7b). Examples where the word-order differs from the subject-object-verb order will be argued to result from move-α.

The difference between Dutch and German on the one hand, and English on the other hand, will then be partly related to the structure of their VPs. English VPs are head-initial, (7a), German and Dutch VPs are head-final (7b). We

[4] The reader is referred to Koster (1975) and the references cited there.

should try to account for this contrast by relating it to some other principle of the grammar. Some authors[5] have argued that the difference between English and Dutch/German is due to the **directionality of government** of the verbs: in Dutch and in German verbs govern to the left, in English to the right. If verbs assign case to the NPs which they govern this difference in directionality of government will determine the respective order of verb and complement.

2.2 *Verb Second*

It would not be correct to say that German and Dutch root clauses always display SVO order: an extension of the data of both languages shows that the subject does not necessarily precede the verb in such clauses.

8a Dat   boek   kocht   Wim   gisteren.
    that   book   bought   Wim   yesterday
    'That book Wim bought yesterday.'
8b Gisteren   kocht   Wim   dat   boek.
    yesterday   bought   Wim   that   book
    'Yesterday Wim bought that book.'

9a Dieses   Buch   kaufte   Karl   gestern.
    this   book   bought   Karl   yesterday
    'This book Karl bought yesterday.'
9b Gestern   kaufte   Karl   dieses   Buch.
    yesterday   bought   Karl   this   book
    'Yesterday Karl bought this book.'

In (8a) and in (9a) the verb is preceded by the direct object, in (8b) and in (9b) by a time adverb. Rather than saying that main clauses exhibit a superficial SVO order we ought to say that in Dutch and in German the verb in the root clauses is in the second position:

10 XP – V – . . .

But not every verb can occur in second position:

---

[5] For example Hoekstra (1984).

11   *Dutch*
11a Gisteren   heeft   Karel   dat   boek   gekocht.
      yesterday has   Karel   that book   bought
      'Yesterday Karel bought that book.'
11b *Gisteren heeft gekocht Karel dat boek.
11c *Gisteren gekocht Karel dat boek heeft.
11d dat Karel gisteren dat boek gekocht heeft.
      that Karel yesterday that book bought has,
      'that Karel bought that book yesterday.'

12   *German*
12a Gestern hat Karl das Buch gekauft.
12b *Gestern hat gekauft Karl das Buch.
12c *Gestern gekauft Karl das Buch hat.
12d dass Karl gestern das Buch gekauft hat.

(11) and (12) show that it is the finite verb which must be in second position. Non-finite verbs occur towards the end of the sentence. The relative position of non-finite verbs with respect to the other constituents of the root clause is no different from their position in subordinate clauses (cf. (11d) and (12d)). We return to the position of sentence-final verbal elements later on.

The distribution of the finite verb in root clauses is referred to in the literature as **verb second** (V2). In Dutch and in German declarative root clauses and in direct *wh*-interrogatives (see (13a) and (14a)), the finite verb occurs in the second position. In direct *yes–no* questions the finite verb occurs sentence-initially (13b/c) and (14b/c):

13   *German*
13a Was kauft Karl?
      what buys Karl
      'What does Karl buy?'
13b Kauft Karl   das   Buch?
      buys Karl   the   book
      'Does Karl buy the book?'
13c Hat Karl das Buch gekauft?
      has Karl the book bought
      'Has Karl bought the book?'

14   *Dutch*
14a Wat koopt Wim?
     what buys Wim
     'What does Wim buy?'
14b Koopt Wim het boek?
     buys   Wim the book
     'Does Wim buy the book?'
14c Heeft Wim het boek   gekocht?
     has   Wim the book   bought
     'Has Wim bought the book?'

Let us try to derive the various word-order patterns using the movement transformations we have postulated throughout this book (see section 1).
Consider first the following:

15a dass Hans das Buch kauft.
     that Hans the book buys
     'that Hans buys the book.'
15b Kauft Hans das Buch?
     buys Hans the book
     'Does Hans buy the book?'
15c Das Buch kauft Hans.
     the book buys Hans

As already announced we want to argue that (15a) is closest to the underlying order of the sentence and that the order verb-subject in (15b) is derived. In other words, the D-structure of (15b) will be (16a):

16a

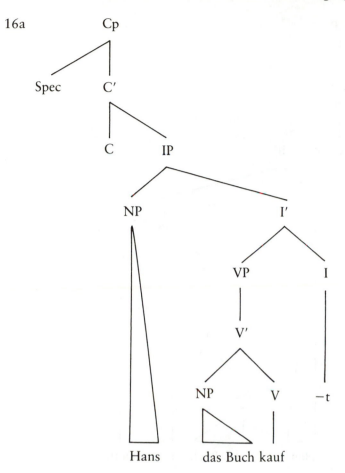

We assume that when VP is head-final, IP is also head-final so that I occurs to the right of VP. This assumption is based on the fact that in the majority of languages that have 0V-order, auxiliaries tend to follow the non-finite verb, an observation due to Greenberg (1963). We shall assume that the position of the auxiliary correlates with that of I.

In (16a) the lexical verb *kauf* must receive its agreement and tense inflection. This is realized on the head of IP: I. In order to pick up its inflection the verb is assumed to move to I, leaving a trace. This is then another application of move-α, specifically of head-to-head movement. The question arises whether the trace of the verb will be properly governed in (16b).

16b

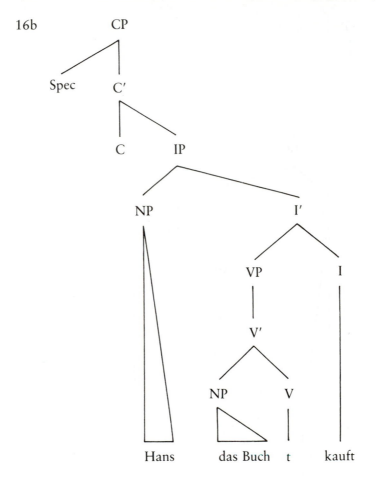

We assume that the moved verb-stem *kauf* and the inflection form one complex head, where V and I are merged. Chomsky (1986b: 68-9) proposes that the trace of the moved verb in (16b) is antecedent-governed. In (16a) VP, which is not L-marked, would be a BC and a barrier. Even if we assume, as does Chomsky, that I, theta-marks VP, it does not L-mark it, because I is not a lexical head. However, in (16b) I dominates *kauft* which contains the V *kauf*. Since *kauf* is a lexical head, Chomsky proposes that I does now L-mark VP: it theta-marks it, by assumption, and it now dominates a lexical head. In (16b) VP is L-marked and hence not a barrier for government from I. The moved V can antecedent-govern its trace.

The word-order in (16b) corresponds to that found in subordinate clauses, where the finite verb is sentence-final.

(15b) illustrates the order exhibited in *yes–no* questions: the finite verb is sentence-initial. In order to obtain this order all we need to do is to move the verb with the inflection from I to another position, C:

16c

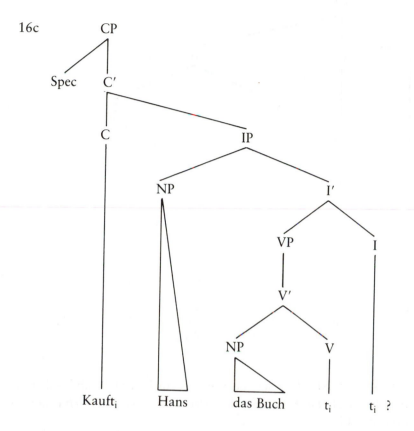

In (16c) the trace of the moved verb under I is antecedent-governed by the antecedent *kauft*; as pointed out before, verb-movement is a local process moving the verb from one head-position to the closest c-commanding head-position.

The next question is how to arrive at the verb second pattern of root declaratives and *wh*-questions, where the finite verb is in second position preceded by an XP. The answer will not surprise anyone: we move another constituent to a position preceding the verb, more specifically to the [Spec,CP] position which is the landing site for *wh*-movement:

16d

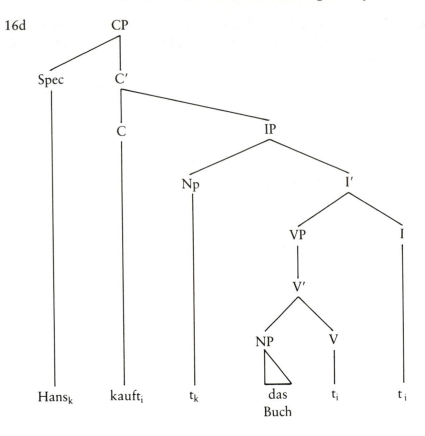

In (16d) the subject NP *Hans* has been moved to [Spec,CP] and will now precede the finite verb *kauft*. In (16e) the direct object NP *das Buch* is moved to [Spec,CP] (cf. (15c)).

16e

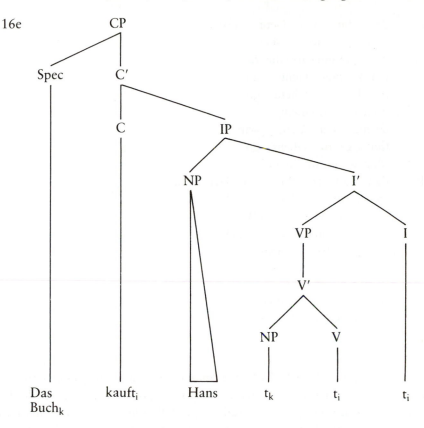

The proposal that the inflected verb moves to C is supported by the observation that in certain Dutch and German dialects C is itself inflected. This shows that there is a clear affinity between verbal inflection and C. In West Flemish the complementizer *dat* which introduces finite subordinate clauses is inflected for person and number.[6]

17a Goa Jan noa Gent?
    goes Jan to Ghent
17b Goan-k (ik) noa Gent?
    go-I (I) to Ghent
17c Goa-me (we) noa Gent?
    go-I (I) to Ghent
17d Goan Jan en Pol noa Gent?
17e Goa-se noa Gent? (3sg fem)
17f Goan-ze noa Gent? (3pl)

---

[6] Cf. Haegeman (forthcoming) and also Bayer (1984a and b) for similar data in Bavarian.

18a . . . da   Jan   noa   Gent   goat.
     . . . that Jan   to   Ghent   goes
     '. . . that Jan goes to Ghent.'
18b . . . dan-k   noa   Gent   goan.
     . . . that-I to   Ghent   go
     '. . . that I go to Ghent.'
18c . . . da-me   noa   Gent   goan.
     . . . that-we to   Ghent   go
     '. . . that we go to Ghent.'
18d . . . dan Jan   en   Pol   noa   Gent   goan.
     . . . that Jan   Pol   to   Ghent   go
     '. . . that Jan and Pol go to Ghent.'
18e . . . da-se   noa   Gent   goat.
     . . . that-she to   Ghent   goes
     '. . . that she goes to Ghent.'
18f . . . dan-ze   noa   Gent   goan.
     . . . that-they to   Ghent   go
     '. . . that they go to Ghent.'

The question must be asked why the finite verb should always move to C in main clauses in Dutch and German, while in English it is only possible if a *wh*-phrase or a negative phrase occupies [Spec,CP]. One observation that may help us to understand this phenomenon is that in Dutch and in German the complementizer *dat/dass* cannot be deleted in declarative sentences, while in English it can:

19a I think John is ill.
19b *Ik denk Jan ziek is.
     'I think Jan is ill.'

This suggests that the complementizer position must be filled in Dutch and German. In subordinate clauses there is a complementizer, in main clauses there is no complementizer, hence the verb must be the relevant lexical filler.

The next question is why C should have to be filled. One possibility that has been proposed is that NOMINATIVE in Dutch and in German is NOT assigned from I, the head of IP, but rather from C. The idea is that C also has inflectional features (which are indeed overtly realized in West Flemish). A constraint specific to these languages would then be that the case assigning C must be lexically filled.[7]

2.3   *Further Arguments for SOV*

The V2-hypothesis for root clauses in conjunction with the hypothesis that the German and Dutch VP is head-final will allow us to derive the word-order patterns for both main clauses and subordinate clauses. We turn to some empirical arguments in favour of the SOV-hypothesis.[8]

2.3.1   NON-FINITE CLAUSES

The SOV hypothesis combined with the V2-hypothesis for root clauses accounts for the fact that a non-finite verb follows its complements. Let us briefly illustrate this point with some examples.

In root clauses with a finite auxiliary and one or more non-finite verbs, the finite auxiliary will move to I and eventually to C; the non-finite verb is not affected by the movement and thus will follow the object:

20a dat Wim dat boek gekocht heeft.
                           -fin   +fin
    that Wim that book bought has
    'that Wim has bought that book.'
20b Wim heeft dat boek gekocht.
              +fin   -fin
    Wim has that book bought
    'Wim has bought that book.'

Consider (21), where the bracketed CP is a complement clause.

---

[7] The following works are but a selection of the literature to be consulted for further discussion: den Besten (1983), Haider and Prinzhorn (1986), Haegeman and van Riemsdijk (1986), Koopman (1984), Platzack (1983, 1986a, 1986b), Schwartz and Vikner (1989) and Weerman (1989). For a different view see Travis (1984, 1986). See also Haegeman (forthcoming).

[8] This section is mainly based on Koster's (1975) discussion of Dutch. Similar discussions of German can be found in Bach (1962) and Bierwisch (1963). For further arguments the reader is referred to the works cited.

21a dat hij gisteren probeerde [CP om het boek voor Marie te kopen].

that he yesterday tried   for the book for Marie to buy

'that he tried to buy the book for Marie yesterday'.

21b *dat hij gisteren probeerde [CP om voor Marie te kopen het boek].

21c *dat hij gisteren probeerde [CP om te kopen het boek voor Marie].

We discuss the relative order of the non-finite CP and the verb *probeerde* in section 2.4. Within the non-finite CP, the direct object NP and the indirect object NP must precede the verb, as predicted by the SOV-hypothesis. Recall that verb second only applies to root clauses.

Consider (22):

22a [VP Een boek schrijven] kan hij wel.

a   book write   can he indeed

'Write a book, he can indeed.'

22b *[VP Schrijven een boek] kan hij wel.

In (22) the entire VP occupies the first position, [Spec,CP]. We assume that VPs, like any other maximal projection, can be subject to move-α and hence may move to the first position. Inside the moved non-finite VP the verb must be final, as expected if VP is head-final.

2.3.2   VERB-PARTICLE COMBINATIONS

There are a number of verbs in Dutch and in German which are composed of two elements: a verb stem and a particle. The relative order of verb and particle in root and embedded clauses offers further evidence for the SOV/verb second analysis as discussed above. Consider the following examples:

23a . . . dat   Jan een   vriend   uitlachte.

. . . that Jan a   friend   out-laughed

'that Jan laughed at a friend.'

23b Jan lachte een vriend uit.

'Jan laughed at a friend.'

24a . . . dass Hans das Buch   zurückgab.

. . . that Hans the book back-gave

'that Hans returned the book.'

24b Hans gab das Buch zurück.
     'Hans returned the book.'

The verb *uitlachen* in (23) is composed of the particle *uit* ('out') and the verb
stem *lachen* ('laugh') and means 'to laugh at', 'to mock'. We assume that the
item *uitlachen* is a separate entry in the lexicon and that it is inserted at
D-structure as one morphologically complex word, which we shall represent as
V*. Though the two elements may be felt to form one lexico-semantic unit, we
see from (23b) that they are separable. Similarly, in (24) the verb *zurückgeben*
('return') consists of two elements: the verb *geben* and the particle *zurück*
('back').

Let us assume that the order exhibited in (23a) and (24a) reflects the
underlying order: the verb and the particle are one lexical unit. In order to
derive (23b) and (24b), in which the verbs are separated from the particles *uit*
and *zurück* respectively, we use our earlier hypothesis that the finite verb
moves away from the particle to end up under C.

Roughly, omitting irrelevant details here, the underlying structure of (23b),
will be (25a) and the S-structure (25b):

25a

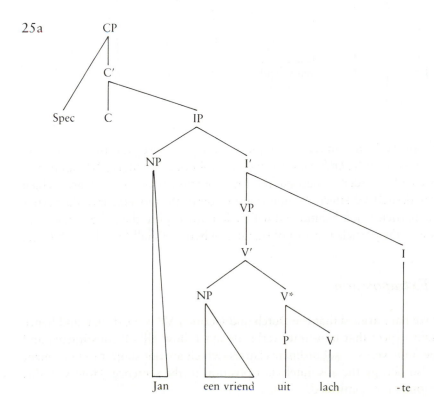

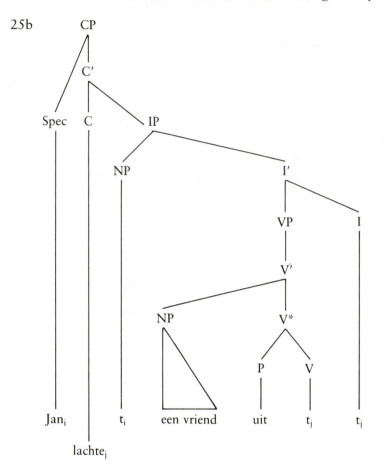

25b

In (25b) the verb *lach-* moves to I to pick up the past tense inflection *-te* to form *lachte*; subsequently, *lachte* moves to C. In addition, the subject NP *Jan* moves to [Spec,CP] in order to become the first constituent of the sentence, which gives the desired V2 effect. An important result of the movement of the verb is that the particle is left behind and will be left-adjacent to the trace of the verb. In this way the particle is a sort of signal of where we shall find the verb trace.

2.4 Extraposition

So far we have argued that the Dutch and German VP is head-final and hence we might expect that non-finite verbs always follow all VP-constituents and that the finite verbs of subordinate clauses (which are not subject to movement to C) also occupy the absolutely last position of the sentence. However, this prediction is not confirmed.

Consider the Dutch examples in (26):

26a dat   Jan   voor   Marie   een   boek   kocht.
    that   Jan   for   Marie   a   book   bought
    'that Jan bought a book for Marie.'
26b dat Jan een boek kocht [voor Marie].

The PP *voor Marie* precedes the finite verb *kocht* in (26a) and follows it in (26b). How can this be made compatible with our proposal that the Dutch VP is head-final? A simple conclusion imposes itself. If the Dutch VP is head-final we shall assume that the order in (26b) is a derived order: the PP *voor Marie* originates to the left of V and is moved to the right, leaving a trace:

26c dat Jan [$_{VP}$ t_i een boek t_k] kocht$_k$ [$_{PP}$ voor Marie$_i$].

We assume that the PP is adjoined to IP. The movement of the PP out of its dominating VP is sometimes referred to as **PP-over-V** (Koster, 1973), sometimes the more general term **extraposition** is used.

An important characteristic of the grammar of Dutch and German is that finite sentential complements follow the finite verb.[9] In (27a), for example, the verb *denkt* takes a sentential complement [*dat Marie ziek is*], which is obligatorily extraposed:

27a dat Jan denkt   [dat   Marie   ziek   is].
    that Jan thinks   that   Marie   ill   is
    'that Jan thinks that Marie is ill.'

The underlying structure of (27a) is (27b). The S-structure is represented in (27c):

27b dat   Jan   [$_{CP}$ dat   Marie   ziek is]   denkt.
    that   Jan   that   Marie   ill   is   thinks
27c dat Jan t_i denkt [$_{CPi}$ dat Marie ziek is].

(28) illustrates extraposition of a non-finite clausal complement in Dutch:

[9] There are various complicating factors with respect to the relative order of finite and non-finite verbs in Dutch and German. We refer the reader to a discussion in Haegeman and van Riemsdijk (1986) and the references cited there.

28a dat Jan gisteren   probeerde om Marie te kussen.
     that Jan yesterday tried   for Marie to kiss
     'that Jan tried to kiss Marie yesterday.'
28b dat Jan gisteren t$_i$ probeerde [$_{CP_i}$ om Marie te kussen].

Not all VP-internal material can be extraposed.

29a omdat   hij het boek kocht.
     because ' he   the book bought
     'because he bought the book.'
29b *omdat hij kocht het boek.

30a omdat   hij de   glazen gebroken ontving.
     because he   the   glasses broken   received
     'because he received the glasses broken.'
30b *omdat hij de glazen ontving gebroken.

31a omdat hij zijn werk ijverig   deed.
     because he   his   job   industriously did
     'because he did his job full of zeal.'
31b *omdat hij zijn werk deed ijverig.

   As the reader can see for himself, the following constituents, among others, resist extraposition: direct object NPs (29b), predicative participles (30b) and adjectives (31b).

   In section 2.3 we argued that a verb such as *uitlachen* in Dutch, which consists of a particle and a verb, should be treated as one complex lexical unit and inserted under the node V*. In root clauses, when the verb element is finite, it must move to C, leaving the particle behind. The particle is found immediately to the left of the trace of the finite verb. This analysis predicts that any material which occurs to the right of the finite verb in a subordinate clause will also follow the particle in a root clause, and conversely that material which could not be extraposed over the V will not be able to follow the particle. This prediction is entirely confirmed in (32) and (33).

32a dat ze gisteren aankondigde [$_{CP}$ dat ze ziek is].
     that she yesterday announced   that she ill   is
     'that she announced yesterday that she is ill.'
32b *dat ze gisteren [$_{CP}$ dat ze ziek is] aankondigde.

32c   Gisteren kondigde ze *aan* [$_{CP}$ dat ze ziek is].
      'Yesterday she announced that she is ill.'

32d   *Gisteren kondigde ze [$_{CP}$ dat ze ziek is] *aan*.

We have seen that finite clauses extrapose obligatorily. Hence we expect that they follow the finite verb in a subordinate clause (32a, 32b) and we also expect them to follow the particle (*aan*) in root clauses (32c, 32d).

33a   dat   hij   het   boek   teruggaf   aan   Marie.
      that   he   the   book   back-gave   to   Marie
      'that he returned the book to Marie'.

33b   *dat hij aan Marie teruggaf [$_{NP}$ het boek].

33c   Hij gaf het boek *terug* aan Marie.
      'He returned the book to Marie.'

33d   *Hij gaf aan Marie *terug* [$_{NP}$ het boek].

In (33a) we see that the PP *aan Marie* may be extraposed over the finite V. Hence it may follow the particle *terug* in the root clause in (33c). Conversely, object NPs resist extraposition (33b) and cannot follow the particle in root clauses (33d).

2.5   Summary: Dutch and German as SOV Languages

Let us briefly sum up the main points discussed so far. We have attempted to provide an analysis of Dutch and German root clauses and subordinate clauses. The claim is that Dutch and German are underlyingly SOV languages, i.e. that their VP and their IP are head-final. The subordinate clause word-order is closest to the underlying order. The root clause word-order is derived by means of a movement of the finite verb into C, referred to as verb second. In addition, another constituent is moved in to [Spec,CP]. Subject to certain constraints, VP-internal material may be extraposed to the right of the VP.

3   Scrambling

The internal structure of the German and Dutch VP has given rise to a lot of controversy. Consider the Dutch examples in (34) and their German parallels in (35).

34a dat   Jan waarschijnlijk met   dit   mes   de   taart   snijdt.
    that Jan probably   with this knife the   cake   cuts
    'that Jan probably cuts the cake with this knife.'
34b dat Jan waarschijnlijk de taart met dit mes snijdt.
34c dat Jan met dit mes waarschijnlijk de taart snijdt.
34d dat Jan met dit mes de taart waarschijnlijk snijdt.
34e dat Jan de taart met dit mes waarschijnlijk snijdt.

35a dass Hans wahrscheinlich mit   diesem Messer die Torte schneidt.
    that Hans probably   with this   knife   the cake cuts.
35b dass Hans wahrscheinlich die Torte mit diesem Messer schneidt.
35c dass Hans mit diesem Messer wahrscheinlich die Torte schneidt.
35d dass Hans mit diesem Messer die Torte wahrscheinlich schneidt.
35e dass Hans die Torte mit diesem Messer wahrscheinlich schneidt.

The examples above suffice to illustrate that both German and Dutch allow striking variation for the order of VP-constituents and adverbials. T! e languages contrast sharply with English where no such liberty is allowed.

36a John will probably cut the cake with this knife.
36b *John will probably cut with this knife the cake.
36c *John will cut probably the cake with this knife.

In English the direct object occurs right-adjacently to V with which it forms V'. V governs and assigns case to the direct object NP. The adverbial *probably* precedes the verb.

In the German and Dutch examples (34) and (35), (i) the adverbials *waarschijnlijk* or *wahrscheinlich* are somet'mes interspersed between the complements of the verb, and (ii) the direct object-NP is not always adjacent to V. The apparent freedom of word-order of German and Dutch sentences has led some linguists to the claim that these are languages without the same rigid structure as English, indeed some have argued that there is no VP at all in German and Dutch.[10] But if we assume that the German and Dutch VP is like

[10] See, for example, Haider (1981, 1982) and Tappe (1982). One of the main opponents to this view has been den Besten (1985). This is not the place to go into the whole debate surrounding the Germanic VP. The interested reader will find an excellent summary of the discussion in Webelhuth (1984/5), who also offers a number of convincing arguments to support the claim that German, and Dutch, have a VP as one of their structural components.

the English VP in its structural make-up then the word-order variation exhibited in (34) and (35) must be explained.

3.1 Scrambling

In this section we shall sketch a way of analysing the data exhibited in (34) and (35). The account is based mainly on work by den Besten and Webelhuth (1987).[11] We shall see that the word-orders can be derived on the basis of the types of movement posited so far. No extra assumptions are needed. Let us first return to the English VP. V takes as its first complement an internal argument to form a V', V' combines with further VP material to form further V projections.[12] The two VP-constituents NP and PP cannot be interchanged in (36b).

Now consider the following Dutch example, based on (34) but without the complicating factor of the sentence adverbial:

37a dat Jan met dit mes de taart snijdt.
    that Jan with this knife the cake cuts
    'that Jan cuts the cake with this knife.'
37b dat Jan de taart met dit mes snijdt.
    that Jan the cake with this knife cuts

If we assume that the structure of the Dutch VP is like in English, except that the Dutch VP is head-final, then we would have to assume that (37a) and (37b) have the underlying structure (38):

38

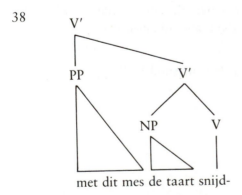

met dit mes de taart snijd-

---

[11] For more discussion of the word-order patterns in German see Stechow and Sternefeld (1988: 452–77) and Uszkoreit (1987: 151–60).
[12] For a different view of VP structure, see Larson (1988).

In order to obtain the reordering of the NP and the PP we will assume that a movement rule moves NP to the left of PP and adjoins it to VP:

39

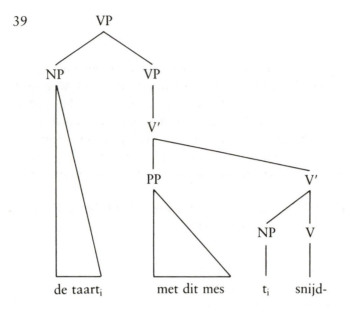

de taart_i   met dit mes   t_i   snijd-

Let us consider also the following examples:

40a dat   hij   waarschijnlijk   de taart   snijdt.
      that   he   probably   the cake   cuts
40b dat hij de taart waarschijnlijk snijdt.

The adverbial *waarschijnlijk* has scope over the entire sentence. We assume that such adverbials are modifiers of INFL and adjoined to I′:[13]

41a   dat [_IP hij [_I′ waarschijnlijk [_I′ [_VP de taart snijd-] -t]]].

[13] For a different analysis, see Haegeman (forthcoming).

41b

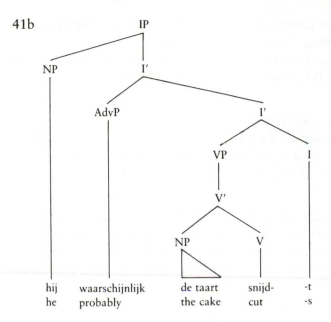

hij	waarschijnlijk	de taart	snijd-	-t
he	probably	the cake	cut	-s

If (41b) is the D-structure for both (40a) and (40b), then (40b) must be derived via an application of move-α: the NP *de taart* is moved out of the VP and adjoined to I':

42a   dat [IP hij [I' de taart₁ [I' waarschijnlijk [I' [VP t₁ snijd-] -t]]]

42b

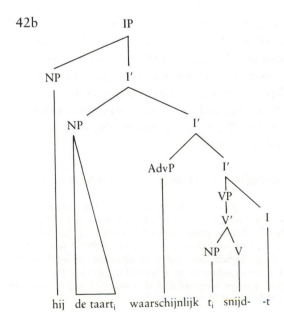

hij   de taart₁   waarschijnlijk   t₁   snijd-   -t

The movement of VP-constituents to derive the various word-orders of VP is referred to as **scrambling**.[14] Scrambling is a property typical of German and Dutch. English VP-constituents are rarely allowed such freedom of movement.[15] The only parallel example would be heavy NP-shift.

43a John bought the book yesterday.
43b *John bought yesterday the book.
43c John bought the most recent book on GB yesterday.
43d John bought yesterday the most recent book on GB.

In (43a) the direct object NP *the book* cannot be moved to the right of the adverbial *yesterday*. On the other hand, this movement is allowed in (43d) where the object is particularly heavy, hence the label 'heavy NP-shift'. Clearly the constraint that only heavy NPs can move does not apply to scrambling in Dutch and German:

44a dat   Jan   het   boek$_i$ waarschijnlijk t$_i$ gekocht   heeft.
     that Jan   the   book   probably   bought   has
     'that Jan has probably bought the book.'
44b dass Hans das Buch$_i$ wahrscheinlich t$_i$ gekauft hat.

Scrambling in German and Dutch can thus not be amalgamated with heavy NP-shift.

One proviso is in order concerning the analysis proposed above. We suggested that the scrambled NP is adjoined to I', i.e. to a non-maximal projection. In the *Barriers* framework (Chomsky, 1986b), this is not expected since adjunction is limited to maximal projections. It is possible that this restriction must be relaxed independently of the scrambling data in Germanic. An alternative proposal might be to reconsider the whole structure of INFL as suggested in work by Pollock (1989). We shall not go into this issue here (see Haegeman (forthcoming) for a discussion).

---

[14] See de Haan (1979) for a first description. De Haan refers to the movement of NPs as in (42b) as 'NP placement'.

[15] One should of course also address the question why scrambling is possible in Dutch and German and not in English. One proposal is that adjunction to IP in English is barred because of the NOMINATIVE case properties of I. Koster (1986) suggests that within its government domain English I does not tolerate an NP with another case. If, as suggested above, C in Dutch and German may be at least partly responsible for NOMINATIVE case assignment, this would mean that I is not the sole NOMINATIVE case assigner. Koster suggests that this makes I in a sense more tolerant of cases other than NOMINATIVE within its domain.

One direct advantage of the scrambling account for the various word-orders found in Dutch and in German is that we can maintain a maximally simple account of case and theta role assignment to the direct object. If the direct object NP uniformly originates in a position adjacent to V and dominated by V' the internal theta role will be assigned inside V' and structural case assignment will respect the adjacency condition. When an object NP is separated from its case assigning verb by intervening material we consider this to be a derived order. In (44), for instance, the direct object NPs (*het boek*, *das Buch*) are case-marked via their traces.

3.2   Scrambling vs. Wh-*movement*

In this section we discuss some properties of scrambling. The account is based on work by den Besten and Rutten (1989).

Scrambling differs from NP-movement and *wh*-movement to [Spec,CP]. NP-movement and *wh*-movement to [Spec,CP] are substitutions, whereas scrambling is an adjunction operation that moves a constituent to an A'-position. The following constituents are scrambled in Dutch:

(i)   NPs
In (45a) the direct object is moved; in (45b) the indirect object is moved; in (45c) a predicative NP is moved.

45a Hij heeft   het   boek$_i$ gelukkig   niet t$_i$ gelezen.
     he has   the   book   fortunately   not   read
     'He fortunately has not read the book.'
45b Hij   heeft   Jan   gelukkig t$_i$ niets   gegeven.
     he   has   Jan   fortunately   nothing   given
     'Fortunately he has not given Jan anything.'
45c Hij is   Einstein$_i$ nu   eenmaal   niet t$_i$.
     he is   Einstein   after all   not
     'After all, he is no Einstein.'

(ii)   PPs

46a Hij   heeft   [aan   Jan]$_i$ gelukkig   niet   t$_i$ een   boek   gegeven.
     he   has   to   Jan   fortunately   not   a   book   given
     'Fortunately he has not given John a book.'

46b Hij   heeft   [met   Marie]$_i$ gelukkig   niet t$_i$ gepraat.
    he   has   with   Marie   fortunately   not   talked
    'Fortunately he has not talked to Marie.'

(iii)   Pronominal elements

47 Hij   wil   het$_i$ waarschijnlijk t$_i$ aan   Maartje   geven.
    he   wants   it   probably   to   Maartje   give
    'He probably wants to give it to Maartje.'

(iv)   Pronouns such as *er*, *daar*, etc. which are complements of prepositions
       and are referred to as R-elements[16]

48 Hij   zal   er$_i$ waarschijnlijk t$_i$ aan   denken.
    he   will there   probably   about   think
    'He will probably think about it.'

That the relevant elements in the above sentences have been moved can be
deduced from the fact that they precede the sentential adverb *waarschijnlijk*. If
we assume that such adverbs are generated outside VP, possibly adjoined to I',
the position of the scrambled elements must result from movement.

Elements that resist scrambling are:

(i)   Particles

49a dat   Johannes   helaas   opgestaan   is.
     that Johannes   unfortunately   up-stood   is
     'that Johannes unfortunately has got up.'
49b Johannes staat   helaas   op.
     Johannes stands   unfortunately   up
     'Unfortunately Johannes gets up.'
49c *dat Johannes   op$_i$ helaas t$_i$ gestaan   is.
      that Johannes up   unfortunately   stood   is

Op is a particle that forms a complex lexical unit with the verb *staan*.
Although, as we have already seen, particles may be separated from their verb

---

[16]   See van Riemsdijk (1978a) for a discussion of the R-pronouns in Dutch.

heads as a result of verb second (section 2.3; cf. (49b)), the particles cannot themselves scramble (49c).

(ii)   Small clauses[17]

50a dat   zij   waarschijnlijk [sc Piet   erg   aardig] vond.
     that she   probably   Piet   very   nice   found
     'that she probably thought Piet very nice.'
50b *dat zij [sc Piet erg aardig] waarschijnlijk vond.

(iii) Predicative adjectives

51a dat   zij   waarschijnlijk [AP erg   aardig] is.
     that she   probably   very nice   is
     'that she is probably very nice.'
51b *dat zij [AP erg aardigi] waarschijnlijk ti is.
51c *dat zij [AP erg aardigi] waarschijnlijk [sc Piet ti] vond. (cf(50))

Both scrambling and *wh*-movement of a constituent to [Spec,CP] move a constituent to an A'-position. The data above show that scrambling cannot be assimilated to *wh*-movement to [Spec,CP]. For instance, predicative adjectives can move to [Spec,CP] while they cannot scramble:

52a *dat zij [AP erg aardigi] waarschijnlijk was.
     that she very nice   probably   was
52b [AP Erg aardigi] was zij   waarschijnlijk ti niet.
     very   nice   was she   probably   not
     'She was probably not very nice.'

There is a gradient with respect to which elements favour scrambling and which do not. Definite NPs, for example, are far more likely to scramble than indefinite ones:

53a dat   zij [NPi dat   boek] nu eenmaal ti gekocht heeft.
     that she   that book   after all   bought   has

---

[17] If small clauses are projections of their predicates then the small clauses in (50) are APs.

53b dat zij nu eenmaal dat boek gekocht heeft.

54a dat zij   nu eenmaal   een   huis   gekocht   heeft.
      that she   after all   a   house bought   has
54b ?dat zij [NP$_i$ een huis] nu eenmaal t$_i$ gekocht heeft.

Unstressed pronouns are usually scrambled:

55a *dat   zij   nu eenmaal   het   gekocht   heeft.
      that she   after all   it   bought   has
55b dat   zij   het$_i$ nu eenmaal t$_i$ gekocht   heeft.
      that she   it   after all   bought   has

56a *dat   zij   nu eenmaal   hem   gezien   heeft.
      that she   after all   him   seen   has
56b dat zij hem$_i$ nu eenmaal t$_i$ gezien heeft.

With strong contrastive stress on the pronoun scrambling is not obligatory:

56c dat zij nu eenmaal HEM gezien heeft.

Again (56) shows that scrambling should not be equated with *wh*-movement to [Spec,CP]. Unstressed object pronouns resist movement to [Spec,CP]:

57a Jan heeft   dat   boek   gisteren   gekocht.
      Jan has   that   book   yesterday   bought
      'Jan bought that book yeterday.'
57b Dat boek heeft Jan gisteren gekocht.
57c DAT heeft Jan gisteren gekocht.
      THAT has Jan yesterday bought
      'John bought THAT yesterday.'
57d *Het   heeft   Jan   gisteren   gekocht.
      it   has   Jan   yesterday   bought

We conclude from the data above that scrambling must be distinguished from movement to [Spec,CP]. While the latter movement is done by substitution, the former is by adjunction. Certain constituents resist *wh*-movement and may scramble, and conversely, certain constituents that can be *wh*-moved do not scramble. Scrambling in German and Dutch is the subject of ongoing research.[18]

3.3   Scrambling as a Stylistic Rule or a Syntactic Rule?

It has sometimes been proposed[19] that scrambling does not apply between D-structure and S-structure, but rather that it is a **stylistic rule** that permutes VP-constituents between the level of S-structure and that of PF.[20] This analysis would distinguish scrambling from movement to [Spec,CP] by locating the two types of movement at different levels of the grammar. Recall that we have adopted the T-model where the grammar is organized as follows:

58

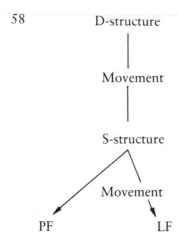

As seen in chapter 9, movement that intervenes between S-structure and LF has no overt manifestation in the surface form of the sentence represented by PF. Movement between S-structure and PF, on the other hand, will have an overt reflex but should not have any impact on the LF representation, i.e. it should not be meaning-changing.

However there are arguments against the proposal that scrambling in German and Dutch takes place between S-structure and PF. One argument is

[18] The reader is referred to Grewendorf and Sternefeld (1989) for a discussion of scrambling.
[19] See Koster (1978a: 232). For a general discussion of the notion stylistic rule see Rochemont (1978).
[20] Chapter 12 (2.2) discusses an example of a PF movement rule in French.

based on the interaction between scrambling as discussed here and the parasitic gap phenomenon discussed in chapters 8 and 9 (section 5). We shall briefly summarize the main points of the discussion here.[21]

Consider (59a), a typical example of a parasitic gap construction. The trace t_i signals the 'real gap' resulting from *wh*-movement of *which articles* and *e* indicates the parasitic gap. We saw that the parasitic gap is dependent on the real gap – (59b) – but not vice versa – (59c) and (59d):

59a Which articles$_i$ did John file t_i without reading e?
59b *Which articles did John file them without reading e?
59c Which articles did John file t_i without thinking?
59d Which articles did John file t_i without reading them?

In chapter 8 it was shown that parasitic gaps must not be A-bound:

60   *Poirot is a man who$_i$ I think t_i runs away when you see e_i.

In (60) t_i is the trace of *wh*-movement of *who*. t_i c-commands the parasitic gap *e* in the *when*-clause. (60) is ungrammatical because e_i is A-bound by the trace. We saw in chapter 9, section 5 that parasitic gaps are licensed at S-structure. Consider the ungrammatical (61a) and its rough S-structure (61b):

61a *Who did you say filed which articles without reading e?
61b *[$_{CP}$ Who$_i$ did [$_{IP}$ you say [$_{CP}$ t_i [$_{IP}$ t_i filed which articles [without [PRO reading e]]]]]]?

In (61a) *who* has moved at S-structure, but *which articles* is *in situ*. The second gap in the *without*-clause is the cause of the ungrammaticality: in (62) we have replaced *e* by a pronoun and the sentence is grammatical:

62   Who did you say filed which articles without reading them?

In chapter 9 we proposed that in order to achieve the paired reading typical of sentences with multiple *wh*-elements, *which articles* is *wh*-raised at LF, leaving a trace, t_j. *Wh*-raising would give us the LF representation (63) for the

---

[21] This section relies heavily on Bennis and Hoekstra (1984).

example in (61a/b). At LF *which articles* will c-command the parasitic gap *e*, but as shown in chapter 9, section 5 this is not sufficient to license the parasitic gap:

63 [Which articles$_j$ who$_i$] did you say t$_i$ filed t$_j$ without reading e$_j$?

For various reasons, which we do not go into here, Dutch does not have many occurrences of parasitic gaps.[22] There are however interesting examples which at first sight cause problems for the idea that parasitic gaps depend on the presence of real gaps.

64a dat Jan die boeken [zonder e te bekijken] weglegt.
that Jan those books [without e to inspect] away-puts
'that Jan puts those books away without looking at them.'
64b dat ik mijn oom [na jaren niet e gezien te hebben] ont-moette.
that I my uncle after years not seen to have met
'that I met my uncle after not having seen him for years.'

The non-overt objects of *bekijken* in (64a) and *gezien* in (64b) are interpreted as coreferential with the NPs *die boeken* and *mijn oom* respectively. These empty categories occur within subordinate clauses from which extraction is not allowed. One way of licensing such empty categories is to argue that they are parasitic gaps, i.e. that they are licensed by the presence of an A'-bound trace. If we assume that the overt object NPs, *die boeken* and *mijn oom*, are in their base-positions then this would be puzzling since in this case there will be no traces available to license the proposed parasitic gaps. In addition, the relevant overt object NPs would be argued to be in A-positions – the base position of object NPs is an A-position. If the direct object NP is in a c-commanding A-position and is co-indexed with the second gap then the overt NP would A-bind the second gap, *e*. If the second gap is claimed to be a parasitic gap then this is problematic: parasitic gaps must not be A-bound. The data in (64), however, can be made fully compatible with our discussion of parasitic gaps in chapters 8 and 9 once we adopt the scrambling analysis to account for constituent order in the Dutch VP and if we, in addition, assume, against Koster (1978), and with Bennis and Hoekstra (1984), that scrambling is a movement rule that operates between D-structure and S-structure.

---

[22] See Bennis and Hoekstra (1984) and Koster (1987) for discussion.

As suggested in the discussion of scrambling above, the NPs *die boeken* and *mijn oom* need not be in their base-position in (64). Given that they precede an adjunct clause, it seems reasonable to argue that they originate in an A-position adjacent to V and have been scrambled leftward out of VP. Roughly, the structure of (64a) would be as in (65):[23]

65

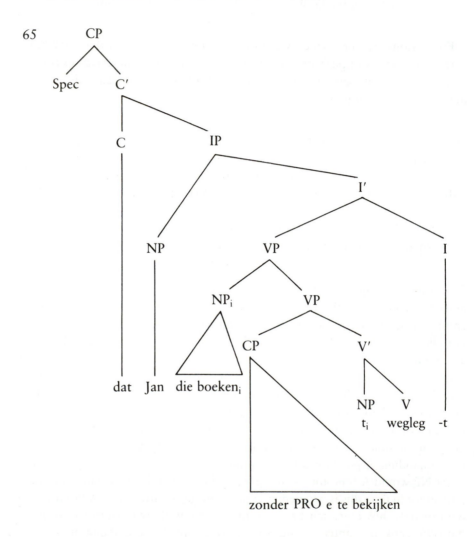

If the NP *die boeken$_i$* originates as the internal argument of V then we can maintain the idea that its case and theta role are assigned by V inside V'. After adjoining the NP to VP there is a VP-internal trace, t_i. This trace will license the parasitic gap e_i inside the *zonder*-clause. But we have argued that parasitic gaps

[23] In (65) the adjunct clause introduced by *zonder* is taken to be a VP adjunct.

are licensed at S-structure, so we must conclude that the movement of the NP *die boeken* has taken place at S-structure. (66) shows that the NP *die boeken* must move in order to allow for the object of the verb *bekijken* to be non-overt:

66a *dat Jan zonder e te bekijken die boeken weglegt.
     that Jan without e to inspect those books away-puts
66b dat Jan zonder ze te bekijken die   boeken weglegt.
     that Jan without them to inspect those books away-puts

In (66a) the parasitic gap in the *zonder*-clause cannot survive because there is no licensing trace. In this case, the object of *bekijken* must be overt.

3.4 Summary

In this section we have seen that the relatively free word-order of the VP constituents in Dutch can be accounted for if we adopt the scrambling hypothesis. Scrambling moves a VP-consituent to an adjoined position. Scrambling is not to be equated with movement to [Spec,CP]. The analysis of parasitic gap phenomena in Dutch shows that scrambling is a syntactic process which takes place prior to S-structure. It is restricted to Dutch and German and not operative in English.

4 Summary

This chapter offers a survey of word-order variation between Dutch and German on the one hand and English on the other. It is argued that the word-order patterns in Dutch and German can be derived on the basis of the movement rules established for English.

To account for the different word-orders in root clauses and in subordinate clauses we propose that Dutch and German are underlyingly SOV languages with head-final VP and IP. The subordinate clause word-order reflects the underlying order. Root clauses are the result of a movement rule, verb second, which places the inflected verb in 'second' position, under C. Verb second is an instantiation of head-to-head movement. In addition, *wh*-movement places a constituent in the [Spec,CP] and extraposition may move PPs and clauses rightward.

The apparent freedom in word-order of the VP-constituents and adjuncts in German and Dutch is related to the rule of scrambling which adjoins a VP-constituent to the left, to VP or to I'. It is shown that scrambling is not to be identified with movement to [Spec,CP]. Parasitic gap phenomena show that scrambling is a syntactic rule and must not simply be considered a stylistic rule of surface reordering of constituents at PF.

5   Exercises

Exercise 1

Discuss the derivation of the following Dutch sentences:

1   Gisteren   heeft   Jan   een   boek   teruggestuurd   over   algebra.
     yesterday   has   Jan   a   book   back sent   about   algebra
     'Yesterday Jan returned a book about algebra.'
2   Wanneer   komt   de   trein   uit   London   aan   in   Gent?
     when   comes   the   train   from   London   to   in   Ghent
     (*aan-komen* = arrive)
     'When does the train from London arrive in Ghent?'
3   Gisteren   heeft   Jan   die   boeken   waarschijnlijk   aan   Marie
     yesterday   has   Jan   those   books   probably   to   Marie
     gegeven.
     given
     'Yesterday Jan probably gave those books to Marie.'

Exercise 2

We analyse sentences with inverted subjects and sentence-initial *wh*-phrases in terms of movement of I to C. A similar analysis is proposed for (1) where a sentence-initial negative element triggers subject-auxiliary inversion:

1a   Never again shall I speak to that man.
1b   Never before have so many been saved by so few.

Which problems does sentence (2) present for this analysis?

2   He said that never again would he speak to that woman.

Exercise 3

Compare the following English and French sentences. What conclusions can you draw with respect to verb movement in the two languages?[24]

1   Il aime le chocolat.
    he likes the chocolate
    'He likes chocolate.'
2   He likes chocolate.
3   Aime-t-il le chocolat?
    likes he the chocolate
    'Does he like chocolate?'
4   Does he like chocolate?

Exercise 4

Consider the following examples:

1a   Into the room came a young woman of twenty-five.
1b   Off went the young man.
1c   Blackstable is a little village in which live fishermen and sailors.

In these examples the subject of the sentence is preceded by the lexical verb. Try to decide whether these examples can be derived by movement of the verb to C as illustrated in section 1. How could one derive such sentences where the subject inverts with the verb?[25]

---

[24]   The reader is referred to work by Pollock (1989) for discussion of the movement of verbs in French and English. This article offers a new analysis of the structure of IP and plays an important role in research in progress.
[25]   See Milsark (1974, 1977) and Rochemont (1978) for discussion.

12 Romance Languages: Subjects and Objects

Contents

Introduction and overview

Introduction and Overview

In this chapter we turn to some of the syntactic properties of the Romance languages. It is inconceivable that we should cover all the properties of Romance languages that have been dealt with in the literature. This would be the subject matter for many large volumes.[1]

The first topic to be addressed is that of non-overt objects as exemplified in Portuguese and Italian. We shall see that the non-overt objects in these two languages have different syntactic properties. The analysis is based mainly on the discussion of empty categories developed in chapter 8. Then we turn to a discussion of clitic pronouns, concentrating mainly on French data.

In section 1 we discuss non-overt object NPs in Romance languages: section 1.1 concerns zero topics in Portuguese, section 1.2 deals with the null object in Italian. Section 2 discusses the clitic pronoun system, with special attention for French subject clitics.

1   Non-overt Objects in Romance Languages

1.1   Null Objects in Portuguese

Consider the following examples from European Portuguese (see Raposo, 1986):

1a A Joana viu-o   na   televisao   ontem é   noite.
    Joana saw him on   television   last   night
    'Joana saw him on television last night.'
1b A Joana viu na televisao ontem é noite.

---

[1] The interested reader is referred to the literature on Romance. Seminal work has been been done, for instance, by Kayne (1975) (on French), Rouveret and Vergnaud (1980), Jaeggli (1981) (mainly on Spanish), Rizzi (1982) (on Italian) and Zubizarreta (1982, 1985, 1987), see also Jaeggli and Silva-Corvalan (1986), etc. Chomsky (1988a) is an introduction to Government and Binding Theory which is mainly based on Spanish data.

1c José sabe que Marie o   viu.
    José know that Maria him saw
    'José knows that Maria saw him.'
1d José sabe que Maria viu.

In (1a) and (1c) the verb *viu* ('see') takes two arguments, one realized by the subject NP, one by the object NP. (1b) and (1d) are at first sight problematic: the external argument is realized by the subject NP, but there is no overt direct object NP. The object of *viu* is 'understood' both in (1b) and in (1d). (1b) and (1d) mean roughly the same as (1a) and (1c) respectively, the complement of *viu* is 'him', 'her', 'it' or 'them'. It is identified as the so-called **discourse topic**, i.e. some specific entity which is salient in the context of the discourse.[2] Because the understood object is interpreted as the discourse topic we call it a zero topic.

Following the reasoning adopted in this book so far, it seems natural to assume that there is an empty category in the object position of *viu* in (1b) and (1d) corresponding to the overt pronoun *o* ('him') in (1a) and (1c). The representation of these sentences would then be (2):

2a A Joana viu e na televisao ontem é noite.
2b José sabe que Maria e viu.

1.1.1 IDENTIFYING THE EMPTY CATEGORY

The question that arises is what type of empty category the *e* postulated in (2) could be. On the basis of the two binary features [± anaphor] and [± pronominal] (see disussion in chapter 8) we assume that there are four types of empty categories.

3a PRO: [+anaphor, +pronominal]
3b *pro*:   [−anaphor, +pronominal]
3c *wh*-trace: [−anaphor, −pronominal]
3d NP-trace: [+anaphor, −pronominal]

PRO is an unlikely candidate for the empty category in (2). We have established (chapter 5) that PRO must be ungoverned at S-structure. The object position in (2) is clearly governed by the verb. Evidence that the position

---

[2] The notions topic, sentence topic and discourse topic are discussed among others in Sperber and Wilson (1986: 216–7)

is governed is that in (1a) and in (1c) there is an overt pronoun in the object position of *viu*. Because such an overt NP must be case-marked, it must occur in a governed position.

NP-trace is also unlikely for two reasons. On the one hand, NP-movement typically extracts an element from a position which is not case-marked (see chapter 6); the object positions in (2) are case-marked. Moreover, the trace of NP-movement is subject to Principle A of the binding theory: it must be bound in its governing category. In (2a) the non-overt object of *viu* is not bound by the subject *Joana*, and in (2b) it is neither bound by *Maria* nor by *José*: we have just seen that the understood object is interpreted as a discourse topic.

We conclude that the two anaphoric empty categories are excluded. Let us turn to the non-anaphoric empty categories. One first hypothesis might be that the empty category is *pro*, the base-generated non-overt pronominal, found typically in the subject position of Italian (see discussion chapter 8):

4a *pro* Parlo italiano.
   I speak Italian.
4b *pro* Lavora benissimo.
   He/she works very well.
4c *pro* Parlano   correntemente   italiano   e   francese.
        speak   fluently   Italian   and French
   'They speak Italian and French fluently.'

If the non-overt object in Portuguese is interpreted as an occurrence of *pro*, our examples in (2) would have the analogous representations in (5):

5a A Joana viu *pro* na televisao ontem é noite.
5b José sabe que Maria *pro* viu.

In chapter 8 we defined the licensing conditions of *pro* as follows:

6   *Pro*-drop parameter
6a *pro* is governed by X^o_y;
6b Let X be the licensing head of an occurrence of *pro*: then *pro* has the grammatical specification of the features on X co-indexed with it.

Condition (6a) can be satisfied in (5): the object position is governed by the V (*viu*). However, it is not immediately obvious how (6b) is to be satisfied, i.e. how the content of the object in (5) can be recovered. In addition, there are

empirical reasons for not equating the empty category in (2) with *pro*.
Consider the following Portuguese examples (Huang, 1984: 541):

7a João$_i$ disse que e$_i$ viu o Pedro.
    'João said that he saw Pedro.'
7b *João$_i$ disse que Pedro viu e$_i$.
    'João said that Pedro saw him.'

8a João$_i$ sabe que e$_i$ gostaria de conhecer a Maria melhor.
    João know that would like to know Maria better
    'João knows that he would like to know Maria better.'
8b *João$_i$ sabe que a Maria$_j$ gostaria de conhecer e$_{i/j}$ melhor.
    'João knows that Maria would like to know him better.'

9a João disse à Maria$_i$ que gostaria de conhecer-la$_i$ melhor.
    João said Maria that would like to know her better
    'João told Maria that he would like to know her better.'
9b João disse à Maria que gostaria de conhecer e$_i$ melhor.
    João said Maria that would like to know better
    'João told Maria that he would like to know her better.'

Let us assume with Huang (1984) that the non-overt subject in the
subordinate clause in (7a) and (8a) is *pro*.[3] Being [+pronominal] *pro* is subject
to Principle B of the binding theory: it must be free in its GC, the lower clause
(see chapters 4 and 8). In (7a) and (8a) *pro* in the subject position can be
co-indexed with the subject of the matrix clause, which is outside its GC. The
non-overt object in the Portuguese examples in (7b) and (8b), however, must
not be co-indexed with the subject in the main clause. This suggests that the
non-overt objects are not subject to Principle B, but rather that they are subject
to Principle C: they must be free everywhere. If we equate the non-overt
objects in the b-sentences with *pro*, the hypothesis we are examining, their
behaviour with respect to binding is unexpected. Similar conclusions can be
drawn from (9). While the overt object pronoun *la* in (9a) can be co-indexed
with the indirect object *à Maria* in the main clause, the non-overt object in (9b)
may not. This again suggests that our proposal that the non-overt object is a
non-overt pronoun, *pro*, is not on the right track.

---

[3] Raposo ((1986, n. 11) and (forthcoming)) suggests that an alternative analysis is
possible.

This leaves only one empty category to consider: *wh*-trace. At first sight, this is an equally unlikely candidate. *Wh*-traces are generated as the result of movement and they are bound by an antecedent in an A′-position. In our examples there is no obvious A′-binder for the trace.

1.1.2 NULL OPERATORS

In chapter 8 we discussed movement of non-overt elements.

10a I know [$_{NP}$ the man [$_{CP}$ O_i that [$_{IP}$ Lord Emsworth will invite t_i]]].
10b John is too stubborn [$_{CP}$ O_i for [$_{IP}$ us to invite t_i]].
10c John bought the dog [$_{CP}$ O_i for [$_{IP}$ Bill to give t_i to Mary]].

In (10a) the trace in the object position of *invite* is bound by a non-overt antecedent in an A′-position, the empty operator O_i. O_i has moved to [Spec,CP], t_i is a *wh*-trace.[4] The empty operator is co-indexed with the antecedent of the relative clause by a rule of predication.[5] In (10a) O_i will be co-indexed with the NP *the man*. A similar analysis applies to (10b) and (10c). Consider the following examples (from Rizzi, 1986a: 514):

11a John bought the dog for Bill to give – to Mary.
11b John bought the dog for Bill to give bones to – .
11c *John bought the dog for Bill to give – to – .

The sentences in (11) have the representations in (12). What seems to rule out (11c) is that there are two simultaneous zero operators:

12a John bought the dog [$_{CP}$ O_i for [$_{IP}$ Bill to give t_i to Mary]].
12b John bought the dog [$_{CP}$ O_i for [$_{IP}$ Bill to give bones to t_i]].
12c *John bought the dog [$_{CP}$ O_i O_j for [$_{IP}$ Bill to give t_i to t_j]].

Let us return to the non-overt objects in Portuguese. By analogy with the examples in (10) and (11) we could perhaps postulate that the non-overt object NPs are *wh*-traces bound by non-overt antecedents, i.e. zero operators. The

[4] Authier (1989) and Stowell (1985) offer more discussion of the status of null operators.
[5] Chomsky (1982: 92–5) suggests that the co-indexation is at LF.

representation of (2a) would then be (13) rather than our earlier hypothesis
(5a):

13   [$_{CP}$O$_i$ [$_{IP}$ A Joana viu t$_i$ na televisao ontem é noite]].

In (13) there is an empty operator in [Spec,CP] which binds a trace in the
object position. We have just seen that the empty operator in relative clauses
(10a) is ultimately co-indexed with its antecedent by a rule of predication.
Recall now that the interpretation of the non-overt object in Portuguese is that
it refers to some discourse topic. Raposo (1986) suggests that the zero operator
in (13) will be co-indexed with a discourse topic.[6] If we adopt the idea that the
non-overt object in European Portuguese is bound by a non-overt operator,
then the ungrammaticality of the examples in (14) follows:

14a   *Quando é que o João vai oferecer à Maria?
      'When is João going to offer it to Maria?'
14b   *Para qual dos filhos é que Maria comprou?
      'For which of his children did Maria buy it?'
      (from Rizzi, 1986a: 513).

The representation of these examples would be as in (15):

15a   *[$_{CP}$ Quando$_i$ O$_j$ [é que o João vai oferecer t$_j$ à Maria t$_i$]]?
15b   *[$_{CP}$ Para qual dos filhos$_i$ O$_j$ [é que à Maria comprou t$_j$ t$_i$]]?

The examples are ruled out on the same lines as (12c): there are two
operators in [Spec,CP], in (15) one is overt and the other is non-overt.

The fact that the non-overt objects are incompatible with overt operators in
[Spec,CP] is another empirical argument for not equating them with *pro*. In
Italian *pro* is admitted in the subject position of a finite clause even if there is
an overt operator in [Spec,CP]:

16   No so [$_{CP}$ *quando* [$_{IP}$ *pro* ha   visto   Maria]].
     not know when   has   seen   Maria
     'I do not know when he saw Maria.'

---

[6] Raposo (1986: 380, 384–6).

Let us return to (7b) and (8b), repeated here for the reader's convenience as (17). According to the empty operator analysis, the S-structure of these examples will be as in (18):

17a *João$_i$ disse que Pedro viu e$_i$.
'João said that Pedro saw him.'
17b *João$_i$ sabe que a Maria$_j$ gostaria de conhecer e$_{i/j}$ melhor.
'João knows that Maria would like to know him better.'

18a *[$_{CP}$ O$_i$ [$_{IP}$ João$_i$ disse que Pedro viu t$_i$]].
'João said that Pedro saw him.'
18b *[$_{CP}$ O$_i$ [$_{IP}$ João$_i$ sabe que a Maria gostaria de conhecer t$_i$ melhor]].
'João knows that Maria would like to know him better.'

In the ungrammatical (18a) the subject of the matrix clause *João* is coreferential with the discourse topic, i.e. with O$_i$ and with t$_i$. The ungrammaticality is predicted by our hypothesis. We have seen that traces of *wh*-movement are subject to Principle C of the binding theory, they must be free. In the representation (18a) t$_i$ is a *wh*-trace and it is not free. (18a) is grammatical if *João* and the zero operator are not co-indexed.

19a [$_{CP}$ O$_m$ [$_{IP}$ João$_i$ disse que Pedro viu t$_m$]].
'João said that Pedro saw him.'

The same reasoning explains the ungrammaticality of (17b) with the representation (18b). (19b), on the other hand, is grammatical: the trace in the object position of *conhecer* is bound neither by *João* nor by *Maria*:

19b [$_{CP}$ O$_m$ [$_{IP}$ João$_i$ sabe que a Maria$_j$ gostaria de conhecer t$_m$ melhor]].
'João knows that Maria would like to know him better.'

So far we have argued that the non-overt object in Portuguese is like a *wh*-trace bound by a non-overt operator. If this is the case then we expect that the other diagnostics identifying *wh*-traces also are valid. Specifically, if the non-overt object results from *wh*-movement then we expect that the distance between the trace and the null operator will be subject to the subjacency constraint (chapter 7). Raposo (1986) shows that this is indeed the case. While extraction from a clause which is the complement of a verb is possible, (20a), it is not possible to extract from a clause which is the complement of a noun (20b) and neither is extraction from adjunct clauses (20c) possible. The reader is referred to Raposo's own article for further discussion.

20a   Eu disse ao António que pedise   ao Manel   que   guardasse t_i
      no   cofre de   sala de jantar.
      I told Antonio that he asked   Manel   to   keep
      in the safe of the dining room.

20b   *Eu informei a polícia da possibilidade de o Manel ter guardado t_i no cofre de sala de jantar.
      I informed the police of the possibility that Manel had kept in the safe of the dining room.
      (Raposo, 1986: 381, example (16c).)

20c   *O pirata partiu para as Caraíbas depois de term guardado t_i cuidadosamente no cofre.
      The pirate left for the Caribbean after he had guarded carefully in the safe.
      (Raposo, 1986: 382, example (19).)

A further argument supporting our analysis is that the non-overt object in Portuguese licenses a parasitic gap (Raposo, 1986: 384):

21a   Vi e_i na TV   sem   reconhecer e_i.
      I saw   e   on   TV   without   recognizing   e
21b   *Vi-os$_i$ na TV sem reconhecer e_i.

We have seen that parasitic gaps must be licensed by another A'-bound trace. In (21a) the second empty category in the object position of *reconhecer* is parasitic upon the existence of the non-overt object of *vi*. This would be compatible with our analysis that there is an A'-bound trace in the main clause of (21a).

1.1.3   THE PRE-MOVEMENT STRUCTURE

We have only discussed the S-structure representation of the Portuguese sentences with non-overt objects. If these sentences illustrate *wh*-movement, the next question is to determine the pre-movement structure, i.e. the D-structure.

Raposo (1986: 385–6)[7] proposes that the pre-movement structure of (1b), repeated here as (22a), is (22b).[8]

22a A Joana viu na televisao ontem é noite.
22b A Joana viu PRO na televisao ontem é noite.

1.1.4 CONCLUSION

In this section we have discussed another occurrence of the zero operator, introduced in chapter 8. In European Portuguese there is a zero operator which is related to a salient element in the discourse and which binds a *wh*-trace in an object position. Let us refer to this phenomenon as the **zero topic operator**.

The non-overt topic operator is not an exclusive property of Portuguese. Campos (1986) shows that the analysis proposed for Portuguese also applies to Spanish. Huang applies a similar analysis to non-overt objects in Chinese and to certain constructions in German (Huang, 1984: 546ff).[9] The non-overt topic operator is not available in English: the English equivalents of (1b) and (1d) are ungrammatical. The discourse topic must be overtly expressed:

23a *Basil saw on television last night.
23b Manuel, Basil saw on television last night.

Whether a language has non-overt topics or not is another instance of parametric variation.[10]

1.2 Non-overt Objects in Italian

1.2.1 THE DATA

Consider the following examples from Italian (Rizzi, 1986a: 503).

---

[7] In chapter 8 we proposed a similar analysis for the null operator in relative clauses (see Jaeggli, 1981).
[8] For further discussion the reader is referred to Raposo (1986) whose analysis differs slightly from our own.
[9] The interested reader is referred to these discussions for details.
[10] Huang (1984) and Raposo (1986) offer two different explanations of the parameter. The reader is also referred to Authier (1989), who compares the null operator in relative clauses and purpose clauses (discussed in chapter 8) and the zero topic operator discussed in the present chapter. Authier provides arguments for keeping the two operators distinct.

24a Questo conduce la gente_i a [PRO_i concludere quanto segue].
     this   leads   people   to conclude what   follows
24b Questo conduce — a [PRO concludere quanto segue].

In (24a) *condurre* takes three arguments, realized by the subject (*questo*), the object NP (*la gente*) and the non-finite clausal complement (*a concludere quanto segue*). (24a) is an example of object control (see chapter 5). The PRO subject of the infinitival clause is controlled by the direct object.

In (24b) the direct object NP is absent, but the sentence remains grammatical and again there is a PRO subject in the infinitival clause. This is rather puzzling. Remember that we have seen in chapter 5 that an object controller cannot be omitted in sentences with obligatory control.

25a This leads people [PRO to conclude what follows].
25b *This leads — [PRO to conclude what follows].

While our discussion predicts that (25b) is ungrammatical, it leaves unexplained the grammaticality of the Italian parallel (24b). In spite of the absence of a direct object in (24b) PRO is understood as being controlled by an implied object. (24b) means, roughly, 'this leads one to conclude what follows'.

1.2.2   CONTROL BY THE UNDERSTOOD OBJECT

Consider the following examples (Rizzi, 1986a).

26a L'ambizione spesso spinge — a [PRO commettere errori].
     the ambition often pushes —   to make   mistakes
26b Un generale può costringere — a [PRO obbedire ai suoi ordini].
     a general   can force —   to obey   his orders
26c In questi casi, di solito Gianni invita — a [PRO mangiare con
     in these cases, generally Gianni invites —   to   eat   with
     lui].
     him

In all the examples above the object controller is understood in Italian. The reader can verify from the English glosses that the direct object cannot be omitted in English. An important feature of the interpretation of the examples is that the controller is obligatorily interpreted as 'one', 'people in general'; it must be 'generic'.

Following the reasoning developed in this book and applied in the above section on non-overt objects in Portuguese, let us postulate that the understood direct object in the Italian examples at issue is a non-overt constituent, an empty category. This hypothesis allows us to maintain the idea that the controller cannot be omitted in sentences with obligatory control. In Italian (24b) we shall say that the controller is present, though non-overt. English does not allow for non-overt objects. Schematically, the Italian sentence will have the representation in (27a) and the English pendant that in (27b):

27a NP V $[e]_i$ a $[PRO_i$ VP]
27b NP V [PRO to VP]

We need to identify now what type of NP *e* in (27a) is.

1.2.3 CONSTRAINTS ON THE INTERPRETATION OF THE NON-OVERT OBJECT

An interesting property of the non-overt object in Italian is that it is apparently plural. Rizzi (1986a) gives the following examples:

28a La buona musica   riconcilia e_i con se stessi$_i$.
 the good music   reconciles   with themselves
 'Good music reconciles one with oneself.'
28b Un bravo psicanalista può   restituire e_i a se stessi$_i$.
 a good   psychoanalyst can   give back   to themselves
 'A good psychoanalyst can give you back to yourself.'

29a Un dottore serio visita e_i nudi$_i$.
 a good doctor   visits   nude [plural]
 'A good doctor examines his patients nude.'
29b Di solito, Gianni fotografa e_i seduti$_i$.
 in general, Gianni photographs seated
 'In general Gianni photographs his subjects seated.'

(28) contains a plural reflexive *se stessi*. According to Principle A of the binding theory, reflexives must be bound in their GC. Since the sentences in (28) are grammatical, we deduce that both (28a) and (28b) must contain an appropriate binder for the reflexive. The subject in these examples cannot be the relevant binder: in (28a) and (28b), the subject is singular, while the

reflexive is plural. From the point of view of the interpretation, the reflexive in these examples is not dependent on the subject. As the English translations show, it is the understood object which binds the reflexive. We conclude that there must be a non-overt binder in these sentences, *e* in the object position, and that this binder is plural.

The examples in (29) contain plural predicative APs (*nudi* and *seduti*). The plural APs could not possibly be predicated of the singular subject NPs, but they relate to the understood plural object. In English the object must be expressed overtly.

30a *A good doctor examines nude.
30b A good doctor examines his patients nude.

(30a) would only be possible with *nude* referring to the subject NP *a good doctor*; in (30b) the object NP is overt and *nude* may relate to it.

The examples in (28) and (29) offer further evidence for a non-overt object in Italian: the non-overt object is not simply 'understood', it plays an active part in the sentence in that it is involved in syntactic processes such as binding or predication.[11]

In the above examples we see that the understood object in Italian is generic. Indeed, the understood object must be interpreted as generic: if we were to try to force a specific interpretation on the implicit object the sentences would decrease in acceptability:

31a *La buona musica ha   finalmente riconciliato e_i con me stesso$_i$.
     the good   music   has finally   reconciled —   with myself

---

[11] In chapter 5 we have distinguished between implied arguments which are not represented as NPs and those which are. Recall that the AGENT in passive sentences, for instance, may be understood while it is not syntactically active:

(ia)   They signed the cheque drunk.
(ib)   *The cheque was signed drunk.

In (ia) *drunk* is predicated of *they*. In (ib) we see that *drunk* cannot be predicated of the understood AGENT of the activity. Rizzi (1986a) shows that while it may be argued that the object in English is also understood (iia) it is not syntactically active since it cannot, as we have seen, control PRO:

(iia) This analysis leads to the adjunction approach.
(iib) *This analysis leads to conclude that scrambling is adjunction.

Rizzi proposes that the internal argument of *lead* in (iib) is saturated in the lexicon so that it cannot be projected in the syntax.

31b *Ieri,   Gianni   ha   fotografato e$_i$ seduto.
    yesterday, Gianni   has   photographed — seated

The intended interpretation for (31a) is that the object is 'me' and the sentence is unacceptable in this interpretation. Similarly, the object of *fotografato* in (31b) is intended to be specific and the sentence is out.

1.2.4   THE IDENTIFICATION OF THE EMPTY CATEGORY

Let us now try to identify the feature composition of the null element in the object position of the Italian sentences discussed here. Again, it is unlikely that an empty category in an S-structure object position could be PRO. The reasoning is the same as that used for the discussion of the Portuguese examples in section 1.1.1: the object NP is governed and we know that PRO must be ungoverned.

Could the empty category be an NP-trace? At first glance, this is also improbable. The examples do not suggest that there has been NP-movement. However, it might be conceivable that we have another instance where a zero element has been moved (see discussion above), in which case, of course, there would be no overt antecedent. However, if the object *e* we have posited were an NP-trace then it ought to be subject to Principle A of the binding theory and it ought to be A-bound in its GC. Thus we would expect that the object in (24b), for instance, will be bound by an element in an A-position, possibly the subject. But clearly the empty object of *conduce* is not bound by *Questo*. Similar arguments can be advanced for the examples in (28). In (28a), for instance, we already have established that the object must be plural, given that it serves as a binder for *se stessi*. Hence, it is not possible that the same empty category would itself be bound by the singular subject NP. Analogously to the Portuguese examples, neither of the empty categories which are [+anaphor] are suitable. This leaves us with two empty categories to consider: *wh*-trace and *pro*, both of which are [−anaphor].

In section 1 we have seen that the non-overt object in Portuguese is a *wh*-trace bound by a zero discourse operator. Could this analysis apply to Italian (32a) which would be represented as (32b)?

32a La buona musica riconcilia con se stessi.
32b [0$_i$ [$_{IP}$ La buona musica riconcilia t$_i$ con se stessi$_i$]].

While such a representation is appropriate for Portuguese, it turns out that for Italian it will not work. Remember that in Portuguese the presence of an overt *wh*-operator in [Spec,CP] was incompatible with the non-overt object (see (14a));

33a *Quando é que João vai oferecer à Maria?
33b [$_{CP}$ Quando$_i$ 0$_i$ [$_{IP}$ é que João vai oferecer t$_i$ à Maria t$_j$]]?

In our Italian examples, the non-overt generic object is fully compatible with the presence of a *wh*-element in the sentence-initial position:

34a Quale   musica   riconcilia   con se stessi?
     which   music   reconciles   with oneself
34b Non so come   queste   parole possano condurre a   concludere
     I do not know how such   words could   lead   to conclude
     quanto   segue.
     what   follows

Another contrast is that while in Portuguese the non-overt object refers to a specific discourse entity and may thus be singular, the Italian non-overt object must be plural and is generic, i.e. non-specific.[12]

This leaves us with one final option: *pro*, the non-overt pronominal found in the subject position of Italian (see the discussion in chapter 8). Under this hypothesis, the examples with non-overt objects in Italian differ from those in Portuguese: in Italian they would have the representations in (35):

35a Questo conduce *pro$_i$* a PRO$_i$ concludere quanto segue.
35b La buona musica riconcilia *pro$_i$* con se stessi$_i$.
35c Un buon dottore visita *pro$_i$* nudi$_i$.

Let us briefly return to the null subject in Italian, illustrated in (36).

36a *pro* Parla italiano.
     'He/she speaks Italian.'
36b *pro$_i$* Vede se stesso$_i$ nello specchio.
     'He sees himself in the mirror.'
36c *pro$_i$* Lavora sempre seduto$_i$.
     'He works always seated.'

---

[12] See Rizzi (1986a) for further arguments.

Unlike the non-overt object postulated in this section, *pro* in the subject position need not have generic reference. In (36) the subject is third person singular and it has specific reference. The *pro* subject may be singular or plural, its features being recovered on the basis of the finite INFL:

37a *pro*ᵢ Vedono se stessiᵢ nello specchio.
    'They see themselves in the mirror.'
37b *pro*ᵢ Lavorano sempre sedutiᵢ.
    'They work always seated.'

Recall that a specific and singular interpretation of the non-overt object is excluded (38):

38a *Ieri sera la buona musica ha riconciliato con se stesso.
    last night the good music has reconciled with himself
38b *Il dottore ha visitato nuda.
    the doctor has visited naked (feminine)

If we postulate that the Italian non-overt object is *pro*, we need to explain the restriction on its interpretation. Let us return to the general question of the licensing conditions of *pro*, given in chapter 8 and repeated in (6) above. In the subject position of Italian *pro* is licensed: it is governed by the INFL node, which is specified fully for the AGR features of the subject. Nothing in (6) restricts the licensing head of *pro* to INFL. Indeed, as stated, (6) leads one to expect that other heads, say V or P, may also be licensers. For the Italian data at hand Rizzi proposes that 'the licensing of *pro* in object position can now be viewed as another instantiation of the licensing schema: in Italian V belongs to the licensing class, in English it does not' (1986a: 519).

However, recall that *pro* must not merely be licensed by a governing head (6a), its content must also be recovered (6b). In the case of the Italian subject *pro* we assume that the features on INFL will identify *pro*. For the interpretation of *pro* in object position in Italian Rizzi proposes that its content can be established through a mechanism of *arb*-assignment which will force the generic or arbitrary interpretation on *pro*.

39 *Arb* **interpretation**
    Assign *arb* to the direct theta role.
    (1986a: 521).

Recall that PRO too may be interpreted as arbitrary:

40   It is difficult [PRO$_{arb}$ to always be happy].

An interesting property of PRO$_{arb}$ in Italian is that it is grammatically plural. In (41) the predicative AP *allegri* is predicated of arbitrary PRO and must be plural.

41   È   difficile [PRO$_{arb}$ essere   sempre   allegri/*allegro].
     is   difficult   to be   always   happy plural/*singular

These data provide evidence for Rizzi's rule of *arb*-interpretation for object *pro*. Recall that we identified plurality as a constant property of the non-overt object in our Italian examples:

42a   La buona musica riconcilia con se stessi/*stesso/*stessa.
42b   Un buon dottore visita nudi/*nudo/*nuda.

In (42a) the reflexive bound by the understood object is obligatorily plural. In (42b) a singular NP *nudo* can be predicated of the subject NP but not of the understood object; *nudi* will be interpreted as related to the implicit object.

We conclude that in Italian the verb is a licenser of *pro*, and that the recovery of the content of object *pro* is not due to inflection, but rather to a rule of *arb* interpretation (39).[13]

1.3   Summary: Non-overt Elements in Object Positions

As the reader can see from our discussion, not all understood objects are instances of the same empty category. In Portuguese, the non-overt objects were interpreted as traces bound by a non-overt topic operator in an A′-position; in Italian, the non-overt object is identified as *pro*, it is licensed by the V and interpreted via rule (39) of *arb* interpretation. Neither type of non-overt object is licit in English.

---

[13]   Rizzi (1986a) contains a discussion of further constraints on V as a licenser of object *pro*.

2   Pronouns and Clitics

In this section we turn to pronouns in Romance languages, specifically to the French pronoun system. We discuss the distribution of the object pronouns (section 2.1) and of the subject pronouns (section 2.2). Some of the properties of the pronoun system of French will also be shown to apply to other Romance languages.

2.1   Object Pronouns and Clitics

2.1.1   FRENCH OBJECT PRONOUNS

Consider the following examples paying special attention to the word-order:

43a Marie   voit   les   enfants.
     'Marie   sees   the   children.'
43b Marie   les   voit.
     Marie   them   sees
     'Marie sees them.'

44a Marie ne voit que les enfants.
     'Marie sees only the children.'
44b Marie ne voit qu'eux.
     'Marie sees only them.'

Like English, French is an SVO language: in (43a) and (44a) the NP object *les enfants* ('the children') follows the verb. However, when the direct object is pronominal, two possibilities arise. Either the object precedes the verb (43b) or it follows it (44b). Depending on its position, the pronoun surfaces in two distinct forms: *les* when it precedes the verb and *eux* when it follows it. The latter form is also used when de pronoun is the complement of a preposition:

45a Marie paie pour les enfants.
     Marie pays for the children.
45b Marie paie pour eux.
     Marie pays for them.

The two forms of the pronoun are in complementary distribution: where *les* is possible, *eux* is not and vice versa:

46a *Marie eux voit.
46b *Marie ne voit que les.
46c *Marie paie pour les.

For reasons that will become clear soon we call *les* the weak form of the pronoun and *eux* the strong form. The examples above already show that the strong form occurs in the same position as full NPs, and that the weak form is excluded from those positions. Neither strong forms nor full NPs are allowed in the pre-verbal position occupied by the weak pronoun:

46d *Marie les enfants voit.

2.1.2 STRONG FORMS AND WEAK FORMS

(47) is a list of the forms of the object pronouns in French. Even though for some pronouns strong forms and weak forms have the same morphological shape we assume that for each of the object pronouns a strong form is paired with a weak one. In the case of *nous* and *vous* we assume simply that strong and weak forms are the same:

47	*Strong forms*	*Weak forms*	*Translation*
	moi	me	me
	toi	te	you
	lui	le	him
	elle	la	her
	nous	nous	us
	vous	vous	you
	eux	les	them

We have seen that the weak object pronoun precedes the verb; we also observe that it cannot be separated from it (48a). The strong form is like any NP: it follows the verb and may be separated from it (48b and c):

48a *Je   le   ne   crois pas.
      I   him   not   believe

48b	Je ne	crois	(souvent)	que	lui.	
	I	believe	(often)	only	him	
48c	Je ne	crois	(souvent)	que	mon	frère.
	I	believe	(often)	only	my	brother

The weak forms cannot be stressed contrastively. The strong forms are like full NPs and can bear contrastive stress:

49a	*Jean	LE	connaît.	
	Jean	HIM	knows	
49b	Jean	ne	connaît que	LUI.
	Jean	only	knows	HIM
49c	Jean	ne connaît	que	SON FRÈRE
	Jean	knows	only	HIS BROTHER

The weak object pronoun is dependent on the presence of the verb: not only can the weak pronoun not be separated from the verb, it cannot occur if there is no verb (see Kayne, 1975: 83):

50a Qui as-tu vu?
    Who have you seen?
50b Lui/elle/eux.
50c *Le/*la/*les.

Consider also French subject–verb inversion in the following examples:

51a Il part demain pour Paris.
    'He leaves tomorrow for Paris.'
51b Part-il   demain   pour   Paris?
    leaves-he tomorrow for   Paris
    'Does he leave for Paris tomorrow?'

52a Il prendra le TGV.
    'He will take the TGV.'
52b Pendra-t-il   le   TGV?
    will take-he   the   TGV?
    'Will he take the TGV?'

53a Il   le   prendra   tôt   le   matin.
    he   it   will take   early   the   morning
    'He'll take it early in the morning.'

53b Le   prendra-t-il   tôt   le   matin?
    it   will take-he   early   the   morning
    'Will he take it early in the morning?'

54a Il n'invite qu'eux.
    'He invites only them.'

54b N'invite-t-il qu'eux?
    'Does he invite only them?'

The finite verb in French inverts with the subject pronoun *il* to form a *yes–no* question. Following our earlier discussion we shall assume that this is an example of movement of the finite verb to the pre-subject C position.[14]

55

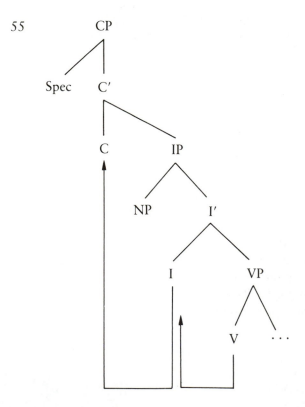

---

[14] Unlike in English full lexical verbs can also be inverted with the subject NP in French. For a discussion of the contrast between French and English, see the important article by Pollock (1989).

In (53b), where the finite verb is preceded by a weak form of the pronoun, the pronoun moves along with the verb. One might propose that the weak form of the pronoun is moved to [Spec,CP], but this will not do given (56):

56   Quand   le   prendra-t-il?
     when   it   will take-he
     'When will he take it?'

In (56) *Quand* is a *wh*-element which is itself moved to [Spec,CP]. This means that *le* cannot also occupy [Spec,CP]. With respect to subject–verb inversion, i.e. movement of V to C, somehow the object pronoun *le* and the verb count as one element. It is proposed that the weak object pronoun attaches morphologically to the head V with which it forms one complex lexical unit. Elements which attach obligatorily to heads are called **clitics**, they **cliticize** onto a head. Cliticization is often interpreted as an instantiation of a movement transformation. Following an analysis by Kayne (1975: chapter 2), we propose that at D-structure (57a) the object clitic is in its theta-position, [NP,V']; at S-structure (57b) the clitic is cliticized onto V with which it forms a complex word dominated by V*. V* is the head of the VP. Informally one might say, that the head V **incorporates**[15] the clitic. Cliticization can be interpreted as another instance of head-to-head movement, where the clitic adjoins to the head.[16]

57a   VP

---

[15] For a detailed discussion of the phenomenon of incorporation, see Baker (1988).
[16] Note the contrast with V to I, and V + I to C: in these cases movement involves substitution.

57b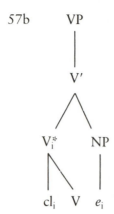

The moved clitic will leave a gap in the base–position. Let us try to determine the type of empty category. The discussion is very tentative. We assume that the merging of the clitic and the verb as one unit means that the pronominal properties of the clitic end up on the node V*, so that V*$_i$, the head of VP, is specified for the features of both V and of the clitic. V*, with its relevant features, governs the empty object position. On this assumption we might say that V*$_i$ in (57b) licenses *pro* in the object position, just like the finite I in Italian licenses *pro* in the subject position. V* is a head, i.e. an X°, which governs the empty position, satisfying the licensing condition for *pro* (6a) and, by virtue of the feature of the clitic, V* can identify the content of *pro* in the object position, satisfying (6b).

57c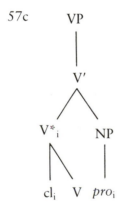

Further research will have to show whether the proposal developed here can be maintained.

2.1.3   OBJECT CLITICS IN ITALIAN AND SPANISH

An alternation between weak clitic pronouns and strong ones with their respective properties is also found in Italian:

58a   Ho visto Gianni.
      'I have seen Gianni.'
58b   L'   ho visto.
      him have seen
      'I have seen him.'
58c   Ho visto LUI.
      'I have seen HIM.'

Consider now the following Spanish examples (Jaeggli, 1981: 14):

59a   Vimos la casa de Mafalde.
      'We saw Mafalde's house.'
59b   Vimos a Guille.
      'We saw Guille.'

60a   La vimos.
      it we see
      'We see it.'
60b   Lo vimos.
      him we see
      'We see him.'

The data above are from standard Spanish: they are similar to those given for French above. However, consider also (61):

61   Lo vi a el.
     him I saw to him
     'I saw him.'

In (61) the direct object is expressed twice: once as a clitic and once as a strong pronoun. This is an example of what has come to be known as **clitic doubling**.

In standard Spanish, only full pronouns are doubled by a clitic (as in (61)); in certain dialects of Spanish, lexical NPs may also be doubled by a clitic. (62) is an example from South American Spanish (Jaeggli, 1981: 14).

62   Lo vimos a Guille.
     him we saw Guille

In both examples of clitic doubling the full pronoun or the lexical NP must be preceded by the preposition *a*. It is proposed that the preposition is needed for case theoretic reasons. The idea is that the clitic itself absorbs the ACCUSATIVE case assigned by the verb and that the preposition will case-mark its complement, the pronoun or the NP.

The doubling phenomena raise some questions for the analysis of clitics proposed in (57). If the clitic *lo* in (61) and (62) has been moved from the direct object position as suggested in the analysis, then we conclude that either the direct object itself (expressed with the preposition *a*) has been inserted AFTER the movement, i.e. at S-structure, or else that the PPs *a el* and *a Guille* are not in the direct object position. We would have to assume that these PPs are base-generated outside V'. Alternatively, these instances of clitic doubling do not involve movement. We leave the discussion here, the reader is referred to the literature on Romance languages.

2.2   *Subject Pronouns in French*

Unlike Italian and Spanish, modern French is not usually considered as a *pro*-drop language. A pronominal subject must be overt. In this section we shall look at subject pronouns in French.

63a   Tu parles beaucoup.
      'You speak a lot.'
63b   *Parles beaucoup.

Like object pronouns, subject pronouns in French have two forms:

64   *Strong forms*   *Weak forms*   *Translation*

Strong forms	Weak forms	Translation
moi	je	I
toi	tu	you
lui/elle	il/elle	he/she
nous	nous	we
vous	vous	you
eux/elles	ils/elles	they

The strong form of the subject pronoun corresponds to the strong form for the object pronoun. We conclude that in French case is morphologically realized on the weak forms of the pronouns only. The strong forms are like full NPs in that they have no overt case-marking. (See chapter 3 for the contrast between morphological case and abstract case). The use of the weak form is illustrated in (65):

65a   Je vais au cinéma ce soir.
     'I go to the cinema tonight.'
65b   Il va au cinéma ce soir.
     etc.

Let us look at some of the properties of the weak subject pronouns:[17]
   (i) Jaeggli (1981: 90) points out that the weak form of the subject pronoun and the verb must be adjacent. The only elements that can intervene are clitics.

66a   *Il, souvent, va au cinéma.
     'He often goes to the cinema.'
66b   *Tu, paraît-il, ne veux pas partir.
     'You, it appears, don't want to go.'
     (examples from Jaeggli, 1981: 90).
66c   Il les voit souvent.
     he them sees often
     'He sees them often.'

NP subjects pattern differently:

---

[17] The discussion is based on Kayne (1975: 84ff) and Jaeggli (1981: 90).

67a   Jean souvent va au cinéma.
        Jean often goes to the cinema.
67b   Marie, paraît-il, ne veut pas partir.
        Marie, it seems, does not want to leave.

   (ii) Weak forms occur on their own; strong forms can be modified:

68a   *Ils deux partiront demain.
        they two will leave tomorrow
68b   Eux deux partiront demain.
        they two will leave tomorrow

   (iii) Weak forms of the pronoun must not be conjoined with full NPs. Strong forms, on the other hand, are like ordinary NPs and can be conjoined:

69a   *Jean et je voulons aller au cinéma.
        Jean and I want to go to the cinema.
69b   Jean et Marie veulent aller au cinéma.
69c   Jean et moi voulons aller au cinéma.

   (iv) When the subject is stressed contrastively the strong form must be used.

70a   LUI partira le premier.
70b   *IL partira le premier.
70c   JEAN partira le premier.

   These data suggest strongly that, like the weak object pronouns, the weak subject pronouns are clitics. Morphologically, the weak subject pronouns in French also behave like clitics: they too form one word with the verb.

71   J'invite Jean.
        'I invite Jean.'

   When there is an object clitic, though, it intervenes between the subject clitic and the verb. Similarly, the negative clitic *ne* intervenes:

72a   Je l'invite.
        I him invite

72b *Le j'invite.

73a Je ne viens pas.
     I not come
     'I don't come'
73b *Ne je viens pas.

(72) and (73) suggest that the subject clitic attaches to the verb after the object clitic and the negative clitic have been cliticized. If both object clitic and subject clitic in (72) cliticize to the verb at S-structure, then we will have to ensure that we obtain the correct ordering.

In *yes–no* questions the subject clitic is not moved along with the verb, in contrast with object clitics or negative clitics:

74a Le prendra-t-il?
     it will take-he
     'Will he take it?'
74b Quand le prendra-t-il?
     when it will take-he
     'When will he take it?'

75a Ne vient-il pas?
     not comes-he
     'Isn't he coming?'
75b Pourquoi ne le prend-il pas?
     'Why doesn't he take it?'

Let us consider how to deal with the cliticization of the subject clitic in (71). Given that the subject clitic must be assigned the external theta role of the verb, we assume that it originates in [Spec,IP]:[18]

[18] Recall that we discussed an alternative analysis for the base-position of subjects in the appendix to chapter 6. Under this assumption, of course, the analysis proposed here must be modified.

76a

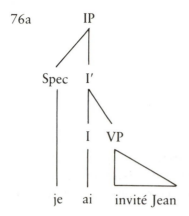

Suppose the subject clitic were to move to the finite verb between D-structure and S-structure. This means that it would have to be **lowered** from the [Spec,IP] position onto I, and the S-structure of such sentences would be (76b):

76b

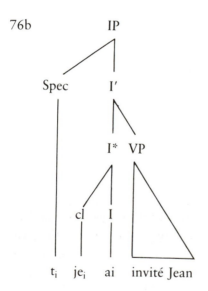

This movement poses a problem. None of the examples of movement we have discussed so far involve a rule which lowers constituents. *Wh*-movement and NP-movement are clearly examples of upward movement: the moved element c-commands its trace. In the case of the movement of the clitic in (57c), V* c-commands *pro* in the object position. But in (76b) the moved element fails to c-command its trace. I*, which we assume will have all the features of the clitic, does not c-command the vacated position in [NP,IP]

either: the first branching node dominating the I* complex is I' which does not dominate the vacated subject position.

Obviously, one might try to circumvent the problems mentioned by means of some auxiliary hypotheses. However, this is not what was proposed in the literature. Kayne (1984: 216, 221, n 19) proposes that both subject and object weak pronouns in French are clitics and will cliticize to a head. He proposes that the pre-verbal object clitics cliticize to the verb at S-structure (as sketched in (57)). However, he argues that the cliticization of the pre-verbal subject is not done at the level of S-structure, i.e. in the syntax proper, but rather at the post-syntactic level of PF. At S-structure, according to Kayne, the pre-verbal subject pronoun is in the [NP,IP] position (as in (76a)). It only cliticizes to the verb after S-structure. While the cliticization of the object clitic in French is an instance of syntactic cliticization at S-structure, the rightward cliticization of the subject clitic is not syntactic but phonetic.[19] As can be seen from the discussion, the movement of the subject clitic to I is apparently not subject to the same conditions as those developed for the movement that mediates between D-structure and S-structure or between S-structure and LF. If the clitic is lowered onto I, then it would be hard to see how its trace can be properly governed, for instance. However, recall that the ECP is checked at LF. Since the movement of the subject clitic to I does not affect LF representations, it will not create a trace that is subject to the ECP.

In the literature the movement that maps D-structure onto S-structure or S-structure onto LF is referred to as 'syntactic'. Movement processes intervening between S-structure and PF are referred to as **PF-movement**.[20]

---

[19] Similar proposals for the treatment of weak pronouns in Germanic are proposed in Haegeman (forthcoming).

[20] Kayne's proposal that French pre-verbal subject pronouns in French cliticize to I at PF does not entail that subject clitics universally are cliticized at PF. Rizzi and Roberts (1990) show that while the rightward cliticization of the French pre-verbal subject pronoun may be a PF phenomenon, the leftward cliticization of the post-verbal subject in the subject–verb inversion pattern is a syntactic cliticization (see also (74) and (75)).

(ia)   Parle-t-il?
        speaks-he
        'Does he speak'
(ib)   Jean parle-t-il?
        Jean speaks-he
        'Does Jean speak?'

The reader is referred to their work for discussion. Rizzi and Roberts (1990) adopt the analysis referred to in chapter 6, section 5, where it is assumed that all NPs in the canonical subject position [NP,IP] are base-generated VP-internally.

2.3 *Movement and the Model of the Grammar*

Let us finally return once more to our model of the grammar developed so far. We have outlined a T-model with the following levels of representation:

77

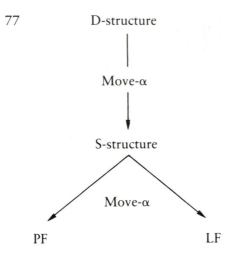

Movement of a constituent may take place between D-structure and S-structure. We have identified various instantiations of move-α: movement of maximal projections (*wh*-movement, NP-movement) and movement of heads (V-movement, clitic movement).

Movement may also take place between S-structure and LF. We have only discussed instances of movement of maximal projections: *wh*-raising, and quantifier raising. Some authors have argued that head-to-head movement is also possible at LF.[21]

In chapter 11 we argued against the idea that scrambling in the Dutch and German VP was an example of movement between S-structure and PF. The rightward cliticization of the weak subject pronoun in French, however, is an appropriate example of movement at this level. Further research into the properties of PF movement will have to establish the kind of constraints that apply there.

---

[21] Baker (1988) and Stowell(1985).

3 Summary

In this chapter we describe and examine some data from Romance languages. Various types of non-overt elements occur in object positions: in Portuguese we have identified a non-overt element which is bound by a non-overt topic operator; in Italian arbitrary *pro* may occur in the object position.

In our discussion of French we concentrate on the cliticization process which affects object clitics and subject clitics. We propose that objects undergo syntactic cliticization while the rightward cliticization of subject clitics is a PF phenomenon.

4 Exercises

Exercise 1

We have already seen two instances of *pro* in Italian where there is no corresponding empty category in English: I licenses subject *pro* and V licenses object *pro*. However, earlier English can be seen to pattern differently from present-day English. Consider the following examples (Rizzi, 1986a: 532, taken from Visser, 1969: 1342ff).

1 When he commaunded to receiue the man . . . into the church again, in what church commaunded he to receiue him?
  'When he orders to receive the man . . . into the church again, in what church does he order to receive him?'
  (1532–3, St. Th. More, *Works* (1557) 826 E7)
2 He had not otherwise forbid to molest them.
  'He had not otherwise forbidden to molest them.'
  (1649, Milton, *Tenure of Kings* (ed. Garnett): 72).
3 I then advised to fly
  (1725, Pope, *Translation Odyssey* (*World Classics*) IX: 133).
4 all the gods . . . , that teach to tame the soil and rule the brook
  (1748, James Thompson, *Castel of Indolence* II, VIII)

Discuss the interpretation of the sentences above paying specific attention to the control properties of the infinitival clause. What conclusions can we draw from data such as those above with respect to parametric variation?

Exercise 2

Consider the following data from earlier French. What conclusions can we draw with respect to the status of the subject pronoun?

1   Par dessus seelerent une pierre . . .
    on top fixed   a stone.
    'they hid the opening with a stone . . .'
    (*Roman du Graal*, pp. 26–7, from Adams, 1987: 11)
2   Et   lors   se porpensèrent li Grieu
    d'un mult   grant enging.
    and then contemplated   the Greeks
    of a very great plan
    (Villehardouin, xlvii, Adams, 1987: 11)
3   Oserai le vous   demander?
    dare (I) it you   ask
    'Dare I ask you?'
    (*Roman du Graal*, p. 21; Adams, 1987: 15)

For further discussion of the French data and interaction with verb movement as discussed in chapter 11, see Adams' article (1987) on the development of French.

Exercise 3

Consider the following data from colloquial German, cited by Huang (1984: 546–7) and taken from Ross (1982).

1a   Ich hab' ihn schon gesehen.
     I have him already seen
     'I saw him already.'
1b   Hab' ihn schon gesehen.
     have him already seen
     'I saw him already.'
1c   Hab' ich schon gesehen.
     have I already seen
     'I saw him/it/her already.'

1d   *Ihn habe schon gesehen.
     him have already seen
1e   *Ich habe schon gesehen.
     I have already seen
1f   *Habe schon gesehen.

2a   Ich trag die schon.
     I wear them already
     'I am already wearing them.'
2b   Trage die schon.
     wear them already
     'I am already wearing them.'
2c   Trage ich schon.
     wear I already
     'I am already wearing them.'
2d   *Die trage schon.
     them wear already.
2e   *Ich trage schon.
     I already wear
2f   *Trage schon.

Try to identify implicit arguments in the sentences above and to determine their status.[22]

Exercise 4

We have been arguing that English is not a null subject language and that it also lacks zero operators. Discuss the relevance of the following data, which are found, for instance, in the register of diaries, for this claim:

1a   Left exhausted after lunch.
1b   Looked at myself in the mirror.
1c   Will do the job my own way.

2a   *He thinks that will leave after lunch.
2b   *They don't know whether will return.
2c   *She left because was tired.

3a   *When will leave?
3b   *What will do?
3c   *This job, won't do.

---

[22] For discussion see Huang (1984).

Compare the data above with the Italian data in (4)–(6):

4a Sono partito stanco.
    am   left   tired
    'I left tired.'

4b Guardavo me stesso nello specchio.
    watched   myself in the mirror
    'I watched myself in the mirror.'

5a Sono partiti perché ero stanco.
    are   gone   because was tired
    'They left because I was tired.'

5b Non so quando ritorneró.
    not know when   shall return
    'I do not know when I shall return.'

6a Quando partirà?
    when   will leave
    'When will he leave?'

6b Che cosa farà?
    what   will do
    'What will he do?'

Would it be legitimate to postulate that the implicit subject in the English examples is *pro*?[23]

Exercise 5

Compare the data in exercise (4) with the French examples below, which all illustrate the register of informal notes:

1 Suis allé au magasin.
    am   gone to the shop

2 *Il est allé au magasin parce que voulais du pain.
    he is gone to the shop   because   wanted   bread

3 Reviendrai ce soir.
    will come back tonight
    'I will come back tonight.'

4 *Ce soir, reviendrai.

[23] See Haegeman (1990) for further illustrations and discussion.

5   *Il pense que reviendrai ce soir.
    he thinks that will return tonight

Do the judgements above justify interpreting the non-overt subject in (1)
and in (3) as *pro*? Compare especially with the Italian data in the
previous exercise.[24]

---

[24] See Haegeman (1990) for some further data and discussion.

Bibliography

Aarts, F. and J. Aarts (1982) *English Syntactic Structure*, Oxford: Pergamon.

Abney, S. (1987) *The English Noun Phrase in its Sentential Aspects*, Cambridge: unpublished MIT diss.

Abraham, W. (ed.) (1983) *On the Formal Syntax of the Westgermania*, Amsterdam: John Benjamins.

Adams, M. (1987) 'From Old French to the theory of pro-drop', *Natural Language and Linguistic Theory*, 5, 1–32.

Akmajian, A. and F. W. Heny (1975) *Introduction to the Principles of Transformational Syntax*, Cambridge, Mass.: MIT Press.

Akmajian, A., R. Demers and R. Harnish (1979) *Linguistics: An Introduction to Language and Communication*, Cambridge, Mass.: MIT Press.

Allwood, J., L.-G. and O. Dahl (1977) *Logic in Linguistics*, Cambridge: Cambridge University Press.

Anderson, S. (1986) 'The typology of anaphoric dependencies: Icelandic (and other) reflexives', in Hellan, L. and K. Koch Christensen (eds) *Topics in Scandinavian Syntax*, Dordrecht: Reidel.

Aoun, Y. (1984) 'A significant generalization in Chinese', in de Geest and Putseys (eds) *Sentential Complementation*, 11–21.

Aoun, Y. (1986) *Generalized Binding, the Syntax and Logical Form of Wh-interrogatives*, Dordrecht: Foris.

Aoun, Y. and D. Sportiche (1983) 'On the formal theory of government', *The Linguistic Review*, 2, 3, 211–36.

Aoun, Y. and N. Hornstein (1985) 'Quantifier types', *Linguistic Inquiry* 16, 623–36.

Aoun, Y., N. Hornstein and D. Sportiche (1981) 'Some aspects of wide scope quantification', *Journal of Linguistic Research*, 1, 69–95.

Authier, J.-M. (1988) 'Null object constructions in Kinande', *Natural Language and Linguistic Theory*, 6, 19–37.

Authier, J.-M (1989) 'Two types of empty operator', *Linguistic Inquiry*, 20, 1, 117–25.

Bach, E. (1962) 'The order of elements in a transformational grammar of German', *Language*, 38, 263–9.

Baker, M. (1988) *Incorporation. A Theory of Grammatical Function Changing*, Chicago: University of Chicago Press.

Baker, M., K. Johnson and I. Roberts (1989) 'Passive arguments raised', *Linguistic Inquiry*, 20, 2, 219–51.

Bayer, J. (1984a) 'Towards an explanation of certain *that*-t phenomena: the COMP node in Bavarian', in de Geest and Putseys (eds), *Sentential Complementation*, 23–32.

Bayer, J. (1984b) 'COMP in Bavarian syntax', *The Linguistic Review*, 3, 209–74.

Belletti, A. (1988) 'The case of unaccusatives', *Linguistic Inquiry*, 19, 1, 1–34.

Belletti, A. and L. Rizzi (1981) 'The syntax of *ne*: some theoretical implications', *The Linguistic Review*, 1, 117–54.

Belletti, A. and L. Rizzi (1988) 'Psych-verbs and θ-theory', *Natural Language and Linguistic Theory*, 6, 3, 291–352.

Bennis, H. (1986) *Gaps and Dummies*, Dordrecht: Foris.

Bennis, H. and L. Haegeman (1984) 'On the status of agreement and relative clauses in West-Flemish', in de Geest and Putseys (eds), *Sentential Complementation*, 33–53.

Bennis, H. and T. Hoekstra (1984) 'Gaps and parasitic gaps', *The Linguistic Review*, 4, 29–87.

Bertocchi, A. and C. Casadio (1980) *Conditions on Anaphora: An analysis of reflexives in Latin*, Papers on Grammar, 6, CLUE, Bologna.

Besten, H. den (1983) 'On the interaction of root transformations and lexical deletive rules', in Abraham, W. (ed.), *On the Formal Syntax of the Westgermania*, 47–131. Also published in *Groninger Arbeiten zur Germanistischen Linguistik*, vols 1–3, pp. 1–78.

Besten, H. den (1985) 'The ergative hypothesis and free word order in Dutch and German', in Toman, J. (ed), *Studies in German Grammar*, pp. 23–64.

Besten, H. den and G. Webelhuth (1987) *Remnant Topicalization and the Constituent Structure of VP in the Germanic SOV Languages*, Paper presented at GLOW, Venice.

Besten, H. den and J. Rutten (1989) 'On verb raising, extraposition and free word order in Dutch', in Janssens et al., *Sentential Complementation and the Lexicon*.

Bierwisch, M. (1963) *Grammatik des deutschen Verbs*, Berlin: Akademie Verlag.

Blom, A. and S. Daalder (1977) *Syntaktische Theorie en Taalbeschrijving*, Muiderberg.

Bloomfield, L. (1935) *Language*, London: George Allen and Unwin.

Borer, H. (1980) 'Empty subjects and constraints on thematic relations', in J. T. Jensen (ed.), *Proceedings of the Tenth Annual Meeting of NELS* (*Cahiers linguistiques d'Ottawa, vol. 9*), Department of Linguistics University of Toronto.

Borer, H. (1983) *Parametric Syntax*, Dordrecht: Foris.

Borer, H. (1986) 'I-subjects', *Linguistic Inquiry*, 17, 375–416.

Borer, H. (1989) 'Anaphoric AGR', in Jaeggli and Safir (eds), *The Null Subject Parameter*, 69–109.

Bouchard, D. (1984) *On the Content of Empty Categories*, Dordrecht: Foris.

Bouchard, D. (1985) 'The binding theory and the notion of accessible SUBJECT', *Linguistic Inquiry*, 16, 117–33.

Bresnan, J. (1970) 'On complementizers: toward a syntactic theory of complement types', *Foundations of Language*, 6, 297–321.

Bresnan, J. (1982) 'Control and complementation', *Linguistic Inquiry*, 13, 3, 343–434.

Brody, M. (1985) 'On the distribution of empty categories', *Linguistic Inquiry*, 16, 4, 505–46.

Burton-Roberts, N. (1986) *Analysing Sentences*, London: Longman.

Burzio, L. (1986) *Italian Syntax*, Dordrecht: Reidel.

Burzio, L. (1989) *The Role of the Antecedent in Anaphoric Relations*, paper presented at Geneva University, March, 1989.

Campos, H. (1986) 'Indefinite object drop', *Linguistic Inquiry*, 17, 354–9.

Cardinaletti, A., G. Cinque and G. Giusti (1988) *Constituent Structure*, Dordrecht: Foris.

Carroll, S. (1983) 'Remarks on FOR–TO Infinitives', *Linguistic Analysis*, 12, 415–54.

Chomsky, N. (1965) *Aspects of the Theory of Syntax*, Cambridge, Mass.: MIT Press.

Chomsky, N. (1970) 'Remarks on nominalisation', in Jacobs, R. and P. S. Rosenbaum (eds), *English Transformational Grammar*, 184–221.

Chomsky, N. (1973) 'Conditions on transformations', in Anderson, S. and P. Kiparsky (eds), *A Festschrift for Morris Halle*, New York: Holt, Rinehart and Winston, 232–86.

Chomsky, N. (1980) 'On binding', *Linguistic Inquiry*, 11, 1–46.

Chomsky, N. (1981a) *Lectures on Government and Binding*, Dordrecht: Foris.

Chomsky, N. (1981b) 'On the representation of form and function', *The Linguistic Review*, 1, 1, 3–40.

Chomsky, N. (1981c) 'Principles and parameters in syntactic theory', in Hornstein, N. and D. Lightfoot (eds), *Explanation in Linguistics*, 123–46.

Chomsky, N. (1982) *Some Concepts and Consequences of the Theory of Government and Binding*, Cambridge, Mass.: MIT Press.

Chomsky, N. (1986a) *Knowledge of Language, its Nature, Origin, and Use*, New York: Praeger.

Chomsky, N. (1986b) *Barriers*, Cambridge, Mass.: MIT Press.

Chomsky, N. (1988a) *Language and Problems of Knowledge. The Managua Lectures*, Cambridge, Mass.: MIT Press.

Chomsky, N. (1988b) *Some Notes on Economy of Derivation and Representation*, ms.

Chung, S. and J. McCloskey (1983) 'On the interpretation of certain island facts in GPSG', *Linguistic Inquiry*, 14, 704–13.

Cole, P. (1987) 'Null objects in universal grammar', *Linguistic Inquiry*, 18, 4, 597–612.

Contreras, H. (1984) 'A note on parasitic gaps', *Linguistic Inquiry*, 15, 704–13.

Coopmans, P. and I. Roovers (1986) 'Reconsidering some syntactic properties of PP-extraposition', in Coopmans et al., *Formal Parameters of Generative Grammar*, 21–35.

Coopmans, P., I. Bordelois, and B. Dotson Smith (eds) (1986) *Formal Parameters of Generative Grammar – Going Romance*, Dordrecht: ICG Printing.

Czepluch, H. (1982) 'Case theory and the dative construction', *The Linguistic Review*, 2, 1, 1–38.

Davis, L. (1986) 'Remarks on the theta criterion and case', *Linguistic Inquiry*, 17, 3, 564–8.

Emonds, J. (1970) *Root and Structure Preserving Transformations*, Indiana University Linguistics Club.

Emonds, J. (1976) *A Transformational Approach to Syntax*, New York: Academic Press.

Engdahl, E. (1983) 'Parasitic gaps', *Linguistics and Philosophy*, 6, 5–34.

Evans, G. (1980) 'Pronouns', *Linguistic Inquiry*, 11, 337–62.

Evans, G. (1982) *The Varieties of Reference*, Oxford: Oxford University Press.

Everaert, M. (1986) *The Syntax of Reflexivization*, Dordrecht: Foris.

Flynn, S. and W. O'Neill (1988) *Linguistic Theory in Second Language Acquisition*, Dordrecht, Boston, London: Kluwer.

Fromkin, V. and R. Rodman (1988) *An Introduction to Language*, 1974, 4th edn, New York, etc. Holt, Rinehart & Winston.

Geest, W. de and Y. Putseys (eds) (1984) *Sentential Complementation*, Dordrecht: Foris.

George, L. (1980) *Analogical Generalization in Natural Language Syntax*, Doctoral dissertation: MIT.

Giorgi, A. (1984) 'Towards a theory of long distance anaphors: a GB Approach', *The Linguistic Review*, 3, 4, 307–62.

Giorgi, A. (1987) 'The notion of complete functional complex: some evidence from Italian', *Linguistic Inquiry*, 18, 511–18.

Goodall, G. (1987) *Parallel Structures in Syntax*, Cambridge: Cambridge University Press.

Grange, C. and L. Haegeman (1989) 'Subordinate clauses: adjuncts or arguments', in Janssens et al. *Sentential Complementation and the Lexicon*, 281–300.

Greenberg, J. H. (1963) 'Some universals of grammar with particular reference to the order of meaningful elements', in J. H. Greenberg (ed.) *Universals in Language*, Cambridge, Mass.: MIT Press.

Greenberg, J. H. (1978) *Universals of Human Language*, 4 vols, Stanford, Cal.: Stanford University Press.

Grewendorf, G. and W. Sternefeld (eds) (1989) *Scrambling and Barriers*, Amsterdam: John Benjamins.

Guéron, J. (1980) 'On the syntax and semantics of PP extraposition', *Linguistic Inquiry*, 11, 637–78.

Haan, G. de (1979, 2nd edn 1981) *Conditions on Rules*, Dordrecht: Foris.

Haegeman, L. (1985) 'The *get*-passive and Burzio's generalization', *Lingua*, 66, 53–77.

Haegeman, L. (1986a) 'INFL, COMP and nominative case assignment in Flemish infinitivals', in Muysken and van Riemsdijk (eds), *Features and Projections*, 123–37.

Haegeman, L. (1986b) 'The double object construction in West Flemish', *The Linguistic Review*, 5, 4, 281–300.

Haegeman, L. (1987) 'Register variation in English: some theoretical observations', *Journal of English Linguistics*, 20, 2, 230–48.

Haegeman, L. (1990) 'Non-overt subjects in diary contexts', in Mascaro and Nespor (eds), *Grammar in Progress*, 167–179.

Haegeman, L. (forthcoming) *Generative Syntax: Theory and Description. A Case Study from West Flemish*, Cambridge: Cambridge University Press.

Haegeman, L. and H. van Riemsdijk (1986) 'Verb projection raising, scope and the typology of rules affecting verbs', *Linguistic Inquiry*, 17, 3, 417–66.

Haider, H. (1981) *Empty categories and some differences between English and German*, Wiener Linguistische Gazette, 25.

Haider, H. (1982) 'Dependenzen und Konfigurationen', *Groninger Arbeiten zur Germanistischen Linguistik*.

Haider, H. (1984) 'The case of German', in Toman (ed.) *Studies in German Grammar*, 65–102.

Haider, H. and M. Prinzhorn (eds) (1986) *Verb Second Phenomena in Germanic Languages*, Dordrecht: Foris.

Haik, Isabelle (1983) 'Indirect binding and referential circularity, *The Linguistic Review*, 2, 2, 4313–30.

Hale, K. (1983) 'Warlpiri and the grammar of non-configurational languages', *Natural Language and Linguistic Theory*, 1, 5–47.

Hale, K. and S. J. Keyser (1986) *Some Transitivity Alternations in English*, Lexicon Project MIT Working Paper, 7.

Hale, K. and S. J. Keyser (1987) *A view from the Middle*, Lexicon Project MIT Working Paper, 10.

Heim, I. (1982) *The Semantics of Definite and Indefinite Expressions*, GLSA.

Hellan, L. and K. Koch Christensen (1986) *Topics in Scandinavian Syntax*,

Dordrecht: Reidel.

Henry, A. (1989) 'Infinitives in a *For to* Dialect', Ms.

Higginbotham, J. (1980) 'Pronouns and bound variables', *Linguistic Inquiry*, 11, 679–708.

Higginbotham, J. (1983) 'Logical form, binding, and nominals', *Linguistic Inquiry*, 14, 395–420.

Higginbotham, J. (1988) 'On the varieties of cross-reference', in Cardinaletti et al. *Constituent Structure*, 123–42.

Higginbotham, J. and R. May (1981) 'Questions, quantifiers and crossing', *The Linguistic Review*, 1, 1, 41–80.

Hoekstra, T. (1984) *Transitivity*, Dordrecht: Foris.

Hornstein, N. (1977) 'S′ and X′ convention', *Linguistic Analysis*, 3, 137–76.

Hornstein, N. (1984) *Logic as Grammar*, Cambridge, Mass.: MIT Press.

Hornstein, N. and D. Lightfoot (1981) *Explanation in Linguistics*, London: Longman.

Hornstein, N. and A. Weinberg (1981) 'Case theory and preposition stranding', *Linguistic Inquiry* 12, 55–92.

Hornstein, N. and A. Weinberg (1988) ' "Logical form" – its existence and its properties', in Cardinaletti et al., 143–56.

Huang, J. (1982) *Logical Relations in Chinese and the Theory of Grammar*, MIT diss.

Huang, J.(1983) 'A note on the binding theory', *Linguistic Inquiry*, 14, 3, 554–61.

Huang, J. (1984) 'On the distribution and reference of empty pronouns', *Linguistic Inquiry*, 15, 531–74.

Huang, J. (1989) 'Pro-drop in Chinese: a generalized control theory', in Jaeggli and Safir (eds), *The Null Subject Parameter* 185–214.

Huddleston, R. (1976) *An Introduction to English Transformational Grammar*, London: Longman.

Huddleston, R. (1984) *Introduction to the Grammar of English*, Cambridge: Cambridge University Press.

Hyams, N. (1986) *Language Acquisition and the Theory of Parameters*, Dordrecht: Reidel.

Hyams, N. (1989) 'The null subject parameter in language acquisition', in Jaeggli and Safir (eds), *The Null Subject Parameter*, 215–38.

Jackendoff, R. S. (1972) *Semantic Interpretation in Generative Grammar*, Cambridge, Mass.: MIT Press.

Jackendoff, R. S. (1977) *X-Syntax: A Study of Phrase Structure*, Cambridge, Mass.: MIT Press.

Jacobs, R. A. and P. S. Rosenbaum (1970) *English Transformational Grammar*, Waltham, Mass.: Ginn.

Jaeggli, O. (1981) *Topics in Romance Syntax*, Dordrecht: Foris.

Jaeggli, O. (1986) 'Passive', *Linguistic Inquiry*, 17, 4, 587–633.

Jaeggli, O. and C. Silva-Corvalan (eds) (1986) *Studies in Romance Linguistics*, Dordrecht: Foris.

Jaeggli, O. and K. J. Safir (eds) (1989) *The Null Subject Parameter*, Dordrecht: Kluwer.

Janssens, J., D. Jaspers, W. Klooster, Y. Putseys and P. Seuren (1989) *Sentential Complementation and the Lexicon. Studies in Honour of Wim de Geest*, Dordrecht: Foris.

Johnson, K. (1985) *Subjects and θ-theory*, MIT ms.

Johnson, K. (1988) 'Clausal gerunds, the ECP and government', *Linguistic Inquiry*, 19, 4, 583–610.

Jones, M. A. (1983) 'Getting *tough* with *wh*-movement', *Journal of Linguistics*, 19, 1, 129–59.

Kayne, R. (1975) *French Syntax*, Cambridge, Mass.: MIT Press.

Kayne, R. (1983) 'Chains, categories external to S, and French complex inversion', *Natural Language and Linguistic Theory*, 1, 109–37.

Kayne, R. (1984) *Connectedness and Binary Branching*, Dordrecht: Foris.

Kemenade, A. van (1987) *Syntactic Case and Morphological Case in the History of English*, Dordrecht: Foris.

Kempson, R. (1988a) 'Grammar and conversational principles', in Newmeyer, F. (ed.) *Linguistics: the Cambridge Survey, Volume II. Linguistic Theory: Extension and Application*. Cambridge: Cambridge University Press, 139–63.

Kempson, R. (1988b) 'Logical form: the grammar cognition interface', *Journal of Linguistics*, 24, 393–431.

Keyser, S.J. (ed.) (1978) *Recent Transformational Studies in European Languages*, Cambridge, Mass.: MIT Press.

Kiss, K. E. (1981) 'Structural relations in Hungarian, a "free" word order language', *Linguistic Inquiry*, 12, 2, 185–214.

Kitagawa, Y. (1986) *Subject in Japanese and English*, University of Massachusetts, Amherst: PhD Diss.

Koopman, H. (1983) 'Control from COMP and comparative syntax', *The Linguistic Review*, 2, 365–91.

Koopman, H. (1984) *The Syntax of Verbs*, Dordrecht: Foris.

Koopman, H. and D. Sportiche (1982) 'Variables and the bijection principle', *The Linguistic Review*, 2, 139–60.

Koopman, H. and D. Sportiche (1987) *Subjects*, Ms UCLA and USC.

Koster, J. (1973) 'PP over V en de Theorie van J. Emonds', *Spectator*, 2, 294–311.

Koster, J. (1975) 'Dutch as an SOV language', *Linguistic Analysis*, 1, 111–36.

Koster, J. (1978a) *Locality principles in syntax*, Dordrecht: Foris.

Koster, J. (1978b) 'Why subject sentences don't exist', in Keyser (ed.), *Recent*

Transformational Studies in European Languages, 53–64.

Koster, J. (1984a) 'On binding and control', *Linguistic Inquiry*, 15, 3, 417–59.

Koster, J. (1984b) 'Infinitival complements in Dutch', in de Geest and Putseys (eds), *Sentential Complementation*, 141–50.

Koster, J. (1986) *The relation between Pro-drop, Scrambling and Verb Movement*, Groningen Papers in Theoretical and Applied Linguistics, TTT no. 1.

Koster, J. (1987) *Domains and Dynasties*, Dordrecht: Foris.

Kuno, S. (1973) *The Structure of the Japanese Language*, Cambridge, Mass.: MIT Press.

Kuroda, Y. (1986) *Whether we agree or not*, Ms. UCSD.

Larson, R. K. (1988) 'On the double object construction', *Linguistic Inquiry*, 19, 3, 335–91.

Lasnik, H. (1986) 'On accessibility', *Linguistic Inquiry*, 17, 126–9.

Lasnik, H. (1988) 'Subjects and the theta-criterion', *Natural Language and Linguistic Theory*, 6, 1, 1–18.

Lasnik, H. and J. Kupin (1977) 'A restrictive theory of transformational grammar', *Theoretical Linguistics*, 4, 173–96.

Lasnik, H. and M. Saito (1984) 'On the nature of proper government', *Linguistic Inquiry*, 15, 2, 235–89.

Lasnik, H. and J. Uriagereka (1988) *A Course in GB Syntax*, Cambridge, Mass.: MIT Press.

Lebeaux, D. (1989) *Parameter-setting, The Acquisition Sequence, and the Form of the Grammar: The Composition of Phrase structure*, Paper presented at the GLOW conference in Utrecht.

Lightfoot, D. (1979) *Principles of Diachronic Syntax*, Cambridge: Cambridge University Press.

Lightfoot, D. (1981) 'Explaining syntactic change', in Hornstein and Lightfoot (eds), *Explanation in Linguistics*, 209–39.

Lightfoot, D. (1989) *How to Set Parameters. A New Account of Word Order Change*, Paper presented at the interdepartmental research seminar in Linguistics. University of Geneva, 11 April.

Lumsden, J. (1987) *Parametric Variation in the History of English*, MIT diss.

Maracz, L. and P. Muysken (eds) (1989) *Configurationality. The Typology of Asymmetries*, Dordrecht: Foris.

Manzini, R. (1983) 'On control and control theory', *Linguistic Inquiry*, 14, 3, 421–46.

Manzini, R. and K. Wexler (1987) 'Parameters, binding theory and learnability', *Linguistic Inquiry*, 18, 3, 413–44.

Marantz, A. (1981) *A Theory of Grammatical Relations*, MIT diss.

Marantz, A. (1984) *On the Nature of Grammatical Relations*, Cambridge, Mass.: MIT Press.

Mascaro, J. and M. Nespor (eds) (1990) *Grammar in Progress, GLOW Essays for Henk van Riemsdijk,* Dordrecht: Foris.

Massam, D. and Y. Roberge (1989) 'Recipe context null objects in English, *Linguistic Inquiry,* 20, 1, 134–9.

May, R. (1985) *Logical Form,* Cambridge, Mass.: MIT Press.

Milsark, G. (1974) *Existential sentences in English,* MIT diss.

Milsark, G. (1977) 'Towards an explanation of certain peculiarities of the existential construction in English', *Linguistic Analysis,* 3, 1, 1–31.

Milsark, G. (1988) 'Singl-*ing*', *Linguistic Inquiry,* 19, 4, 611–34.

Mohanan, K. P. (1982) 'Grammatical relations and anaphora in Malayalam', in Marantz, A. and T. Stowell (eds), Papers in Syntax, MIT Working papers in Linguistics.

Mohanan, K. P. (1985) 'Remarks on control and control theory', *Linguistic Inquiry,* 16, 637–48.

Muysken, P. (1983) 'Parametrizing the notion head', *The Journal of Linguistic Research,* 2, 57–76.

Muysken, P. and H. van Riemsdijk (1986) 'Projecting features and feature projections', in Muysken and van Riemsdijk (eds), *Features and Projections,* 1–30.

Muysken, P. and H. van Riemsdijk (eds) (1986) *Features and Projections,* Dordrecht: Foris.

Nakajima, H. (1984) 'COMP as subject', *The Linguistic Review,* 4, 121–52.

Newmeyer, F. (1980) *Linguistic Theory in America,* New York: Academic Press.

Newmeyer, F. (1983) *Grammatical Theory,* Chicago: University of Chicago Press.

Obenauer, H. (1985) 'On the identification of empty categories', *The Linguistic Review,* 4, 135–202.

Pankhurst, J., M. Sharwood Smith and P. van Buren, (eds) (1988) *Learnability and Second Languages,* Dordrecht: Foris.

Perlmutter, D. M. (1989) 'Multi-attachment and the unaccusative hypothesis: the perfect auxiliary in Italian', *Probus,* 1, 63–120.

Pica, P. (1984) 'Introduction à l'étude des réfléchis à longue distance', in Couqueaux, D. and Ronat M. (eds) *La Grammaire Modulaire,* Paris: Minuit.

Platzack, C. (1983) *Germanic Word Order and the COMP/INFL Parameter,* Working Papers in Scandinavian Syntax, 2, University of Trondheim.

Platzack, C. (1986a) 'The position of the finite verb in Swedish', in Haider and Prinzhorn (eds), *Verb Second Phenomena in Germanic Languages,* 27–47.

Platzack, C. (1986b) 'COMP, INFL and Germanic word order', in Hellan and Christensen (eds), *Topics in Scandinavian Syntax,* 185–234.

Platzack, C. (1987) 'The Scandinavian languages and the null-subject parameter', *Natural Language and Linguistic Theory*, 5, 377–402.

Poggi, L. (1983) *Implicazioni Teoretiche della Sintassi dei Pronomi Clitici Soggetto in un Dialetto Romagnolo*, Tesi di laurea Universita della Calabria.

Pollock, J.-Y (1989) 'Verb movement, UG and the structure of IP', *Linguistic Inquiry*, 20, 365–424.

Postal, P. M. (1971) *Cross-over Phenomena*, New York: Holt, Rinehart & Winston.

Postal, P. M. (1974) *On Raising*, Cambridge Mass.: MIT Press.

Postal, P. M. and G. K. Pullum (1988) 'Expletive noun phrases in subcategorized positions', *Linguistic Inquiry*, 19, 4, 635–70.

Prewett, J. (1977) 'Reflexivization and *picture* noun phrase constructions', in L. Hutchinson (ed.) *Minnesota Working Papers in Linguistics and Philosophy of Language*, 4, 121–54.

Quirk, R. and C. L. Wrenn (2nd edn 1957) *An Old English Grammar*, London: Methuen.

Quirk, R., S. Greenbaum, G. Leech and J. Svartvik (1985) *A Comprehensive Grammar of the English Language*, London: Longman.

Raposo, E. (1986) 'On the null object in European Portuguese', in Jaeggli and Silva-Corvalan, *Studies in Romance Linguistics*, 373–90.

Raposo, E. (1987) 'Case theory and INFL to COMP: the inflected infinitive in European Portuguese', *Linguistic Inquiry*, 18, 1, 85–109.

Raposo, E. (forthcoming) *On Null Objects and Subjects in European Portuguese*.

Reinhart, T. (1981) 'Definite NP anaphora and c-command', *Linguistic Inquiry*, 12, 605–35.

Reuland, E. (1983) 'Governing -*ing*', *Linguistic Inquiry*, 14, 101–36.

Riemsdijk, H. van (1978a) *A Case Study in Syntactic Markedness*, Dordrecht: Foris.

Riemsdijk, H. van (1978b) 'On the diagnosis of *wh*-movement', in Keyser (ed.), *Recent Transformational Studies in European Languges*, 189–206.

Riemsdijk, H. van and E. Williams (1981) 'NP-structure', *The Linguistic Review*, 1, 171–217.

Riemsdijk, H. van and E. Williams (1986) *Introduction to the Theory of Grammar*, Cambridge, Mass.: MIT Press.

Rizzi, L. (1978) 'A restructuring rule in Italian syntax', in S. J. Keyser (ed), 113–18; also in Rizzi (1982a), 1–48.

Rizzi, L. (1982a) *Issues in Italian Syntax*, Dordrecht: Foris.

Rizzi, L. (1982b) 'Violations of the *wh*-island constraint and the subjacency condition', in Rizzi (1982a), 49–76.

Rizzi, L. (1982c) 'Negation, *wh*-movement and the null subject parameter', in Rizzi (1982a), 117–84.

Rizzi, L. (1986a) 'Null objects in Italian and the theory of *pro*', *Linguistic Inquiry*, 17, 501–58.

Rizzi, L. (1986b) 'On the status of subject clitics in Romance', in Jaeggli and Silva-Corvalan (eds), *Studies in Romance Linguistics*, 391–419.

Rizzi, L. (1990). *Relativized Minimality*. Cambridge, Mass: MIT Press.

Rizzi, L. and I. Roberts (1989) 'Complex inversion in French', *Probus*, 1, 1–30.

Roberts, I. (1983) 'Oblique Case in the History of English', *Southern California Papers in Linguistics* 10: 143–59.

Roberts, I. (1987) *The Representation of Implicit and Dethematized Subjects*, Dordrecht: Foris.

Robins, H. (1967, 2nd edn, 1979) *A Short History of Linguistics*, London: Longman.

Rochemont, M. (1978) *A Theory of Stylistic Rules in English*, Amherst: University of Massachussets PhD diss.

Ross, J. R. (1967) *Constraints on Variables in Syntax*, MIT diss.

Ross, J. R. (1982) *Pronoun Deleting Processes in German*, Paper presented at the Annual Meeting of the LSA San Diego.

Rouveret, A. and J. R. Vergnaud (1980) 'Specifying reference to the subject', *Linguistic Inquiry*, 11, 1, 97–202.

Safir, K. (1985) *Syntactic Chains*, Cambridge: Cambridge University Press.

Safir, K. (1986) 'Relative clauses in a theory of binding and levels', *Linguistic Inquiry*, 17, 663–90.

Safir, K. (1987) 'The anti-c-command condition on parasitic gaps', *Linguistic Inquiry*, 18, 4, 678–83.

Schwartz, B. D. and S. Vikner (1989) 'All verb second clauses are CPs', *Working Papers in Scandinavian Syntax*, 43, 27–50.

Sells, P. (1984) *Syntax and semantics of resumptive pronouns*, University of Massachusetts, PhD diss.

Smith, N. V. and D. Wilson (1979) *Modern Linguistics*, London: Penguin Books.

Sobin, N. (1987) 'The variable status of COMP-trace phenomena', *Natural Language and Linguistic Theory*, 5, 33–60.

Sperber, D. and D. Wilson (1986) *Relevance*, Oxford: Basil Blackwell.

Sportiche, D. (1981) 'Bounding nodes in French', *The Linguistic Review*, 1, 2, 219–46.

Sportiche, D. (1988a) 'A theory of floating quantifiers and its corollaries for constituent structure', *Linguistic Inquiry*, 19, 3, 425–49.

Sportiche, D. (1988b) *Conditions on Silent Categories*, ms.

Stechow, A. von and W. Sternefeld (1988) *Bausteine Syntaktischen Wissens*, Opladen/Wiesbaden: Westdeutschen Verlag.

Stowell, T. (1978) 'What was there before there was *there?*' In D. Farkas, W. Jacobson and K. Todrys (eds) *Papers from the Fourteenth Regional Meeting*, Chicago Linguistics Society.

Stowell, T. (1981) *Elements of Phrase Structure*, MIT diss.

Stowell, T. (1982) 'The tense of infinitives', *Linguistic Inquiry*, 13, 3, 561–70.

Stowell, T. (1983) 'Subjects across categories', *The Linguisitic Review*, 2, 285–312.

Stowell, T. (1985) 'Null antecedents and proper government', *Proceedings of the Fifteenth Annual Meeting of NELS, GLSA*, University of Massachusetts, Amherst.

Stuurman, F. (1985) *Phrase Structure Theory in Generative Grammar*, Dordrecht: Foris.

Tappe, T. (1981) *VP and coherent infinitives in German*, ms, University of Göttingen.

Taraldsen, K. T. (1981) 'The theoretical interpretation of a class of marked extractions', in A. Belletti, L. Brandi and L. Rizzi (eds), *Theory of Markedness in Generative Grammar*, Proceedings of the 1979 GLOW Conference, 475–516, Scuola Normale Superiore, Pisa.

Thiersch, G. (1978) *Topics in German Syntax*, MIT diss.

Timberlake, A. (1979) 'Reflexivization and the cycle in Russian', *Linguisitic Inquiry*, 10, 1.

Toman, J. (ed.) (1985) *Studies in German Grammar*, Dordrecht: Foris.

Travis, L. (1984) *Parameters and Effects of Word Order Variation*, MIT diss.

Travis, L. (1986) *Parameters of Phrase Structure and V2 Phenomena*, ms, McGill University, presented at the Princeton Workshop on Comparative Syntax, March.

Uszkoreit, H. (1987) *Word Order and Constituent Structure in German*, Stanford: Center for the Study of Language and Information.

Valin, R. Van (1986) 'An empty category as the subject of a tensed S in English', *Linguistic Inquiry*, 17, 3, 581–6.

Vergnaud, J.-R. (1985) *Dépendences et niveaux de représentations en syntaxe*, Amsterdam: John Benjamins.

Visser, F. Th. (1963) *An Historical Syntax of the English Language*, vol. 1, Leiden: Brill.

Visser, F. Th. (1969) *An Historical Syntax of the English Language*, vol. 2, Leiden: Brill.

Webelhuth, G. (1984/5) 'German is configurational', *The Linguistic Review*, 4, 203–46.

Weerman, F. (1989) *The V2 Conspiracy; a Synchronic and Diachronic Analysis of Verbal Positions in Germanic Languages*, Dordrecht: Foris.

Wekker, H. and L. Haegeman (1985) *A Modern Course in English Syntax*, London: Croom Helm.

Wexler, K. and P. Culicover (1980) *Formal Principles of Language Acquisition*, Cambridge: Mass.: MIT Press.

Williams, E. (1980) 'Predication', *Linguistic Inquiry*, 11, 1, 203–38.

Williams, E. (1981) 'Argument structure and morphology', *The Linguistic Review*, 1, 1, 81–114.

Williams, E. (1982) 'The NP cycle', *Linguistic Inquiry*, 13, 277–96.

Zagona, K. (1982) *Government and Proper Government of Verbal Projections*, University of Washington at Seattle: PhD diss.

Zribi-Hertz, A. (1984) 'Orphan prepositions in French and the concept of null pronoun', *Recherches Linguistiques*, 12, 46–91.

Zubizarreta, M.-L. (1982) *On the Relationship of the Lexicon to Syntax*, MIT diss.

Zubizarreta, M.-L. (1985) 'The relationship between morphophonology and morphosyntax: the case of Romance causatives', *Linguistic Inquiry*, 16, 247–89.

Zubizarreta, M.-L. (1987) *Levels of Representation in the Lexicon and in the Syntax*, Dordrecht: Foris.

Index